D0542890

SHARING THE PROMISED LAND

Also by Dilip Hiro

Non-Fiction

Dictionary of the Middle East (1996)
The Middle East (1995)
Between Marx and Muhammad: The Changing Face of Central
Asia (1994)
Lebanon, Fire and Embers: A History of the Lebanese Civil
War (1993)
Desert Shield to Desert Storm: The Second Gulf War (1992)
Black British, White British: A History of Race Relations in
Britain (1991)
The Longest War: The Iran-Iraq Military Conflict (1989)
Islamic Fundamentalism (1988)
Iran: The Revolution Within (1988)
Iran under the Ayatollahs (1985)
Inside the Middle East (1982)
Inside India Today (1977)
The Untouchables of India (1975)
Black British, White British (1971)
The Indian Family in Britain (1969)

Fiction

Three Plays (1987)
Interior, Exchange, Exterior (Poems, 1980)
Apply, Apply, No Reply and A Clean Break
(Two Plays, 1978)
To Anchor a Cloud (Play, 1972)
A Triangular View (Novel, 1969)

SHARING THE PROMISED LAND

An Interwoven Tale of
Israelis and Palestinians

DILIP HIRO

Hodder & Stoughton

With thanks to Macmillan Ltd for use
of seven maps on pages viii and ix.

Copyright © 1996 by Dilip Hiro

First published in Great Britain in 1996
by Hodder and Stoughton
A division of Hodder Headline PLC

The right of Dilip Hiro to be identified as the Author of
the Work has been asserted by him in accordance with the
Copyright, Designs and Patents Act 1988.

10 9 8 7 6 5 4 3 2 1

All rights reserved. No part of this publication may be
reproduced, stored in a retrieval system, or transmitted,
in any form or by any means without the prior written
permission of the publisher, nor be otherwise circulated
in any form of binding or cover other than that in which
it is published and without a similar condition being
imposed on the subsequent purchaser.

A CIP catalogue record for this title
is available from the British Library.

ISBN 0 340 63526 6

Typeset by Palimpsest Book Production Limited,
Polmont, Stirlingshire
Printed and bound in Great Britain by
Mackays of Chatham PLC, Chatham, Kent

Hodder and Stoughton
A division of Hodder Headline PLC
338 Euston Road
London NW1 3BH

CONTENTS

LIST OF ILLUSTRATIONS

Portrait of Rabbi Zvi Yahuda Kook
Israeli soldiers and Palestinian demonstrators, near Psagot
    Jewish settlement, the West Bank, January 1995
The Tomb of the Patriarchs/Ibrahimi Mosque, Hebron
A Jewish mother and child at the room connecting the tombs
    of Abraham and Sarah

Section II
Rabbi Moshe Levinger, Hebron
Wall mural in Gaza city
Empty villas in the Beit El Jewish settlement on the West
    Bank
Israeli soldiers killed in a bombing attack at Beit Lid, Israel,
    in January 1995
A Palestinian refugee house at Jalazoun camp on the West
    Bank
Palestinians killed at Noble Sanctuary/Mount Moriah, Jeru-
    salem, in October 1990
Memorial to six Fatah activists, Gaza city
The tomb of Dr Baruch Goldstein in Kiryat Arba
Islamic banner at a book exhibition at Al Najah University,
    Nablus
The Palestine Mosque, Gaza city
Harb Abu Namous and family, Gaza city
Sewerage on a road in Rafah, the Gaza Strip
Palestinian woman at Rafah, Gaza Strip
Wax models of Anwar Sadat, Shimon Peres and Menachem
    Begin at Lod International airport, 1977
Yitzhak Rabin and Yasser Arafat shake hands watched by
    President Bill Clinton, Washington D.C., September
    1993 (*G.P.O., Jerusalem*)
Shimon Peres and Yitzhak Rabin with Yasser Arafat and
    Ahmad Qrei, Erez checkpoint, Gaza Strip, January 1995
    (*G.P.O., Jerusalem*)
Binyamin Netanyahu, June 1996 (*G.P.O., Jerusalem*)

(All pictures are by Dilip Hiro unless stated.)

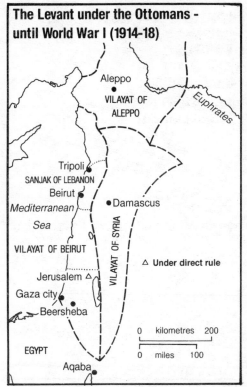

The Levant under the Ottomans - until World War I (1914-18)

Aleppo

VILAYAT OF ALEPPO

Euphrates

Tripoli

SANJAK OF LEBANON

Beirut

Mediterranean

Sea

Damascus

VILAYAT OF BEIRUT

VILAYAT OF SYRIA

Jerusalem △

△ Under direct rule

Gaza city

Beersheba

EGYPT

Aqaba

0 kilometres 200

0 miles 100

ISRAEL 1949 UN Armistice Lines

LEBANON

SYRIA

Mediterranean

Sea

Nazareth

Jenin

Tel Aviv (1)

WEST BANK

Amman

Jerusalem (2)

Hebron

Dead Sea

GAZA STRIP

Gaza

I S R A E L

J O R D A N

Beersheba

SINAI/ EGYPT

0 kilometres 50

0 miles 50

N

Eilat

Aqaba

..... Armistice Lines

(1) Internationally recognised capital of Israel

(2) Self-declared capital of Israel

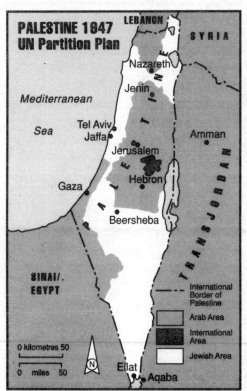

PALESTINE 1947 UN Partition Plan

LEBANON

SYRIA

Nazareth

Jenin

Mediterranean

Sea

Tel Aviv

Jaffa

Jerusalem

Amman

Hebron

Gaza

Beersheba

P A L E S T I N E

T R A N S J O R D A N

SINAI/, EGYPT

Eilat

Aqaba

0 kilometres 50

0 miles 50

N

—·— International Border of Palestine

Arab Area

International Area

Jewish Area

JERUSALEM 1949 Armistice Lines

0 kilometres 3

0 miles 2

N

.... Armistice Lines

— — — Municipal Boundary: Jordanian East Jerusalem

— — Municipal Boundary: Israeli West Jerusalem

To Ramallah

W E S T

B A N K

Mt. Scopus (Israel)

To Tel Aviv

Jordanian East Jerusalem

To Jericho

Israeli West Jerusalem

Beit Safafa

To Bethlehem

W E S T

B A N K

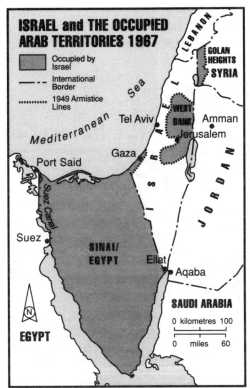

ISRAEL and THE OCCUPIED ARAB TERRITORIES 1967

Occupied by Israel

— ·· — International Border

·········· 1949 Armistice Lines

LEBANON

GOLAN HEIGHTS

SYRIA

Sea

Mediterranean

Tel Aviv

WEST BANK

Amman

Jerusalem

Gaza

JORDAN

Port Said

Suez Canal

Suez

SINAI/ EGYPT

Eilat

Aqaba

SAUDI ARABIA

EGYPT

N

0 kilometres 100

0 miles 60

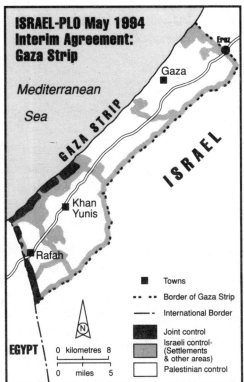

ISRAEL-PLO May 1994 Interim Agreement: Gaza Strip

Erez

Gaza

Mediterranean Sea

GAZA STRIP

ISRAEL

Khan Yunis

Rafah

EGYPT

■ Towns

· · · Border of Gaza Strip

— · — International Border

Joint control

Israeli control- (Settlements & other areas)

Palestinian control

N

0 kilometres 8

0 miles 5

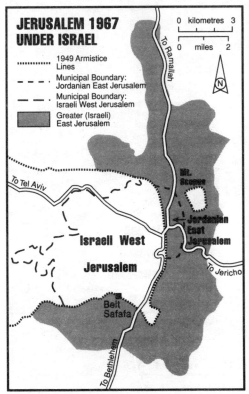

JERUSALEM 1967 UNDER ISRAEL

·········· 1949 Armistice Lines

— — — Municipal Boundary: Jordanian East Jerusalem

– – – Municipal Boundary: Israeli West Jerusalem

Greater (Israeli) East Jerusalem

0 kilometres 3

0 miles 2

N

To Ramallah

To Tel Aviv

Mt. Scopus

Jordanian East Jerusalem

Israeli West Jerusalem

To Jericho

Beit Safafa

To Bethlehem

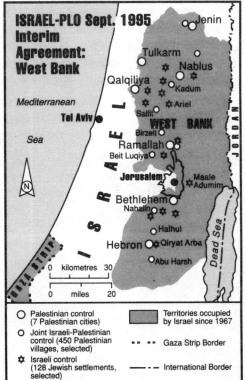

ISRAEL-PLO Sept. 1995 Interim Agreement: West Bank

Jenin

Tulkarm

Nablus

Qalqiliya

Kadum

Ariel

Salfit

WEST BANK

Birzeit

Mediterranean

Sea

Tel Aviv

Ramallah

Beit Luqiya

JORDAN

Jerusalem

Maale Adumim

Bethlehem

Nahalin

ISRAEL

Halhul

Hebron

Qiryat Arba

Abu Harsh

Dead Sea

GAZA STRIP

0 kilometres 30

0 miles 20

N

○ Palestinian control (7 Palestinian cities)

◐ Joint Israeli-Palestinian control (450 Palestinian villages, selected)

✡ Israeli control (128 Jewish settlements, selected)

Territories occupied by Israel since 1967

· · · Gaza Strip Border

— · — International Border

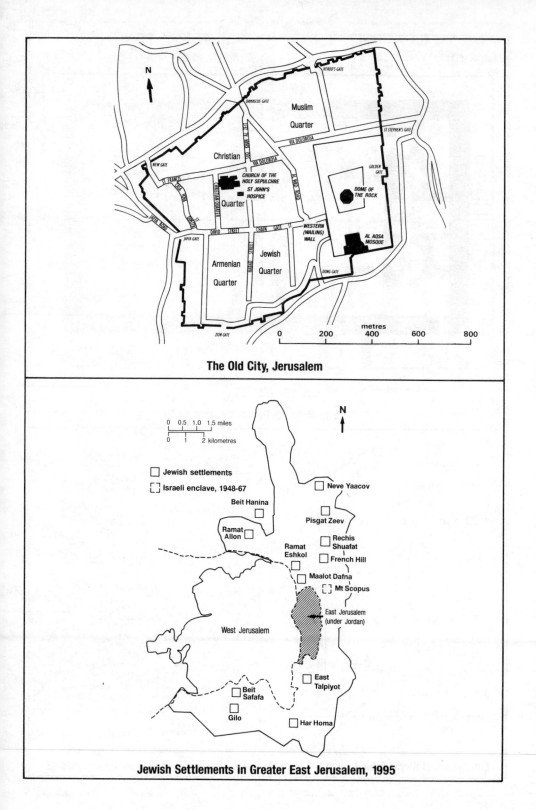

The Old City, Jerusalem

N

Muslim
Quarter

HEROD'S GATE

DAMASCUS GATE

ST STEPHEN'S GATE

VIA DOLOROSA

Christian

VIA DOLOROSA

NEW GATE

GOLDEN
GATE

ST FRANCIS

CHURCH OF THE
HOLY SEPULCHRE
ST JOHN'S
HOSPICE

DOME OF
THE ROCK

CHRISTIAN QUARTER RD

AL WAD ROAD

Quarter

JAFFA ROAD

WESTERN
(WAILING)
WALL

AL AQSA
MOSQUE

DAVID STREET   CHAIN GATE ST

JAFFA GATE

Armenian

Jewish

DUNG GATE

Quarter

Quarter

ZION GATE

metres

| 0 | 200 | 400 | 600 | 800 |

Jewish Settlements in Greater East Jerusalem, 1995

N

0   0.5   1.0   1.5 miles

0   1   2 kilometres

□ Jewish settlements

⌐⌐ Israeli enclave, 1948-67

□ Neve Yaacov

Beit Hanina

□ Pisgat Zeev

Ramat
Allon

□ Rechis
Shuafat

Ramat
Eshkol

□ French Hill

□ Maalot Dafna

⌐⌐ Mt Scopus

East Jerusalem
(under Jordan)

West Jerusalem

□ East
Talpiyot

Beit
Safafa

□ Gilo

□ Har Homa

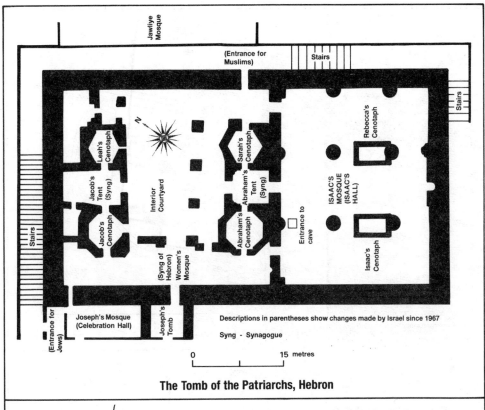

The Tomb of the Patriarchs, Hebron

Jawliye Mosque

(Entrance for Muslims)

Stairs

Stairs

Rebecca's Cenotaph

Leah's Cenotaph

Sarah's Cenotaph

Jacob's Tent (Syng)

Interior Courtyard

Abraham's Tent (Syng)

ISAAC'S MOSQUE (ISAAC'S HALL)

Jacob's Cenotaph

Abraham's Cenotaph

Entrance to cave

Isaac's Cenotaph

Stairs

(Syng of Hebron) Women's Mosque

(Entrance for Jews)

Joseph's Mosque (Celebration Hall)

Joseph's Tomb

Descriptions in parentheses show changes made by Israel since 1967

Syng - Synagogue

0   15 metres

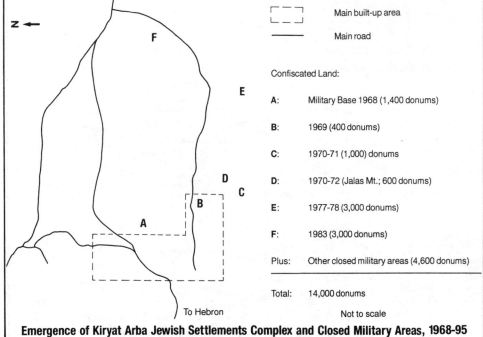

Emergence of Kiryat Arba Jewish Settlements Complex and Closed Military Areas, 1968-95

Z ←

F

E

D

C

B

A

To Hebron

- - - - Main built-up area

——— Main road

Confiscated Land:

A:	Military Base 1968 (1,400 donums)
B:	1969 (400 donums)
C:	1970-71 (1,000) donums
D:	1970-72 (Jalas Mt.; 600 donums)
E:	1977-78 (3,000 donums)
F:	1983 (3,000 donums)
Plus:	Other closed military areas (4,600 donums)
Total:	14,000 donums

Not to scale

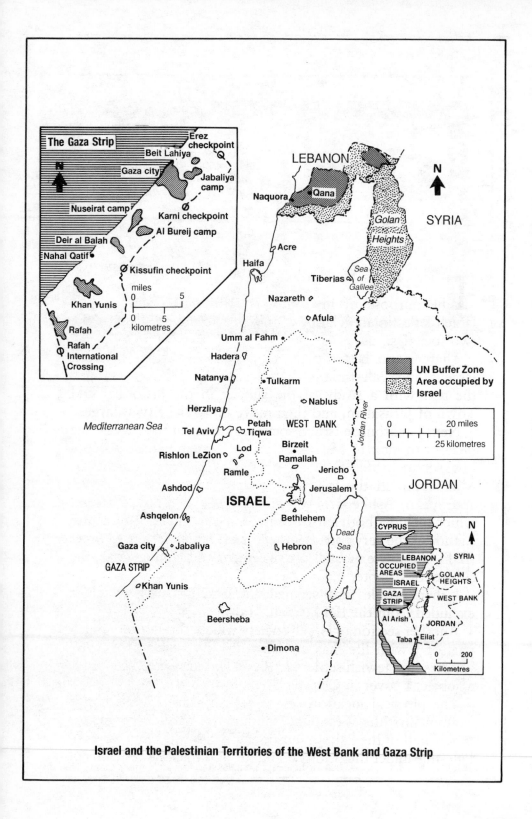

The Gaza Strip

Erez checkpoint
Beit Lahiya
Gaza city
Jabaliya camp
Nuseirat camp
Karni checkpoint
Al Bureij camp
Deir al Balah
Nahal Qatif
Kissufin checkpoint

miles
0   5
0   5
kilometres

Khan Yunis
Rafah
Rafah International Crossing

LEBANON
Naquora
Qana
Golan Heights
SYRIA
Acre
Haifa
Tiberias
Sea of Galilee
Nazareth
Afula
Umm al Fahm
Hadera
Natanya
Tulkarm
Herzliya
Nablus
Mediterranean Sea
Tel Aviv
Petah Tiqwa
WEST BANK
Lod
Birzeit
Rishlon LeZion
Ramallah
Ramle
Jericho
Ashdod
Jerusalem
JORDAN
ISRAEL
Bethlehem
Ashqelon
Dead Sea
Gaza city
Jabaliya
GAZA STRIP
Hebron
Khan Yunis
Beersheba
Dimona

Jordan River

UN Buffer Zone
Area occupied by Israel

0   20 miles
0   25 kilometres

CYPRUS
N
LEBANON
SYRIA
OCCUPIED AREAS
GOLAN HEIGHTS
ISRAEL
GAZA STRIP
WEST BANK
Al Arish
JORDAN
Taba
Eilat
0   200
Kilometres

Israel and the Palestinian Territories of the West Bank and Gaza Strip

PREFACE

The purpose of my book is to describe and analyse Israeli-Palestinian relations, and provide anatomies of the two societies.

There is no better place to examine relations between Israelis and Palestinians than Jerusalem. I therefore open the text with a study of the subject in the historical Old Town of Jerusalem, and then move on to the city at large.

Next I anatomize Israeli society, starting at the edges – the ultra-Orthodox in Mea Shearim, Jerusalem – then proceed inwards to profile Oriental Jews, also called Sephardim or Mizrachim. In the following chapter, my focus is on the (European) Ashkenazim-dominated secular political centre, which includes both left-of-centre Labour and right-of-centre Likud. At the very core of society is the Israeli Defence Forces (IDF), the single most effective cement and homogenizer, the subject of Chapter 6.

I then profile that segment of Israeli society which is excluded from the IDF, Israeli Arabs.

Another section of Israeli society which, though very much part of Jewish life, has chosen to to live beyond the 1967 borders: the Jewish settlers in the West Bank and Gaza Strip, a subject I cover in Chapter 8.

The physical location of the Jewish settlers leads me to examine first the West Bank community, which accounts for nearly half of the Palestinians living within the boundaries of Palestine under the British mandate, and then the residents of

Gaza. In the latter case I enclose a history of the Palestinian intifada (1987–93) without which there would have been no mutual recognition of Israel and the Palestine Liberation Organization in 1993.

My focus then shifts to the Palestine Liberation Organization. Next I turn to the Palestinian Authority and its teething troubles. A study of the Islamic opposition – Hamas and the Islamic Jihad – in the following chapter completes my anatomy of the Palestinian society today.

The penultimate chapter in a way reflects the one on Jerusalem's Old Town, both being rooted in religion. Here I have Jewish and Islamic fundamentalists debate their respective viewpoints within the context of the Divine Promises as recorded in the Old Testament.

Reflecting the title of the concluding chapter, I close my text with a summary of the past and a surmise of the future.

A word about the terms used. An Israeli citizen's identity document mentions 'Nationality: Jew/Arab; and Citizenship: Israeli'. Which term should be qualified – Jew or Arab, or Israeli – and when? It is a complex issue; and everyday terminology is far from logical or consistent. The Israeli state emphasizes Jewishness no matter where a particular Jew lives. So Israeli officials describe, say, Saul Bellow, an eminent novelist, as an American Jew rather than Jewish American. At home they apply the same logic when categorizing those Palestinians who stayed behind in Israel in 1948, calling them 'Israeli Arabs', not 'Arab Israelis'. In the media the terms 'Israeli' and 'Jew' are used interchangeably even though one-sixth of Israelis are not Jewish. In the same way a Palestinian is taken to be a Muslim even though in the Palestinian territories one-tenth of them are Christian. By and large I have stayed with the prevalent convention despite its deficiencies. But when I discuss Israelis in a religious context, say, I qualify them as Jewish or Muslim or Christian.

The dates in brackets after the first mention of a monarch specify when he/she reigned. But corresponding figures for non-hereditary personalities indicate their years of birth and death.

Finally, a word about spellings. Since standard ways of transliterating Arabic and Hebrew words require acutes, graves, ogoneks and so on, and these are not used in the English-language news agencies or newspapers, I have opted for the spellings current in the English-language print media. Within this context I have been consistent – using, for instance, Halacha, not Halakha; Muslim, not Moslem; and Quran, not Koran. The 'al'/'el' in Arabic and 'ha' in Hebrew mean 'the'. For the sake of consistency, I have used the Hebrew definite article always as a combined prefix – HaAretz, not Haaretz or Ha'aretz.

I spent the first three months of 1995 in Israel and the Palestinian territories.

Dilip Hiro

London
June 1996

INTRODUCTION

Israel is exceptional.

You realize this at the start of your journey from abroad. At London's Gatwick airport each airline is identified on the electronic indicator by a letter from the alphabet. But not so the one flying to Israel. The symbol for Monarch, the airline destined for Tel Aviv, Flight MON 4778, on my day of travel, a cold January morning in 1995, was *. Fair enough. Except that nowhere was there a sign leading towards *. The signposting dealt exclusively with the alphabet.

I was supposed to check in three hours before the departure time. I was already late. And nervous. Desperate, I button-holed a young, plump man in a boiler suit collecting luggage trolleys. He approached the multicolour monitor leisurely, stared at the signs for a while, and said: 'A' zone. How did he guess? More pertinently, why did not the airport authorities put 'A' against MON 4778? The trolley man pointed the way to the 'A' zone. I rushed. Before I could get my bearings I was face to face with a posse of police officers wielding sub-machine-guns. 'Tel Aviv?' asked a thin, clean-shaven cop. I nodded yes. He gestured vaguely in the direction of a blank wall. A seam in the wall opened – to reveal an enormous elevator. Lifting my battered suitcase, I stumbled in. The middle-aged men and women around me chattered in Russian. When the elevator reached its destination, we faced not a series of check-out counters, but a vast, white-painted underground bunker with makeshift walls, which blocked the vision of the visitor. Even my untutored mind concluded that the place had been designed to withstand a bomb blast with a minimum of damage to itself and the passengers.

Israel's uniqueness strikes you again, in a different context, as you consider its ancient name (Hebrew, Prevailing with God), and remember that it was established only in 1948. It is a young state, Israel, and a largely immigrant one, populated by the Jews from more than 100 countries.

The mosaic nature of Israel dawned on me one blustery winter afternoon in south Tel Aviv in a café-bakery on Jerusalem Boulevard. Sitting there along with my Hebrew interpreter, Rafi, I was overwhelmed not just by the aroma of cakes and pastries emanating from the incongruously tidy rear of the establishment, but also by the sheer variety of the colour and texture of the desserts in trays of black plastic or varnished wood, stored on the glass-fronted shelves along the walls and displayed in the shop window.

'The ones you see there,' said Rafi, pointing to a distant tray, 'are *rogalakh*, from Poland.' 'Your part of the wood,' I muttered, clutching my cup of coffee to warm my hands. 'My mother's,' Rafi said. 'You forget that my father was born in Britain.' I nodded. He turned towards the shop window. 'That's *shtrodel* there, from Central Europe.' 'Thought Poland was part of Central Europe,' I said. 'Poland is Poland,' came the reply. Rafi turned his face to the trays stacked up behind the cash register. 'Those are *latkes levivot*, from East Europe.' At my behest, he beckoned the young man with a cadaverous face and shining black hair, his hand on the cash register. He came over and sat down in a chair, placing his hairy hands on the white, Formica-topped table. He turned out to be the owner. Where was he from, I wondered aloud. 'Turkey, Izmir,' he replied. His name was Yaacov Nouri. 'What was his favourite cake?' I enquired. '*Uga marokait*,' he replied instantly. 'Sounds Moroccan,' I guessed. 'So it is,' Rafi said. 'I love it, made with pure honey,' Yaacov added, gesturing. He got up and fetched a couple for us. With their dark brown exterior they looked like éclairs. I took a bite, gingerly, at first, then voraciously. So did Rafi. 'Different cakes from different Jewish communities in the world,' Rafi summed up. 'Do they share a common dessert?' I enquired. 'Yes,' replied Yaacov. '*Ozne haman*.' 'The one every Jew eats at the time of the Purim festival,' Rafi explained. 'It marks the liberation of the Jews from the evil designs of Haman, the Prime Minister of King Ahaseurs of Persia.' 'In the fifth century BC,' added Yaacov.

The state policy of 'the ingathering of Jews from the four corners of the world' runs hand in hand with the emphasis that is laid, in official and private circles, to link the Jewish past with the present. Every year on 9 Av, the day the Second Temple was destroyed by the Roman army of Titus in AD 70, the Jews in Israel fast and pray. They shut their eateries, cinemas and theatres. The media devote the day to examining the reasons why the Second Temple fell and the Jews lost their political sovereignty. What lessons can today's Jews draw from that disaster? Are there any parallels between what was and what is? Are contemporary Jews in Israel sliding into the sort of irreconcilable feuding which paved the way for the Jews' defeat and humiliation in the ancient era?

A linkage between the present and the distant past informed and inspired the early Zionists. Their decision to revive Hebrew – long dead as an everyday, spoken language – is a case in point. They were moved as much by negative reasons as positive. They viewed Yiddish as the language of the ghetto, which needed to be abandoned. Thus, revival of Hebrew, a classical language, used for many centuries only in the Jewish liturgy, became closely associated with Zionism. One of the early acts of the pioneering Zionists in Palestine was to set up a Hebrew school. The cementing role of Hebrew among the Zionist settlers of Palestine can hardly be overstated. In a larger context there is correlationship between the rise of Jewish nationalism and the emergence of Hebrew as a living, contemporary language over the past century. During that period Hebrew has flowered as the language of the Jews, first in Palestine, and then in Israel, and now possesses a substantial body of modern literature.

Besides Hebrew, many other aspects of Israeli life today can best be understood in the historical context of Zionism. It started as a religious ideology, and then acquired a

political counterpart. While, from the early twentieth century
onwards, political Zionism forged ahead, religious Zionism
did not disappear. Indeed Zionism evolved as a catch-all
ideology with several strands. As its varied adherents journeyed to Palestine and settled there, they put a different
spin on it – socialist, nationalist, Messianic and religious
fundamentalist.

The metamorphosis of Zionism over time is neatly captured by the Histadrut (Hebrew, Federation). It was established in Palestine in 1920 as an umbrella organization to
encompass all labour-pioneer groups of Zionist persuasion,
with its membership limited to Jewish workers, artisans
and traders. Within a few decades, Histadrut had been
transformed into a multi-faceted body, which combined the
seemingly contradictory roles of a trade union federation
with the ownership of vast industrial and construction
companies and banks, and supplemented it with providing
health insurance and social welfare to most Israelis. Today
Histadrut's commercial and industrial activities are on such a
scale that it employs one-fifth of the total Israeli workforce.

Initially, in the political Zionist camp socialists were the
dominant force. They believed in social equality and dignity
of labour. They put these concepts into practice in Palestine.
A result was the kibbutzim (Hebrew, agricultural communes)
movement, which preceded the 1917 Bolshevik Revolution.
Today egalitarian socialism has disappeared from the political landscape of Israel. Its citizens exalt private enterprise,
and are as addicted to individual gain and consumerism
as Americans. Yet Israeli state and society fondly preserve
kibbutzim, which are struggling to survive in radically altered
circumstances.

Whatever else has changed in the country, the old drive
and enterprise has not. One sees the results of this restless
energy in various spheres of Jewish Israeli life – economic,
social, military and political.

Travelling by bus on a sunny, late February morning from
Jerusalem to Haifa – via Lod, Petah Tiqwa, Kfar Seva,
Hadera, Ein Hod – I witnessed first hand the outcome of the
marriage of natural fecundity and human enterprise in the

coastal strip between the Mediterranean Sea and the inland hills: orchards, fields, and vast, plastic-covered greenhouses, like clouds anchored to the earth. It was as if the coastal plain, 130 kilometres from north to south, Haifa to Ashdod, and some 24 kilometres east to west, had been transformed into one gargantuan garden. Yet the area is also home to nearly two-thirds of the Israeli manufacturing industry, which ranges from food processing to fighter aircraft, and furniture-making to silicon chips. Between my last visit to Israel in the late 1970s and now, the Ben Gurion Airport at Lod had grown from a medium-sized, passenger-friendly facility to a vast complex of buildings, runways and parks, dotted with multicolour billboards, advertising beer, videos and cigarettes. Much else, happily, was still on a human scale. The apartment blocks that filled the towns and cities were seldom higher than four or five storeys. Here and there were homes with slanting red tiles, reminders of Britain, my country of domicile. But unlike in Britain, everything was new here. New, clean and smooth. It was as if I were traversing a large, rural county of an American state, lapped by the Atlantic, on a Greyhound bus. The feeling of being in the United States – as represented by its quiet, rural, small towns – was unmistakable. Later, when I looked up the figures on the Israeli economy, I realized that there was more to my feelings than mere impressions. With a per capita income of $11,675 in 1993, Israel's living standards were about two-thirds of America's. They were almost on a par with those in Britain, a country with two and a half centuries of industrial revolution behind it.

In its drive to develop the coastal belt, Israel has not neglected its arid zone, the Negev. Successful research at the Beersheba University, for instance, has led to an agricultural technique of growing tomatoes and melons on saline water. It was a research institute at the Sede Boqer Kibbutz in the Negev that perfected the technique for using solar energy to heat domestic water. Today the sun reflectors, installed on ceilings almost universally, have made Israeli buildings stand apart in the Mediterranean region.

Like most industrious people, Israelis play as hard as they

work. Since the religious injunctions of the Sabbath require the shutdown of all bars, restaurants, cinemas, theatres and nightclubs, and since the Jewish day begins with the sunset, Israeli enjoyment clusters around Friday afternoon and Saturday night. Little wonder that the Ben Yehuda Mall, the pedestrian precinct closed to vehicular traffic in downtown Jerusalem, comes vibrantly alive on Friday afternoons, with pop music blaring out of loudspeakers at its junction with Jaffa Road.

Loitering around the Ben Yehuda Mall in my shirtsleeves one Friday afternoon in March (spring arrives early in Jerusalem, sometimes a month before the vernal equinox), I felt part of the relaxing, local crowd. The open-air cafés and restaurants, with their clientele spread out on the cobbled streets, were doing brisk business. Pretty, aproned waitresses with ponytails rushed from table to table, and from the customer to the kitchen and back again, adroitly threading their way through furniture and humans, balancing trays as well as their agile bodies. The miscellaneous stores selling clothes, music cassettes, books, electronic gadgetry, shoes, mobile phones, jewellery, take-away pizzas and so on were full. A stubbled old man, dressed in an oversize, camel-colour coat, played a violin to no one in particular. Across the street, a big, black-bearded man, sweating profusely, beat rhythmically a huge medieval wooden instrument, newly restored, with a well-polished baton. When he stopped, a small, appreciative audience clapped. Watching the informally dressed people around me, mostly young and white, often tanned, laced with a dash of blond hair or African kink, I surmised I could be anywhere in a European city of the Mediterranean on a spring Saturday afternoon. Suddenly an exotic sight pulled me up short. A hefty young man, covered in a long white prayer shawl, wearing a *kippa* (Hebrew, skullcap) – his left arm bandaged with a dark leather strap carrying sacred Jewish prayers on parchment tucked inside a small leather box, his forehead strapped tightly with another talisman-like box bearing prayers – intoned a prayer from a printed sheet, watched by two bearded men, one older than the other, the proprietors of the religious paraphernalia. They were laying the *tefillin* (Hebrew, phylacteries), an integral part of saying the Jewish prayer properly, on the young man. In the midst of a hedonistic Jewish multitude gratifying its material needs and cravings, I witnessed a lax Jew being led into the fold of the pious and the religious. Only in Israel, I concluded, does one encounter scenes such as these, religion creeping up at an odd moment and an odder place.

Though created by Jews and described as the Jewish state in the Declaration of the Establishment of the State of Israel (commonly, but wrongly, called the Declaration of Independence) in 1948, Israel is not a religious state. The term 'Jewish' in the Declaration is unqualified. So the State of Israel, strictly speaking, is neither religious nor secular. In practice, though, lacking a state religion, it claims to be secular. Yet its state symbol is religious: the Jewish menorah; and its flag carries the Star of David, a religious emblem. 'The belief of the Jew in his nation is of its essence religious,' notes Colin Thubron, a British writer. 'To judge it in practical or patriotic terms is to mistake its nature.'[1]

The symbiosis between religion and nationalism is aptly captured by the Western (Wailing) Wall in Jerusalem's Old City. In contemporary Israel it is both a holy shrine and a national monument – the site used for celebrating high Jewish holidays as well as staging patriotic rituals such as the swearing in of military officers. The area around the Western Wall is festooned with Israeli flags at all times. Above all, the Wall appears in the second stanza of the Israeli national anthem, 'HaTikva' (Hebrew, The Hope), thus:

> As long as our eyes perceive the beloved Wall
> And tears are shed over the ruins of the Temple
> Our hope is not lost.

On a closer inspection the Declaration of the Establishment, 1948, too inextricably links religion and nationalism. 'The State of Israel will be open for Jewish immigration and for the Ingathering of the Exile', it says. This statement was formalized into the Law of Return, 1950. In effect, this law says that Israel is to be open to Jewish immigrants only.[2] It confers on every Diaspora Jew an inherent right to become an Israeli citizen.

What about the non-Jews living in Israel ever since its founding? For every five Jews then, there was one Muslim or Christian Arab. Did the State of Israel wish to distinguish between one citizen and the other? Yes. Though citizens of Israel, the Arabs were a threat to the fledgeling state so there had to be a way of telling them apart. And it was institutionalized, innovatively, in the classifications to be recorded in the identity card which every adult Israeli citizen was required to carry. *Leum/Quomieh* (Hebrew/Arabic: Nation or Nationality): Jew or Arab; *Izrahut/Janatieh* (Hebrew/Arabic: Citizenship): Israeli. Common citizenship but different nationality. So Jews and Arabs were, and are, treated separately as ethnic groups, not religious. (In any case, since a minority of Arabs are Christian, a strictly religious divide would have become complicated.) Having accepted Arabs as a nationality on a par with Jews, the State of Israel found itself placing Arabic on a par with Hebrew. Thus there are two official languages in Israel: Hebrew and Arabic. That is the theory. Which in practice should mean that all road signs must be in both languages. In reality they are not. None the less, on a higher, abstract plane, the thinking behind the concepts of citizenship and nationality is remarkable, and once again innovative.

For those who think of Jews as a race, a trip to Israel can be an eye-opener. Here you have Jews who are white, European; Jews who are brown, Middle Easterners; and Jews, chiefly from Ethiopia, who are African. At a Jewish settlement on the West Bank I met Ania, the Jewish maid of a leading settler, who, being a member of a Mizo tribe from the Indo-Burmese border area, was a Mongol.

Religiously, Jews in Israel are officially divided into Sephardim (Hebrew, from Spain) and Ashkenazim (Hebrew, from Germany), each sect having its own chief rabbi. Since most Jews of European ancestry, settled in the West and Australasia, belong to the Ashkenazi synagogue, the term Ashkenazim denotes both sectarian affiliation and geographic origin. Not so with the Jews from the Middle East and North Africa. They are described as Sephardim in sectarian terms, and Mizrachim (Hebrew, Orientals) in geographical. Today Mizrachim and Ashkenazim are almost equal in size.

The ingathering of these diverse strands of the world Jewry in Israel has been far from smooth. The Zionist movement was almost wholly Ashkenazi. Its pioneers settled in Palestine, and set the foundations first of the Yishuv (Hebrew, Settlement), the pre-state Jewish community, and then of Israel in the mould of their European background. So when the Jews from the Middle East and North Africa, with Arabic as their mother tongue, arrived in large numbers soon after the establishment of Israel, there was much misunderstanding and tension. The only way, Mizrachi/Oriental Jews soon realized, they could find acceptance and integration into the Israeli society was by abandoning most of what was 'oriental' about them. They did, reluctantly. They and, more particularly, their children underwent westernization, imparted to them formally through the educational system and informally through the state-run broadcasting media. In other words, the intermingling of different cultural and artistic mores that occurred due to the arrival of Diaspora Jews from the West and the East occurred, essentially, on western terms. Today in the cultural sphere western dominance is most obvious in Hebrew literature and in classical music. But pop is more of a hybrid, with the Arab/Oriental music having an edge over the European. Only in cuisine have oriental dishes come to hog the mainstream.

Besides the educational system what helped to acculturate the Mizrachim was the three-year-long conscription into the military, which applied to all Jewish Israelis, male or female. This was a by-product of an innovative system which the founders of the State of Israel devised. They decided to combine maintaining a small standing army with military training for all Jewish Israelis. Such an approach yielded them the best of both worlds: low cost of defending the country, and the creation of a universally trained society which could be fully mobilized within a day or two. The shared experience of serving in the Israel Defence Forces (IDF) became the cement that joined Israeli society across sectarian and ethnic divisions.

Since national security is at the top of the national agenda, the IDF and military service rank high in individual and collective consciousness. Yet merely serving in the IDF is not enough to maintain a highly motivated, mobilized society. The founders of Israel realized this. They were aware, too, of the need for forging and maintaining a national consensus, with no quarter given to scepticism and doubt, surrounded as the fledgeling Jewish state was by rabidly hostile Arab neighbours. Consensus was best achieved by reiterating the moral righteousness of Zionism and Israel.

The most effective tool was, and remains, history – the prism through which Jewish Israelis, like all other people the world over, gain sight of their self-image. 'The Israeli public has been given a one-dimensional version of their own history – beginning with the Jewish colonization of Eretz Israel (Hebrew, Land of Israel) – but especially regarding the events of the [1948] War of Independence and thereafter,' writes Yossi Melman, a senior journalist at *HaAretz* (The Land), a much respected Israeli daily, and the author of *The New Israelis*. 'Like mainstream American historiography, which has painstakingly avoided the embarrassing truth about the massacring of the Native Americans, Israel's history too has been painted in black and white. Israeli myth has its own good guys and bad guys ... [T]he Israeli spin on their own history tells of an unfailingly righteous nation that has always only desired peace. This same legend speaks of how Israel has looked untiringly to open windows of opportunity. But the Arabs, the bad guys, closed the windows and went to war.'[3]

Israel's military doctrine, conceived chiefly by David Ben Gurion (1886–1973), the most eminent of the founders of Israel, and backed by the United States, was, and remains, that the IDF must always maintain qualitative superiority in military hardware and training over the neighbouring Arab states. In other words, Israel should be so militarily powerful that its strength should deter the Arabs from attacking it. Even in 1948 the IDF performed so well in its war with the armies from Egypt, Syria, Jordan, Lebanon and Iraq, that it ended up controlling nearly 75 per cent of Palestine compared to about 54 per cent allocated to the Jews by the United Nations partition plan of November 1947.

During the 1956 Suez War, and later, the IDF proved its prowess in conducting tank warfare. And in the June 1967 War the Israeli air force performed with spectacular brilliance. All in all, Ben Gurion's doctrine was impressively effective for a quarter of a century. The Arab countries did not strike the first blow in 1956 and 1967. Even when Egypt and Syria initiated armed hostilities in 1973 they struck Israel in the Arab territories occupied by it since 1967. That conflict ended in a draw. In contrast, when Israel invaded Lebanon in 1982 its advance was so swift that it reached Beirut within a week. The overall fatalities sum up the picture aptly. In its four major conventional wars with Arabs, from 1948 to 1973, Israel lost a total of 9,520 lives versus the Arab loss of 46,850, a ratio of 1:5.

From humble beginnings, Israel, a country of 4.35 million Jews (who are subject to conscription) today, has built up its defences to the extent that it is currently the ninth most powerful military power on earth. Aside from the five permanent members of the United Nations Security Council, it is the only state that possesses an arsenal of at least 200 nuclear weapons.

However, such massive strength does not make Israel immune from 'the enemy within', the title borne by the Palestinians living under the Israeli military in the West Bank and Gaza Strip since 1967. Twenty years later they demonstrated – to the chagrin of Israeli politicians – the impotence of the IDF soldiers to put down a popular civilian uprising, commonly known as intifada (Arabic, shaking off).

The young Israeli conscripts and the older reservists were ill trained to contain widespread civil unrest, which continued, intermittently, for nearly six years. The IDF was not alone. It worked in conjunction with the police and the security service, called Shin Beth (Hebrew acronym of Sherut Betakhon, Security Service) or Shabak (Hebrew acronym of Sherut Betakhon Klali, General Security Service). Having grasped the vital role played by the Shin Beth's Palestinian agents, the intifada leaders turned their attention to their own 'enemy within' during the latter part of the intifada, and initiated a programme of assassinating the agents. It proved effective. They succeeded in destroying the Israeli network of 20–25,000 Palestinian agents in the West Bank and Gaza Strip. With this, it became a formidable task for the IDF to re-impose full control over the occupied Palestinian territories. As it was, its resort to the curfews, firings on the demonstrators, house searches, beatings and torture, and house demolitions in the Occupied Territories to crush the intifada had a deleterious effect on the democratic, law-abiding ethos of Israel. This happened because the IDF, a largely conscript army, is drawn from Israeli society at large. After active duty in the IDF for three years, at 18, every Israeli male must serve annually for at least a month until he is 54. Because of the intifada the period of reserve duty was extended, often doubled. Among other things this damaged the economy.

Thus the long-running intifada brought to the surface the contradiction that had existed all along between the realization of the Zionist dream – Jewish settlement of Palestine and the ingathering of the world Jewry in Eretz Israel – and its cost to those who lived in Palestine, the Palestinians, in the loss of their homes and their forced exile. Return and construction by one people took place at the expense of expulsion and destruction of the other.

The man who brought this home to me, inadvertently, was an unassuming fisherman in Jaffa, named Muhammad Suri. I met him by chance on a cloudy, but pleasant, February afternoon as, accompanied by Rafi, I explored the old Arab Quarter of historic Jaffa, now part of the Tel Aviv-Yafo metropolis. He was standing by himself, sipping beer from a bottle, at the supermarket where, noticing the signs in Arabic, we had struck up a conversation with the plump manageress wearing a blue skirt and white blouse. A thin, gaunt-faced man, Suri was glad to talk – in fluent Hebrew.

Suri invited us to his home, an old, stone building with steps leading to a platformed threshold. Over cups of Turkish coffee in his front room, he told us that he was born in Acre in 1953 and that his father, a fisherman, migrated to Jaffa when he was five. He was attached to the place, where he had grown up, and to the country, where they had been fishermen for many generations. Referring to the recently arrived Russian immigrants, who were being housed in the Arab Quarter, he alleged official pressures to ease him out of his house. 'I was born in this country, and my father and his father and his father were born here,' he said, raising his voice. 'I'll stay whatever the pressure from the Government. I'll never leave.' Had anybody mentioned his leaving the country? 'No,' he replied. 'But when you have most of your near and dear ones exiled, you have that fear hovering over you all the time.' Where were his blood relations now? He began naming names and where they lived. It got too complicated; and I said so, politely. Suri retreated to his living room, and emerged, holding an old pocket diary. It had the names and phone numbers of his uncles, aunts, cousins – all those with deep roots in Acre – who, in his words, had been 'expelled before and during the 1948 War'. The list was long and varied. It showed Suri's blood relations scattered across the continents: Kuwait city; Miya Miya refugee camp near Sidon, Lebanon; Damascus; Jarash, Jordan; Tunis; Gaza city and Khan Yunis in the Gaza Strip; Copenhagen; Nablus in the West Bank; and Charleston, South Carolina, USA.

Mentally recalling the list of the Jewish Israelis I had interviewed recently, I discovered a symmetry in the ingathering in Israel of the Jews from Poland, Russia, Britain, Turkey, Iran, Morocco, India and the United States of America with the dispersion of Muhammad Suri's relatives from Palestine to Kuwait, Jordan, the West Bank and Gaza Strip, Denmark, Lebanon, Syria, Tunisia and America.

Indeed, of the 6.5 million Palestinians today, roughly a half are in the Diaspora. Of those who live in the Palestine of the British mandate (1922–48), a quarter are in the pre-1967 Israel, classified as 'non-Jews' in official documents and carrying identity cards which describe them as Arab Israelis. The rest are in the West Bank, the Gaza Strip and Greater East Jerusalem under overall Israeli control.

Of these, the residents of the Gaza Strip, about a million

strong, constitute the bottom of the heap, crammed as they are into an area 45 kilometres by eight kilometres – about two-fifths of which, being under Israeli control due to the settlements populated by a mere 4,000 Jewish Israelis, is closed to them. This becomes obvious the moment you cross the military checkpoint from Israel into the Gaza Strip. It is like driving from the affluent suburbs of Los Angeles into the shanty towns of the Bangladeshi capital, Dhaka.

Our taxi drove along a narrow ribbon of a road flanked by wide sandy borders. The buildings were made of breeze blocks, single-storeyed, with an occasional multi-storey structure breaking the monotony. The ribbon widened into a dual carriageway with a sand-covered barrier in the middle, and a narrow pavement on both sides of the road. Suddenly the taxi began making waves in a vast pool of brown water, the result of the previous day's downpour. The driver, a veteran of countless trips between the Gaza Strip and Israel, manoeuvred his sturdy Mercedes-Benz like a pilot guiding a ferry across a treacherous river. In Gaza city he had to be equally deft to steer his vehicle through narrow, winding streets, often used as playgrounds by children. The political graffiti on the walls reminded the visitor of the turbulent past of the territory.

Nearly a half of Gazans live in refugee camps, a hotchpotch of makeshift houses made solid, dirt tracks, and tall, forbidding watch towers. The temporary arrangements made in 1948, meant to last a few months, perhaps a few years, have been turned into permanent, higgledy-piggledy settlements. The inhabitants, young and old alike, make scant distinction between private and public. They have no road sense because there are no roads worth mentioning – only dirt tracks and pot-holed streets, which turn into an unending string of brown puddles after the slightest downpour. Open malodorous channels carry domestic sewage. The garbage disposal is accomplished by an army of goats who can be seen, at all times of the day, attacking the stinking heaps with unflagging gusto. Donkey carts abound. The overall impression is of desolation and dirt: garbage scattered all over, stones, concrete blocks, cinders, torn polythene bags, empty plastic and glass bottles. In the air and on the ground there is a pervasive sense of things left undone, half done – unpaved, unswept streets, rotting piles of garbage, chaotic traffic of men, animals and motorized vehicles on pot-holed roads and dirt streets. All this translates, money-wise, into a per capita income of $930 a year, a measly eight per cent of the figure for an Israeli.

While West Bankers were given opportunity, twice, by the Israeli authorities to elect their representatives to run municipal affairs, Gazans were not. The Gaza Strip thus represented the Israeli military occupation in its rawest form. It was only logical that the intifada should erupt there in the winter of 1987. So deep and abiding was the hatred of the Israeli troops among Gazans that when four winters later there was heavy snow, followed by floods, the IDF came to Jabaliya Camp to help evacuate the residents and save their lives, the people pelted them with stones. The IDF retreated.

The intifada stemmed from 20 years of collective and individual frustrations and humiliations that the Palestinians had endured in their dealings with the Jews and the Israeli authorities, military and civilian. Many of the leaders of the intifada – backed by the secular Palestine Liberation Organization as well as the religious Islamic Resistance Movement, known by its Arabic acronym Hamas – were young educated Palestinians, fluent in Hebrew and familiar with Israeli norms, who took over the communal leadership from the pliant, older generation of Arab notables. The intifada caught the imagination and commitment of most Palestinians. In its first four years, it resulted in the arrest of one out of six male Palestinians. And on average one Palestinian died daily, mostly as a result of firings by the Israeli military or border police.

Until the intifada, Palestinians had put faith in other Arabs to deliver them from the Israeli occupation, and restore *status quo ante*. Ever since the founding of Israel in 1948, Palestinians had hoped that one day a powerful Arab leader on a white horse would arrive and deliver them. This was not to be. Slowly, painfully, they realized that only they could

liberate themselves and establish a nation-state, and that they
had to rely on themselves.

Before reaching that conclusion and acting on it, they
went through different phases since the 1948 Arab-Israeli
War – popularly called *Al Nakbat al Falastin* (Arabic, The
Palestinian Disaster) – which set asunder their society into
three components: the remnants (inside Israel), the refugees
(scattered in the neighbouring Arab states), and the inhabitants of the West Bank (under Jordanian jurisdiction) and
the Gaza Strip (under Egyptian administration).

The remnants conducted politics in traditional Palestinian
ways inside Israel within the limits imposed by the authorities. The exiles participated in the politics of the countries
where they lived. Within a decade, however, they as well as
the remnants inside Israel turned increasingly radical and
adopted rejectionist policies. Their vehement criticism of the
Arab states for their failure to liberate Palestine led the Arab
League to sponsor the formation in 1964 of the Palestine
Liberation Organization.

The June 1967 Arab-Israeli War, which resulted in a swift
and humiliating rout of the Arabs, was the turning point.
With the West Bank and Gaza Strip lost to the Jewish state,
and the Arab neighbours of Israel reeling from their defeat,
the Palestinians and the PLO emerged as the leading players
in their struggle for recovering their land.

They followed a twin-track strategy: attacks on Israeli
and Zionist targets; and the building of a network of
Palestinian organizations – from trade unions, students'
associations, women's groups to doctors' and engineers'
syndicates; and from schools and hospitals to the veterans'
welfare programmes. There was a whole paraphernalia of the
militias of the various groups affiliated to the PLO. Among
other things, the PLO set up the Palestine National Fund
to meet its financial requirements. It was funded by grants
from Arab and other friendly states, and an income tax on
the Palestinians living in the Diaspora. There were uncanny
parallels here with the Zionist movement before the founding
of Israel.

The sharper the reality of the PLO and the Palestinians, the greater the resistance of the Israeli leaders to acknowledge it. Prime Minister Golda Meir (1898–1978) said in 1969 that there were no Palestinians while her aides described them as South Syrians. After her, Prime Minister Yitzhak Rabin (1922–95) graduated to referring to them as 'the so-called Palestinians'. To Prime Minister Menachem Begin (1913–92), in the late 1970s, they were 'the Arabs of Eretz Israel'.

By then the Arab League had recognized the PLO as the sole representative of the Palestinian people, and accorded it full membership; and the United Nations had given the PLO an observer status. The PLO, based in Beirut since 1972, had become a 'state within a state' within Lebanon, helped by the fact that Lebanon slid into a civil war in 1975. The PLO had all the instruments of a state, including foreign missions in scores of countries, but no land of its own.

Israel regarded the PLO's high profile in an adjoining country, which it also used as a base for attacks on Israeli targets, as an intolerable challenge. The result was a fully-fledged invasion of Lebanon by Israel in 1982, and the expulsion of the PLO from Beirut.

With the PLO now banished to distant Tunis, the Palestinians living in the West Bank and Gaza Strip lost any hope they had of being liberated by an outside power. The onus was on them, and them alone. They met the challenge. In five years they were up in arms against their occupiers, the Israel Defence Forces. They mounted their intifada. It was their struggle and it was headed by local leaders. The PLO backed it. So did Hamas, based in the Occupied Territories. The intifada continued, off and on, for several years.

It ended in September 1993 with the signing of an accord between Israel and the PLO in Washington. The agreement was a compromise. The PLO accepted Israel's right to exist in security, and the Jewish state recognized the PLO as the representative of the Palestinian people living in the Occupied Territories of the West Bank and Gaza Strip. Their right to self-rule was to be put into practice, in stages.

Which side compromised more and which less remains a point of debate. What is indisputable, though, is that the overall achievement of Zionism and Israel has been stupendous. In 1897 when the first Congress of the (World) Zionist Organization, meeting in Basle, Switzerland, resolved to 'create for the Jewish people a home in Palestine secured by public law', nobody, except possibly the convenor of the assembly, Theodor Herzl (1860–1904), seriously hoped to see this goal achieved. It was only after the collapse of the Ottoman Turkish empire, whose Arab domain included Palestine, in October 1918, coupled with the declaration a year earlier by the British Foreign Secretary, Arthur James (later Lord) Balfour, favouring 'the establishment in Palestine of a National Home for the Jewish people', that the situation changed dramatically. Once Britain had been given a mandate over Palestine by the League of Nations in 1922, the pace of systematic Jewish immigration accelerated. By the time Britain handed over the 'problem of Palestine' to the United Nations, the successor to the League of Nations, in 1947, the Jews were 30 per cent of the population, four times more numerous than three decades before.

'The international achievement of Zionism is in having taken hold of Palestine from within Palestine and, no less important, having made the native Palestinian population seem like the outsider,' writes Edward W. Said, an eminent Palestinian intellectual and professor at Columbia University, New York. 'Most of the time thereafter, Palestinians have found themselves in the situation of someone outside looking in, and finding that fact of banishment to be the main defining characteristic of [their] existence . . . We have now become disinherited outsiders.'[4]

These words were fresh in my mind when I arrived one cold, sunny morning in March at the Deheisheh Refugee Camp on the outskirts of Bethlehem along the road to Hebron. Surrounded by a five-metre-high steel-wire fence, the camp was hard to miss. Equally hard to miss was the stench, the result of broken sewerage pipes, that hung over it like a cloud. Yet the camp dwellers assured me that the air was not as malodorous that day as on others.

Home to over 8,500 Palestinians, Deheisheh is unwieldy, the dwellings of its residents, often large, extended families, branching out like wild plants, into rooms, halls and niches held together by cement and rusting steel plates. None of them had running water. The only flowing liquid, in public, was the sewage, making its way between the dwellings, when it could, by the force of gravity. The camp dwellers, displaced from their native homes by the violence of the past, talked fondly of their birth places in Palestine. Muhammad Yusuf Suleiman, a neat man of 55 with a clipped salt-and-pepper beard, who had been living in the camp since 1954, said: 'I come from the village of Deir Aban in Ramle district [now in Israel]. I still have land there. I hope to return before I die.' His naïvety, without the slightest hint of irony, was touching. In his freshly pressed traditional Arab dress, he seemed a man from the distant past.

Not so Milhem Elian, the owner of an almost empty clothes shop in a narrow, winding street. Brought to the camp in 1949 by his parents at the age of 18 months, Elian, a tall, well-built man with thinning hair, in dark brown pants and blue bush-shirt, had known no other place. The experience had hardened him. He claimed to be the first camp resident to be imprisoned by the IDF in 1967 soon after Israel occupied the West Bank. He had married and raised a family. 'We live in a room not large enough for chickens,' he said. 'Six people in a room, six metres by five. But one Jew and his wife have a whole villa to themselves. You can go and see for yourself – at the [nearby] Efrat settlement.' He pointed, vaguely, southwards. 'These Jews come from abroad, from Russia, from Argentina and America, take our land and live like lords while we [the native born] are forced to live like animals.'

I took Elian's advice and journeyed a few kilometres south. On the hills overlooking the highway stood a new settlement – gleaming in the afternoon sun, white stone buildings with red-tiled roofs. This was Efrat. Having arrived from an over-crowded, stench-filled refugee camp, I found the air at Efrat particularly bracing. There were only a few people about in the smoothly paved streets. Many of the freshly painted houses, detached or semi-detached, were indeed empty.

What had the people claiming an almost continuous political-cultural history since the advent of Islam in the region – displayed dramatically in the form of the golden Dome of the Rock, built in AD 691, on Mount Moriah – done to find themselves refugees in their own land? The question kept nagging me.

Reading my notes of the visits to the Palestinian refugee camps and the Israeli absorption centres for new immigrants, I was struck by the stark contrast between these places. I was deeply impressed by the meticulous care the Jewish Agency and the Israeli Ministry of Immigration and Absorption took in preparing the immigrant before his aliya (Hebrew, ascent) to Israel, and the systematic follow-up that ensued. At the absorption centres at East Talpiyot, Jerusalem, the talk was all about getting a job for the newly-arrived immigrant, fitting it into his/her life, and the pros and cons of certain houses and neighbourhoods of Jerusalem. When the focus turned to subjects more social than personal, it was the Palestinian terror that got mentioned invariably, and the continuing, frustrating elusiveness of a comprehensive peace with the Arabs.

The priorities were altogether different in the Palestinian refugee camps. The camp dwellers talked of joblessness, survival, making ends meet. They reminisced about their home villages now in Israel. They complained of the indignities they had suffered at the hands of the IDF or the police. They described their imprisonments and detentions during the intifada, and their injuries, resulting from IDF firings. They related how their land had been confiscated by the Israeli authorities, a process which continued unabated, the peace accord or not, and had by now placed nearly two-thirds of all West Bank land into the Israeli hands. They described the juggernaut of the Jewish settlements ravaging the West Bank, and the unrelenting Judaization of their places and their everyday life.

So what solution do they have in mind? Repossession of the land and realization of the Palestinian statehood. 'An independent and sovereign Palestinian state is required at this stage to fulfil our history as a people during the past century,' writes Edward W. Said. 'The inventory of what we are and what we have done and what has been done to us can never be completely justified, or even embodied, in a state. The converse of this view – that a state *can* rectify, defend against, and embody the memory of a past history of suffering – has seemed to Palestinians to account for Israeli theorizing, and for Zionist practice in creating a state apart for Jews.'[5]

If such a state comes into being some day – against persistent and heavy odds – it would be less than a quarter of the Palestine under British mandate, and would cover about half of the area allocated to the Arab Palestinians by the 1947 United Nations partition plan.

1

THE WALLED HEART OF JERUSALEM:

A Battleground

The Old Town, the heart of Jerusalem, sacred to every other human being on earth, is bounded by magnificent, crenellated walls. There is nothing more bracing than a march along its ramparts on a spring morning, I was told. The thought of circling the religious nucleus of Jerusalem – where Abraham prepared to sacrifice his sons Isaac and Ishmael (called Ishaq and Ismail respectively by Muslims), the Jews built their two Temples, Jesus Christ preached his doctrine and died of crucifixion, and Prophet Muhammad broke his miraculous night journey from Mecca to Heaven – kept me awake overnight.

Predictably, my point of ascent was the Damascus Gate – known among Jews as Shaar Shechem, Gate of Shechem/Nablus, and among Arabs as Bab al Amoud, Gate of the Column (now extant) – the threshold to the Old Town, the undisputed leader of the gates, an emblem of authority. I ambled along westward, to the Jaffa Gate, and then the Dung Gate, beyond which the town walls were sealed. I saw Islamic minarets rise above church bell-towers, and Israeli flags flutter in the air. Despite the television aerials sprouting from variously shaped roofs – flat, domed, spiked, slanting – like so many weeds on a wilting lawn, I found the Old Town's ambience decidedly medieval. After all, the massive stone walls were erected in 1537–40 by Ottoman Sultan Suleiman the Magnificent (r. 1520–66), preserving approximately the shape that the settlement had in 1187 when Saladin (Salah al Din Ayubi) recaptured it from the Crusaders, and began reconstructing it. Malik al Muazzam Isa razed the old boundaries in 1219, allowing the town to expand. But its sack by the Mongols in 1244 set the clock back again. It was only under the Mameluke sultans (r. 1248–1517) that the settlement witnessed sustained reconstruction and expansion. By the time the Ottoman Turks seized the Old Town it was furnished with mosques, religious schools, pilgrims' hostels, orphanages and hospitals. All along it enclasped the holiest of holies of the major monotheistic faiths: the Dome of the Rock and Al Asqa (Arabic, The Distant) Mosque, the Church of the Holy Sepulchre, and the ancient Western Wall.

Viewing the Western Wall (HaKotel HaMa'aravi, in Hebrew) from the Dung Gate along the southern rampart, I saw men and women worshipping stones. Or was I imagining? I hazily remembered reading that some ultra-Orthodox Jews regarded revering the stones of the Wall as a form of idol worship. Later when I mentioned this to Rafi, my Hebrew interpreter, he said dismissively: 'Crackpots!'

One cloudless day in March, accompanied by Rafi, I visited the Kotel, the popular term for the Western Wall. A supporting wall, running north to south, and fronted by a vast plaza of bright stone, it is enclosed. Access to it is gained strictly through police checkpoints, furnished with metal detectors, which, unknown to all save the exceptionally curious, are switched off on the Sabbath.

We approached the monument from the Jewish Quarter, standing on an elevated ground to its west, and descended many steps of stone on to a rectangular plaza, large enough to hold a congregation of over 100,000, sloping gently eastwards. The warm afternoon sun behind us shone on a wall (in front of us) some 90 metres long and 22 metres high, austere, except for occasional prickly capers between its ashlars swaying in mild wind, like tufts of hair on a featureless face. This was the Kotel. It was divided unevenly by movable steel-wire fences, about a metre high, laid perpendicular to the monument, with women on our (smaller) right side, and men on the (larger) left. Another temporary barrier running parallel to the Kotel regulated the approach to it, with an opening at each of the two opposite ends, a makeshift gate. Here a plump, spectacled man gave us thin cardboard *kippas*, skullcaps. 'Throughout the day and night, rain or shine, there is somebody present here, facing the wall in prayer,' he said. 'There are more people inside the tunnel,' Rafi added – pointing to a vaulted entrance into the wall behind the gatekeeper that joined the Kotel at a right angle – 'praying at all hours.'

I found men, young, old, middle-aged, in black coats and hats at prayer in assorted ways. Some gently pressed the Kotel with their palms, an evocative gesture, whispering all the while. Others, gathered in small groups, chanted their devotions from books, swaying back and forth. Some kissed the smooth, weather-beaten stones. I counted 12 courses of massive, shiny stones – chiselled by the masons of King Herod Antipas (r. 4 BC – AD 40) – topped by many layers of stones of much smaller sizes.

The Jews revere the Kotel as the only surviving fragment of their Second Temple, destroyed by Roman Emperor Titus 30 years after Herod's death. It is in reality a retaining wall on the western side built to buttress the windy rock, called Mount Moriah, on which the Temple stood.

What is so sacred about the Kotel, and why do the Jews come here? Rafi and I buttonholed the devout as they left.

'This is where Abraham offered to sacrifice his son, Isaac; this is where Jacob was on his way,' said Joel Beinin, a tall, graceful, black-coated man in his middle age, thickly bearded, wearing a ferral hat. 'This is where Solomon built the First Temple; and this is where it was destroyed after 400 years, and the Jews came back from Babylon and built it again,' he continued. He was apparently referring to the flattened summit, Mount Moriah, not to the part of a buttressing.

'Holiness is never far from here. King David had promised that it [the Mount] would never be ruined, and it has never been [for long]. The courtyard was 250 metres long in those days; this is part of its outer [western] wall which survived.'

There are legends about why the Western Wall survived. One version has it that different sections of the Second Temple were raised by different social classes, with the Western Wall of its courtyard erected by the poor. When Titus went on a rampage in Jerusalem, setting it alight, angels blessed the Western Wall with their wings, declaring: 'This work of the poor shall be indestructible.' And it was. Exactly when the Kotel became sacred is shrouded in mystery. There is a reference to its holiness in the twelfth century by Benjamin of Tudela. After the destruction of the Second Temple, the Jews were permitted to enter Jerusalem only on 9 Av, the anniversary of the sacking of the Second Temple. Since the pilgrims would go up in silence and descend in tears, the Wall acquired the epithet, Wailing. The purpose of the pilgrimage thus became lamenting the razing of the Temples. (Every so often, I was told, you see a Jew crying quietly, re-enacting the grieving of his ancient forebears.) Now, with an open, unhindered access to the Wall, the purpose of the pilgrimage has changed drastically.

'Coming here is like going to the king's palace,' said Joel Landover, a tall, 52-year-old accountant in a business suit. 'When you go inside [the synagogue] under the vaults you are near the holy of the holies, and nearest to God, so you can add more to your prayer and say what you cannot at home.'

Accompanied by Rafi, I entered the synagogue in the wide, vaulted tunnel about 300 metres long, deftly lit to produce eternal sunshine, an element which added to the congeniality of the place. The groups of worshippers, donning black hats or (sometimes) kippas, in grey or charcoal-black business suits, gathered around tables stacked with prayer books, invoking the Lord; others facing the Wall, sitting in tubular steel chairs with sky-blue seats, immersed themselves in the scriptures; others offered prayers in front of an ark, containing a sacred Torah scroll behind a black cloth embellished with golden Hebrew lettering. 'Reading prayers from a book concentrates the mind,' Rafi explained. 'If the Jews are gathered in a group to pray then the books become like music score sheets.' Facing the ancient monument, lined up against another wall, running parallel, were five shelves of prayer books of assorted sizes, hardbacks, some of them tattered through over-use, classified on one side 'Ashkenazi Version' and on the other 'Sephardi Version'. Deeper into the tunnel the worshippers, singing Psalms, were lost to the world. Which psalm was the most popular, I asked Rafi. 'Offhand, I'd say 137.' Prompted by me Rafi recited it:

By the rivers of Babylon, there we sat down, yea, we wept, when we remembered Zion.
We hung our harps upon the willows in the midst thereof.
For there they that carried us away captive required of us as a song; and they that wasted us required of us mirth, saying, Sing us one of the songs of Zion.
How shall we sing the Lord's song in a strange land?
If I forget thee, O Jerusalem, let my right hand forget her cunning.
If I do not remember thee, let my tongue cleave to the roof of my mouth; if I prefer not Jerusalem above my chief joy.
Remember, O Lord, the children of Edom in the day of Jerusalem who said, Rase it, rase it, even to the foundation thereof.
O daughter of Babylon, who art to be destroyed; happy shall he be, that rewardeth thee as thou has served us.
Happy shall he be, that taketh and dasheth thy little ones against the stones.[1]

It was a very moving text, I remarked, as Rafi returned to his normal, laid-back demeanour.

On turning around and leaving the cavernous synagogue, I changed not just light and air, but the very essence of my existence: it felt as if I had touched solid ground after spinning around in outer space.

Rafi and I resumed our humdrum conversation with the

faithful. Nahum Shahak, who disguised his thinness with baggy dark trousers and an oversize black coat, told me about the ancient shrine itself. 'The lower stones of the Wall are original,' he said. 'The other stones were put in by Sir Moses Montefiore [of London] in the nineteenth century.' He was wrong about Sir Moses. The 20-odd layers above the Herodian bottom were built and rebuilt first by the Crusaders and then Ottoman sultans, the rulers of Palestine from December 1516 to December 1917, all of them using smaller stones than the original.

'I pray for half an hour by myself, and don't participate in communal chanting like others,' said Micah Watt, a plumpish, ruddy-cheeked, middle-aged resident of Jerusalem's ultra-Orthodox neighbourhood of Mea Shearim. 'Also I don't make a request. Real ultra-Orthodox don't address notes to God. There is no such tradition in Judaism.'

Watt was referrng to the practice of supplicants pressing their scribbled prayers and pleas on folded paper between the cracks of the Herodian stones, treating the Kotel as a post-box to God. The practice dates back to the eighteenth century. Now the religious authorities have given it a hi-tech touch. They have installed a fax machine, I was told, for the convenience of those faraway believers, at home and abroad, who are too busy or depressed to make the pilgrimage and do the deed with their own hands. Every few days the caretakers remove the notes, which have survived wind, rain and dew, and bury them ceremoniously in consecrated ground.

There is much ritual in Judaism, and I witnessed it as a wizened old man in a colourful skullcap noticed the *kippa*-less thatch of Rafi's wavy hair, an unmistakable sign of secularism, and confronted him with a set of phylacteries, *tefillin*. A bashful Rafi submitted. 'The idea behind the *tefillin* is to have the prayer boxes touch your arm, representing force, and your head, representing intellect,' Rafi said. 'You must say at least three prayers like this daily – on waking up, between nine o'clock and noon, and at sunset.'

Rafi then perked up as he described a ceremony at the Wall he remembered with fondness and pride. It was against the backdrop of the Wall that he had paraded on his graduation in the Israeli Defence Forces in his late teens. Was it before or after the hand-grenade attack at the Western Wall, I wondered. 'Before,' he replied grimly. 'That was awful. The Islamic Jihad terrorists. It was the graduation ceremony of the Givati Brigade, if I remember it right, on the Feast of the Tabernacles, in [October] 1986. The terrorists threw hand grenades at the parade from the Temple Mount.' How many? 'I don't know,' he said. 'A few. But enough to cause a carnage. About 70 soldiers were injured. And one man died, a spectator. The outrage was unspeakable. The Government caught the perpetrators though. Three of them, I think, two were brothers, young Palestinians. After that the Government tightened up security all around the Wall.' There was a long pause. 'There have been happier times, secularly speaking, at the monument,' Rafi continued. 'Like when Yehudi Menuhin gave a concert here to celebrate the Israeli-Egyptian Peace Treaty in 1979, and my parents and I came here from Tel Aviv to listen.'

In short, the Western Wall today is as much a national monument as religious – along with the Yad Vashem, the Museum of Holocaust and Heroism, in West Jerusalem. The many Israeli flags pinned to the Wall precinct flaunt the shrine's national significance. '[F]or centuries this [Wall] was the focal point of their mourning [of] the destruction of the Holy Temple, and the exile and dispersion that followed,' write Michael Romann and Alex Weingrod, Jewish Israeli academics. 'Since Jerusalem's unification under Israeli sovereignty in 1967, the Kotel represents their triumphant return and control over the entire city [of Jerusalem].'[2]

Rafi and I retreated to the Jewish Quarter to revive ourselves with cappuccino and dainty Jewish cakes. We sat in wooden chairs on cobbled stones on HaKaraim Street, not far from Batei Machse Square, beyond which ran Habad Street/Suq al Huzor, the eastern boundary of the Jewish Quarter. Bounded by this street to the east and Chain Gate Street to the north, it measures 12 hectares, about an eighth of the Old Town. Its chronicle is long and chequered.

Though the Second Temple was razed in AD 70, the Jews were expelled from Jerusalem only after their revolt collapsed in AD 135. They were permitted to return in the fifth century. During the Crusades (1099–1187) they were as much victims of Christian zealotry as were Muslims. The defeat of the Crusaders, who had ended the Jewish presence in Jerusalem, by Saladin in 1187 brought relief to the Jews. But it was only after the walls had been demolished in 1219 by Malik Isa, and the settlement had been sacked by the Mongols a quarter of a century later, followed by the rule of the Mamelukes, that the Jews got a chance to strike roots in Jerusalem. In the early fifteenth century they began renting property from Muslim landlords. According to al Obeidiah of Bertinoro, who visited Jerusalem in 1488, there were about 200 Jewish families settled in the town, with their own synagogue named after Rabbi Moshe Ben Nahuman, and known in Hebrew by his acronymn RMBN, Ramban, who had visited the town in 1267. The Jews now had two religious monuments: the Wall, separated from the nearest houses by a three-metre-wide alley in an area called the Magharebi (the Arabic term used for the Western Arab world of North Africa) Quarter, and the Ramban synagogue. (In contrast Christians possessed 118 buildings related to their religion, and Muslims about 480.)

After the Ottoman conquest of Palestine in late 1516, some of the Sephardic Jews who had settled in Turkey after their expulsion from Spain in 1492, moved to Jerusalem. This led to the construction of four Sephardi synagogues – Elijah, Emtzai/Khal Zion (also called Central), Istambouli and Yohanan Ben Zakkai – in the late sixteenth century. There were 324 Jewish property owners. In the early nineteenth century the population of Jerusalem was nearly 8,000, about a quarter of whom were Jews. Following the rebellion by their Egyptian Governor, Muhammad Ali, in 1831, the Ottomans imposed direct rule over Jerusalem and its environs. The improved security caused an increase in the local population. The Ottomans granted equal rights to non-Muslims, and appointed them to the local municipal council. The first reliable demographic figures became available after Sir Moses Montefiore of London conducted a protostatistical census in 1839. It revealed 3,000 Jews, with varied backgrounds, among a total of some 10,000 residents. By the mid-nineteenth century there were over a score of synagogues in the Jewish Quarter.

Once houses were raised for Jews outside the ramparts in the New Town, from 1860 onwards, the number of Jews in the overcrowded, unsanitary Old Town declined. A combined census of the Old and New Towns in 1875, sponsored again by Sir Moses Montefiore, showed 10,000 Jews out of a total population of 20,000. Due to the Jewish immigration inspired and encouraged by the Zionist Organ-ization (later World Zionist Organization), an international body founded in 1897, the number of Jews in the two Towns rose sharply. In 1905 two-thirds of the total population of 60,000 was Jewish, with most of the Jews residing outside the historic, walled settlement. When during World War I the British captured Jerusalem in December 1917, there were 14,000 Jews living in the Old Town. The Western Wall was in the Magharebi (Arabic, western) Quarter – inhabited by the Arabs of North African descent, some of whom had lived there since Saladin's victory – which opened to the outside world through the Gate of the Magharebi Quarter, now popularly known as the Dung Gate.

During the British mandate, a form of trusteeship, which formally commenced in 1922 and lasted 26 years, relations between Jews and Arabs soured. Due to the Arab-Jewish rioting in 1921, 1926 and 1929 – stemming from the protest by the native Arabs against the escalating Jewish immigration under the British auspices – the number of Jews in the Old Town shrank to 5,600. It declined further after the eruption of the Arab Revolt in 1936 which continued for three years, and which led the British to move the Jews out of the non-Jewish Quarters into the Jewish Quarter for their own safety. The Jews either kept their real estate empty or leased it to Arabs, and many moved to the Jewish neighbourhoods of the New Town. (However, due to the long-established tradition of 'key-money', the Jewish occupancy was often based more on purchasing tenancy rights by paying 'key-money' rather than acquiring outright ownership. Also in most instances the land on which the real estate was built belonged to local patrician Arab families.)

Long before the United Nations General Assembly adopted a resolution for partitioning Palestine into Arab and Jewish sectors in November 1947, Jerusalem was virtually split into two parts – Arab East and Jewish West – with their inhabitants clashing frequently. By the time the British left in May 1948, there were only 1,700 Jews in the Jewish Quarter of the Old Town, and another 300 elsewhere in Arab East Jerusalem.

During the 1948 Arab-Israeli War fighting erupted in the Old Town. The inhabitants of the Jewish Quarter confronted the Jordanian army, and suffered 86 deaths and much damage to private and public property, including synagogues and yeshivas (Hebrew, sitting), religious academies. Finally some 2,000 unarmed Jews gathered at the four Sephardi synagogues to surrender to the Jordanian army, and were later transferred to Israel. (On the other side, some 20,000 Arabs fled Jewish West Jerusalem, controlled by Israel.) The Arab residents of the Old Town sacked the Jewish Quarter; and the victorious Jordanian army demolished the synagogues and yeshivas based in the area.

The Old Town, measuring almost one square kilometre, was about one-seventh of the Arab East Jerusalem under Jordanian control. Though Jordan's truce agreement with Israel, enforced in April 1949, required it to give Jews access to the Western Wall, it did not do so. Equally, it barred Israeli Arabs, whether Muslim or Christian, from visiting their holy places in the Old Town of Jerusalem or Bethlehem. On the eve of the June 1967 Arab-Israeli War, the population of East Jerusalem was over 60,000.

On 7 June, the third day of the Six Day Arab-Israeli War, the Israelis captured the Old Town. General Moshe Dayan, the Israeli Defence Minister, instantly recognizable by his black eye-patch, was among the first Jews to pray at the Western Wall. After prayers he inserted a petition beseeching God: 'Let peace reign in Israel.' He then declared: 'We have come back to our holiest of holy places, never to be parted from it again.'[3]

After sunset on 10 June, Saturday, while the war was still in progress, according to Meron Benvensiti, an Israeli historian and former deputy mayor of Jerusalem, the residents of the Magharebi Quarter were given three hours to evacuate their buildings adjacent to the Western Wall. 'Bulldozers . . . began to topple the one- and two-storey houses by floodlight,' writes Benvensiti. 'By morning a space of more than one acre had been cleared in front of the Western Wall . . . It was then decided to demolish the entire Magharebi Quarter [consisting of 80 houses, shops and a plastic factory, and 619 residents].'[4] The levelled ground was later turned into a plaza.

On 27 June, a little over a fortnight after the end of the Six Day War, Israel's parliament, the Knesset (Hebrew, Assembly) expanded Jordanian East Jerusalem from 6.5 square kilometres to nearly 74 square kilometres (including the Mount Scopus enclave, measuring 2 square kilometres, that Israel had retained during and after the 1948 War), and annexed it, and claimed unification of West and East Jerusalem into a single city under Israeli sovereignty. Due to the flight of about 30 per cent of the 60,000 residents of (Jordanian) East Jerusalem during and after the war, its population declined to 44,000. But the addition of the huge adjoining area to Jordanian East Jerusalem raised the total population of 'Greater East Jerusalem' to 71,000, as recorded by an Israeli census in September 1967. According to the new Israeli law, all of the new East Jerusalemites became 'permanent residents' of Israel, and received Israeli identity cards, which entitled them to social security and healthcare benefits and voting rights in municipal elections. It also gave them the option of abandoning their current Jordanian citizenship for an Israeli one. With a few exceptions, they ignored the offer.

In April 1968 the Government set up a public company, the Jewish Quarter Restoration and Development Corporation (JQRADC), to revive and resettle the quarter. Its activities covered an area larger than the old Jewish Quarter. This was, in the words of Amos Elon, 'a defiant assertion of a presence even more than a restoration of what had been lost'.[5] It occurred at the cost of expropriation of land and houses of 5,500 Palestinians.[6]

The new real estate was sold exclusively to Jews. Non-Jews could not buy, or even rent, property in the enlarged Jewish Quarter. The Palestinians challenged the official decision on two separate grounds, in 1968 and 1974: first to resist eviction from their homes they had occupied since 1948 or earlier in the old Jewish Quarter; and then to buy property in the new one. Both times the Israeli High Court of Justice ruled in favour of the Government.

In each case it was Muhammad Burqan who moved the court. He was evicted from his family home in the pre-1948 Jewish Quarter in the mass expulsion of 1968. The High Court turned down his appeal against the JQRADC. It argued that the JQRADC's refusal to permit an Arab Jordanian citizen to remain in his home was not an act of discrimination in view of Jordan's expulsion of the Jews and the demolition of their Quarter in the Old Town in 1948. Furthermore the court rationalized the restoration of an exclusively Jewish Quarter beside the Muslim, Christian and Armenian Quarters in the Old City in terms of history, politics and national security. (However, despite their names, the Muslim, Christian and Armenian Quarters were not exclusive: each of them contained more than one religious or ethnic group.) In 1974, when the JQRADC put Burqan's renovated house up for sale he tried to buy it back. But he was barred. The ban was sustained by the High Court. Advancing a broad politico-historical argument, the court stated that since there had 'always' been a distinctive Jewish Quarter in the Old Town, there should once again be such a neighbourhood. As the 'non-Jews' had three other quarters (Armenian, Christian and Muslim) to themselves, it concluded, the Government could keep the Jewish Quarter free of non-Jews.[7] The residents of the new Jewish Quarter were so zealous about keeping it pure that when the remains of a twelfth-century church were found in the midst of their district in the mid-1970s, some of them vandalized the plaque on the partially restored site, forcing the authorities to replace the old sign, 'St Mary of the Germans', with 'archaeological garden'.[8]

It is worth noting that the legal restrictions on non-Jews

regarding owning or renting real estate in the Jewish Quarter do not apply to Jews wishing to buy or rent non-Jewish property in the non-Jewish quarters either inside the Old Town or outside.

The restored Jewish Quarter is starkly different from the others. Its quiet, children-free streets, newly paved and lighted, its arched passageways, and its houses made of new stone, often in neoromantic style, and fitted with vaulted windows, give it an appearance of an expensive, gentrified district, tarted up with art galleries, souvenir shops, studios and craft boutiques. Its public places, dominated by new or restored synagogues and yeshivas of imposing proportions, rob the district of the intimacy, warmth and a touch of chaos that are the hallmarks of the Muslim, Christian and Armenian Quarters. Its population density of 71 per acre is only two-fifths that of the Muslim Quarter, home to some 20,000 people.

The Batei Machse Square, an open space signposted by a Greek column, a possible relic of the Herodian times, aptly captures the comparative spaciousness of the Jewish Quarter. The sun was setting behind the ramparts of the Old Town as we loitered around the square. Just as the muzzeins called the faithful to prayer a peal of church bells sonorously stirred the calm air. Near the far wall a couple of bearded old Jewish men sat on benches gazing at the children at play. We wandered over, and read the inscribed engraving on the wall:

Thus saith Lord of Hosts; There shall yet old man and old women/ dwell in the streets of Jerusalem, and every man with his staff in his/ hand for every age.

And the streets of the city shall be full of boys and girls playing. Zechariah.

An estimated 2–2,500 Jews are permanently resident in the Jewish Quarter. A proportion of the apartments, highly priced by any standard, are owned by Jewish Americans, who only occupy them for part of the year. There are seven yeshivas, some of whose students live in the quarter. Most of the permanent residents are middle-class professionals, almost invariably practising Orthodox or ultra-Orthodox. At the corner of the Batei Machse Square and HaMekubalim Street, a large leaflet, stuck between notices for flat-sharing, herbal medicine and curry food, neatly summed up the ambience of the quarter:

> The Time for Your Redemption has Arrived!
> What is the Messianic Era?
> What does 'MASHIAIH' mean?
> Why is Now an 'Era of Miracles'? Consider
> * The Unforseen Collapse of the Iron Curtain & its Satellite regimes
> * Ingathering of 100s of thousands of suppressed and stricken exiles, converging in the Holy Land from undreamt of directions
> * In the Persian Gulf . . . lightning-quick victory and the Divine Protection of Israel.
> What can I do?
> Listen to the Lubanvitcher Rabbi, Rabbi Menach M. Schneerson, who has appealed to every individual.

Since there are no legal restrictions on Jews to buy or rent non-Jewish property in the non-Jewish quarters in the Old Town (or outside), there are Jews who reside outside their quarter. Almost invariably they are ultra-nationalist, determined to 'redeem' all of the Old Town from its Christian and Muslim inhabitants. Since 1978, often working in covert collusion with the Israeli Government – run by the right-wing Likud (Hebrew, Unity) either as the leading coalition partner or as an equal with left of centre Labour from 1977 to 1992 – they have made inroads into the Muslim and Christian Quarters. Their secular argument is that Jews can, and should, live anywhere in united Jerusalem. But they are vehemently against giving Muslim or Christian Arabs the same right.

Jewish Penetration Of Non-Jewish Quarters

By 1990, five Jewish groups were actively involved in the

process of 'redemption' of non-Jewish real estate in the Old Town: Atara Le Yoshna (Hebrew, To Ancient Throne), a consortium of Jewish property companies closely linked with the Israeli Custodian of Absentee Property and the Israel Land Administration; Atreet Cohanim Yeshiva (Hebrew, Crown of Priests Religious Academy), initially associated with Atara Le Yoshna; the Ne'emanei Har HaBeit (Hebrew, Faithful of the Mount of the House [of God], popularly known as Temple Mount Faithful); Shuvia Banin Yeshiva; and Rabbi Israel Ariel's Temple Institute. Of these Atreet Cohanim emerged as the most active and controversial.

In December 1978, on the eve of the Jewish festival of Hanuchha, eight young Orthodox Jews announced that they had established Atreet Cohanim Yeshiva in the Muslim Quarter to study the ancient priestly texts in anticipation of the imminent coming of the Messiah and the rebuilding of the Second Temple at the original site, on Mount Moriah. They were led by Matityahu HaCohen Dan, a bearded, extrovert Orthodox Jew, who had served in the IDF. They held seminars on the priestly rites of the two ancient Temples, and referred to the Babylonian exile of the Jews when, guided by God, Hagai tested priests, *cohanim*, on the sacrifices at the Temple and the laws governing it as a prelude to the reconstruction of the Second Temple. Confident that a similar event would occur in our times, they argued that if the Jews were ill-prepared, physically and spiritually, for the arrival of the Messiah then they were unfit to beseech God that he should send the Messiah. The announcement of the founding of the Atreet Cohanim Yeshiva occurred several weeks after Prime Minister Menachem Begin had signed the Camp David Accords, with Egyptian President Anwar Sadat at the behest of the United States, an event which divided the right-wing forces, with the ultra-nationalists denouncing it as a sell-out.

However, had the Atreet Cohanim Yeshiva limited itself to scholarly studies it would have drawn little attention. But the ambitions of Dan – who was close to Ariel Sharon, the ultra-nationalist Likud leader who, from May 1977 to June 1981 was both Agricultural Minister and chairperson of the cabinet's (Jewish) Settlement Committee – went beyond scholarship. He aimed to engender a palpable Jewish presence around the Haram al Sharif (Arabic, The Noble Sanctuary), the site of the Dome of the Rock and the Al Asqa Mosque, as a step towards raising Jewish consciousness about the Third Temple to be built where the Dome of the Rock had stood since the late seventh century. 'Of course we want to take the place of the Muslims on the [Temple] Mount and clear away their mosque[s],' wrote Menachem Bar Shalom, Atreet Cohanim's public relations director, to a supporter in Sarasota, Florida, in March 1986.[9]

Atreet Cohanim was guided by the ideas of Rabbi Avraham Yitzhak HaCohen Kook, the founder in 1921 of Merkaz Harav Kook Yeshiva in Jerusalem, which provided religious teachers, rabbis, for the Yishuv (the Jewish community in Palestine). Kook's ideology fitted the thinking of neither the secular Zionist pioneers, committed to creating a nation of Jews in Palestine through human endeavour, nor the ultra-Orthodox, who believed in the divine intervention re-establishing the Jewish state of Israel. Actually it married the secular and religious schools of Zionism, and presented the concept of Eretz Israel as an integral part of Judaism along with the cardinal tenets of God, the Torah, and the redemption of the Jews whose continued lack of piety had held up the arrival of the Messiah. After his death in 1935, his son, Zvi Yehuda Kook, headed the Yeshiva, and became the interpreter of his ideas – especially after the founding of Israel in 1948. He reaffirmed his father's assertion that only after the Jews had returned to Eretz Israel, resettled the land, and adopted the way of life prescribed by the Torah, would the Messiah come. He and his disciples believe that since Eretz Israel was given to the Jews by God they must secure it and defend it by any means necessary.

Matityahu Dan set up a subsidiary of the Atreet Cohanim, called the Jerusalem Reclamation Project (JRP), in the early 1980s, with the objective of 'redeeming' all of the nearly 1,100 properties in the Muslim Quarter, occupying almost half of the Old Town.

During the next decade, the JRP acquired 123 properties

for an estimated $18 million. The finance was provided overtly by rich Jewish militants living in North America who responded partly to the appeals for funds made by Israel's chief Ashkenazi rabbi, Abraham Chana Shapira, and covertly (as revealed later by the Israeli press, including the *Jerusalem Post*) by the Housing Ministry of Israel from at least 1986 onward.[10]

Initially the JRP conducted its dealings in low key. Since most of the Muslim residents of the Old Town had retained their Jordanian citizenship they were subject to Jordan's laws, including the one which made it a capital offence to sell property to Jews. In order to help them circumvent this law, the JRP often used Lebanese Christians of right-wing persuasion as intermediaries. Later the JRP combined force with subterfuge. 'Given a foothold in an area or even a courtyard, expansion into adjoining property can begin,' wrote Graham McNeill, a British researcher. 'The most typical method used is to force an entry to "create facts on the ground" and then to take legal course to prove previous Jewish ownership or occupancy – as was the case with St John's Hospice, the Rsass Building in Aqabat Khalidieh, and the Diskin Orphanage and Kindergarten in Aqabat Saraya. Such cases, complicated by confusion over previous tenants, legality of leases and subleases as well as loss of documents, can and do run for years, incurring massive legal costs.'[11] Emboldened by its successes, the JRP moved into the Christian Quarter, with the Atreet Cohanim activists occupying St John's Hospice in the Christian Quarter on the eve of Easter in 1990. This set alarm bells ringing in the Christian circles, worldwide, and made the JRP lower its profile.

By then the JRP's holdings included a museum, several yeshivas and synagogues, dormitories for yeshiva students – including one in Tariq Bab al Hadid/The Iron Gate Street (86 students), another on the top floor of the multi-storey house of Ariel Sharon in Al Wad Street, and another in the apartments of Beit Rand, a three-storey building next to Suq al Qattanin (Arabic, Cotton Merchants Market); and more than 50 apartments.

The leading Arab residents, Muslim and Christian, detected

a pattern in the acquisitions of the JRP and the Atara Le Yoshna, which concentrated on Al Wad Street – the main artery of the Muslim Quarter, running north to south from the Damascus Gate to the Western Wall – and Chain Gate Street, running east to west, near the Western Wall and leading to Mount Moriah. 'Both sides of Al Wad Street are being slowly taken over by the Jews, with the house of Ariel Sharon [guarded at all times by Israeli soldiers] forming a strategic location,' said George Hintlian, an Arab Christian resident of the Armenian Quarter.[12]

It was the Sharon affair in October 1987 which had alerted the Arab Palestinians inside the Old Town and outside. After the JRP had announced that it had 'rented' its recently acquired large, multi-storey house – strategically spanning Al Wad Street – in the Muslim Quarter to Sharon, then Minister of Trade and Industry, Sharon held a much-publicized house-warming party, attended by 700 prominent Israelis, including Prime Minister Yitzhak Shamir (1915–), and occupied the top floor apartment. He draped the house with a gigantic Israeli flag, which ended just above the pinnacle of the massive archway, and installed a huge menorah on the roof. The incensed Palestinians rioted, but in vain. The Government responded by placing a permanent military guard on the premises. The incident made the Palestinians realize that the Jewish Israelis held nothing sacrosanct about them and their way of life. It was one of the factors which stoked Palestinian anger which erupted into an intifada two months later.

One sunny afternoon Rafi and I stopped under the archway formed by Sharon's house. Rafi began reading the graffiti written on the stone walls by bored IDF guards: 'Let the green beret [border police under IDF command] let in the Old City, Judea and Samaria, and they will fix the intifada'; 'Starting November '92 three years of boredom [during conscription]'; and so on. As Rafi translated the graffiti to me, a couple of IDF soldiers eyed him from a distance, then slowly walked up to him to discover a young man, looking very Jewish, with fashionably permed hair, wearing unmistakably Israeli clothing – jeans and a check shirt under a loose, mauve-coloured sweater. They stopped, with an indulgent smile spreading over their young, clean-shaven faces. Rafi chatted with them, and discovered that Sharon only slept there a few nights a month, a token presence. The cost of this exercise to the Israeli tax-payer, I discovered later, was put at $250,000 to $500,000 a year.

Rafi and I ambled down Al Wad Street southward and faced a sign: 'Yeshivath Torah Hagin (founded 1886) Rabbi Isaac Winograd/Igud Lohamey Yeriteh Synagogue' – at the site of old Yeshiva Torah Chaim (also written as Haim). We entered a battered door, walked several metres on the empty ground floor past a rickety cycle, and went upstairs. On the first floor, to the right we saw two houses which seemed Arab, and to the left was a closed door which, once opened, led to a stairs and the balcony of the Yeshiva (also written as Yeshivath). As we reached the top of the steps, I saw a young student packing an Uzi collapsible sub-machine-gun under his clothes as he prepared to go down.

We were soon chatting in fluent English with the principal of the Yeshiva, Rabbi Shlomo Haim Aviner across a long, Formica-topped table in what appeared to be a makeshift dining hall. A thin-faced man of 52, with a long beard and grey, bespectacled eyes, Aviner looked neat in his white shirt, light brown pants and cream-coloured skullcap. Born in Lyons, France, he had graduated in mathematics and nuclear physics, and then studied electronics. He emigrated in 1966. 'After arriving in Israel I felt that moral edification was important,' he said. 'I needed spiritual science.' He worked on Kibbutz Levi for seven years (1966–73), fought in the 1973 Arab-Israeli War, and then enrolled at Rabbi Kook's yeshiva. After graduation in 1978 he decided to live on a Jewish settlement on the Occupied (Syrian) Golan Heights, where he became a rabbi. Four years later he was appointed to the present job.

An urbane, soft-spoken man, he enchanted me with a simple, humanistic statement. 'It takes five years to become a teacher, 10 to become a rabbi, 15 to become a judge, and 20 to become a Jew,' he said. 'But it takes 25 years to become a human being.'

He was well versed on the origins of his yeshiva and the premises it occupied. 'The original Torah Hagin Yeshiva was established [in 1886] after the pogroms in Russia in the 1880s. After the pogrom in 1929 here it was closed down. All the Jews were concentrated in the Jewish Quarter by the British mandate authorities in 1936. Following the 1967 War the Jewish presence was recreated in this [Muslim] quarter. At our yeshiva we follow the ideology of Rabbi Zvi Yehuda Kook, who died in 1982. We don't seek draft exemption for our students on religious grounds. Some enrol after the IDF, others get deferment. Our 100 unmarried students are from all over the country. We have 50 married students, mostly from Jerusalem. Some live in the Old City and others in the New City.' (My later enquiries revealed that this yeshiva followed a policy of accommodating its students in the vicinity, in the Muslim Quarter. In 1982, as part of their extra-curricular activities, the students started tunnelling under Mount Moriah, hoping to find a chamber where King Solomon was supposed to have stored several golden vessels used for rituals at the First Temple. They were detected by the Arabs guarding the Mount, who raised the alarm. Rioting followed. The authorities decided to seal the tunnel.)

'After 1967 we only had a synagogue here, and in 1981 we started a yeshiva here [the original yeshiva having moved elsewhere after 1929]. When we restarted the yeshiva in 1981 there was a negative response from the Arab neighbours. But now we have good relations with them.' The image of one of his students packing a sub-machine-gun under his clothes whizzed past my mind.

'All yeshivas were destroyed after the [1948] War of Independence,' Aviner continued. 'After the War our neighbour was an Arab. He closed down the yeshiva and stored the holy books in a back room. When the Jordanian soldiers ransacked the place, he kept quiet about the scriptures. This Arab became the guardian of our yeshiva. After the 1967 War he took the key of his back room to the military governor of Jerusalem. When they opened it there was 20 centimetres of dust on the books. He saved all the books and no damage was done.'

'What was the name of this Arab?' I asked.

Aviner looked puzzled for a moment, then waved his hand, dismissively: 'I don't know.' He paused. 'You can ask his wife downstairs.'

I wondered quietly if Aviner would pass his own 'human being' test according to which it took longer to become 'a human being' than 'a Jew'.

After leaving Aviner, Rafi and I knocked on the door of the 'good Arab', who, by Aviner's account, lived just a floor below. A plump, middle-aged Palestinian woman invited us in. It transpired that the name of the 'good Arab' was Abu Wahid al Bikri al Lakhim, that he had died in 1990, and that his wife, too, had passed away soon after. Our enquiry was over within a few minutes. Yet Aviner, who had crossed the Arab's threshold twice daily for 13 years, except on the Sabbath and holidays, had never bothered to find out his name, or noticed that his wife, too, had died. (According to David K. Shipler, the Jerusalem bureau chief of the *New York Times* from 1979 to 1984, al Lakhim had stored some 20,000 books, including Hebrew commentaries on the Talmud, published in Warsaw in the 1820s, and the Holy Ark.)[13]

Had I read what Aviner had told an American journalist and author, Robert Friedman, about Arabs, before I arrived at his yeshiva, I would have been better prepared. ...ner's view, Palestine was a barren and empty land until the Jews returned,' writes Friedman. '"The Arabs are squatters," Aviner told me. "I don't know who gave them authorization to live on Jewish land. All mankind knows this is our land. Most Arabs came here recently ... But even if some Arabs have been here for some 2,000 years, is there a statute of limitations that gives a thief the right to his plunder?"' There was more. '"We must settle the whole Land of Israel, and over all of it establish our rule," Aviner said. "In the words of Nahumanides [son of Rabbi Moshe Ben Nahuman, who visited Jerusalem in 1267]: 'Do not abandon the land to another nation.' If that is possible by peaceful means, wonderful, and if not, we are commanded to make war to accomplish it."'[14]

Among other things, in the words of Friedman, 'Rabbi

Aviner believed that a Jewish communal presence in St John's Hopsice ... could be the springboard for a more substantial Jewish presence in the Christian Quarter.' With over 5,000 residents, the Christian Quarter was the second most populous.

Aviner's statement alluded to the JRP's take-over of St John's Hospice, which came to light on 11 April 1990, during the Easter Holy Week and (Jewish) Passover, when about 150 armed Jewish settlers, allied with the Atreet Cohanim Yeshiva, moved into the 70-room, two-storey hospice constructed in the late-nineteenth century in Suq Khan al Zeit near the Church of the Holy Sepulchre. A property of the Greek Orthodox Church, the hospice had been leased since 1932 to Martyos Matossian, an Armenian, who rented rooms to visiting pilgrims and local Arab families. The Church attempted to evict Matossian in 1980, and finally won an eviction order six years later. Matossian appealed. Aware of the long-running dispute, the JRP intervened to benefit from it. One of its rich patrons in the United States offered to buy Matossian's lease for $5 million, but he rejected it, aware of the risks of making deals with Jews. The JRP then engaged a Lebanese businessman, Nabil Sahnawi, owner of a Panama-registered company, SBC, which specialized in hotel management, to approach Matossian with an offer of $3.5 million to purchase the lease for St John's Hospice. Matossian agreed. The two parties signed the deal in Geneva in June 1989, with the case against Matossian still pending in the Israeli court.

A group of Atreet Cohanim Yeshiva affiliates, calling itself 'No'et David', planned to move into the hospice on the eve of the next Passover which happened to coincide with the (Christian) Holy Week. Arriving at the premises armed, the Jewish settlers began throwing into the street not only furniture but also the smashed remnants of crucifixes and religious paintings. They then embossed a Jewish identity on the building by covering the Byzantine cross at the front of the building with a wooden plank and painting a blue star of David on it. They renamed the hospice No'et David (Hebrew, David's Homestead).

The next day, Thursday, following the tradition of Jesus bathing the feet of the Twelve Disciples, the Greek Orthodox Patriarch, His Beatitude Diodoros I, aged 78, dressed in his official robe of gold cloth, and wearing a crown, washed the feet of his priests, and blessed the faithful by dipping a bouquet of flowers in the dirty water and sprinkling them with it. Then, instead of leading the congregation to the Greek Orthodox monastery, as is the custom, the Patriarch headed for St John's Hospice, now guarded by scores of armed Israeli border police, who had been seen on the previous day assisting the Jewish settlers to move in. There the Patriarch and his flock joined the protesting Arabs who were shouting pro-Palestine Liberation Organization slogans. This went on a for a while. Then a young, black-robed Greek Orthodox cleric, raised shoulder high by the demonstrators, reached the plaque bearing the Star of David, and pulled it down. Without warning, the police fired tear gas. In the resulting stampede, many clergymen, including the Patriarch, were knocked down, and trampled. Within minutes the news was flashed across the globe by the worldwide news agencies.

Consequently, the protest that ensued was not only local and national but also international. On 27 April, Friday, all churches in Israel and the Occupied Territories shut their doors and protested by ringing funeral peals. It was unprecedented for the Church of the Holy Sepulchre to close down, something its caretakers had never done since the Crusaders' defeat in 1187. While Ariel Sharon dismissed the protestation as anti-Semitic and inspired by the terrorist PLO, John Cardinal O'Connor in New York portrayed the St John's Hospice take-over as part of a plot to buy up Christian property in the Holy Land. During the controversy that simmered on for several months, David Levy, the then Housing Minister, revealed that his ministry had secretly paid $1.8 million to Himnutta Company, a subsidiary of the Jewish National Fund, which owned all land in Israel, for transfer to SBC to help it buy the sublease of the hospice. (In another context, a link had developed between the Housing Ministry and the Custodian of Absentee Property, an office created by the Absentee Property Law, 1950. Though the

Custodian was an appointee of the Finance Ministry, over the years he had taken to working with the Housing Ministry, which was directly involved in creating Jewish settlements in the Occupied Arab Territories.)[15]

In the court the Greek Orthodox Church reasoned that since its lease with Matossian forbade subleasing, his contract with SBC was illegal and invalid. Upholding the argument, the court decreed that the settlers must leave the hospice. However, it allowed 20 maintenance and security employees of SBC to stay on pending further litigation. In reality these SBC employees turned out to be none other than the members of the original 'No'et David' group affiliated to the Atreet Cohanim Yeshiva. They brought in their families stealthily and settled down.

Nearly five years later when one morning in February, aided by an ultra-nationalist Jewish contact, I managed to visit the place, discreetly guarded from a window on the top storey, by a small group of young armed men equipped with mobile phones and walkie-talkies, I found that about 20 rooms were occupied on that floor. Once the heavily locked door had been opened by the guards from the inside, we went past prams and cycles parked on the ground floor, then up the stairs. Two young women were looking after children whose parents had apparently gone to work or study at the local yeshivas. There were cooking facilities. The evidence I saw did not support the official position that only 20 professional security men and maintenance workers in the pay of SBC lived there.

Most probably, the residents were in daily touch with the Atreet Cohanim Yeshiva whose registered office in Chain Gate Street was located behind a green, steel-plated door in the modern-looking Ma'aravim Complex of several apartments and a synagogue and another yeshiva. Next to the bank of letter-boxes in the wall to the right, were three young security guards, one of them wearing a white baseball cap, standing, with his back to the door, facing another colleague, equipped with a mobile phone and an Uzi sub-machine-gun, looking ahead, and the third sitting at a desk turning the pages of a book in Arabic. I had arrived there in the company of Rafi. 'Could we talk to an official of the Atreet Cohanim Yeshiva?' he asked. 'It is part of our security contract that journalists are not to be allowed,' replied the guard wearing a baseball cap. I ran my eye over the letter-boxes. Besides Atreet Cohanim Yeshiva were: Synagogue of the Association of the Fighters of the Old City, and four other comparatively unknown organizations.

Outside, across the narrow cobblestone Chain Gate Street, in the Haim Olam (Hebrew, Light of the World) Compound, signposted in red, past the gently rising courtyard filled with a series of clothes-lines, and a row of Palestinian houses to the right, inside a multi-storey building was the Yeshiva Shuvia Banin. It belongs to the ultra-Orthodox sect of Bratsilvic, founded in 1815 by Rabbi Nahuman of Bratslav, Ukraine. Unlike other ultra-Orthodox sects its adherents do not have a living chief rabbi. Instead they follow the founder by reading and interpreting his copious volumes.

'We learn our books all the time,' said Tsafair Arnon – fat, bearded, black-coated, looking older than his 35 years – his words filling the small, crowded office with his foul mouth odour. 'We start our lessons at two a.m.' Why? 'Because our founder said that midnight is the Holy Hour and early morning is the time we are nearest to God. As most of our 170 students live outside the Old City, in Mea Shearim, we get up around midnight. Then we walk through the Muslim Quarter, in groups, not alone, to reach our yeshiva. We are used to it. This is our home even though there is danger.'

How did it come to be your home? 'For the last 100 years Jews have lived here in this [Muslim] Quarter. About 60 years ago this was an Orthodox [religious] school. Many Jews from Europe helped it with money. The students and teachers left after the 1929 riots, but some of them returned. Before 1948 Arabs and Jews lived door to door. But after the 1948 War all the Jews left. But this place [in the Muslim Quarter] was not occupied. In 1967 it was still empty. There were times of tension here like when somebody [Michael Rohan] tried to burn down the Al Aqsa Mosque in 1969. The Jews came to this building in 1981 when it was used by members of the Gush Emunim [Hebrew, Bloc of Faithful]. Some of them slept here. The whole place was in ruins. We [Bratsilvic] came here in 1982. The Arabs did not want us to move in.' Besides the historic animosity between Arabs and Jews, I learnt later, there was the practice of the Bratsilvic climbing up to the roof of their yeshiva and singing religious incantations loudly and collectively in the middle of the night.

'We used to come here on foot from Mea Shearim [where 3–4,000 Bratsilvic families have their central synagogue], go through the Damascus Gate and the [Arab] market,' Arnon continued. 'Arabs used to kick us, beat us. In 1984 one young yeshiva student, Eli Umedi, was murdered. The situation got tense. Then we took "revenge action".' Here he broke into a knowing smile. Did they beat up Arabs with lead pipes and chains? Arnon was non-committal, still smiling. 'Anyway, then the Arabs relaxed. Later [in October 1987] Sharon set up his house on Al Wad Street, and was given a military guard. That helped. Then intifada came [in late 1987], with our [Muslim] neighbours rioting and Arab boys throwing stones. So we let some unmarried students live here since we had some rooms. But now that's stopped.'

Actually the violence ceased only after another killing of a Jewish settler, Elhanoun Aron Atalai, a student of Atreet Cohanim Yeshiva, in the Muslim Quarter in 1991 in the midst of the intifada – followed by the instant confiscation of the Muslim property near the spot by the Israeli authorities, and severe retaliatory measures against the local Palestinians. Later I saw the memorial to Atalai near a Palestinian cafeteria, inscribed thus:

Here was murdered
Elhanoun Aron Atalai
by the wretched people
on the night of 14 Adar Tashima (1991)
'In his blood we will live & Jerusalem we will build
Remember what Amaleks [biblical enemy of Israelites]
did to you'

Parallel to this reality on the ground exists another – on the roofs of the Muslim Quarter. Jaafar (pseudonym), a plump, middle-aged, well read Palestinian, introduced me to it one drizzling afternoon. We went up the steps of a black-painted wrought-iron staircase at the end of Suq al Huzor/Habad Street. On the flat roofs of the shops and houses were scattered several steel barriers, weather-beaten, stamped POLICE in English and Hebrew. In the middle-distance I saw a watch-tower manned by a young guard armed with a machine-gun and a mobile phone. A bearded, bespectacled man in a black coat with a mobile phone in hand, and a woman in a blouse and skirt, wearing a pancake hat, walked slowly by. 'They have mobile phones and walkie-talkies,' Jaafar whispered. Who are 'they'? 'The Jewish settlers,' came the reply. 'There were three fatal stabbings of the Jews between 1982 and 1991. But that did not stop the settlers or the Government penetrating the Muslim or Christian Quarters. The question for them was: how to make secure the movement of Jewish settlers in the non-Jewish quarters. The answer: by skipping the use of streets and bazaars to get around.' So were there now well-trodden 'roofways' being used by the Jews in the non-Jewish quarters? 'You see one in front of you. Here. Before a Jew leaves his house he phones and checks with the guard over there, telling him his destination, and the guard checks at the other end. And so on.'

Jaafar then descended to the reality of the ground, taking me to a few Palestinian homes where the residents found themselves living cheek by jowl with the newly arrived Jewish families. In one place, the Palestinians, sharing a common entrance at the street level, which opened into a small courtyard, claimed that their Jewish neighbours, upstairs, pelted them with life-threatening rubbish. I looked up. The protective steel-wire net, fitted above the courtyard, was littered with metal rods and pipes, and heavy stones.

A stickler with words, and fluent in Arabic, Hebrew and English, Jaafar took childlike delight in pointing out the inconsistencies in the names of streets and bazaars. Behind a rainstorm drainpipe by a bakery, he read aloud David Street in Hebrew and English in black letters against a white marble background, and Suq Alloon (Alloon Market) in Arabic. He showed me a street named Arman (i.e., Armenian) in Arabic and English and Haim Olam in Hebrew. Granted that streets, markets and gates tend to carry multiple names in the Old Town, there was more to Jaafar's examples than met the eye. Because Arman Street divides the Armenian Quarter, the second smallest with an estimated population of over 4,000, from the Jewish Quarter, the insertion of a different name comes in Hebrew. But since David Street is a main shopping artery, popular with western tourists, it is important to advertise that name in English, leaving its original title intact only in Arabic, a language of little consequence, in the Israeli view, to foreign pilgrims and tourists.

In David Street/Suq Alloon we passed a sturdy, middle-aged Palestinian with a hang-dog expression in a light grey jacket, selling film rolls. 'An informer,' Jaafar whispered. We were soon at the Omar ibn Khattab Square that leads to the Jaffa Gate. To the left was a large, forbidding stone structure with incredibly thick walls, built by the Ottomans, which was now the local headquarters of the Israeli (civil) police and border police. Across its electronically controlled steel-bar barrier there was a restaurant undergoing renovation. 'Its owner is an Israeli informer,' Jaafar said matter-of-factly.

We retraced our path through David Street/Suq Alloon and continued westward, entering Chain Gate Street, named after the main (Chain) Gate to the Haram al Sharif, the Noble Sanctuary. As we proceeded to the Islamic shrine, I recognized the Shuvia Banin Yeshiva, the green steel door of the Ma'aravim Complex, and the Young Israeli Synagogue, written in blue letters in English, etc. Jaafar added the dormitories of the Bar Ilan University to the list, pointing out that these premises as well as Shuvia Banin Yeshiva were on the southern side of the street, facing the Western Wall Plaza. We reached the end of the street, and faced the twin, green gates – the Chain Gate (Bab al Silsile) and the Knife Gate (Bab al Sikine) – standing in a vaulted veranda. Jaafar turned me sideways, and translated a large sign in Hebrew fixed to the mosaic lintel of a distinguished early-fourteenth-century building: 'The Western Wall Look-Out of the IDF'. 'The building has its own gate opening into the Haram,' said Jaafar. 'That gives the IDF free access to the whole esplanade. Under the Jordanians it was a school. That made sense as the building is called Tankiziya Madrasa [Arabic, Religious School] after its builder, Saif al Din Tankiz al Nasiri. During the British mandate it was the house of Haajj [Muhammad Amin] Husseini, head of the Supreme Muslim Council.' Now I was able to place the machine-gun-bearing Israeli soldier poised on a roof next to the Western Wall I had noticed on the day I interviewed the pilgrims to the Wall. He had climbed up there from here, a historic madrasa.

The Noble Sanctuary/Temple Mount

Jaafar and I entered the open courtyard of the Haram al Sharif where the octagonal Dome of the Rock (Qubbat al Sakhra) stood, majestic, on a large stone platform, held up by the buttressing Herodian walls, many metres above the vast courtyard of the same era – to be approached by a long flight of steps, framed in a tall arcade with three arches. The golden cupola of the Dome of the Rock shone brilliantly in the afternoon sun as it had done for more than 13 centuries. Encompassed by freestanding archways on the four sides of the raised, rectangular platform on which it is founded, the Dome of the Rock, Islam's first aesthetically outstanding accomplishment, struck me as a perfectly harmonious blending of shape and colour. The glazed Persian tiles covering the outside walls were a sumptuous blend of blue, lapis lazuli, cobalt, emerald, green, ochre and mauve, a feast to the eye, assembled to create abstract, yet wondrous, mosaics. Verses from the Quran in graceful Arabic calligraphy, white letters on blue, embellished the upper edge of the octagon.

Legend has it that its builder, Caliph Abdul Malik ibn Marwan (r. 684–705), wished to raise the newly emerged Islamic faith to the same level as its forerunners, Judaism and Christianity, and outdo the already existing Church of the Holy Sepulchre, then called the Church of Resurrection. Today the Dome is by far the most glaring landmark of Jerusalem, its most insistent and stunning image. Though an indisputable Islamic shrine, it covers the (World's) Foundation stone of the Jews, equally revered by Muslims, and is constructed in the Christian-Byzantine style of the late seventh century most likely on the area where the Second Temple of the Jews had stood. It thus represents a unique synthesis of the major monotheistic creeds.[16]

If the Dome of the Rock is a diamond, sharp, concentrated, brilliant, the Al Aqsa Mosque is like a necklace – long, laid out – built to accommodate more than 5,000 worshippers. Situated to the south of the Dome, on the edge of the vast esplanade, the Al Aqsa looks plain, its unglamorous exterior lifted by the silver dome at the southern end, and the portal of seven arched gateways under a crenellated parapet at the northern – facing the Dome across a medieval fountain, a string of tall, dark green cypresses, and a flight of well-trodden steps to the terrace. Originally constructed in AD 715 by Caliph al Walid ibn Abdul Malik as the mosque for the Haram al Sharif (the Dome of the Rock is a shrine, not a mosque where sermons are preached after the Friday prayer), it has been destroyed and reconstructed a few times.

Inside, the Al Aqsa is divided into a central nave and two transepts, a division laid out by seven lines of columns, pillars of stone and marble, adorned with stylized capitals of various origins, many of them Christian, the legacy of the period when the Crusaders (in the late eleventh century) converted the premises into a church. Today, besides the compulsory *mihrab* (Arabic, prayer niche), recess in a wall, pointing to Mecca, it has two more – dedicated to Moses and Jesus – once again symbolizing a synthesis of the major monotheistic faiths. Compared to the Dome of the Rock, the Al Aqsa is spartan, an impression unshaken by its luxurious carpets, glittering chandeliers, and a carved ceiling, painted in gold and blue in the 1930s, a contrast to the gold, green, and blue mosaic work of the dome dating back to 1189 under Saladin. Another contribution of Saladin, a carved wooden pulpit, installed there in October 1187 after his victory over the Crusaders, was burnt down as a result of arson on 21 August 1969. The Israeli authorities arrested a young Australian, Michael Dennis Rohan, a member of the Christian fundamentalist Church of God, the next day, and he reportedly confessed to the crime. The arson was seen throughout the Arab and Muslim world as a Zionist attempt to destroy the Islamic monuments in Jerusalem as part of a plan to denigrate and destroy Islam. It led to an international outcry among Muslims. King Faisal of Saudi Arabia channelled it to convene a meeting of the heads of 29 Muslim-majority countries in September; and this in turn led to the founding of the Islamic Conference Organization, the first international body of Muslim states.

Pinpricks continue, Jaafar told me. Indeed as he and I emerged from the Al Aqsa Mosque, we saw commotion on the Haram: Israeli police, Arab guards, photographers, and a small group of men being taken away. 'Crazy fanatics,' said Jaafar. Who? 'The men they've arrested. Nutcases, the disciples of Yehuda Etzion, who insist on praying on the Haram al Sharif,' came the swift reply. 'That's the starting point for reclaiming the Haram for the Jews, and building the Third Temple there.' Wasn't the Haram al Sharif forbidden to the Jews, with government notices saying so at the gates to the Mount? Jaafar smiled a cynical smile. 'Did you see any?' he asked. Nothing in English, but what about Hebrew? 'Nothing in Hebrew either, believe me,' he replied. There was a strong reason behind the ban, wasn't there? 'Tell me,' Okay said Jaafar, here goes: 'The inner sanctum of the Jewish Temple is to be entered by the High Priest only, and that also only on the Passover. Since nobody knows where exactly that inner sanctum was on the Mount Moriah, Jews are forbidden to walk on it lest they should by mistake traduce that particular spot. Hence all of the Mount is out of bounds to Jews.' There was a pause. 'That makes all IDF soldiers non-Jews,' Jaafar said, still smiling. How? 'Because all IDF recruits are brought here as part of their training, to familiarize them with every bit of Israel. And this' – here he stamped the hallowed ground – 'is Eretz Israel'.

This was exactly the line of Yehuda Etzion who was arrested on the Mount on 11 April 1995, I discovered later. His picture showed him to be a bespectacled, balding, clean-shaven man of medium height, dressed in jeans and a flannel shirt. Born in 1951 in Israel, Yehuda Etzion grew up in an ultra-nationalist household. His father, Abraham Mintz, was a member of Lehi (Hebrew acronym of Lohemei Herut Israel, Fighters for Free Israel), a militant Zionist organization, which resorted to terrorism in the 1940s. After graduating from a yeshiva attached to the Bnei Akiva (Hebrew, Children of Akiva, an eminent rabbi in Roman times), the youth section of the National Religious Party (NRP), he became a founder first of the Gush Emunim, which led the Jewish settler movement in the Occupied Territories of the West Bank and Gaza Strip, and then the Elon Moreh Gariin (Hebrew, cell). From Elon Moreh, a Jewish settlement near Nablus, he organized the establishment of Ofra settlement near Al Bireh in 1976. It soon became the operational headquarters of the Gush Emunim. He was a member of the Gush secretariat until 1978. Then he turned even more religious and more right wing.

The trigger for Etzion, as with the founders of the Atreet Cohanim Yeshiva, was Prime Minister Menachem Begin's accord in September 1978 to vacate Egypt's Sinai Peninsula in exchange for a peace treaty with Cairo. They all believed in the Eretz Israel which lay between 'Two Rivers [the Nile and the Euphrates]'. Rejecting the ideology of Rabbi Zvi Yehuda Kook and the NRP, which accepted the State of Israel as a step towards the final redemption of the Jewish people, he developed his own thesis. He argued that since the leaders of the State of Israel, guided by secular democratic principles, had committed a series of blunders, it was perfectly legitimate to sketch out the full scenario of redemption now. It would include the Kingdom of Israel, a priestly kingdom based on the Temple Mount, which would encompass all the land between the Nile and the Euphrates. It was a duty of the true believers to struggle to achieve this aim, he reasoned. In his scenario Etzion assigned a central role to the Temple Mount. '[King] David's property in the Temple is therefore a real and eternal property,' he stated. 'The expurgation of the Temple Mount will prepare the [Jewish] hearts for the understanding and further advancing of full redemption. The purified mount shall be – if God wishes – the hammer and anvil for the future process of promoting the next holy elevation.' The reason why the process of Jews' redemption had stopped was that their enemy, the Arabs, possessed the Temple Mount, he argued. Only by retaking the Mount from them could the Jews restart the stalled process of redemption. As the Israeli Government had failed to do so, it was incumbent upon the true believers to act.[17]

Etzion's stance on the Temple Mount was remarkably close to the position taken earlier by the Chief Rabbinate of the State of Israel. On 22 Adar 5736 (1977) it stated: 'The Temple Mount is Mount Moriah, the site of the Temple and of the Holy of Holies, the place where the Lord G-d of Israel chose to house His Name, which was sanctified by ten holy blessings by David, King of Israel: the Jewish People's right to the Temple Mount is an external and inalienable right, over which there can be no concessions.'[18] This statement about Mount Moriah, which is weighed down with legendary significance of the highest kind, skated over certain historical facts. The legend has it that Adam was created here from a spoonful of dust, and it is to this spot that he returned on his flight from Eden 'to till the earth whence he was taken' (Genesis 3:23). It is the traditional site of the Holy Rock where Cain murdered Abel, Noah made his sacrifice, and Abraham prepared to offer God his son (Isaac, according to Jews and Christians/Ismail according to Muslims). As for recorded facts, after the two Jewish Temples, Roman Emperor Hadrian (r. 117–38) erected a temple to Jupiter here. But by the time Byzantine Christian rule was well established in Jerusalem some centuries later, the site was used as a dump. It was left to the Muslim conqueror of Jerusalem in AD 638, Caliph Omar ibn Khattab (r. AD 634–44), to clear the area, and build the Dome of the Chain on it. None of this mattered to the Jewish ultra-nationalists, like the joint heads of the Chief Rabbinate (in 1977) or Etzion.

Soon after the Egyptian-Israeli Peace Treaty went into force in March 1979 Etzion met Menachem Livni, an austere-faced engineer, a reserve major with an expertise in explosives, who lived in the Jewish settlement of Kiryat Arba next to

Hebron, and was close to the ultra-nationalist Rabbi Moshe Levinger. Livni had recently come under the influence of Yeshua Ben Shoshan, an ideologue, who reasoned that the existence of the 'Abomination' – the term he used for the Dome of the Rock – on the Temple Mount lay at the root of 'all the spiritual errors of our generation' and was 'the basis of the hold of Ishmael [the Arabs] in Eretz Israel'.[19] In other words, the Dome of the Rock symbolized powerlessness of the Jews.

In early 1980 Etzion, Livni and Ben Shoshan called five other Jews of similar views for a meeting in Kiryat Arba. Etzion convinced the gathering that demolishing the Islamic monument on the Temple Mount would unfreeze the process of redemption. In more practical terms, he foresaw the demolition of the Dome of the Rock triggering an apocalyptic conflagration between Israel and its Arab enemies which, he confidently forecast, would result in an ignominious defeat of the Arabs, the expulsion of the Palestinian Arabs from Judea and Samaria, and pave the way for the reconstruction of the Third Temple as a prelude to the rise of the sacred Kingdom of Israel. Though committed to reviving the process of redemption, Livni did not share the overly optimistic scenario of Etzion regarding the consequent war. In the end the consensus was that since the operation was highly complex, work could begin immediately on fleshing out the details, with the final decision to be left for later.

Livni considered but soon discarded the idea of strafing the Dome of the Rock: even a slight error would have endangered the lives of the Jews praying at the nearby Western Wall. He therefore planned a ground attack. He spent two years devising a plan. Starting with a detailed layout of the Dome of the Rock and the construction of a working model, Livni organized a theft of large quantities of explosives from an arms factory on the Golan Heights as well as their testing in the Negev Desert. The explosives were used to produce 28 precision bombs. Determined not to endanger Jewish life or property in the adjoining area, Livni meticulously calculated how the Dome of the Rock would break up under the impact of the explosives and how far the shrapnel would descend.

A group of some two-dozen bomb-laden participants was trained to scale the walls of the Old City to reach the esplanade of the Temple Mount stealthily. But, in case they were detected by the Arab guards, they were to be armed with tear-gas canisters and Uzi sub-machine-guns fitted with silencers.

Intent on frustrating the Israeli plan to evacuate the last Jewish settlement in the Sinai by April 1982 as part of the Egyptian-Israeli Peace Treaty, the conspirators wanted to strike before the deadline. Livni wanted a religious go-ahead in the form of approval by a (sympathetic) rabbi. (Etzion was not a qualified rabbi.) He purportedly failed to get it. At the final meeting of the eight activists only Etzion and Ben Shoshan voted in favour of going ahead. So they decided to postpone the project.

Starting spring 1983 there was an escalation in ter-rorist actions by Palestinians and Jewish Israelis, with Hebron emerging as a particular hot-spot. In March 1983 Palestinian assailants killed a Jewish yeshiva student in the centre of Hebron. In July six Jewish settlers from the nearby Kiryat Arba mounted a daylight machine-gun and grenade attack on the students of the Islamic College in Hebron, killing four and wounding 33. (Livni provided logistical support for the operation.) This action split the Gush Emunim-sponsored settler movement and underground, and enabled the Shin Beth to infiltrate the Jewish Underground (HaMachteret HaYehudit), a generic term.

What further activated the Jewish Underground, of which Livni and his close associates were part, was a bomb explo-sion in December 1983 in Jerusalem which killed six Jews and wounded 41, the most serious incident of its kind over the past five years. In retaliation the Jewish Underground rigged 14 grenades at the entrances to mosques, churches and Arab homes in and around Jerusalem. Some exploded causing injuries. In early March 1984 four Jewish soldiers in civilian dress ambushed a bus from Ramallah to Jerusalem, injuring eight Palestinians.

More seriously, later that month, the activists of the Baalei Teshuva (Hebrew, Knights of Return) cult based in Lifta village near Jerusalem, fervently committed to building the

Third Temple, tried to implement their plan to blow up the Dome of the Rock in the middle of the night. Armed with ladders, ropes and explosives, they scaled the (generally deserted) eastern wall of the Old Town, and moved quietly to within 100 metres of the shrine. But they were noticed by an Arab guard, who raised the alarm. In their haste to escape they abandoned most of their gear behind, and with it enough clues to the police detectives to end up in jail.

Another, more serious plan by Livni and his co-conspirators got prematurely exposed because of the abortion of a terrorist attack on the Palestinians. On the night of 26 April 1984, a dozen members of the Jewish Underground rigged explosives, obtained from the seized Syrian mines stored on the Golan Heights, to the fuel tanks of five buses parked outside the scattered residences of their Palestinian drivers in East Jerusalem, to explode at 4.30 p.m. the next day, Friday, when no Jews were expected to be in the streets. The bombs never exploded. All of the conspirators were picked up by the Shin Beth, whose agents also arrested 24 others allegedly involved in terroristic activity. The list included not only relatives of the members of Israel's parliament and senior Israeli officials administering the Occupied Territories, but also some high-ranking IDF officers. During the subsequent questioning some Shin Beth agents feigned sympathy for their charges, and won their confidence. They thus gained further intelligence on the Jewish Underground's activities, including a detailed plan to destroy the Dome of the Rock. Those involved in the Dome demolition project, led as before by Livni, were by and large experienced IDF men, trained to implement plans with military precision. The evidence submitted by the authorities in court showed that arms and explosives had been procured; some 30 precision bombs, assembled from the explosives taken out of the captured Syrian mines stored on the Golan Heights and taken to Kiryat Arba, had been hidden in scattered places; and trial runs had been conducted. As before the plotters had acquired tear-gas canisters and silencers for their Uzi sub-machine-guns.

'Had they not been arrested before they had a chance to blow up the shrine, their act would probably have brought a reign of warfare and terrorism upon Israel and Jews everywhere,' wrote David K. Shipler of the *New York Times*. 'One official in the prime minister's office [then Yitzhak Shamir, the Likud leader] even estimated that Israel could not have survived the Muslim onslaught that would have come if the Dome had been destroyed.'[20]

The trial of the suspects ran from May 1984 to July 1985 in Jerusalem. The judge found 18 of the accused guilty, and sentenced them to prison terms ranging from 4 months to life while at the same time commending them for 'their pioneering ethos and war records'.

On the day he received a jail sentence of seven years, Yehuda Etzion arrived in court with the picture of the (future) Third Temple superimposed on the Dome of the Rock, with the rest of the esplanade cleared of all other Islamic monuments. Addressing journalists he called on the Israeli Government to make 'purifying the Temple Mount' its 'overriding goal'.[21]

This picture is commonly displayed in the yeshivas in Jerusalem, and is sold freely in the Jewish Quarter of the Old Town. I bought a copy at the Temple Institute at 24 Misgav Ladach Street, run since its founding in 1985 by Rabbi Israel Ariel. The small museum has a large model of the Third Temple, and displays the vessels and priestly robes to be used there. 'We have prepared 60 of the 90 vessels required for the Third Temple,' said Efrat Liebowitz, a young, chubby-faced woman in white blouse and long black skirt, selling literature at the Institute. 'We are also preparing garments for the priests and the High Priest. Work goes on in several yeshivas in the Old Town. We have scholars weaving prayer shawls and studying Talmudic texts about restoring sacrificial slaughter in the Temple. We don't know when the Messiah will come, but we should be ready.'[22]

I needed to visit the Haram al Sharif to interview pilgrims. On the morning I spent outside the Al Aqsa Mosque conversing with the faithful about their views on the Haram al Sharif and the significance of praying at the Al Aqsa, my find of the day was Ali Salamin, a resident of the Shuafat district of East Jerusalem. A 35-year-old man of medium height, stout, with a thick black beard, balding, dressed in khaki pants and a grey shirt, Ali spoke fluent English, having worked for several years with the Arabian-American Oil Company in Saudi Arabia. Surprisingly well-informed on Islam and its antecedents, he talked about the Haram al Sharif as if it were a grand stage on which prophets and warriors had re-enacted a historical pageant of monotheism.

Standing in front of a small monument resting on 11 columns, east of the Dome of the Rock, he said, 'This is what Caliph Omar ibn Khattab built after capturing Jerusalem [in AD 638] as a scale model for the Dome of the Rock.' What is it called? 'The Dome of the Chain, Al Quttab al Silsile. During Prophet Solomon's rule those who held on to the chain, hanging from the roof of his palace, dropped dead if they told a lie.' It sounded more like a legend, I thought. 'The work on the Dome of the Rock began in AD 684 and finished seven years later,' Ali continued.

Looking up at the Dome of the Rock, Ali began reciting the Quranic verses that embellish the exterior of the drum and the top of the walls, those on the drum being the seven verses from Chapter 17, The Night Journey, Verse 1:

> Glory be to Him, who carried His servant by night
> from the Holy Mosque to the Distant Mosque
> the precincts of which We have blessed
> that we might show Him some of Our signs.
> He is the All-hearing, the All-seeing.

'In AD 621 [a year before Muhammad's migration from Mecca to Medina] God took Prophet Muhammad from the Holy Mosque in Mecca to the Distant (Al Aqsa) Mosque here,' Ali explained. 'Historically speaking, it remains the first *qibla* (Arabic, direction for prayer) of Muslims. They faced in its direction while praying. After it had been the first *qibla* for 18 months, God told Muhammad to make Mecca the first *qibla*. After the Prophet's death [in AD 632] in Medina, his burial place became the second holiest shrine in Islam. Then came Al Aqsa.'

Ali looked up again, and resumed translating the verses from The Night Journey in the Quran:

And We gave Moses the Book, and made it
a guidance to the Children of Israel:
'Take not unto yourself any guardian
apart from Me.'

The seed of those We bore with Noah; he was
a thankful servant.

And We decreed for the Children of Israel
in the Book: 'You shall do corruption
in the earth twice, and you shall ascend
exceeding[ly] high.'

So, when the promise of the first of these
came to pass, We sent against you
servants of Ours, men of great might, and they went
through the habitations, and it was a promise
    performed.

Then We gave back to you the turn to
prevail over them, and We succoured you
with wealth and children, and We made you
a greater host.

If you do good, it is your own souls
you do good to, and if you do evil
it is to them likewise. Then, when
the promise of the second came to pass,
We sent against you Our servants
to disconcert you, and to enter the Temple,
as they entered it the first time,
and to destroy utterly that which they ascended to.

'You notice what the Quran says about Beni Israel, Children of Israel, who were later called Jews,' Ali remarked. 'Our war with the Jews is not religious though, it is political.' I nodded. Why the title, The Night Journey? 'It is the journey Prophet Muhammad made at night on his winged steed, al

Buraq, the Lightning, from Mecca to the Haram al Sharif to Heaven.'

Entering the Dome was like stepping inside a cornucopia of colour and light, matter and design, its patterned yellow and red stucco centre glowing like the sun, trapped, the stained-glass windows in the drum filtering in a soft greenish-blue light, the base of the drum resplendent with golden mosaics, the whole structure supported by an inner circle of four sturdy granite piers and 12 veined marble pillars, and an outer circle of twice as many piers and columns as the inner one – the columns being of various hues whose Byzantine gold-leaf capitals and the occasional crosses etched on their stems bore witness to their pre-Islamic origins: remains of the Herodian Temple or the churches destroyed by Persian Emperor Chosroes II in AD 614. The octagonal shape of the building surmounted by a dome modelled on the then existing Church of Resurrection (later renamed Holy Sepulchre) – that is, a circle within an octagon – was symbolic in ancient times of the centre of the world. Thus the Dome of the Rock is a synthesis in form and concept of Judaism, Christianity and Islam.

Directly underneath the Dome was the Rock, camel-brown, roughly 18 metres by 12 metres, sunk for most part like an iceberg into the ground – the Rock of Foundation of the Jewish legend, dating back to the time when the upper world was split from a shard from the pit of Chaos below, the inner sanctum of the Jewish Temple, which the Jews later visited annually (at Passover) to mourn and anoint, which then later served as an altar to Baal and Jupiter, and which Muslims renamed the Rock of Heaven.

I found it protected by an encircling parapet from over-zealous pilgrims intent on ensuring heavenly prospects in after-life by acquiring a bit of its hallowed mass, illuminated by soft, subdued light, some of it shining through a gaping hole in its body – the result, I surmised, of the millions of gallons of blood that had flown over the spot from the sacrificed bodies of animals as part of the ritual in the Jewish Temple. All things considered, I concluded, the Holy Rock had maintained its legendary status as the Centre of the World with admirable integrity, only occasionally surrendering a sharp edge or two.

We circled round the Rock over carpeted marble floor, stepping in and out of the light filtering through the stained-glass windows, marvelling at the overall harmony of space and matter, colour and design. Despite the rich oriental carpets, the golden friezes, the inlaid carvings, the mother-of-pearl inlays, the blue and white striped arches between the columns under which the faithful prostrate five times a day facing Mecca, the shrine felt warm, welcoming.

I followed Ali as he descended to a softly lit chamber with unfissured walls. 'The Rock of Heaven is washed twice a week with rosewater,' said Ali. 'When Prophet Muhammad climbed up the ladder of light to the heaven, guided by Archangel Gabriel, the Rock rose to follow the Prophet. But Gabriel held it back and left his fingerprints on it.' What happened to the winged steed, al Buraq, that brought Prophet Muhammad to the Haram? 'The Prophet prayed at the Haram al Sharif, tethered al Buraq by the Western Wall, then walked to the Holy Rock, and ascended to the heaven.' (Later Ali took me to a site just a few metres east of the Western Wall, marked 'Al Buraq Mosque' in tiny letters, leading to an underground cellar, bare, save for a small, framed sign ALLAH in white letters against a black background on a wall and threadbare carpets on the floor lighted up by strip neon-light.) 'Under the Rock is a cave with shrines to Prophets Abraham and Khadr (Elijah, to Muslims),' continued Ali. Why Abraham? 'According to the Quran, Prophet Abraham was the first Muslim.' How? 'Muslim means the one who submits – to the will of God. And Prophet Abraham was the first to do so and convey His message that there was only One God.' Ali's explanation sounded a little pat. 'Beneath it is the Well of Souls (Bir al Arwah), where spirits of the past are waiting for the Judgement Day,' Ali concluded. So here was the complete history of humankind – from the Creation to the End of Days, I thought.

My next interviewee was Abdul Rabbo, a craggy-faced 80-year-old, in a business suit with a black and white checked *kiffayeh*, head dress, a resident of Al Muqabar neighbourhood of East Jerusalem. 'There is a mosque in Jabal al Muqabar, but I come to Al Aqsa. One prayer here is equal to 500 prayers elsewhere. Here I am nearest to God, and after prayers I feel elevated.' His sentiments paralleled the ones I had heard earlier at the Western Wall.

There was another Palestinian from Al Muqabar outside the Al Aqsa Mosque: Abdul Karim Karaki. A small, powerfully built man of 52, bearded, he was smartly dressed in a black and white tweed jacket and dark grey pants, and carried a mobile phone. A guard at the Haram al Sharif, he had held that position for 20 years. Surely I could check with him Jaafar's claim that IDF soldiers came to the Haram regularly. 'All the time,' Karaki replied instantly. 'They come and go as they please. They don't even pay the entrance fee like the others.'

Here was also my chance, I thought, to question somebody who was present on the fateful morning of 8 October 1990 in the midst of the crisis created by the Iraqi invasion of Kuwait two months earlier.

The Temple Mount Faithful (TMF), a group of about 1,000 Jews led by Gershon Salomon, committed to reclaiming the Temple Mount/Haram al Sharif in order to build the Third Temple there, had declared that on the Feast of Tabernacles, due on 8 October, Monday, they would lay a foundation stone for the Third Temple. In the past whenever TMF members had tried to enter the courtyard on the Temple Mount in large numbers, the authorities had compromised by letting a few do so through the Israeli controlled Magharebi Gate under heavy guard to pray for a while and then depart. This time, however, in mid-September the Israeli High Court banned the TMF from entering the area. But the TMF let it be known that it would defy the court order. Responding to this, in his sermon on the preceding Friday the preacher of the Al Aqsa Mosque, Shaikh Fadlallah Silwadi, called on his co-religionists to congregate at the Haram on the following Monday morning to frustrate the TMF's plans.

That morning TMF activists, after assembling at Silwan village, just outside the southern walls of the Old Town, began marching towards the Mount as planned. Word reached the 3,000-strong Palestinians assembled on the Mount. They became agitated, and around 10.45 a.m. surged towards the Western Wall and the Israeli police station. They threw stones which landed in the Western Wall Plaza where Jewish worshippers were gathered. The Israeli security forces fired tear gas shells at the Palestinians.

After the first round of stones and tear gas, one or more of the following incidents triggered a massive burst of fire from the Israeli police and troops: (a) a gun dropped by a fleeing Israeli soldier was picked up by the rioting Palestinians, and this alarmed the soldier's colleagues who started firing; (b) Israeli soldiers from the Mahkame observation post built into the Western Wall shot dead a Palestinian youth waving a Palestinian flag, which enraged the crowd; and (c) a few of the armed Jewish settlers from the Occupied Territories present at the scene began firing their personal weapons.

Whatever the primary cause, by 11.30 a.m., following the Israelis' use of tear gas, plastic bullets and live ammunition, 17 Palestinians lay dead, and another 150 were wounded. Since most of the Jewish worshippers, having said their prayers (prescribed for the period of 9 a.m. to 12 noon) had left the Western Wall by the time the stone-throwing started, only about 20 of them were hurt. 8 October 1990 became the bloodiest day of the Palestinian intifada, and indeed of the 23 years of Israeli occupation of the West Bank, Gaza Strip and East Jerusalem.

'I was on duty that morning,' said Abdul Karim Karaki. 'Thousands of people were praying inside and outside the Al Aqsa. There was shooting by the IDF, also by the police. Some Palestinians died near the ablution place [outside the Mosque]. I closed the door of the Al Aqsa [to protect the worshippers]. The whole thing went on from about 10.30 a.m. to evening. The security forces threw 200 gas grenades inside the Al Aqsa and outside. Seventeen people were killed on the Haram, and another four in the demonstrations that broke out in Saladin Street outside the Old City. A policeman fired a shot at my head, but I am short, and there was a tall man behind me. He got hurt.'

Karaki pointed out the bullet marks on the walls and gates of the Al Aqsa. Then he took me inside and showed me a large glass container, full of spent gas cartridges, nailed to a pillar. 'A souvenir of the Israeli security forces,' he said, bitterly. 'I feel sad that the Al Aqsa was captured by the Jews in 1967. We Muslims feel that our country fell under occupation in 1967. Something terrible happened. Until today I am not reconciled to the fact that my country is occupied. And haven't we suffered? Since 1986 my family has never sat together in full because somebody is always missing, in jail. It was only a few days ago that my son was released after three years in jail, a political prisoner.' How often did he pray at Al Aqsa? 'At least once a day. And I pray to God daily to send somebody like Saladin to liberate the Al Aqsa Mosque, the way Saladin did, from the Crusaders.'

Karaki directed me to the Islamic Museum to see for myself the Muslim martyrs of 8 October 1990. Near the entrance on the cream-coloured wall was a large framed picture. Underneath the Islamic invocation of Allah (in Arabic), on both sides of the image of a powerful fist, emerging out of a tree trunk, holding the barrel of a gun against the background of the Dome of Rock, were 17 oval-shaped colour photographs of the dead, an inscription describing them 'Martyrs of the Al Aqsa'. Save for a woman and a child of indeterminate sex, they were all male, most of them young, teenagers even, a few old, and the rest middle-aged.

Looking at them reminded me of another framed picture on another wall: the colour photographs on the front page of the *Yediot Aharonot* (Hebrew, Latest News) on 23 January 1995 displayed on the greyish wall of a Jewish school in the Beit Vagan district of West Jerusalem, the victims of the double suicide bombing by two Islamic Jihad activists at the Beit Lid bus station near the Mediterranean port of Natanya the day before. The faces in that picture were uniformly young, the faces of IDF conscripts. For the terrorists had struck a well chosen target: on a Sunday morning at a busy bus station when hundreds of young soldiers were on their way to their bases after the Sabbath.

Both sides, locked in a grim, protracted struggle, had

created a long list of martyrs. And they had been conducting their conflict at many layers, with a bewildering variety of weapons: military hardware, suicide bombings, bulldozers, terrorism, stones, subterfuge, knives, tear gas, metal rods, deception, money, diplomacy, courts, propaganda.

As I would travel to the West Bank and Gaza Strip and visit some Jewish settlements there, the parallels between the situation there, and the one existing between the Jewish settlers in the Old Town's Muslim Quarter and the Muslim Palestinians, would become obvious. And I would think of the Walled Town as a microcosm of what was happening at large in Israel and the Palestinian Territories.

2

JERUSALEM:

Yerushalayim/Al Quds

Danny Jacobi sounded friendly over the phone, and showed a welcome understanding of how a newly arrived visitor feels in a sprawling city of hills like modern Jerusalem. He simplified the tricky task of gaining entry into a government establishment several storeys up in a tower block in the Jewish neighbourhood of Ramat Eshkol (Hebrew, Eshkol Hill) in Greater East Jerusalem. 'I'll meet you at the supermarket near the office,' he said in fluent English. 'It's part of a large shopping centre, and it's the only supermarket.'

I arrived early and walked around the spacious shopping mall. It was well planned, taking up a central position in the midst of residential and office blocks. I detected a whiff of a fortress mentality among the planners, the soft belly of commerce protected by watch-towerlike structures. Not far was an alien, if not murderously hostile, territory – I was to discover later.

Jacobi was punctual. A pleasant-looking, broad-shouldered, bespectacled man, in his mid-30s, with thick black hair, wearing a tweed jacket and well-pressed trousers, he was every boy's image of an ideal schoolteacher. And that is where I was. Not exactly a school, but the Ministry of Education – more specifically that section of the Ministry which produces its own text books, and vets (some would say censors) others before they can be published by private companies.

I spent a useful hour with him during which he plied me with history books in Hebrew. As I prepared to leave I asked him if he would please phone a taxi company to pick me up. 'Where do you want to go?' he enquired, as he lifted the receiver. The American Colony Hotel. He put the receiver down. 'No taxi will take you there,' he announced with a finality that baffled me. I expressed surprise. 'Well, I have a friend, an archaeologist, at the Rockefeller Museum. He tells me that they really had to shop around to find a Jewish cab company which would accept their calls.' But the Rockefeller Museum was near the Damascus Gate, only a few kilometres from here, and so was my hotel, in Jerusalem, not in the West Bank, I protested. 'It's in East Jerusalem,' he explained. But Ramat Eshkol, too, was in East Jerusalem. 'Ah,' he replied, 'Ramat Eshkol is a Jewish neighbourhood in East Jerusalem.' A Jewish neighbourhood or Jewish settlement? 'Settlements are in the West Bank,' he pointed out. 'Here we have neigh-bourhoods,' he added, straight-faced. The settlements were only in Judea and Samaria, you mean? 'We now say "in the Administered Territories",' he said. 'Or just the Territories.' Not always though. 'No,' he agreed.

Before the 1967 Arab-Israeli conflict the land where Ramat Eshkol stood was part of the Palestinian territory under Jordanian control. Soon after, having annexed Jordanian East Jerusalem and vast tracts around it, altogether measur-ing twice as much as West Jerusalem, the Labour-led Israeli Government combined its reconstruction of an expanded Jewish Quarter in the Old City, and the Mount Scopus enclave (which it had retained during 1949–67) and its sur-roundings, with the settlement of Ramat Eshkol (named after Levi Eshkol (1895–1969), a Labour Prime Minister), French Hill (re-named Givat HaMivtar) and Maalot Dafna. Even though, legally speaking, Jerusalem Municipality, which had until then run West Jerusalem since 1949, was in charge of the local affairs of the unified Jerusalem after 28 June 1967 – such as land development, housing and so on – it was the central government, also based in West Jerusalem, which decided what was to be done in the expanded city, where and how. The overall objective was national: to install a profligating Jewish population in the formerly Palestinian region of the city and its surroundings to such a degree so as to destroy any chance of splitting the metropolis again.

The plans to establish Ramat Eshkol, French Hill and Maalot Dafna followed the pattern of the earlier Israeli blueprints to found self-contained, middle-sized towns (population 10–30,000): residential quarters serviced by a comprehensive socio-economic infrastructure. Care was taken to ensure that the new settlements were inhabited only by Jews, that the newly created service facilities catered only for them, and that there was absolutely no need for the Jewish residents to have dealings with the surrounding Palestinian population.

Over the next quarter of a century the Israeli Government duplicated these plans as it set up more settlements inside the (enlarged) Greater East Jerusalem. It did so against the backdrop of events in the international arena. Responding to the launching of a Middle East Peace Plan by US Secretary of State, William Rogers, in December 1969, it decided in early 1970 to fortify the core of Jerusalem by founding Jewish settlements at strategic points overseeing the main roads from the Occupied West Bank into the city. (A similar intent had led the Israeli administration earlier to rebuild and vastly expand the newly relocated Hebrew University and Hadassah Hospital on Mount Scopus, and reinforce them with government buildings nearby: to oversee the Old Town and northern East Jerusalem.) Thus arose Ramat Allon (on the north-western edge), Neve Yaacov (on the north-eastern edge), East Talpiyot (in the east) and Gilo (on the southern edge). Israel ignored the United Nations Security Council Resolution 298 in 1971 which declared invalid its actions to alter the status of Jerusalem, including 'expropriation of land

and properties, transfer of populations and legislation aimed at the incorporation of the occupied section [of the city]'.

In 1980, as the Israeli Knesset embarked upon consolidating its earlier annexation of Greater East Jerusalem, culminating in its adoption of a 'basic law' which stated that 'united Jerusalem is the capital of Israel', the United Nations Security Council reiterated the international position clearly in March 1980 in its Resolution 465, passed unanimously. Referring to its resolutions 237 [1967], 252 [1968], 267 [1969], 271 [1969] and 298 [1971] on the subject, it affirmed once more that 'the Geneva Convention Relative to the Protection of Civilian Persons in Time of War, of 12 August 1949, is applicable to the Arab territories occupied by Israel since 1967, including Jerusalem'.[1] This Convention forbids the occupying power to change the demography of the territory under its occupation through such means as deportation or transfer of 'parts of its own civilian population into the territory it occupies', and discriminatory treatment of the occupied people on the grounds of race, religion, national origin or political affiliation.[2] The Security Council re-stated its earlier position on 30 June 1980 in its Resolution 476, adopted by 14 votes with one abstention (the United States of America), specifically expressing 'grave concern' at the 'legislative steps initiated in the Israeli Knesset with the aim of changing the character and status of the Holy City of Jerusalem'. The Likud-led Israeli Government responded by setting up a Jewish settlement at Pisgat Zeev between Neve Yaacov and French Hill, thus fashioning a continuous residential belt from Mount Scopus to Neve Yaacov with the strategic aim of separating the enlarged city's eastern sector from its West Bank hinterland.

Israeli Governments, whether Labour or Likud, realized these plans by expropriating 30 per cent of Greater East Jerusalem, measuring 73.7 square kilometres. More than four-fifths of the expropriated land was Palestinian. The authorities classified a further 46 per cent of the land as 'green zones', thus denying the right of the Palestinian owners to build there, and used up another 6 per cent in road building, thus leaving the native Palestinians with

only 12 per cent of the land for development.[3] While
the Jewish settlements were established in such a way as
to split Palestinian villages and neighbourhoods from one
another, an elaborate road system was constructed to link
the settlements, further isolating Palestinian centres of the
population. So while the Jewish settlements scrambled the
old Israeli-Jordanian frontier, they created a host of new,
informal borders. 'The interface that divides these areas [from
its Arab environment] is further dramatized by the massive
supporting terraces surrounding the Jewish neighbourhoods
– they present a kind of "solid front" facing the adjacent
Arab areas,' write Michael Romann and Alex Weingrod.[4]
By taking a long view of Mount Scopus from the vicinity
of the Old Town, one can easily verify the statement made
by Romann and Weingrod. Alternatively, one has only to
stand on the south-western edge of the sprawling Hebrew
University on Mount Scopus to realize the strategic advantage
the area has over the Old Town and the rest of (former
Jordanian) East Jerusalem.

A dramatic weakening of the Arab camp, resulting from the
Iraqi invasion of Kuwait in August 1990 and the subsequent
Gulf War in early 1991, made little difference to Israel's
policy of strengthening its hold over Jerusalem. The Likud-led
Government responded to the convening of the Middle East
Peace Conference in October 1991 by establishing yet two
more Jewish settlements – Har Homa on the southern edge of
the east, and Rechis Shuafat next to the Palestinian village of
Shuafat.

As a result of almost a quarter century of Jewish colonization, leading to a dozen settlements, more than 38,000 newly
built, government-subsidized housing units were allocated to
the Jews. The corresponding figure for the Palestinians was
555. (Despite the finding of a municipal inquiry in 1981
that the Palestinian Arabs needed 18,000 new housing units,
the authorities issued permits for only 10,000 housing units
during the next dozen years, thus sharpening the disparity in
the housing density that already existed between Arabs and
Jews: 2.2 persons per room to one person per room.) The
Israeli Government combined the offer of subsidized housing

to its Jewish citizens with exemption from municipal tax for five years followed by a lower rate of taxation. Consequently, the Jewish population in Greater East Jerusalem soared from nil in 1967 to 76,000 in 1983, and then doubled during the next decade.

Following the accord between Israel and the Palestine Liberation Organization in September 1993, the climate for further expropriation of the Palestinian land by the Israeli authorities changed somewhat. When, in April 1995, the plans of the Jerusalem Municipality under the mayorship of Ehud Olmert, a Likud leader, to confiscate 53 hectares of Palestinian land in the villages of Beit Hanina (on the north-western edge) and Beit Safafa (in the south above Gilo) – later backed by the Labour-led national administration headed by Prime Minister Yitzhak Rabin – were put into effect there was much protest by the Palestinians and others in the region, but in vain. Only after the Israeli Arab Members of the Knesset (MKs) threatened to withdraw their support from the Labour-led Government and bring it down did the Rabin Government relent. It was the first time since 1967 that the Israeli authorities had backed down on the issue of land expropriation in the annexed Greater East Jerusalem.

By then the officials at both local and national levels had taken to emphasizing that the Jewish population of Greater East Jerusalem now exceeded its Arab counterpart, numbering 161,000, having surpassed it two years earlier, when the Jewish population of West Jerusalem totalled 251,000. Unsurprisingly, the Palestinian demographers disputed the statistics, claiming that they had been been doctored.[5] These claims became more insistent after Ehud Olmert of Likud (Hebrew, unity) defeated the long-time mayor, Teddy Kollek, a Labourite, in November 1993, and the local and national authorities intensified advance publicity for the 15-month-long 'Jerusalem 3000' festivities, commencing on 4 September 1995, the Jewish New Year. The occasion was King David's conquest of the Jesubite stronghold of Jerusalem in 996 BC. Leaving aside the scholarly disputation about the date – which in the absence of recorded documents cannot be determined accurately (as is also the case, for example, with the birthdate of Jesus Christ) – there were more mundane considerations. The 15-member European Union boycotted the celebrations, objecting to the festival's exclusivist theme of Jerusalem as a strictly Jewish and Israeli city. So did the United States: its ambassador to Israel stayed away from the opening ceremony. The Palestinians were not invited; but had they been they would have ignored the gesture. As in the case of the annual Jerusalem Liberation Day, while the Hebrew media greeted the launch of the Jerusalem 3000 festival – marked by a sound and light and fireworks spectacular – with special radio and television programmes and newspaper supplements, the Arabic media said or wrote nothing about it. When questioned on the subject by international news agencies, Faisal Husseini, the best known leader of the Greater East Jerusalem Palestinians, said: 'These celebrations not only disclaim Jerusalem's Arab and Islamic identity, they glorify the occupation. Jerusalem was not built 3,000 but 5,000 years ago. The recent occupation is trying to celebrate the old one [by King David].'[6] Husseini's words were lost on most Jewish Israelis who supported three 'forevers' regarding Jerusalem: 'forever Israel's capital', 'forever under exclusive Jewish control', and 'forever united'.

'Forever united' implies that the city had been united when all of it came under the control of Israel in 1967. A close examination reveals that this unity is mainly administrative, and that even in administration – whether local or national – there are several areas of ongoing division and difference between Arabs and Jews.

When the Israeli Government annexed the Jordanian Jerusalem and its vast environs in 1967, it planned to absorb its residents in the same way it had the Arabs who stayed behind in Israel in 1948. But this did not work. Unlike the Palestinian Arabs in 1948, East Jerusalemites possessed Jordanian citizenship, and had their own established institutions, secular and religious. Almost unanimously they rejected the option of abandoning their Jordanian nationality for Israeli. So the Israeli Government lowered its sights and decided on absorbing them as residents of the city, not the

State of Israel, and gave them the right to vote in local elections, not national. (The Israeli identity cards issued to them carried special serial numbers, noting their status as 'Arab Jerusalem Residents'; and the Ministry of Interior set up a separate section to deal with such matters of theirs as births, deaths and marriages, permission to travel abroad, and the resettlement of their close relatives from outside Greater East Jerusalem.) East Jerusalemites hardened their non-co-operation with the Israeli authorities by creating additional independent institutions and voluntary organizations of their own and strengthening the existing ones.

However, the Israeli innovation of local voting rights to Greater East Jerusalem Arabs began to work. With the proportion of the eligible Arab voters for the mayoral poll rising steadily from 7.3 per cent in 1973 to 18.4 per cent in late 1983, the Israeli authorities had good reason to believe that the situation was steadily improving.

There were other encouraging indicators. A survey of high school pupils in 1982 revealed that approximately two-thirds of the Jewish students and just over a half of the Arab students had visited both parts of Jerusalem during the past month. But their feelings varied. Whereas only one per cent of the Jewish pupils visiting East Jerusalem felt 'very uncomfortable', the figure for male Arab students visiting West Jerusalem was 35 per cent. Also Arabs were much more interested in knowing the other side better than Jews.[7]

In retrospect, from the Israeli viewpoint, this situation turned out to be the apex. With the eruption of the Palestinian intifada in late 1987, the percentage of the Arabs participating in the mayoral election a year later plummeted to below five per cent, and lingered there at the subsequent poll in 1993 – a year which marked another milestone in the Arab-Jew relationship. The Israeli Government, responding to a series of Palestinian terrorist actions, closed pre-1967 Israel to the Palestinian residents of the West Bank and Gaza Strip, thus undermining its long-held official position – as illustrated in the official maps of Israel since 1977 – of not recognizing these frontiers. The intifada, backed by all Palestinian groups of various political hues based at home and/or abroad, and the Tunis-based PLO, increased self-reliance among Palestinians. Therefore in all spheres of life – political, socio-cultural and economic – the size and number of independent Palestinian organizations rose sharply.

But even during the period of increasingly peaceful co-existence, marked by rising economic and social intercourse, under Israeli rule in the early 1980s, there was scant mutual comprehension or understanding. In 1983, a highly promising year for Israelis, a wide chasm existed between the two sides. This was well illustrated in May of that year. Because of the strictly lunar calendar followed by Muslims, and a complicated solar calendar, with a 19-year cycle, followed by Jews, the Israeli Jerusalem Liberation Day and the Islamic (Prophet Muhammad's) Night Journey and Ascension (al Isra wal Miraj) celebration fell on the same day in late May.

Aware of the significance of the day, Jewish Israeli daily newspapers brought out special supplements on Jerusalem. In West Jerusalem, the Jews celebrated the liberation of (part of) Jerusalem in 1967 with folk dancing, performed deftly by several thousand well-rehearsed, gaily dressed school students and youths along the main thoroughfares of West Jerusalem, applauded by a good-humoured, clapping audience of families in holiday mood. The procession wound its way through the central business district to Jaffa Road, the main commercial artery of the western sector. The celebratory song and dance resumed later in the Old Town at the Western Wall – where the plaza was festooned with Israeli flags – with most of the participants this time being adults, who concluded the day by thanking the Lord in their prayers at the Wall.

On the esplanade at the top of the Western Wall, barely a few hundred metres away from the dancing and singing congregation of the Jews, another scene was in train. Having offered their noon prayers on this holy day of the Night Journey and Ascension inside and outside the Al Aqsa Mosque, thousands of worshippers listened to the religious sermon by the prayer-leader and speeches by local Muslim personages. Reminding their audience of the supreme significance of

the site of the Holy Rock of Heaven from where Prophet
Muhammad ascended to paradise – an event which imbued
Jerusalem with divine holiness, and conferred on it the Islamic
name of Al Quds (The Holy) or Beit al Muquddus (The Holy
House [of God]) – the speakers called on them to safeguard
the city and its sacred shrines from the Zionist enemy. Then
followed two short plays performed by young Palestinians.
They captured well the frustration and humiliation of the
Palestinian existence under the Israeli military occupation,
and found resonances among the pious audience.

Characteristically, neither side reported the activities of
the other. The Arabic press printed not a word about the
Jerusalem Liberation Day. Equally, both the privately owned
newspapers and the publicly run radio and television on the
Jewish Israeli side ignored the Islamic holiday. The two
events might as well have happened at the opposite poles
of the earth.

By all accounts the bitter, protracted Palestinian intifada,
which erupted in 1987, reversed the process of reconciliation
between the two communities, and stoked inter-communal
alienation and enmity.

Today many conversations and reports in Israel and the
Palestinian Territories often refer to 'before the intifada'
and 'after the intifada'. 'Jews once filled East Jerusalem's
restaurants and went bargain shopping on Saturdays in the
Old City market and on Salah al Din Street, East Jerusalem's
main commercial street,' noted Yossi Halevi in the *Jerusalem
Report* in mid-1993. 'Arabs considered it a mark of status
to buy clothes in "Sharia Yafo" [Arabic, Jaffa Road], the
term they use for all of West Jerusalem. In summer tents
were erected near the Damascus Gate, and Jews and Arabs
came to eat slices of watermelon and watch kung fu videos
... Now the Damascus Gate watermelon stands have been
replaced by [north-south] Route One, Arabs buy their clothes
in Ramallah, and Jews shop for bargains and eat [exclusively]
in West Jerusalem.'[8]

To be sure, the reversal of the process of mutual acceptance
and trust came about in stages – in response to violent acts
from both camps: individual Palestinian terrorist actions

on one side and state violence on the other. A sensational fire-bomb assault on a Jewish driver in the Palestinian district of Wadi Joz in 1988 resulted in the Jews staying away from Arab neighbourhoods. The situation worsened sharply in October 1990 after firings by the Israeli police and military on the Temple Mount and Salah al Din Street had killed 21 Palestinians. The retaliatory Palestinian actions, often stabbings, resulted in the murders of three Jewish men in Baqaa later that year and four Jewish women in Kiryat HaYovel early the next year. Jewish Israeli vehicles, easily identified by the Hebrew stickers, became targets of arson attacks, with 450 cars meeting such a fate in 1992, and another 190 during the first half of 1993.

A pattern of mutual, self-reinforcing fear became established. Jews kept away from the Arab sector, apprehensive of terrorism and occasional antagonistic demonstrations that erupted in the Palestinian areas. It became a common practice among Jews to enter the Old Town not from the 'Arab' gates on the north and east, but from the gates on the western side of the walled town: Jaffa, Zion and Dung Gates. Arabs kept away from the Jewish sector, mindful of the constant harassment by the Israeli civil police (blue uniform), and the border police (dark green uniform) under the command of the Israeli Defence Forces, who checked their identity papers and searched them humiliatingly. The chance of body search and arrest rose sharply if they were detected in West Jerusalem at the time of a bomb explosion or some other terrorist action. The young, able Palestinian men in their 20s and 30s, the most productive in any society and most mobile, were the most vulnerable to Israeli police and military harassment. Those Palestinians who were obliged to traverse a Jewish neighbourhood en route to their place of employment during daytime took to rushing through the area, avoiding eye-contact. Barring emergency, most Jews and Arabs withdrew to their respective neighbourhoods after dark, the only Jews in the Palestinian districts being the Israeli border police on patrol.

The brief decline in tension which followed the signing of the Israeli-PLO accord in September 1993 proved short-lived.

Following the killing of 29 Muslim Palestinians at prayer in the Ibrahimi Mosque/Tomb of the Patriarchs in Hebron by a Jewish settler in early 1994, a series of suicide bombings by militant Islamists revived fears among Jews.

This showed in such activities as tourism, as I discovered during a tour of Jerusalem and Bethlehem in early 1995, organized by a company based in Tel Aviv. The tour guide, a plump, middle-aged, dark-haired woman (of Italian origin) in a striped sweater, with a bubbling sense of humour, repeatedly warned her charges, collected in Tel Aviv and West Jerusalem, 'never, ever' to go into East Jerusalem, 'never, ever' to stray away from her in the Old Town outside the Jewish Quarter.

What I witnessed was only one, apparent layer of mutual distrust and fear between Jews and Arabs. There are others, often more profound, which are not so apparent, and require inquiry and research. In commerce and industry there is still an ongoing exchange and intercourse between the two sides in Jerusalem. In the non-political arena Jews and Arabs remain separated by language, religion and other cultural-ethnic aspects of life as strongly as before. In the political sphere, too, they remain apart since Palestinians refuse to participate in local elections and are totally unrepresented at the city hall. The century-old struggle between Jew and Arab for land continues, with the Jewish Israelis, having gained the upper hand in 1948, continuing to further their position, and the Arab Palestinians trying to resist as hard as they can.

More specifically, the two camps, their perceptions shaped by recent history, approach the issue of Jerusalem differently. Jewish Israelis see the city central to their state. 'Jerusalem is the heart of the Jewish people, the focus of its yearning, the land of its vision, the cradle of its prayers,' said Prime Minister Yitzhak Rabin, inaugurating the 'Jerusalem 3000' festivities in September 1995. Israelis point out that even though from 1948 to 1967 West Jerusalem (area 35 square kilometres) adjoined the armistice lines with Jordan, and its link with the rest of Israel through a narrow corridor was precarious, their leaders moved the government and parliament to the city, and saw its population soar from

84,000 in 1948 to 200,000 on the eve of the June 1967 War. Their annexation of a vastly expanded East Jerusalem received an almost universal backing among Jewish Israelis. Since then Jewish citizens have come to consider the Jewish settlements within the newly created Greater East Jerusalem as an integral part of Yerushalayim and Israel, and categorize them differently from those in Judea and Samaria (that is, the West Bank).

In contrast, Palestinians regard the city under Jordanian control from 1948 to 1967, measuring 6.5 square kilo-metres, as their 'Al Quds'. When the exiled mayor of 'their Jerusalem', Rouhi Khatib, aged 80, returned home in May 1993, after a 26-year exile in Jordan, thousands of Palestinians turned out to accord him an enthusiastic welcome. Upholding this position, they place all Jewish settlements built outside their Al Quds on a par with others established elsewhere in the West Bank. The maps published by Palestinians, whether in Arabic or any other language, are consistent and unambiguous on this point. In line with the resolutions adopted repeatedly by the United Nations Security Council, the Palestinians regard all these Jewish settlements as contravening the Fourth Geneva Convention, 1949, and therefore illegal.

Palestinians have been helped, inadvertently, by the build-ing of a north-south highway, cutting through the heart of the city. Though the primary purpose of constructing the six-lane highway, Route One, connecting Hebron in the south with Nablus in the north, completed in the spring of 1993, was to connect the Jewish settlements in the north-eastern part of Greater East Jerusalem with the city centre, it has come to symbolize the frontier between the Jewish West Jerusalem and the Arab East Jerusalem. Save for a few minor deviations, Route One runs along the pre-1967 no man's land between the armistice lines of Israel and Jordan. Today it has recreated a wall – invisible to visitors but very real to local residents – with the Jewish sector to its west, and the Arab to its east.

In a sense Route One formalized what had existed all along not only in terms of international law, as determined by the United Nations, but also the practices of the Israeli Government, local and national.

The western states, including the United States, Britain and France (three of the five permanent members of the United Nations Security Council), which posted diplomatic representatives in the city maintained parallel consulates in West Jerusalem and East Jerusalem. These consulates functioned independently of their respective embassies in Tel Aviv, and reported directly to the Foreign Ministry at home. The two American consulates, for instance, were in direct touch with the State Department in Washington. That is, these and all other members of the United Nations (with the exception of Costa Rica and El Salvador) continued to respect *corpus separatum* status of Jerusalem as spelled out in the United Nations General Assembly Resolution 181 adopted in November 1947, and maintained their embassies in Tel Aviv. The UN resolution specified partition of Palestine, then under British mandate, into a Jewish sector, an Arab sector, and an internationally-administered sector, consisting of Jerusalem and its environs, to be open to both sides.

The continued *corpus separatum* status of Jerusalem is just the latest of its many unique features.

One such feature is its name: 'Yerushalayim' to Jews, meaning 'Founded by [God] Shalem', and 'Al Quds' to Muslims, meaning (in Arabic) 'The Holy'. It is an apt illustration of the deep divide that exists between the two ethnic groups. The Israeli postal authorities use a date stamp with 'Arushalayim' in Arabic, a word which has no currency elsewhere either in writing or speaking. Of the seven gates of the Old Town only two carry the same name in Hebrew and Arabic: the New Gate (Shaar HaHadash/Bab al Jadid) and Herod's Gate, called Flower Gate in both Hebrew and Arabic. The rest have different names in the two languages: St Stephen's Gate (Shaar HaArayot, Lions' Gate; Bab Sitna Mariam, Lady Mary Gate); Damascus Gate (Shaar Shechem, Shechem/Nablus Gate; Bab al Amoud, Gate of the Column); Jaffa Gate (Shaar Yafo, Jaffa Gate; Bab al Khalil; The Khalil/Hebron Gate); Zion Gate (Shaar Ziyyon, Zion Gate; Bal al Nabi Daoud, The Prophet David Gate); and

Dung Gate (Shaar HaAshpot, The Dung Gate; Bab Harat al Magharibi, Gate of the Occidental [People's] Quarter). When, following its capture of East Jerusalem in 1967, the Israeli authorities changed the name of Port Said Street, running along the northern wall of the Old Town towards West Jerusalem, to HaTsanhanim (The Paratroopers') Street to honour the paratroopers who took East Jerusalem from the Jordanians, the Palestinians refused to give currency to the name. It was the same when it came to neighbourhoods. For instance, the Palestinians have stuck to the traditional Jabal al Muqabar (Arabic, Mountain of Evil Counsel) for the district just beyond the southern fringe of the former Jordanian Jerusalem, and have refused to use the Israeli title of East Talpiyot.

While it is true that despite their differing ethnic identity, Jews and Arabs apply to the same Israeli administrative agency – be it police or income tax authority – the actual arrangements are almost always segregated. This pertains as much to education, health care, national insurance allowances, income tax assessment and payment, labour exchanges, and construction licences as it does to local fire fighting and bus services.

In the important area of maintaining law and order there is of course only one authority: the Israeli police. By taking over wholesale the government machinery of Jordan in East Jerusalem, the Israeli authorities acquired the central police station, situated in the Old Town, and absorbed it into its own system. This required Arab policemen to serve under Jewish officers. Their jurisdiction covered the former Jordanian Jerusalem, which included all of the Old Town. This lasted as long as the expanded Jewish Quarter in the Old Town was being rebuilt. By the time the renovated Jewish Quarter was occupied by Jews in the mid-1970s, the central police station of West Jerusalem had quietly placed it under its own jurisdiction, thus ensuring that Arab policemen were kept out of intra-Jewish affairs. The converse does not apply. Jewish police and border police regularly patrol Greater East Jerusalem, and carry out such routine tasks as fining Arab motorists or taxi-drivers.

There are separate income tax offices, labour exchanges and planning offices for Jews and Arabs.

The segregation in the educational system is total, with Arab and Jewish students pursuing different curriculums in separate schools imparting education in Arabic or Hebrew. When, in the immediate aftermath of the annexation of Greater East Jerusalem, Israel altered the inherited Jordanian system into the Israeli Arab system, most Greater East Jerusalem parents withdrew their children and enrolled them either into the private school system, run mainly by Christian institutions, or the West Bank municipal school system, which had continued more or less as before 1967, with the final graduation examination conducted by the Jordanian Education Ministry. This made Israel reverse its policy and revert to the pre-1967 curriculum (except for the compulsory teaching of Hebrew), while administering the Palestinian schools under the joint supervision of the municipality and the Ministry of Education. Even then only about a half of Greater East Jerusalem students enrolled in the Israeli-supervised system, the other half opting either for the private system or the one run by the United Nations Relief and Work Agency (UNRWA) for Palestinian Refugees. A marked difference in the educational achievement of the Jewish students of the city – whether in the Western or Greater Eastern part – and the Arab students had developed. Over 90 per cent of the former finished the final twelfth grade as against 50 per cent of the latter.[9]

As in education so in health care. The Israeli system, catering for Jews, stands apart from the Palestinian system, caring for Muslims and Christians. Health care for Jewish residents is provided by the state-subsidized national health service, largely financed by the Kupath Holim (Hebrew, Sick Fund) of the Histadrut[10] which is rendered by local hospitals and clinics. The Palestinian system, inherited from Jordan, which lacked a state-sponsored medical care programme, relies heavily on Muslim and Christian religious charities as well as the United Nations agencies. Even when the membership of Histadrut entitles Palestinians to state-sponsored health care, they receive this service in clinics in Greater East Jerusalem which, staffed with Arabic-speaking employees, are situated in Palestinian districts, and cater only for them. Nothing sums up the strict division of the medical care system better than the existence of two ambulance services, the Red Shield of David and the Red Crescent, and two blood banks, one Jewish and the other Arab.

'Generally speaking, Jews are never hospitalized in an Arab institution, even in those urgent or emergency cases where this might appear to be the best option,' write Michael Romann and Alex Weingrod. 'Should a Jew be injured in the Arab section of the city, a Jewish ambulance will invariably be called in, and it will take him to the nearest Jewish hospital.'[11]

In another common emergency, fire, the same practice prevails. The main criterion for dispatching the first fire-fighting engine to the site of fire is the ethnic composition of the area – not the distance of the fire from a fire brigade station.

While the Israeli authorities merged the fire fighting facilities by subordinating the East Jerusalem station to its West Jerusalem counterpart, they left the bus transport systems of the two sectors alone – up to a point. They limited the franchise of the Palestinian bus company, to the Arab sector while enlarging that of the Jewish bus company by letting it ply not only along the routes between West Jerusalem and the Jewish settlements in Greater East Jerusalem but also certain sections of the Arab sector itself, thus undermining the position of the Arab bus company. Overall, Jews have the facility to reach any Jewish destination, be it in West Jerusalem or Greater East Jerusalem, by using a Jewish bus. The same statement cannot be made about Palestinians since there are no Palestinian destinations within West Jerusalem, and Arab buses are not allowed to ply in that sector. When a Palestinian decides to use a bus to reach his/her place of work in West Jerusalem, he/she cannot do so by riding an Arab vehicle all the way. He/she must use a Jewish bus before or after crossing Route One. With their different colours, the two bus systems are instantly recognizable.

In the case of taxis, for many years Arab-owned and operated vehicles carried license-plate numbers starting with '666' whereas Jewish-owned and operated cabs had license plate numbers starting with '66'. After the annexation of Greater East Jerusalem, the authorities duplicated the practice of allocating different serial numbers to Arab residents for their identity cards to the vehicle licence plates. As and when the ethnic ownership of a vehicle changed, its licence plate too had to be altered. However, over the years inter-ethnic trans-actions became so frequent that the authorities discontinued the practice of replacing the license plate. Thus, in this minor matter, ideology gave way to pragmatism.

Yet in most day-to-day affairs which matter most to residents, administrative pragmatism and sensitivity have yet to prevail over popular Jewish prejudice against the Arab minority even when it comes to implementing official policies. The status of Arabic is an apt example. Officially Arabic is on a par with Hebrew, and all Israeli laws are translated into Hebrew. But such a basic document as the telephone directory of Jerusalem is issued only in Hebrew, with an option to the subscriber to ask, specifically, for a copy in English. There is no officially printed directory in Arabic, which is the mother tongue of nearly 30 per cent of the city's population. Characteristically, when an enterprising Arab businessman printed a directory in Arabic, he included only Arab subscribers.

What Palestinians find particularly onerous is the absence of Arabic signs even in those administrative centres which the authorities have established exclusively for them. Israeli bureaucrats, whether at the national or local level, show scant consideration for Arabic-speaking citizens, and seldom bother to post signs in that language. Even the municipality of united Jerusalem, run for more than a quarter of a century by Teddy Kollek, considered a liberal in ethnic matters, failed to treat Arabic consistently on a par with Hebrew, as a state law requires.

In the national context, the authorities lost little time to align the socio-religious status of Muslim Jerusalemites with that of Muslim Israelis. In the spheres of polygamy and permissible age for marriage, they modified the Muslim canon law, called the Sharia (Arabic, road/path) to bring it in line with the law of Israel, and prohibited polygamy and marriage below 16 years for males.

For Muslim Jerusalemites the question of challenging these official actions did not arise. Their highest religious body, the Supreme Muslim Council (SMC), refused to acknowledge the authority of Israeli government, which retaliated in kind, and ignored its existence. The Supreme Muslim Council, originally established by the British in Palestine in 1920, dissolved itself when the British departed in May 1948. Following the 1948 Arab-Israeli War, Jordan set up a special ministry in the capital to fill in the gap left by the demise of the SMC. When Jordan lost the West Bank, including its Al Quds, to Israel in June 1967, the religious personages of the territory revived the Supreme Muslim Council. It immediately began supervising Islamic sites and dealing with religious issues in Al Quds and elsewhere in the West Bank. It was financed by Jordan, and Israel made this arrangement official. The Supreme Muslim Council has its own network of Sharia courts and judges – and so has Israel, where the state president appoints Sharia judges, and the Ministry of Religious Affairs runs Sharia courts whose verdicts are implemented by civil authorities. But the laws and procedures of the two systems are dissimilar, and the Israeli Government ignores the workings of the courts run by the Supreme Muslim Council, based in the Old Town of East Jerusalem. However, over the decades the two sides have worked out a *modus operandi*. In routine cases of marriage, divorce or wills, a Muslim Jerusalemite approaches a Sharia court based in pre-1967 Israel, and gets its approval. He then registers the document with the Israeli bureaucracy.

The continued non-co-operation of the Supreme Muslim Council with the Israeli authorities is the norm so far as Palestinians are concerned. A whole range of Palestinian voluntary organizations have maintained this stance from the day of occupation by Israeli military. This applies as much to the associations of lawyers, teachers, engineers, pharmacists, businessmen and hoteliers as taxi-drivers. They have all followed a consistent line on their relations with the corresponding Jewish organizations: rebuffing any moves by the latter to merge and form associations covering all of united Jerusalem.

Since the Palestinian rejection of the Israeli rule rests on the international legal position regarding the occupier and the occupied, the stance of Arab attorneys towards the legal system of Israel is of paramount significance. They continue to boycott Israel's courts, and refuse to apply for the membership of the Israeli Bar Council, a *sine qua non* for practising law in Israel, and ignore the authorities' gesture of conferring on them the Bar Council membership unilaterally. Consequently, when Palestinians decide to challenge any government action they end up hiring liberal-minded or iconoclastic Jewish lawyers.

The differences and splits existing in the public domain are reflected in the private sphere, from shop signs to booking airline tickets, from purchasing a packet of cigarettes to buying a car. The residents of united Jerusalem can be distinguished not just by their names or dress, but by such clues as the cigarettes they smoke, the buses or cabs they ride, or the cars they drive. Anybody smoking Alia, Farid or Imperial cigarettes can be taken to be a Palestinian. On the other hand, it is hard to find Palestinians who drive a Subaru, a Japanese car popular with Jews, since they prefer such European models as Fiat, Peugeot and Mercedes-Benz.

Jerusalem's travel agents and tour operators are plugged into different centres, those in the west connected to their head offices in Tel Aviv, which harbours the country's only civilian international airport, and those in the east linked with Amman, as in the pre-1967 period. This is not something which immediately becomes apparent to foreign visitors. Equally, until and unless they visit Arab and Jewish homes and are extraordinarily observant, they would not know that cooking-gas containers in Jewish households are painted silver-white whereas those in Arab homes are painted blue.

But what strikes even a casual visitor to the city immediately are the shop signs: they are either in Hebrew alone or in Hebrew and English, or they are in Arabic or in Arabic and English. The only, insignificant exceptions he/she will detect are in some of West Jerusalem's driving schools, law firms, and furniture and garment stores, which carry signs in Hebrew and Arabic.

He/she will also be able to tell straight away by looking at the clientele of a café or restaurant whether it is in an Arab or Jewish locality. The almost total absence of women in such a place means it is in an Arab neighbourhood. And a sexually mixed gathering – outside of the ultra-Orthodox districts of West Jerusalem – unquestionably signals a Jewish environment.

This social difference is one of the reasons for the wide chasm that lies between the leisure activities of the two communities, and the means employed to publicize them. A supplement in the *Jerusalem Post* on Fridays is full of information about cinema, theatre, music, nightclubs, art galleries, public lectures, museums, cafés and restaurants – all of them in West Jerusalem. There is not a word about cultural or other activities in East Jerusalem. A similar clutch of information, along with advertisements by stores and restaurants, is supplied by *Events in Jerusalem*, a publication given away free at all four- and five-star hotels in West Jerusalem as well as the American Colony Hotel in East Jerusalem. It contains useful telephone numbers of embassies, hospitals, airlines, leading hotels and such international institutions as the Young Men's Christian Association (YMCA) and the Young Women's Christian Association (YWCA).

The information about the YMCA came in handy to me as I had misplaced the number of Peter, a British specialist on the Middle East, who, before we parted at the Ben Gurion Airport, had told me that he was staying at the YMCA only a few hundred metres from the American Colony Hotel, my abode. Armed with the phone number of the YMCA in *Events in Jerusalem*, I called. The receptionist said that they had no guest by that name. That surprised me: Peter had planned on staying for a few weeks. It was several days later that I realized that the YMCA I had phoned was in West Jerusalem, not East. So once I had obtained the new telephone number I called. I found Peter. It was then that I realized that the receptionist at the YMCA (West) did *not* say: 'Could your friend be staying at the YMCA in East Jerusalem?'; or

'Have you tried the YMCA in East Jerusalem?' Apparently the ongoing animosity between Jews and Arabs has rubbed off even on those who, technically at least, belong to the *same* organization, which happens to be neither Muslim nor Jewish.

Among other things the Palestinian intifada widened the cultural gap that has always existed between Arabs, an oriental people, and the Zionist Jews who began arriving from Europe from the early twentieth century onwards. Respecting the Islamic ban on alcohol, most Muslim Arabs either do not drink or at least do not do so in public. And, reflecting the deprivation and suffering that came in the wake of the intifada, Muslim Palestinians voluntarily abstained from drinking in the open, and so did their Christian fellow-men. The call to abstaining from enjoyment in public also applied to cinema, the only popular form of entertainment. As a result the three cinemas in East Jerusalem closed down, never to reopen. In contrast, night-life in West Jerusalem, more subdued than in Tel Aviv due to the sacredness of the city, became more lively than before. On the other side, the only public entertainment available to East Jerusalemites were occasional plays performed by two highly political theatre companies.

Though Greater East Jerusalem has become an ethnically mixed area due to the Jewish settlements set up since 1967, and extensive economic ties have developed between the two communities, there has been no discernible shift or relocation of commercial quarters on either side of Route One. Each of the ethnic groups continues to maintain its own exclusive central business district – the Jaffa Road area in West Jerusalem and the Salah al Din Street area in East Jerusalem; and its own commercial centre of gravity.

Once a visitor to the city has crossed Route One from the west to the east, or the other way, he/she immediately notices the change in sights, sounds and smells. The shopping area in West Jerusalem could be anywhere in the European region of the Mediterranean. And the one in East Jerusalem is reminiscent of similar districts in Damascus or Amman: the street-stall holders selling kebabs grilled on red-hot charcoal; the newsagent displaying newspapers and precariously-bound books in Arabic only; the drivers of large, shared taxis called *sheroots*, merrily shouting their destinations; a young, lithe waiter, fast on his feet, delivering hot beverages in tiny cups or glasses to his scattered customers; an older man, donning the traditional *kiffayeh*, lugging a samovar of Turkish coffee: all the traditional images of the Orient are here, within shouting distance of Salah al Din Street, just north of the historic Damascus Gate, the approach to which is taken up by Palestinian women in colourful, sequin-embellished dresses, selling vegetables and fruit.

How a (European) Jew, a journalist, arriving from West Jerusalem sees the scene is well captured by Yossi Halevi in the *Jerusalem Report*. 'Walking along Salah al Din a Jew feels disoriented by strangeness,' he reported. 'The magazine covers at news-stands show pictures of evidently well-known men and women he can't identify; the bookstalls offer almost nothing except Islamic piety and political rage; iced carob juice is dispensed from a large brass samovar on a peddlar's back and fava beans floating in vats of steaming water sold as an accompanying snack; groceries stock Shomar-brand mango wafers and lablabs with chillies from the Al Juneidah Dairy – companies and products unknown in West Jerusalem.'[12]

This is a far cry even from the small Jewish shops along Cardo in the Old Town's Jewish Quarter, which cater for the tourists and which, in their cleanliness and orderliness, are far removed from the hustle and bustle of the medieval market of the Arabs with its aromatic spice shops and sacks of musky nuts and dried fruit.

Different days of the Sabbath – Friday, commencing with the sunset on Thursday, for Muslims; and Saturday, commencing with the sunset on Friday, for Jews – add another dimension to the differences between the two communities. The contrast becomes sharper during the holy month of Ramadan, when Muslims fast between sunrise and sunset, especially on Fridays.

I witnessed the phenomenon one Friday in February

(1995), which almost coincided with the month of Ramadan. On my way to Jaffa Road from the American Colony Hotel in the early afternoon, my taxi got caught in a traffic jam. I left the cab and heaved myself up the hill past the New Gate of the Old Town, and turned right into Jaffa Road. The small bookshop of Sematizsky, the most extensive chain of its kind in Israel, was crowded. It was hard to be able to stand up and open a book at the same time. I had scarcely found one volume I was seeking (shop assistants in Israel do anything but assist customers), and begun the search for the next, when an alarm went off, telling us to hurry up and leave. I had planned to get some photocopies done, but that shop had already closed. Within the next half an hour the area became almost deserted as I ambled along to keep an appointment with a Christian Palestinian at a cafeteria near the Jaffa Gate about a kilometre away. After a few cups of coffee and a long conversation, as we walked towards the Haram al Sharif/Noble Sanctuary, we encountered wave after wave of the Muslim faithful who, having finished the afternoon prayers and listened to the sermon, were repairing to their homes in the Old Town and outside – watched gingerly by young machine-gun-toting Israeli soldiers as well as agents of the Shin Beth. The following afternoon, Saturday, I took a stroll in the Jaffa Road area, and counted the number of persons I encountered: 15 in as many minutes. In sharp contrast, the business in the Damascus Gate area, despite the languor caused by the fasting during daytime, was brisk, with hundreds of people about. I was struck not only by the contrast in the weekly rhythm of life of Jews and Muslims, but also by the proximity of the two different ways of life.

During my visits to the Old Town and its environs, I noticed Arab souvenir shops, whether outside or inside the Old Town, selling a paraphernalia of objects made to appeal to Jewish pilgrims and tourists, including Stars of David, menorahs, and maps, guides and picture books with overtly Zionist text and images. At one such store I bought a map of the Old City published by the Jewish Quarter Tourist Administration which, among other things, showed the Jewish Quarter extending all the way from the western rampart to Via Dolorosa – in the process reducing the Muslim Quarter, the largest of the four neighbour-hoods, to about the universally accepted size of the Jewish Quarter, the smallest of the lot. In stark contrast, West Jerusalem souvenir stores, catering among others for a substantial body of non-Jewish visitors and pilgrims, do not carry any Muslim or Christian religious symbols or objects.

More than religious tolerance or intolerance is involved. This contrasting behaviour reflects economic imbalance between the two groups. The financially weak Muslim and Christian Palestinian merchants are not in a position to adhere strictly to their nationalist views and religious affiliation, and ignore the custom provided by Jewish visitors and pilgrims. Contrary is the case on the other side. The economically strong Jewish traders can afford to overlook the non-Jewish customers and refrain from stocking Christian and Muslim religious souvenirs, thus maintaining their religio-cultural purity.

A similar situation prevails in the wider market of employment. Jews are better educated and better off materially than Arabs. They control a very wide range of manufacturing and service industries, and have proportionately less people in manual and semi-skilled pursuits than Arabs. Their business establishments, especially in hotel and catering and the construction industry, draw on the Palestinian pool of unskilled and semi-skilled labour. There is no counter-movement: that is, there are no Arab employers engaging Jews in menial and semi-skilled jobs, or even in highly skilled positions. Among Jews it is mostly salesmen, suppliers and debt-collectors who need to travel to Arab districts, and they do so by car. On the other side, acute economic necessity leads Arabs to be dependent on Jews. And to earn their livelihood Arab employees have to journey to Jewish neighbourhoods and perform their jobs there. Lacking the means to own a car, they have no choice but to use a bus, the only public transport available, which has to be Jewish beyond Route One in West Jerusalem.

All this takes place within the context of well-defined,

deeply entrenched residential segregation, which is a hall-mark of Jerusalem. The 28-year-long reunification has not resulted in the emergence of a single ethnically-mixed district. The decision of some liberal-leftist Jewish families to take up residence in East Jerusalem in order to spawn a mixed environment led nowhere. By the early 1980s they had retreated to West Jerusalem.

The only desegregated pattern to be found is in the sphere of public buildings used for administrative purposes. After capturing East Jerusalem from Jordan in June 1967, the Israeli authorities seized most of the Jordanian municipal and government buildings, and used them mainly for the same purpose as before. The only other Israeli agency which managed to establish itself in East Jerusalem was Histadrut, the multi-purpose labour federation, which also provides health care under its Kupath Holim scheme. It established administrative offices and health clinics to cater for its Arab members. Persistent attempts by private Jewish capital, especially in the hotel and tourist industry, failed to gain a foothold in the Arab East Jerusalem. (Equally, such was the strength of Jewish opposition that there was no known case of Greater East Jerusalem Arab enterprise branching out in West Jerusalem or in any of the Jewish settlements in Greater East Jerusalem.) Having witnessed and experienced the consequences of the sale of agriculture land to immigrant Zionist Jews in Palestine since the early 1900s, most Palestinians in Greater East Jerusalem resolved to resist the encroachment of Jewish capital into the urban property market. In any case there was no reciprocity. Though there was no administrative or judicial ban on selling or leasing Jewish real estate to Arabs outside the Jewish Quarter of the Old Town in the rest of Jerusalem, this never happened. 'Transactions [from Arabs to Jews] which do occur are always complicated, secretive and costly,' noted Michael Romann and Alex Weingrod. 'Needless to say, under the circumstances of "United Jerusalem" Jewish land is never sold or in other ways transferred to Arab ownership.'[13]

Ethnic neighbourhoods in Jerusalem are instantly identi-fied by locals. And even for a visitor, untutored in Hebrew or

Arabic, it does not take long to learn to differentiate between Arab and Jewish areas. The tell-tale signs are easy to spot: architecture, pattern of land usage, intensity of development, and level of such civic facilities as street pavements and lighting, and parks and playgrounds.

In both major categories – residential and business – a Jewish neighbourhood stands apart from its Arab counterpart. Its residential section consists primarily of apartment tower blocks, built in a modern style, and rising as high as eight storeys. In contrast, an Arab district tends to be made up mostly of low-rise buildings, no more than two storeys high, constructed in a traditional style. Whereas the business section of a Jewish neighbourhood is mostly concentrated in the centre of the district, the business facilities in an Arab neighbourhood are more evenly spread out. The contrast in the provision and quality of civic services and facilities is equally striking. Parks and playgrounds are aplenty in West Jerusalem, and rare in the East. It is almost impossible to find unpaved streets in either West Jerusalem or the Jewish settlements in the East. On the other hand it is not uncommon to come across dirt tracks in the midst of middle-class Arab localities.

This disparity stems from Israeli policies and practices. Urban development in the Jewish neighbourhoods of Jerusalem, whether in the West or Greater East, is subject to statutory regulations. These ensure certain standards of building construction, occupancy and infrastructural facilities for the neighbourhood. While the Israeli authorities have been fully armed with overall plans for establishing and developing the Jewish settlements in Greater East Jerusalem, they have never had any planning scheme for the Arab sector of the eastern zone. In the absence of such a document, Israeli bureaucrats do not bother to apply the statutory regulations to the building construction and other related matters in the Arab areas, and grant or reject applications for building haphazardly. Little wonder that between 1967 and 1984, the most intensive years of a government-financed construction boom in greater East Jerusalem, nearly 90 per cent of non-residential building – industrial plants, businesses and public offices –

took place in Jewish neighbourhoods.[14] The overall result was a further consolidation of spatial segregation between the two groups.

Due to the tax exemption given to the Jews deciding to move into newly created Jewish settlements in Greater East Jerusalem, a typical Jewish resident of the city paid less in taxation than his Arab counterpart. Indeed while Arabs were about 30 per cent of the total population of (Greater) East and West Jerusalems, their share of the municipal taxes was 26 per cent.[15] But what they got in return from the municipality in services was only a fraction of what they paid in tax.

Among those who exposed this inequity was Amir Cheshin, a balding, heavily built, middle-aged man, who for over 10 years was mayoral adviser on Arab Affairs. 'Last May [1994] I leaked an unpublished report,' he told me. 'It compared municipal expenditure in West Jerusalem to that in [Greater] East Jerusalem.' Including the Jewish settlements or excluding? 'Excluding.' What were the conclusions? 'In East Jerusalem only between two to 12 per cent of the total municipal budget items for services are invested in the infrastructure, depending on the budget item.' What were the figures for West Jerusalem? 'Two and a half times as high. The report revealed that in half of the Arab neighbourhoods in [Greater] East Jerusalem there is no organized sewerage system, and in the remaining half the system badly needs repairs.' What about water supply and drainage? 'The same. About a half of the water-supply system requires replacing. And drainage problems are severe, I tell you.' And the street lighting and road maintenance? 'Bad. Why don't you go and look for yourself.' Where? 'Try an area which is partly Jewish and partly Arab. Try a couple.'[16]

I did: one to the north of the American Colony Hotel, and the other to the south. In the north, I focused on Lohame HaGetaot (Hebrew, Fighters of the Ghetto), which forms the boundary between the Jewish neighbourhood of Givat HaMivtar, also known as French Hill, and the Arab village of Isawiya. I discovered the street at the Jewish end lined with trees on both sides, but as I walked downhill towards Isawiya, the trees disappeared.

Next I studied the southern village of Abu Tur, named after Ahamd al Turi, a legendary eleventh-century warrior who, driven by his zealotry, attacked the Crusaders from the back of a bull. Situated south of Hinom Valley, which skirts the southern rampart of the Old Town, and extending eastwards to the Arab village of Silwan, Abu Tur is spread out along Jerusalem's most spectacular heights. The 1948 Arab-Israeli War split the village, most of it ending up under Jordanian control, and the rest becoming part of the no-man's land between the armistice lines. It was reunited after the 1967 conflict, and partly rebuilt. Its scenic location attracted middle-class Jews who moved into the apartments constructed along the western edge of Abu Tur. The Jewish population rose steadily, reaching 5,000 in 1983 and rising to nearly 6,000 a decade later, and living in the uphill section of the village. The Arabs, nearly twice as numerous, were confined downhill in the eastern sector of Abu Tur. While the Jewish zone became progressively posh the Arab zone became increasingly overcrowded since the residents there were repeatedly denied permits to build new housing. The contrast between the two sides was well captured by the state of Ein Rogel Street, the spatial dividing line. As in the case of Givat HaMivtar-Isawiya, I found the Jewish section of Ein Rogel Street smoothly paved and well maintained, and its Arab section in disrepair.

As for civic services, little had changed since a study of Abu Tur by Michael Romann and Alex Weingrod in 1983. Arab and Jewish pupils attended separate schools, with Arabic and Hebrew as the respective language of instruction. Arab families availed of medical care facilities provided by Arab health clinics and hospitals located in Greater East Jerusalem while Jewish households made use of either the health clinic based in their sector by Histadrut or hospitals situated in West Jerusalem. Though in theory the local community centre, run by the municipality and charged with providing entertainment and adult education, was open to both ethnic groups, in reality it catered for local Jewish inhabitants only.

Such studies are of more than academic interest. For they

point the way to the pattern of the future – peaceful co-existence between Arabs and Jews, between Palestinians and Israelis, in the city and beyond.

As for Jerusalem, whether united in more than an administrative sense or not, there is another aspect which transcends the problematic Arab-Jew relationship. It concerns the intra-Jewish relationship between secular and modern Orthodox Jews on one side, and between the secular and the ultra-Orthodox, concentrated in the Mea Shearim neighbourhood, on the other.

3

MEA SHEARIM:

A Fortress of Jewish Ultra-Orthodoxy

I met David Asher in a small, open-fronted café near the bended junction of a narrow street in Mea Shearim (Hebrew, Hundred Gates) in north Jerusalem. Furnished with small, white-topped Formica tables and black wooden chairs, with each table bearing not a menu but an after-meal prayer, elegantly printed on a four page folder with embroidered borders, the café, harbouring an appetizing whiff of aromatic smells of freshly cooked food, was uncluttered and spotlessly clean. In a well-pressed pair of black trousers and a white shirt, his head covered with an enclasping black cap, which covered most of his furrowing forehead, David, a man of medium height, with a trimmed salt-and-pepper beard, too looked neat, exuding the confidence and easy manner that comes with owning and running a successful establishment.

'I was born religious,' he began. Where? 'Uzda, Morocco. My father was Moroccan, my mother Algerian. They came to Israel in 1948. I grew up in Jerusalem in Baqaa [village] near Talpiyot. Did my army service, then travelled – all over, ended up in New York. I lived in the Village.' Doing what? 'From 1973 to 1989 I worked with WEVD Radio, the Hebrew language station. I was the producer, and my woman the news-reader, the DJ. We were busy, happy sometimes, not happy other times. But in New York I lost all my Jewish identity. Our Torah says not to do things like eating pork etc. I did all those things and more.' Drugs? He smiled an enigmatic smile. What happened after 1989? 'Returned home, Jerusalem, my roots. I was single: by then my relationship had ended. Now I am back to being a proper religious Jew. I follow the Torah, and feel healthier, cleaner, clearer.' Sitting upright in his chair, he threw a quick glance at his trim body as if to verify his statement. 'Some of my friends have become religious [like me],' he continued. Why so? 'Why? Look around.' He turned to Rafi, my interpreter. 'The crime rate in Israel is zooming. Drugs, AIDS. There's no communication between parents and children. Not like when I grew up. We respected our parents even when we didn't agree with them.' Is it like that in Mea Shearim now? 'Yes,' he replied, his dark eyes brightening up. 'Mea Shearim is a strong area of Judaism, a strong area. Most of it is full of synagogues and yeshivas.' At least it was well demarcated, I remarked. 'How do you mean?' he said, firing his first question. I opened my notebook, and read aloud the large notices in English I had copied earlier at an entrance to the district:

MODEST DRESS SKIRTS REACHING UNTIL BELOW THE KNEE
DEAR VISITOR, YOU ARE QUITE WELCOME TO MEAH SHEARIM BUT PLEASE DO NOT ANTAGONIZE OUR RELIGIOUS INHABITANTS BY STROLLING THROUGH OUR STREETS IN IMMODEST CLOTHING. OUR TORAH REQUIRES THE JEWISH WOMEN TO BE ATTIRED IN MODEST DRESS. MODEST DRESS: DRESS SLEEVES REACHING UNTIL BELOW THE ELBOWS (SLACKS FORBIDDEN), STOCKINGS, MARRIED WOMEN HAVING THEIR HAIR COVERED ETC., ARE THE VIRTUES OF THE

JEWISH WOMAN THROUGHOUT THE AGES.
PLEASE DO NOT OFFEND OUR RESIDENTS
AND CAUSE YOURSELF ANY UNNECESSARY
INCONVENIENCE. WE BEG YOU NOT TO
INFRINGE UPON OUR WAY OF LIFE AND
HOLY CODE OF LAW. WE BESEECH YOU TO
USE DISCRETION BY NOT TRESPASSING OUR
STREETS IN AN UNDESIRABLE FASHION.
THE MEN ARE REQUESTED NOT TO ENTER
BAREHEADED. Thanking you in advance for
complying with our request and wishing you blessings
from above for your good deeds
Committed for guarding modesty – Meah Shearim and
Vicinity, Jerusalem The Holy City

'See, always so polite,' David beamed. 'Thanks, please, blessings. It all comes from having a community that is self-
supporting, and cares for the weak and needy. There is a
stable family life here. Divorce is rare. People live frugally,
with lots of books and just a few pieces of furniture. They are
not consumerists. We have self-help groups, and they supply
anything, from baby clothes to cooking utensils, to poor
families.' People certainly looked less frantic, I said. 'That's
because we lead our lives according to the Torah. Everything
should be run the way Torah says – at least in Jerusalem.' It's
a holy place. So only holy people should run it. At the Town
Hall in Jerusalem they don't read even one sentence from the
Torah.' That was odd, I remarked, because after the election
of Ehud Olmert [in 1993] as mayor, the City Hall had started
the Torah culture and Torah education departments. 'That's
the least Olmert could do, seeing how the Haredim (Hebrew,
Those who fear [God]), the ultra-Orthodox, put him there.
They're so well organised they'll put [Binyamin] Netanyahu
in the driving seat when the time comes, you'll see.' Meanwhile,
Olmert would better take the path of *teshuva* (Hebrew, return
[to strict Judaism]) himself, I said. 'Yes, why not?' replied Asher.
'I did. That path is open to all Jews, whether Ashkenazi' – he
turned to Rafi – 'or Edot Mizrachim (Hebrew, Eastern Peoples)
like me. A "Born Again Jew".'

The label Haredim/ultra-Orthodox applies to those Jews who adhere to a strict interpretation of the Halacha (Hebrew, The Way) Jewish Law. Full observance of the Halacha involves following all 613 religious prohibitions and obligations that regulate Jewish life, from trivial daily bodily functions to the organization of life in society – and separation between Jews and Gentiles. There are two major and one minor schools within ultra-Orthodoxy: Hassadim (Hebrew, pious), Mitnagdim (Hebrew, opponents), and Bratslavic, named after the Ukrainian town of Bratslav.

In Mea Shearim the signs of Jewish ultra-Orthodoxy were everywhere. Adult males, bearded to the man, maintained the tradition of donning the garb of the East European ghetto – black trousers, thin long black coats and wide black hats – their strained faces a reminder of the past, their dolefulness relieved by the lustre of their heavy-lidded, grey or blue eyes. Their sidelocks, shaped into ringlets, dangled like black ropes from their black hats. The few women about wore long-sleeved dresses, their skirts falling well below the knees and covering the upper part of their heavy stockings, their hair shielded from the gaze of lustful men by a scarf or a wig. 'Many of the companies selling products in our neighbourhood have to redesign the packaging to see that there were no naked women or women dressed immodestly,' Rubin Cardova, a tall Romanian Jew, wearing a black *kippa* over his light-brownish hair, explained outside his sweetshop. 'Otherwise they will not be able to sell the product here.' He offered us a few sweets. 'For the same reason television is off limits. You never know when a semi-clad woman would appear – in a commercial or a news item or a play or soap opera. It's the same with most Israeli publications – lots of nudity and lasciviousness.'

That explained another social phenomenon in Mea Shearim and other ultra-Orthodox neighbourhoods in Jerusalem – Beit Israel, Geula and Har Nof – and elsewhere: wallpapers. At a busy intersection near Cardova's shop, underneath the large sign in Hebrew and English – 'KUPATH [FUND] RABBI MEIR BAAL HANES' – the stone wall of the two-storey building was plastered with posters and fliers, some in blood red, others in green, still others in yellow, and news-sheets. A few bearded men, one of them resting his back against the saddle of his leaning cycle, pored over the contents of the printed papers.

In the absence of television aerials the burden of modernity was borne by the sun-powered water-heaters clutched to the red-tiled roofs. Other than that Mea Shearim has kept its decrepit charm and character – conspicuously missing from the newer parts of Jerusalem – with dark, weather-worn houses, their rickety balconies turned into cages by unpainted steel rods, laid out on both sides of narrow streets, choked with cars and vans.

Driven out of the Old Town of Jerusalem by overcrowding and poor sanitation, the Jews set up a new colony to the north in 1875, naming it Mea Shearim. The settlement, heavily gated to keep the brigands out, was initially open to all Jews. It was only from the early twentieth century that it turned increasingly ultra-Orthodox.

Today, besides the general gloominess of the houses and shops, the evidence of the early history of Mea Shearim is provided by the backyards built to accommodate, temporarily, the new Jewish immigrants. Wide and leisurely, harbouring sagging washing lines, and furnished with steps leading to the back landing on the first floor, these backyards transport the visitor to an age when land was cheap and time moved slowly. During my rambling through the district, I came across a semicircular sign in Hebrew and English over the entrance to a synagogue at the end of a string of shops, behind rolls of wallpaper and an array of upright brooms:

1898 SYNAGOGUE & FOUNDED 1898
ROTHERS ISSACHAROFF & BABAIOFF.

The Hassadim, the leading ultra-Orthodox sect, was established by Israel Baal Shem Tov (1698–1740), a pious Jew, who, rebelling against the literalism of the Talmud (Hebrew, Learning), attempted to help religious but illiterate Jews to relate to the Jewish law and doctrine through emotional means. He devised a method of total surrender by the believer to God through mystical elevation, involving singing and dancing. Despite being branded heretic by the Talmudists in 1781, the size of the Hassadi community grew, especially in Poland and Russia. As the leader of his group of disciples, a Hassadi rabbi acted as an intercessor between them and God, offering inspired advice on all matters of life – including marriage, business and personal problems. Later, as literacy grew among Jews, the leaders of the sect corrected the initial dramatic lurch towards mysticism and restored a greater respect for the study of the Torah. They studied as industriously as others, but maintained an intimacy in communal life through such practices as congregational singing and dancing. But this balancing act was not enough for some who wanted a total return to the study of the Torah as a means to getting closer to God. They were called Mitnagdim. They thrived in Vilna, Lithuania. To distinguish themselves from the Hassidim, they hid their sidelocks behind their ears. Further division came when the followers of Rabbi Nahuman of Bratslav, Ukraine, who established his school in 1815, deviated from the practice of having a living chief rabbi.[1]

At the beginning of the twentieth century a small minority of the Hassidim and the Mitnagdim migrated to Palestine, preferring to live in Jerusalem's Mea Shearim district. Later, led by Rabbi Abraham Karelitz, most of the Mitnagdim immigrants left Mea Shearim for the Bnei Beraq agricultural settlement near Tel Aviv. Over time, like other sects, the Hassidim fell victim to hair-splitting factionalism, and broke up into four sub-sects, named after places in Poland: Belz, Gere, Lubavitch (also known as Habad) and Vishnitz. Today the male followers of these sub-sects can be differentiated by the presence or absence of sidelocks, and subtle differences in the dress: wearing or not wearing the prayer shawl over the shirt; tucking or not tucking trousers into ankle socks, and how far; the side of the hat where the bow is tied, and so on.

Politically, the ultra-Orthodox supported Agudat Israel (Hebrew, Union of Israel). It was formed in Katowice, Poland, in 1912 largely by the ultra-Orthodox Jews of Germany, Poland and Ukraine, to address Jewish problems from a religious perspective. A member had to accept the supremacy of the Torah in Jewish life. Its adherents in Palestine boycotted the quasi-official organs of the Yishuv, the Jewish community. They did so primarily because the creation of Israel through human endeavour – such as the one by Zionist pioneers in Palestine – ran counter to their belief that Israel, as a 'peoplehood', would be redeemed by the Messiah, and secondarily because they were opposed to women's suffrage. They considered Jews as a religious, not ethnic, entity, and believed that the Jewish problems could only be solved by the Torah. When its members in Palestine accepted funds from the Jewish National Fund, established by the World Zionist Organization, then called the Zionist Organization, to set up kibbutzim and yeshivas, there was a split. The majority opted for co-operation with Zionists on the basis that Zionism could be put to the service of Judaism practised according to the Halacha. The minority, arguing that the Zionist effort to establish the Jewish homeland in Palestine was a 'negative event' because it derived from the working of human, not divine, will, formed the Neturei Karta (Aramaic, Guardians of the [Holy] City). It became the best known of the anti-Zionist sub-sects within Hassadim, the others being the Satmar Hassidim (named after a place in East Europe) and the Toldot Aharon (Hebrew, History of the Lost), the last being highly conspicuous because of the striped coats worn by its male adherents.

In return for endorsing the United Nations partition plan for Palestine in 1947, as urged by David Ben Gurion, the foremost socialist Zionist figure-head, Agudat leaders secured from him a written promise that in the future Jewish state laws will be promulgated regarding observance of the Jewish Sabbath and dietary laws, rabbinical courts, and the status of the Chief Rabbinate. Ben Gurion took this decision against the background of the recent discovery of the Holocaust, the Jewish genocide, after World War II – primarily affecting the East European Jewry – which had softened the earlier hardline secularism of his socialist Zionist colleagues, making them receptive to the idea of retaining the traditions of East European Jewry, including ultra-Orthodoxy and the Council of Torah Sages.

Once Israel was founded in 1948, Agudat decided to participate in the state's affairs, including participation in parliamentary elections, thus conferring an ultra-Orthodox recognition on the Zionist state. On the eve of the first general election in 1949 it combined with its sister organization Poale Agudat Israel (Hebrew, Workers of the Union of Israel) to form the Agudat bloc. This bloc then allied with the Mizrahi bloc – Mizrahi (Hebrew, acronym of Merkaz Rouhani, Spiritual Centre) and Poale HaMizrahi (Hebrew, acronym of Workers of Spiritual Centre) – to constitute the United Religious Front (URF). In a parliament of 120, the URF won 16 (Mizrahi bloc 10, Agudat bloc six), and joined the Government headed by David Ben Gurion of Mapai (Hebrew, acronym of Mifleget Poalei Israel, Israel Workers Party).

Mizrahi was the vehicle of Orthodox Jews, who were not as strictly committed to following the Jewish law and tradition as the ultra-Orthodox. But, like the ultra-Orthodox, they believe that the Jewish law, Halacha, does not change with times, and that only exceptionally well-qualified authorities can interpret it. They engage in daily worship as well as participate in traditional prayers and ceremonies, study the Torah, and observe dietary laws and the Sabbath. They separate men and women in the synagogue where music during the communal service is banned.

Mizrahi was formed in 1902 by a group of rabbis in Vilnius, Lithuania, to counter growing secularization of the education of Jews in Europe, and marked the rise of religious Zionism as a distinct faction within the Zionist movement, represented by the World Zionist Organization. The party advocated founding a Jewish national home in Palestine based on the Torah. Its overall thesis was that while 'the great redemption' was in the hands of the Messiah, Zionism was helping to realize 'a small redemption'. In Palestine Mizrahi ensured that the Chief Rabbinate was organized within the framework of the elected assembly representing the Yishuv, thus laying the foundation for a link between official, secular authority and religion, which was to continue after the establishment of Israel. Its members abandoned the ghetto clothes and prayer shawl, rooted in their East European history, and adopted the everyday western dress of socialist Zionists. To distinguish themselves from their secular co-religionists, they took to wearing a multicolour, knitted, crocheted skullcap. In 1922 the younger members of Mizrahi formed Paole HaMizrahi which focused on workers in the Orthodox community.

Accepted as part of the broad stream of Zionism, the dominant socialist Zionists shared power with Mizrahi. The provisional Government of Israel, formed in May 1948, included one Mizrahi minister. Later, as constituents of the United Religious Front, both Mizrahi and Paole HaMizrahi joined the Government after the 1949 General Election. By securing the Ministry of Religious Affairs, the Mizrahi bloc put its stamp on the religious aspect of Israeli state and society during the important formative years. In 1950 it steered major laws on the Sabbath, dietary practices in public institutions, rabbinical courts, and the status and functions of the Chief Rabbinate. Since then the Mizrahi bloc – later renamed Mafdal (Hebrew, acronym of Mifleget Datit Leumit, National Religious Party) – sharing power in all the coalition governments, whether headed by a left-of-centre or right-of-centre party, for nearly the next four decades, and always controlling the Ministry of Religious Affairs, has been the dominant force in the religious institutions of Israel. Under its guidance the religious affairs ministry decided how to finance rabbinical councils and rabbinical courts, and influenced the composition and working of the powerful Chief Rabbinate, consisting of two joint Chief Rabbis (of Ashkenazim and Sephardim) and a 10-member Chief Rabbinical Council. Over the years Orthodox rabbis, often politically loyal to Mafdal, have successfully challenged the legitimacy of certain non-Orthodox marriages, divorces and conversions in Israel.

However, in the early days of Israel, being part of the United Religious Front, the Mizrahi bloc shared some of the authority flowing from the religious laws with its partner, the Agudat bloc. For instance, the power of enforcing the kashrut/kosher aspect of the dietary law was vested in Eda Haredim (Hebrew, Pious People). Allied with the Toldot Aharon sub-sect, it is the most extreme group, and has been known to burn down bus stops in ultra-Orthodox quarters carrying advertisements that offend its sense of modesty.

The Sabbath, lasting from Friday sunset to Saturday sunset, is enforced strictly in Israel. During Sabbath there is no public transport and no delivery of telegrams. Newspapers do not appear on a Saturday. Since the Ministry of Religious Affairs is in charge of Jewish shrines such as the Western Wall, treated as an Orthodox/ultra-Orthodox synagogue, men and women are segregated at the Wall. Also the enforcement of the Sabbath at the shrine is strict. Hardly had I written down the approximate length and height of the Western Wall on my first visit, on a Saturday, than a bearded man in black upbraided me with a fierce whisper: 'Shabbot [Sabbath]!' The degree of Sabbath observance by individual Jews varies. The general guidance comes from the Chief Rabbinate and is an ongoing process. In 1992, for instance, it ruled that the faithful could use the telephone so long as they avoided physical contact with the instrument. This led many observant Jews to use a pencil to dial calls.

All this goes on in the context of the lack of a written constitution in Israel. The statement in the Declaration of the Establishment of Israel in May 1948 that a constitution would be drafted by the following October remains unfulfilled to this day. Among other things the relationship between the state and the synagogue has yet to be defined constitutionally. The continuing vacuum has been filled by the 'status quo' laws, drafted and implemented by the Ministry of Religious Affairs controlled almost invariably by a religious party, and the rulings of the Chief Rabbinate.

Most observers believe that the decision of the Israeli state to make the Halacha binding in such areas of life as marriage, divorce and death (burial without religious rites and cremation are forbidden) has a general backing among secular Jews. By and large secularists perceive it as an effective way of avoiding conflict between civic and religious centres of power in these personal matters of import.

'Secular [Jewish] Israelis have a need, so it seems, to maintain religious institutions which will keep the faith on their behalf but, at the same time, by the extremist nature of these institutions, make sure that the majority of [Jewish] Israelis have nothing to do with them,' writes Rabbi Dow Marmur. 'In this way the dominant religion of the Jewish state has become institutionalized vicarious Judaism.'[2]

The sharing of authority and responsibility between religious and civil leaderships extends to other important areas such as education. In Palestine each of the three groupings of Zionists – socialist Mapai, Orthodox Mizrahi and ultra-Orthodox Agudat – set up its own educational system. After the founding of Israel, the Mapai-dominated Government disbanded the Mapai network and transformed it into a secular, state system, but left intact the Mizrahi- and Agudat-run schools and yeshivas, with the schools to be financed fully, and the yeshivas partly, by the public exchequer, as institutionalized in the Compulsory Education Law, 1949.

However, in the early formative days of Israel, the religious parties wanted more. In mid-1951 the United Religious Front brought down the Government led by David Ben Gurion on the issues of educating immigrant families and the URF's degree of control over religious education in secular, state schools.

In the Ashkenazi tradition, a yeshiva, an old institution, was a community affair, with the local rabbi acting as its head, and its student body drawn locally and taught part-time in Yiddish. But in the eighteenth century, after the Lithuania-based Mitnagdim's return to intensive study of the Torah, their yeshivas in Lithuania and Belorussia emerged as regional boarding schools, drawing bright students from a large area. Most of these students, engaged in full-time study and worship, were aged 15 to 24, and unmarried. Believing that these studies were central to ensuring the survival of Jews, the rabbinical teachers disallowed the teaching of any secular subject. Later, in 1878, kollels (Hebrew, including) emerged as post-yeshiva institutions for brilliant married students who wanted to continue Torah studies. When Orthodox and ultra-Orthodox Jews from East Europe began migrating to Palestine in the early twentieth century, they transplanted these all-male institutions there. In their educational system aside from yeshivas, too, they maintained separation of sexes.

With a dramatic upsurge in the Jewish immigration from Arab countries in Israel between 1950–53, the popularity of single-sex schools rose since the parents born in the Arab Middle East disapproved of their daughters attending mixed-sex schools. During the period 1948–53 the number of pupils in Agudat schools shot up, from nearly 7,000 to over 24,000.

The establishment of Israel as a social welfare state created conditions which proved conducive to the consolidation and expansion of the religious communities, especially the ultra-Orthodox, whose male members are encouraged to spend a lifetime in study and worship, centred around home, yeshiva and synagogue. With the safety net of state allowances guaranteeing a minimum living standard, the leaders of the ultra-Orthodox community were able to transform the voluntary ghetto of the past into a formally demarcated territory where they were able to enforce a rigidly Judaistic way of life.

In the religious educational field, within a generation of Israel's existence, almost all ultra-Orthodox males had either graduated from yeshivas, or were enrolled there or at kollels. That is, the self-contained ultra-Orthodox educational system, totally divorced from its secular counterpart, now completely socialized the children of the community. Also the social mores of the tightly-knit community were such that young people married early, between 18 and 22, and became parents within a few years. They thus became socially and economically dependent on the extended family in a community, which provided mutual assistance and cared for its weaker members, and was committed to a life-long study of the Torah (for its male members) – a contrast to the achievement-oriented rat race of the outside world. However, when having fathered half a dozen children, mature yeshiva and kollel graduates tried to find jobs (to supplement the earnings of their wives) they found their choice limited: rabbis or rabbinical judges, or religious functionaries to supervise Jewish dietary laws, check slaughter houses etc. Equally seriously, as the size of the ultra-Orthodox community, opposed to birth control, increased, the burden of supporting an ever burgeoning body of religious scholars by the state and private charity, mainly by the co-sectarians in North America, became unbearable. Under the circumstances Agudat's political agenda narrowed to maintaining ultra-Orthodox yeshivas and kollels with public and private funds, a far cry from the early days of Israel.

The Agudat bloc contested the 1951 election separately, and won five seats. It joined the Government, but quit in protest against the passing of a law prescribing conscription for women. While existing separately, the two Agudat parties stayed in opposition during the era of the Labour-dominated Governments which ended in 1977. Later they contested the parliamentary poll jointly, and their achievement varied from two seats (1981) to six (1988).

Since the emergence of Israel, the aggregate popularity of the religious parties has remained remarkably stable. But there has been a shift within the camp. Of the 16 seats secured by the religious groupings in the 1949 parliament, 10 belonged to the Orthodox Mafdal, and six to the ultra-Orthodox groups. In 1988 the proportions reversed – with the ultra-Orthodox parties claiming 13 of the 18 seats won by the religious groups – and remained so thereafter.

The influence of the ultra-Orthodox parties increased after the 1981 poll. They held the balance of power between Labour (47 seats) and Likud (48 seats). To gain their backing, Likud Premier Menachem Begin allocated extra funds to their educational and cultural institutions, exempted ultra-Orthodox women from military service, and made draft deferment for yeshiva students easier.

With the 1984 and 1988 general elections again producing close results between Labour and Likud, the leaders of the ultra-Orthodox and Orthodox groups were able to extract many concessions from the front-runners, even though in the end the result was a national unity government.

Besides the funding of yeshivas and kollels, the subject which has most interested ultra-Orthodox leadership is the exemption or deferment of military service for its yeshiva students. The idea was first aired during the 1948–9 Arab-Israeli War. Prime Minister David Ben Gurion agreed to exempt them from compulsory draft on the basis that, given the paucity of such students, their deaths in combat could undermine Torah studies in the future. His decision then affected some 500 young men. By the early 1990s the total population of yeshivas and kollels exceeded 100,000 (some 30,000 more than the aggregate student body of the Israeli universities), with about 20,000 enrolled in ultra-Orthodox institutions. Leaving aside the question of the numbers involved, the ultra-Orthodox highlight the spiritual essence of their reasoning. Intensive, full-time study of the Jewish law and tradition is imperative to ensure spiritual survival of Jews, they say, pointing to the Old Testament, which records that Levis, the priests, were exempted from fighting by Moses during the four decades of the Jewish wanderings in the Sinai Peninsula.

However, there is a practical dimension to this. The ultra-Orthodox leadership is apprehensive that exposing its young men and women to a two- to three-year-long experience in the secular environment of the military would pollute the self-enclosed world and its value system in which they had been raised, and undermine the continuity and strength of its community by causing defections. Also the very idea of the mixing of young men and women, a common practice in the IDF, is anathema to the ultra-Orthodox. Indeed, in 1953 the ultra-Orthodox frustrated the implementation of a law conscripting women into the armed forces. Its female members threatened to court arrest rather than serve in the military. The Government backed down, but insisted that a woman draftee would have to appear before a committee to be tested on her religious knowledge. Later, in 1981, Premier Begin discontinued this practice, and gave an option to ultra-Orthodox women to do community service for two years.

As for males, those joining a yeshiva get a deferment from the military service straight away, and continue studying so long as the IDF does not need them. This applies to all yeshiva students, ultra-Orthodox or not. As a rule, the non-ultra-Orthodox yeshiva students serve in the armed forces. In contrast, most married ultra-Orthodox men make sure to remain registered with a kollel until they are at least 24 and have fathered a couple of children. In that case, even if the draft call comes through, the actual time served in the IDF is four months or less. In the mid-1990s the need for human power in the military was on the decline; and the IDF, which had reduced the service period for women from 24 to 20 months, saw no need to draft the ultra-Orthodox.

The overall impression among the non-ultra-Orthodox, who formed 90 per cent of the total Jewish population in 1994, was that the ultra-Orthodox were deliberately avoiding the patriotic duty of military service, an immoral, unethical thing to do. They were also critical of ultra-Orthodox intolerance and zealotry in enforcing a strict observance of the Sabbath. This manifested itself publicly and regularly, with the police in Jerusalem closing as many as 130 streets and roads to vehicular traffic on the Sabbath and other Jewish holidays in order to prevent the ultra-Orthodox stoning passing cars and trucks in 'religious self-defence'.

The number of such streets in Jerusalem has been on the increase, reflecting the movement of the ultra-Orthodox from their traditional neighbourhoods into adjoining areas. This is due to large family size in the neighbourhoods like Mea Shearim, where the housing density, at three persons to a room, is three times the figure for the Jewish population elsewhere in the city. Also there is a steady infusion of the ultra-Orthodox from outside the city because there are better facilities, public and private, for them here than anywhere else in the country, except Bnei Beraq, a city of 125,000 near Tel Aviv, which is a stronghold of the Mitnagdim sect. A pattern is already discernible. A few ultra-Orthodox families move into a new street, followed by others, and start pressuring their neighbours to observe the Sabbath strictly – not to drive or play the radio loudly or work in the back garden. Finally they shut the street down on the Sabbath, thus getting the police involved. With their power increasing at City Hall the ultra-Orthodox feel increasingly bold.

Mirroring the increase in their size, the ultra-Orthodox have acquired a greater political clout than before. In the quarter century since the 1967 War, when Israel captured East Jerusalem, the percentage of the ultra-Orthodox among Jews doubled, from 15 to 30. But due to large families, more than half of Jerusalem's Jewish pupils below 10 were ultra-Orthodox.

In the November 1993 elections to the City Hall and mayor's office, two-thirds of the 86,000 votes for the successful Likud candidate, Ehud Olmert, came from the ultra-Orthodox electors. Overall, the ultra-Orthodox parties secured eight seats in the 30-member municipal council, with another five going to the Orthodox Mafdal, the religious parties thus forming the largest single bloc of 13 – versus the total strength of 10 for Labour and the leftist Mertez (Hebrew, vitality). Together with seven members of the Likud and the secular nationalist Tzomet (Hebrew, Crossroads), the right-wing-religious alliance controlled two-thirds of the seats in the City Hall. One of the first acts of the new council was to double the budget for the ultra-Orthodox schools. Another was to make it easier for the ultra-Orthodox to secure housing loans.

Nationally, the budget in 1992 raised allocations to ultra-Orthodox educational and cultural institutions to an unprecedented $246 million, a 500-fold increase in less than a decade. This happened despite the fact that the two ultra-Orthodox parties, which won parliamentary seats, took contrary stands on forming a coalition with Labour after the June 1992 poll.

On the eve of this election, at the behest of Bnei-Beraq-based Rabbi Eliezer Schach, the head of prestigious Ponivezh Yeshiva, Agudat Israel, Poale Agudat Israel and Degel HaTorah (Hebrew, Flag of the Torah) combined to form the Yahadut HaTorah HaMeuhedet (Hebrew, United Torah Judaism). It won six seats.

An equal number of seats were secured by another ultra-Orthodox group, Shas (Hebrew, abbreviation of Shomere Torah, Guardians of Torah). The nucleus of its support was the ultra-Orthodox community within the Edot Mizrachim, the term used for the Jews of Middle Eastern or North African origin.

When Mizrachim arrived in Israel in the early 1950s they were dispersed to development towns in the Negev and Galilee. There they were approached by both the Orthodox Mafdal (then functioning under a different name) and the ultra-Orthodox Agudat. To the new arrivals Mafdal appeared as part of the governing Zionist establishment, representing a modern religious culture rooted in Palestine-Israel, and not in the East European Diaspora (as was the case with the ultra-Orthodox Agudat), into which they wished to integrate. On the other hand, Mafdal coupled its political activity with religion, using the local Ashkenazi synagogue as a party branch. Since the Mizrachim invariably belonged to the Sephardi synagogue they felt alienated.

This made ultra-Orthodoxy attractive to some Mizrachim. Earlier, a minority of Mizrachi parents, approached by ultra-Orthodox yeshiva graduates to send their children to Agudat-run schools and yeshivas, where sexes were separated, had joined the ultra-Orthodox camp. The other point of convergence between the two sides was religio-cultural. They both believed in saint worship and ritual practices at saintly tombs. Many of the Mizrachim joined ultra-Orthodox yeshivas which were run invariably by Ashkenazim.

Over time Mizrachim realized that Ashkenazim were unprepared to regard them as equals academically or socially. They also noticed Ashkenazi reluctance to marry Mizrachim. The resulting disappointment found resonances in the office of the Sephardic Chief Rabbi, occupied during 1973–83 by Iraq-born Ovadia Yosef.

Finally, Mizrachi disaffection took a political turn. In the local election in Jerusalem in 1982 the Mizrachi ultra-Orthodox, encouraged by Chief Rabbi Yosef, offered their own list of candidates, which was in competition with the two lists of Ashkenazi ultra-Orthodox, both backed by the highly respected Rabbi Schach. The Mizrachi list did surprisingly well.

This led to the formation of Shas in late 1983. It received the blessing of Rabbi Yosef, who visualized it as a vehicle for righting the wrongs being done to Mizrachim by Ashkenazim. He encouraged Rabbi Arye Deri, a young Moroccan-born graduate of the Ponivezh Yeshiva in Bnei Beraq, to join Shas. In the 1984 election Shas, led by Deri, won four seats. It joined the national unity administration, and Deri became a cabinet minister at 29. The Government allowed Shas to establish its own educational network, thus raising the total of such systems to four, three of them religious.

In 1988 Shas secured six seats, and became the largest religious group in parliament. Its leading figures, Rabbis Arye Deri and Yitzhak Peretz, became ministers, one of them taking over the important interior ministry in the national unity administration that followed. Though the party's backing came almost exclusively from Mizrachim, its leadership, having graduated from Ashkenazim-run yeshivas and kollels, was beholden to Rabbi Schach. The resulting twin-headed leadership continued until March 1990. In that month, encouraged by Rabbi Yosef, Shas withdrew its backing from the national unity government with a view to later entering into a coalition with Labour. But at a rally in Tel Aviv, with Yosef present on the dais, Schach publicly nullified the Shas-Labour agreement, thus publicly snubbing Yosef. It was the most humiliating experience for Yosef yet. But it terminated the dual leadership of Shas, with the party now deciding to rely exclusively on Yosef, who had set up the Council of Torah Scholars to guide Shas on major issues (just as the Council of Torah Sages had done for Agudat for decades).

During the campaign for the June 1992 election, Rabbi Schach said publicly what he had all along thought privately. 'The time has not yet come for Sephardim to take positions of leadership,' he told an election rally. 'They need to follow Ashkenazi guidance.' Sephardim had not been so blatantly insulted in a long time. This goaded Rabbi Yosef – who had earlier threatened to resign from Shas whose (political) leader, Deri, was under police investigation for charges of embezzlement of public funds and bribe-taking – to withdrew his threat, and become the top campaigner for the party. Despite the loss of the backing of the venerable Schach, and the staining of its image due to bribery charges, Shas improved its overall vote, and retained its six seats.

Whereas the United Torah Judaism, following the instruction of Rabbi Schach, stayed away from coalescing with Labour, the Shas parliamentarians led by Deri joined the coalition at Yosef's behest. Yosef thus emerged as the most powerful rabbi in the country. In the process he liberated the religious Mizrachim from the domination of their Ashkenazi counterparts.

Born in Baghdad in 1920, Ovadia Yosef was raised by his parents in Jerusalem, which has been his base ever since. A brilliant yeshiva student, he became an author at 18, and went on to publish nearly 30 more volumes on religious matters. Significantly, he retained the traditional Sephardi rabbinical dress of a gold-embroidered black robe and a blue turban-shaped hat. The dark glasses he wears, which enhance his distinctive appearance, are a medically prescribed device to protect his failing eyesight caused by diabetes.

Throughout his career as a Sephardi rabbi, he suffered slights and insults at the hands of the Ashkenazi religious establishment. It dismissed him as 'a donkey bearing books', describing him as more a memorizer of the sacred texts than an original thinker or interpreter. But he sharpened his knowledge and understanding of the Torah, and started to make his mark in the early 1960s, journeying up and down the country, urging his audiences in synagogues and cinema halls to take up study of the Torah. He began attracting more people to his meetings on the Torah than even the most important politician could manage. Yet, even when he rose to be the Chief Rabbi of Sephardim – on a par with the Chief Rabbi of Ashkenazim – he was excluded from the Council of Torah Sages, an exclusively Ashkenazi body, the final spiritual and political authority among the ultra-Orthodox Jewry, which guided Agudat Israel. Among

Yosef's memorable rulings, when holding the high office, was the one which declared that the Falashas of Ethiopia were fully Jewish. The other was that Sephardi soldiers should pray separately to preserve their own ritual rather than join the Ashkenazim in a common service. Indeed his independent-mindedness went down so badly with his Ashkenazi counterpart, Chief Rabbi Shlomo Goren, who had a reputation for pomposity and surliness, that Joseph Burg, the Mafdal Minister of Religious Affairs, steered a bill through parliament in 1983 limiting the tenure of a chief rabbi to 10 years, thus making both Goren and Yosef step down later that year.

Unlike Goren, a hardliner, Yosef has taken a middle position on the thorny issue of Israel and the messianic redemption: 'While the restoration of Jewish sovereignty has religious value, it is premature to speculate about its messianic significance.' Equally, on making peace with Arab neighbours, he has been dovish. At a conference on the Jewish law in August 1989, he declared it religiously permissible to return parts of the Land of Israel if that would 'prevent war and save lives'.

Having seen his picture on the walls of several shops, cafés and restaurants in different Israeli cities, I was curious to encounter him in the flesh. So I went to the Yasdim synagogue in the Bukharan Quarter of Mea Shearim in Jerusalem one Saturday night. The place was packed, as was the small adjoining room, with the admirers glued to the video-screen. Following the custom, the congregation passed around mint and basil branches to taste the sweetness of the just-ended Sabbath. The moment Rabbi Yosef arrived, flanked by aides, pin-drop silence ensued. As he cut through a parting knot of people, the faithful touched his robe and then placed their fingers on their lips, as if he were a Torah scroll. Having seated himself in a chair, the size of a throne, he started talking without much ado in a colloquial idiom, conversationally, as if addressing each of the members of the audience personally.

Emulating his example, other ultra-Orthodox Sephardi rabbis too speak colloquial Hebrew when addressing their congregations. This is in marked contrast to Ashkenazi ultra-Orthodox rabbis who speak literary Hebrew and remain aloof from their audiences. The Sephardi ultra-Orthodox also broke the traditional taboo against television, freely using the medium to give interviews and propagate their views to large audiences, attempting all the time to draw secular Jews back to the religious fold. At well-orchestrated rallies in sports stadiums, in between popular religious music, they lambast the emptiness, corruption and decadence of Israeli secular life and offer to fill the vacuum with a genuine Torah way of life. Their secular critics accuse them of cynically exploiting the gullible among the electorate and point to the charges of corruption and bribery levelled against the party's political leader, Deri.

None the less, it was undeniable that the arrival of Shas on the political stage changed the nature of religious politics. 'Mizrachim's drive for [political] self-help resulted in the creation of Shas,' said Dr Meir Buzaglo, a slim, balding, Morocco-born Jew in his mid-30s with dark tinted glasses, who teaches philosophy at the Hebrew University of Jerusalem. 'Shas has its institutions and organization, and it provides good education in its schools. Actually Shas started with education mainly in poor [Mizrachi] neighbourhoods. Because of Shas the political stereotype of Mizrachim broke down. Until then Mizrachi opinions were solicited from taxi-drivers [most of whom are Mizrachim]. Now in the media the Shasnik is one among the few images of the Mizrachi. Several stereotypes are better than one. And with separate elections for parliament and prime minister in the future, more and more Sephardim will split their votes – give one to Likud or Labour for prime minister, and the other to Shas.'[3]

4

MIZRACHIM/SEPHARDIM:

Coming of Age

The first thing one does, when arranging to meet a stranger at a public place, is to ask over the telephone: How do I recognize you? So I did, from my hotel room facing the panoramic bay in Haifa in February 1995. 'I am tall, well built, balding, Middle Eastern looking, and I'll be wearing a leather jacket,' came the reply from my prospective Hebrew interpreter, David Siso. 'Middle Eastern looking', I repeated the phrase in my mind a few times. He meant he looked like an Arab, having originated in an Arab country. That is, he was an Arab Jew – just as there are European Jews and American Jews. But nobody in Israel uses the label 'Arab Jew': it is seen as a contradiction in terms. The words in vogue are Mizrachim and Sephardim. Though used interchangeably in the everyday language of Israel, and also in journalistic and academic writings at home and abroad, the terms have different meanings. 'Sephardim' applies to a religious school within Judaism whereas 'Mizrachim' is a geographical term which covers all those Jews not originally from Europe/the West. But the two terms share the same counterpart: Ashkenazim, which is used in both contexts, religious and geographical. Hence the confusion.

My 70 kilometre bus journey with David Siso from the coastal plain of Haifa to Mount Meron was pleasant and uneventful. As we began our slow ascent in the mountainous Galilee on our way north-eastwards toward Safed (officially called Zefat), the administrative headquarters of the region with a long-established Jewish community and a centre of Jewish mystical tradition, *kabbala* (Hebrew, received [tradition]), since the sixteenth century, the landscape became scenic, the shrubbery of the plain turning into woodlands. Each year hundreds of thousands of Jewish Israelis visit the area not to admire the nature's bounty, although some do, but to visit the shrines of many eminent rabbis of the past – revered by their followers as *tsadik*s (Hebrew, saints), morally pure men who possessed miraculous powers – buried in the woods surrounding Safed.

Mount Meron is the site of the shrine of Rabbi Shimon Bar Yohai, the reputed author in second-century Palestine of the Book of Zohar (Hebrew, Splendour or Enlightenment), regarded as the single most influential work of Jewish mysticism. On 7 Adar, the Lag Ba'Omer festival, 33 days after the Passover (often in April), up to 200,000 believers, mainly Mizrachim, gather to pay homage to Rabbi Bar Yohai. Among them were many of the close relatives of Siso, all of them of Iraqi origin, he told me, although for him it was his first, rather moving, visit. In between the annual festival, the faithful arrive daily in hundreds, even thousands, to pray and call upon the saint to intercede on their behalf with the Almighty in their moments of crisis, financial, emotional, physiological. The practice is commonplace among Mizrachim. In contrast, among Ashkenazim only the small Hassadi sect members appeal to the *tsadik*s in this way.

We went past the open blue iron gate on the left, reserved for males, under one of the twin-arched stone entrances of considerable span, and entered a courtyard leading to the shrine, consisting of many cosy, sun-filled rooms. Accosted by a plump, bearded man in black, intent on collecting funds, I pumped him for basic historical information. 'The shrine was built by Rabbi Abraham Galanta 500 years ago,' he said. 'Rabbi Shimon Bar Yohai was buried here more than 1,800 years ago. The Jews come here to pay respects, mostly those who believe in *kabbala*.'

Inside, every room had prayer books on shelves stacked against whitewashed walls. A pilgrim would pick up a book, approach the saint's tomb and recite prayers. The four sides of the grave, raised a metre above the stone floor, were covered in black cloth with Hebrew inscriptions embroidered in gold, with the one side reserved for women blocked from view from all others. Having prayed in front of the shrine, his head covered with my folding tweed cap, Siso glanced at the scribbled entreaties left next to the contribution box. 'Meir Amitel will be undergoing surgery on Thursday. Please pray for him,' said one.

In a nearby room an elderly Jew sitting on a well-polished wooden bench was engrossed in the scriptures. Next door, in a small hall, yeshiva students were at work. Aside from them everybody else seemed relaxed. 'Until a few years ago people were eating inside the shrine, and smoking, and sleeping,' said Shaul Katchta. A slim, oval-faced Mizrachi owner of a kiosk, his skull covered with a knitted cap, he sold us sandwiches and soft drinks. 'Now the shrine is much cleaner, and there is better discipline,' he continued. 'It has become a property of a Mizrachi group, based in Safed.'

How effective are the appeals to Rabbi Bar Yohai? 'I have been married 16 years, and had three daughters,' replied Katchta. 'When my wife was pregnant last time, I prayed at the shrine for a son. We got a son. If you really believe in it, and pray seriously, it works.'

To most Ashkenazim this is unfamiliar territory, with their rabbis openly critical of such practices, finding no antecedent in classical Jewish theology or tradition, pointing out, for instance, that the burial place of Moses is unknown. (However, the burial places of Abraham, Isaac and Jacob and their wives are known, and are much revered.) They blame the influence of Christianity and Islam on Judaism for saint worship among Jews, which became established in the eighteenth century. The fact that some of the Jewish shrines in the Galilee carry inscriptions in Arabic lends weight to their reasoning.

For me the whole argument came together when I surveyed the sprawling stone building from an elevated vantage point. The series of white domes, each covering a room, was strongly reminiscent of Muslim shrines I had visited. But for the Hebrew signs and inscriptions I could have been at one of those Islamic monuments.

Though the life and works of Rabbi Bar Yohai date back nearly two millennia, the Jews of Morocco, the largest community from North Africa, have recreated in Israel the legend of a much more recent saint, popularly known as Baba Sali. His grizzled, ascetic face adorns many Mizrachi homes and shops. He was a legend in his life-time in Morocco, and was given a posthumous lease of fame and adulation by his son Baruch Abu Hatzeira who, having re-interred him in Netivot – a development town 15 kilometres east of the Gaza Strip, populated by some 13,000 Moroccan Jews – declared in the early 1980s that his father's sainthood had reincarnated itself in his body and soul. This gave an opportunity to Moroccan Jews to continue the tradition. They flock to Netivot in huge numbers on Baba Sali's birthday in January and, much to the amazement and disgust of many Ashkenazim and most secularists, turn the occasion into a hybrid of an open-air Arab bazaar, scooping up specially blessed amulets to beat the evil eye, and listening to pop artists singing the praises of Baba Sali and Baba Baruch. 'Were David Ben Gurion to know of this he would turn in his grave,' said a Mizrachi educationalist of Moroccan origin to me later, as he picked up a book and cited the veteran Israeli leader: '"The Moroccan Jew took a lot from the Moroccan Arabs. The culture of Morocco I would not like to have here."'[1]

On Mount Meron I conversed with Siso as we munched Katchta's delicious sandwiches. 'On arrival in Israel, Mizrachim were sent off to development towns, to the fringes of Israel,' said Siso. 'They were Europeanized in a rough way. My grandfather, Eliezer, was a rabbi in Baghdad, a highly respected man. He and the whole family were sprayed

with DDT (dichloro-diphenyl-trichloro-ethane) [disinfect-
ant] before being allowed to disembark from the ship. He
never forgave them for that. The Ashkenazi immigration
clerks changed our names if they found them unfamiliar or
difficult to pronounce. The name of my mother [then eight
years old] was Faiwaza. The immigration clerk changed it
instantly to Zvi. Her parents did not know what was
happening, they did not know Hebrew.'

In what other ways were they Europeanized? 'They arrived
wearing local dresses. That was not on so far as the Ashkenazi
bureaucrats were concerned. They made the Mizrachim dis-
card their traditional clothes, and put them all into western
khaki clothes, men and women alike. For Jews like my
grandfather it was difficult. The parents lost control of their
family. Since they did not know the [Hebrew] language they
had no control over their children, who were being taught in
Hebrew; they became helpless.'

The migration of Jews from some 10 Arab countries in
the Middle East and North Africa occurred in the wake
of the Arab defeat in the 1948–9 Israeli-Arab War, which
created anti-Jewish feeling in the Arab world, resulting in
riots and other violence. Mizrachi Jews began arriving in
large numbers in Israel from 1949 onwards, and a regulated
inflow continued for a decade, by which time it totalled more
than half a million people.

They arrived in the Jewish state which had been founded by
Ashkenazim in the image of their East European background.
Of the 717,000 Jews in Israel in 1948, four-fifths were
Ashkenazim, and they were preponderant in every stratum
of society, from manual workers to the elite. The long-
established small Mizrachi communities in Jerusalem, Safed
and Tiberias – tracing their roots to the period when, following the 1492 Edict of Expulsion in Spain, the Jews migrated
to other countries along the shores of the Mediterranean,
including Ottoman Turkey, which possessed Palestine (in
the process acquiring the name Sephardim, from Sephard,
Spain) – had nothing to do with Zionism.

'After the establishment of Israel, when Ben Gurion saw
about three-quarters of a million Jews, mostly European,

versus about twice as many Arab Palestinians, he became quite desperate,' said Sami Chetrit, a tall, muscular man in his mid-30s, with a receding hairline and a post-graduate degree in political science from Columbia University, New York, who headed a specialist Mizrachi school in south Tel Aviv. 'Only the European survivors of the Holocaust came to Israel because they had no other choice. "We have the state we longed for, but the people we wanted are not here," Ben Gurion said in 1952. His pleas to American Jews to come to Israel had failed. Their leaders had told him: "We are not Zionist in your sense of the word. We can be Zionist as American patriots. We'll give you financial support." All the American Jews who had been to Palestine during the Second World War had returned home, nobody settled here.'[2]

What was the reaction in Israel when the Jews from the Middle East and North Africa began arriving? 'When the European Jews were faced with us, Arab Jews, in the early 1950s, they panicked,' replied Chetrit. 'If you read the papers and magazines of that time, everybody was in panic – not only officials and politicians but also journalists, thinkers, academics. They feared that their European culture would be overwhelmed by Arab culture. Dusting Arab Jews with DDT [before being let in] was symbolic.'

The reality for Mizrachim was such that Ashkenazim fears were misplaced. They were small in numbers with low standards of formal education, untutored in the language of their newly adopted country, and without effective leadership. Their political and commercial elite had opted to migrate to the West. Having had almost no grounding in the concept and practice of Zionism, and lacking any previous contacts, political or filial, with the Zionist groups, who now exercised power in Israel, they found themselves dumped in temporary housing or shunted off to development towns in far-off zones and given poorly paid jobs or assigned the task of establishing new co-operative farms, *moshavim* (Hebrew, settlements or colonies), with limited funds. The infusion of this underclass into Israeli society inadvertently enabled the earlier settled Ashkenazim to move upwards socially and economically.

Even though by the mid-1960s, due to the high rates of

immigration and births, Mizrachim surpassed Ashkenazim in numbers, they lagged behind in all other aspects of society and state. In contrast to the cultural and local autonomy they had enjoyed in most Arab countries – recognized as they were as *dhimmis* (Arabic, derivative of *ahl al dhimma*, people of *dhimma*, legal equality of an individual) along with Christians – they were controlled in Israel by *nikhbidin* (Hebrew, notables) who were tied to the political parties, bureaucrats and other organs of the state.

The behaviour of the dominant Mapai (later Labour) party towards Mizrachim varied between patronizing and bullying. The Zionists from East Europe, like all other Europeans, held oriental culture in low esteem, and made no allowance for the common Jewishness they shared with Mizrachim. Mapai/Labour activists, given to glib stereotyping, often described Mizrachim as 'a lost generation of the desert' which, by persisting in its old ways, was seriously undermining Israel's European culture, social as well as political. They concentrated heavily on socializing their children.

'The Government implemented the system devised by S. Eisenstadt in the 1950s,' said Chetrit. 'His strategy was absorption [of Arab Jews] through modernization. He equated modernization with Europeanizing so far as Arab Jews were concerned. By letting them absorb European culture we should modernize them, with focus on education, he said. Since Mizrachim were excluded from the decision-making process Ashkenazim decided our fate. In the process they destroyed our Arab culture. So what we have today is that half of the Israeli Jewish society has lost its heritage, its culture.'

The strategy was effective but the human price was high. 'Young people from Morocco or Yemen were encouraged to shed their culture, with their distinctive folklore, and music and dress,' notes Stephen Brook, a Jewish British writer. 'Everything that had been familiar to these people was taken away from them, and in its place they had to assume the styles and values of an essentially secular Zionism that bore little relation to the way they had been raised . . . For many Oriental Jews the problems of adaptation proved too great. Slums developed in the new towns and in the old cities. Without a proper job, heads of family lost both their self-respect and the respect of their children, and the entire family structure began to fall apart. Children, unanchored, often turned to crime.'[3]

Yet the Ashkenazi establishment remained sceptical. 'Maybe in the third generation something will appear from the Oriental Jew that is a little different [from the first generaion],' Ben Gurion said in the late 1960s. 'But I don't see it yet.'[4]

To be sure, the newcomers did not always endure the jibes and humiliation silently. In July 1959 the Mizrachim rioted in Haifa. The spark was the obstreperous resistance of a drunken, disorderly Moroccan Jew in the Old City's Wadi Salib district, populated by poor North African immigrants, to arrest by the police, which resulted in his being shot dead. The word spread quickly, and the next morning the rioting Mizrachim burnt down the offices of Histadrut. Protest violence spread to areas outside Haifa. This was the first incident of its kind, and had a salutary effect on the Ashkenazi establishment. Or did it, I asked Sami Chetrit. 'Not really if I can generalize from the experience of my family,' he replied. 'We came to Israel from Morocco in 1963 when I was four. We were shunted off to Ashdod, a development town, full of Mizrachim. My father, Meir, had bad experiences. He was highly qualified and had a well-paid job in the interior ministry of Morocco. He is fluent in Arabic, Hebrew and French. Yet the Ashkenazim here treated him like shit. Their attitude was "All Mizrachim are the same".'

Serious reconsideration of the national policy of westernization of Mizrachim had to await developments in the race relations of the United States in the mid- and late-1960s. Taking their cue from the revival of ethnic pluralism in America – a country of immigrants like contemporary Israel – the Ashkenazi decision-makers began moderating their stance on the hegemony of European culture. As a result the Ministry of Education and Culture came up with a programme of Mizrachi and Sephardi heritage to embellish the secular school curriculum with Mizrachi history, literature and folklore.

By now the authorities were dealing with the second generation of Mizrachi immigrants. Emulating the example of a radical Afro-American group, called the Black Panthers, some of them initiated a protest movement in the late 1960s in Israel, and named it the Black Panther Party (BPP). It focussed on the discrimination and economic disadvantage suffered by Mizrachim, and criticized *inter alia* the building of fresh apartments for the new immigrants, now mainly Ashkenazi, while ignoring the problem of poor housing for Mizrachi citizens. By staging large demonstrations in Jerusalem, which often turned violent and embarrassed the governing Ashkenazim-dominated Labour Party, it acquired a high profile. But, due to the splits which developed in its leadership, it failed to win a single seat in the December 1973 General Election.

In that poll, the two-month-old right-wing Likud bloc, led by Menachem Begin, secured 39 seats, partly because of the large backing it won from Mizrachi voters. Over the years, recoiling from the mistreatment received from the ruling Labour establishment, Mizrachim had begun supporting the opposition Herut (Hebrew, Freedom), headed by Begin. Though an Ashkenazi, Begin increasingly convinced his Mizrachi audiences that as a politician treated as a pariah by the highminded, elitist Labour leadership since the founding of Israel, he and his party (and its antecedent Revisionist Zionists) stood in the same 'excluded' column as they did. Once David Levy, a 32-year-old Moroccan Jew who made his livelihood as a building worker, had become the first Mizrachi to be elected to parliament on the Herut ticket in 1969, Begin had someone in the party leadership with whom ordinary Mizrachim could instantly identify. Begin himself adopted the Mizrachi habit of saying 'Be Ezrat Hashem (Hebrew, By help of the Lord)' – the Jewish equivalent of Inshallah (Arabic, God willing). He urged Mizrachim to maintain self-respect, and promised them official treatment on a par with Ashkenazim as Jews and as Israelis. These factors helped Herut's successor, Likud, to improve its parliamentary strength at the next poll in 1973. Begin went out of his way to boost the importance of David Levy.

The rise in Likud's votes in the May 1977 election was marginal, from 30.2 to 33.4 per cent, but it emerged as the largest group in parliament because of the split in Labour. Significantly, the breakaway Democratic Movement for Change, led by Yigal Yadin, promised to improve the lot of Mizrachim, thus further reducing the proportion of Mizrachim who backed Labour. It won 15 seats at the expense of Labour. The success of Likud in forming the next Government was greeted with jubilation by Mizrachim, who taunted Labour leaders. 'At last we have paid you back for the DDT,' they would tell them.

Of the 20 ministers in Begin's cabinet, five were Mizrachi. This was in stark contrast to the total of three Mizrachim ministers appointed during Labour's 29 years in power.

Desirable though this was, the arrival of the Mizrachim on the national political stage did not overnight dissipate the long-held Ashkenazi prejudice against them. A year after the swearing-in of the Begin government, the Israeli military chief of staff said: 'It will take years and years before Oriental Jews, even those acquiring full education [here], will manage to cope with the mentality of the West.'[5]

Having won the support of a majority of Mizrachim, Begin took steps to consolidate and expand it. He exceeded his promise of providing 9,000 civil service jobs to Mizrachim. His police minister, a Mizrachi, opened the doors of the force to fellow-Mizrachim, thus recasting the image of police as Mizrachim-haters.

Labour leaders, now languishing on opposition benches in parliament, went out of their way to court the Mizrachi electorate. During the three election campaigns in the 1980s both Labour and Likud wooed Mizrachim. But, by winning about two-thirds of the Mizrachi vote in the 1988 poll, Likud remained far ahead of its rival.

Just as the defeat of Labour in the 1977 election had partly to do with the Mizrachi factor, so too had the failure of Likud at the 1992 poll. Whereas the predominantly Mizrachi faction of Levy in Likud secured one-third of the seats in the central committee on the eve of the 1992 election, the Likud list of parliamentary candidates, inspired by the party's newly elected Ashkenazi leader, Binyamin Netanyahu (1950–), failed to reflect this fact. As a consequence, a substantial minority of traditional working-class Mizrachi electors abstained, and many middle-class Mizrachi voters switched to Labour.

Overall, though, in the political-administrative sphere at the local and national levels, Mizrachim had advanced substantially during the quarter century after they became a demographic majority in Israel around 1965. Studies showed that at lower levels of power, whether elected or bureaucratic, the Mizrachi proportion was roughly in line with the community's numerical strength. At the national level, in the 1992 parliament, one-third of the members were Mizrachi, with the proportion on Labour benches being about 40 per cent. By then they had produced a president of the republic, Yitzhak Navon; two deputy prime ministers (including David Levy); an army chief of staff (Moshe Levy); and a secretary-general of Histadrut (Yisrael Kessar), who was also an unsuccessful candidate for Labour leadership.

Furthermore, by then the idea of a Mizrachi political party had been tried, successfully. This happened in a round-about way. In August 1980, Aharon Abu Hatzeira, a Mizrachi Minister of Religious Affairs in the Begin Government (1977–81), was charged with corruption. After he was compelled to resign he left Likud and set up Tami (Hebrew, acronym of Tenuat Masoret Israel, Movement for Tradition of Israel), a Mizrachi party, which won three seats in the 1981 poll. It joined the coalition government led by Begin, and Abu Hatzeira became Minister of Labour and Welfare. While in office he got a four-year suspended sentence for fraud. In the 1984 General Election Tami secured only one seat partly because another Mizrachi party, Shas, also entered the electoral fray. Since then Shas has become a fixture of the Knesset.

Indeed, despite all the progress made by Mizrachim in the political arena, Shas is the only group which is led at the top by them. All other political parties are led by Ashkenazim. They also still maintain a monopolistic hold over such powerful economic institutions as the Government's economic ministries, public sector undertakings, Histadrut's vast industrial complex, and the leading collective organizations in the private sector.

Equally importantly, there is almost total absence of Mizrachim in the intellectual, opinion-forming and policy-making apparatus of the state and society: academics, senior journalists, columnists, top officials. This was a personal discovery. Halfway through my field research in Israel, which included interviewing leading officials, academic specialists, senior journalists, opinion formers and other intellectuals, I realized that, contrary to the promise I had made to my publisher that about half of my Jewish interviewees would be Mizrachi, I had not encountered a single such person. How was I to fill this gap?

I mentioned my problem to David Eppel, an amiable, bearded, middle-aged senior editor of British origin at the Israel Broadcasting Authority in Jerusalem, and asked if there was a Mizrachi journalist in his organization. Having answered me in the negative after a long pause, Eppel became pensive, as if saying, 'How incurious of me that I hadn't even thought of this – absence of Mizrachi journalists'. But Avi Gus, his round-faced, clean-shaven, bespectacled colleague of East European origin, a senior editor in the Hebrew news section, became tense and defensive. 'I speak Arabic and I am an expert on Middle East politics,' he said, implying that the only purpose for which a Mizrachi journalist could be employed would be to have him deal with Arabic language broadcasts and/or specialize in Middle Eastern events. Then, having assured me that there were no differences between Ashkenazim and Mizrachim, Gus added: 'A large number of those in jail are Mizrachim, and a high percentage of criminals are Mizrachim. They have a lower educational level and lower income level.'

Why? I asked Professor Sammy Smooha at the sociology department of the Haifa University on Mount Carmel in March 1995. An Iraqi Jew, distinguished looking, with grey, swept-back hair, and steel-rimmed glasses, surrounded by neatly arranged shelves of books and boxes, he seemed effortlessly implanted into his large, dimly lit office on the tenth floor.

'For obvious reasons, Mizrachim started out with a severe handicap, social, economic and cultural,' Smooha began. 'Forty years on, there is still a visible socio-economic gap between Mizrachim and Ashkenazim. The Mizrachi per capita income is two-thirds the figure for Ashkenazim. Mizrachim are the dominant majority in the poor and working classes whereas Ashkenazim are predominant in the upper middle and upper classes. It is a vicious circle. Because most Mizrachim live in poor neighbourhoods in cities and in development towns, their schooling is poor. They end up in a vocational school, not a grammar [i.e., academic] school. Statistics show that two-thirds of Mizrachi students go to vocational schools whereas two-thirds of Ashkenazi students go to academic schools. You see that clearly in the percentage who matriculate [high school graduation at 18]. For Ashkenazim the figure is 46, and for Mizrachim 25.'

And at universities? 'There Mizrachim are only 20 per cent of the student body and Ashkenazim over 70 per cent even though the two communities are almost equal in size,' continued Smooha. 'The additional hurdle for Mizrachim is the university entrance exam. It tests the applicant's general knowledge of western culture, where Mizrachim are at a disadvantage.'

What has been the government response? 'It recognizes that there are differences in the academic achievement of the two communities,' replied Smooha. 'But it insists on calling Mizrachim "culturally disadvantaged", not "socially or ethnically disadvantaged". The Zionist state is in a bind. There is no place for ethnicity within Zionism. Yet, in a predominantly immigrant society of Israel ethnic differences exist. The Ashkenazi establishment tries to close its eyes to it, insisting that even if there is a problem it is receding fast. That's its first, superficial response.'

Is there anything deeper? 'Very much so,' said Smooha firmly. 'But you have to push the Ashkenazi establishment, as I've done, sting them. Then you get to the second layer, at the truth. You find that Ashkenazim have very deep feelings, prejudices and convictions. You find them full of insecurity, apprehension, and fear that they might lose control [over Mizrachim], hatred even. They feel that Mizrachim are ungrateful for what has been done for them; they are inferior, overdemanding, overdependent on state [benefits]; they are responsible for their own backwardness because they are not trying hard and expect the authorities to spoon-feed them, that somebody should do something for them all the time; and they are always complaining. They nurture unjustified feelings of deprivation instead of working hard, postponing their immediate gratification by investing in further education; and even now middle-class ethics and values elude them.'

Strong language, all the more so, coming as it did from a soft-spoken academic who had spent a lifetime studying the subject. Smooha's specific argument boiled down thus: 'The Government's solutions are compensatory education and social welfare. But experience has shown that these steps are just enough to arrest further widening of the gap, but not enough to reduce the gap itself. The Government action is well short of a comprehensive social policy. It amounts to tinkering with the problem, not tackling it head on.'

How about a quota system as in the United States? 'There is no question of an affirmative action or allocation of positions, a quota system, says the Government,' came the reply. 'It argues that meritocracy is the order of the day, and that we have a qualitative edge over Arabs due to high educational standards, and so we cannot lower standards.'

My interviews with Mizrachi educationalists revealed that the 'compensatory education' was not the panacea it was made out to be by education ministry officials, and that the problem was deep-rooted, tied as it was with self-esteem of Mizrachi students, the history books they had to read, and so on.

Instead of carping about the inadequacy of the governmental action, a group of Mizrachi educationalists and intellectuals set up a non-profit organization, called Kedma (Hebrew, Going East) in 1993.[6] It started two schools for disadvantaged Mizrachi students in HaTikva district of Tel

ASHK: Because we are not Arab.

MZRH: We are – Arab Jews.

ASHK: Arab Jews? Don't make me laugh.

MZRH: If you can be a European Jew, or an American Jew, why can't I be an Arab Jew, since my country of origin is Arab?

ASHK: Not so long as they are our enemies.

MZRH: But you can't go on living surrounded by Arabs and Arab Jews, and hope to maintain a dominant position in several different ways.

ASHK: Militarily, we can maintain that position for a long time, I'm sure, assuming the Americans will back us. Culturally, there are problems, I agree. Already, look at our cuisine.

MZRH: More Mizrachi than Ashkenazi. The only facet of life where we have prevailed.

ASHK: An important facet, though. Food – like sex.

MZRH: Intermarriage, you mean.

ASHK: Yes. Nearly a quarter of all Jewish marriages are now mixed. It's quite an achievement.

MZRH: But there's a difference. Ashkenazim are less inclined to marry Mizrachim than the other way around.

DH: What about the children? Which synagogue do they belong to: Sephardi or Ashkenazi?

MZRH: By and large they'd follow the father's affiliation.

DH: And that's official.

ASHK: What do you mean?

DH: That this classification of Sephardim and Ashkenazim is recognized officially, that the state puts its stamp on this difference.

MZRH: Sure, you can see it even at the Western Wall synagogue – with the prayer books on one side of the shelves marked 'Sephardi Version' and on the other 'Ashkenazi Version'.

ASHK: That's why whenever the subject of legislation on religion comes up in the Knesset, many Ashkenazi MKs [Members of Knesset] say: 'Let's do away with this dual system, the Chief Rabbi of Ashkenazim and the Chief Rabbi of Mizrachim.'

MZRH: Let me remind you that it was the Zionists from East Europe who insisted on having their own chief Ashkenazi rabbi. And they finally convinced the British after their mandate started in 1922, and got him.

ASHK: That was a long time ago.

DH: Does that mean that before 1922 there was only one chief rabbi and he was Sephardi?

MZRH: Yes.

ASHK: So let's have just one chief rabbi again.

MZRH: No way. This is the one official institution which recognizes our separate identity, where you Ashkenazim cannot dominate us. So we will never let it be abolished. Never.

DH: The religious affiliation is only one aspect of ethnic identity. Others are language, dress, cuisine and music.

ASHK: And folklore and tradition.

MZRH: There is unity on dress and cuisine, almost. Not so in the language and music, though. We speak Hebrew differently and we use it less formally than Ashkenazim do. And our folklore and tradition are different from yours.

ASHK: But the differences are getting less and less. More things unite the two communities now than divide them.

MZRH: I'd put it differently. So long as one group stereotypes another, you can say that they are ethnically different.

DH: Example?

MZRH: Television drama. You see Mizrachi men portrayed with open neck shirts, showing hairy chests, and wearing chains, whereas Ashkenazim are shown cool and better-dressed.

ASHK: That's a flimsy argument.

MZRH: All right. Let's try something heavy. A typical Ashkenazi stereotypes a Mizrachi as backward and

irrational; and when he sees that 'other' backing Likud
– an intransigent party in his view – that confirms his
stereotype.

ASHK: What about the typical Mizrachi?

MZRH: Yes. He does something similar. He stereotypes
an Ashkenazi as a wishy-washy liberal, who belongs to
the Labour camp, which shunned and insulted him in
the past, and still does not like him to get too close.

ASHK: But we all share the same political culture. We all
believe in democracy and freedom of expression and
electoral politics.

MZRH: While we share a common political value system
we have distinct subcultures.

ASHK: We share common political values today because
of the hard decisions the Labour Zionist leaders took
in the early days of the Mizrachi mass immigration.

MZRH: The immense price you extracted from us, treating us like dumb cattle!

ASHK: Sometimes you have to be cruel to be kind. There
was no way we were going to let your backward,
feudal way of life overwhelm our own modern democratic system.

MZRH: That was never a serious possibility. You had all
the levers of power.

ASHK: We were not prepared to take a chance.

MZRH: Yet our subcultures are still different, no doubt
about it.

DH: How?

MZRH: Take religious rites and liturgy. Sephardim are
different from Ashkenazim.

ASHK: Only because the Diaspora Jews were affected
by the music of the communities among whom they
settled. The musical traditions in Europe were different from those in the Arab countries along the
Mediterranean.

MZRH: Whatever the historical reasons, they are different. Also Mizrachim are more pragmatic than
Ashkenazim when it comes to religious observation
and interpretation. Look at the religious rulings issued

by the two Chief Rabbis – the Sephardi is always more practical, down-to-earth. Also you often find Mizrachim going to the beach or watching television at home after attending synagogue on Saturday morning. And you see only a very small proportion of them in the Orthodox or ultra-Orthodox camp. And fewer still are secular.

ASHK: That's changing.

MZRH: Not really. The vast bulk of Mizrachim belong to the traditional religious category, *masorti*, and there they'll remain for a long time to come. In another important area, the family, there are obvious differences too. The average Mizrachi family is larger than Ashkenazi.

ASHK: The fertility rates are beginning to equalize. Mizrachi families are not as large as they used to be. And now you have more and more ultra-Orthodox couples, mostly Ashkenazi, having 10 to 12 children.

MZRH: Maybe. There's also the traditional role of women in the family and the custom of maintaining strong ties with the extended family.

ASHK: That's of course a typically oriental way of life. But with an increasing proportion of mixed marriages, this pattern is bound to change.

MZRH: Perhaps . . . Finally, being predominantly working class or lower-middle class, Mizrachim have developed over decades what Professor Smooha calls 'proletarian patterns of adaptation'. These set them apart from Ashkenazim who are rarely working class.

ASHK: All western societies have a class system.

MZRH: So do Arab societies.

ASHK: Most Arabs are still our enemies. So why keep on harping about the Ashkenazi-Mizrachi problem among Israeli Jews? By focussing on it you're inhibiting the solution. And by talking about differences within us you're weakening the Jewish nation, strengthening misconceptions and providing fuel to the enemies of Israel.

MZRH: That's your way of manipulating us, making us

feel we're unpatriotic, even subversive. It's your way of keeping us, Mizrachim, down, to maintain the status quo – whereby you set the national agenda and take the important decisions, and all we can do is react, if that.

ASHK: You're being paranoid.

MZRH: I'm being perceptive.

ASHK: If so, why can't you see that the Government has got alleviating policies in place: compensatory education and urban renewal? And they're working, slowly maybe, but definitely working. And mixed marriages are on the rise. With time the problem will disappear.

MZRH: So you have been saying for nearly a hundred years.

ASHK: A hundred?

MZRH: Ever since 1897 when the Zionist settlement of Palestine started. Remember the Zionists brought in Yemeni Jews into Palestine in 1907 for manual work? And where were they accommodated? On the fringes of the settlements. Segregated housing among Jews!

ASHK: That's stretching it a bit, don't you think? Our starting point should be the large scale immigration of Mizrachim in the early 1950s.

DH: Maybe the founders of Israel set an unrealistic timetable for it.

MZRH: There's more to it than that.

ASHK: Our starting point is *Kibbutz Galuyot*, Ingathering of Diaspora Jews, and *Mizug Galuyot*, Integration of Diaspora Jews. We Zionists maintain that the idea of Jewish ethnicity is a heritage of the Diaspora, and we want to do away with the Diaspora and its legacies. We don't want to perpetuate these differences.

MZRH: But you cannot abolish reality. If it tells you time and time again that ethnic differences are deep-rooted, you must face up to them.

ASHK: Yes, we always have to start with the past, I know. But we have a design for the future.

DH: Which is?

ASHK: To create the New Jew, not Ashkenazi or Mizrachi, just the New Jew – the smart, confident Jew – an antithesis to the miserable Jew of the ghetto, who was kicked around and persecuted. That is why official Zionism considers Ashkenazi and Sephardi categorizations as well as the Yiddish ghetto and the Jewish inferiority complex as negative characteristics of the Diaspora, which must be renounced.

MZRH: Early on the Zionists attacked Yiddish Diaspora culture as well as Mizrachi Diaspora culture. But then they changed tack.

ASHK: How?

MZRH: Look at the Israeli literature in Hebrew. It's *all* translated from Yiddish. There is no translation of Jewish literature in Arabic or Persian.

ASHK: This is something we should seriously look into. And you're more likely to get a positive response from a Labour government than Likud on a subject like that.

MZRH: Since you mention politics, Israeli leaders should worry that the ethnic divide has been strengthened by a political divide. In the 1988 election 80 per cent of Mizrachim voted either for Likud or some other secular or religious right-wing group.

DH: That many?

ASHK: Yes, and it's the other way around for Ashkenazim and Labour and other leftist groups. As for Likud alone, I'd say about 65 per cent of Mizrachim voted for it.

DH: How do you explain that?

MZRH: Simple. History. Labour ran the Government and other institutions when Mizrachim arrived and were badly treated. So they turned to the opposition Likud, which was then called Herut.

DH: That seems only a partial explanation. You can go for a party as a vehicle of protest that far. But there has to be something more profound which has sealed a solid pact between Mizrachim and Likud for all these decades.

ASHK: Actually several studies have been made and erudite papers written on the subject.

DH: Is there a consensual thesis?

ASHK: Yes. Something like – Likud is a modern version of Revisionist Zionism of Vladimir Zeev Jabotinsky [1880–1940] with its emphasis on political power, military might, Eretz Israel, Jewish nation and an abiding suspicion of non-Jews. That is one stream, and it established itself in Palestine. Then you have Mizrachim who had grown up in a feudal, authoritarian Arab environment, and brought with them elements of authoritarianism, fanaticism, piety and irrationalism. Though the socio-political institutions in Israel tried to moderate these tendencies among Mizrachi, the process was slow. These two strands from separate sources came together in Israel at a time when the Ashkenazi pioneers began losing their values of egalitarianism and dignity of labour, and became venal and corrupt. In 1977 a new compendium of forces assumed power. Exercising power singly or jointly over the next quarter century, it has shifted the political centre of gravity towards inflexible nationalism and hardline religion at the expense of the humanistic, pragmatic and conciliatory political culture of Israel during the first two decades of its existence.

MZRH: That is an amalgam of the papers published by Professors Erik Cohen and Shlomo Avineri, both of them blinkered Ashkenazim.

DH: Dismissing them as blinkered Ashkenazim does not get us far.

MZRH: Professor Smooha has rubbished this thesis so well that I can only summarize his argument laid out in his paper 'Jewish Ethnicity in Israel'.[8] The basic assumption on which Cohen and Avineri construct their theses is wrong. Mizrachim are not shaping Israeli politics singly or jointly. Ashkenazim continue to dominate politics, and set the agenda and take policy-making decisions. Look at the Mizrachi MKs in

Labour, almost 40 per cent; and look at the Mizrachi
Labour cabinet ministers – only three out of 13 – less
than a quarter. Neither Labour nor Likud examines
national issues from a Mizrachi viewpoint.

ASHK: Nor do they look at these from an Ashkenazi
viewpoint.

MZRH: They don't have to – if the vast majority of
decision-makers are Ashkenazim themselves. Even
Likud does not have a comprehensive policy on
Mizrachim.

ASHK: But it has successfully projected a Mizrachi as a
top-ranking leader: David Levy.

MZRH: Look at the way the Ashkenazi establishment
derides him. Scandalous. Is there any other leader of
his rank who is the butt of so many jokes – about
his working-class background, his lack of English
and so on.

ASHK: Israeli politics is a rough business.

MZRH: There is another misconception popular among
Ashkenazim. They think of Mizrachi political culture
being nationalist, extremist and anti-Arab.

ASHK: Isn't it?

MZRH: No, if you look deeply enough. Just as in the
religious sphere, so in politics, Mizrachim are by and
large pragmatic. They have always regarded Likud as
a vehicle for upward mobility, socially and politically
– not as a source of ultra-nationalism, to be imbibed
like mother's milk.

ASHK: So why are they so solidly opposed to peace with
the Palestinians?

MZRH: They are not.

ASHK: You can't be serious.

MZRH: Remember how they reacted to Begin's Peace
Treaty with Egypt in 1979? They backed it all the
way. And who agreed to the international Middle
East Peace Conference in Madrid in October 1991,
which got the whole peace process going? Likud Prime
Minister Yitzhak Shamir.

ASHK: Are you then debunking the thesis of Ben Dror

Yemeni, a Mizrachi columnist in the *Ma'ariv* [Hebrew, Afternoon prayer]?

MZRH: Which is?

ASHK: He argues that Mizrachim are anti-Palestinian.

MZRH: But on socio-economic grounds – not ideological, as is the case with Likud hawks and religious hardliners. Mizrachim are against those who compete with them for jobs and those below their socio-economic status – that is, the Palestinians. That attitude keeps them in the Likud camp which has long been their preferred choice. So once again you see their actions stemming from direct experience, rather than some high-faluting ideology.

ASHK: That's a highly dubious interpretation.

MZRH: Are you familiar with Yemeni's study of Mizrachi students at university?

ASHK: No.

MZRH: It showed that when Mizrachi students enter a university they are almost all Likud. But year by year they change and become liberal and leftist. They examine their socio-political problems and realize that the conflict with Arabs at home and in the region is at the centre of the socio-economic disadvantage they are suffering. They become liberal on the peace issue, and begin to re-examine their own background. Before entering university they would force their parents at home to switch off Arab music. But university education provides them with tools to examine themselves and their background constructively. And they also acquire self-confidence to appreciate their own culture.

DH: You mean the situation can change politically only if the educational level of Mizrachim rises, and that is not happening.

MZRH: Exactly.

DH: So back to square one, Mizrachi under-achievement in education.

ASHK: It's never back to square one, really, as life always goes forward. Since 1989 there has been an influx of ex-Soviet Jews into Israel on a massive scale: 540,000 so far [early 1995]. And another 350,000 are expected by the end of the decade.

MZRH: We know that has already pushed the Ashkenazi proportion up to 52 per cent.

ASHK: There is more.

MZRH: Where?

ASHK: Nowhere in particular. But in general, yes. Examine the bare facts: worldwide there are 10.5 million Ashkenazim, but only 2.5 million Mizrachim.

MZRH: But in Israel, the heart of Judaism, we are almost neck and neck with you, 2.1 million each.

ASHK: Except that for this heart of Judaism to thrive, it must receive sustenance from the Jewish hinterland. And that hinterland is almost totally Ashkenazim.

MZRH: I know Four out of five Ashkenazim live in the Diaspora, whereas four out of five Mizrachim are in Israel.

ASHK: You have a knack for presenting Mizrachim in a good light.

MZRH: And you Ashkenazim.

ASHK: I am only stating bare facts. Then there is the money factor; very important. Ashkenazim in Israel and the Diaspora have the money. You don't.

MZRH: Oh, we have some, too. Not as much as you. After all you are four times more numerous than us. But, like you, most of our rich Mizrachim live in the Diaspora.

ASHK: Only they haven't been as generous to you as our kith and kin have been to us.

MZRH: That'll change.

ASHK: But that won't put you on top in Israel. You didn't make it even when you had numbers on your side. Now that you're on a downward spiral in numbers, there is no way you can seriously challenge Ashkenazi superiority in Israel's economy and politics.

5

THE SECULAR CENTRE:

Pragmatic Politicians

Tucked into a side of a hill, called Hanasi, on the western edge of Jerusalem, the Knesset, the powerhouse of Israeli politics, is both a unique building and a unique institution.

A single chamber parliament, it is the supreme authority in Israel. It can, like its British counterpart, pass any law it wishes, which cannot be amended, vetoed or overturned by any other authority, executive or judicial. But, unlike the British parliament, neither the Prime Minister nor the President or monarch, or any other top state official, can dissolve it. Only the current Knesset can do so. And only it has the power to order new elections. During the first ten years of Israeli history (when a parliamentary poll was held in January 1949, July 1951 and July 1955), it functioned without a fixed term or tenure, with each Knesset deciding its own life span. Only in 1958 did it legislatively fix its term at four years with a proviso for advancing elections to an earlier date. Since then it has become customary to allow up to five months for the election campaign after the four year term.

Viewed as a tourist site, from the street level of Ruppin Road that loops around the Knesset's southern side, its multi-storey structure of pink stone looks grand – its rows of columns majestically holding up the straight roof and forming a line of sentinels around the precious core. But the face it projects to those who work there, or visit it for education or business, is altogether different. They have to enter the building from the north side through its vast backyard, the flattened top of the hill, part of Kiryat Ben Gurion, a complex of multi-storey, buff-coloured stone buildings housing the prime minister's secretariat, and ministries of interior and finance.

One afternoon in February 1995 Rafi and I drove up Hanasi Hill and found a parking place outside the northern gate of the Knesset hugging a low-level, nondescript building. The line of visitors was orderly but long. As we had an appointment with Dr Yoram Lass, a Labour MK (Member of Knesset), we went swiftly through security checks, in the process obtaining permission to carry a camera inside the Knesset, a privilege limited to journalists and writers. We were soon treading a long pathway, one of several running parallel, leading to a bare, rectangular stone structure, capped with a flat cement concrete roof, with a low rectangular opening fashioned in the middle of the front wall. It was a long walk in the open to the Knesset proper – an effective precaution against a suicide bomber rushing into the building, I thought. The apparent bunker-like design of the Knesset stemmed, it seemed, from the overriding consideration of making it withstand bombing raids. The building was conceived and constructed between 1949 and 1967 when Israeli West Jerusalem hugged the armistice line with Jordan. Until 1966 a converted bank building in the downtown area of West Jerusalem housed the Knesset.

At the entrance of the Knesset proper, we faced another set of security guards. They cleared us and directed us to the office of Dr Yoram Lass. Every time we left or entered a different floor, the ever alert guards checked our passes. Inside, the general gloom of the building – white, unadorned walls, dirty green carpets, and dark corridors illuminated by neon strip-lighting – was relieved by an occasional bank of red chairs with matching cushions lined up against a wall. Different floors were occupied by individual MKs, the leaders of the parties represented in the Knesset, and the ministers and deputy ministers.

We waited in the cramped office of Dr Yoram Lass, complete with its ubiquitous personal computer, where Rafi chatted amiably with his secretary, a small young woman with thin legs, whom he had known for some years. Dr Lass, a tall, slim man with glasses, looking elegant in his navy-blue blazer, arrived, apologizing for being late.

He led us to the cafeteria reserved for MKs and other privileged persons such as journalists and lobbyists. It was a fine establishment, bright and airy, with its large glass windows facing the street and the Valley of the Cross, each table topped with a blue cloth and a slender vase of flowers. It buzzed with activity, its businesslike ambience thankfully free of frenzy. There were about a hundred people at the tables being served by a host of efficient waiters and waitresses. We planted ourselves by a glass window, and I took up a seat which faced the street. But Dr Lass was more interested in watching the television consoles, placed at strategic points inside the cafeteria, flashing the proceedings in the chamber. The house was discussing the role of social workers that afternoon, and Dr Lass had been scheduled to speak. 'Not to worry,' he said. 'The cafeteria is almost an extension of the chamber.' Rafi smiled his rare smile. 'That's why people say that more important decisions are taken inside the cafeteria rather than the chamber.' Dr Lass looked away as if trying to catch the attention of a waiter.

Did some of his constituents come to meet him here, I asked Dr Lass. 'No,' he replied. 'There are no constituents in the way there are in Britain or America. You can say that an MK represents every Israeli voter in general but no one in particular.' So the whole country is a single constituency with 120 MKs? 'Yes, it's a pure system of proportional representation, where a voter casts his ballot for the party of his choice, and not for an individual candidate. The system goes back to the pre-state days when the Zionist pioneers were anxious to have all viewpoints, no matter how odd, represented in their Elected Assembly, *Asafat HaNivharim*,' explained Dr Lass.[1]

Several flaws of the system had become apparent over the decades, I remarked: the leaders of the major parties had often to buy the backing of the small factions to form a coalition government; an MK was not accountable to his or her voters but to his peers in the party, which was not required to follow a legislated system for making up its list of candidates; and there was much temptation for an MK to switch parties for material or political gain. 'The Knesset hasn't remained static on the matter,' said Dr Lass. 'In 1990 it passed a bill which specified that any MK quitting his party must lose his parliamentary seat. It also raised the electoral threshold from 1 per cent to 1.5 per cent. That reduced the number of parties in the Knesset from 15 to ten in the 1992 election.' Which meant less haggling between the leading parties and the small groups, I said. 'Haggling nonetheless,' interjected Rafi. 'In the spring of 1990 it took three months to put together the next cabinet. Shimon Peres failed to do so because of a diktat issued to two MKs by a rabbi in Brooklyn.' Rafi returned to sipping his aromatic filter coffee, an example of the fine food and drink served at the cafeteria. 'That's when the idea of a directly elected prime minister was first floated,' Dr Lass said. 'Had [Prime Minister] Yitzhak Shamir not been so resistant to it, we would have had our first popularly elected premier in 1992, instead of 1996.'

How did a particular party go about making up its list of 120 candidates for the Knesset? 'It used to be a centralized affair, resting solely with the central committee in the case of the Labour Party, and its antecedent, Mapai,' came the reply from Dr Lass. 'Then it was shared by the central committee and the district branches of the party. In 1991, when the party was in opposition, its convention adopted the primary system of fixing the Knesset list and electing the party leader. The list was divided into national primaries and regional primaries, the first category was for those known nationally, and the second for those known locally. For this each of the 152,000

Labour members had two votes – one to be used for the national list candidates and the other for the regional list.' But there had to be some kind of *a priori* division between the national and regional lists, I remarked. 'Yes, in the Knesset list of 120 party representatives, the first 10 were chosen on the national basis. The eleventh was from the Tel Aviv region, the twelfth from the Haifa region, the thirteenth was national and so on – with the twentieth being an [Israeli] Arab, and the thirtieth being a Druze and so on.' What was the voter turn-out? 'Seventy per cent, just a bit less than the 77 per cent turn-out in the General Election that followed four months later [in June 1992].' (So close are the two foremost secular parties, Labour and Likud, in their organizational structure and the strategic thinking of their respective leaderships, that the right-wing Likud adopted the primaries system when it had to choose its next leader. In that hotly contested election, held in March 1993, Binyamin Netanyahu won – defeating David Levy, a senior Likud figure of Sephardi origin, and Benny Begin, a son of former Prime Minister, Menachem Begin.)

So at last the voters in the Tel Aviv region knew if one of the party candidates selected from their area was now an MK or not, I remarked. 'Yes, but that did not mean they would make a point of approaching him or her with their problem just because they lived in the same region,' Dr Lass insisted. 'They would seek out any MK of the party they had voted for, preferring to go for someone they had easy access to. Or sometimes they go for an MK who specializes in a particular area.' Like? 'I am a doctor and teacher of medicine, and I specialize in public health,' he replied. 'I did a post-graduate degree in medicine at Harvard University from 1971–3. Then private practice. From 1982–7 I was social director at the Medical College of Tel Aviv. Then from 1987–9, I was director-general for public health at the Health Ministry. So people approach me mainly in health matters – by phone or letter. I have my own mail-box.' How did he divide his week? 'I spend Monday to Wednesday in Jerusalem because the Knesset meets on these days. But a lot more work gets done in the standing committees of the Knesset.' How many such committees were there? 'Nine, with 19 members each. They're like the American Congressional committees. And they work six days a week. Many MKs travel around the country and meet the people. I do. Because we don't have a particular constituency to nurture in order to get re-elected, we try to have a high profile in the public eye.' How? 'The media. It's extremely important for a sitting MK to be in the news, to be seen and heard in the media.'

How strict was party discipline among MKs? 'Not as strict as in the British Parliament with its two- and three-line whips, but not as loose as in the American Congress,' said Dr Lass. 'There are subjects of major importance, and minor. On minor matters we have freedom of voting in the chamber. But the subject of war and peace, the future of the Palestinian territories, these are major issues. The party caucus meets once a week, and we discuss all such matters freely. But the final majority vote is binding on all party MKs.' The other subjects of weighty import, it emerged, were: absorbing Jewish immigrants from the former Soviet Union, relations between the Israeli state and Judaism, reforming the electoral system, economic liberalization, and the treatment of Israeli Arabs. When an MK defied the majority decision on a major issue, what was the penalty? 'In theory he could be thrown out of the party,' replied Dr Lass. 'In practice, the issue gets fudged.'

Lass's name came up on the television console. The three of us got up. As Dr Lass rushed to the chamber Rafi and I walked a short distance to the press gallery with its entrance facing the cafeteria. Here a television camera was locked on to the proceedings; but I was forbidden to take still pictures. At the far end, in an arclike formation, was the public gallery behind bullet-proof glass. It was fairly full. The debating chamber, built like a circle with its top cut off, was made of stone. Its walls were bare, save for a profile of Theodor Herzl, the founder of the (World) Zionist Organization in 1897, which was not far from my seat. Under the Herzl image, to its left, was the chair of the Speaker, at the centre of a dais, now occupied by a vice-Speaker, an MK of the ultra-Orthodox Shas party, a fact highlighted by the black skullcap he wore. On each side of him was a voting panel, with green, red and yellow lights, signifying yes/no/ abstaining votes. On the dais just to the right of the Speaker was a podium with a microphone where Dr Lass was now addressing his audience of six other MKs, including one minister, each of them occupying an individual seat, equipped with microphone. The minister sat on the innermost ring of a series of concentric tiers on the ground floor below the dais. Everybody in the chamber, including the minister, was informally dressed, open-neck shirts being the norm.

Having said his piece, Dr Lass left the chamber and met us outside. It was time for 'photo opportunity'. I suggested a lower floor where above a bank of red chairs against a wall the faces of the four founders of Israel beamed at the onlooker.

The most familiar image to Dr Lass, Rafi and me was that of David Ben Gurion (Prime Minister, 1948–53, and 1955–63), dressed in a black suit and tie, folded arms resting on his desk, his squat, chubby face with its balding head adorned by tousled tufts on the sides, looking appropriately solemn.

By all accounts Ben Gurion is regarded as the foremost founding father of Israel, whose legacy has been continued by subsequent generations of Israelis. During the formative years of the Jewish state he took all the important decisions, thus defining the nature of state and society that were to emerge over the next several decades. He was both the prime minister and the defence minister. He also took charge of foreign affairs, immigration and economic development. Israel has not since then experienced such concentration of power in the hands of a single politician even though the list of the major problems facing it has not altered much – except its foreign policy, which after the first two years of its existence became firmly pro-American.

Since Ben Gurion's life encapsulated Zionist history in Palestine and the first decade and a half of Israel, it deserves outlining in some detail. Born David Green in Plonsk, Poland, into a lawyer's family, he went to Warsaw University in 1904, and joined the Poale Zion (Hebrew, Workers of Zion). Two years later he left for Palestine where he became a farm hand. He was a co-founder of the Poale Zion journal, *HaAhdut* (Hebrew, The Unity). In 1912 he enrolled at Istanbul University to study Turkish laws and government. The outbreak of World War I brought him back to Palestine. In 1915, following deportation as a troublemaker by the Ottoman authorities, he sailed for New York. There he joined an American battalion of the Jewish Legion being formed as part of the British army. Trained in Canada, he arrived in Egypt as a member of the 40th Royal Fusiliers.

In the post-war Palestine the Poale Zion split, with its leftist section leaving in 1919. Its rightist, nationalist section, led among others by Ben Gurion, combined with the followers of Berle Katznelson, the founder of the Agricultural Workers' Union, to form Ahdut HaAvodah (Hebrew, The Unity of Workers). Soon Ahdut HaAvodah and Poale HaTzair (Hebrew, The Young Worker) took a lead in constituting an umbrella organization to encompass all labour-pioneer parties of Zionist persuasion: Histadrut. With successive elections to Histadrut conferences showing Ahdut HaAvodah and Poale HaTzair to be the main parties, pressure grew on their leaders to seek a merger. They did. The result was the founding of Mapai in January 1930 under the stewardship of Chaim Arlosoroff. Following the murder of Arlosoroff in 1933, Ben Gurion was elected head of Mapai, a position he held for the next three decades. Two years later he became the leader of the executive committee of the Jewish Agency for Palestine, which had been recognized by the British mandate as the official representative of the Jews in Palestine.

Ben Gurion had little time for those Jewish organizations which seceded from the (World) Zionist Organization. When the Revisionist Zionists, headed by Vladimir Jabotinsky, broke away from the Zionist Organization in 1935, Ben Gurion was among those who argued that the Revisionists had ceased to be Zionists and turned into fascists.

Differing with his colleagues in the Mapai leadership, Ben Gurion favoured the proposal made in 1937 by the Peel Commission, appointed by the British Government, to partition Palestine into a Jewish state on the Galilee and part of the coastal plain, occupying about a quarter of Palestine, and an Arab state to be attached to the adjoining Transjordan. He favoured building a Jewish state on whatever land the Zionist pioneers could secure in Palestine. In the end nothing came of the Peel Commission report because the Palestinian Arabs rejected it.

Along with his Mapai colleagues Ben Gurion opposed the British White Paper of 1939 which limited Jewish immigration into Palestine to an annual average of 15,000 for the next five years. But he could not remain anti-British once World War II had erupted in September 1939. He encouraged fellow Jews to join the British Africa Corps. In May 1942, as Chairman of both the Jewish Agency Executive and the (World) Zionist Organization in Palestine, Ben Gurion convened an extraordinary American Zionist Congress at Biltmore Hotel, New York. It coupled its call for unrestricted Jewish immigration to Palestine with a demand that 'Palestine be established as a Jewish Commonwealth integrated into the structure of the new democratic world'.

After the end of the war in Europe in May 1945, backed by Jewish Agency funds, Ben Gurion, in his role of Histadrut chief, began purchasing arms in Europe. In December 1946 the 22nd (World) Zionist Organization, meeting in Basle, Switzerland, endorsed the 1942 Biltmore Hotel resolution, and appointed Ben Gurion head of the WZO's defence department. This enabled him to bring various Jewish armed militias in Palestine under a single command. The single most important fighting force was the Haganah (Hebrew, Defence). Formed in 1920, the Haganah grew dramatically in the mid-1930s. During the latter, post-1938 phase of the Arab Revolt (1936–9), when the Palestinian Arabs attacked not only British targets but also Jewish settlements, the British mandate fostered and armed the Haganah. As a result, the Arabs lost 3,232 lives versus the Jewish loss of 329 and the British loss of 135. Following the outbreak of World War II, the British legalized the Haganah, which instructed its members to join the Jewish units within the British army. More than 40,000 Palestinian Jews, men and women, did so. However, once the war ended, the Haganah turned against the British, still committed to limiting Jewish immigration to Palestine, and engaged in the smuggling of illegal Jewish immigrants.

Early in 1947, noticing the convergence of the American and Soviet positions on the partition of Palestine, the national council of the Yishuv, Jewish community in Palestine, led by Ben Gurion, began formulating plans to consolidate the Jewish sector in Palestine, militarily and otherwise. By the time the United Nations adopted the partition plan in November 1947, the Yishuv had a large professional army in the form of the Haganah, supported by 79,000 reserves, armed police and home guards.

With the rejection of the United Nations partition plan by the Palestinian Arabs, the scene was set for civil conflict between the Jews and the Arabs. It got going by January 1948. On the Jewish side, aside from the Haganah, two other Zionist militias were active. These were Irgun Zvai Leumi (Hebrew, National Military Organization), popularly known as Irgun, founded by the Revisionist Zionists in 1937, now led by Menachem Begin (Prime Minister 1977–83), and its small ultra-radical breakaway faction, Lehi, formed by Avaraham Stern in 1940, now headed by Yitzhak Shamir (Prime Minister 1986–92) and Nathan Yellin-Mor. Ben Gurion's repeated attempts to bring the Irgun and Lehi under his control failed. He was particularly concerned about the Irgun whose leader, Begin, he regarded as a serious rival. (Nobody could have guessed then that between them, these militia leaders together would govern Israel for 25 years – divided almost evenly between the Haganah chief and his two rivals – and that this period would span more than half of Israel's first 45 years.) When Begin turned out to be the chief planner of the attack on 9–10 April 1948 on the Arab village of Deir Yasin near Jerusalem, which resulted in the massacre of 254 men, women and children, Ben Gurion used the event to discredit Begin.

By then, at Ben Gurion's behest, the Jewish Agency for Palestine had transferred all its executive powers to the people's administrative committee of the Yishuv assembly's national council. It was this committee of 13, headed by Ben Gurion, and functioning as the provisional government, which issued the Declaration of the Establishment (*HaKomemiyut*) of the State of Israel in Tel Aviv on 14 May 1948. Twelve days later it formally set up the Israel Defence Forces (IDF), consisting of 30,000 fully mobilized troops, with Ben Gurion as the Defence Minister. The IDF was engaged in combat with 26,000 Arab troops – comprised of 7,000 Egyptians, 4,000 Iraqis, 5,000 Jordanians, 2,000 Lebanese, 4,000 Palestinian irregulars and 4,000 Syrians. The Arab-Israeli War I was on.

By the time the conflict ended on 7 January 1949, it had passed through four periods of active combat: 14 May to 11 June; 9 to 18 July; 15 October to 6 November; and 21 November 1948 to 7 January 1949. The first truce, arranged by the United Nations, came into effect on 11 June. It required the warring parties to cease all military activity including importing weapons. Ten days later, defying the decision of the cabinet majority, the Irgun, led by Begin, insisted on unloading arms and volunteers aboard the freighter *Altalena*, which had reached Tel Aviv from Europe, to reinforce and re-arm its troops scattered along the beaches between Tel Aviv and Haifa. When the Irgun commanders tried to steer the ship to the shore, Ben Gurion ordered the IDF to shell it. (The IDF commander to implement the order was Yitzhak Rabin, later to become the Prime Minister and/or Defence Minister.) Some 40 Irgun soldiers were killed, with many more receiving injuries. The ship sank, and most of the arms and ammunition were destroyed. Though devastated by the event, Begin decided against striking back and starting a civil war. He disbanded the Irgun in September during a lull in the Arab-Israeli fighting.

By acting boldly in the midst of a crisis and succeeding, Ben Gurion managed to secure the Israeli Government a monopoly of armed might, thus strengthening both its power and legitimacy. But the *Altalena* incident intensified the ill-will that had existed all along between him and Begin. They severed all contact, and stopped talking to each other.

In later years Prime Minister Ben Gurion would never address Begin directly in the Knesset, referring him to as 'the member sitting to the right/left of So and So . . .'

Under Ben Gurion's command the IDF performed well in the Arab-Israeli War I, securing for Israel an area 21 per cent larger than the 54 per cent of Palestine allocated to the Jews by the United Nations partition plan. The Israeli dead amounted to 6,000 whereas the figure for the opposing side was 18,500, of which 16,000 were Palestinian Arabs, including those killed during the civil conflict from January to mid-May 1948. Among other things Ben Gurion ensured that the IDF remained free of party politics, where promotion was based exclusively on merit, with no consideration given to the party affiliation of the officer. This tradition has continued and played an important role in maintaining high morale in the IDF.

Following negotiations between the warring parties on the Greek island of Rhodes, Israel concluded armistice agreements with Egypt on 24 February 1949, Lebanon on 23 March, Jordan on 3 April and Syria on 20 July. Iraq, which lacked common borders with Israel, signed no such agreement with it.

In the Janaury 1949 election, Mapai, headed by Ben Gurion, emerged as the largest party. It won 46 Knesset seats out of 120. Ben Gurion became the Prime Minister. He formed a coalition government with the help of the religious parties, functioning under the umbrella of the United Religious Front (16 seats).

As described earlier, the Ben Gurion Government passed laws on the observance of the Jewish Sabbath and dietary injunctions, rabbinical courts and the status of the Chief Rabbinate along the lines agreed in principle during the pre-state days.[2] In the Jewish personal law, the administration gave monopoly powers to the Orthodox school, ignoring altogether the Conservative and Reform schools. It decided that only a marriage or divorce conducted in the Orthodox manner was valid, and that a Jew could not be buried until and unless he/she underwent an Orthodox Jewish ceremony. However, those who insisted on a secular service could be buried within the premises of any of the many secular kibbutzim scattered around the country.

The relationship between the state and Judaism was of such paramount importance that it needed to be tackled in the constitution which, according to the Declaration of the Establishment, was to be drafted by October 1949. This was not to be. Though the elections in January 1949 were indeed for the Constituent Assembly, this body adopted a Transition Law the next month. It declared Israel a republic, to be headed by a president who would be elected for a five-year term by the Knesset, a single chamber parliament of 120 members, where the leader of the largest group would become the prime minister. The Constituent Assembly then transformed itself into the First Knesset.

The absence of a written constitution provided Ben Gurion with much leeway. While he kept his promise on the religious matters that had been settled during the pre-state period, he was not prepared to yield to the URF in other religious areas. Indeed his disagreement with the URF on the degree of governmental control over religious education in schools caused the downfall of his government in mid-1951.

However, new elections did not change much. Mapai won 45 seats, and the constituents of the United Religious Front, 15. The result was another Ben Gurion coalition government including the religious parties.

In the economic field, aware of the non-socialist programmes of his partners in the Government, Ben Gurion, more a social democrat than a doctrinaire socialist, readily diluted such egalitarian policies of Mapai as income redistribution and economic planning. He became an ardent proponent of a mixed economy.

Above all else, Ben Gurion gave top priority to building up the military strength of Israel but under civilian leadership. This policy has been the bedrock of the Jewish state ever since. He lost no time in introducing universal conscription for men and women, followed by annual reserve duty for several weeks by men. He visualized the IDF as the chief socializing agent of Israeli adults, an institution without class differences, which would help integrate newly arrived Jewish immigrants.

Ben Gurion decided to double the Jewish population, standing at 759,000 in late 1948, within a decade. In the event Israel achieved this figure four years earlier. The passing of the Law of Return in 1950, guaranteeing every Jew the right to settle in Israel – followed by the Nationality Law, 1952, conferring automatic citizenship on those who had arrived under the Law of Return – was an effective means to this end. Intent on encouraging populating the inhospitable Negev Desert, Ben Gurion set up his private home at Sede Boqer, a new kibbutz in the area.

The attitude of Ben Gurion to those Palestinian Arabs who remained in Israel was a mixture of disdain and hostility. 'He retained the negative view of the Arab personality and character derived from the stereotypes existing not only in the Yishuv but in the West as a whole,' writes Professor Don Peretz in *The Government and Politics of Israel*. 'Although widely read in the classics of several non-Jewish cultures, Ben Gurion never regarded Islamic philosophy or literature as of major significance. He learned Greek and Spanish, but never thought it worthwhile to master Arabic. His attitudes toward Middle Eastern culture were revealed in his evaluation of Oriental Jewish culture and in his policies toward Israeli Arabs. They could not really join the mainstream of life in the Jewish state.'[3] As Defence Minister, Ben Gurion put Israeli Arabs under military administration. His device for dealing with Israeli Arabs was to set up a special department on Arab affairs, headed by an Israeli Jew, in the prime minister's secretariat.

Ben Gurion played a crucial role in deciding the basic orientation of Israel's foreign policy. Though he excluded the 19-member bloc of strongly socialist, pro-Moscow Mapam (acronym of Mifleget Poalei Meuhudet, United Workers' Party) from his government, he was aware of the goodwill that existed towards the Soviet Union in large segments of the Israeli labour movement. Aside from the Marxist ideology, this had to do with the Soviet actions before the founding of Israel and the 1948 Arab-Israeli War. Having backed the partition of Palestine at the United Nations General Assembly in November 1947, Moscow had acted to neutralize western influence in the prospective Jewish state. It arranged arms supplies to the Zionists in Palestine through the branches that (the staunchly anti-British) Lehi had established earlier in Czechoslavakia, Hungary and Romania. The first clandestine shipment of arms from East Europe arrived in Palestine in March 1948. The flow continued for about a year, well after the end of the Arab-Israeli War. On the other hand, Washington was generous to the newly established Jewish state, and provided it with $200 million in credits and grants during its first year of existence.

What turned Ben Gurion firmly pro-West was the most significant underwriting of Israel's continued existence yet in the form of the Tripartite Declaration by the United States, Britain and France on 25 May 1950. The signatories pledged to oppose any attempt to change by force or threat of force the armistice boundaries of Israel set in January 1949. Such a guarantee of its frontiers by the western powers, coupled with a promise to supply it with weapons on the basis of 'a balance of forces between it and the Arab states', pleased Ben Gurion greatly. He showed his gratitude to Washington by backing it unconditionally at the United Nations on the issue of the war between North Korea and South Korea which broke out a few weeks later. By signing a treaty of friendship, commerce and navigation with the United States in October 1951, he formalized close ties with Washington, a state of affairs which has continued since then – barring a few periods of strain, especially after the 1956 Suez War, when Ben Gurion refused to withdraw unconditionally from the Sinai as required by the United Nations Security Council.

Taken together Ben Gurion's actions turned the prime ministry into the most powerful office in the country, far ahead of the presidency of the republic. He was able to do so by chanelling all his extraordinary energy and dynamism into the job, seizing opportunities as and when they arose, and making full use of his control over several networks, domestic and foreign.

In the course of his years as the chief executive of his

country, he made his loyalty to Mapai subservient to his loyalty to Israel, and went on to develop his ideology of *mamlachtiut*, statism. In response, large sections of Israeli society, enchanted by his charisma and vigour, came to regard him as the leading national figure who stood above party politics. Oddly, this popular perception rubbed off on Ben Gurion's party, Mapai, which was regarded informally as *the* national party by all other political groups.

Equally oddly, the actual electoral appeal of Ben Gurion was not widespread. At his best he secured only 38 per cent of the popular vote for Mapai. His impact on his colleagues and the party bureaucracy too was limited. His relationship with Mapai's old guard – Moshe Sharett (1894–1965, Prime Minister 1954–5), Levi Eshkol and Pinchas Sapir – was problematic.

Failing to find rapport with his peers, Ben Gurion turned his attention to younger party activists, some of whom came to share his newly coined ideology of statism. Among his young followers and advisers, whom he promoted in the IDF and the Government, were Moshe Dayan and Shimon Peres (1923– ; Prime Minister, 1984–86, 1995–6). Interestingly, most of them came from the military where they had been either officers (Dayan) or high-level technocrats (Peres). Among other things they extended the concept of pioneering, applied initially to agriculture, to such areas of human endeavour as science and technology, thus terming scientists and technicians too as pioneers. They argued that specialization and efficiency ought to be valued as much as manual labour in agriculture. In retrospect, this was the beginning of the trend whereby Mapai/Labour began moving away decisively from its traditional association with labourers and workers. This trend developed to the point when within a generation of Israeli history, the Labour Party ceased to be the favourite of working-class voters.

Having played a leading role in shaping the basic outline of Israel's internal and external policies, Ben Gurion resigned as Prime Minister in December 1953, and retired to his private home at Sede Boqer in the Negev. But not for long. In early 1955 Moshe Sharett, his successor, drafted him in to the cabinet as defence minister when the incumbent, Pinchas Lavon, resigned in the midst of a scandal concerning the exposure and arrest of an Israeli sabotage team recruited within Egypt's Jewish community.

In response to the execution of two ring leaders of the Jewish espionage-sabotage cell in Egypt, Ben Gurion ordered a massive attack on an Egyptian military camp in the Gaza Strip, which resulted in 39 Egyptian deaths. The escalating tension resulted in Ben Gurion replacing Moshe Sharett as the Prime Minister in late 1955 after parliamentary elections in July in which Mapai won 40 seats.

Within a year Ben Gurion was involved in invading and occupying the Sinai Peninsula in collusion with Britain and France in the Suez War, called the Sinai Campaign by Israelis. He capitalized on the crisis that started with a diplomatic row between Egyptian President Abdul Gamal Nasser (1918–70) and the United States, and then extended to Britain and France.

On 19 July 1956 the United States informed Egypt that it was withdrawing its aid offer for the Aswan High Dam, thus undermining the loan from the World Bank for Reconstruction and Development which was predicated on the US assistance. In response, a week later President Nasser nationalized the Suez Canal, owned jointly by Britain and France. Following a debate on the matter at the United Nations Security Council, Egypt agreed on 11 October to the principles regarding running the Canal, including maintaining its status as an international waterway. This was not enough to satisfy Britain and France, the dominant foreign powers in the Middle East since the collapse of the Ottoman empire in 1918. Determined to cling to their power and influence in the region, they had initiated clandestine talks with the Ben Gurion administration at the highest level to bring about the downfall of Nasser through armed intervention. On 24 October the three Governments signed a secret agreement to attack Egypt.

On the night of 29–30 October Israel invaded the Sinai. At 1800 on 30 October Britain and France gave a 24-hour ultimatum to Egypt and Israel to cease hostilities and withdraw their troops 16 kilometres from the Suez Canal so as not to jeopardize freedom of shipping. As Israel's forces were some 48 kilometres from the Canal, it accepted the ultimatum. Egypt rejected it. Fighting between the two sides continued. With the deadline ending at 1800 on 31 October, Britain and France bombed Egypt's airfields, virtually destroying its air force, and continued attacking Egyptian military facilities for the next 36 hours. Cairo ordered its forces, sent earlier across the Canal into the Sinai, to retreat and thus avoid being encircled by the enemy. They did so by 2 November. On that day the United States co-operated with the Soviet Union at the United Nations Security Council to sponsor the Uniting for Peace resolution which condemned aggression against Egypt. The next day, while continuing to consolidate its position in the Sinai, Israel completed its occupation of the Gaza Strip. On 4 November the United Nations General Assembly voted to set up a United Nations Emergency Force (UNEF) to supervise the truce. On 5 November British and French paratroopers landed at the northern (Port Said) and southern (Port Suez) ends of the Canal. Israel, advised by London and Paris, attached unrealistic conditions to accept the United Nations Security Council ceasefire resolution. Soviet Premier Marshal Nikolai Bulganin addressed a letter to his Israeli counterpart Ben Gurion: 'It [the aggression] is sowing a hatred of the state of Israel among the peoples of the East such as cannot but make itself felt with regard to the future of Israel, and which puts in jeopardy the very existence of Israel as a state.'[4]

On the night of 5–6 November, British and French forces landed in the Port Said area, and after seizing the town started moving south along the Canal, which had been blocked by the Egyptians with sunken ships. The newly re-elected American President Dwight Eisenhower applied economic pressure on Britain, with the US Federal Reserve Board selling large amounts of British pounds, thus undermining the pound-dollar exchange rate. Yielding to the American-Soviet pressures, the invading governments accepted a ceasefire from midnight on 6–7 November. By then Israel had occupied

Gaza and most of the Sinai, including its south-eastern tip, Sharm al Shaikh, at the mouth of the Gulf of Aqaba.

By then Egypt had lost 1,650 troops and 215 aircraft while Israel's losses were 190 men and 15 warplanes. (At 26 men dead and five aircraft lost, the British and French losses were minimal.)

General Moshe Dayan, a protégé of Ben Gurion and the IDF chief of staff since 1953, provided brilliant leadership during the nine-day conflict. Dayan was born in 1915 in Degania kibbutz near the Sea of Galilee. He joined the Haganah when in his teens. Due to lack of fluency in English he discontinued his studies at the London School of Economics in 1935–6, and returned to Palestine, where he participated in the Haganah operations to counter the Arab Revolt, 1936–9. Following a change in the British mandate policy at the start of World War II, the authorities suppressed the Haganah, and sentenced Dayan to five years' imprisonment. After his release in early 1941, he led a British reconnaissance unit into Syria then under the pro-Nazi French regime. He was wounded and lost his left eye. He started wearing a black patch, which later become his universally recognized trademark. During the 1948–9 Arab-Israeli War, after his battalion had captured Ramle and Lod, Dayan was appointed commander of the Jerusalem area, a prestigious position. Under the benign guidance of Ben Gurion, in charge of the Defence Ministry, Dayan rose rapidly in the military hierarchy. After serving as head of the southern command, 1950, and the northern command, 1952, he won promotion to chief of army operations, a position he held for a year.

Following the ceasefire in the Suez War, Dayan fully supported the hardline position that Ben Gurion took regarding evacuating the Sinai. Once the UN Emergency Force (UNEF) to supervise the truce began arriving on 4 December, Britain and France prepared to leave. They finished the withdrawal by 23 December, handing over their positions to UNEF. Though Israel agreed to withdraw on 8 November it did not actually do so until 8 March 1957 – and that too only after Ben Gurion had secured commitments from the United

States on three counts: it would stand by the Israeli right of passage through the Gulf of Aqaba; ensure that the Gaza Strip was not used again for launching guerrilla attacks against it; and assist Israel, secretly, in its nuclear research programme. On Israel's insistence UNEF troops were posted in the Gulf of Aqaba region, to safeguard Israeli shipping, and in the Gaza Strip exclusively on the Egyptian side. In exchange Egypt was allowed to return to Gaza to administer it.

Whatever the political and diplomatic consequences of the Suez War, it accelerated Israel's policy of shoring up its military, and gave further impetus to its top leaders to acquire nuclear weapons of their own. Both these aims were achieved during the next decade. An official acknowledgement of this came, inadvertently, in the late 1960s in reference to the unprecedentedly harsh way Israel responded to the guerrilla actions in 1965–6 by the Palestinians operating from Jordan and Syria. 'The reprisal actions of 1965–6 differed from those which preceded the Sinai campaign,' stated *The Paratroopers' Book*, the semi-official history of the IDF's airborne corps. 'The operations were no longer acts of vengeance, savage and nervous, of a small state fighting for its independence. Rather, they were blows struck by a state strong and sure of itself, and which did not fear the army it confronted.'[5] Though by the mid-1960s Ben Gurion, leader of a small group called Rafi (acronym of Reshima Poalei Israelit, Israeli Workers List), was out of power – having resigned in 1963 after realizing that he lacked the kind of authority he had exercised before – his doctrine had become a cornerstone of the state's military policy. Also for the next few decades the group of his young protégés such as Moshe Dayan and Shimon Peres continued to dominate Israeli public life.

True to his combative nature, Ben Gurion campaigned against his successor, Levi Eshkol (Prime Minister 1963–9), a veteran Zionist pioneer from Ukraine, who had been active in Mapai-Histadrut-Haganah politics. During the 1948–9 Arab-Israeli War, he became director-general of the Defence Ministry under David Ben Gurion, focusing on the war's economic and financial aspects. In 1951 he was elected to parliament on the Mapai list, and kept his seat until his demise. After a year as Minister of Agriculture and Development, he served as Finance Minister, a position he retained until he succeeded Ben Gurion as Prime Minister and Defence Minister in 1963.

Lacking the domineering personality and style of Ben Gurion, Eshkol opted for ruling by consensus within his cabinet. Among other things he tried to normalize life in Israel. He liberalized the economy, which had been run on a war footing since 1948. He detached the broadcasting department from the Prime Minister's secretariat, transforming it into an independent authority. Later, in 1969, at his behest the Knesset passed a law establishing television, which had until then been considered a corrupt medium by the largely puritanical Labour leadership. He removed (in December 1965) the travel limitations that had been imposed on Israel's Arab citizens since 1948.

By sponsoring a cabinet decision to bring the remains of Vladimir Jabotinsky from New York to Israel for reburial in Jerusalem, Eshkol lowered tensions between the Government and the right-wing opposition led by Begin, a follower of Jabotinsky. This was the first sign of a thaw between the centre-left and right of Israeli politics, a definite departure from the Ben Gurion legacy.

Aware of the declining popularity of Mapai, Eshkol encouraged the party leadership to form an alignment, *maarach*, between Mapai and the leftist Ahdut HaAvodah-Poale Zion. This was ratified by the Mapai convention in February 1965. Disagreeing with this, Ben Gurion and his rightist-inclined followers left Mapai and offered their own list, Rafi, in the November 1965 election. Rafi got 10 seats and the Mapai-Ahdut HaAvodah-Poale Zion Maarach 45. Ben Gurion's personal popularity proved unequal to the institutional strength of his former party. Eshkol headed the government formed after the poll.

It was during Eshkol's premiership that Israel went to war with its Arab neighbours, and won a stunning victory. The crisis that preceded the conflict, which before its outbreak had been portrayed by Israeli officials as a life-and-death struggle for the Jewish state, brought the traditional, secular left-of-centre and right-of-centre of Israeli politics together – thus setting a pattern which was to be repeated in peace time in the 1980s. Later the ease with which some leading figures of the (nominally) opposing camps switched sides illustrated the remarkable change that had occurred in Zionist politics within Israel. The sharp lines which in pre-state days divided labour Zionists from ultra-nationalist Zionists became so blurred that crossing from one side to the other aroused no lifting of eyebrows among politicians or the public.

Nothing illustrated this better than the relationship between Yitzhak Rabin, who was to become Labour Prime Minister, and Ariel Sharon, an ultra-nationalist hawk, whose actions as Defence Minister in the early 1980s even his staunchly right-wing Prime Minister, Menachem Begin, found hard to condone. During the 1956 Suez War, as the commander of a brigade, Sharon, then 28, engaged in combat which had not been authorized by his superiors, and thus destroyed his chances of advancement in the IDF. But soon after Rabin became the IDF chief of staff in 1964, he promoted Sharon to head the IDF's training department, and then conferred on him the rank of brigadier general in 1967. One of the first decisions Rabin made after becoming the Prime Minister the first time around, in 1974, was to appoint Sharon as his special adviser.

June 1967 War: A Milestone

The third Arab-Israeli War in June 1967 was a milestone for Israel in more ways than one. Having invaded and occupied 68,300 square kilometres of Arab territory in Egypt, Syria and the remnants of the British mandate Palestine – two and a half times its own area – Israel could no longer portray itself as a small, weak and fledgeling Jewish state surrounded by powerful Arab neighbours determined to exterminate it. Domestically it altered the Israeli political landscape radically. It revived the old debate about the Zionist aims and ways of achieving them, thus opening up avenues for Menachem Begin and his party that had for long been closed. It marked the end of an era, where established political parties made a successful use of co-opting ethnic and communal leaders of the newly arrived immigrants who now formed a substantial majority in the national population of 2.38 million. And Israeli Arabs ceased to live under military control. More specifically, Israel's spectacular victory gave rise to the Moshe Dayan phenomenon, and provided a vehicle later for the political careers of his chief of staff, General Yitzhak Rabin (Prime Minister, 1974–77, 1992–95), and his chief of operations, Ezer Weizman (1924– ; President, 1993–), who had masterminded the country's military air strategy which was to yield stunning results. All of them happened to be *sabra* (Arabic, cactus; that is, prickly on the outside but soft and sweet on the inside), a term used in Israel for the Jews born in Palestine.

The war, though lasting only from 5 to 10 June 1967, had a long fuse. Taking seriously Israel's threats of overthrowing it, the nine-month-old radical regime of pan-Arabists (of Baathist persuasion) in Syria, which had been actively aiding Palestinian guerrilla activity against Israel, signed a defence treaty with Egypt in November 1966. Early in April 1967 Israel attempted to cultivate disputed Arab land in the Syrian-Israeli demilitarized zone, thus triggering a confrontation. On 7 April 1967, the IDF escalated the already tense situation by bombing the Syrian Heights, buzzing the outskirts of Damascus, and engaging in dogfights in Syrian airspace. A month later Syria informed Egypt's President Nasser of Israeli troop concentration along its border. On 16 May, while promising to aid Syria, Nasser dispatched Egyptian troops to eastern Sinai as a precaution against an Israeli attack.

This signalled the start of an acute crisis. On 18 May Nasser demanded the withdrawal of the United Nations Emergency Force, which had been patrolling the truce lines since the end of the 1956 Suez War on the Egyptian side only. The UNEF withdrew immediately. On 22 May, having stationed Egyptian troops in Sharm al Shaikh at the tip of the Tiran Straits, Nasser blockaded the Gulf of Aqaba and the sole Israeli port of Eilat.

Within Israel there was a rising feeling among the populace that the Eshkol administration was behaving timidly. Following the 1956 Suez War it had been made to believe that the closure of the Straits of Tiran by Egypt would be considered an act of war. Now, on the morrow of Nasser's action, Eshkol called on the international community to restore the status of the Straits and the Gulf of Aqaba as an international waterway open to free navigation. The same day his Foreign Minister, Abba Eban, left for Paris, London and Washington to resolve the crisis by diplomatic means. Nothing tangible emerged out of these endeavours.

As tension rose in the region Premier Eshkol, who also held the defence portfolio, maintained, at least in public, his willingness to continue diplomatic efforts to dissipate the crisis. There was growing impatience among politicians and the public. During their consultations with Eshkol, two leading opposition leaders from the contrasting poles of the political spectrum – Menachem Begin, the head of Gahal, Gush Herut-Liberalim (Hebrew, Freedom-Liberal bloc), and Ben Gurion, the leader of Rafi – proposed that he should cede his defence portfolio to Moshe Dayan, a Rafi MK. The leadership of his own Mapai Party instructed Eshkol to give the defence portfolio either to Dayan or Yigal Allon. But Eshkol's choice of Allon was vetoed by a coalition partner that threatened to bring down the Government. Eshkol was reluctant to appoint Dayan Defence Minister. He had clashed with Dayan in 1964 when the latter was Agriculture Minister in his Government, and forced him to resign, thus crippling the rise of Dayan, who had joined the Mapai after retiring from the military in 1958. Dayan's subsequent defection to Ben Gurion's Rafi Party left him languishing on the opposition benches in the Knesset elected in 1965.

In order partly to mask his humiliation, Eshkol appointed Dayan as Defence Minister in the course of forming a national unity administration, which included all political groups except Maki (Hebrew acronym of Miflaga Kommunistit Israelit, Israeli Communist Party) and Rakah (Hebrew acronym of Reshima Kommunistit Hadash, New Communist List). The new government formed on 1 June included six representatives of Gahal, including Begin, who was appointed a minister without portfolio.

On the Arab side in the region, reflecting the popular mood in his country, King Hussein ibn Talal (r. 1952–) of Jordan, hitherto hostile to Nasser, rushed to Cairo on 30 May to conclude a mutual defence pact, and place his forces under Egyptian command.

Israel had earlier told its superpower ally, the United States, that it would go to war if one or more of the following events occurred: departure of the UNEF, blockading of the Tiran Straits, signing of a Jordanian-Egyptian defence pact, and dispatch of Iraqi forces to Jordan. By the time the national unity government was sworn in on 1 June all but one of these eventualities had come to pass. Three days later Iraqi troops entered Jordan after it had joined the Egyptian-Syrian-Jordanian defence pact. On 5 June a surprise, pre-emptive attack by Israel on the Egyptian air bases at 7.46 a.m., when all Egyptian pilots were having breakfast, heralded the start of the shortest Arab-Israeli armed conflict.

Israel simultaneously attacked all 17 Egyptian airfields and destroyed three-fifths of Egypt's warplanes, consisting of 365 fighters and 69 bombers. In the ground fighting in the Sinai, Egypt lost 550 tanks. Later in the day Israel struck at the Jordanian and Syrian air forces on the ground with equally deadly efficiency. It rejected the United Nations Security Council call for an immediate ceasefire on 6 June.

On the Egyptian front, Israel captured the Gaza Strip on 6 June, the day Egypt decided to withdraw its 80,000 soldiers and 1,000 tanks from the Sinai Peninsula. Having occupied most of the peninsula by 8 June, Israel reached the Suez Canal the following day. On the Jordanian front the Israelis captured East Jerusalem as well as Bethlehem, Hebron, Jenin and Nablus by 7 June. It then accepted a UN-sponsored ceasefire on this front. The Syrian front witnessed artillery duels on the first four days. Israel violated the UN-sponsored truce on the fifth day, 9 June, by launching an offensive to capture the Golan Heights. It achieved this aim by the evening of the sixth day, 10 June, when the final ceasefire came into effect. In the naval battle, the Israelis captured

Sharm al Shaikh on 7 June, thus ending the blockade of the Straits of Tiran.

The Arab losses in men and weapons were heavy. The Egyptian dead amounted to 11,500, with a majority dying of thirst in the Sinai, the Jordanian to 2,000, and the Syrian to 700. The Israeli death toll was 778 dead. Whereas Egypt lost 264 aircraft and 700 tanks (out of 1,200); Jordan 22 aircraft, including all of its 18 warplanes, and 125 tanks (out of 287); and Syria 58 aircraft (out of 90) and 105 tanks (out of 750); the corresponding figures for Israel were: 40 aircraft (out of 260) and 100 tanks (out of 1,100).

The brilliant Israeli blitzkrieg in June 1967 was a personal triumph for Dayan. He became the most popular and charismatic of the younger generation of Israeli leaders. By joining the newly formed Labour Party in 1968, Dayan returned to the political mainstream. As defence minister Dayan was in charge of administering the Occupied Arab Territories. His power and influence grew. When Premier Eshkol died in February 1969, he was a candidate for the post of Prime Minister, his serious rival being Yigal Allon, Deputy Prime Minister, who had been a military star of the 1948 Arab-Israeli War. To spare the one-year-old Labour Party a traumatic experience of a bitter battle for the top job, the party leadership drafted Golda Meir (Prime Minister, 1969–74), then in retirement, as the premier. In the Meir cabinet Dayan retained both his Defence Ministry and the autonomy with which he ran it. In the matters of defence and military administration of the Occupied Arab Territories, his authority was equal to, if not greater than, the Prime Minister's. He took a hawkish line on the Occupied Territories, and used threats to establish a breakaway group of his own to impose his views on his Labour colleagues.

Not surprisingly, later Dayan became the first top-ranking Labour leader to cross the floor and join the cabinet headed by the Likud chief, Begin, without many qualms. Though Rabin, one of Dayan's two *sabra* peers, remained consistently loyal to the Labour Party during his later, political career, as defence minister in the national unity governments in the 1980s, he became well known for establishing a special relationship with Prime Minister Yitzhak Shamir, the Likud leader. As for Ezer Weizman, he was the first top-ranking military officer who opted for the right-wing Gahal, led by Begin. Later he acquired the unique distinction of masterminding the election campaigns of *both* Likud (a success) and its rival Labour (a failure).

Born in a prominent Jewish family in Palestine, Ezer Weizman was a nephew of Chaim Weizman, the first President of Israel. He enrolled in the Royal Air Force during World War II, and became a pilot. Following demobilization, he joined the Irgun. During the 1948–9 Arab-Israeli War, he was one of the first Israeli pilots. After the military conflict he became a senior officer in the Israeli air force, rising to commander of the air force, 1958–66. It was under his command that the air force perfected its plan to destroy the air power of its Arab neighbours, which it implemented efficiently during the June 1967 Arab-Israeli War, when Weizman was the IDF's chief of operations.

A spectacular victory in the armed conflict helped to cement the national unity coalition. It was unanimous in its decision to extend Israeli laws to occupied East Jerusalem. The differences that arose between the coalition partners, and within Mapai, on the future of the rest of the Occupied Arab Territories were contained by postponing the formulation of a coherent policy on the subject. The consensual climate proved conducive to consummate, in early 1968, the previous decision to amalgamate Mapai with Ahdut HaAvodah-Poale Zion (and Rafi as well) to form the Israeli Labour Party with the resultant parliamentary size of 55 members. Meir inherited this strength when she became the premier in February 1969.

Meir, a Ukrainian Jew, who had grown up in the United States, arrived in Palestine in 1917 as the wife of Morris Meyerson, a book-keeper. She was active in Histadrut-Mapai politics. Following the arrest by the British in 1946 of Moshe Sharett, head of the Jewish Agency's political department, dealing with foreign affairs, she replaced him. International relations remained her strong card, and she served as Israel's Foreign Minister from 1956–66. After she resigned from the cabinet, she was drafted as secretary-general of Mapai to heal internecine wounds caused by the departure of David Ben Gurion. When Mapai transformed itself into the Labour Party in 1968, she retired from public life, only to be redrafted this time as the Prime Minister.

The consensual politics that Meir inherited in the form of a national unity government were undisturbed by the elections of October 1969. While Labour allied with Mapam to sponsor a joint list of candidates, Gahal offered a manifesto which was not much different from Labour's. The various parties virtually retained their previous strengths in the new Knesset, and the national unity administration that followed had the same composition as the one before. It was not until Meir accepted the peace plan of US Secretary of State, William Rogers, in July 1970 that Gahal objected and left the Government. Now within her Labour-dominated cabinet she had to find a balance between Dayan (defence), Yigal Allon (education, and deputy premier) and Shimon Peres (without portfolio, 1969; transport, 1970–4).

On the singularly important issue of the future of the Occupied Arab Territories, Dayan set the pace. He used his office to create Jewish colonies in the Occupied Arab Territories. In April 1973 he mounted a campaign to annex the West Bank, the Golan Heights and parts of the Sinai. A few months later he unveiled a plan to build a port city of Yamit in the Rafah approach, straddling the international border of Egypt and the Gaza Strip. When the moderate Finance Minister, Pinchas Sapir, denied him necessary funding, tensions within Labour rose. A ministerial committee, chaired by Israel Galili, a minister without portfolio and long-time confidant of Meir, adopted a document drafted by Galili. It gave a green light for 'an urban centre' at Yamit and largescale acquisition of land in the Occupied Arab Territories by the Israeli Government and private Jewish organizations. Most Labour moderates saw the Galili Document as a go-ahead for 'creeping annexation' of the Occupied Arab Territories. Yet one of their principal leaders, Sapir, endorsed it, afraid that failure to do so would lead to the defection of Dayan and his faction, and the collapse of the Meir Government.

The Western
Wall and the
Dome of the
Rock, Old
City,
Jerusalem

A close-up of
the Dome of
the Rock,
with the
verses from
Chapter 7,
'The Night
Journey', of
the Quran
inscribed in
Arabic along
the top of its
walls, Old
City,
Jerusalem

Jews at
prayer inside
the
synagogue
adjacent to
the Western
Wall,
Jerusalem

Palestinian flags flutter against the background of a large Israeli standard hung from the roof of the house occupied by Ariel Sharon in the Muslim Quarter, Old City, Jerusalem, since October 1987

Graffiti in the Muslim Quarter, Old City, Jerusalem. The large sign to the left of the outline of the Dome of the Rock – Muhammad (in Arabic) – is a transfiguration of the original Star of David

A steel wire-mesh installed over the small courtyard of a house by an Arab family on the ground floor as a safeguard against heavy objects thrown by the Jewish family living upstairs in the Muslim Quarter, Old City, Jerusalem

Inside the Torah Chaim Yeshiva in the Muslim Quarter, Old City, Jerusalem. *Inset:* Rabbi Shlomo Haim Aviner, head of the Torah Chaim Yeshiva

Israeli soldiers posted round the clock at an intersection in a market in the Muslim Quarter, Old City, Jerusalem

An office of the United Nations Truce Supervision Organization, established in June 1948, along the ceasefire line running through Jerusalem, February 1995

A street scene in ultra-Orthodox quarter of Mea Shearim, Jerusalem

An overview of the 500-year old shrine of Rabbi Shimon Bar Yohai on Mount Meron near Safed, popular with Sephardic Jews

Dr Yoram Lass, member of the Knesset, against the portraits of Israeli leaders – with David Ben Gurion on the extreme right – at the Knesset, Jerusalem

Moshe Dayan and Yitzhak Rabin in a market in the Muslim Quarter, Old City, Jerusalem, after the capture of East Jerusalem and the West Bank from Jordan in June 1967 – as depicted in the Wax Museum, Tel Aviv

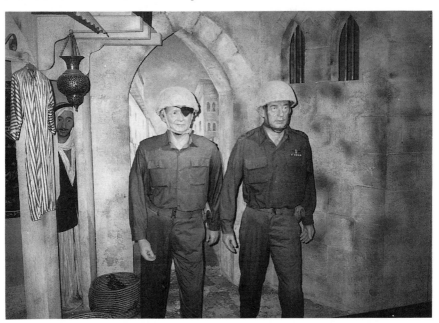

Emile Shukri Habibi, a former Arab member of the Knesset and a writer, at his office in Haifa

Fayaz Qawasmeh, the owner of Nahar al Khalil (Hotel), Hebron, where Moshe Levinger and others rented rooms in April 1968, in his villa, February 1995

Pinchas Fuchs and wife at the Elon Moreh Jewish settlement near Nablus
Inset: Portrait of Rabbi Zvi Yahuda Kook at the public relations office of the Kiryat Arba Municipal Council

Israeli soldiers stop Palestinian demonstrators from approaching the Psagot Jewish settlement on top of the hill near Al Bireh, January 1995

The Tomb of the Patriarchs/Ibrahimi Mosque, Hebron

A Jewish mother and child praying in the room interconnecting the tombs of
Abraham and Sarah. Its walls are decorated with tiles inscribed with
Quranic verses. The Arabic inscription on the plinth on the left of the door
reads, 'In the name of Allah, the Merciful, the Compassionate . . .'

Later the party secretariat adopted it as its official platform for the General Election due in late October.

Attention of all political parties was focused on the impending parliamentary poll – with the newly formed Likud (Unity) bloc, consisting of Gahal and a few small secular ultra-nationalist groups, emerging as a serious challenger to the Labour-Mapam alliance – when Israel was attacked by Egypt and Syria on 6 October 1973, on the eve of the Jewish festival of Yom Kippur (Hebrew, Day of Atonement).

October 1973 War: A Nasty Jolt

Unlike the 1956 and 1967 military conflicts, when Israel had taken the initiative, this time Egypt and Syria mounted pre-planned attacks on the Israeli forces, but not in the pre-1967 Israel. They did so in the Arab Occupied Territories with the aim of regaining the Egyptian and Syrian lands. They took this initiative three years after the Rogers peace plan, which secured a ceasefire in the Arab-Israeli War of Attrition (1969–70), had failed to pave the way for the recovery of their territories through diplomatic means. The Arab move, which came during the fasting month of Ramadan, took Israelis completely by surprise, who were about to begin their three day Yom Kippur holiday, and whose military took 72 hours to get fully mobilized instead of the planned 36 hours. The war, which lasted until 25 October, became known as the October 1973 War, or the Ramadan War (among Arabs) or the Yom Kippur War (among Israelis).

Between 6 and 8 October, while the Egyptian Second Army crossed the Suez Canal at Kantara and Ismailia in the central sector, the Third Army did so at Port Suez in the south. On the Golan Heights front the Syrians captured Mount Hermon and made gains at Khushniya. The Israelis were unable to check the advance of the Egyptian and Syrian forces. On 9 October the United States began an arms airlift using the planes of the Israeli airline El Al. That day the Israeli military was mobilized fully. The Soviet Union began airlifting arms to Egypt and Syria, with the latter getting two-thirds of the

shipments. Between 10 and 12 October the Israelis counter-
attacked on the Golan front, and advanced east of the armistice line north of Qunaitira to Saasa, despite an offensive
by Egypt meant to relieve the Syrians. The following day
Washington started using American aircraft to carry weapons
to Israel. On 15 October the Israeli offensive along the Suez
Canal, led by General Ariel Sharon, succeeded in creating
a wedge between the two Egyptians armies north of the
Great Bitter Lake of the Suez, and established a bridgehead
near Deversoir on the western bank. That day Soviet Prime
Minister Alexei Kosygin flew into Cairo. Between 15 and
19 October, repeated Syrian attempts to regain the Golan
Heights were frustrated by the Israelis. On 16 October an
oil embargo imposed against the military backers of Israel
– principally the United States, Holland and Portugal – by
the Organization of Arab Petroleum Exporting Countries
went into effect. Three days later, on 19 October, having
expanded the bridgehead, the Israelis pushed southwards
on the Egyptian soil in order to surround the Egyptian
Third Army along the eastern bank. On that day Kosygin
left Cairo after Egyptian President Anwar Sadat had agreed
to let Moscow try for a ceasefire *in situ*. On 21 October
Henry Kissinger, US Secretary of State, arrived in Moscow
to negotiate a deal with Soviet leaders. By then America
had airlifted 20,000 tonnes of weapons to Israel, plus 40
F-4 Phantom bombers, 48 A4 Skyhawk ground attack jets,
and 12 C-130 transporters. (By the end of the airlift on
15 November, 33,500 tonnes of US arms were shipped to
Israel.) The Soviet weapons shipments to Egypt and Syria
totalled 15,000 tonnes. On 22 October, following Kissinger's
successful talks in Moscow, a truce, specified by the United
Nations Security Council Resolution 338, went into effect
at 18.52 Greenwich Mean Time. But soon after the Israelis
broke the ceasefire on the Golan front, and regained Mount
Hermon.

On 23–4 October, violating the truce on the Suez front,
the Israelis rushed to Adabiya in the Gulf of Suez to
encircle the Egyptian Third Army. But their attempts to
seize Port Suez failed. The Israeli breach of the ceasefire

angered the Soviet Union. On 24 October it put on alert seven airborne divisions for airlifting to Egypt if the Israelis went ahead with surrounding the Egyptian Third Army. The following day Washington put its military, worldwide, on 'stage three alert', and its 82nd Airborne Division and the nuclear-armed warplanes of the Strategic Air Command on 'heightened alert' in anticipation of Moscow's possible direct intervention in the Arab-Israeli War. Against this backdrop, later that day the United Nations Security Council Resolution 340, renewing its ceasefire call, went into effect, and marked a formal end of the hostilities.

During the warfare, as signatories to the Joint Defence and Economic Co-operation Treaty of the Arab League, nine Arab states – Algeria, Iraq, Jordan, Kuwait, Libya, Morocco, Saudi Arabia, Sudan and Tunisia – dispatched 50,000 troops and air units to Egypt and Syria, including 30,000 Iraqi troops sent to Syria.

The human fatalities were: Egyptian 9,000, Syrian 3,500, and Israeli 2,552. The weapon losses were: Egypt 300 aircraft; Syria 160 aircraft; Egypt and Syria combined, 1,800 tanks; and Israel 114 aircraft, 800-plus tanks.

The war shattered the invincible image of Israel and Dayan. Though Dayan recovered from the initial shock, and the Israeli military performed well later, the label of failure stuck to him. However, the Jewish state's turn-around stemmed directly from Washington's massive airlift of arms and ammunition to it. Israel obtained the crucial American aid urgently by threatening to use its nuclear weapons as a last resort and readying its delivery systems for the purpose.

This and other crucial decisions were made by Meir and her 'kitchen cabinet' at an all-night session on 8–9 October 1973 at her Tel Aviv office next to the Defence Ministry's vast underground headquarters. Besides Meir and Dayan, the participants included General David Elazar, the IDF chief of staff; Yigal Allon, Deputy Prime Minister; Israel Galili; and Brigadier-General Israel Leor, the Prime Minister's military aide. The meeting began with an assessment by Dayan. He predicted an imminent collapse of the IDF since its present arms and ammunition stocks were expected to last only about a week, and the sole source of further military supplies was the United States. Therefore the meeting focused on how to get Washington to airlift emergency military supplies. It decided to arm its nuclear weapons arsenal, then estimated to contain more than 23 atomic bombs, to be used against the Egyptian and Syrian targets (such as their military headquarters) in the eventuality of the IDF's complete collapse; and to inform the United States of this immediately, demanding a prompt airlift of weapons and ammunition to enable Israel to mobilize its collapsing troops for a major counter-offensive and fullscale warfare for an extended period. Urgent orders went out to the regional IDF commander (a) to make operational nuclear missile launchers at a hillside of Kfar Zechariah, situated in the Judean hills south-west of Jerusalem, where nuclear weapons were stored in bunkers, and (b) to mount the stored atomic bombs on specially adopted F-4 Phantom bombers stationed at the Tel Nof air base near Rehovot. By deciding to let the missile launchers be placed in the open, the Israeli leaders made sure that their presence would be noted by both the American and the Soviet spy satellites. The Israeli ploy worked. Following an urgent meeting between Simcha Dinitz, the Israeli ambassador to the United States, and Kissinger at the White House on 9 October morning, Washington told Israel that it would immediately make good its arms and ammunition losses.[6]

However, the nuclear brinkmanship was not over yet. When the US military went on alert on 25 October in response to possible Soviet entry into the Middle East conflict, Israel reverted to its earlier nuclear alert. But, with the ceasefire taking hold, Washington returned to the normal state after a day, and so did Israel.

Besides decimating Dayan's political future, the war brought about more lasting changes in Israeli society. It ended the political convention which drew a line between foreign and defence affairs and domestic politics. It also severely shook Israeli citizens' confidence in their leaders and their crisis management skills. The radical right, secular and religious, capitalized on popular disappointment with the Labour political establishment, and transformed it into a protest movement and a strong lobby to compel the administration to accelerate the colonization of the West Bank.

The IDF's unpreparedness for war, combined with reports that top Israeli officials, including Dayan, had ignored intelligence reports that Egypt and Syria were planning an attack, provided additional ammunition to the opposition Likud in its attack on the ruling Labour alliance. The latter tried to deflect it by following a twin-headed strategy. The Meir government appointed an inquiry committee, chaired by Shimon Agranat, head of the Supreme Court. And it presented the Middle East Peace Conference, to be held on 22 December 1973 in Geneva, as a major breakthrough to peace and security. In the event this meeting achieved nothing. It adjourned after a day due to the impending Israeli General Election on 31 December.

In that poll the Labour-Mapam bloc lost five seats, retaining 51, while Likud gained eight, to score a total of 39. This encouraged the religious parties, holding 15 seats, to take a hard line in their negotiations with Meir, on joining a coalition government. An exasperated Meir formed a minority administration with the support of 58 MKs. It did not last long.

The report of the Agranat Commission on the October 1973 Arab-Israeli War, published in March 1974, blamed General David Elazar for what went wrong, and cleared Moshe Dayan, the Defence Minister. However, when Elazar resigned, pressure on Dayan to follow suit mounted. He refused. To get around the problem, in April Meir offered the resignation of her full cabinet to President Ephraim Katzir (1916– , r. 1973–8).

Unsurprisingly, Dayan did not enter the race for the Labour Party leader, leaving the contest to Yitzhak Rabin and Shimon Peres to be settled by the 600-odd members of the party's central committee. Rabin, backed among others by Meir, defeated Peres by 298 votes to 254.

What particularly favoured Rabin was the fact that he was not part of the Government at the time of the October 1973 War whereas Peres was Transport Minister. Rabin was then

Israeli ambassador to the United States. At the same time, as the IDF chief of staff during the lightning Israeli victory in the June 1967 War, he was regarded highly as a soldier.

Born into a middle class Jewish family (of Russian origin) in Jerusalem, Rabin graduated from an agricultural college in 1940. The next year he joined Palmah (Hebrew, acronym of Plugot Mahatz, Shock Units), the strike force of the Haganah, and trained under Yigal Allon, a leader of the leftist Ahdut HaAvodah. Rabin participated in the successful Allied campaign in 1941 in Syria then under a pro-Nazi French Government. In the 1948–9 Arab-Israeli War, he commanded a brigade which saw combat on the Jerusalem and Negev fronts.

After the military conflict Rabin headed the IDF's tactical operations branch, 1950–52, under chief of staff Yigal Yadin. Following his graduation from the British Staff College in 1953 and promotion to major-general, Rabin served as chief of the IDF's manpower branch, 1954–6, commander of the Northern Command, 1956–9, chief of operations, 1959–61, deputy chief of staff, 1961–4, and chief of staff, 1964–8. Even while serving as ambassador to America, 1968–73, he advised Prime Ministers Eshkol and Meir on important military matters.

Once back home, Rabin joined the Labour Party. He was elected to the Knesset in the December 1973 poll. He was given a labour portfolio in the cabinet formed by Golda Meir in March 1974. Following her resignation soon after, Rabin challenged Peres for party leadership, and won, despite the latter's long standing in Israeli politics.

Though Rabin gave Peres the important defence portfolio, their relations remained strained. In 1976, in contravention of the party policy of not allowing Jewish settlements near Palestinian urban centres on the West Bank, Peres compromised with the ultra-nationalist Gush Emunim when they set up a settlement in Kadume near Nablus, an act which Rabin found unforgivable.

Overall Rabin's mind-set was that of a soldier, and it never changed. Though he formally retired from the IDF at the age of 46, he did not really abandon his military uniform. Being a born soldier, he was more at ease implementing policies and orders rather than conceiving them. He lacked imagination. In contrast Peres, an intellectual at heart, was known as a man of vision, political and technological.

Born Shimon Persky into the household of a timber merchant in the small town of Vishniva, Poland, Peres was 13 (in 1936) when his family migrated to Palestine. After studying at an agricultural school, he joined the Alumot kibbutz. A sensitive youth, fond of reading and of poetry, he was also a good organizer. He served as secretary of the labour Zionist youth group, HaNoar HaOved (Hebrew, The Young Worker), 1941–4. Active with the Haganah since 1941, he became its manpower chief in 1947, and later also its weapons procurer. By the time the 1948–9 Arab-Israeli War ended, he was in charge of the Israeli navy. He became a favourite of Premier Ben Gurion.

Between 1953 and 1959 he served as the Defence Ministry's director-general. He established Israel Aircraft Industries, which went on to manufacture jet aircraft and guided missiles and sophisticated avionics. In 1956, having persuaded France (then colluding with Israel against President Nasser of Egypt) to ship weapons to Israel secretly, he succeeded in getting Paris to sell it a nuclear reactor, a deal which developed into a much wider co-operation in the development and manufacture of nuclear weapons at Dimona in the Negev Desert. During the visit of the West German Defence Minister, Franz Strauss, to Israel in 1958, Peres persuaded him to supply weapons clandestinely to the Jewish state. In such dealings, which contravened international embargos, Peres was involved in the forging of documents, falsifying the names of the end-users of weapons, and creating fictional purchasing and selling firms.

Peres entered the Knesset in 1959 on a Mapai ticket, and has since then retained a seat. During his tenure as Defence Minister, 1960–65, he first persuaded President John Kennedy to end the US arms embargo and sell Israel defensive weapons such as anti-aircraft missiles, and then prevailed upon President Lyndon Johnson to sell Israel offensive weapons such as tanks and fighter aircraft. Meanwhile, a reprocessing plant to transform uranium into weapons-grade plutonium was completed at Dimona in 1962. The French presence there continued until 1966. In early 1968 the Dimona plant began producing four to five nuclear arms annually.[7]

When Ben Gurion left Mapai in 1965 to set up Rafi, Peres followed him, becoming Rafi's secretary-general. But when the Labour Party was formed in 1968 by amalgamating Mapai, Ahdut HaAvodah-Poale Zion and most of Rafi, he left Rafi, and became deputy secretary-general of the new party. The next year he joined Golda Meir's cabinet first as a minister without portfolio, and then moved to the Transport Ministry, 1971–4.

As Defence Minister in the Rabin administration, Peres did much to rebuild the IDF after the traumatic experience of the October 1973 War. This helped him to sustain a substantial faction within the Labour Party. Consisting largely of elements who had been Ben Gurion loyalists, it was considered rightist. The faction headed by Yigal Allon, the veteran Ahdut HaAvodah leader, was leftist. In between was the one, the largest of the three, loyal to Rabin, who had been adopted as the favourite son by the old guard Mapai politicians. But Rabin, a newcomer to politics, lacked experience and confidence to be able to impose his will on the more seasoned politicians like Peres and Allon.

During Rabin's premiership as the annual inflation rate soared to 50 per cent, and popular discontent grew, his government became less and less secure. The year 1976 proved to be one of rising social tensions, and the forerunner of a series of financial scandals. Asher Yadlin, appointed by Rabin as Governor of the Bank of Israel, was indicted on charges of bribery and fraud committed during his directorship of Histadrut's Sick Fund, and later confessed that he had channelled the embezzled funds to the Labour Party's coffers. In May, in a milieu of strikes and worker unrest, policemen were subjected to grenade attacks by the slum dwellers of Tel Aviv. Six months later, following a 20 per cent increase in food and transport charges, workers staged a series of strikes. In December the ruling coalition fell apart, and a new poll was announced for 17 May 1977.

Factionalism within Labour on the issue of the Occupied Arab Territories intensified. In January 1977, following a financial scandal, housing minister Avraham Ofer – who had conducted Rabin's successful campaign for party leader in 1974 – committed suicide. Rabin's inexperience in civil administration, poor communicating skills, and continued strained relations with Peres hurt his government's popularity. Yet, in a new challenge by Peres to his leadership in early 1977, Rabin scraped through by 1,445 votes to 1,404 in an electoral college of 3,000. Then came a revelation which made his position untenable. In March it was revealed that, during his ambassadorship in America, his wife, Leah, had maintained an active account with an American bank in Washington, an illegal act. The next month he resigned as party leader. The party delegates then elected Peres as his successor.

In the May 1977 poll the Labour-Mapam bloc's strength fell to 32. It ceded its traditional leading position in the Knesset to Likud which won 43 seats. The result became known popularly as a *Ma HaPach* (Hebrew, The Upheaval). It signalled the end of an era.

1977 Election: The Unveiling of a New Era

Fifteen of the 19 seats that Labour lost went to the Democratic Movement for Change (DMC) formed only in October 1976 by Yigal Yadin, an eminent Labour leader, who had become the IDF chief of staff at the age of 32. The DMC fought the election on the platform of reforming the electoral system, improving the lot of Sephardi Jews, and cleansing the administrative and political apparatuses which had been soiled primarily by the corrupt and nepotistic ways of the Labour establishment.

Summing up the social situation, Eric Marsden, a senior British journalist based in Jerusalem, wrote: 'Israel has been governed [for three decades] by interlocking groups of ministers and senior officials, many of them from an elite of about 250 families who rose to prominence in the [Zionist] pioneering days. Along the way many establishment members, and more particularly their sons, have changed direction. There are many instances of fervent egalitarian socialists from kibbutzim whose sons have become capitalist entrepreneurs, technocrats or army leaders, with a right-wing outlook, while still paying lip service to the Labour movement.'[8]

As such the emergence of Likud as the largest bloc in the Ninth Knesset ahead of the Labour-Mapam bloc by 11 seats, seemed apt in more ways than one. Headed by Menachem Begin – who had by then won the respect even of his opponents as an honest, ascetic patriot and an able leader – Likud had presented itself to voters as an orderly and principled entity. Its election campaign had been masterminded by Ezer Weizman, who had been per-suaded to return to the political bloc led by Begin, with whom he had fallen out some months earlier. For his brilliant success, Begin rewarded him with the Foreign Ministry.

Menachem Wolfovitch Begin was born in Brest-Litovsk (then in Poland, later in Russia). He obtained a law degree at the University of Warsaw in 1935. At 16, he joined Betar (acronym of Brit Trumpeldor, Covenant of [Yosef] Trumpeldor), the youth organization and chief socializing agent of the Revisionist Zionists, known for its emphasis on iron discipline and militarism. More radical than Vladimir Zeev Jabotinsky, the (Polish) founder of the Revisionist movement, which combined its ultra-nationalism with con-servative socio-economic policies, Begin challenged him in 1938 after being promoted to commander of Betar in Poland. On the eve of the Nazi invasion of Poland in 1939, Begin fled to Vilnius, Lithuania, then under Soviet rule. In September 1940 he was sentenced to eight years' hard labour in a Siberian camp for engaging in illegal Zionist activities. But, after the Soviet Union had joined World War II on the Allied side in mid-1941, Begin was released, and drafted into the Free Polish Army. He arrived in Palestine in May 1942 as a soldier of that force. Here he renewed contacts with the local Betar.

After his demobilization from the Free Polish Army in December 1943, Begin was appointed commander of the Irgun, the militia of the Revisionists. Declaring an armed struggle against the British mandate in January 1944, he went underground. The Irgun resorted to bombing British installations. Begin repeated his anti-British call in October 1945, five months after the end of the war in Europe. The Irgun's terroristic actions led the British to declare an award of £10,000 [worth $300,000 today] for his arrest. In July 1946 the Irgun bombed the British mandate government offices in the King David Hotel, Jerusalem, killing 91 British, Arab and Jewish officials and staff. Following this, the Haganah, the main military force of the Jewish community in Palestine, stopped co-operating with the Irgun. A year later the Irgun hanged two British sergeants in retaliation for the execution of three of its members, an act which aroused public anger in Britain. The Irgun participated actively in the ethnic conflict which erupted after the rejection by the Palestinian Arabs of the United Nations partition plan in November 1947. The massacre of over 250 Arab men, women and children during a raid by 132 Irgun and Lehi militiamen on 9–10 April 1948 on Deir Yasin village near Jerusalem, planned chiefly by Begin, increased panic among Palestinian Arabs, and turned their mass flight from the prospective areas of the (planned) Jewish state into a stampede.

Later, led by Begin, the Irgun ranks refused to be absorbed into the Israel Defence Forces formed by the provisional government of David Ben Gurion in late May 1948. They continued to participate in the war against the Arab states as a separate entity. This went on until 21 June when Ben Gurion ordered his forces to destroy the freighter *Altalena*, anchored off Tel Aviv, loaded with weapons and volunteers for the Irgun. While refraining from hitting back at Ben Gurion's forces, Begin did not disband the Irgun until three months later. Soon thereafter former Irgun ranks and the Revisionist Zionists re-emerged as the Herut party under Begin's leadership.

In 1949 Begin was elected to the Knesset, and maintained his membership until 1984. In the first five general elections, 1949–61, his Herut faction won about 12 per cent of the vote, emerging as the largest opposition group in the parliament. Leading his party in an authoritarian way, Begin brooked no challenge.

Membership of the Knesset failed to mellow Begin, who stuck to his populist demagoguery and extremist rhetoric of the pre-state period. He was vehemently opposed to the idea of accepting reparations, totalling $2 billion, from the West German Government for the brutal atrocities against Jews committed by Nazi Germany during 1933–45, considering it as an inadequate step by the Germans. He expressed his opposition by inciting a mob to attack the Knesset (then based in downtown Jerusalem). In retaliation, in January 1952, the Knesset suspended him for 15 months.

This had a chastening effect on Begin. But it took him several more years to fully understand and accept the norms and practices of a democratic system operating through a popularly elected parliament. It was only in the mid-1960s, when he was over 50 years old, that he mellowed enough to compromise his extremism and form an alliance with Liberals, which was named Gahal. Winning more than 21 per cent of the vote, it secured 26 Knesset seats in the general election of November 1965. An advocate of conservative socio-economic policies, Gahal was opposed to a strong public sector created by Labour. Its other main plank was a commitment to recreating the biblical Eretz Israel.

Given its size, Gahal became the leading choice for partnership in the national unity government that Prime Minister Levi Eshkol formed on the eve of the June 1967 Arab-Israeli War. Begin was given a cabinet post but no specific portfolio.

Israel's stunning victory in that conflict was perceived by rightists, both religious and secular (such as Gahal supporters), as an event of legendary proportions, tantamount to a divine intervention. More specifically, it lent credence to the grand, ultra-nationalist scenario of recreating the Kingdom of Israel, and gave fresh impetus to militaristic patriotism, the fountain-head of Revisionist Zionism. It made Begin buoyant.

Gahal retained its 26 Knesset seats in the 1969 poll and its place in the national unity government that followed. Begin stayed in the cabinet until July 1970 when, protesting against the majority decision to accept an American peace plan which envisaged Israel's withdrawal from Sinai, he resigned, and resumed his opposition role. But Gahal's sharing of power for three years lent it and its leader, Begin, legitimacy and respectability they had lacked before. This would contribute to their electoral victory in 1977.

When the surprise Arab attack on the Israeli forces in October 1973 shook popular confidence and respect for the Labour establishment, Gahal benefited. On the eve of the December 1973 poll, Begin combined Gahal with the smaller Free Centre, the State Party (a remnant of Rafi) and the Eretz Israel movement to form the Likud bloc – an enterprise in which Ariel Sharon, an ultra-nationalist, played a substantial role. The major element that brought these factions together was their commitment to incorporate the Occupied Territories of the West Bank and the Gaza Strip into Israel. Ideologically, Likud was an alliance of the conservative, capitalist and ultra-nationalist trends within secular Zionism.

Likud's first performance at the poll showed that, at 30.2 per cent of the popular vote, the cumulative strength of its constituent forces was only 8.5 per cent behind the liberal, social democratic forces, represented by the Labour-Mapam alliance. In the subsequent 1977 election, backed by 33.4 per cent of the voters, Likud emerged 7.4 per cent ahead of its rival. In a way, this was an aggregate measure of the right wing drift of Israelis, which had begun soon after the founding of Israel nearly three decades before.

As the leader of the largest group in the Knesset, Begin was invited to form the next government. By coalescing with the religious parties, holding 17 seats, he secured the aggregate backing of 60 MKs, thus bypassing Labour's breakaway Democratic Movement for Change, led by Yigal Yadin.

Installed in the country's most powerful office, Begin

exercised authority in a manner reminiscent of David Ben Gurion, his *bête noire*: highly personal and domineering. At the same time, he refrained from making a clean break with the Labour-dominated era. He retained virtually all of the senior civil servants and ambassadors even though most of them had been Labour appointees, but reminded them that the power to take major policy decisions rested with him.

As a firm believer in the recreation of the biblical Eretz Israel, Begin was quick to remove the ambiguities and doubts in the previous Labour Governments' stance on the Occupied Arab Territories. He unequivocally rejected the possibility of giving up any territory of the Palestine under British mandate. His government started publishing maps of Israel without the 1949 armistice lines. Within weeks of taking office Begin journeyed to the controversial Elon Moreh settlement near Nablus. The ultra-nationalist Jewish colonizers, organized under the banner of Gush Emunim, had been allowed to settle there in December 1976 by the previous Labour defence minister, Peres, after their several earlier attempts to do so had been foiled by the IDF. During his visit to Elon Moreh to unveil a synagogue during the Jewish festival of Sukkot in July 1977 he declared: 'There will be many more Elon Morehs.' On the other side, Begin refused point blank to recognize Palestinians as a distinct entity in the peace talks Israel wished to have with its adversaries. Aware that his stands on these issues were not much different from Moshe Dayan's, he offered the foreign ministry to Dayan, a Labour MK. Dayan accepted, thus giving the Begin administration a majority of one in the Knesset.

Outside of the Eretz Israel of the Old Testament, Begin was willing to trade land for peace in his dealings with Egypt and Syria. Yet, when Egyptian President Anwar Sadat took his dramatic, unilateral step in November 1977 to address the Knesset in Jerusalem to declare his acceptance of Israel's existence, the response of Begin was tepid. Among those who were concerned about this were 350 reserve army officers. In the spring of 1978 they addressed a letter to the Prime Minister urging him to pursue the path to peace seriously and vigorously. Their action led to the formation of Peace Now

(Hebrew, Shalom Achshav) group as a mass-based lobby for peace, which organized rallies and demonstrations.

In the Egyptian-Israeli negotiations that followed, Begin allowed both Dayan and Weizman important roles. The result was the Camp David Accords, hammered out at the American presidential retreat of Camp David, Maryland, in September 1978 between Begin and Sadat, with the assistance of US President Jimmy Carter. They laid out the framework for (a) a peace treaty between Egypt and Israel, and (b) a resolution of the Palestinian problem.

The highlights of (a) were as follows. Egypt would regain Sinai, in stages, in exchange for an agreement to conclude a peace treaty and establish normal diplomatic and economic relations with Israel. The time-frame for 'total peace for total withdrawal' was three years after the signing of the treaty. The highlights of (b) were the following. Over a five-year transition period the Palestinian residents of the West Bank and the Gaza Strip would gain autonomy and see the end of Israeli military rule, while Israel would retain sovereignty over the land and water of these territories and maintain military camps there. During the transition period there would be talks on the final status of these territories between Israel, Egypt, Jordan (if it wished), and the elected representatives of resident Palestinians.

This breakthrough with Egypt won Begin the 1978 Nobel Peace Prize which he shared with Sadat. The two leaders signed the Egyptian-Israeli Peace Treaty at the White House in Washington on 26 March 1979. By removing the Arab world's most populous and strategic country from the anti-Israeli camp, Begin deprived the Arabs of the military option in their continuing conflict with the Jewish state.

Unlike in the case of Egypt, there was no compelling reason for Begin to tackle peacefully the Palestinian problem. He deliberately prevaricated, leaving the Palestinian autonomy provisions in the Camp David Accords unimplemented by the deadline of May 1980. This brought about the resignation of Weizman, who thought that his move would trigger the fall of the Begin administration. It did not. Nor had the earlier resignation of Dayan shaken the Government.

Begin had allocated the Foreign Ministry to Yitzhak
Shamir, a hawk. Following his electoral success in July
1981, with Likud improving its strength by five to 48,
largely due to an expanding base among Sephardi Jews,
Begin re-appointed Shamir as Foreign Minister and gave
Ariel Sharon the Defence Ministry he had long coveted.
With three important ministries run by ultra-nationalists,
the Begin administration moved decidedly rightwards. It
capped its formal annexation of Greater East Jerusalem
(in mid-1980) with the annexation of the Golan Heights
in December 1981. This was followed by a fullscale invasion
of Lebanon, which occurred within six weeks of the final
Israeli withdrawal from the Sinai in late April 1982 as part
of the Egyptian-Israeli Peace Treaty. The architect of this
major military enterprise, which resulted in thousands of
mainly civilian fatalities among Lebanese and Lebanon-based
Palestinians, was Ariel Sharon who had the backing of
Begin. They initiated a war when neither Israel's security nor
its existence was under any serious threat. They emerged
as strong proponents of a military interventionist policy,
first adopted and executed by Premier David Ben Gurion
in 1956 – albeit in collusion with Britain and France –
which culminated in the Suez War. That time around the
Israeli attempt at hegemony in the region was contained
by the unified stand taken by the two superpowers, the
United States of America and the Soviet Union. This time
the Lebanon War and the subsequent unforeseen mishaps,
combined with the Byzantine nature of politics in Lebanon,
then in the throes of a long-running civil conflict, created deep
fissures within Israeli society itself. The conclusion that most
Israeli politicians were obliged to draw was unambiguous.
There are limits to the power, military and political, of Israel,
a small country – however determined and well armed – to
impose its will on a whole region. The immediate price that
Begin and Sharon paid for their flawed action was public
censure followed by loss of influence, if not power. While
Begin withdrew from public life altogether within a year of
the end of the Lebanon War, Sharon continued his political
career – away from the defence ministry.

Born Ariel Shinerman in a Zionist family in Kfar Malal, Palestine, Sharon joined the Haganah as a youth. After participating in the 1948–9 Arab-Israeli War, he continued his military career, working as an intelligence officer. He established Unit 101, composed exclusively of volunteers, to carry out swift cross-border reprisal attacks – one such operation against an Egyptian military camp in the Gaza Strip in early 1955 resulting in two-score Egyptian deaths. When Unit 101 was incorporated into the paratroopers later in the year, Sharon became a paratrooper commander. During the 1956 Suez War, he exceeded the orders he had received as a brigade commander, and engaged in a battle which caused many casualties. This slowed down his rise in the military hierarchy. Only when Yitzhak Rabin became chief of staff in 1965 was Sharon promoted to run the IDF's training department, and later elevated to brigadier-general.

During the June 1967 Arab-Israeli War Sharon commanded a division on the southern front, capturing the Umm Katif range in the Sinai. In 1969 he was put in charge of the southern command. His iron-fist policy towards the Palestinian resistance to the Israeli occupation of the West Bank and the Gaza Strip earned strong condemnation of Palestinians and became a source of controversy among Israelis. In mid-1973 he quit the army, and entered politics by joining Gahal. He was instrumental in the creation of Likud out of the merger of Gahal, the Free Centre, the State Party and the Eretz Yisrael movement. In the October 1973 Arab-Israeli War he commanded a division which established a bridgehead over the Suez Canal. However, his later command of the division proved controversial.

After being elected to the Knesset in December 1973 on the Likud ticket, he resigned after some months to serve Labour Prime Minister Rabin as a special adviser. In 1976 he formed his own group – Shlomzion (Hebrew, Peaceful Zion) – which won two seats in the May 1977 poll. He then amalgamated it with the Herut faction of Likud, and became Minister of Agriculture in the Likud-dominated government. Later he also became chairman of the cabinet's (Jewish) Settlement Committee. In both capacities he gave much impetus to the

Jewish colonization of the West Bank and the Gaza Strip. He believed in territorial maximalism and achievement of political ends through military means. He got his chance to put his beliefs into practice, dramatically, after the July 1981 elections when Premier Begin named him defence minister.

Once Sharon and Begin had withdrawn Israeli troops from the Sinai in April 1982, they finalized their plans to attack Lebanon. On 6 June 1982 the IDF marched into southern Lebanon with the ostensible aim of clearing the area of the Palestinian commandos and making northern Israel safe from their artillery and rocket fire. But, when the United States did not object too much, Sharon and the IDF chief of staff, Raphael Eitan – who was later to join the ultra-nationalist Tehiya [Hebrew, Renaissance] party[9] – implemented a more ambitious plan. Its objectives were to bring about the evacuation of all foreign forces from Lebanon, then in its seventh year of a civil war (1975–90), including those of the Palestine Liberation Organization, headquartered in Beirut since 1972, and the establishment of a new Lebanese regime under Bashir Gemayel, a right-wing Maronite (Catholic) Christian warlord, with a view to having it conclude a peace treaty with Israel. In short, the game plan of Sharon and Begin was not merely to pacify the northern Israeli frontier but to rearrange the regional political landscape, and thus establish Israel as the unrivalled power broker in the region.

Commanded by Sharon, on 13 June 1982 IDF troops entered Beirut, then divided into Christian East and Muslim (Lebanese-Palestinian) West. In collusion with the Maronite Christian Phalange militia, the IDF besieged some 500,000 Lebanese and Palestinians in the eight square kilometres of West Beirut. For a month Sharon tried, unsuccessfully, to secure the unconditional PLO surrender by a combination of artillery fire, air raids, and severing of water and electricity supplies as well as food and fuel. Following a ten-day truce, the IDF staged an intense bombing of West Beirut for a week, and then subjected it to a more intensified bombardment from the air, land and sea, with Sharon ordering saturation bombing for 11½ hours, non-stop, using phosphorous shells and concussion and cluster bombs. His actions aroused widespread condemnation in the Arab and the western worlds, and angered Washington. It pressured Premier Begin to intervene. He did. As a result the 63-day siege of West Beirut ended, and peace returned to the beleaguered city on 13 August.

Following US mediation, on 21 August contingents of about 1,000 men from the US, Britain, France and Italy – forming the Multi-National Force for peacekeeping – were deployed in West Beirut to ensure the safe withdrawal of PLO and Syrian troops. On 1 September the last of the 8,144 PLO commandos, 3,500 (Syrian-controlled) Palestine Liberation Army soldiers, and 2,700 Syrian troops left West Beirut. The Multi-National Force withdrew soon after.

At their peak, the IDF deployed 76,000 troops, the PLO fighters and their Lebanese allies amounted to 18,000, and the Syrian units to 25,000. With 15,700 Lebanese, Palestinians and Syrians dead, including 1,110 PLO fighters and 1,350 Syrian troops versus 350 Israeli fatalities, the human losses were grossly uneven. So, too, were the weapons losses: Syria 92 aircraft and 42 tanks; the PLO 20 tanks; and Israel 2 aircraft and 2 tanks.[10]

Sharon, backed by Begin, now set out to become the kingmaker in Lebanese politics in getting Bashir Gemayel elected President later that month (September). He succeeded, only to see his protégé killed – as a result of a huge bomb explosion at Gemayel's Phalange party headquarters – on 14 September, before he could take office. In retaliation, Sharon allowed his Maronite Christian allies a free hand to murder some 2,000 Palestinians in the refugee camps of Sabra and Shatila in Beirut. This outraged not only many Lebanese, Palestinians and Syrians but also large segments of Israeli society.

In an unprecedented move, on 25 September, responding to a call by the Peace Now group, some 400,000 Israelis demonstrated in Tel Aviv, demanding an inquiry into the Sabra and Shatila massacres and a recall of the Israeli troops from Lebanon. The Begin Government appointed an inquiry commission chaired by the head of the Supreme Court,

Yitzhak Kahan. Yielding to popular pressure, Sharon ordered the withdrawal of IDF troops from Beirut on 29 September. The western Multi-National Force re-entered the city.

Following a critical report by the Kahan commission, Sharon was forced to resign as Defence Minister in February 1983. But he retained a place in the cabinet as a minister without portfolio. With thousands of IDF troops posted in Lebanon, where feelings against the Israeli occupiers were running high, they became targets of ambushing, sniping and booby-trapped vehicles, in a growing campaign of armed resistance by the Lebanese. By spring the steadily rising list of Israeli fatalities had topped 150, pushing the grand total of IDF dead in Lebanon above 500. This turned Israeli public opinion against continued military presence in Lebanon. It demoralized not only the IDF command but also Prime Minister Begin. Unable to bear responsibility for continued Israeli deaths, he resigned on 29 August 1983, thus ending his six-year premiership in ignominy. A politician who had achieved power with a bang went out with a whimper.

In the Likud leadership contest that followed, Yitzhak Shamir defeated David Levy. At 68, Shamir was the oldest politician to become Prime Minister. Born Yitzhak Yzernitzky in a religious family in Poland, Shamir joined the Revisionist Zionist youth movement, Betar. He moved to Palestine when he was 20 (in 1935), and two years later joined the Irgun. When the Irgun split in 1940, with Avraham Stern forming Lehi, Shamir opted for the new group. Following Stern's assassination in 1942, he became one of the three commanders of Lehi in charge of organization and operations, which included the assassination in 1944 of Lord Moyne, the British resident minister in the Middle East. Arrested by the British in 1946, Shamir was dispatched to a detention camp in Eritrea. He escaped after four months, and found his way to Paris, where he lived until the founding of Israel in May 1948.

Following his arrival in Israel, Shamir enrolled in the political wing of Lehi, the Fighters Party. In 1955 he joined Mossad (Hebrew, Institute, its official title being HaMossad LeModiin Ve Tafkidim Meyuhadim, Institute for Intelligence and Special Tasks), the Israeli foreign intelligence agency, and served in various senior positions until 1965.

After running a mattress factory for five years, he re-entered politics by joining the Herut party. Three years later he became chairman of the Herut executive; and in the December 1973 election he won a seat in the Knesset. In parliament he served as Speaker, 1977–80. An ultra-nationalist, he opposed the Camp David Accords negotiated by Prime Minister Begin, the leader of both Herut, to which Shamir belonged, and the larger Likud bloc. Yet, after Weizman resigned as Foreign Minister in 1980, Begin offered the Foreign Ministry to Shamir, and he accepted it. When he succeeded Begin three years later he retained the foreign affairs portfolio.

Shamir inherited the ill-effects of the Lebanon War: a deleterious involvement in the imbroglio of Lebanese politics, and hyperinflation which among other things had led to the collapse of several banks. On the positive side he inherited a draft Lebanese-Israeli peace treaty mediated by the United States, which had been initialled by the two sides in May 1983.

But the final signature of the treaty by Lebanon's President, Amin Gemayel (r. 1982–8), after the Lebanese parliament had ratified it, eluded Shamir. Indeed it never materialized. Once the western Multi-National Forces withdrew from Lebanon in February 1984, President Gemayel felt exposed, and found himself at the mercy of the powerful Syrian President Hafiz Assad (r. 1970–), who was deadly opposed to the treaty. Gemayel decided to annul it, and the Lebanese parliament did so in early March.

Meanwhile, the toll of Israeli fatalities in Lebanon rose steadily. At home, hyperinflation was compounded by a chronic balance of payments deficit. The roots of the twin crisis lay chiefly in the larger issue of war and peace: the October 1973 Arab-Israeli War which necessitated massive rearmament during and after the conflict, financed mainly by American credits; the expense of the evacuation of the Sinai following the 1979 Egyptian-Israeli Peace Treaty, funded largely by US loans; and the cost of the Lebanon War against the background of rising inflation. The rise in the military budget from 1974 onwards had gone hand in hand with increased expenditure on social welfare. The authorities managed this by borrowing heavily at home and abroad, and by curtailing investment. Most of these developments occurred against the background of the official decision – taken in the course of fiscal reform in 1977 – to abolish exchange controls. By the early 1980s the problem of huge Israeli loans and balance of payment deficits loomed large. As confidence in the Israeli economy plummeted capital outflow increased, deepening the crisis further. The situation grew worse as the Government resorted to ever rising deficit budgeting, reaching 10–15 per cent of the annual Gross Domestic Product by the early 1980s, expecting to spend itself out of the crisis. Inflation, which reached triple figures annually in 1979, escalated into hyperinflation, running at 400 per cent a year, after 1983.

Shamir's inability to resolve the economic crisis and devise a way out of the Lebanese quagmire encouraged a small religious group in the Likud-led administration to break ranks, and vote for a no-confidence motion against the Government, thus forcing a parliamentary poll a year ahead of schedule.

The 1984 election campaign was thus dominated by the two issues on which the Likud bloc was weak. Unsurprisingly it lost six seats, retaining 41. It now fell behind the Labour-Mapam bloc at 44 (which was three less than before).

There were two main reasons why the Labour-Mapam bloc overtook Likud. The Democratic Movement for Change, a major factor behind Labour's defeat in 1977, disintegrated, following its controversial decision to join the Begin administration, with its leader, Yigal Yadin, retiring from public life in 1981. The disaffected Labour voters returned to their traditional party whose leaders, now confined to the opposition benches and deprived of the chances of corruption and embezzlement of public funds, had improved Labour's popular image. And, shaken by the anti-Labour feelings prevalent among Sephardi voters, which came to surface when Likud assumed office in 1977, the Labour hierarchy went out of its way to open its doors to Sephardim. Though this did not impress the largely sceptical Sephardim, it helped to stem the desertion rate.

However, having decided to exclude the (Marxist) Hadash (Hebrew acronym of Hazit Demokratit le Shalom ve Leshivyon, Democratic Front for Peace and Equality) and two Arab groups, Peres, leader of the Labour-Mapam bloc, could not muster a majority in the Knesset. Likud's Shamir needed to bargain with seven groups or individual MKs to manage a majority, and found the task daunting. Peres and Shamir then discussed forming a national unity government, an arrangement they justified in the light of the looming economic crisis, no less damaging to Israel than a threat of war. Disagreeing with Peres, six Mapam MKs quit the Labour-Mapam bloc, and joined the opposition. It took Shamir and Peres several weeks to devise a common set of policies on the economy, the Lebanese War and the Middle East peace process, and secure the consent of the religious parties to be included in the national unity government. The question of who should lead the new cabinet for the first half of the four-year term was settled by Ezer Weizman, who headed a group called Yahad (Hebrew, Together). It was to be Peres. In return Peres appointed him a minister without portfolio, but with a seat in the inner political cabinet. Thus rewarded, Weizman and two other Yahad MKs joined Labour, raising its strength to 41, on a par with Likud. Shamir served as deputy premier and Foreign Minister until 1986 and then became the Prime Minister. Following the November 1988 poll, returning 39 Labour MKs and 40 Likud, the national unity concord was renewed. It lasted two years.

National Unity Governments: 1984–90

Between them the two major secular blocs, one right-of-centre and the other left-of-centre, exercised power jointly for six years. The three Governments they formed included the leading figures of both. Likud's Shamir and Sharon became a constant feature, as did Labour's Peres and Rabin (who ran the Defence Ministry throughout) – and Weizman.

They monopolized the prime ministry as well as the crucial defence, foreign and finance portfolios. And they – all of them Ashkenazim – were members of the powerful inner political cabinet.

Working in conjunction with Rabin, his Defence Minister, Peres devised and implemented a three-stage Israeli withdrawal from Lebanon, starting in early February 1985 and ending on 6 June, exactly three years after Israel's invasion of its northern neighbour. But the evacuation was not total. Israel retained a wide security belt inside Lebanon, to be guarded by 1,000 IDF troops and 3,000-strong Israeli-run Christian militia, called the South Lebanon Army. Overall, Israel lost almost as many soldiers (300) in the aftermath of its invasion of Lebanon as during the war itself (350).

The disentangling of Israel from Lebanon almost coincided with the launching on 1 July 1985 of the Economic Stabilization Programme (ESP), which had been worked out in co-operation with trade unions and employers. It froze prices and wages as well as currency devaluation, and introduced the New Israeli Shekel (equal to 1,000 Old Israeli Shekel). By raising interest rates sharply it introduced a tight money policy. The ESP was so severe that it resulted in a 30 per cent fall in real wages in three months. But it held, and it worked. By the end of the year, the annual inflation was down drastically – from 250 per cent to about 20 per cent. The success of the ESP enabled the Government to sharply reduce, and then eliminate, the budget deficit. Confidence in the Israeli economy returned, and with it foreign capital.

On stepping down as the Prime Minister in October 1986, Peres took over the Foreign Ministry from Shamir, hoping to revive the moribund Middle East peace process. He saw an opportunity in the plan agreed by Yasser Arafat (1929–), Chairman of the PLO, and King Hussein of Jordan in early 1985. It envisaged the Palestinians exercising their right to self-determination within the framework of a confederation of Jordan and Palestine – and a joint Jordanian-Palestinian delegation to participate in the regional peace talks to be organized under the United Nations auspices. Following his clandestine meetings with King Hussein in London, Peres signed a secret memorandum of understanding with him in early 1987. But it was overruled by Prime Minister Shamir. He stuck to the 1978 Camp David Accords, which stipulated Israel retaining sovereignty over the land and water of the West Bank and Gaza Strip, and which did not recognize Palestinians as a separate entity. In April 1987 the Palestine National Council cancelled Arafat's agreement with Jordan. This finally destroyed any prospect of a negotiated solution to the Palestinian problem, and was a crucial factor in the eruption of the intifada in December.

The speed with which the intifada spread from the Gaza Strip to the West Bank, its severity, the overwhelming, enthusiastic backing it won, and the unprecedented unity it engendered among different Palestinian factions, secular and Islamic, puzzled and upset the Yitzhak Shamir administration. The task of crushing the Palestinian uprising fell primarily on Yitzhak Rabin, the Defence Minister. Emulating his former military adviser, Ariel Sharon, now his colleague in the inner political cabinet and as the Minister of Trade and Industry, Rabin pursued an iron fist policy to smash the intifada. Besides the conventional means of firings, curfews, harassment, arrests and house searches and demolitions, his strategy included such tactics as breaking bones of the protestors.

Prime Minister Shamir remained as unyielding on the peace process as before. In early 1988 he rejected the peace proposals of George Shultz, US Secretary of State, as impractical. The Shultz plan specified a six-month period for talks between Israel and a joint Jordanian-Palestinian delegation to work out the details of a transitional autonomy arrangement for the West Bank and Gaza Strip, which would last three years, during which a final settlement would be negotiated. These talks would run concurrently with an international peace coference, involving the five permanent members of the United Nations Security Council and all the interested parties, on the basis of the Security Council Resolutions 242 and 338. Since the Shultz plan lacked any provision for a Palestinian state, the PLO rejected it. Then, in July 1988, with King Hussein finally cutting the remaining administrative and legal links with the West Bank, Shamir's strategy of persuading Jordan to join the enlarged Camp David Accords became redundant. On the other hand it paved the way for the Palestine National Council to issue a declaration of independence for Palestine 'on our Palestinian land', renounce violence and terrorism, and accept the existence of Israel at its session in Algiers in November 1988. Though this had no immediate impact on the Jewish state, it led to Washington establishing low-level diplomatic contacts with the PLO.

The general election in Israel held in November once again produced a stalemate, with Likud and Labour almost equal in strength. This happened despite the fact that Peres, having realized his three successive failures at the polls, put Weizman in charge of the party election campaign. As before, a major liability of Peres in television interviews was his shifty look: it undermined his credibility with many voters. His unblinking stare, which gave him a shifty appearance, was due to the fact that while the lower part of his face moved as he spoke the upper part remained static – a rare physiological disorder for which there was no cure. Over the years Peres had engendered an image of himself as a victim in a society that craved heroes. Many interpreted his self-control as inability to speak from the heart, which seemed to dovetail with his innate insincerity. To the bulk of Sephardim, forming a majority of the electorate, Peres remained the epitome of arrogant Ashkenazi superiority and privilege. They saw him as a suave intellectual, who lacked the common touch and could not be trusted. Peres's hopes that Weizman, masterminding the Labour election campaign, would do for his party what he had accomplished for Likud in 1977 were dashed.

Shamir retained his premiership in the next national unity government, and Rabin his defence portfolio. But Peres was moved to finance. As before both Weizman and Sharon retained their places in the inner political cabinet. Working together to repress the intifada, Rabin and Shamir, the political boss of the Shin Beth, grew close. In the spring of 1989 they offered a plan to hold local elections in the West Bank to resolve the Palestinian crisis. The Palestinian leadership, determined to continue the uprising, rejected it, reiterating its demand of immediate Israeli withdrawal from the Occupied Territories.

At the same time the PLO was open to talks with any top Israeli politician in power genuinely interested in discussing the Palestinian national rights. One such leader was Ezer Weizman, whose dovish views on the subject went back to the late 1970s. He held a clandestine meeting with a PLO official in Geneva in the winter of 1989. Soon after Premier Shamir, who controlled Mossad, exposed Weizman's action, charging, rightly, that he had violated both the Israeli law, which forbade contacts with the PLO, and the official policy of boycotting the PLO. Weizman resigned.

Shamir's obduracy on the twin issues of the intifada and the regional peace process led Peres to conspire with Shas, the ultra-Orthodox party, having six MKs, to bring down the national unity government, with a view to forming a Labour-dominated administration with a narrow majority. In March 1990 the Shamir Government fell. But, as described earlier,[11] Rabbi Eliezer Schach publicly nullified the Shas-Labour agreement.

Then Shamir set out to court the secular ultra-nationalist groups – Tehiya (3 MKs), Moledet (Hebrew, Homeland; 2 MKs) and Tzomet (2 MKs) – as well as a radicalized National Religious Party (5 MKs). It took him nearly three months of tortuous horse trading to assemble them and three others into a coalition with a bare majority in the Knesset. The end result was the most right-wing and ideological govern-ment in Israeli history. It enabled Ariel Sharon to fashion an unbeatable alliance of his radical faction within Likud and the secular ultra-nationalists without. As the Housing Minister in Shamir's new cabinet, Sharon accelerated the building of Jewish settlements on the West Bank. But the pursuit of radical, ultra-nationalist policies in the face of continued Palestinian intifada and a moderated stance of the PLO proved counter-productive. It brought about a reaction from the electorate the bulk of which preferred politics of the secular centre. The consequence was the return to power of Labour in 1992 – an event which, like its counterpart a quarter century before, was popularly called *Maa HaPach*, The Upheaval.

But this was not the only dramatic development in the Israel of the 1990s. The country also experienced Jewish immigration on a scale it had not done for nearly four decades. This time the source was the Soviet Union, with the second largest Jewish population in the world after the United States. During 1989, with the tide of Soviet Jewish immigration building up due to Moscow's relaxed policies – raising the total of immigrants from 13,300 in 1988 to 199,500 two years later – a new factor entered the regional politics.

THE DRAMATIC 1990s

The Iraqi invasion and occupation of Kuwait on 2 August 1990 benefited the right-wing Shamir Government. It diverted the attention of US President George Bush's administration away from pressuring Israel to advance the regional peace process. By linking Iraq's evacuation of Kuwait with the Israeli with- drawal from the Occupied Arab Territories, Iraqi President Saddam Hussein won the backing not only of the PLO and its leader, Yasser Arafat, but also an overwhelming majority of ordinary Palestinians. This in turn undermined the position of Israeli doves and strengthened the ultra-nationalist camp.

Bush succeeded in assembling a coalition of 28 countries, including the six Arab Gulf monarchies, Egypt, Morocco and Syria, to confront Iraq, militarily, on 15 January 1991. Two days later Iraq fired a dozen ground-to-ground missiles at Israel. A couple of these landed in Tel Aviv where the Iraqi target was the defence ministry headquarters. The actual damage done was small, both in human injury and in loss of property. Yet thousands of Tel Aviv residents fled. Industry, commerce and education came to a standstill. Those who stayed wore gas masks and stayed in specially sealed rooms during Iraqi bombardment. Though the Israeli Defence Minister, Moshe Arens, threatened retaliation in public, the Government bowed to American pressure, and did nothing. Had Israel intervened in the conflict most of the Arab and Muslim countries in the anti-Iraqi coalition would have withdrawn, thus weakening it, militarily, diplomatically and morally. When Iraq hit populated areas of Tel Aviv with three missiles on 22 January, Premier Shamir told Israeli television, 'It isn't a question of ping-pong: you hit me, I'll hit you.'[12] However, it emerged later that, following the example of Golda Meir in 1973, Shamir had put Israel on full nuclear alert and (according to US satellite pictures) ordered missile launchers in Kfar Zechariah armed with nuclear weapons to be deployed in the open, facing Iraq. The nuclear alert remained until the Gulf War ended on 27 February.[13] Had Iraqi missiles, armed with poison gases, hit Israeli targets and caused largescale deaths, Israel would have retaliated with its atomic weapons, so ran a widely held conjecture.

As it was, Iraq's unprovoked attacks on Israel enhanced sympathy for it in western capitals. West Germany offered emergency humanitarian aid of $170 million, followed by a further package, including financial assistance in the building of two submarines, which raised the total to $670 million. Washington gave Israel $650 million to cover its Gulf War-related expenditure.

Shamir's public restraint during the Gulf War, which led to the decimation of the Arab world's most militarily powerful state, well known for its anti-Zionist doctrine, raised his international status. This was helped further when Shamir agreed to participate in a Middle East Peace Conference, an idea actively pursued by James Baker, US Secretary of State. But Shamir did so only after all Israeli preconditions had been met: the exclusion of the PLO from the talks; the inclusion of the Palestinian residents in the Occupied Territories, unconnected with the PLO, in a joint Jordanian-Palestinian delegation; any settlement with the Palestinians to include a transitional period of autonomy under the Israelis; and the negotiations to be bilateral, with no third country acting as a mediator or arbiter. In return Israel conceded the principle of land for peace as contained in the United Nations Security Council Resolution 242. The Middle East Peace Conference opened in Madrid in late October 1991.

But before then, like Begin, his eminent predecessor, Shamir allowed himself to be dragooned into an extremist enterprise of Ariel Sharon, inadvertently digging his own political grave. In summer 1991 Sharon announced largescale plans to colonize the West Bank to emphasize Israel's resolve to hold on to the Occupied Territories (irrespective of the outcome of the forthcoming regional peace conference), involving a trebling of the confiscation of the Palestinian land in the previous year and a quadrupling of the funds for the construction of Jewish settlements along with the necessary roads and infrastructure. This angered Washington.

Later, when Shamir requested the Bush administration to become Israel's guarantor for the $10 billion loan it planned to raise in international finance markets to settle the recent Russian immigrants, the White House replied that it would do so only if Israel froze all Jewish settlement activity. Shamir refused to accept the American condition. The relations between Israel and the United States became strained.

While Shamir and his ultra-nationalists were busy running the Government, Labour leaders, languishing in opposition, pondered the party's inability to improve its electoral appeal. They decided to decentralize it. Its 1991 convention adopted the primaries system for both the party's leader and Knesset list. This showed clearly that Labour was serious about democratizing itself. And when the new arrangement led to Yitzhak Rabin replacing Shimon Peres as the party leader, it confirmed the changed image Labour wanted to project. To re-invent itself the party entered the Knesset elections of June 1992 as the Labour Under Rabin Leader (HaAvodah Be Reshut Rabin). Unlike visionary Peres, the down-to-earth Rabin inspired trust among Israelis of all classes and ethnic background. His long, distinguished military career, topped more recently by six continuous years as the defence minister, had embossed on the national psyche the image of a man totally devoted to the security of Israel – a state of affairs which Likud and ultra-nationalist politicians found hard to challenge or undermine. The Labour Under Rabin Leader won. It secured 44 seats versus Likud's 32 and formed the Government in coalition with the left-wing Meretz (official title, Meretz-Israel HaDemokratit, Vitality – The Democratic Israel) with 12 seats and Shas with six seats.

The 1992 Upheaval

There was much in common between this Upheaval and that of a quarter century ago. Just as in 1977 it was not Likud which won but Labour which lost, chiefly because of the breakaway Democratic Movement for Change; this time, of the eight seats that Likud lost, five went either to ultra-nationalist secular groups or the radicalized National Religious Party.

Like Labour in 1977, the Likud had become tarnished with allegations of corruption and embezzlement of public funds. In March 1992 a report published by the state comptroller charged several Likud luminaries with corruption and misuse of public funds. Shamir's refusal to support electoral reform in the form of direct election of the prime minister in 1992 made him appear as part of the *status quo*, and hurt his popular standing. His decision to forgo a US loan guarantee in order to expand Jewish settlements in the West Bank alienated the Russian immigrants, the majority of whom voted Labour. On the other hand, the expenditure of vast sums on absorbing the large influx of (Russian) Ashkenazim at the expense of social welfare, which mainly benefited the underprivileged class, lost Likud some of its normal support among the largely working class Sephardim.

The other major factor to alienate Sephardi voters was the rampant factionalism within Likud, divided between groups led respectively by Shamir, Ariel Sharon and David Levy, and which worked against Levy. On the eve of the party's selection of the Knesset list by the 3,300-strong central committee in March 1992, the Shamir and Sharon factions combined to keep out Levy's predominantly Sephardi nominees. They succeeded. Levy protested loudly and publicly, accusing his rivals that they had turned Likud into 'a white elitist party in which Sephardim do not have a chance'.[14]

Three years later, in his interview with me in the Knesset cafeteria, Levy was still critical of his rivals' behaviour on the eve of the 1992 poll. A well built, bespectacled man of 58, capped with a thick mane of grey hair over an unlined, open face, Levy looked suave in his well-cut business suit and tie. 'Due to the economic liberalization and deregulation, initiated by the Likud Government in 1977, many of the economic problems arising from a highly centralized government run by Labour for three decades were solved,' he said. 'Also young leadership came up in Likud, from the Sephardi development towns. But the factionalism of the party's old guard blocked the progress of these young activists.'

Levy has a particular rapport with the inhabitants of the Sephardi-dominated development towns. He lived in one, Beit Shean, after arriving in Israel from Morocco in 1957. He made his living as a construction worker, a fact which his detractors constantly refer to. Politically active with Herut, he became mayor of Beit Shean in the mid-1960s, and then an MK in 1969. After the Likud victory in 1977, Premier Begin appointed him Minister of Immigration and Absorption, and them moved him to the housing portfolio. Following the 1981 poll, Begin named him Deputy Prime Minister, the first Sephardi to achieve this office. But when he challenged Shamir for the Likud leadership in 1983 he lost. It was seven years later that Premier Shamir, heading a government with a thin majority, included him in the cabinet, offering him the foreign portfolio. His working-class Sephardi background and lack of knowledge of English (he is fluent in French) are the butt of many jokes, undoubtedly concocted by Ashkenazi politicians and journalists.[15]

These unflattering jokes about Levy reached a peak when he challenged Binyamin Netanyahu, his deputy at the Foreign Ministry in 1990–91, for Likud leadership in March 1993. Netanyahu made his impact on international television channels during the Gulf War. His youthful, good looks, and facility with producing 'sound bites', made him an instant television personality. Given Levy's lack of English, Netanyahu was in constant demand to explain Israeli policies during the Gulf conflict.

Born in 1950 in Jerusalem into the family of a right-wing academic Bentzion, he left for the US when his father got a teaching job there in 1964. He returned to Israel to do his military service, and became a commander in the Sayeret (Hebrew derivative of reconnaissance) Matkal (Hebrew acronym for 'general staff'), an elite commando force, then resumed his university education at the Massachusetts Institute of Technology (MIT) in Cambridge, Mass. After obtaining his master's degree in business administration, he held consulting and management jobs in the United States and then in Israel. In 1982, on the recommendation of Moshe Arens, the Israeli ambassador to the United States, who had an aeronautical engineering degree from the MIT, Premier Begin appointed Netanyahu Israel's ambassador to the United Nations. After serving there for two years, Netanyahu returned to Israel, and became director of the Jonathan Institute, which specialized in researching terrorism. Elected to the Knesset on the Likud ticket in 1988, he served under Levy. When Premier Shamir insisted on having Netanyahu as the chief Israeli spokesman at the Middle East Peace Conference in Madrid in October 1991, Levy stayed away from the gathering. Soon after he got Netanyahu transferred to the prime minister's office. In the Likud leadership contest in March 1993 Netanyahu had the advantage of the expertise and funds from his Jewish American friends. Out of 142,000 of 216,000 Likud members, 52 per cent favoured Netanyahu, and only 27 per cent Levy (the rest were divided between two other candidates). Yet the ill-feeling between the upstart Netanyahu and the veteran Levy persisted, and ran deep.

The feud between Netanyahu and Levy had a parallel on the other side of the political spectrum with the Peres-Rabin rivalry. For nearly 20 years these Labour politicians, devoid of any fundamental differences of policy or ideology, were locked in a personal struggle for power, and engaged in ongoing, underhand intrigue and back-stabbing. Labour's electoral victory in June 1992 did not lead to an immediate reconciliation between the two. Though Premier Rabin gave Peres the foreign portfolio, he allowed him to deal only with the less important, multilateral talks with the Arab countries – concerning refugees, water resources, the economy, ecology and regional security and disarmament – which had been initiated by the Madrid conference.

But unlike Shamir, who after losing power revealed that he had planned on dragging out the peace talks for the next 10 years, both Rabin and Peres were serious about peacemaking. The Labour-dominated Government's lifting of the ban on contacts with the PLO in January 1993 set the scene for secret talks between the two sides. Initiated by two Norwegian intermediaries, Terje Rod Larsen and Mona Juul, these took place in Norway. Though Peres was involved directly through his deputy, Yossi Beilin, the final decisions always rested with Rabin. The resulting accord, called the Declaration of Principles (DOP), based on mutual recognition of Israel and the PLO (as the representative of the Palestinian people), and providing for limited autonomy for Palestinians in the Gaza Strip and the West Bank town of Jericho, was concluded at the White House in Washington on 13 September 1993. After the document – popularly called the Oslo Accord (since it was initialled in Oslo on 30 August 1993) – was signed by Peres and Mahmoud Abbas (for the PLO), prodded by President Bill Clinton, Yasser Arafat and Yitzhak Rabin, life-long enemies, shook hands in the presence of worldwide television channels.

With this most widely seen handshake in history, Rabin and Arafat inaugurated a new chapter in the history of the region.

The Declaration of Principles contained the following timetable:

By 13 December 1993: the two sides to agree a protocol on the withdrawal of Israeli forces from the Gaza Strip and Jericho.

By 13 April 1994: Israel to complete military withdrawal from the Gaza Strip and Jericho, and transfer power to the Palestinian Authority to be nominated by the PLO.

By 13 July 1994: following a modalities agreement on the election to the Palestinian Council and a Comprehensive Interim Agreement, specifying the structure and powers of the Council, the poll will be held after Israeli forces have been redeployed outside West Bank population centres to the specified locations. Israel's (military-run) civil administration in the Occupied Territories will be dissolved, with its powers transferred to the Palestinian Authority.

By 13 December 1995: Israel and the Palestinian Authority to start talks on the permanent settlement, including Jerusalem, Palestinian refugees, Jewish settlements, borders and relations with neighbours.

By 13 December 1999: the permanent settlement to take effect.

In the event the Israelis and the Palestinians transformed the Declaration of Principles into a working document in Cairo on 4 May 1994. It gave rise to the Palestinian Authority, headed by Arafat. On 1 July he left the PLO headquarters in Tunis to administer the Gaza Strip and Jericho. Later that month Peres became the first Israeli foreign minister to visit Jordan openly, and saw his peace efforts culminate in a Jordanian-Israeli Peace Treaty in October, signed by Rabin and King Hussein of Jordan in the presence of President Clinton. Later Rabin, Peres and Arafat shared the 1994 Nobel Peace Prize in Oslo, Norway.

The opposition to the Israeli-PLO Accord came from both the Israeli right wing, secular and religious, and the radical Palestinian groups, secular and religious. On the Palestinian side Hamas and the Islamic Jihad combined their verbal opposition with terroristic attacks against Israeli targets inside Israel and the Occupied Territories, which escalated after the killing of 29 Muslim worshippers at the Ibrahimi Mosque/Tomb of the Patriarchs, Hebron, in February 1994. Rabin responded to every such incident by sealing off the West Bank and the Gaza Strip, thus depriving tens of thousands of Palestinians of their livelihood. After a Hamas suicide bomber had killed himself and 22 Israelis on a bus in Tel Aviv in October 1994, the next major terroristic action occurred three months later. Two Islamic Jihad suicide bombers killed themselves and 21 Israeli soldiers at a bus stop at Beit Lid near Natanaya, central Israel. Every such incident slowed down the negotiations between the Palestinians and the Israelis on the Comprehensive Interim Agreement.

Meanwhile, anger and apprehension among some 120,000 settlers in 128 Jewish settlements in the West Bank built up. They responded by setting up a co-ordination committee. At its meeting in Ariel in late July it adopted a plan to disrupt the redeployment of the IDF in the West Bank. It involved blocking all highways in Judea and Samaria (i.e., the Occupied Territories); erecting 'outpost settlements' (with five Jews, a tent and a flag, qualifying as a settlement) overlooking the blocked highways; and assembling at pre-determined sites if dislodged by the IDF. This plan was to be complemented by a series of simultaneous demonstrations at main crossroads beyond the Green Line (i.e., pre-1967 Israel).

Considering the settlers' co-ordination committee plan deficient in dramatic impact, Eliakim Haetzini, an ultra-nationalist resident of Kiryat Arba, and a former Tehiya MK now leading the Zo Aretz Enu (This Our Land) movement, proposed passive resistance in the tradition of Mahatma (Mohandas K.) Gandhi and Martin Luther King. Acting in unison, the Zo Aretz Enu activists blocked most Israeli highways during the afternoon rush hour in early August. The action succeeded in impinging on the public mind. But it did not swell the Zo Aretz Enu ranks. Israeli drivers, with a reputation for impatience, took unkindly to the experience of wasting a couple of hours on their way home from work.

The settlers' co-ordination committee implemented its plan of occupying strategic hilltops overlooking main highways in the West Bank. The success of their plan depended very much on the response they aroused among the Jewish Israelis across the Green Line. And their stance in turn depended very much on the terrorism committed by radical Palestinians. After the suicide bombing in January 1995 there was a lull for six months, and this helped to soothe Israeli feelings. Then came a suicide attack in Ramat Gan near Tel Aviv on 24 July, claiming seven lives. It gave some impetus to the ultra-nationalist settlers' plans, but not enough.

While pressing on with arduous, all-encompassing negotiations with the Palestinians with ever-shifting deadlines, Rabin refrained from taking tough action against the Jewish settlers. Except for the IDF's disbanding of 1,000 Jewish ultra-nationalists, mainly from the Efrat settlement near Bethlehem, from the land belonging to the nearby Palestinian village of Al Khadr on 31 July, Rabin decided to ignore the settlers' campaign. So did most of the media. Even the suicide bomb-attack by a female Hamas terrorist killing five people, including herself, on a bus in Jerusalem on 21 August, failed to generate interest in the ultra-nationalist agitation. Indeed, overlooked by the media and police, they appeared increasingly ludicrous to most Israelis as they camped on treeless hilltops in scorching summer heat.

Another ploy to arouse popular protest and derail the Israeli-PLO talks, initiated by Ariel Sharon, too failed. In late August Sharon, whose obesity is legendary, led a group of other ultra-nationalists in a seven-day hunger strike inside a tent pitched near the Prime Minister's residence. He failed to ignite much media interest or attract a long list of concerned political allies to his tent.

Finally, the staging of funeral processions mainly by Jewish Israeli teenagers on 13 September, the second anniversary of the Israeli-PLO Accord, by the settlers' co-ordination committee at the locations of the Palestinian terrorist attacks, failed to capture the popular imagination, and stop the peace process.

Indeed the two sides, led respectively by Arafat and Peres, initialled the Comprehensive Interim Agreement on extending the jurisdiction of the Palestinian Authority to the West Bank, and the holding of elections to the Palestinian Council, on 24 September after a series of non-stop marathon sessions. It was a complex document of 300 pages and many detailed maps.

Four days later Rabin and Arafat signed the Second Israeli-PLO Accord, popularly called the Oslo II Accord, at the White House in Washington in the presence of President Clinton. With this the Israeli-Palestinian peace process became almost irreversible.

While any criticism from the radical Palestinian side was muted the reaction from the Israeli right wing was sharp and shrill. On 5 October thousands of Jewish Israelis demonstrated in Jerusalem against the Oslo II Accord. They burnt effigies of Rabin dressed in a Nazi Gestapo uniform. Later Likud leader Binyamin Netanyahu addressed the demonstrators whose favourite chant was: 'Rabin is a traitor.' He reiterated his earlier statement that if Likud were elected to power it would scrap the Oslo II Accord. In the debate on the subject that followed in the Knesset, Likud MKs kept up their attacks on the latest Accord, some of them declaring, 'There will be no Israel [left] after this peace agreement.'

The tone and content of these speeches, slogans and images had been set two years earlier, in the wake of the Oslo I Accord. A week after the agreement was initialled in Oslo, tens of thousands of protestors demonstrated outside Rabin's office. Their most popular banner read: 'Wanted for Treason: Yitzhak Rabin and Shimon Peres.' Soon caricatures of Rabin in a Nazi officer uniform or an Arab dress appeared on walls in Israel and the Jewish settlements in the Occupied Territories.[16] They became a common feature at the rallies and demonstrations organized by the ultra-nationalists.

Most speakers at these rallies argued that since the Rabin Government had the support only of 55 out of 112 Jewish MKs it lacked legitimacy.[17] The anti-Rabin and anti-Peres rhetoric and sloganeering gathered pace in the summer and autumn of 1995 as the Jewish settlers in the West Bank and their sympathizers in the pre-1967 Israel whipped up feelings against the Government. They routinely labelled Rabin not just a political rival but a traitor to Israel and the Jewish people, who had collaborated with rabid Muslim terrorists, and had agreed to hand over parts of Eretz Israel to them.

Among those who regularly participated in such demonstrations was Yigal Amir, a 27-year-old law student at the Bar Ilan University of Ramat Gan, who lived in a northern suburb of Herzliya, named after Theodor Herzl, the founder of the (World) Zionist Organization. The discussions of Amir – who had earlier spent five years at the Yavne Yeshiva in Ashdod, combining his military service and religious studies – with his colleagues at the university were always based on the Torah. He would tell friends that since Rabin had given away parts of the Eretz Israel to the Arabs it was a *mitzvah* (Hebrew, positive obligation) of a pious Jew to kill him. He began stalking Rabin in June 1995.

The rising vociferousness of the right-wing opposition goaded the Peace Now group to muster its forces in a city with a long record of secularism and moderation: Tel Aviv. And to counter the right-wing assault on his peacemaking, Rabin agreed, unprecedentedly, to address the Peace Now rally at the Malkhei Israel (Hebrew, Kings of Israel) Square, in the shadow of the Town Hall, in the company of Peres, on 4 November (Saturday) evening after sunset. The event attracted some 150,000 people.

Apparently the ambience of the large assembly so moved Rabin that he agreed, again unprecedentedly, to join in the singing of the Song of Peace, 'Tnu la shemesh l'alot, La boker le ha'in' (Let the sun shine, let the morning rise), a routine exercise at the Peace Now rallies, by reading the words hastily written down for him:

> Let the sun shine, let the morning rise,
> The purest of prayers will not bring us back.
>
> He whose life has been extinguished,
> And has been tucked into the earth,
> Bitter tears will not wake him up,
> Will not bring him back here.
>
> Nobody will bring us back,
> From the deep pit of darkness,
> Nor can the joy of victory,
> Nor songs of glory.

> Don't whisper a prayer,
> It is better to sing a song of peace,
> With a great shout.

Ironically, these were to be the last words in public of Rabin, a man who never ceased to think or act like a soldier. These were the words of a song written after the 1967 Arab-Israeli War, which was banned two years later from Israeli radio stations. A pacifist work, it was perceived as undermining the willingness of young Israelis to fight. Soon after its establishment in 1978, the Peace Now group adopted it as its theme song. Its popularity soared after the Israeli invasion of Lebanon in 1982.

At 9.50 p.m. as Rabin walked along a darkened passageway leading to the concourse, where his car was parked, Yigal Amir fired two shots from his gun and killed Rabin. 'I acted alone on God's orders and I have no regrets,' Amir told the police. 'I had planned to kill Peres and Rabin together, but Peres left alone before Rabin.'

The event shocked Israel and the rest of the world. More than a fifth of Israel's popultion of five million filed past Rabin's body as it lay in state in the Knesset plaza or paid respects to the cortège as it covered the 60-kilometre journey from Tel Aviv to Jerusalem. Rabin's funeral on 6 November was attended by some 60 heads of state, including those of Egypt and Jordan.

'Yitzhak Rabin was a son of this rocky soil, of Jerusalem, a first generation son,' wrote Aharon Megged, an Israeli novelist. 'He was not "like" anyone [else]. Not Ben Gurion, not Sharett, not Eshkol, not any of the previous leaders of the nation . . . Not a "man of vision" nor a "man of letters", nor a riveting speaker, and really, neither a diplomat or politician of great sophistication, even when he reluctantly filled all these roles. In everything he did, whether in war or politics – he was determined to carry out the mission he took upon himself [or that was placed upon him] as an outstanding soldier: with all the ability, talent and wisdom with which he had been graced . . . [Characteristically] [i]t wasn't pictures of [Baruch] Spinoza [1632–77], of Maimonides [1135–1204] or of [Theodor] Herzl that adorned the walls of his office, but rather a photograph of his own commander, Yigal Allon ... The security of Israel flowed in the veins of Yitzhak Rabin.'[18]

Peres as the Premier

As expected, Shimon Peres succeeded Rabin as the premier. Rabin's assassination, and Labour's often repeated argument that 'verbal violence' of Likud and other right-wing groups had created an environment conducive to the tragic murder, put Likud and Netanyahu on the defensive.

A faction within the Peres Government wanted to capitalize electorally on the feeling aroused by Rabin's assassination among Israeli voters by advancing the polls for the Knesset and premiership not normally due for about a year. Its argument did not prevail. Such a move would have appeared too opportunistic to most voters. Also the electoral campaign would have overlapped the implementation of the Oslo III Accord, due to start in mid-November and culminate in the elections to the Palestinian Council and the Palestinian Authority's presidency on 20 January.

Once the IDF troop deployment had been carried out according to the Oslo III Accord – highlighted locally and internationally by the IDF's evacuation of Bethlehem during the Christmas season – most Palestinians as well as Israelis were convinced, at least for the time being, that the peace process was being consolidated.

On 5 January 1996 came the news of the assassination – by means of a booby-trapped mobile telephone – of Yahya Ayash, the Palestinian master bomb-maker, who was held responsible for assembling explosives for suicide bombers since October 1994. The success that the Shin Beth had in recruiting a Palestinian agent, Kamal Hamad, an uncle of the man in whose house Ayash had taken refuge in the Gazan village of Beit Lahiya, and planting a miniature bomb in Ayash's cellular telephone impressed on the public once again that the arm of Israeli intelligence and security agencies was very long indeed. Shin Beth officials proudly claimed responsibility for Ayash's murder: they thus wished to restore their reputation which had been tarnished severely by Rabin's assassination two months earlier. Significantly, having refused to accept the resignation of Karmi Gillon, the Shin Beth chief, after Rabin's assassination in early November, Peres did so on 8 January. In his resignation letter, Gillon claimed that 'the organization was on the right track, ready for all its missions [such as the killing of Ayash]'.

Expectedly, the elections to the executive and legislative organs of the Palestinian Authority resulted respectively in the victory for Arafat by an overwhelming plurality and for his Fatah movement by a two-thirds majority. This in turn led the Peres administration to reconsider the poll dates for Israelis. In early February it found 59 per cent of the voters backing the Oslo Accords, with only 24 per cent opposing, and Peres leading his rival, Netanyahu, by 18 points. On its advice, the Knesset decided to call the parliamentary and premiership polls on 29 May 1996.

By all accounts, these elections were to be the most significant since the founding of Israel in May 1948. And, contrary to earlier estimations, they were also to be one of the most unpredictable due to the events that followed the announcement of the polling date.

The four suicide bombs between 25 February and 4 March in Jerusalem, Tel Aviv and Ashqelon, which consumed 59 lives, spoiled the neat calculations of Peres and Labour. The first three attacks were claimed by Hamas, and the last one by the Islamic Jihad. By thus illustrating that Israelis were far from secure, the Islamic extremists undermined Peres's popularity. His lead over Netanyahu in the opinion polls fell to the extent that for the first time he lagged a few points behind his rival.

This happened despite the fact that Peres acted swiftly and forcefully. After the first bombing on 25 February, Peres ordered the closure of the West Bank and Gaza Strip, and imposed a naval blockade of the Gaza Strip to prevent Islamic radicals escaping by sea. At a meeting with Arafat at the Ezer checkpoint of the Gaza Strip, Israeli chief of staff, Amnon

Shahak, virtually ordered Arafat to arrest the 15 listed Hamas leaders.

Following the second suicide bombing in downtown Jerusalem on 3 March, Peres put Israel on a virtual war footing. He created a special anti-terror command. He ordered the building of a two-kilometre-wide fence, equipped with electronic surveillance devices and patrolled by motorized IDF units, along the 350 kilometre border dividing the West Bank and Israel, allowing only 18 crossing points. When Arafat telephoned Peres after the bombing, the latter reportedly shouted at Arafat: 'If you cannot do the job, we will do it – don't tell me you are doing enough. Finish off Hamas! A few arrests here, a few arrests there – that is not enough.'[19] As Defence Minister, Peres ordered the IDF to impose internal closure of the West Bank, with all movement between population centres banned. Further Israeli action followed after the fourth suicide bomb, this time in Tel Aviv, on 4 March, the Purim festival day. Following an emergency cabinet session, Peres declared: 'Israel will go into any corner where terror has taken root.' In an interview with the British Broadcasting Corporation's World Service, Israeli Foreign Minister, Ehud Barak, former chief of staff, said: 'There is a 50:50 chance of Israel going into the Palestinian Authority areas.' By re-entering the Palestinian cities in the West Bank and Gaza in tanks and armoured personnel carriers, Israel would have scrapped the Oslo Accords. But the feelings in the Jewish state were running high. 'Israelis are now united in their conviction that Arafat cannot deliver the security they long for,' wrote Zeev Schiff, a veteran military analyst. 'These attacks prove that Israelis must not rely on Arafat for their security. Even when he tells us he is arresting the heads of the terrorist groups, we know that he is not serious.'[20] A measured view was offered by Karmi Gillon, former Shin Beth chief. 'Arafat is taking measures against suicide bombers who are en route to carry out attacks in Israel, and he tries to eliminate suicide attacks,' he said. 'But he is not putting enough pressure on the Hamas leadership.'[21] On the other hand Israeli President Ezer Weizman declared: 'If we cannot find the needle we must burn the haystack.' Yielding to the mounting pressure, Arafat stated: 'I will co-operate fully with Israel to wipe out terrorism.' He immediately banned six Palestinian militias, including the two belonging to Hamas and the Islamic Jihad. By then the IDF – authorized by the Oslo II Accord to maintain overall security in 465 Palestinian villages and refugee camps in the West Bank – had re-entered the West Bank areas it controlled jointly with the Palestinian Authority, conducted mass interrogation, arrested scores of Islamists, and sealed many houses.

There was little doubt that the (Izz al Din) Qassam Brigade, the military wing of Hamas, wanted to have an impact on the Israeli polls; and it figured that by wrecking the chances of Peres it would also weaken Arafat, and create a political vacuum among Palestinians to be filled by Hamas. Such an estimation seemed logical enough. But when the Palestinian Authority's Preventive Security Service chief, Colonel Jibril Rajoub, tried to propagate the idea that there was a formal collusion between Hamas and Likud, his move backfired. Soon after arresting Muhammad Abu Wardeh, a student of Ramallah Teachers Training College, for allegedly recruiting two Hamas suicide bombers, Rajoub invited the Israeli Television to interview him on 5 March. In his interview, Abu Wardeh 'revealed' that the Hamas bombings were 'part of a political agenda to help Likud win the next general election'. This did not quite tie in with what Abu Wardeh had said earlier in the day in his interview with the 'Voice of Palestine' of the Palestine Broadcasting Authority. 'The true reason for the new wave of bombing was to avenge the murder of Ayash,' he explained. 'The people who did these actions came from the areas under Israeli occupation. You know I have no idea about the people involved in the suicide attacks, but I can say it is all the fault of the Israelis. It started after they killed Yahya Ayash.' Little wonder that many Israelis did not take seriously the theory of collusion between Hamas and Likud. 'This is a clear attempt by Arafat and Rajoub to save Prime Minister Shimon Peres from losing the next election,' said Tsiahi HaNegbi, a Likud MK.

If there was a political collusion of any sort, it was between the Peres Government and Arafat's Palestinian Authority.

Though their intelligence services concluded that the order to the Qassam Brigade to mount suicide attacks on Israeli targets inside Israel had come from that section of the Hamas leadership that was based in Damascus, they deliberately played this down. This had to do with Peres's strategy on peace with Syria. Having unilaterally suspended talks with the Syrians in progress at a venue in the Maryland state of the United States following the suicide bombings in late February, Peres did not wish to further rebuff President Hafiz Assad by highlighting anti-Israeli activities in Damascus. Instead he escalated his attacks on Iran as the prime instigator of terrorism against Israel.

Arafat joined the Israeli chorus of combating terrorism. In his inaugural address to the Palestinian Council in Gaza city on 7 March, he proposed a worldwide campaign against terrorism. The idea caught the imagination of the US President whose staff and Secretary of State, Warren Christopher, organized a 'summit of the peacemakers' six days later, a record, at the Egyptian port of Sharm al Shaikh, to be jointly hosted by Presidents Hosni Mubarak and Bill Clinton.

Besides the host countries the summit was attended by 26 states and the Palestinian Authority, including Britain, Canada, France, Germany, Italy, Japan, Russia, Spain and Turkey. Of the 22 Arab League members, 14 attended, the notable absentees being Syria and Lebanon. After a four-hour meeting, the summit communiqué was read out by Clinton. 'The summit had three fundamental objectives: to enhance the peace process; to promote security; and to combat terror,' he said. These were to be pursued by 'political and economic means', by closer co-operation and by 'establishing a working group to seek practical methods for co-ordination'.

But the true purpose of the exercise – to bolster Peres's electoral chances – was not mentioned by Clinton, or any other leader. The 24 hours that Clinton spent in Israel following the summit – during which he promised Israel an additional $100 million to counter terrorism by purchasing advanced bomb detecting devices, X-ray systems, robots to handle suspected bombs and radar censors to combat terrorists – left little doubt as to the main thrust of his summitry.

Thus reassured, Peres terminated the internal closure of the West Bank on 15 March. But he decided to continue the closure of the Green Line, the pre-1967 border of Israel, and keep the Palestinian workers out of Israel. Periodic mass arrests, which had pushed the total of suspected Islamic radicals to 1,000 by the end of March, continued. So too did the blowing up of the houses of the recent and past suicide bombers, since such acts produced dramatic television footage and impressed Israeli voters.

This occurred against the background of simmering violence along the Israeli–Lebanese border, where Israel's occupation of Lebanese territory since June 1982 had engendered armed resistance from Hizbollah (Arabic, Party of God), a militant Shia Muslim organization formed in late 1982. The conflict between the two sides had waxed and waned.

The formal understanding reached between them in July 1993 – that so long as Israel refrained from attacking Lebanese civilians inside and outside its occupation zone, Hizbollah would not fire rockets at north Israel – broke down on 30 March 1996. The shelling that day by the IDF – in response to a series of Hizbollah attacks inside the occupation zone which had killed six Israeli soldiers during a fortnight – left two Lebanese civilians dead. Hizbollah targeted northern Israel with its Katyusha (Russian, Little Katherine) rockets. When a bomb, purportedly planted by the IDF, killed two Lebanese boys in a village near the occupation zone on 8 April, Hizbollah fired more Katyushas into north Israel. Two days later a Hizbollah suicide bomber killed one Israeli soldier and injured three.

On 11 April Peres responded by ordering a major military operation, code-named Grapes of Wrath. It involved simultaneous Israeli attacks on south Beirut, the Beqaa Valley in the east, and Nabatiya in the south as well as shelling of the United Nations buffer zone, established in southern Lebanon after the Israeli invasion of March 1978. Israel imposed a naval blockade from Tyre to Beirut. Warned by the IDF, some 400,000 Lebanese civilians from the affected area in Lebanon fled. On the other side, to escape Hizbollah's rockets, 20,000 of the 24,000 residents of Kiryat Shimona abandoned their homes. To damage Lebanon's reconstruction efforts, Israel hit a power station on 15 April.

Three days later came a distressing deviation from the above pattern of fighting. At 1.55 p.m. Hizbollah fighters fired two Katyusha rockets and eight mortars from a cemetery about 350 metres behind the United Nations post, harbouring civilian refugees, on a hilltop in Qana. Eighteen minutes later, assisted by an overhead pilotless drone, providing real-time photographs of the ground, the Israeli gunners fired six 155 mm shells which exploded on impact inside the United Nations compound, and another six which burst several metres above the ground, wounding the survivors of the earlier, direct hits. Of the 869 refugees sheltering in the large prefabricated conference room, 102 died, and another 200 received injuries. The United Nations commander immediately informed the headquarters at Naqoura, which contacted the Israeli liaison office. But it was not until 2.25 p.m. that the Israeli firing stopped, with 28 more shells falling around the United Nations perimeter at Qana.

The massacre of over 100 Lebanese civilians shocked the world, and induced active diplomacy by the United States and France to end the violence. As a result a truce came into effect on 27 April after the July 1993 (unsigned) agreement between Israel and Hizbollah was renewed. This allowed both parties to attack military targets within the occupation zone, but forbade them to target civilians outside the area. It also set up a ceasefire monitoring group, made up of America, France, Israel, Syria and Lebanon.[22]

Peres claimed that as a consequence of the Grapes of Wrath operation, the situation along the Israeli–Lebanese frontier had become 'calm'. But most observers concluded that Israel's surgical attempt to crush Hizbollah had ended with a negotiated agreement which left it intact. What motivated Peres was to impress the Israeli voters that he could be tougher than Rabin when it came to punishing Israel's foes. Whereas Rabin's blitz against Hizbollah in July 1993, lasting a week, had caused the deaths of 123 civilians and 16 Hizbollah militia, and the displacement of 200,000 people, his operation had lasted 16 days, and resulted in the killing of 160 civilians and 50 Hizbollah fighters, the homelessness of

400,000 civilians, and damage worth $500 million. Under his command the IDF had responded to the 1,000-plus Katyusha rockets from Hizbollah with 23,000 artillery shells and 523 air strikes.

Peres hardened his stance elsewhere as well. On 1 April he declared that he would hold a referendum on any final settlement with the Palestinians. Arafat protested, arguing this was 'completely against what had been agreed upon', and that there had been no referendum on Israel's peace treaties with Egypt and Jordan. Peres ignored the criticism, aware that attacks by Arafat were an electoral asset for him.

Yet he needed Arafat's co-operation in getting the Palestine National Council to amend its Charter.[23] Arafat concurred with Peres's preference that the PNC should annul the old Charter, with its threats to Israel's existence, rather than deliberate over its wording. So the PNC, meeting in Gaza city, adopted a resolution which called for the Charter to be made consistent with the PNC's November 1988 resolution, which explicitly recognized Israel, the Oslo Accords of September 1993 and September 1995, and the United Nations Security Council's resolutions relevant to Palestine, especially 242 and 338, and instructed its legal committee to present a modified version of the Charter within six months. The vote was 504 for and 54 against. 'I am very happy to have fulfilled my commitments [to Israel]', said Arafat. The vote took place on 24 April, the Day of Establishment of Israel. When Peres was told of it, he said: 'It's the most significant ideological change in the Middle East in the last 100 years'.[24] In contrast, Netanyahu was sceptical. He hammered away his argument that the Oslo Accords had created more Israeli dead, not less, and described Peres's overemphasis on peace as a sign of defeatism, an unIsraeli characteristic.

The prime peace broker, President Clinton, had no doubt about the change in the Palestine National Charter. He awarded Arafat by holding a 45-minute meeting with him at the White House on 1 May, the first such encounter. But he did so only after having a series of meetings with Peres. He was pleased when on 5 May Israeli and Palestinian negotiators, led respectively by Uri Savir and Mahmoud Abbas, met in

Taba in accordance with the 1993 Oslo Accord. Having decided 'the nature and venue of talks', they adjourned to sometime after the Israeli election.

On 13 May, to bolster Peres's electoral chances, Arafat agreed to let him postpone the IDF evacuation of most of Hebron, originally due by 28 March, to mid-June.

Aware of the fatal impact that another suicide bomb attack inside Israel would have on his electoral fate, Peres ordered a complete sealing of Israel from the Palestinian territories 72 hours before the poll. There was no further explosion. Yet he lost.

THE 1996 UPHEAVAL

In the prime ministerial contest, Binyamin Netanyahu won by 1,501,023 votes to Shimon Peres's 1,471,566, a majority of one per cent. The voter turn-out of 79.3 per cent was marginally higher than the one in the 1988 poll at 78.8 per cent.

In the final analysis, the outcome was decided by two groups, both equal in size electorally (at 11 per cent of the total), inclined to vote en bloc, and existing outside the Israeli mainstream: ultra-Orthodox Jews and Israeli Arabs. Whereas over 90 per cent of the better organized ultra-Orthodox, living in tight, urban communities, exercised their ballot almost wholly for Netanyahu, only 77 per cent of the scattered and loosely organized Israeli Arabs did so, almost totally for Peres. Urged by their communal leaders to cast their ballot for Peres, 'the peacemaker', Israeli Arabs turned out in higher numbers, proportionately, than in the past six General Elections; but an unusually large percentage – seven, to be exact – could not bring themselves to vote for Peres, 'the perpetrator of the Qana massacre', and deposited blank ballots. With their invalid votes amounting to 31,500 – higher than Netanyahu's majority of 29,450 – they robbed Peres of victory.

Aware of the crucial role that ultra-Orthodox Jews were set to play in the tight race, Netanyahu focused on winning their support in the last days of the campaign. He took to wearing a skullcap, something he had not done before; and, like Menachem Begin, began lacing his speech frequently with 'BeEzrat HaShem'. He tried to paint the Labour–Meretz opposition as an alliance dominated by atheists. He succeeded in persuading most rabbis that Likud's continuing commitment to recreating Eretz Israel was preferable to Labour's adoption of territorial compromise. A mere 36 hours before the polling, he obtained the endorsement of Rabbi Yitzhak Kaduri, a 106-year-old ultra-Orthodox patriarch, who, placing his frail hands on Netanyahu's head, said: 'May God grant that next week you become the Prime Minister.' The flashing of this image on television and newspapers finally tipped the balance for Netanyahu.

This was the culmination of a campaign where Likud posters proclaimed 'Netanyahu is Good for the Jews', implying that Peres was the candidate of the Arabs. Along with this stridency in the streets went telegenic Netanyahu's impeccable style on television – a contrast to Peres's stodgy manner. Netanyahu repeated endlessly short, simplistic slogans, concentrating on the emotional issues of the future of Jerusalem and the Jewish settlements. He put Peres on the defensive, charging that the latter would uproot Jewish settlements, divide Jerusalem and allow Palestinian refugees to return, thus endangering 'demographic security' of Israel, and that already he had 'sub-contracted' Israeli security to Arafat. In this debate Netanyahu was, inadvertently, aided by the media.

'Israeli news coverage and attention focused largely, and at times obsessively, on Jewish security – on charges that Mr Arafat was not extraditing terrorists, on disputes over whether he had actually dropped calls for Israel's destruction from the PLO Covenant,' noted Serge Schmemann, the Jerusalem bureau chief of the *New York Times*. 'Polls repeatedly showed that most Israelis were convinced that Mr Arafat was not living up to the agreements, though Israel was at least as culpable by ignoring its contractual obligations to release female prisoners, to make a transit road from Gaza to the West Bank, or to withdraw the military from Hebron. But by failing to counter a one-sided perception of the agreements, Mr Peres in effect ensured that every terror attack would be perceived as a huge violation and as evidence of government incompetence. Instead of trying to spell out his vision, Mr Peres was trying to prove that he was tough enough to handle the security risks, taking extraordinary measures against the Palestinians, unleashing a vicious raid into Lebanon, and asserting that Hamas, Islamic [Jihad] Holy War and Hizbollah – three very different organizations – were an amorphous source of anti-Israeli terror backed by Iran, a claim for which the Government never produced any strong evidence. The problem was that once Mr Peres began trying to out-tough Mr Netanyahu, voters were bound to ask why they should not vote for Mr Netanyahu.'[25]

Since Labour and Likud concentrated heavily on the prime ministerial poll, the small, established parties benefited at their cost, except Meretz, which lost three seats. The other major factor was the introduction of two votes for each elector. Many voters split their ballots, giving one to Labour or Likud in the prime ministerial contest, and the other to a small party which held greater appeal for them.

In the religious spectrum, Shas (10 MKs) gained four seats, a symptom of growing political self-confidence among Mizrachim; and the National Religious Party (9 MKs), three. With the United Torah Judaism maintaining its previous size of four, the total of the religious factions came to 23, a record. Equally, by closing their ranks, the non-Zionist Israeli Arabs augmented their strength to eight: the United Arab List – composed of the Arab Democratic Party and the Islamic Movement – four; and the Democratic Front for Peace and Equality, four out of a total of five, the remaining member being Jewish. (See further, pp. 246–7 and 254–8.) Among the new entrants was Yisrael BeAliya (Hebrew, Ascent into Israel), a party of ex-Soviet Jews, with seven MKs, led by Natan Shcharansky. The other was the four-member Third Way, headed by Avigdor Kahalani, who broke away from Labour in protest at the party's agreement, in principle, to vacate the Golan Heights for peace with Syria. This was part of the reason why Labour's strength fell from 44 to 34. Likud, which contested the Knesset election in alliance with Tzomet, headed by Raphael Eitan, and Gesher (Hebrew,

Bridge), formed by David Levy in June 1995, found its size reduced to 22 from 32 – with Gesher gaining five, and Tzomet five (down from eight).

The 18-member Coalition Government that Netanyahu formed on 18 June included Likud (with its parliamentary leader, Moshe Katzav, as Minister of Tourism and Deputy Premier), Gesher (with Levy as Foreign Minister and Deputy Premier), Tzomet (with Eitan as Agriculture Minister and Deputy Premier), the NRP (with its leader, Zevulun Hammer, as Education Minister and Deputy Premier), Shas, the UTJ, Yisrael BeAliya and the Third Way.[26] It won a vote of confidence by 62 votes to 52.

Netanyahu's Cabinet stated its policy guidelines as follows. One, retain Israeli sovereignty over the Golan Heights. Two, strengthen and develop Jewish settlements, and ensure that in the final agreement on Palestinian 'self-government', they retain their 'affinity' with Israel. Three, oppose the formation of a Palestinian state. Four, oppose return of Palestinian refugees to 'any part of the Eretz Israel west of the Jordan River'. Five, thwart any attempt to undermine the unity of Jerusalem and prevent any action which runs counter to exclusive Israeli sovereignty over it. Six, ensure that the IDF is authorized to 'go anywhere [in Eretz Israel]' to guarantee the security of Jews.[27]

These guidelines did not augur well for comprehensive peace and reconciliation in the region. But they had the backing of 55.5 per cent of Jewish Israelis who had voted for Netanyahu. By so doing they had ignored an important conclusion that had led the earlier Likud Government, headed by Yitzhak Shamir, to join the peace process at the Madrid conference: history had shown that Israel's doctrine of total self-reliance in security was virtually unattainable, and that it needed the co-operation of Arab neighbours to feel truly secure. Any attempt to revert to the doctrine of one hundred per cent self-reliance in defence and security would mean further bolstering of military and Shin Beth. As it was, the Israel Defence Forces had been the single most important feature of the state and society since the founding of Israel.

6

THE ISRAEL DEFENCE FORCES:

The Sword and Social Cement

Between the American Colony Hotel, the oldest establishment of its kind in Jerusalem, and the Central Command roundabout just past the American Consulate in East Jerusalem – a brisk three-minute walk, uphill, along Nablus Road – lie the opposite ends of a long, chequered chapter in the history of the holy city and of Palestine/Israel. The mansion now accommodating the American Colony Hotel was built by the Ottoman sultan in the mid-nineteenth century to house his governor of Jerusalem, which was under his direct rule. And at the end of the walled American Consulate, a mini-fortress complete with an electronically-controlled steel gate, in the shadow of Palestine Potteries across the narrow road, stands an Israeli war memorial, with its back to the busy road junction (named after Pikud HaMerkaz, The Central Command), a branch of which leads to the Damascus Gate of the Old Town.

At the apex of a triangular platform of stone, seven metres sideways and four metres along the base, stand two tablets. The small one on the ground records the date of the battle and the name of the combat unit; and the other, large one, standing upright, with a flagpole rising from its spine, displays the names of the IDF soldiers who fell.

(THE VERTICAL TABLET)

The logo of the
Parachute Regiment

(List of 25 names)
Shlomo Epstein (Moma)
Aiviho Peled

fell in the Six Day War
during fighting in the streets of Jerusalem
to liberate
'Urban Line' – Mandelbaum
Pass and Rockefeller Museum
and brought it to the liberation of the Old City
Jerusalem – Yaer Tashkaz [i.e. June 1967]

(THE GROUND TABLET)

27 Yaer Tashkaz
6.6.67
Here fell
Zahal[1] Fighter
Battalion 28 Platoon A
May the Souls be
Held in Peace

This is one of over 900 war memorials erected all over Israel. Altogether they commemorate the deaths of over 15,000 Jewish Israeli soldiers who died during or shortly after the seven wars – four Arab–Israeli wars (1948, 1956, 1967 and 1973), two Israeli invasions of Lebanon (1978 and 1982), and the War of Attrition (1969–70) – in which Israel was involved since its founding in 1948. That gives Israel one war memorial for every 17 dead. The figure for the United States is one memorial for 15,000 killed, and in Europe 10,000.

Little wonder that the Remembrance Day in Israel is an important event, especially in the calendar of schools and colleges. Most educational institutions have a Remembrance corner where the names of the former students who fell in the wars since 1948 are chiselled into a memorial stone. Due to the injunction against images in Judaism there are no statues or other sculptural representations of the dead.

The significance of the Remembrance Day also derives partly from its timing. It falls on the eve of 14 May, the anniversary of the establishment of the Jewish state. Since 14 May 1948 fell on 5 Iyar 5708 AM (Anno Mundi, Year of the World), and since Israel follows the Jewish calendar, which differs from the Christian, the actual (Christian) dates vary from year to year. The rationale for the Israeli Government's decision to declare 4 Iyar as the Remembrance Day was simple: to draw the causal connection between those who died fighting for the founding of the Jewish state and its continued existence.

Sirens signal the start of the commemoration of the Remembrance Day – a two-minute silence – followed by the lighting of the remembrance torch at the main town square, a few speeches and the communal singing of the national anthem, *HaTikva*. Except for the difference in the date (11 November being the Remembrance Day in Europe and the Veterans' Day in the United States), these celebrations follow the same pattern in Israel as in western countries.

However, the Remembrance Day is preceded by a week by the Holocaust Day, commemorating the six million Jews killed by the Nazis in Europe during World War II, an occasion of especial significance to schools, the main socializing agency. 'The overall purpose of the Holocaust Day is to inculcate the feeling among students that they are descendants of the Holocaust,' explained Michael Yaron, an inspector at the Ministry of Education and Culture in Jerusalem. A plump, pleasant-looking man, and a son of a Jewish couple who had arrived in Palestine from Germany in the mid-1930s, he had been a history teacher for 28 years. 'What we try to do is to make schoolchildren feel psychosis, feel that they are the descendants of the victims, an integral part of the people who actually suffered the Holocaust. Jewish students absorb this view and feeling through education and through visits to Yad Vashem [the Holocaust museum in Jerusalem]. They do so through other means as well: television documentaries, movies, radio programmes. On the Holocaust Day the children read poems etc. They also try to find a Holocaust survivor and invite him to address them. And the official choice of the date was made to link the Holocaust with the Independence and Remembrance Days that follow soon after.'

There is yet another anniversary that is unique to Israel – or, to be specific, individual Israeli urban centres. Each of the country's cities and major towns adopts a specific unit of the IDF, and then makes it a point to celebrate its birthday in a big way. The armoured corps, with its birthday in October, has been adopted by Tel Aviv. On that day armoured personnel carriers and tanks fill the city's main Malkhei Israel Square, and their crews happily welcome visitors to inspect their machines and chat with them. The adults arrive invariably with their children, who are the prime target of the IDF. The purpose of the exercise is to put on display part of the IDF mainly for the school-going youngsters in a relaxed, civilian, almost carnival-like atmosphere, and motivate them to serve in the military not as an unavoidable chore, but as a thrilling, patriotic rite of passage.

'For its first three decades, Israel's education was primarily designed to indoctrinate and encourage the country's youth into volunteering for the elite and commando units,' notes Yossi Melman. 'These special forces make a big point of emphasizing their unique abilities. Their soldiers receive special decorations, medals, wings and different uniforms. Schoolchildren, from early on, are fed on heroic stories, and they learn to worship these elite units.'[2]

Military draft, introduced under the Compulsory Service Law 1949, was part of David Ben Gurion's ideology of statism, which emerged out of his growing conviction that a highly centralized form of government was the best way Israel could overcome the centrifugal tendencies inherent in a society composed predominantly of recently arrived immigrants. Along with military conscription went a uniform system of education, health care and trade union services, all provided by centralized national agencies.

The main burden of devising and strengthening the public agencies to absorb the large influx of immigrants and impart on them the still evolving Israeli identity fell on the nearly 760,000 Jews who were there at the founding of Israel in 1948. Between then and 1954, they had to cope with the daunting job of receiving and absorbing an almost equal number of Jewish immigrants. The adults among the new arrivals could not be socialized through education, and that task fell largely on the IDF. By all accounts it performed the job well. Since then the IDF has become a vital agency of socialization and social development.

Indeed the IDF has imparted certain national characteristics: directness, no-nonsense approach to life, a certain distaste for luxury. Israelis are direct, some would say brusque; and they do not stand on ceremony. They consider social niceties a waste of time and effort. The roots of this behaviour lie in the IDF. 'When I reported at the base on my first day in the IDF, the reception clerk gave me a form to fill in,' recalled Rafi Singer. ' "Thank you," I said. "Never say 'Thank you' in the army," said the clerk curtly.' Israelis also believe in getting things done. There is much value attached to initiative and innovation, whether in military life or civilian. Finally, the IDF imbibes a spartan lifestyle. The furnishings in a typical, lower- or middle-class Israeli home are an apt illustration of this attitude.

There are still other implications of the universal draft. In most (western) societies youth in the late teens tends to challenge traditional values and the establishment. In Israel they join the IDF, and find themselves having to shoulder responsibilities, which involve life and death. By being absorbed early on into the established order Israeli youths grow up conservative.

Also Jewish Israelis arrive at universities more mature than in any other country. As someone who made several visits to the country's prime institution of higher education – Hebrew University in Jerusalem – I can vouch for that.

The main campus of Hebrew University on Mount Scopus is an architectural oddity. It has large areas of gardens and shrubbery laid out next to cavernous rooms bored into a hillside at different levels. Like a snake in the snakes-and-ladders game, every so often the campus turns on itself, leaving the visitor baffled. But, like the Knesset, the repository of political power, the Hebrew University, a storehouse of intellectual power, boasts a fine, spacious cafeteria. Its round tables with shining, copper-colour tops, and black plastic chairs fill not just its small bright interior but also the large, often sunny, cobblestoned courtyard.

It was in this open space one cloudless afternoon in March 1995 that I had a long conversation with a group of students about the Israel Defence Forces. Male and female in equal numbers, they were all in their mid-20s, with an honourable IDF record (with one of them, Esther, from a family of professional army officers), and an extraordinary grasp of spoken English.

'Since your childhood you are brought up [at home and school] to serve your country in the army,' said Ana. Slim, oval-faced and olive-skinned, she was a middle-class resident of Natanya, and had graduated from a grammar high school. 'The IDF service is a rite of passage towards a full citizenship of Israel. The main point to remember is that the IDF is a popular, living institution. It is everywhere, and it's very Israeli.'

'The first thing that strikes a visitor to Israel like me is the ubiquitousness of gun-carrying soldiers, male and female,' I said. 'You see them everywhere, in the street, in all public places – at bus stations, especially on Sundays.'

'Getting back to their bases after the Sabbath,' explained Ana. 'You don't have to be a foreigner to notice soldiers in the street. We do that as we grow up. As a child and a teenager you see them all the time, and you know that when you are 18 you'll put on the military uniform whether you like it or not.'

'There are other ways in which the IDF predominates but which we don't see every day,' said Eli. A small ring in his left ear signalled a laid-back attitude to life which he, refreshingly, combined with a sharp mind and a close-shaven, squarish face. 'About a third of Israel's beaches are closed to civilians, because they are for exclusive IDF use. And large parts of the Negev are closed to the public because they are used for military exercises.'

'The main difference though is between the open bases and closed bases of the IDF,' said Ana.

'I grew up on closed bases as my father is a career military officer,' said Esther. Wearing a large white sweater, which flattened her already scanty breasts, she had shining grey eyes in a chubby face. 'When you are drafted you are asked to state your preference for a closed or open base. Depending on what is available, your preference may be met or not. In my case it was granted. All the time I was on a closed base. I was an officer – very tricky to be friendly with your troops and at the same time issue orders. In the army you learn to take responsibility, and mature early. You also know that you're doing a certain job in the IDF, and that somebody else will take over from you when you leave, and thus maintain continuity.'

'At closed bases there are opportunities for women to take officer courses,' said Ana. 'I took this course, and became an officer within a year. Then they transferred me to an open base which I did not like. There was none of the camaraderie and dedication you find on the closed bases. People there were not interested [in their jobs]. They were the Unit 805.'

Everybody smiled, except me. I looked at Ana enquiringly.

'8 a.m. arrive; zero, do nothing; 5 p.m. finish,' she explained. 'The clock watchers, the ones who did not take the IDF home.'

'You could say I was like that,' said Sarah. Buxom and black-haired, Sarah covered her shyness with dark, round glasses. 'I was on an open base near my home town, five minutes by bus. I did clerical jobs. I was secretary to a lieutenant-colonel. For me it was just a job. The only difference was that I was in uniform and that I earned only $100 a month, which was very cheap to the IDF. But then as an IDF soldier you get concessions in travel, theatre tickets etc. Also the IDF organized day trips to Jerusalem, visits to the theatre, concerts and so on, and organized discos. There was social life attached to the IDF.'

'An opportunity to meet the opposite sex?' I asked.

'Yes,' said Eli. 'One out of five serious romances starts in the IDF.'

'If I had to get involved with a guy from the IDF he'd better be from an elite unit,' said Ana.

'It's hard to get into elite units unless you come from a kibbutz,' said Micah. Heavily built and slow in speech, he had a long, horsy face, and a fine record in the air force. 'Also it depends on what you mean by elite,' he continued. 'The air force thinks it is elite. But not everybody in the air force is a pilot, you know. Anyway, being in the air force I was on a closed base, and lived a highly-regulated life.'

'What impact do the paraphernalia of the IDF – the uniform, the stripes, the sub-machine-guns – have on the recruit?' I enquired.

'When I first put on the uniform and carried a gun, I was very proud to be marching up and down, to show everybody that I was serving my country,' Micah replied. 'When I returned home [in a Tel Aviv suburb] on a Friday afternoon I was proud of how well I was doing [in the IDF]. This went on for about six months, maybe a year. After that it wore off. Then when I passed the officer training course, and got my stripes, and I saluted the flag I really felt proud of the IDF and my country.'

'What does carrying a gun do to you?' I asked.

'A gun gives you power, power to kill,' said Ana. 'The initial impact is strong. But as Micah said the effect wears off.'

'As an IDF reserve officer in the air force, I am allowed to carry a pistol,' said Micah. 'But I don't. Some of the reserve officers do, though. It all depends on your personality.'

'Whether you are a show-off by nature or not?' I said.

'You could put it that way,' replied Micah.

Despite a constant flow of filter coffee to the company, at my expense, I could detect a certain flagging of energy. But I could not let them go until they had addressed an important issue: the role of the IDF as a socializing agent.

'Is the IDF an equalizing institution?' I asked. 'Does it expose the conscript to those sections of society he or she is unlikely to meet in unregulated, civilian life?'

'In different departments on a base there are different groups,' replied Esther. 'In my department we were all Ashkenazim, middle class, with good academic backgrounds. We did not mix with others, like Sephardim.'

'It depends on whether the base is open or closed,' said Eli. 'On an open base, you are out of the premises come 5 p.m., and you go your way. But on the closed bases you have comradeship, a tight life spent together with others, and there you meet different sections of society and learn more about them.'

'The IDF exposes the draftee to experiences he would not normally have,' said Sarah. 'There is mixing in so far as in the IDF you come across people who have not done their matriculation [high school graduation]. Outside the army you don't come across such people, but in the army you do. However, there can be proper mixing only between middle class and high class, but none between lower class and middle class.'

'How important was the IDF to you in strictly personal terms?' I enquired.

'Crucial,' Ana replied. 'Only when the military service is done, can you get along with your life.'

'The IDF is important for jobs,' said Micah. 'Certain jobs are given only to those who have served in the IDF. Also if you haven't served in the IDF you are not entitled to certain social security and mortgage benefits.'

'You could say there is a clear dividing line between those who have done the IDF service and those who have not,' said Eli. 'IDF personnel enjoy social esteem, whereas the non-IDF are marginalized.'

'For a young person the social aspect of life is important,' said Esther. 'Friends always ask, which unit did you serve in?'

'The prestige and advantage of the IDF service depends on

where the conscript serves – in a combat unit, intelligence unit, non-combat unit, desk job, kitchen, storekeeping etc.,' explained Micah. 'The combat unit has the highest rating, and the competition to get in is tough. You can have ten applicants for each place. The kids from the kibbutzim are strong here. They have a background of communal life, and they adjust easily to the IDF life.'

'What about the reserve duty?' was my last question.

'We have none,' said Sarah.

'For men it goes on until they are 51,' said Micah with a sigh. 'Nobody likes the reserve duty. It is such a chore. It became more of a chore during the intifada, which went on and on. It turned the IDF into a police force, charged with restoring law and order. Which is not the IDF's job, really.'

'Also the length of the reserve duty went up,' said Eli. 'Too many complications and unforeseen situations came up at all levels – in the field and at the high command level. A new set of problems arose, disciplinary, moral-ethical, ending up in military trials.'

During the six years the intifada lasted, according to Premier Yitzhak Rabin, 250,000 IDF troops underwent posting in the West Bank and the Gaza Strip.[3] That amounted to one in three of all male Jewish Israelis, aged 18 to 50.

The severity and pervasiveness of the Palestinian intifada in December 1987 caught the IDF command, administering the occupied West Bank and the Gaza Strip since June 1967, by surprise. Yet its initial reaction was to treat the phenomenon as short-term rioting, limited mainly to the Palestinian refugee camps and their surroundings, and led by a rag-bag collection of malcontented youths, well versed in throwing stones and petrol bombs. It responded to it as in the past. It dispatched conscript troops to the disturbed areas with a mandate to restore 'normal conditions'.

This response had partly to do with the IDF's experience in 1970 of tackling increased acts of sabotage and terrorism by the Palestinians in the Gaza Strip, the territory which was the first to erupt into an intifada 17 years later. As the head of the southern command from 1969 to 1973, Ariel Sharon was in charge of administering the Gaza Strip, which was placed under emergency regulations about a year after its capture by the IDF in the June 1967 War. The rise in Palestinian resistance there could be judged by the claim made by the Popular Front for the Liberation of Palestine (PFLP) that it had launched 89 armed operations in the Gaza Strip. Sharon used strong-arm methods to repress the Palestinian resistance, and got the situation under control by 1972. His success stemmed partly from the events beyond his control. Due to the defeats that Palestinian commandos suffered at the hands of the Jordanian army in September 1970 and July 1971, the PFLP leadership had to quit Jordan; and this weakened, and later exposed, its links with its underground activists in the (adjoining) West Bank as well as the Gaza Strip.

However, the major difference between the events of 1970–72 and now was that this time around the intensified Palestinian resistance was home-grown: it was not directed by parent organizations operating abroad, and was not dependent on their state of being. Yet, as Defence Minister, Yitzhak Rabin ordered the IDF in January 1988 to 'strike the intifada off the agenda'.[4] It soon proved to be an ineffective gesture.

Often lacking riot control equipment, the IDF soldiers and their officers were untrained in policing, a task they were now assigned. As a result they frequently over-reacted. This in turn led to charges of use of excessive force, and gross violation of the rules of engagement they were required to follow. Some of the IDF officers and soldiers found themselves being tried in military courts under the glare of publicity. Facing legal dilemmas, tinged with morality, and unwilling or unable to interpret liberally, or innovatively, the IDF's written rules of engagement to resolve each and every eventuality, most unit commanders chose to avoid confrontation with the perpetrators of the intifada. The end result was that the Palestinians lost much of their fear of the IDF, and the Israeli public lost its faith in the military's ability to restore the *status quo ante* quickly. 'For an army and society long accustomed to military campaigns which were for the most part short and often glamorous, the protracted [IDF] failure to carry

out those instructions [of Rabin] was a sobering experience,'
noted Professor Stuart Cohen of Bar Ilan University, Ramat
Gan, a suburb of Tel Aviv.[5]

By the end of the Gulf War in early March 1991 when
the intifada, now in its fourth year, had forced the political
issue of the Palestinian self-determination to the fore, and had
combined rioting with large scale non-violent resistance in the
form of strikes, boycott of Israeli goods and mass resignations
from government jobs, the Israeli military leadership had
publicly concluded that it faced a unique challenge.

This was one of the several problems the IDF command
had to cope with. It found itself having to devote a dis-
proportionate amount of its time and expertise to tackling
the intifada at the expense of its mainstream problems
and concerns centred around defending the country against
external aggression. Posting of conscripts and reserves in
the West Bank and the Gaza Strip took them away from
their professional courses of training and exercises. The
alternative activity of tackling disturbances of public order, a
psychologically demanding undertaking, began to demoralize
the ranks and their field commanders. Also the very concept
of deploying IDF soldiers in small units to quash a civilian
insurgency ran counter to the Israeli military doctrine of
creating a professional force operating in large units equipped
with high-technology weaponry.

Later the IDF high command tried to overcome its dilemma
by taking compensatory steps. In active co-operation with the
Shin Beth, it increased surveillance of suspected Palestinian
activists. It bolstered the border police. Though nominally
a police force, with a large intake of loyal Druze Arab
citizens, the border guard was under a military command.[6]
It also established a separate elite unit, *Mista'arvim* (Hebrew,
Masqueraders), to locate the Palestinians suspected of having
committed violent crimes, and to execute them. Consisting
of conscript volunteers, this unit became the police, judge,
jury and executioner. Over the months the trigger-happy
operations of these death squads created unease among the
more sensitive MKs and members of the Government, who
demanded their dissolution.

The unsatisfactory state of affairs was summarized in the spring of 1992 by Zeev Schiff, the country's foremost military commentator, thus: 'One cannot help feeling that [continued] confrontation with citizens, and with a [Palestinian] people subject to Israeli conquest, has generated a distortion in the IDF. Our elite forces, the flower of our youth, should not be focusing their attention on the slaying of wanted suspects – even if they are murderers. Their eyes should be on other targets and on different enemies.'[7]

In a sense, Israel's military chronicle was running parallel to its political history. Just as in politics, so in the military, old certainties were gone, opening the way for devising and implementing other doctrines such as containment and extended containment of the enemy, instead of outright defeat or decimation. And just as in political chronicling, so in military history, June 1967 was a watershed, followed by the surprise of the October 1973 Arab attack.

Once Israel had consolidated itself in the late 1940s, its military-political hierarchy adopted and refined the doctrine of precipitate action against its enemies. It applied this doctrine both as a form of reprisal, and as a pre-emptive strike; and did so in the widest possible context.

Israel acted in this way, successfully, in the mid-1950s when dealing with the Palestinian guerrilla attacks mounted from the Egyptian-administered Gaza Strip. This was a reactive response. In contrast, Israel's invasion and occupation of Sinai in 1956 was an example of a successful pre-emptive strike, worked out in advance with Britain and France. About a decade later came another instance of an effective application of the precipitate action by Israel, taken in retaliation, to counter Palestinian commando actions launched this time from Syria. And Israel's performance in the June 1967 War was the most spectacular example of its continued adherence to the concept of determined, precipitate action in its pre-emptive version.

Since Israel was, unprecedentedly, put on the defensive in the 1973 Arab-Israeli War, there was no question of employing the well-tried doctrine. But it was applied once more, in its retaliatory version, to countering the persistent Palestinian guerrilla threat from south Lebanon, which reached a peak in early 1978. It materialized in the form of an Israeli blitz-krieg in south Lebanon in March 1978. The military action succeeded in emptying the border area of armed Palestinian activity, and provided the IDF with a rationale to carve out a self-declared security zone inside Lebanon, to be patrolled by its troops and an Israeli-trained and financed Lebanese force, called the South Lebanon Army. The next, dramatic military move by Israel was pre-emptive – the clandestine bombing in June 1981 of the Iraqi nuclear reactor being assembled near Baghdad.

In retrospect, this proved to be the last successful application of the doctrine of precipitate armed action with specific military aims by the Jewish state. (Israel's restraint in the face of Iraqi missile attacks during the 1991 Gulf War, for whatever reasons, marked a definite break in its long-established policy of precipitate action, pre-emptive or retaliatory, against its enemies. The IDF high command had now to consider seriously such doctrines as extended containment. As it was, a potential for its application existed not only in a foreign context but also in a domestic one – with respect to the Palestinian intifada.) Had Israeli Defence Minister Ariel Sharon stuck to this tried and tested doctrine in his invasion of Lebanon in June 1982, he would have vacated Beirut after the last PLO fighter and the Syrian soldier had left the city on 1 September. But he did not. He went on to play the king-maker in the Byzantine politics of the Lebanon, and landed the IDF and Israel in a mess. It was another three years before the Jewish state was able to extricate itself from the quagmire of its own making.

The military events in Lebanon in 1982–5 had a profound effect on the state and society in Israel. 'Israeli over-confidence of 1967 was shattered partially in the 1973 War and then more fully in the 1982 Lebanese invasion,' said Benny Morris, a Jewish Israeli historian. A plumpish, bespectacled man in his mid-40s, with an open, friendly face and wavy black hair, Morris is a fellow at the Hebrew University's Truman Institute, a building tucked away from the teaching heart of the university, and the author of *The Birth of the Palestinian*

Refugee Problem, 1947–1949. 'The 1973 and 1982 Wars together shattered the invincible image the IDF had acquired in 1967. Due to this ordinary people, journalists and academics began to question the IDF and the generals. Serious questioning of Israeli policies and popular history began in the mid-1980s.'

The mid-1980s also marked the (unannounced) end of the era of heroes in Israel. The heroic period was remarkable for the ease with which successive Israeli governments presented the periodic regional hostilities as wars of survival for the Jewish state to the populace. Along with this presentation ran the official line which highlighted Israel's right to make itself secure behind internationally accepted borders while striving hard to seek peaceful co-existence with its Arab neighbours. The Israeli authorities' continued success in convincing the public of the Jewish state's righteousness rested on fostering and maintaining a wide consensus at home. They attained it by employing a combination of tools, some of which, such as news management, were designed to achieve immediate, or short-term, results, while others, such as education at schools and the IDF, were tailored for the long term.

Those in charge of education in Israel, and their predecessors – the Zionist pioneers in Palestine – were aware of the significance of historical myths and heroes in the national culture. 'The Zionist movement from the very beginning felt an urgent need to develop a new set of Jewish heroes who would compensate for 2,000 years of passive behaviour in the Diaspora,' said Dr Reuven Gal, director of the Israeli Institute for Military Studies, who had served as the chief pyschologist of the IDF for many years. 'There was a stress laid on military valour and prowess, ranging from pre-Diaspora Jewish historical figures like the Maccabees and the defenders of the Masada, up to modern warriors like [Yosef] Trumpeldor and beyond. They form an important part of the army's educational process, in which new recruits are taken to places like Tel Hai [Trumpeldor's burial place] and Masada to give them positive examples of behaviour in combat.'[8]

Yosef Trumpeldor (1880–1920) is the most celebrated

hero in the Zionist annals in Palestine. After his death in 1920, the labour battalions formed by fresh immigrants from southern Russia were named after him as was the youth organization of Revisionist Zionists – Betar, the acronym of Berit Trumpeldor, the Covenant of Trumpeldor. Born in southern Russia, Trumpeldor became the first Jewish commissioned officer in Russia after his outstanding performance in the 1904–5 Russo-Japanese War. In 1912 he migrated to Palestine and worked on a kibbutz. During World War I he first joined the Zion Mule Corps, part of the British armed forces, and then travelled to London to form Jewish battalions within the British military. After the February 1917 Revolution in Russia he returned to his native land where he set up a Zionist pioneer organization to prepare Jewish youth for migration to Palestine. In late 1919 he returned to Palestine. In January 1920 the Jewish settlements in the upper Galilee, then part of Syria and under French control, became embroiled in the anti-French campaign by local Arabs. The Zionist leaders advised the Jewish settlers to evacuate the area until order had been restored. Disregarding this, Trumpeldor and his followers travelled to Tel Hai, near presentday Kfar Giladi, to assist its Jewish settlers. In the subsequent bloodshed, on 1 March 1920 Trumpeldor became one of eight Jewish fighters to succumb to Arab bullets. His last words, reputedly, were: 'It is good to die for our country.' This line is engraved on the pedestal of a roaring stone lion that stands where Trumpeldor and his comrades fell. Trumpeldor became the archetypal Jewish settler who ploughed during the day and, armed with a rifle, guarded the settlement at night. On his death anniversary thousands of schoolchildren are bussed to Tel Hai for a commemorative service.

In contrast, Masada refers to an event that took place in AD 73 at the fortified castle of Masada built by the Roman King Herod the Great (r. 37–4 BC) on a rock 460 metres high on the fringe of the Judaean Desert overlooking the Dead Sea. Following the Jewish revolt in Palestine in AD 66, a large contingent of Jewish zealots captured the Masada fortress and set up a base there. Having crushed the Jewish uprising in Jerusalem in AD 70, the Romans besieged the Masada fortress. The Jewish zealots refused to surrender. Finally, when the Romans broke through and seized the castle, they found that of the 960 Jews, all but seven (two women and five children) had killed themselves, preferring death to surrender. Over the centuries the event aroused mixed feelings among Jews since Judaism disapproves of self-annihilation and requires that suicides be buried outside the fence of a cemetery. But after Jewish immigration into Palestine accelerated after World War I, the intellectuals among the Zionist pioneers began re-examining the mass suicide at Masada. They gave it a different spin: fighting to the end was preferable to surrendering and losing independence. An eminent Zionist poet, Yaacov Lamdan, coined the line in 1927: 'Never again will Masada fall!' This became a rallying cry of the Zionists in Palestine, and Masada a leading symbol of Jewish heroism performed in pursuit of attaining and maintaining independent statehood. Since the establishment of Israel, a visit to Masada is mandatory for the youth movements of all Zionist political parties. And the IDF brings recruits to Masada to take their oaths of allegiance.

The IDF, the successor to the Haganah, the main military arm of the Jewish immigrants, began performing well from its birth on 4 June 1948, three weeks after the outbreak of the Arab-Israeli War I. It reduced the Arab-ruled area to a mere 22 per cent of British Palestine, about half of what the United Nations partition plan had allocated the Arabs. This provided much grist for the heroic mill. 'Due to the Holocaust the Jews and the Zionists lacked confidence,' said Benny Morris. 'They created myths about the 1948 War and the events surrounding it partly to bolster their own ego.'

Today even the title of this armed conflict remains controversial. It is known among non-Israelis as the First Arab-Israeli War, the 1948–9 Arab-Israeli War or the Palestine War. But Israelis call it the War of Independence.

If it was a War of Independence, when exactly was it declared, by whom and against whom? This was the question I posed to several Jewish Israelis: old and new historians, journalists and university students.[9]

Amos Elon is a doyen of traditional Israeli historians, with a biography of Theodor Herzl and the translation of Herzl's copious diaries (from German to Hebrew) to his credit. A tall, slim, bespectacled man in his late 60s, with a lean face and receding grey hair, he looks professorial. On a table of his well-appointed, book-lined apartment in Jerusalem are pictures of him with President Anwar Sadat of Egypt, Crown Prince Hassan ibn Talal of Jordan, and Yasser Arafat.

ELON: The War of Independence started with the United Nations partition plan in November 1947. After the partition plan Arabs stopped everything, began attacking the Jews. The lines were drawn. That was the beginning.

DH: That was a civil war, won't you say?

ELON: Yes.

DH: By their very nature civil wars just break out, they are not declared. But as a conventional armed conflict, a war of independence must be declared.

ELON: Calling it the War of Independence was a retroactive action. This name was put on it later.

DH: If this war was declared by the Zionists against the British, the foreign rulers of Palestine, then it finished on 14 May 1948 when the British left.

ELON: No need for this line of inquiry. Actually the term was borrowed later to appeal to the American people. It was a public relations job.

DH: Which transformed the Declaration of the Establishment of the State of Israel in Tel Aviv on 14 May 1948 into the Declaration of Independence.

ELON: I had not thought of it like that before.

At Hebrew University, Taniya Alfersey, a pretty, slim history student, with permed blonde hair and dangling earrings, summed up the prevalent view thus: 'It started as the War of Independence from the British. Then it became the War of Independence from the seven Arab armies which attacked Israel in May 1948.' (She said seven armies, presumably because the Arab League, which declared war against Israel, had seven members then. But two of them, Saudi Arabia and North Yemen, did not participate.)

'There are three terms in use: War of Independence (Milhemet HaAtzmaut), War of Liberation (Milhemet HaShihrur), and War of Establishment (Milhemet HaKomemiyut),' said Benny Morris. 'The War of Establishment is the most accurate. But because it is neutral, it is not very appealing. The War of Independence is the most satisfying psychologically. Every [Jewish] Israeli can identify with the War of Independence. Americans had a War of Independence.' (But the American War of Independence is popularly called the American Revolution. It was declared by the Thirteen Colonies against Britain in April 1775, followed by the adoption of the Declaration of Independence on 4 July 1776. It ended in October 1781.)

On the floor above Morris's office, I put the question to Professor Moshe Ma'oz, a specialist on Middle Eastern history. A man of medium height and strong build, dark skinned, Ma'oz, in his early 60s, was wearing an open neck shirt, corduroy trousers, sandals and dark glasses. 'The War of Independence was never declared,' he said. 'It was *post factum*. It never was for independence from a foreign power. It was a defensive war against the Arab invasion. The terms used were Milhemet HaAtzmaut (independence) or HaShihrur (liberation).' I pursued the matter. 'If it was a war of liberation or independence, it could not be against the Arabs because the Arabs were not the rulers of Palestine,' I argued. 'It is a mess,' said Ma'oz. 'That is why I use a neutral term, the War of 1948.'

In Haifa I raised the matter with Ilan Pappe, a 'new historian' at Haifa University, and the author of *The Making of the Arab-Israeli Conflict, 1947–51*.[10] A small man in his late-30s, with a round, clean-shaven face, Pappe radiates boundless energy, physical and intellectual. 'There are four terms in use: War of Independence, War of Liberation, War of Establishment, and War of Post-Mandate Palestine,' he explained. 'And there are two phases of the war. The first phase began in early 1946 when the conflict was between the Jewish Agency and the British mandate. You could stretch it, and call it a war of independence. But because of the Arab involvement, it was more a civil war than a conventional war. The second phase began after 14 May 1948. The Arab League did not declare war against Israel until *after* it had been established. So you could not call it the War of Independence, because Israel was independent when a conventional war started on 15 May 1948.'

For a written, quasi-official version of the War of Independence, I turned to *The Political Dictionary of the State of Israel*.[11] Describing the United Nations General Assembly resolution on the partition of Palestine on 29 November 1947 as the starting point of the conflict, it divides the War of Independence into five phases, two of which precede the establishment of Israel: (i) 29 November 1947 to 31 March 1948; and (ii) 1 April to 14 May 1948. During Phase i, states *The Political Dictionary*, the Haganah concentrated on the defensive measures against attacks by the Palestinian irregulars assisted by a foreign Arab volunteer force, which entered Palestine in January 1948, and which reached the strength of 5–8,000 by April. Though the British, with 100,000 troops, were the strongest party, they concentrated on protecting their own forces and installations. During Phase ii, the Jewish High Command decided to 'seize the initiative in order to gain effective control of the territories allotted to the Jewish state [by the UN plan] and to establish secure communications with Jewish settlements outside it'.

By most accounts, the conventional war went through four phases: (i) 14 May to 10 June 1948, followed by a 28-day UN truce; (ii) 9 to 18 July 1948, followed by a UN truce of unspecified duration; (iii) 15 October to 6 November 1948, followed by a UN truce in the south on 6 November, and in the north and centre on 30 November; and (iv) 21 November 1948 to 7 January 1949, when the warring parties accepted the United Nations Security Council resolution of 16 November calling for the signing of armistice agreements.

According to the popular and official Israeli version of the events, on 15 May 1948, a day after Israel's establishment, the armies of five Arab countries – Egypt, Transjordan, Iraq,

Syria and Lebanon – invaded the newly born state. The Egyptian army was only 35 kilometres from Tel Aviv when, according to the *The Political Dictionary*, it was stopped by 'a hastily mobilized blocking force, assisted by the first fighter planes which had arrived from Czechoslovakia'. Basically, it was touch and go for a fledgeling republic of three-quarter million Jews, invaded by five enemy states with an aggregate population of 40 million. If Israel survived, and succeeded in concluding armistice agreements with these countries, it was a miracle – a repetition of the Old Testament confrontation between diminutive David and giant Goliath.

The prevalent view is well reflected in Amos Elon's *The Israelis: Founders and Sons*. 'The invading Egyptian force comprised a number of infantry brigades, roughly totalling 10,000 men,' Elon writes. 'Their infantry was supported by a small air force, heavy artillery, tank and armoured units. The fledgeling Jewish state, barely a few days old, was as yet unequipped with anything but the most primitive weapons. The total strength of the invading Arab armies has been estimated at 23,500. They were amply equipped with British and French-made tanks, airplanes, heavy artillery, spare parts, and ammunition. Their four-pronged invasion was unco-ordinated but simultaneous. The Israelis at this stage had some 3,000 "regulars" under arms and 14,000 inadequately trained recruits, only 10,000 rifles with 50 rounds of ammunition each, four ancient cannons smuggled in from Mexico, [and] 3,600 sub-machine-guns.' Elon also cites [Abdul Rahman] Azzam Pasha, an Egyptian diplomat and secretary-general of the Arab League, the collective of seven independent Arab states formed in 1945, threatening 'the Jews of Palestine with a bloodbath in the manner of Genghis Khan and Tamerlane'.[12] Whatever the rhetoric used by the Arab leaders inside and outside Palestine, the final decision to attack the Zionist state collectively came on 12 May (after Jordan and Egypt had been persuaded to join the plan), only three days before the actual fighting. Though King Abdullah of Jordan was (nominally) the supreme commander of all the Arab forces, there was no central command. The four Arab countries adjoining Israel mounted unco-ordinated attacks.

Since 1971, when Elon first published his book, which deals with the 1948–9 Arab-Israeli War only in passing, three important, scholarly works by a group of young Jewish Israeli historians have appeared. Besides the books of Benny Morris and Ilan Pappe mentioned earlier, there is *Collusion Across the Jordan* (1988) by Avi Shlaim. In it Shlaim deals at length with the tortuous clandestine talks between the Zionist leaders in Palestine and Emir Abdullah of the Emirate of Transjordan (later, from December 1948 onward, King Abdullah of the Hashemite Kingdom of Jordan).

These scholars have benefited by the declassification of archival material chiefly in Britain and Israel where a 30-year moratorium on state secrets prevails. In the case of military matters Israel follows a policy of a 50-year moratorium. However, due to frequent overlap between the Foreign and Defence Ministries of the country, previously unavailable military information became available from 1978 onwards. Also material from the Arab side, often in the form of diaries, letters and memoranda, began appearing from the late 1970s. Lastly, several Palestinian documentation centres in Lebanon, mostly in Beirut, and the West Bank made their documents available to researchers. 'Considering the richness and originality of the [research] material,' noted Ilan Pappe, 'it is obvious why the historiographical portrait of the [1948–9] war required drastic change.'[13]

According to Pappe, on 15 May the five Arab League members added 23,500 troops (Egypt 10,000; Transjordan 4,500; Syria 3,000; Iraq 3,000 and Lebanon 1,000) to some 12,000 irregular Arab forces, most of them Palestinian, already engaged in the fighting with the Zionists, which had erupted in January 1948. Pappe's grand total of 35,500 on the Arab side is slightly higher than the figure of 30,280 provided by Morris. On the Zionist/Israeli side, starting with the adult membership of Haganah at 35,000 in May 1947, Morris concludes that on the eve of the war in May 1948, Haganah had 'mobilized and deployed in standing military formations' 35,780 troops.[14] It is noteworthy that this figure is considerably higher than 27,400 'first line troops' of Israel provided by Walid Khalidi, editor of *From*

Haven to Conquest: Readings in Zionism and the Palestinian Problem until 1948, published by The Institute of Palestine Studies, Beirut, in 1971.[15] The comprehensive information in this book on the manpower and weaponry of the Arabs in Palestine, the Zionist forces, and the Arab Expeditionary Force to Palestine, contained in Appendices VIII, IX-A and IX-B, is culled from many published sources.

Khalidi's figures for the weapons possessed by the Zionists in April 1947 tie up neatly with Morris's statistics pertaining to September 1947. The respective figures (with Morris's numbers in parenthesis) are: rifles 10,000 (10,489); sub-machine-guns 1,900 (2,666); light machine-guns 444 (700); medium machine-guns 186 (186); two-inch mortars 672 (672); and three-inch mortars 96 (92). Morris adds that between October 1947 and July 1948, the Haganah's arms factories produced 16,000 sub-machine-guns, 210 three-inch mortars, 3,000,000 9 mm bullets, and 150,000 grenades. Furthermore, 'thousands more weapons were purchased, or stolen from the withdrawing British, during the first months of the war.'[16]

Official Israeli historians point out that at the start of the war Haganah did not possess tanks or artillery. According to Khalidi, the Arab side altogether had 102 artillery pieces while the Israelis had four. But whereas the Arabs had only 40 three-inch mortars, the Israelis had 803 two-inch, three-inch and six-inch mortars. In the hilly terrain of Palestine, a mortar is a better 'artillery' weapon than a cannon. As for armour, the Arabs deployed 22 light tanks and 101 armoured cars. But these weapons were vulnerable since the Israelis possessed 75 anti-tank rifles.[17]

On the crucial point of air power, Khalidi quotes chapter and verse to show that by 23 April 1948 the Zionists/Israelis had signed a contract with the Czech Government for 10 Messerschmitt ME 190 fighters, and received them all by 20 May. Indeed, *The Political Dictionary*, as cited earlier, refers to the deployment of air power by Israel in the early days of the war. Going by the material published in Khalidi's book, the Arabs and the Israelis (with their strength given in parenthesis) were evenly matched in the air: fighters 10 (10);

heavy transporters nil (3); medium transporters 15 (10); light transporters 12 (9); and trainers 21 (25).[18]

As for manpower, only Jordan's Arab Legion, commanded by British General John Glubb, was professionally led. The Lebanese and Syrian troops were former territorial militiamen. The Egyptian and Iraqi troops were badly led, and were equipped with poor British-supplied arms. Little wonder that the Arab offensive lost momentum by early June. As a result, a UN-brokered truce for four weeks followed. By now, whereas the strength of the regular Arab troops reached 35,000, the Israel Defence Forces numbered 65,000.

The ceasefire worked more in favour of the Israelis than the Arabs. Britain abided by the UN embargo on arms sales to the warring parties, thus depriving Egypt, Iraq and Jordan of their sole source of weapons and ammunition; but Czechoslovakia and other East European states, encouraged by the Soviet Union, successfully ignored the ban, and continued supplying military hardware to Israel. (While clandestinely receiving weapons from abroad for the Haganah/IDF, Premier David Ben Gurion, who was also the Defence Minister, forced the Irgun, led by Menachem Begin, to desist from taking delivery of the arms and volunteers from East Europe that had arrived by ship near Tel Aviv. By so doing Ben Gurion accomplished two major objectives: he showed that he was enforcing the UN embargo, and he demolished the power base of his political rival, Begin.)[19] Equally important was the fact that, unlike Israel, none of the Arab countries had arms manufacturing facilities of its own.

No wonder that in the 10-day fighting that erupted on 8 July the Israelis did well. This time the Arabs accepted a ceasefire of unspecified period to give a chance for mediation efforts of the UN, entrusted to Count Folke Bernadotte, a member of the Swedish royal family, to succeed. The IDF was now 90,000 strong. After Bernadotte had produced a comprehensive peace plan in early September, which *inter alia* specified the Negev, then under IDF control, as Arab territory, he displeased Israel. (He was assassinated on 17 September by three activists of Lehi, popularly known as the

Stern Group, or Stern Gang, after their leader, Avaraham Stern. (In mid-October the IDF unleashed a series of offensives. During the next three weeks it gained territory in the north, centre and south. The ceasefire that followed on 6 November was short-lived. Another succession of assaults that the IDF staged from 21 November onward did not cease until the final truce was signed on 7 January 1949. 'In these offensives, the IDF beat the Transjordanian and Egyptian armies and the ALA [Arab Liberation Army] in the Galilee, and conquered large parts of the territory earmarked in 1947 by the United Nations for a Palestinian Arab state,' writes Benny Morris.[20]

Undoubtedly, overall, the IDF performed brilliantly. Yet, as Karl von Clausewitz, a Prussian general and a writer on military affairs, has stated, war is diplomacy by other means. So in the final analysis, the IDF gains were the end result of non-military achievements of the Zionists in Palestine and elsewhere. Conversely, the Arabs inside and outside Palestine came out worse in the war because of what had preceded the hostilities. '[T]he fate of Palestine, and hence that of the Palestinians, had been determined in the session rooms and corridors of the UN, in the meetings of various international inquiry committees and inside the discussion halls of the Arab League long before even one shot had been fired,' concludes Pappe. 'It was the Jewish success first in building the infrastructure for a state and then in winning the diplomatic campaign that decided the battle long before it started; as it was the inadequacy of the Palestinian leadership and the meandering politics of the Arab League that helped explain the consequences of this war [of 1948–9].'[21]

None the less, the events of the Arab-Israeli War I showed Ben Gurion that it was possible for Israel to create and maintain 'qualitative superiority' in military hardware, training, mobilization and motivation over the combined strength of its neighbouring Arab enemies. Out of this experience emerged Ben Gurion's military doctrine of 'qualitative superiority' over the Arabs. He held it firmly. Once he introduced the nuclear arms factor into the equation, with the assistance of the French starting in 1957, he laid an unshakeable foundation for the continued implementation of his doctrine. The generosity of the United States, which escalated after the installation of John Kennedy in the White House in 1961, has ensured that the doctrine remains as valid today as it was when first conceived by Ben Gurion.

Indeed, Ben Gurion's thesis was twin-headed, devised to meet the Arab threat both abroad and at home. His solution for the Palestinian Arabs who refused to leave Israel was to ensure that they were concentrated in certain areas and that these were administered by the IDF, the agency that safeguarded the external security of the Jewish state.

7

THE DOUBLE MARGINALS:

Israeli Arabs

After my few attempts over the telephone had failed to locate Dr Adel Manna at the Truman Institute of Hebrew University where, according to one of his senior colleagues, he shared an office with two other researchers, I drafted Rafi, my Hebrew interpreter who studied international relations at the university, to assist me in my search.

When I mentioned the name, Adel Manna, Rafi immediately said, '*But* he is an Arab'. I was dumbstruck. Had I managed to collect my wits quickly I would have asked Rafi, 'Isn't an Israeli Arab allowed to be on the teaching or research staff of Hebrew University?' 'In theory, yes,' he would have replied. 'But in practice . . .'

The facts on the ground came to me from Dr Manna when I finally tracked him down, and he came to have tea with me at the American Colony Hotel. 'Though 1,200 of the 25,000 students at Hebrew University are Arab, there are only two Arab professors, both of them in the medical faculty,' he told me. 'As a researcher at the Truman Institute, I'm the only other Arab on the university's teaching-research staff.

Nationally, of some 6,000 professors, only 12 are Arab, that is 0.2 per cent, most of them at Haifa University.'

A light-skinned man of medium height and intelligent looks, Dr Adel Manna, 47, clean-shaven, balding, and wearing thin-framed glasses, has a quintessentially professorial appearance. After studying Middle Eastern history at Haifa University, he pursued further studies at Hebrew University. (Introducing him in an article in the *Jerusalem Report* of 17 June 1993, the magazine's correspondent mentioned that Manna had his Hebrew University diploma 'prominently displayed' at home, and that Hebrew books, 'including an 11-volume series on Israeli history', lined his shelves.) Manna later won a scholarship at Oxford University in Britain. He has since then taught history at Haifa and Hebrew Universities in Israel as well as at the West Bank universities of Birzeit and Al Najah (in Nablus).

History has placed Manna and some 800,000 others – called Israeli Arabs – at the margins of two societies: Israeli and Palestinian. 'Israeli Arabs are double marginals: marginal to Palestinians and marginal to Israeli Jews,' he said. 'Yet they are the most open-minded people because of what they are. They are Palestinian by nationality, and they are also Israeli citizens. They know the Jewish society well, their language, culture, day-to-day life. That makes them an ideal bridge between Israeli Jews and Palestinian Arabs.'[1]

The fate of a double marginal, especially one as perceptive and well-read as Manna, is unenviable. The conflict of being a Palestinian Arab and an Israeli citizen at the same time starts to nag early on. 'I was born in late 1947 in the village of Majd al Kurum [between Acre and Safed] in western Galilee,' Manna said. 'My father had land there. During the 1948–9 War our village surrendered. Still, the Israelis decided to expel lots of people from our village to Wadi Ara [some 30 kilometres south] and to the East and West Banks [of Jordan River]. The Israelis put young men above 16 and young couples under 30, including my parents, in buses [to get rid of child-bearing couples], and said to them: "Go to [King] Abdullah [of Jordan]." My family stayed in Nablus, then moved to Amman, then to

Syria and finally Lebanon. We lived in Beirut, then moved to Ein Hilwa refugee camp, near Sidon. We lived there until early 1951. Then my father and 15 others and their families hired a boat from Sidon port. We landed at a point north of Acre. Since my father had papers pertaining to the November 1948 Israeli census, he was allowed to stay in Israel. But half of our village, including my uncle, is still in the Ein Hilwa refugee camp.'

For every three Arabs who were registered during the first Israeli census, one was left out because he/she lacked a 'permanent dwelling'. This claim was made to me by Emile Shukri Habibi (1921–96). A Christian Arab born in Haifa, Shukri was an eminent public figure who successfully combined politics with literature and journalism. A bear-like figure with heavy shoulders and a sad, moustached face, he chain smoked, using a small plastic cigarette-holder. His office at Arabesque Publishing House, occupying two rooms in a whitewashed, barrack-like building in an Arab quarter of Haifa, was sparse. 'My father was the *mukhtar* (Arabic, leader) of his community in Haifa,' Habibi said. 'We were nine brothers and sisters. Nobody remained in Israel [in 1948] except me and my sister. Others were forced to leave – for Lebanon, Syria and Jordan. One becomes accustomed to such separation. Yet the dream of reunion never dies. It's one of the main elements of the collective consciousness of Israeli Arabs. The other element of this consciousness is that we consider this to be our homeland. We have become a minority in our homeland because of Israel, and because of the expulsion of most Arabs from the land. Unlike the Palestinians who became refugees, we stayed put. We were prepared to die in our homeland instead of going into the Diaspora. Today we are protected by the knowledge and confidence of being the original inhabitants of this country. We never feel like foreigners even when we are discriminated against. They, the Israeli Jews, are the foreigners, we say.'[2]

Having worked as a news reader in the Arabic section of the Palestine Broadcasting Station, from 1941–3, Habibi resigned to work full-time for the Palestine Communist Party (PCP). In 1945 he was one of the co-founders of the League of

National Liberation (LNL), a leftist Arab group. Four years later he played a leading role in the creation of Maki, Israeli Communist Party, out of the merger of the PCP and the remnants of the LNL. Maki recognized the State of Israel without accepting the Zionist doctrine of a link between the Jews in Israel and in the Diaspora. It backed the right of the Palestinian Arab refugees to return home, and the founding of the Palestinian state in the territory allotted to the Arabs in the United Nations partition plan of November 1947. In the First Knesset (1949–51), it won four seats, improving its strength steadily to six in the Third Knesset (1955–9). Habibi became an MK in 1951 and maintained a seat in the Knesset for more than 20 years.

'Israeli Arabs had to fight for their rights in their homeland,' Habibi continued. 'The Jewish state treated us as *mekhots la garder* (Hebrew, outside of fence), outcasts. Until 1954 the Israeli Government actively encouraged Arabs either to leave or convert to Judaism. It wanted a Jewish state clear of all Arabs. For those Arabs who remained, the state policy was not to recognize them as a national group, but to fracture them into religious minorities: Muslim [75 per cent], Christian [15 per cent], Druze. Even among Muslims the Israelis tried to separate the bedouin [Arabic, nomads] from the rest. In 1956 the Druze were allowed to join the IDF. They are Arabic speakers, but they have been so brainwashed that they feel more Israeli than the Jews. Until 1966 Israeli Arabs [concentrated in the Galilee and the Little Triangle – formed by the villages of Jaba, Ijzim and Ein Ghazal along the Haifa–Tel Aviv highway – and the Negev] were under military rule when they could not travel without the military governor's travel pass, just like Africans in [the white-ruled] South Africa. Most of our fertile land was confiscated "for security reasons". We could not depend on aid from the Arab world. Maki helped us to be practical and to depend on ourselves. We did. Maki was the only political organization which opposed military administration of the Arab-inhabited areas and discrimination against Arab citizens. Along with the progressive forces in the Jewish population we fought back vigorously for Arab rights, and secured an end to the military rule and land confiscations in 1966 [in December 1965, to be precise]. The fact of our persistence is tantamount to a miracle. We paid dearly for our struggle. We never had the illusion that someone on a white horse will come and deliver us, and learnt early on to rely on ourselves, exclusively.'

Why did the Israeli Government end the military administration of the Arabs in 1966? Was it the comparatively liberal policy on Arabs by Prime Minister Levi Eshkol who succeeded Ben Gurion in 1963? Was there a greater sense of security among Jewish Israelis? Or a combination of both?

'Until 1966 Israeli Arabs' movements were restricted in order to control our labour so that we could not go and sell our services in Haifa, for example,' explained Atallah Mansour. A tall, vigorous, bespectacled man of 61, moustached, with greying hair and a paunch, Mansour has a strong face and an equally strong manner. A Hebrew-language journalist since 1954, Mansour has a colourful background. Born in Nazareth in a Christian family, he joined the auxiliary Arab organization of Mapam, United Workers Party, a left-wing Zionist party, and its kibbutz Shaar HaAmakem (Hebrew, Gate of the Valley) 25 kilometres from Nazareth. He published his first book, a novel based on his experiences at the kibbutz, in Hebrew. His latest volume, *Subtenants* (1991), examines the Israeli policy towards Arab citizens. 'In the mid-1960s the Jewish immigration dropped; in fact there was more outflow than inflow,' Mansour continued. 'That's when the Government lifted the military administration of us, so that we could fill the labour shortage caused by the outflow. We got this information from the horse's mouth as they say. The Government opened some archives in the late 1980s on the Israeli Arabs. Towards the end of 1990 we [Israeli Arabs] held a seminar here [in Nazareth], and invited top Israeli officials on Arab affairs. They argued, and we got the facts from their discussion. For example, on the eve of the [first] general election in 1949, the Israeli leaders debated "Should Arabs be allowed to vote?" "No," said many, "they are not part of the Jewish state." Others said, "The world would think that we were following a divide and rule policy towards the local Arabs." And so on. As the discussion was in progress somebody entered the room, and announced that Mapam and Maki [the Communists] had already included Arabs in their electoral lists. Too late, if Mapam, a Zionist party, has Arabs on its [auxiliary] list then other [Zionist] parties cannot keep them out of their lists. So we cannot deny them voting rights. That was the consensus that emerged. That's how we came to possess the basic right of voting.'[3]

While military administration was the overt face of the Israeli rule, education was the subtle, long-term tool employed by the state to socialize the Arab minority in the way it wanted. From the start the central government acquired exclusive control over education in Israel. Its Ministry of Education and Culture set up separate departments for Hebrew and Arabic schools, which imparted education up to high school graduation, called matriculation. At the university level the medium of instruction was exclusively Hebrew.

'Arab education system in Israel is a system for controlling the Arab population,' said Dr Majid Al Haj, a senior lecturer in sociology at Haifa University. A strongly built, fleshy-faced man in his early 40s, with a shining black thatch of hair and moustache, Dr Al Haj had turned his office on the 24th floor of the 29-storey skyscraper, housing Haifa University on Mount Carmel, into a comfortable, tastefully furnished drawing room. 'The Arabic language schools are controlled by the Ministry of Education – the curriculum, text books, budget, appointment of principals and teachers, everything. In the Arabic system there are the state and private sectors. But the Arabic private sector is controlled by the Government even though it is financed by private sources, whereas the Hebrew private sector is not controlled by the Government even though it gets public funds. In the Hebrew system there are the state secular, the state religious, and the private religious sectors. About 25 per cent of the Hebrew schools are in the private sector. Even though they get public funding they are autonomous. For example, the policy of teaching Arabic as a compulsory subject from the seventh to the ninth grade, introduced in 1994, does not apply to the private sector in the Hebrew schools.'4

The tight control over the Arabic language schools resulted, willy nilly, in engendering a generation of schizophrenic Arabs. Among them was Dr Manna. 'As kids we had to celebrate the Feast of Independence, decorate the school and so on,' he said. 'The Day of Independence, based on the Jewish calendar, varies from year to year [in the Christian calendar]. We had to sing songs on that day, including the national anthem *HaTikva*, The Hope. It goes: "As long as still within our breasts,/The Jewish heart beats true./As long as there is hope in the heart,/As long as the soul is longing for Zion. After 2,000 years of exile,/This hope can materialize in the land of our fathers." This is what Arab children were required to sing, a Zionist hymn. At school we had this, and at home my father would tell me: "On this day the Jews expelled us from our own homes, our own land." For us it was a personal trauma. But I had to sing songs which boiled down to: the Jews came and liberated us! But liberated us from whom, from ourselves? I'd ask. The Arab teachers would not say anything. They could not, for fear of losing their jobs. And my father would say: "This is politics. We are a minority here. We cannot say much. The Palestinians who resisted are refugees now. My own brother is a refugee in the Ein Hilwa camp."'

The subject of Palestinian Arabs and what happened to them before and after the 1948 War kept coming up. 'I studied Middle East history at Haifa University, from 1969 to 1972,' said Dr Manna. '"The Palestinians were expelled," I'd say in a discussion in a history class. "No, we wanted the Palestinians to stay," the Jewish students would say, "but their leaders told them to leave, and the Arab countries promised that they'd bring them back when the Zionists had been defeated." I would tell them my personal experience. "I'm not making an abstract historical point," I'd say. But it was no use.'

A pioneering study of the Palestinian refugees was made by Benny Morris and published in 1987. His research was based on archival material released mainly by the Israeli and the British Governments. Morris set out the competing claims thus: 'The general Arab claim, that the Jews expelled Palestine's Arabs, with premeditation and preplanning, as part of a grand political-military design, has served to underline the Arab portrayal of Israel as a vicious, immoral robber state. The Israeli official version, that the Arabs fled voluntarily (not under Jewish compulsion) and/or that they were asked/ordered to do so by their Palestinian and Arab states' leaders, helped leave intact the new state's untarnished image as the haven of a much-persecuted people, a body politic more just, moral and deserving of the West's sympathy and help than the surrounding sea of reactionary, semi-feudal, dictatorial Arab societies.'[5]

Morris divided the period under study – December 1947 to July 1949 – into two parts: up to June 1948, when some 400,000 Palestinians became refugees; and the rest of the period, when about 300,000 Palestinians became refugees.

'To what extent was the Arab exodus up to June [1948] a product of the Yishuv [Jewish community in Palestine] or Arab policy?', Morris asks. 'The answer is as complex as was the situation on the ground. Up to the beginning of April 1948, there was no Yishuv policy or plan to expel the Arab inhabitants of Palestine, either from the area destined for Jewish statehood or those lying outside it . . . The prospect and need to prepare for the invasion gave birth to Plan D, prepared in early March. It gave the Haganah brigade and battalion-level commanders *carte blanche* to completely clear vital areas; it allowed the expulsion of hostile or potentially hostile Arab villages . . . The matter was never discussed in the supreme, political, decision-making bodies, but it was understood by all that, militarily, in the struggle to survive, the fewer Arabs remaining behind and along the front lines, the better, and, politically, the fewer Arabs remaining in the Jewish State, the better.'[6]

What about the Arab side? 'The records are incomplete, but they show overwhelming confusion and disparate purpose [among Arab leaders inside and outside Palestine], "policy" changing from week to week and area to area,' Morris concludes. 'No guiding hand or central control is evident.' As to April [1948] and the start of the main exodus, he adds, 'I have found no evidence to show that the [Palestinian] AHC [Arab Higher Committee] issued blanket instructions, by radio or otherwise, to Palestine's Arabs to flee ... The absence of clear, public instructions and broadcasts for or against the Haifa exodus over 22–30 April is supremely instructive concerning the ambivalence of [Haajj Muhammad Amin] Husseini and the AHC at this stage towards the exodus.' What about the neighbouring Arab states? '[They] did not appeal to the Palestinian masses to leave but neither, in April, did they demand that the Palestinians stay put,' Morris states. 'Hence the spate of appeals in early May by Transjordan, the AHC and various Arab leaders to the Arabs of Palestine to stay put, or if already in exile, to return to their homes. But the appeals, given the war conditions along the fronts, had little effect ... Besides, in most areas the Haganah physically barred return.'[7]

As for the period after June 1948, which involved fighting between Israel and Arab forces in July, October and December 1948–January 1949, Morris concludes: 'From July onwards there was a growing tendency in the IDF units to expel ... just as the pressures on the remaining Arabs by leaders inside and outside Palestine to stay put grew and just as their motivation to stay put increased ... Ben Gurion clearly wanted as few Arabs as possible to remain in the Jewish State. He hoped to see them flee. He said as much to his colleagues and aides in meetings in August, September and October. But ... Ben Gurion always refrained from issuing clear or written expulsion orders; he preferred that his generals "understand" what he wanted done.'[8]

Morris caps his conclusions thus: 'In general, in most cases the final and decisive precipitant to flight was Haganah, IZL [Irgun], LHI [Lehi] and IDF attack or the [Palestinian] inhabitants' fear of such attack.'[9]

His book has been widely acclaimed as a refreshingly objective piece of well-documented history, and he is regarded as an important member of the rising group of new historians. 'But,' he told me in early 1995, 'old historiography is quite strong. Most school and college textbooks follow the traditional view. My book was translated into Hebrew and published only in 1991, four years after the English edition. During the first year [of the Hebrew edition] people kept saying, "The Palestinians left because their leaders told them to etc.", but now nobody challenges what I've said in my book. However, I agree that the trickle-down is slow. It will only happen through universities. Today's students are tomorrow's teachers. And my book is being used at universities.'

There is a long way to go before an equitable balance is struck between competing Israeli and Palestinian versions of history. In any case Israel's state educational system, which covers most of the country's educational institutions, functions within its State Education Law of 1953. The object of state education, for Jew or non-Jew, according to this law, is 'to base elementary education . . . on the values of Jewish culture and the achievements of science, on love of the homeland and loyalty to the State and the Jewish people'.[10]

One result of this doctrine is inordinate distortion and lop-sidedness of history and facts in textbooks. The lopsidedness of the system was pointed out to me by Said Barghouti, the inspector for history education in Arabic high schools in Israel, based in Nazareth. 'In the Arabic schools 20 per cent of history texts are about Jews whereas in the Hebrew [state] schools only 2 per cent of history concerns Arabs,' he said. A thin, dark, tallish, immaculately dressed man of 47, balding, with a cadaverous face, Barghouti talked to me in his unfinished, unheated office, with book-lined shelves, on the second floor of a multi-storey building in Nazareth on a cold February evening.

While referring to the Jewish immigration to Palestine under the Ottomans and the British, history books in Hebrew invariably say: 'the Jews immigrating to Eretz Israel, Land of Israel'. The fact remains that no such entity existed before 1948, and what came into being on 14 May 1948 is Medinat Israel (Hebrew, State of Israel), not Eretz Israel.

'I went through an educational system where the term Palestinian or Palestine was not used in a textbook or by a teacher, only the term Eretz Israel was used,' continued Barghouti, an undergraduate of Haifa University (1970), who obtaineed an MA in history from Hebrew University. 'Until 1966 when the military rule was in place in the Arab areas, if a schoolteacher said the word "Palestine" he got into trouble. Only after 1976, when a new curriculum was adopted, the term "Palestine" was allowed to be used in Arabic schools. The new curriculum still required that from the third grade Arab children should study the Old Testament and Israeli history and literature.'

The system thus created a generation of Israeli Arabs who were culturally shipwrecked. 'I grew up knowing a lot about Zionist culture and literature but nothing about Palestinian history, culture etc,' recalled Manna. 'On the other side, in the Hebrew schools Jewish students study Jewish history, Zionist-Arab conflict etc.; they learn very little about Palestine and Palestinians. In the Arabic system, history textbooks in secondary schools give the history of Palestine under the Ottomans until World War I, then the history of the Zionists. They ignore the history of Palestine and the Palestinian identity. They educate the Arab students for Israeli citizenship, and so the students know nothing about their own cultural and historical identity. This was Israel's way of controlling its Arabs, brainwashing them. It worked – up to a point. But when your textbooks and education prove inadequate to explain everyday reality and the evolving political-military situation, you lose confidence in the educational system.'

Undoubtedly, the wars of 1967 and 1973 and the intifada of 1987 impinged strongly on the communal consciousness of Israeli Arabs. 'After the 1967 War the brunt of discrimination shifted to the Palestinians in the West Bank and Gaza,' said Habibi. 'The Israelis could not rule by force all of the Palestinians, inside and outside Israel, together. At the same time contacts between the Palestinians across the Green Line [the pre-1967 border] increased. There were all those filial links. Politically, the Palestinian intifada was a watershed. It erupted when fellow Palestinians realized what we had done some 40 years before: you have to depend on yourselves and not wait around for a man on a white horse to come and deliver you.'

The Palestinian intifada accelerated politicization of Israeli Arabs, who had for long felt leaderless. With the traditional upper- and middle-class leadership gone into exile in 1948, the remnant of the Palestinian Arab community, now confined almost wholly to rural areas in the Galilee, found itself in a weak position. Except for Maki, a non-Zionist, fringe group, it was barred from national Israeli politics. For many years the mainstream Zionist parties excluded Arabs. Even the left-wing Mapam allowed Arabs to enrol in its auxiliary Arab organization, not the main body. Only in 1958 did it permit Arabs to take up direct membership. 'On the Israeli Arab side, there was fear of being involved in politics,' explained Manna. 'The general perception was that if you became too involved in politics then calamity would strike you as happened in 1948. Therefore Israeli Arabs kept low political profiles. They realized that they were second-class citizens, and that this was a Jewish state and an ethnic democracy. They learnt this the hard way. Between 1948 and 1966, any Arab who did not vote for a Zionist party was considered anti-Israeli.'

Given the secrecy of the ballot, how would anybody know the pattern of voting by any particular group, I asked. 'Most of us live in wholly or predominantly Arab villages and towns,' Manna said. 'So anybody can judge from the results of individual polling stations as to how the electors had voted. The Zionist parties can see whether or not the Arabs had voted for their affiliated Arab list – a practice which continued into the early 1980s. And they know that by controlling individual *mukhtars* and heads of *hamulas* (Arabic, extended families), they secure votes *en bloc*. Generally speaking, Arabs voted for the Zionist party which controlled either the Ministry of Education [for jobs as teachers] or police [for travel permits and security clearance]. If an Arab did not vote for a Zionist party he could not get a job [as a teacher] and a permit to travel to work, and could end up in jail. He knew that he had to have good relations with the police and Shin Beth, and the civil service. So during the 1950s and 1960s more than two-thirds of Arabs voted for the Zionist parties. They even voted for the [ultra-nationalist]

National Religious Party because it controlled the police, interior and education ministries. If you wanted to be a teacher, the only white-collar job available, you needed [security] clearance from the police and Shin Beth. So, all told, the first and second generations of Israeli Arabs were subdued.'

It was only in the mid-1970s that the situation changed. Labour, the successor to Mapai, permitted Arabs to join the main party in 1971. Initially it only accepted Arabs who had an IDF background (i.e., Druzes) or were bedouin. Labour and Mapam continued to run separate Arab lists in the Knesset elections. In the 1969 poll the Labour-affiliated list won 40 per cent of the Arab vote. But the separate Arab lists of Labour and Mapam lost their popularity. The last time Labour got a seat for its Arab list was in the December 1973 election. The October 1973 Arab-Israeli War, in which the Egyptian and Syrian armies performed well, helped to restore a feeling of dignity which Israeli Arabs had lost as a result of a series of disasters they and the Palestinian Arabs had suffered over the past quarter of a century.

Israel's performance in the October 1973 War made the local Arabs realize that the Zionist state was not invincible. This encouraged them to increase their support for Rakah, New Communist List, particularly when it was the only party in the December 1973 poll to demand an unconditional Israeli withdrawal from the Occupied Territories, and the recognition of the national rights of the Palestinians. With 37 per cent of the Israeli Arabs backing it, Rakah's strength in the Knesset rose to four.

The other factors which impinged on the communal psyche of Israeli Arabs were the growing nationalist movement in the occupied West Bank and Gaza Strip, and the rising prestige and international recognition of the Palestine Liberation Organization, culminating in its being given an observer status at the UN in late 1974.

In that year the elected representatives of Israeli Arabs formed the National Committee for Heads of Arab Local Authorities. Of the 99 Arab local authorities, three were municipalities, 58 local councils and 38 regional councils.

The central administration looked on the new body with a benign eye, hoping to build it up as a rival to Rakah. But by spearheading the protest against the Government's takeover of 2,000 acres of Arab land in the Galilee area, through a one-day strike on 30 March 1976 – named the 'Day of the Land' – Rakah increased its popularity, and frustrated the official plan. With the aggregate loss of some 90 per cent of their land through government confiscations since 1948, the feelings among Israeli Arabs were running high. Their demonstrations on the Day of the Land were violently broken up by the police, resulting in the deaths of six Arabs and injuries to 70. This radicalized the National Committee, which decided to adopt a programme of a joint campaign for Arab civil rights and Palestinian self-determination.

As a result, the total Arab vote for the Zionist parties fell to 37 per cent (with Labour receiving a mere 11 per cent) whereas it rose to 50 per cent for the (Marxist) Democratic Front for Peace and Equality (DFPE), popularly called Hadash – formed by the alliance of Rakah and the Black Panther Party, consisting of Sephardic Jews – which won five Knesset seats.[11] Only after this electoral setback did Labour properly open its doors to Arab citizens. However its policy of maintaining a separate Arab affairs department, often headed by an Ashkenazi Jew, continued until late 1994. Even now, unlike in Jewish towns and villages, there are no Labour Party branches in Arab-dominated towns and villages.

Rakah leaders actively promoted the national rights of the Palestinians. One of them, Emile Touma, was secretary of the Arab People's Conference in Support of the Palestine Revolution. In mid-1980, after there had been no progress on the Palestinian front as agreed by Israel in the 1978 Camp David Accords, the Arab People's Conference sponsored a manifesto which combined its twin-headed demand for equality for Arab citizens and an Israeli-Palestinian peace based on self-determination for Israelis and Palestinians with a call on the Israeli Government to negotiate with the PLO on the subject of a Palestinian state. The manifesto was signed by thousands of Israeli Arabs, and this worried the Government led by Likud Prime Minister Menachem Begin.

It banned the congress of the Arab People's Conference on the eve of its assembly in December 1980 called to endorse the manifesto.

Israeli Arabs were deeply antipathetic towards Likud. At the next General Election in 1981 as many as 29 per cent of them backed Labour in order to keep Likud out. Labour's gain was at the expense of the DFPE whose vote stabilized around a third of the total in the three General Elections held in the 1980s.

The 1987 intifada, and the iron fist policy towards it adopted by Yitzhak Rabin, Labour Defence Minister in the national unity government, alienated many Arab members of the party. Israeli Arabs showed their support for the Palestinian intifada by going on a general strike on 21 December. Among those who issued the call for the strike was Abdul Wahab Darawshe, a Labour MK. He left Labour, and formed his own Arab Democratic Party (ADP), the first group of its kind. It called for the withdrawal of Israel from all Arab territories occupied in 1967, and the convening of an international conference on the Middle East attended by all concerned parties, including the PLO, as the sole representative of the Palestinian people, on an equal footing. In the 1988 poll, when 58 per cent of the Arabs voted for non-Zionist groups, the ADP secured one seat.

Year 1987 also witnessed the expansion of the National Committee for Heads of Arab Local Authorities into the Supreme Surveillance Committee of Arab Affairs, with the addition of Arab representatives of all political groups, including the Zionist parties. The Supreme Surveillance Committee resorted to demonstrations and strikes to further the rights of the Arab citizens. In addition to the already established Day of the Land, it declared Days of Equality (24 June 1987), Peace (21 December 1987) and Housing (15 November 1988).

The daily diet of news on the intifada raised the nationalist consciousness of Israeli Arabs. They underwent a process described as 'Palestinianization'. 'We began to say "We are Palestinian",' recalled Atallah Mansour. 'Though our identity document says *leum*, nationality, Arab, we insisted that our nationality was Palestinian, and our citizenship Israeli. This put us in a bind as Israel and the PLO were at war then.'

With no let up in the intifada the Israeli Arab interest in the fate of the Palestinians remained high. Through voluntary charity organizations they provided monetary and other assistance to the Palestinian victims of the Israeli policies and actions. When in December 1992 Premier Yitzhak Rabin deported over 400 Hamas and Islamic Jihad men to south Lebanon, Israeli Arab leaders called a one-day strike. It got the almost unanimous support of the community. The DFPE's Arab MKs, Tawfiq Zayyad and Hashem Mahameed, visited the West Bank and Gaza Strip, and strongly condemned Rabin's move. Leading Israeli Arab personalities set up a protest tent outside the Prime Minister's office, a move which received the backing of Jewish leftists.

'The intifada proved to be a real, live political educator of Israeli Arabs,' said Dr Majid Al Haj. 'They did not need schooling to come to grips with their identity. They now learnt their history from other sources: political parties, parents, books at home, the street and the media. In this regard Arabic schools are lagging behind society at large.'

Along with an explosion of comment and analysis on the Palestinian affairs in the broadcasting media there was by the late 1980s a plethora of published material on Palestine and Palestinians in the form of pamphlets and books. The access to history books written by Arabs became fairly commonplace.

Given the frequency with which the current Palestinian intifada was being compared to the 1936–9 Arab uprising in Palestine, such titles as *Al Muqawam al Arabiye fi Falastin (1917–1948)* (The Arab Resistance in Palestine, 1917–1948) by Naji Alwash, published in Beirut, were popular. In a 30-page chapter (pages 110–39), before dealing with the Arab Revolt of 1936–9 proper, Alwash sets up the scene. In it he gives the central place to Izz al Din Qassam (1881–1935), the first Arab leader in Palestine to preach and practise the doctrine of armed resistance to the British mandate and the

Zionist immigration in Palestine, a struggle in which he lost his life. The fact that Hamas and the Islamic Jihad, the Islamic groups active within the intifada movement, had now named their armed wings after Qassam made biographical information about him topical and relevant.

Born into a religious family in Jabla, northern Syria, Qassam received an Islamic education in Latakia, and joined Al Azhar University in Cairo. There he came under the influence of Muhammad Abdu, an Islamic thinker. On his return to Syria he worked as a preacher. When the French mandated Syria in 1920 he preached against the foreign rule on his return to Syria where he taught at the Ibrahim ibn Adham theological college. Following his participation as a leader in an armed uprising against the French mandate in 1922, he was sentenced to death *in absentia*. He fled to Haifa. There he gave religious sermons and ran a night school for adults. As a marriage steward for the Haifa Muslim court he travelled often to surrounding rural areas, and established a rapport with peasants and workers.

According to Alwash, in 1926 Qassam was elected head of the newly formed Association of the Muslim Youth in Haifa, which proved to be a rich recruiting ground for his own Qassam Group. Two years later he began organizing secret meetings. 'Qassam was a religious man, a preacher, eloquent, with a rich vocabulary, a man of knowledge in many areas,' continues Alwash. 'He placed his skills and knowledge at the disposal of his religious centre in Haifa. He began to inspire his audience to revolt against repression and against foreign rule ... He realized that the traditional leadership was ineffective in countering the threat posed by the British mandate and Zionist colonization because it did not identify with the masses. It was more interested in looking after its own interests. He decided to establish a revolutionary and principled movement based on the Islamic faith and secret organization of its own. He took to holding clandestine meetings. His movement was based on the following principles: resistance should be based on Islamic precepts as well as practical and political principles, which should be applied to raise the members' political consciousness and national identity as well as their understanding of the cultural aspects of Islam; Britain was the root cause of the oppression of the Palestinian Muslims as Zionism was linked with British imperialism, and so the focus should be on the anti-mandate struggle with the objective of stopping the Zionist movement from colonizing any more land in Palestine; and an armed revolution will be able to end the British mandate, and that such a revolution requires the setting up of a secret organization, training fighters in military warfare, and encouraging popular participation in the resistance.'

Before launching his armed campaign Qassam tried to enlist the backing of the traditional leadership headed by Haajj Muhammad Amin Husseini in Jerusalem, writes Alwash. In 1935 he sent one of his aides, Mahmoud Salim, to Husseini calling on him to issue a revolutionary declaration like the one Qassam had issued in the north. Husseini replied that the time was not conducive for such acts, and that political efforts should be made in peaceful ways.

Qassam now unveiled his plan to set up five committees (continues Alwash): the Islamic propagation committee to prepare the people for revolution by all possible means, have an ongoing communication with them, and hold educational meetings; the committee for military training; the committee for procuring and storing of arms; the committee for monitoring and surveillance of the enemy; and the committee for foreign affairs, to establish and maintain links with Arabs in the neighbouring countries.

Matters came to a head after the eighteenth anniversary of the Balfour Declaration on 2 November 1935 when the Nablus committee of the Palestinian leaders decided to call a strike. By 11 November strike committees had been formed in Jerusalem, Jaffa and other places. On the night of 12 November Qassam addressed a secret meeting of his followers, the Qassam Group, mainly unemployed peasants, in Haifa. Two hundred of them had received military training, clandestinely, with weapons they had bought with their own funds. After the meeting Qassam and a large group of his followers, including Mahmoud Salim, headed inland for the wooded hills of Jenin, planning to hide in caves during daytime and attack British and Zionist targets at night. On the night of 13 November, according to Alwash, a Jewish settlement near the village of Boris was attacked by 'an unknown group'. The next morning when a mixed British patrol of three – a Briton, an Arab and a Jew – was sighted in the area, Salim opened fire and killed 'the Jewish spy'. Soon the Jenin area was saturated with armed police, British and Arab, looking for the band which had killed the Jew. By 20 November the area was 'like a war zone'. The armed forces were able to trace the Qassam Group in the valley near the village of Yaabad. The group resisted. When called to surrender, Qassam replied: 'Never. This is a jihad for God and the country.' The final skirmish lasted overnight. By the following morning Qassam and four of his companions were dead. The rest of his group were captured.

Qassam's rebellion failed to make a dent in the British mandate's hold over Palestine. Yet, following his death (martyrdom to his followers), popular pressure grew on different Palestinian groups to close ranks and unitedly challenge the British rule and the Zionist colonizers. The result was the formation of the Arab Higher Committee, and the eruption of the Arab Revolt under its leadership in April 1936, which lasted three years.

The easy availability inside Israel of material such as the above – in stark conflict with the official chronicle, which either ignored Qassam or made a cursory reference to him – began to worry liberal-minded Jewish Israeli educationists and policy-makers. Something needed to be done, they concluded. The initiative to update the curriculum at Arabic schools as well as history textbooks in the light of the dramatic change that had occurred outside schools came from the fellows of the Truman Institute at Hebrew University in 1991. Important Arab officials of the Ministry of Education, which controlled 437 Arabic schools with some 200,000 students, were invited to participate. But the textbook project really got going only after the Labour victory in the General Election of June 1992. In the new cabinet the Ministry of Education went to Shulamit Aloni, a member of the left-wing Meretz, and then to her party colleague, Amnon Rubinstein. They backed the idea of changes in the curriculum and textbooks for the Arabic sector.

Both Dr Adel Manna and Said Barghouti were commissioned to write history books. 'It was agreed at the outset that the official curriculum should familiarize the [Arab] student with "What is a Palestinian Arab?,"' said Barghouti. 'It is a daunting task in several ways. We, Arabs in Israel, are still grappling with our identity. Arabs have lived here, in this land, as Arabs for 3,000 years – since the rule of King Solomon. And as Muslim Arabs we have an almost continuous history here of more than 1,300 years. Our collective problem stems from the rise of Israel, the national state of the Jewish people, in 1948. And my problem as the author is how to narrate a national history of Arabs which is part of the State of Israel, which is the state of Jews. We, Arab educators, are wrestling with this intractable problem. We can find some space within the dichotomy that Israel is a Jewish national state, but it is also a democratic state. As Arab educators we use the democratic charter of Israel to build our curriculum, to help sharpen our communal identity.'

As the author of a book on history, Barghouti had to work within the long-established rules of the Education Ministry and its department charged with writing and supervising textbooks. The Ministry's own books compete with the ones produced in the private sector, but the latter must conform to the Ministry's guidelines and must have its approval before they are published. Though in the Hebrew system there is an expanding private sector, it is almost non-existent in its Arabic counterpart. The Ministry's new textbook project goes through two stages. First, the editorial committee of the Ministry publishes a limited edition of a book, and circulates it among educationists and specialists for their comments. Once these are received and discussed, the text is finalized; and a commercial edition appears.

Barghouti, an employee of the Education Ministry since 1972, encountered opposition to the way he handled the chapter, 'The Palestinian Problem' in *Social-cultural Changes in the Middle East, Vol. III*, (pp. 318–63) in its initial, limited edition version. To do justice to the 1917 Balfour Declaration which, by all accounts, is the seed that grew into the plant called Israel 31 years later, Barghouti devoted five pages to the subject. His editorial committee cut his text down to a single page. 'All my references to Arab land expropriations by Israel were excised,' he said. 'I was told, "If you write about land expropriations this will create hostility against the Jews at the present time".'

While working on *History of the Middle East, Vol. II*, Barghouti ran into trouble on his definition of Zionism. 'Zionism is a belief that Jews constitute a nation which has its own identity and that they have the right to be a free nation like others and that they have the right to return to the land they consider as the land of their ancestors, which they call the Land of Israel,' he wrote. The editorial committee at the Ministry rejected this, regarding it as too qualified – 'they consider as the land of their ancestors'. So the final version read: 'Zionism is a movement which had been created in order to achieve the historical right of the Jews to return to their own land and build their own state.'[12]

On the other hand, said Barghouti, 'We state that Arabs in Israel are an integral part of the Palestinian nation. It is the first [official] textbook to say so.'

Life became much easier for Israeli Arabs when Yasser Arafat and Yitzhak Rabin shook hands at the White House in Washington after the signing of the Israeli-PLO Accord in mid-September 1993. They no longer had to try to maintain conflicting loyalties to two warring parties.

'Today we are the most enthusiastic supporters of the Israeli-PLO Accord of September 1993,' said Emile Habibi. 'We, the Israeli Arabs, forming one-sixth of the national population, are a strong force for co-existence between Palestinians and Israeli Jews. We also know that we will benefit from the peace process more than any other section of the Palestinian people.'

But a pact between Israel and the PLO has created a different set of choices for Israeli Arabs. 'Now there is the Palestinian Authority and a Palestinian flag, and there will be a Palestinian state one day,' said Atallah Mansour. 'But we are in Israel and not in Palestine. We are not going to migrate to the future State of Palestine. So we ought to integrate with the Israeli mainstream.'

The ongoing debate among Israeli Arabs revolves around the question whether they should back mainstream Zionist parties or non-Zionist groups like the Democratic Front for Peace and Equality and the Arab Democratic Party. The result of the 1992 Knesset poll showed the community to be evenly divided on the subject. Though Rabin managed to form a government without including the DFPE (three MKs, two of them Arab) and the ADP (two MKs), his administration lost its majority after he had compelled the Shas leader, Rabbi Arye Deri, to resign his ministerial post following renewed police charges of corruption against him. The fact that Rabin did not then invite the DFPE or ADP to join the coalition, while enjoying their support, strengthened the hands of those Israeli Arabs who favoured Zionist parties. Their argument was that so long as Israeli Arabs supported non-Zionist groups they would be confined to the margins of Israel's national politics.

Deep division within the community adversely affects its overall strength in the Knesset. Of the 2,657,000 Israelis who voted in the 1992 election, 282,700 were Arab, which translated into a ratio of 1:9. At that rate the Arabs should have had 11 MKs. In reality they had only eight, including two Druzes, one of them a member of Likud.[13]

On the other hand, the legitimization and empowerment of the PLO opened new vistas for the DFPE and the ADP, and certain individual Israeli Arabs. Dr Ahmad Tibi, a moon-faced, bespectacled native of the Arab town of Taiba east of Natanya, who runs a gynaecology clinic in East Jerusalem, became a close adviser to Arafat. This has caused much adverse comment in the Jewish Israeli media. 'Israel does not want Israeli Arabs to be too involved in the peace process because they know the Jews better than any other Arabs: their strengths, weaknesses, tricks, real interests, operating methods etc.,' said Dr Adel Manna. 'That is why most Israelis are upset at the high-profile involvement of Ahmad Tibi as Arafat's adviser.'

None the less, at crucial moments Israeli Arab politicians have played a central role in Palestinian politics since the Israeli-PLO Accord. For instance, when tension between the PLO and Hamas rose dangerously high in the Gaza Strip in November 1994, following the fatal shooting of a dozen Palestinians by the Palestinian Authority police, the Israeli Arab MKs intervened, successfully, to lower temperature.

Six months later these MKs intervened on behalf of the Palestinians dramatically, and in the Knesset itself. In late April 1995 the Israeli Government unveiled plans to confiscate 130 acres of Palestinian land in Greater East Jerusalem to build housing for Jews. Protest by the Palestinian Authority and others got nowhere. On 17 May, when 14 of the 15 United Nations Security Council members backed a resolution criticizing the Israeli move, the US, determined to aid Israel, exercised its veto for the first time since the end of the Cold War in 1991. The Rabin administration was all set to go ahead with its confiscation plans when the DFPE and the ADP MKs tabled a no-confidence motion in the Knesset on 22 May. As the Government had the backing only of 58 MKs in a house of 120, its downfall was assured since the opposition declared its support for the no-confidence motion. Fearing this, Premier Rabin climbed down, and the Government 'suspended' its land confiscation plans.

Outside the Knesset, the Supreme Surveillance Committee of Arab Affairs, commonly regarded as the parliament of the Arabs in Israel, remains committed to its two major aims: (a) peace and furtherance of Palestinian national rights; and (b) closing the economic gap between Arabs and Jews in Israel.

Since September 1993 there has been discernible progress on (a). But the socio-economic chasm between the two communities in Israel remains wide. Figures for 1991 revealed that whereas the monthly income of a four-member Jewish family was $1,419, that of an Arab family was $815. While nearly 50 per cent of the Arab families lived below the official poverty line, the corresponding figure for the Jews was one-fifth of the Arabs'. Unemployment among Arabs at 20 per cent was twice the rate for Jews. A similar ratio prevailed in infant mortality. The difference in the level of local public services could be gauged by the per capita local government budget: Arab $42; Jew $133. Whereas the gap between the two ethnic groups in secondary education, ending in matriculation, was not much – Arabs 45 per cent, Jews 65 per cent – at the university level Arabs lagged behind Jews by 3:1.[14] 'At 5 to 6 per cent of the university enrolment, the Arabs are only about a third of their demographic proportion,' said Dr Adel Manna. Yet over 40 per cent of Arab university graduates were either jobless or employed in semi-skilled work. The situation is unlikely to change since large swathes of industry, science and research, tied to the vast military establishment, remain closed to Israeli Arabs because of their lack of service in the IDF. In theory, they can volunteer for the military on an individual basis. But it is common knowledge that the IDF leadership is opposed to having large Arab contingents in the army (Druze males, who are drafted, are only 5 per cent of the overall Arab population), and the Arabs do not want to expose themselves to a situation which requires them to fight fellow Palestinians or other Arabs. Only when there is a comprehensive peace between Israel and its Arab neighbours can one realistically expect Arab citizens of Israel to serve in the IDF like their Jewish counterparts.

Meanwhile continued unemployment and under-employment among Arab university graduates is providing a fertile ground for the rise of Muslim fundamentalism, which is represented in Israel by the Islamic Movement. Its roots go back to the mid-1930s when the Egyptian-based Muslim Brotherhood established branches in Palestine. Dormant for three decades after the emergence of Israel, the religio-political movement revived as a result of renewed interest in Islam among those Israeli Arabs who joined Islamic colleges on the West Bank after 1967. Some 100 members of an organization, called the Usrat al Jihad, Family of the Jihad, led by Shaikh Abdullah Nimr Darwish, were arrested in 1981 on charges of possessing illegal arms. Darwish was a resident of the village of Kfar Qassim, the site of a massacre of 47 unarmed Arab men and women by the IDF on the eve of the Suez War on 30 October 1956. After their release from jail in the mid-1980s the followers of Darwish formed the Islamic Movement with the objective of returning society to the pristine precepts of Islam. It set up grass roots organizations such as community centres, libraries and clothing workshops. It recognized the State of Israel *de facto* but not *de jure*, and called on its supporters to boycott the Knesset poll in 1988. But it participated in the 1989 local elections. Securing 20 per cent of the popular vote, it won control of six local councils, including Umm al Fahm (population, 30,000), the second largest Arab town after Nazareth.

Islamic Movement members were as interested in the fate of the Palestinians in the Occupied Territories as were the secular Israeli Arabs. Both sections of the community were horrified by the massacre in Hebron of Muslim Palestinians at the Tomb of the Patriarchs/Ibrahimi Mosque by Baruch Goldstein, a resident of the adjoining Kiryat Arba settlement, in late February 1994, during the fasting month of Ramadan. They responded with almost the same vigour as did the Palestinians. In the Arab towns like Nazareth (with 60 per cent Muslim population), Jaffa and Rahat (in Negev), the three-day protest turned violent. In Rahat one Arab was killed by police firing. The mourners at his funeral chanted, 'In blood, in spirit, we'll redeem you, O martyr!' – a chant which had not been heard inside the pre-1967 Israel before. This aroused apprehension in the minds of many Jewish Israelis that an Arab intifada from within the Israeli borders was in the making. Such fears proved ill-founded, but the events following the Hebron massacre made many on the opposite sides of the ethnic divide reassess their long-term relationship.

Summing up the overall Israeli Arab scene, Atallah Mansour, a veteran journalist with 35 years of service with the prestigious *HaAretz* daily, said: 'While most Israeli Arabs want reconciliation and co-existence, there are small groups like the Islamic Movement which say, "We'll get all of [British mandate] Palestine".'

In a sense the supporters of the Islamic Movement in Israel

are mirror-images of the members of those ultra-nationalist Jewish groups who wanted all of British mandate Palestine as their Land of Israel. Acting on this belief, some 300,000 Jews, religious and secular, have settled in the areas beyond the pre-1967 borders of Israel, with almost a half of them in the West Bank.

8

NEW FRONTIERSMEN:

Zealots on the Hills

I employed the foot-in-the-door technique when it came to interviewing Rabbi Moshe Levinger in Hebron in March 1995. Rafi and I broke away from the group of visitors from Tel Aviv, who were being given a guided tour of the Jewish Quarter, the Avraham Avinu complex – the largest of the four Jewish enclaves in downtown Hebron, and located next to the vegetable market – by Naom Arnon, the spokesman for the Kiryat Arba settlement but a resident of the nearby Beit Hadassah (Hebrew, House of Hadassah) Jewish enclave. Levinger's two-storey stone house was easy to find. Standing on the far side of a small square, next to the rebuilt synagogue with a white dome, it lay in the path of a pedestrian approaching the enclave from a lane of shuttered, squalid Arab shops – some of them carrying the graffiti in Hebrew, 'Mavet la Aravim (Kill the Arabs)' – and a military command post bristling with gun-carrying soldiers, that branched off a busy main road where it curved sharply uphill. The entrance to Levinger's house was through a side alley, under a cove.

A young daughter of Moshe Levinger answered the door bell, and Rafi explained the purpose of our call. She disappeared – for a long while. It gave me time to read the tablet on a wall facing the square declaring that the new complex had been completed by the Ministry of Housing in 1989 (when a national unity government, including Labour and Likud, was in power). At the strategic points inside the enclave and on its periphery – the rooftops of the houses and the surrounding, shuttered Arab shops – I noticed troops armed with sub-machine-guns. Every time I looked up I saw a young soldier with a gun on a rooftop, alert as a hawk. Levinger's daughter returned. Yes, he would see us, but he needed a while to get ready.

There were another daughter and a son at home. The remaining eight children of Moshe Levinger, aged 59, and his wife, Miriam, 57, were away. The elder daughter, who had once worked as a psychologist at Dimona, told me how crazy Indian Jews living there were about Hindi movies which they watched compulsively on rented VCRs (video-cassette recorders). We waited in a large open plan hall, harbouring a kitchen on the far side and a library of books, all of them in Hebrew, in a near corner. The shelves occupied the walls on the side of the alleyway and the entrance cove. A large table, surrounded by chairs, filled the rectangular space formed by the library walls. Born in Jerusalem, of a father of German origins, a professor, Levinger had grown up surrounded by books, I was to learn later.

Moshe Levinger is a man of medium height, bald, with a long white beard and a slight paunch. He was wearing a faded grey sweater over a white shirt, light blue trousers, a black skullcap and black-framed glasses. We sat around the library table to talk. 'Hebron has a special place in Judaism,' he began. 'In the [Hebrew] Bible we see that God permits three patriarchs [Abraham, Isaac/Yitzhak and Jacob] to settle in Hebron. These men led our world. Of the 18 Jewish prayers, the first prayer is about the patriarchs. Therefore it is our [religious] duty to rebuild villages and towns here, because they belong to us, Jews. All this is in the territories which are the heart of the Land of Israel, which God promised to the

Jewish people. We pray and resolve to return to our Holy Country, Israel. We say in our prayers Eretz Israel as our country. If the Jewish congregation is in Holland or Egypt, outside our Holy Country, they all say the same thing: they feel outside of their homeland, hoping and praying it [the Holy Country] will become our home. There is no period in our history when we said that our connection with Tel Aviv or Herzliya or Natanya or Haifa was stronger than our connection with Beit El (Hebrew, House of God), Hebron, Nablus, Beit Lehem [Bethlehem], Tekoa. These holy cities are the heart of Eretz Israel. They formed our first congregation during the First Temple and the Second Temple periods. We had connections [with the people] over the mountains, who were sometimes Philistine. But the Jews lived in Judea and Samaria. Therefore we think that it is a mistake to think that this is an Occupied Territory. It is the heart of our country. Abraham came to this place under the command of God. God instructed him – first to Shechem [Nablus], then Beit El where a tabernacle was built. Another tabernacle was at a place which is now modern Ramallah. To say Nablus is an Arab city is a lie. Nablus is more Jewish than Tel Aviv. Our connection with Hebron is stronger than with Tel Aviv.'

For Levinger these were not just mere words. He had acted on his belief. He is the leading pioneer of Jewish settlement in the West Bank, having begun the process within a year of the Israeli capture of the West Bank from Jordan in June 1967. 'At the time of the Passover in 5728 [April 1968] we came here, about four families, all together 50 people, to Park Hotel. It was a hotel only in name, it was empty. We rented the whole place. We paid for it, four shekels per bed. The hotel had 40 beds in all. Later people said that I was a poor trader, that I should have bargained and got the rate down to three shekels a bed [since we were renting all the rooms]. If I had been a better trader I'd have brought it down to three shekels.' Levinger's mundane attitude to an event which has since then acquired mythical proportions surprised me; also his reference to shekels was wrong, because the Israeli currency then was the lira. 'Anyway, in spring 1968 four Jewish families, led by me, came to Hebron. Today 1,000 families live in Hebron and Kiryat Arba. We did not know at the beginning how much time it will take to settle here. But we are a people of 3,000 years ago. We have a long perspective. In another 30 years the Jewish community here will be bigger than it is now.'

The history of the Jewish community in Hebron – as told by Naom Arnon, 35, a muscular, bearded man of East European origins, to the Jewish visitors from Tel Aviv; and in a booklet, *Hebron Massacre 1929*, edited by Rachavam Zeevi, a reserve general and leader of the right-wing Moledet group, that Arnon gave me – could be summarized as follows. For about 500 years the Jewish community in Hebron lived in peace with its Arab neighbours. This changed in 1929 when the community was 900 strong. It lived in four neighbourhoods: Beit Hadassah, the Jewish Quarter, Admot Isaiah, and Shava Yeshiva. 'In [August] 1929 burning, murdering etc. happened, Arabs slaughtered us,' Arnon told his audience. 'The Jewish Quarter was totally destroyed, and 67 Jews were murdered. The British mandate did not do anything. Actually, the British police evacuated the Jewish community from Hebron. The Jewish houses were given to Arabs.' (A pertinent fact often mentioned in many Zionist chronicles that the Jews in Hebron had rejected the offer of the Haganah militia for protection went unmentioned. Also, according to Eliakam Haetzini, a leader of the Jewish settlers in Kiryat Arba, some of the Jews who had been evacuated in 1929 returned, and remained until 1937 [the first phase of the 1936–9 Arab Revolt].) 'After the 1967 war the Israeli Government should have returned Jewish families to Hebron,' said the booklet edited by Zeevi. 'Unfortunately this did not happen. In the spring of 1968 Jews rented the Park Hotel . . . Later on the Labour Government built Kiryat Arba [nearby] in 1971. Further construction took place in 1975–76 [under Labour] and again in 1979–80 [under Likud].' Arnon provided the update. 'This was the old Jewish Quarter,' he said, gesturing with his right hand. 'In [April] 1979 one Kiryat Arba mother, Sarah, went to bury her son, named Abraham, in the Jewish cemetery in Hebron [near the bend on the main road], but was barred. This angered the Jews in Kiryat Arba. In protest several Jewish women of Kiryat Arba, led by Miriam Levinger [Moshe's wife], barricaded themselves inside Beit Hadassah [then an abandoned building]. They demanded a renewed Jewish presence in the city. The government of Menachem Begin besieged the building.' This caused visible astonishment among Arnon's audience, one of whom, a thin man in a dark grey suit, was videotaping the event. Prime Minister Begin apparently reckoned that such a move would exacerbate the already tense relations between Arabs and Jews in Hebron and its surroundings. 'But the Government changed its mind after the Palestinian terrorists machine-gunned six Kiryat Arba Jews just outside the Beit Hadassah in May 1980,' continued Arnon. 'It allowed the Jews to move into downtown Hebron. Today about 50 Jewish families live in the town plus 120 yeshiva students.'

A prominent sign on a wall saying 'Bnei Akiva', the name of the youth movement of the National Religious Party, indicated the presence of yeshiva students, and also signalled that the predominantly Orthodox Jewish community living in Hebron backed the ultra-nationalist NRP.

The Bnei Akiva and Jerusalem's Merkaz HaRav Kook Yeshiva, run by Rabbi Zvi Yehuda Kook, the leading ideologue of the Orthodox NRP, were the main forces behind the Jewish colonization of the West Bank, before they together formally set up the Gush Emunim in early 1974. Rabbi Zvi Kook's father, Rabbi Abraham Yitzhak HaCohen Kook, the first Ashkenazi chief rabbi of Palestine, from 1922 onwards, was renowned for deviating from the official Orthodoxy, which held that redemption of Jews and Israel would come only through divine intervention, and not human endeavour, and rejected Zionism as a Jewish version of secular nationalism, an offspring of the eighteenth-century Enlightenment and the 1789 French Revolution. Instead, Abraham Kook offered a synthesis of 'the divine concept' and 'national sentiment' which, he stressed, could underline the evolving institutions of the Yishuv, the Jewish community in Palestine. In a single generation the Yishuv graduated into the State of Israel, which Abraham Kook did not live to see. His son, Zvi, the leading interpreter of his ideology, argued that secular Zionists, despite their irreligiosity, were the inadvertent bearers of a messianic redemption, and that the State of Israel was an unwitting instrument of divine will. The predecessor of the NRP, the Mizrahi, affiliated to the (World) Zionist Organization, was an influential group within religious Zionism, and stressed messianism and mysticism. 'Zionism will wither away if you cut it from its mystical-messianic roots,' said Rabbi Moshe Levinger, a former student of Rabbi Zvi Kook at the Merkaz HaRav Kook Yeshiva. 'Zionism is a movement that does not think in rational terms – in terms of power politics, international relations, world opinion, demography, social dynamics – but in terms of divine commandments. What matters only is God's promise to Abraham as recorded in the Book of Genesis.'[1]

It was therefore not surprising that Rabbi Zvi Kook's definition of Eretz Israel coincided with the Revisionist Zionists', and included present day Jordan. A few weeks before the June 1967 Arab-Israeli War, Kook lamented the truncated nature of the State of Israel. '"Where is our Hebron?,"' he asked. 'And where are our Shechem [Nablus] and our Jericho? Where are they? Can we ever forsake them? All of Jordan – it is ours. Every single inch, every square foot . . . belongs to Eretz Israel. Do we have the right to give up even one millimetre?'[2]

Following Israel's spectacular victory in the Six Day War, Kook attributed it to divine intervention. His followers called 1967 the Year One of the Era of Redemption. One of his star students, Moshe Levinger, pioneered a Jewish settlement near Hebron. In early 1974 he was among the group of Kook's acolytes who met in the Kfar Etzion settlement, halfway between Bethlehem and Hebron, and established the Gush Emunim. The choice of Kfar Etzion was symbolic. Founded as a Zionist settlement in 1927, it fell into the hands of the Jordanian army in 1948, and was then retaken by Israel in 1967. The message of the newly formed Gush Emunim was simple: Kfar Etzion was not negotiable, nor was the rest of Judea and Samaria, its names for the West Bank.

Gush activists emulated the tactics that Levinger and his colleagues had successfully deployed in Hebron and Kiryat Arba in order to establish Jewish settlements in the West Bank. They combined their colonizing endeavour – centred around a strategy of intermittent confrontation and bargaining with the Government – with building up an organizational infrastructure. They opened numerous branches throughout Israel, and infiltrated local parents-teachers' associations and synagogue management committees, in order to gain followers and prospective settlers. The new recruits were not always religious Jews of the Orthodox variety.

Indeed all along the new Jewish colonizers included a substantial body of secular Jews. Prominent among the early settlers was Eliakam Haetzini. He was in fact as much of a pioneer as Moshe Levinger. He was one of the Jews who rented rooms at an Arab hotel in Hebron in April 1968, having responded to the newspaper advertisements inserted by Levinger about his project, with the two of them planning their project in Haetzini's law offices in Tel Aviv.

Robust in appearance, Eliakam Haetzini is a bespectacled man with a grey thatch of hair, whose energetic elocution (in English), accompanied by gesticulation, belies his age. His parents came to Palestine from Keil, Germany, in 1938 when he was 12. He trained as a lawyer, and ran a successful practice at Ramat Gan (near Tel Aviv) before moving to Kiryat Arba. His house on Givat Mamre (Hebrew, Hill of Mamre), with a large terrace, providing a panoramic view of the surroundings, including Hebron, was comfortable, and its reception room impressively spacious. His eclectic library included not only a collection of plays by George Bernard Shaw but also *Suleiman the Magnificent* by Harold Lamb, and *Spartacus*, a novel by Howard Fast, an American Communist writer. Haetzini is a leader of Tehiya, a secular right-wing group. Formed in October 1979 by Galia Cohen and Moshe Shamir, after they had left the Likud in protest at the Israeli-Egyptian Peace Treaty of March 1979, which involved returning all of occupied Sinai to Egypt and uprooting the Jewish colonies set up there, Tehiya wanted Israel to annex the West Bank and Gaza, and accelerate the

Jewish settlement programme there. Its share of Knesset seats in the elections held in the 1980s varied between three and five. But it failed to win a single seat in 1992.

'I was one of the 20–30 people who rented rooms at Nahar al Khalil [the name of an Arab hotel] owned by Fayaz Qawasmeh, in Hebron,' Haetzini began. 'Hebron is a special place for Jews, the place of Abraham and King David. Anyway, after the Passover I returned to my villa in Ramat Gan. After a clash [at the Hebron hotel] the Jewish party was allowed to remain at the [nearby] military camp, in caravans. First the [national unity] Government [of Levi Eshkol] was taken aback. Then the [national unity] Government [of Golda Meir] said in October 1969 that it would build something for the settlers in a suburb near Hebron. Kiryat Arba means four towns, referring to the four hamlets that existed near Hebron in biblical times. The construction of houses began in 1971. I was among the 150 pioneers who took up residence in Kiryat Arba. I rented out my villa in Ramat Gan, and gave up my lucrative legal practice.' He turned to his wife, a plump, matronly figure, hovering in the background. 'She was not sure because of the children's education. But they had a truly Zionist education here in body and soul. We are here because this is the heart of the Land of Israel where the Bible really took place: Judea and Samaria, Beit El and Hebron, where our prophets and kings were born and bred; not in Tel Aviv. The coastal plain was on the margin. Historically it was in Philistine hands. King David came from Beit Lehem (Bethlehem), a Hebrew name. Daily more and more Jews are realizing this. That is why today Kiryat Arba has 6,500 Jews, about a third of them [secular] non-observant, like me. It started with 400 donums [40 hectares] in 1971, now it has 4,000 donums [400 hectares]. There are now three parts to Kiryat Arba. Besides the original Kiryat Arba, there are Givat Mamre, where I am now, and Givat Avot [Hill of Fathers], the latest addition.' His wife brought coffee and cakes.

'Mind you,' Haetzini continued, 'there have been ups and downs. In the village of Rojeib near Elon Moreh [near Nablus], the Government took over private Arab land for security purposes. The Arabs went to the High Court, arguing that this was only a pretext, and that the Government will settle civilians. General Chaim Bar Lev gave an affidavit in which he agreed with the Arabs. So the court ruled in favour of them in early 1980. Unlike many others in Kiryat Arba, I was pleased. I told them that taking over Arab land for security reasons means that once the military leaves, the civilians must leave with it, so says the Hague Convention. But in Kiryat Arba we did not come for military purposes but as part of the process of the return of the Jews. So we are here for good, come what may. Still 15 of us went on hunger strike for 45 days, and only then did the authorities agree to give us land *not* taken over for security reasons.'

On the whole though the Government, then headed by Menachem Begin, was supportive of the Jewish settlers. Indeed, within three years of this administration, which assumed office in May 1977, the Gush Emunim established 20 colonies on the West Bank. Begin's Likud Government had, in most analysts' view, inherited 'an equivocal' policy pursued by its forerunner, the Labour Party. However, the end result of this equivocating stance was that during the decade the Labour-led administrations occupied the West Bank and Gaza, 34 Jewish settlements had sprung up, with less than half in the Jordan Valley, which the IDF leaders wished to control in order to make Israel militarily secure. While proclaiming that it was holding the Arab territories conquered in the 1967 War merely as leverage to obtain peace treaties from its Arab neighbours, Israel under Labour began a colonizing process in the West Bank.

This had partly to do with domestic politics. Intense rivalry between Moshe Dayan, the hero of the 1967 conflict and the Defence Minister, and Yigal Allon, Deputy Prime Minister, translated into competition to show who was more hawkish on the issue of the Occupied Territories. In the tussle that ensued between the Jewish settlers in Hebron and the IDF (run by Dayan), Allon overtly and covertly helped the settlers, thus paving the way for the official establishment of Kiryat Arba, which followed the cabinet's decision to that effect in October 1969. Allon's plan for the Occupied Territories, unveiled the next year, was designed to ensure Israel's security (by making the Jordan Valley its international border) while keeping the increase in the Arab population within the enlarged Israel to absolute minimum. The plan proposed Israel annexing a wide strip of land along the Jordanian border north of Jerusalem, two-thirds of the area of the West Bank south of Jerusalem, and the southern half of the tiny Gaza Strip, and ceding the rest of the Palestinian territory to Jordan, with no role for the Palestinians at all. Not to be outdone, Dayan initiated his own programme of colonizing the West Bank.[3] The existence of a national unity government, which included the Likud until August 1970, helped the hawkish faction within Labour. Later, since the National Religious Party, committed to annexing the Occupied Territories, was still in the cabinet, it ensured that those who set up unauthorized Jewish settlements were treated lightly.

Once Likud became the leading partner in the administration, in which the NRP held important ministerial posts, the pace of colonization accelerated. A small, but highly significant, indicator of the change was the routine use of the term 'Eretz Israel', instead of the official 'Medinat Israel', by Likud Premier Menachem Begin. The settlement drive really got going after the Israeli-Egyptian Peace Treaty of March 1979. By neutralizing the Arab world's most populous and powerful state, this treaty removed the threat of war against the Jewish state by an alliance of its remaining Arab neighbours. The next five years witnessed the most intense construction activity in the West Bank and Gaza. Then there was a slowdown primarily because of the economic crisis caused by hyperinflation, and secondarily because of Israel's inability to extricate itself from the Lebanese quagmire. But the official commitment to establishing new settlements and enlarging the present ones remained. Even when Shimon Peres was the Prime Minister in the national unity government during 1984–6, five new settlements went up. Little wonder that continuing growth in the size of the Jewish settler community showed no sign of decline. In 1977, when Labour lost to Likud, there were 5,000 Jewish settlers in the Occupied Territories; a decade later the figure had reached nearly 60,000. The Jewish settlements, each of them administered by an elected council headed by a mayor, were grouped in regional councils, which were then brought together under the umbrella of the Council of the Jewish Communities in Judea, Samaria and Gaza.

Meanwhile, Israel's strategy of confiscating Palestinian land and acquiring ownership of water resources in the Occupied Territories continued. The Israeli Government and private Jewish bodies possessed only 1 per cent of the land in the West Bank in mid-1967 following Israel's annexation of Greater East Jerusalem. Nearly a quarter of a century later, in the autumn of 1991, the situation was summed up by Yossi Halevi of the *Jerusalem Report* thus: 'Of the West Bank's roughly 5 million donums [500,000 hectares], some 1.5 million donums are [Israeli] government-owned for either military or civilian use. Ownership of an additional million donums is being contested between the [Israeli] government and local Arabs, according to Uri Ariel, secretary-general of the Council of the Jewish Communities in Judea, Samaria and Gaza. The rest of the land [50 per cent] is privately owned by Arabs.'[4]

At that time Israel was ruled by a Likud-dominated right-wing administration headed by Premier Yitzhak Shamir, who was committed to the Jewish settlement of the West Bank and Gaza. As mentioned earlier,[5] he backed the largescale colonizing plans of his housing minister, Ariel Sharon, unveiled in the summer of 1991, which annoyed the George Bush administration in the US. Washington translated its feelings into action by refusing to underwrite the $10 billion loan the Israeli Government wanted to raise in the international financial markets (a commitment which would have cost the US taxpayers $800 million) to absorb the large intake of Soviet Jews. Shamir, standing by his ideological commitment to settle Jews in Judea and Samaria, chose to put his plan for raising international loans on hold. Colonizing of the West Bank and Gaza went on. While this reassured the ultra-nationalists within the Likud and outside, the Government's failure to secure international loans had a negative impact on the Soviet/Russian immigrants. This was one of the factors that led to the defeat of Likud in the 1992 General Election. It once again underlined the importance that Jewish settlements in the West Bank had in Israeli politics.

Meanwhile, the Jewish settler community in the West Bank and Gaza continued to grow. During the Gulf War in early 1991 the Council of the Jewish Communities in Judea, Samaria and Gaza claimed that it represented 92,000 settlers. Since public expenditure on the Jewish settlements was undertaken by different ministries – housing and construction, agriculture, energy, education and culture, immigration and absorption, and transport – it was easy for the Government to bury the figures in the general budget of each ministry. So no official statistic on the total amount spent on Jewish settlements was available. But, according to Meron Benvenisti, who has maintained a database on the West Bank for many years, the total government expenditure on Jewish settlements during 1967–92 amounted to $5 billion, or about $50,000 per settler. Between 1990 and 1991 the figure jumped from $530 million to $830 million, amounting to 2.8 per cent of the national budget.[6] The official settler population statistic for 1993 was 116,400. The signing of 'The Declaration of Principles on Interim Self-Government Arrangements' by Israel and PLO in September of that year made scant difference to the growth. By agreeing not to challenge the Israeli occupation law during the interim agreement, the PLO let Israel continue creating 'facts on the ground' in the Occupied Territories. As a result, by early 1995 Israel had confiscated a further 6,778 hectares (68 square kilometres) of Palestinian land in the Occupied Territories, and allotted 15 square kilometres to stone quarries, and 12 square kilometres for 'nature reserves' which, going by the past record, were apparently widely expected to be used for future Jewish settlements.[7] The Jewish construction activity had used up 763 hectares (eight square kilometres) of Palestinian land.

In the larger, political context, Israel's recognition of the PLO as the representative of the Palestinians (who had until then been officially represented by the non-PLO Palestinian delegates in the joint Jordanian-Palestinian delegation to the

Middle East Peace Conference), which preceded the signing of the Israeli-PLO Accord, opened a new chapter in the historical conflict between Zionist Jews and Palestinian Arabs. Since it tilted the balance towards the latter, it buoyed the mood of the Palestinians. Conversely it depressed the Jewish settlers in the West Bank and Gaza.

This change manifested itself on the ground, especially in Hebron, a historical flashpoint. Ever since 1967 the Jews had won the right to pray inside the Tomb of the Patriarchs, known as the Ibrahimi (derivative of Abraham) Mosque among the Palestinians, albeit only on the Sabbath. The city's Palestinians had deeply resented the re-establishment of the Jewish enclaves in their midst in 1979–80. And the decision of Rabbi Meir Kahane to take up residence in 1980 at the adjacent Kiryat Arba settlement, already the base of Rabbi Moshe Levinger, heightened tension.

Born Martin David Kahane in 1932 to the family of a rabbi in Brooklyn, New York, Meir Kahane joined the Betar, the youth movement of the Revisionist Zionists, as a teenager. He obtained a law degree from New York University, and was ordained as an Orthodox rabbi. He combined his religious work with editing the Brooklyn-based *Jewish Press*. His increasingly militant views led him to establish in the mid-1960s the Jewish Defence League which resorted to such violent acts as bombings in the cause of defending Jews. He coupled this with harassing the Soviet missions in New York to highlight Moscow's ill-treatment of Jews. Declaring that the only way a Jew could escape imbibing Gentile values was to live in Israel, he migrated there in 1971. After the October 1973 Arab-Israeli War, he became virulently anti-Arab. In 1976 he set up his own political group, Kach (Hebrew, Thus), which became known widely by its symbol of a clenched fist. Kahane regarded Jews to be an exclusivist community, opposed to social or sexual intercourse with non-Jews, and insisted that only Jews had the right to live in the biblical Land of Israel. He therefore advocated expulsion of Arabs from the West Bank and the Gaza Strip as well as Israel. 'Our final aim is to expel all Arabs from the Land of Israel,' Kahane said in June 1980.

'We want the [Israeli] Government to make the Arabs feel as miserable as possible by cutting off social benefits . . . [If that fails] we're calling on the Government to organize a Jewish terrorist group that would throw bombs and grenades and kill Arabs.'[8] However, Kahane and his Kach activists did not wait around for official action. They resorted to beating up Arabs in their homes, smashing cars and shop windows in Arab towns, insulting, harassing and threatening them. Such activities brought Kahane 62 arrests until mid-1980, but only two convictions.

Among his followers was a fellow-resident at Kiryat Arba, Dr Baruch Kapal Goldstein. Born in 1957 in Brooklyn, New York, Goldstein was educated at Flatbush Yeshiva, then Yeshiva University, and finally Albert Einstein College of Medicine in the Bronx, New York, where he received a medical degree. In 1983 he migrated to Israel, where he chose to live in Kiryat Arba, and served in the IDF. He became a close colleague of Meir Kahane.

Unlike the Jewish settlers elsewhere, who avoided contact with Palestinian Arabs, the residents of both Kiryat Arba and the Jewish enclaves in Hebron went out of their way to impress their presence on the Arabs of Hebron. As Yisrael Medad, one of the settlers, recalled in the mid-1990s, 'On Sabbath we used to demonstratively stroll in prayer shawls through the Arab market.'[9] This was partly to browbeat the local population, and partly to underline the point that the Jews, expelled in 1929, had returned.

As stated earlier, in the rising tension between Arabs and Jews in the Occupied Territories, starting in spring 1983, Hebron emerged as a hot spot.[10] In March 1983 Palestinian assailants fatally stabbed a Jewish yeshiva student in downtown Hebron. In retaliation half a dozen Jewish settlers from Kiryat Arba killed four students of Hebron Islamic College. A climax came in April 1984 with the arrest of Jewish extremists who had plotted to blow up the Dome of the Rock in Jerusalem. It was against this background that Kahane was elected to the Knesset on the Kach ticket in July 1984. He had received the backing of Jewish Israelis such as Dr Baruch Goldstein and Yona Khaykin, a computer programmer, living in Hebron's Jewish Quarter. 'We came to Hebron [from Boston, USA] out of a sense of adventure and outrage,' said Khaykin. 'The adventure is building a Jewish kingdom. The outrage is that Arabs are still here.'[11]

The Knesset membership gave a sort of respectability to Kahane and his ideology which they had lacked before. Israel's fiasco in Lebanon following its invasion of that country in 1982, and the economic crisis caused by hyperinflation in the mid-1980s, created a feeling of despair in the country, especially among the young, which Kahane was able to channel into his anti-Arab campaign. A poll of young Jews aged 15–18, taken in April 1985, showed 42 per cent backing the idea of expelling Arabs from Israel, the West Bank and Gaza. A survey of Israeli voters in October revealed a 9 per cent support for Kahane, an eight-fold increase in a year, which would have given his Kach group 11 seats in the Knesset.[12] This worried the major parties, Labour and Likud, which then shared power in a national unity administration. At their behest the Knesset passed a law which barred a political party preaching racism from contesting elections. On the eve of the November 1988 parliamentary poll, the Government ruled that Kach was racist and could not participate in the forthcoming election. When Kahane challenged this in the Supreme Court, he lost. Had Kach been allowed to enter the race, it would have won six Knesset seats. In October 1990 Kahane was assassinated in New York while he was addressing a meeting.[13]

Among those who were shattered by this news was Baruch Goldstein. He now joined the Kahane Hai (Hebrew, Kahane Lives) group, headed by the deceased leader's son, Baruch Kahane. Goldstein got elected to the local council of Kiryat Arba on the Kahane Hai ticket, the only candidate of its kind. But such was the popularity of Kahane's ideas in Kiryat Arba that, to the delight of Goldstein, the local council decided to name the settlement's principal square, situated near its main, gated entrance, after Meir Kahane. A memorial tablet read: 'In memory of Rabbi Meir Kahane, a lover of Israel, a giant in Torah, heroic in deeds, murdered in sanctification of the Divine Name.'

Being a doctor and a local councillor, Goldstein was popular among the Kiryat Arba residents, many of whom worked in Jerusalem, and travelled by bus. After dark the hour-long drive along a partly narrow, winding road, flanked by terraced hills, running through Palestinian villages, towns and refugee camps, was hazardous. The Israeli buses, easily identifiable by their make and markings, and their yellow licence plates, were targets of Palestinian attacks by rocks and petrol bombs, an activity which escalated during the intifada that erupted in late 1987.[14] Those Kiryat Arbans who got injured in these instances of violence were treated by Goldstein.

In line with other Jewish settlements, Kiryat Arba was strongly opposed to the Israel-PLO Accord of September 1993. It saw this as a betrayal of the concept of 'redeeming' the land of all of biblical Eretz Israel. On the other side, radical Palestinians perceived it as a betrayal of the historic rights of the Palestinian people to all of Palestine under British mandate, and vowed to continue the intifada. So tension escalated in the Occupied Territories.

The pattern of the past repeated itself. A typical example was the fatal stabbing of Chaim Mizrahi, a resident of the Beit El Jewish settlement by a Palestinian in late October 1993. Its chief rabbi, Zalman Melamed, invoked the Judaistic doctrine of *pikuach nefesh* (Hebrew, preservation of soul), which states that saving (Jewish) life overrides all aspects of the Halacha, Jewish Law. (This Judaistic doctrine is open to different interpretations, depending on whether or not a religious authority decides to interpret human life *per se* or narrows it to Jewish life.) The Beit El residents took the cue and went on a rampage, smashing the cars of the Palestinians living in the proximity of the settlement, hoping thus to deter future attacks on Jews. The overall pattern of inter-ethnic violence – outside of the official Israeli action and reaction – was stray armed assaults on vulnerable, individual Jews by young Palestinians; a communal response by the Jews, who damaged Palestinian cars and property, overturned vegetable and fruit stalls in Arab markets, and blocked major West Bank roads with burning tyres; and an escalation by

Palestinians in the form of hurling rocks and petrol bombs at Jewish buses and cars, invariably carrying yellow Israeli license plates.

There were periodic variations to the general pattern. For example, in mid-December 1993 the Jewish settlers killed three Palestinians as they were returning home from work outside the village of Tarqumiya near Hebron. A month later a group of militant Palestinians engaged in a gunbattle with IDF soldiers in Hebron, and lost four men. Tension rose as the Muslim fasting month of Ramadan, considered holy, started on 11 February. Two days later a group of Hamas activists, posing as Israeli collaborators, lured a Shin Beth agent to a rendezvous in Ramallah, and killed him. To most Kiryat Arbans, including Goldstein, this was a new and menacing development. They were not reassured when on 16 February IDF soldiers shot dead a wanted Palestinian radical in the village of Halhoul near Hebron – an event that triggered serious Palestinian rioting in the village.

Midway through Ramadan, on 25 February, was Purim, a Jewish festival which celebrates the Israelites' vengeance against the Amaleks, a fierce bedouin tribe of Syria, descended from Esau (Genesis 36:12), whose members attacked them in the Sinai during their wanderings (c. 1700–1250 BC), and whose destruction was enjoined by the Old Testament. On the eve of Purim, Goldstein went to the Tomb of the Patriarchs/Ibrahimi Mosque to hear the scroll of Esther, which states *inter alia* that Haman, Persian King Xerxes's (r. 486–65 BC) Prime Minister, who wanted to annihilate the Jews, was a descendant of Agag, an Amalek king (3:1). Halfway through the service, conducted in a room inside the complex, some Arabs in the surrounding area shouted 'Itbah al Yahud (Kill the Jews)'. Goldstein felt humiliated. As a follower of Kahane, he believed that Amalekites were not just a particular tribe at a particular time and place, but an ongoing anti-Jewish entity which perpetuated itself by acquiring different forms in different generations. Having appeared as Nazis in Germany in the pre-1945 world, the Amaleks had taken on the form of the Arabs, especially Palestinian Arabs. It was a religious duty of pious Jews to confront and annihilate presentday Amaleks, Kahane had stressed, thus decimating evil, and paving the way for the coming of the Messiah.

Early next morning around 5 a.m., on Purim, 14 Adar 5754 AM (Anno Mundi), Goldstein returned to the Tomb of the Patriarchs/Ibrahimi Mosque clad in the army uniform he kept at home for reserve duty, which now concealed his Gail assault rifle and several magazines. To the soldiers on duty he was a familiar figure, and they let him pass without search. Inside hundreds of Muslim Palestinians were offering their dawn prayer. Goldstein walked into the prayer hall, and standing behind a pillar fired 111 bullets from his assault rifle. The result was 29 people dead and 67 injured. He was beaten to death by the outraged Palestinians.

The massacre sent shock waves at home and abroad. The PLO suspended its talks with Israel on the implementation of the Declaration of Principles it had signed five months earlier. The Israeli Government of Yitzhak Rabin, deeply embarrassed, was quick to condemn the killings. President Ezer Weizman called the Hebron slaughter 'the worst thing that has happened in the history of Zionism'. Numerous private and official Israeli and Jewish organizations expressed sorrow, and denounced the slaughter and its perpetrator. However, many of the condemnations by individual Jews and voluntary Jewish bodies apportioned equal blame to Goldstein and the Israeli authorities which, they said, had abandoned the Jewish settlers.

A similar division existed among the residents of Kiryat Arba. Several of them, acolytes of Kahane, publicly argued that the people Goldstein killed were not innocent men at prayer in a place of worship, but modern day Amaleks, the followers of Adolf Hitler and Yasser Arafat; and by avenging the Amaleks, he had sanctified God's name, *kiddush HaShem* (Hebrew, sanctification of the Lord), a central mission of the Jews.[15] Among those who adopted this stand were the leaders of Kahane Hai and other fringe ultra-nationalist groups, now banned, who, having gone underground, gave interviews to radio stations in Israel from undisclosed locations. Their position was in contrast to the central thrust of the mainstream Israeli press commentary which condemned the Hebron massacre as the crazed work of a psychopath rather than a politically motivated outrage.

Admiration for Goldstein did not cease with public eulogies at his funeral which, despite heavy rain, was attended by more than 1,000 Kiryat Arbans. The elementary state secular school's management instructed teachers to limit remarks about the Hebron massacre to Goldstein's 'saintly nature' and his self-sacrificing devotion to his medical practice. At Hebron's Talmud Torah elementary school, children were regularly bussed to Goldstein's grave to recite Psalms in his memory. A local poll revealed that 63 per cent of Kiryat Arbans wanted the Government to recognize Goldstein's widow, Miriam, as a 'war widow', since he was killed by Arabs.[16]

In contrast, my Hebrew interpreter, Rafi, felt too embarrassed to translate the inscription engraved on Goldstein's grave, its large horizontally laid white stone, shining in the March sun, surrounded on a windblown hillock by several black plastic chairs. He needed persuading to do so:

Here is buried
The Saint Dr Rabbi Baruch Kapal Goldstein
May the Lord avenge his death
He is the son of Rabbi Israel
Who is still alive
(May he live long)
He is the seventh generation of
Rabbi Shneor Zalman Goldstein
He gave his life for the sake of
The People of Israel, their Torah and Community
His hands were clean
And his heart pure
He was born on 5 Teveth 1947 [5707 AM] (Tafshen
   Yad Zion)
He was murdered for sanctification of the Lord on 14
   Adar 1994 [5754 AM]

A young couple, speaking Russian, arrived. The man, wearing a skullcap, placed a small stone on the grave and kissed it. Rafi squirmed with embarrassment. Five months earlier, in October 1994, an unknown admirer of Goldstein had left a leaflet behind: it declared, 'According to the Halacha, [Premier] Yitzhak Rabin deserved the death penalty for treason.' This was soon after the authorities had arrested about a dozen Kiryat Arbans, including Lt Oren Edri and Rabbi Ido Alba, on suspicion of forming a terrorist group to kill Arabs for attacking Jews. Citing the Gemara, in tractate *Eruvin*, Rabbi Ido Alba said in an interview with the *Jerusalem Post* of 18 January 1995: '[I]t decrees that one must wage war against Gentiles who attack Jews, or who even try to harm the Jewish community. My only "crime" is that I believe that one must carry out what is written ... According to the Torah, we are in a situation of *pikuach nefesh* in time of war, and in such a situation one may kill any Gentile. According to the Halacha, there is no such thing as innocent. No Gentile on the side that is at war against us is innocent.' After these arrests signs appeared in the settlement naming suspected informers of the Shin Beth. Planting informers in Kiryat Arba was comparatively easy. Unlike at other Jewish settlements, the local council there did not screen its prospective residents. This had to do with the biblical tradition, which maintained that Hebron was a 'town of refuge', where even a Jewish murderer, pursued by the avenging family of the victim, could take sanctuary. As it was Kiryat Arba's current residents included Menachem Livni, the mastermind behind the plan in 1984 to blow up the Dome of the Rock.[17] Following a presidential pardon after he had served only seven years of a life sentence for murder, Livni was now head of the settlement's 'science think-tank', engaged in developing scientific and technological patents.

Rafi and I had arrived at Goldstein's grave after spending time with Naom Arnon at the public relations office of the Kiryat Arba settlement, a sturdy, two-storey stone building. The ante-room of Arnon's office had a black and white print of Rabbi Avraham Yitzhak HaCohen Kook. A man with an aquiline nose and a flowing salt-and-pepper beard, wearing a round fur hat, popular with an ultra-Orthodox sect, gazed from a black-framed picture, surrounded, exotically, by a full-size wooden plough nailed to the wall, and two animal saddles, hanging by chains from the roof. In the lobby a Jewish history of Hebron was on display on a wall. 'Genesis:23 has all the [historical] details,' Arnon told us in his modest office. 'Genesis:49 refers to the Jacob's Well. According to Judges:3, twelve spies were sent by Moses to Canaan to evaluate the Promised Land. Ten of them said "We don't have the power to occupy the Promised Land". But Kaleb and Joshua disagreed. They encouraged the Israelites to conquer the Promised Land, and succeeded. See how history repeats itself.' Arnon paused, allowing us time to absorb the significance of his statement. 'One of the pictures on the wall you saw explains that Aviner, a general of King Saul, was buried in Hebron. King David had his capital in Hebron for seven and a half years before moving it to Jerusalem.'

Walking around Kiryat Arba, I felt I was in one of the posher Jewish suburbs of Greater East Jerusalem: street after street of four storey apartment blocks of cream-coloured stone, interspersed with playgrounds and grassy slopes. Among other things I now understood how and why the Jewish settlers, being 5 per cent of the overall population of the West Bank and Gaza, were consuming 40 per cent of the water.[18]

By visiting Kiryat Arba, a Jewish settlement in the Judean section of the West Bank established during the Labour rule, I had complemented my earlier trip to an equally important settlement of Elon Moreh in the Samarian zone of the West Bank, which too had been established when Labour was in power. Here Rafi and I had placed ourselves into the hands of Pinchas Fuchs.

Pinchas Fuchs was a small, slim man of 53, with shining grey eyes flickering behind his glasses, and a luxuriant white beard. On the mild February morning, when I met him, he was wearing a blue-striped button-down shirt, with a breast pocket armed with a ballpoint pen, dark blue pants, with four white tassels hanging from its waist, black shoes and white socks. A leading member of the Elon Moreh (Hebrew, Acorn/Valley of Moreh) Jewish settlement, home to 1,500 people from a score of countries, he took foreign visitors around the settlement. Over time, it soon dawned on me, he had perfected a system of conducting a tour which was as thorough as it was economical in time and effort. A sprawling settlement atop a stony mountain, it needed such an approach; and Fuchs was well qualified to provide it. A PhD in chemical engineering from City University of New York, with an undergraduate degree from Yeshiva University, Brooklyn, he worked (from home) for a computer firm, based in Natanya, 40 kilometres west, and knew how to devise most efficient systems.

An urban man to his fingertips, born and raised first in Newark, New Jersey, and then in New York, how did Fuchs and his family end up on top of a desolate mountain near Nablus in the West Bank? Through a series of decisions, none too dramatic when seen in isolation.

In 1976 he and his family of three joined some 5,000 other American Jews who made the aliya to Israel that year. On arrival he started working as a chemical engineer in Rehovot, south-east of Tel Aviv. He and his family would have continued to live in Rehovot, a pleasant place of 60,000 souls, reminiscent of small-town America, had he not visited an old friend, Avi Yoram, at the army camp of Kadume, 10 kilometres west of Nablus. Yoram was one of the pioneers who had struggled hard to set up a Jewish settlement near Nablus – Shechem of the biblical times – after the victory of Israel on the West Bank in 1967. After frustrating their repeated attempts, the Labour government, headed by Yitzhak Rabin, relented and, as a compromise, allowed the agitators to live in caravans inside Kadume army compound. Finally in early 1977 it permitted the settlers to move out and establish a settlement at Elon Moreh. The inside story of that U-turn by Labour, revealed since then, showed Shimon Peres actively helping the Gush Emunim agitators, overtly and covertly, in order to undermine the standing of Rabin who, by defeating him, narrowly, in the leadership contest, had won his abiding animosity. This was a re-run of the bitter rivalry that had existed a decade earlier between Yigal Allon and Moshe Dayan, which shaped the decision of the Labour-led national unity government of Golda Meir in the case of Hebron-Kiryat Arba. The net losers in both cases were the Palestinians.

Though, thanks to the scandal about the illegal bank account in the United States of Yitzhak Rabin's wife, Leah, Peres led Labour to fight the May 1977 parliamentary poll, he lost – to the right-wing Likud. That set the seal on Elon Moreh. The jubilant settlers welcomed the new Prime Minister, Menachem Begin, at the Sukkot festival in July. An equally jubilant Begin declared: 'There will be many more Elon Morehs.' And there were.

Early the next year Begin gave permission for another Jewish settlement in the area, near the Palestinian village of Rojeib, five kilometres from Nablus. Following Yoram's trail, Fuchs joined 14 other Jews and their families to resettle the Promised Land at Rojeib. Instead of pitching tents they parked their caravans on the site. The Palestinians protested. They appealed to the High Court. They won. The court ruled against the state confiscation of the Palestinian land, arguing that the Government had failed to establish the security ground for its action. (Had it confiscated land on the basis of 'public purpose', instead of 'security purpose', it would have probably won.) 'So the IDF threw me out of my own house in Israel!' said Fuchs, still scandalized.

Having lost the new site in early 1980, the caravan-owning families moved to Elon Moreh, a much larger assembly of caravans. Three years were to elapse before there were buildings ready for occupation. Thus solidified, Elon Moreh expanded steadily. Indeed under the fiendish energy of Ariel Sharon, a right-wing politician of enormous (physical and political) weight, heading the Israeli housing ministry from May 1990 to June 1992, the settlement, injected with caravans shipped in from all over the world, ballooned.

Today Elon Moreh is a well-run community, with an impressive infrastructure: schools, local authority offices, regional council offices, an infirmary, three synagogues and well-stocked shops. It is home to a spice mill and a meat processing plant. Together these establishments provide livelihoods to a high proportion of the settlers. The rest work nearby, none in Tel Aviv or Jerusalem, which are too distant for daily commuting.

A nine-member council, elected annually and headed by the mayor, administers the settlement. One of its offices, housed in a semi-dark Nissen hut, where I met Fuchs, felt like a bunker. A bespectacled, middle-aged woman in a print dress, wearing a pancake hat, operated a telephone exchange and a radio transmitter, glued to a mauve-coloured steel desk, with military precision. A poster in blue and red on a bare wall called on the reader to 'Wake Up from the Nightmare of the Peace Process'.

Unusually among the Jewish settlements on the West Bank and Gaza Strip, Elon Moreh has no perimeter fence. 'If we put up a fence then the Arabs will plant olive trees two inches from it, even though olive trees are not native to this area,' Fuchs explained. 'Moreover, once you erect a fence you define the boundaries, like a prison. All of Eretz Israel is ours.' Who decided about the fence? 'We put the matter to the vote here in 1991, and the people rejected the idea,' Fuchs replied, triumphantly.

The absence of a fence, however, did not mean absence of security. A barrier at the entrance to the settlement was a dramatic reminder to the newcomer of the residents' concern for security. 'At night a spotlight is focused on the valley downwards,' said Fuchs. 'There is a beltway around the settlement, and it's patrolled by an army Jeep – with a soldier sitting in the open-ended back, with his machine-gun pointed outwards. There is an army post, with walkie-talkies, in constant contact with the defence ministry in Tel Aviv.' Later, near the army post, I saw a three-man unit in a Jeep, with a young, sunken-eyed soldier in an olive-green uniform sitting at the open end, his machine-gun pointing outwards. He waved warmly at Fuchs, his weapon stirring the stale, afternoon air. Fuchs waved back, reassured.

Security, local and national, was very much on the mind of Fuchs – and also ancient history – as he surveyed the scene from the Elon Moreh peak at an altitude of 760 metres above sea level. He pointed to the Mount Ebal (Hebrew, curse) summit, altitude 850 metres, the highest in the northern West Bank (which he called Shomorin, the Hebrew name for Samaria), crowned with a darkly-painted steel tower. 'See the antenna?' he asked. 'It picks up as soon as a Jordanian aircraft takes off in Jordan. The flight time between Amman and Tel Aviv is 2.5 minutes, exactly. Without that antenna there'd be no warning to the IDF. None whatsoever. The antenna is also at the centre of telephone communications in the region.' Beyond Mount Ebal, he continued, was Natanya, and then the Mediterranean Sea. He turned 90 degrees. 'To the north lies Lake Tiberias, the Sea of Galilee.' Another 90-degree turn. 'East,' he said, facing a hesitant sun. 'You can see into the Jordan Valley, also Mount Hermon, though they're shrouded in fog this morning.' I looked. I saw an Israeli army base in the valley.

Having finished his geography lesson Fuchs turned to history. 'After crossing the Jordan Valley our patriarchs would take this road to Shechem, the main artery connecting it with Jerusalem and Hebron,' he said confidently. 'Abraham had taken the same road [pause] probably. Jacob took the same road. And several centuries later Joshua trod the same road to return to the Promised Land.' The matter-of-fact manner in which Fuchs talked was impressive and irritating in parts. To all purposes, the events of the ancient age, dating back three to four millennia, were as real to him as the ones printed in today's *Yediot Aharonot* or *Ma'ariv*. Later, in the cosy kitchen of his two-storey home, furnished with all modern conveniences, he could not read a passage from the Old Testament without relating it to the present. While reading Genesis 23:15 – 'And Abraham weighed to Ephron . . . 400 shekels of silver' [to pay for the Machpelah cave to bury Sarah] – he looked at me, and said: 'See, Abraham paid for the land, it says here in black and white. Can the Arabs today show that they paid for the land they claim to be theirs? Can they?' Faced with such a rhetorical question, all I could do was to fix my eyes firmly on my notebook and scribble furiously. 'You do know your Torah well,' I muttered, lifting my eyes briefly.

'I ought to,' he said. 'I read it daily. I know it by heart, almost.'

While spending the day with Fuchs I could not help noticing his propensity to direct our conversations into a biblical context. He told me of the six-week-old murder of Ofra Felix, a young daughter of a local settler. She was on her way home from the Jewish settlement of Beit El, and was killed near Shilo. 'Our first tabernacle was built near Shilo,' Fuchs said. And Beit El had special resonances for him. It was there, he told me, that Jacob, having received the divine promise of the land ('whereon thou liest') in his dream, anointed a stone pillar on the spot, and named it Beit El. 'Genesis 28: 18–19,' Fuchs concluded, with a flourish.

The Jewish settlement in Beit El, only 19 kilometres from central Jerusalem, established in the proximity of the twin Palestinian towns of Ramallah and Al Bireh, was founded in the same year Fuchs joined the settlers' movement: 1978. But, a strictly religious settlement, it took only those Jews who were Orthodox, often affiliated to the National Religious Party. The initial population of 30 families had mushroomed to 600, a total of 4,000 people, including 150 yeshiva students; and the enlarged settlement had officially split into two: Beit El Alaf and Beit El Beth.

Since Beit El is considered by the Israeli Government as part of the Jewish belt it wishes to surround Jerusalem with, it belongs to a different category, in official reckoning, from Kiryat Arba and Elon Moreh.

Here our guide was Zeev Libinskin. A plump, hairy man of medium height, 40, he sported a dense, black beard, and was dressed in grey trousers, white shirt and a blue baseball cap. He had something in common with Rabbi Moshe Levinger and Rabbi Shlomo Aviner, a resident of Beit El and the head of the Yeshiva Torah Chaim in the Muslim Quarter of Jerusalem's Old Town: he was, like them, a graduate of the Merkaz HaRav Kook Yeshiva. 'Its policy is to encourage its students to spread out in Judea and Samaria, and set up settlements there,' Libinskin told us. That is why, he explained, he was in Beit El, his place of abode since 1980. But, like Rabbi Aviner, he worked in Jerusalem at a yeshiva, in its public relations department.

Before reaching Beit El settlements, I saw a vast, fenced army base, with rows of Nissen huts, tall communications towers and military stores. All the soldiers from our bus, which had originated in Jerusalem, got off near the base. It was indeed the headquarters of the military government of Israel in charge of administering the occupied West Bank. Outside the base, but inside the Beit El settlement, near its unfenced entrance were four vast shooting ranges, gouged out of a side of a small hill. 'Tut . . . tut . . . tut!' – all day long the firings punctuated the air.

'How do you cope with this constant barrage of arms fire?' I asked the thin, shy manager of the recording studio of Channel 7, a private right-wing radio station based in Beit El Beth. 'We have a perfectly soundproof studio,' he replied. 'In any case most of our programme consists of playing popular music from tapes or records. As for interviews, we conduct most of these over the telephone.' Since the Israeli Government does not allow private radio or television stations transmitting facilities inside the country, Channel 7 was able to function by broadcasting from a ship off Tel Aviv outside the territorial waters of Israel. 'We have 25 per cent of the audience, most of it young,' the studio manager claimed. 'We're a thorn in the Labour government's side, and we love it.'

The Yitzhak Rabin administration came in for criticism from Libinskin too as he took us around the settlement in his van. 'This government says that our presence here is an impediment to peace,' Libinskin averred in his monotonous voice. 'We say that only our presence here would ensure peace.' He halted in an area full of nicely finished houses, all topped with the unmistakable sun-reflectors for heating water. 'There are 40 newly built empty house here,' he began. 'The Government does not want us to sell these. But we are putting pressure, and it is likely to bend.'

Libinskin's optimism was well founded. A cool examination of the policies pursued by the Labour-led administration revealed an equivocal position on the Jewish settlements.

Four months after Rabin's cabinet assumed office in July 1992, it declared a halt to all publicly funded construction in the West Bank and Gaza, thus removing the hurdle holding up the US administration's willingness to be a guarantor of Israel's $10 billion loan in world markets. As for privately financed construction in the Occupied Territories, it told the building contractors that they would need an approval from a Special Cases Committee chaired by Noah Kinarti, the chief adviser to Rabin on Jewish settlements, well known for his hawkish views on the subject. Also it remained an official policy to allow the 'thickening' of Jewish settlements along the Green Line, the pre-1967 frontier of Israel, as a prelude to an (undeclared) plan to annex the area as part of the final status agreement with the PLO.

It soon emerged that Noah Kinarti was quite liberal in issuing 'special permits' to private builders. And the hawkish Housing Minister, Binyamin Ben Eliezer, was only too willing to provide the infrastructure of roads, electricity, water and sewerage facilities. 'Even where [Jewish] settlers broke into completed houses that the Government had deliberately left unsold, Ben Eliezer has supplied the infrastructure,' revealed Leslie Susser, an Israeli journalist, in early 1995. 'Despite the "freeze", enough houses have been built for the Jewish population in the [occupied] territories to grow by more than 10 per cent to over 140,000 (a figure based on households paying municipal taxes) – since the September 1993 signing of the Declaration of Principles with the Palestinians.'[19]

This revelation came in the wake of a successful demonstration in January 1995 by the inhabitants of the Palestinian village of Al Khadr, along with leftist Jewish Israelis, against the building of 500 houses on the nearby Givat Tamar (Hebrew, Hill of Tamar) two kilometres from Efrat, a large Jewish settlement between Bethlehem and Hebron. The Palestinians claimed that the Givat Tamar belonged to Al Khadr village. Reports in the Israeli press disclosed that Premier Rabin's special adviser on Jewish settlements, Kinarti, had approved the project in January 1993, and that Rabin had endorsed it in August. When the matter became public in December 1994, the left-wing Meretz ministers objected to the bureaucratic Special Cases Committee, and got Rabin to replace it with a ministerial committee to vet new construction, with a view to making it hard for the Jewish settlers to get building permits. Faced with a highly publicized protest on Givat Tamar, Rabin backtracked. But later, at his behest, the newly appointed ministerial committee gave a go-ahead for a 270-house project on Givat Zayit, a hill closer to Efrat.

A random survey undertaken by the *Jerusalem Report* in February 1995 revealed that ongoing Jewish settlement activity was in progress almost everywhere in the West Bank, particularly in the following three sectors: the area around Jerusalem, the Kfar Etzion bloc near Bethlehem, and the zone north-east of Tel Aviv, where Israel, at its narrowest, is 14 kilometres wide. Outside of these areas, construction was either in progress or in the offing at 14 other settlements, divided roughly around Nablus (Elon Moreh, Kadume and Eli), Jerusalem (Dolev, Nahliel, Kokhay HaShahr, Pisgat Zeev and Maaleh Adumim), and Hebron (Kiryat Arba, Telem, Adora, Otniel, Shima and Pnei Hever). As a result house prices in the settlements near Jerusalem and Greater Tel Aviv – such as Alfei Menashe and Ariel (population 12,000) – had risen by 40 per cent over the previous six months.[20]

These developments stemmed from an unpublicized, multi-prong strategy of Rabin, which was geared to achieving both short-term aims (tied to the September 1993 Accord with the PLO) and long-term aims (to be secured through the final status agreement with the PLO). An acolyte of Yigal Allon, Rabin was still wedded to the concepts underlying the Allon Plan of 1970: to treat the Jordan Valley as the security perimeter of Israel; and to gain control of as much of the land and water of the West Bank as possible while avoiding the thankless task of administering hostile West Bankers and Gazans. (The third concept of returning the truncated West Bank and Gaza to Jordan in exchange for a peace treaty had become redundant.) In the quarter century that had passed since then, Israel had obtained majority control of the West Bank's land and water. It had also implanted some 135,000 Jews into the territory, plus another 160,000 in Greater

East Jerusalem. Having conceded the principle of self-rule for Palestinians, to be administered by the PLO, Rabin seemingly realized the potential of using the 128 Jewish settlements in the West Bank for two distinct purposes: (a) a means of ensuring Israel's security along the lines laid out by Allon, and (b) a rationale to annex parts of the West Bank adjoining Israel. Regarding (a), ministerial studies had concluded that 14 Jewish settlements in the Jordan Valley and another group of two dozen around Jerusalem, including the Kfar Etzion bloc, would be enough to underwrite the security of the Jewish state and its capital. As for (b), a study by an Israeli think-tank had concluded that by annexing about one-tenth of the West Bank along the Green Line, Israel could reclaim some 70 per cent of its Jewish citizens now settled in the Palestinian territory. To align plans (a) and (b), a formula would have to be found which confers on the Jordan Valley's Jewish settlements a status that lies midway between being an integral part of Israel and an integral part of the Palestinian entity. This will be one of the more testing problems facing the Israeli and PLO negotiators if and when they embark on devising the final status accord.

For the period of the interim agreement, which ends in May 1999, Rabin decided against moving any settlers. Despite repeated calls from various quarters, including the Peace Now group, to remove the 400-odd Jewish settlers from downtown Hebron in the wake of the Ibrahimi Mosque massacre in early 1994, he stuck to his position. Indeed he went on to combine increased Israeli military presence in the West Bank with an accelerated programme of road building to interconnect the Jewish settlements into integrated blocs, and to provide them with approach roads, bypassing Palestinian population areas, to Jerusalem. The overall purpose was to prevent scattered Jewish communities from turning into besieged outposts. But the dovish ministers put a different spin on it. 'The IDF cannot redeploy [as a precondition for holding elections to the Palestinian Council] without building new roads – for military purposes as well,' explained Shimon Peres, the Foreign Minister, engaged in face-to-face talks with Yasser Arafat, in early 1995. Along with this activity went Rabin's policy of quietly issuing 'special permits' to private building companies to construct more houses in the Jewish settlements, and reclassifying certain settlements as 'development areas', thus entitling their residents to tax concessions. This was part of the reason why the Jewish settlers' anti-Government agitation in the summer of 1995 fizzled out.

On the other hand, by doing what it did, the Israeli Government created hundreds of Palestinian enclaves – shown graphically in the maps accompanying the Israeli-PLO agreement signed in September 1995 – which made the prospect of a viable Palestinian state in the future a virtual impossibility.

But Labour and Meretz supporters argued that the only other alternative the PLO had was to negotiate with a future Likud-led administration. That party's stance remained hard-line. Its interpretation of the United Nations Security Council Resolution 242, the foundation of the Middle East Peace Conference held in 1991, was that the resolution mentioned 'territories for peace', not 'the territories for peace'. Having given up Sinai, forming 88 per cent of the total conquered Arab territories, Israel need not withdraw from the rest. The hawkish position within Likud, summarized by Ariel Sharon, was: 'Peace for peace; Israel should not offer Arabs more than what they are offering Israel – an end to hostilities.'

Once the freshly elected Prime Minister, Binyamin Netanyahu, and MKs had been sworn in, after the May 1996 elections, the new government adopted the Likud line on the peace procss, replacing Labour's 'territorial compromise' for peace with Likud's 'peace for peace'.

This signalled a firm setback for the Palestinians and their territorial aspirations.

9

THE WEST BANK:

A Diminishing Heritage of Palestinians

It is rare to have an individual whose life roughly mirrors the chronicle of his/her country or territory; and rarer still to encounter such a person. But I was lucky. I found Badran Bader Jaber in Hebron: he fitted the bill.

I met him in February 1995 at the University Graduates Association building – a nondescript two-storey structure near the dilapidated offices of the local municipality along King Abdullah Road – with a spacious foyer filled with massive, deep-seated couches and divans, upholstered in brown plastic. Two contrasting images dominated the semi-lit hall: a large painting in black with touches of red, signifying blood, portraying the massacre at the Ibrahimi Mosque/Tomb of the Patriarchs a year earlier, and another, a pleasing pastoral scene in green and golden yellow. Badran Jaber arrived, carrying a walking stick curled at the top – a good-looking man of average height and medium build, with receding grey hair and a moustache. He was wearing grey trousers, a tweed jacket and a dark tie. A veteran of a score of hunger strikes in jail, he looked older than his 47 years, 26 of which he had endured under Israeli occupation. He had spent 10 in prison, and another four under 'town arrest', his current status.

'I was born in Hebron, and am a graduate of Jordan University, Amman, 1969,' Jaber began. 'That year my elder brother, Fathi, was arrested by the Israelis, and sentenced to 25 years in jail. But he was released in 1985 in a prisoner exchange [between Israel and the Popular Front for the Liberation of Palestine-General Command led by Ahmad Jibril]. In between, I was jailed four times.'

1969: on 5 June, the second anniversary of the June 1967 Arab-Israeli War, West Bankers staged a general strike in protest against the Israeli occupation.

'My first arrest came in 1972,' Jaber continued. 'I spent four months under interrogation. Then I served six months under administrative detention. This is the measure introduced by the British mandate during emergency. You are detained for up to six months at a time without any charges being pressed against you. I was released in 1973.'

1973: in August the Palestine National Front (PNF), consisting of Palestinians of all political hues and non-political professionals, was formed clandestinely as an autonomous West Bank and Gaza affiliate of the Palestine Liberation Organization, which was banned. The stand-off between the Israelis and the Arabs in the October 1973 War gave a boost to the PNF. Between then and April 1976, the PNF staged demonstrations and strikes, which paralysed the Occupied Territories periodically. The Israeli Government, headed by Yitzhak Rabin, with Shimon Peres as Defence Minister, responded by army firings (which took a toll of 30 Palestinian lives in the first half of 1976), long curfews, arrests and administrative detentions, deportations and house demolitions.

'My next arrest came in 1975,' Jaber went on. 'One day, returning home from my country cottage, I saw some *fedayeen* (Arabic, self-sacrificers; fig. commandos) outside Hebron. They arrested me because they said that I did not report the presence of *fedayeen* to the IDF. I served three and a half years behind bars.'

1976: Prime Minister Rabin called elections to 24 municipalities in the West Bank in the expectation that the PNF would boycott the poll, thus enabling 'co-operating Palestinians' to assume local power. But the PNF contested the poll, and won 18 of the 24 municipalities, including almost all major towns and cities.

1978: following the signing in September 1978 of the Camp David Accords by Premier Menachem Begin of Israel and President Anwar Sadat of Egypt, which included limited autonomy provisions for the Palestinians (as residents, divorced from the land where they lived and deprived of sovereignty), the next month nationalist West Bankers publicly formed the National Guidance Committee. It was headed by 22 local mayors and leaders of trade unions and professional syndicates. Among other things it resisted the Israeli-sponsored Palestinian armed militia, called Village Councils. The military regime reacted with draconian press censorship, widespread arrests and deportations.

'I was hardly out for two years when I was picked up again by the IDF in 1980,' continued Jaber. 'The interrogation in prison went on for three months.'

1980: by then the Israeli military regime had dissolved most of the PNF-controlled local councils. In May 1980 it deported the mayors of Hebron (Fahd Qawasmeh) and the nearby Halhoul (Muhammad Milhem) as punishment for a Palestinian terrorist attack in Hebron, resulting in six Jewish deaths. Early the next month bomb attacks by Jewish terrorists on the mayors of Nablus and Ramallah – Bassam Shakaa and Karim Khalaf respectively – maimed them.

1981: on 8 November 1981 the Likud Government headed by Begin, with Ariel Sharon as Defence Minister, issued Order 947 to set up Civil Administration in Judea and Samaria under the Head of Civil Administration to be appointed by the Area Military Commander. The first head was Menachem Milson, professor of Arabic literature at Hebrew University, Jerusalem. West Bankers responded with strikes and demonstrations which were curbed by the IDF. A lull followed. Then in spring 1982 Palestinian protest revived, with schools and universities in the forefront. As before the Israeli Government responded with military gun-fire, largescale arrests and beatings, and house demoli-tions. In May 1982 it banned the National Guidance Com-mittee. The Occupied Territories were quiescent when Israel invaded Lebanon the following month. During 1977–82 West Bankers and Gazans mounted an average of 500 pro-tests annually. As for fatalities, the IDF killed 92 Palestinians between 1968 and 1983; and the Palestinians 36 Israelis, including 14 civilians.[1]

'My next imprisonment started in May 1985,' Jaber went on. 'I was accused of working as a member of a political organization. They said that someone told them that I had a leaflet by the Popular Front for the Liberation of Palestine, and that I gave it to a man in 1980. And they arrested me in 1985![2] I spent time in Ramallah and Hebron jails, and in Jneid near Nablus. In Jneid we went on hunger strike for 23 days to get back our rights. After the [Israeli] Minister of Police had a meeting with us in jail, they granted us all our rights in 1987, even our copy books. But they refused to let us transfer anything to the outside. For security reasons. I had made a copy book out of a dictionary of English to French and made it into an Arabic-French dictionary. I spent about 12 months working on it 14 hours a day. They confiscated it. More than once I have dreamt that I had it and that I took it to my colleagues at the school where I teach [sociology and geography] and said to them, "This is what I did in jail".'

1984–7: as the Israeli Government found itself unable to extricate itself from the quagmire of the Occupied Lebanon, Palestinians stepped up their protest. From late 1984 onwards there were random assaults on IDF soldiers and Jewish settlers, particularly in Hebron, Nablus and

Gaza. Enraged Israeli mobs took to meting out summary justice by lynching individual Palestinians in Israel and the Occupied Territories. In early August 1985 defence minister Yitzhak Rabin officially unveiled an 'iron fist' policy. The result was widespread arrests and administrative detentions, frequent closure of schools and universities, and demolition of the houses of the Palestinians suspected of anti-Israeli violence. In response West Bankers and Gazans mounted large demonstrations in the winter of 1986–7 and the following spring. During 1982–6, the average of annual protests varied between 3,000 and 4,400, a manyfold increase over the period of 1977–82.[3]

'I was arrested again in February 1988, the same administrative detention exercise,' said Jaber wearily. 'I was sent to the Ansar III detention camp south of Beersheba, because all the jails in the West Bank and Israel were full up.[4] There were tents everywhere at the Ansar III. We were in a military security zone, near a base. You could hear planes landing and taking off. There were some 5,000 prisoners and detainees. They elected me their leader. When [Defence Minister] Rabin visited Ansar III they told him about me. So when my maximum six month period [of adminstrative detention order] expired, they immediately slapped another one on me. This thing went on until November 1990.'

1988–90: this was the most virulent period of the intifada.[5]

'Since November 1990 I have been carrying this green ID instead of the normal orange ID [for West Bankers],' Jaber concluded, flashing his card. 'I can't leave Hebron. And this entitles an Israeli policeman or soldier to interrogate me and detain me for up to 96 hours without charge.'

I returned to Hebron about a month later, and interviewed Badran Jaber specifically to get his version of how the Jewish settlement in and around Hebron had come into existence. He drew a sketch on a piece of paper and marked the keys. Here is his account (see map on p.xii):

MARK (A): 'During the 1967 Six Day War, on 9 June, the IDF entered the Ibrahimi Mosque using armed force,' Jaber began. 'In early 1968 they set up an IDF base east of Hebron, for army purposes and manoeuvres. They closed the area of the Wadi (Arabic, Valley) al Hussein. [Defence minister] Moshe Dayan came here, and called the local leaders. He told them that the area would be closed, not confiscated, for military purposes. Our leaders consulted many lawyers, including Bahri Jalal Tamimi, the legal adviser to Hebron municipality. He said that the IDF had the authority to do what it was trying to do. We tried to return to our land and farm, but were barred.'

MARK (B): 'After the Battle of Karameh in Jordan [in March 1968] there was danger of the *fedayeen* striking in the West Bank. In April 1968 there was an incident at Fayaz Qawasmeh's hotel with the Jewish settlers. That is why the IDF moved the settlers from his hotel to the military base. The IDF had two pre-fabricated buildings for the settlers. It was the IDF's solution for the Qawasmeh's hotel incident. Later three donums (one-third of a hectare) of our [Bader] family land was confiscated. They did it for establishing Kiryat Arba. In mid-1969 Moshe Dayan had a meeting with the local leaders. He told them: "This is the city of our patriarchs. We are sons of Abraham, we have a place inside Hebron and near the tombs of the Patriarchs." Later the IDF moved the settlers from its base and took them to Kiryat Arba, which carried the sign: "Here will be built soon a big settlement." We tried to protest. But it was no use.[7] In 1970 they confiscated the industrial area, and joined it with Kiryat Arba. 400 donums [120 hectares]. They closed off a new area east of Kiryat Arba. The [1970] Black September events depressed the general Palestinian mood.'[8]

MARK (C): 'In 1970–71 the Israelis began using the IDF field for military training. They took over 1,000 donums [100 hectares]. They bulldozed trees, fences, summer cottages, everything, including my summer cottage, for military purposes. In 1971 they began to build sections A and B of this sketch – houses for settlers. In 1972 came the infrastructure: water, electricity, sewerage, streets, shops, clinics, police station, schools, kindergarten, telephones etc. There was much protest by Hebron people, but it was unsuccessful. The

Black September events had so destroyed our morale that the Palestinian activists could not guide the people forcefully.'

SECTION (D): 'In 1971–2 they confiscated the highest hill in the Hebron sector, Jalas Mountain, for a transmission tower. The area belonged to my relative, Abdul Hamid Jaber [then aged over 80], who owned more than 300 donums [30 hectares]. He was approached by the IDF, but he refused even to rent the plot. The other side of the Jalas Mountain belonged to the Morar family. It suffered the same fate as Abdul Hamid Jaber, who died in 1984. Of the cultivated land confiscated by the IDF were 17 donums [one and a half hectares] belonging to the family of my wife Hamida.'

SECTION (E): 'Within four years, by 1976 [under Labour rule], they completed the infrastructure, and brought in about 2,500 people. [Likud won power in May 1977.] In 1977–8 the Israelis took over more than 3,000 donums [300 hectares] north-west of Kiryat Arba: in Khalil al Dabe, Wadi al Ghurous, Buquan al Ful, Al Bouareh, Ein Bani Salim and Aroud Farahi. They [later] called the settlement Givat HaSinai – after the Sinai which Israel evacuated following the [1979] Egyptian-Israeli Peace Treaty. In 1982 they brought many settlers from Yamit settlement in Sinai after it had been dismantled [in April of that year].'

SECTION (F): 'In late 1983 the Israelis took over 3000 donums [300 hectares] at Tsagrat al Abid, including the Jordan Co-operative Housing Unit set up by the Jordanian Government, seven to eight houses. The IDF confiscated the area between Hebron and Saeer village, which is 11 kilometres from the centre of Hebron. In 1984 when the Palestinian lawyers, including Ali Safaraini of Ramallah and Elias Khouri of the Arab Lawyers League, looked up the regulation section for building at the Civil Administration Headquarters at Beit El they found that the IDF had cordoned off many plots without even informing the owners. The IDF had confiscated uncultivated land and not bothered to even inform the owners. They call it "Closed Military Area".'

All told?: 'By now the Kiryat Arba complex plus Givat HaSinai plus the closed IDF areas totalled 14,000 donums [1,400 hectares]. In 1968 the total was 1,400 donums [140 hectares]. Israelis start with a small stone and build it up into a mountain. The breakdown is: Kiryat Arba, Givat Mamre and Givat Avot together, 4,000 donums [400 hectares]; the closed military area, 6,000 donums [600 hectares]; and Givat HaSinai, 4,000 donums [400 hectares].

'But there is no end,' said Jaber. 'On 9 March [1995] the IDF confiscated 700 donums [70 hectares] of agricultural land in Wadi al Ghurous and Wadi al Hussein along with the vineyards opposite Tel Avot, to expand Tel Avot, a settlement with red-tiled houses you can see from Hebron.

'So far 65 per cent of the cultivated land of the Palestinians in the area has been confiscated by the IDF,' said Jaber, summing up. 'The trees in these lands include olives, grapes, figs, almonds, apricots, pistachios. It was like a part of Heaven, with different colours of the trees blossoming. When I was in my early teens [1957–61, under the Jordanians], I'd steal ripe fruit at night. Those were the days of my boyhood! There was a swimming pool. There was a natural spring. We would play and swim. Girls would pass and we would whistle. Those were the days!'[9] For the first time a smile flickered past his face.

Suddenly, what Rafi and I had seen a few days earlier, on our trek from Eliakam Haetzini's house in Givat Mamre to Kiryat Arba proper, a distance of two kilometres, became comprehensible. We went past a paratrooper base, consisting of some 30 large khaki tents – each tent equipped with an exhaust funnel for the heater – and a battery of water tanks for bathing. On the opposite side of the main road, a bus route, behind a stone embankment, were old Arab houses. As we plodded uphill along a curve, we went past a vineyard on the same side of the road as the IDF base. In the middle distance I saw an Arab working the soil with a donkey-driven plough. The original Kiryat Arba settlement had expanded so much from its initial modest beginning, I realized now, that it had now circumscribed Palestinian houses and fields. This also explained why the sprawling Kiryat Arba and its suburbs were not fenced all around. The fencing was robust and unbroken where the settlement faced Hebron proper, but disappeared from its ever-expanding rear.

This intermixing of the Muslim Arab and the Jew reaches its apotheosis at the Tomb of the Patriarchs/Ibrahimi Mosque in downtown Hebron, a derivative either of the Hebrew root hbr, meaning friend, or the Arabic word haber, meaning granary. The first surmise seems more apt: Muslim Arabs call the town Al Khalil al Rahman, The (Beloved) Friend of (God) the Merciful, or Al Khalil for short – a reference to Prophet Abraham/Ibrahim, whom Prophet Muhammad called the First Muslim, since he was the first to preach monotheism. The Tomb of the Patriarchs – containing the graves of Abraham and Sarah, Isaac/Yitzhak (Hebrew, laughter) Ishaq and Rebecca, and Jacob/Yaacov (later called Israel) and Leah – is the second holiest shrine of the Jews, after the Western Wall. The site, known officially among Muslims as Al Haram al Khalil, the Sanctuary of the Friend (Abraham), and popularly as the Ibrahimi Mosque, is the fourth holiest shrine in orthodox Islam – after Mecca, the birthplace of Prophet Muhammad; Medina, the deathplace of Muhammad; and Jerusalem, the site of the Al Aqsa Mosque from where Prophet Muhammad undertook a journey to Heaven and back. Muslim tradition has it that Prophet Muhammad visited the Al Haram al Khalil on his night flight from Mecca to Jerusalem.

Situated at the entrance to the fertile northern highlands from the arid southern region, Hebron was a strategic settlement, and a thriving town, when Abraham's wife Sarah died there in c. 1800 BC. Genesis 23:7–14 describes Abraham's purchase of the Cave of Machpela (the word may be related to the Hebrew word for 'double' or 'of doubles'), from its owner, Ephron son of Zohar, to bury Sarah.

Around 1250 BC, Moses led the Israelites from Sinai to the Hebron region. His successor, Joshua, conquered Hebron and other Canaanite areas in c. 1200 BC. His capture and destruction of Hebron is described in Joshua 10:36–7. But Hebron revived. After King Saul (r. c. 1020–10 BC), David (r. c. 1010–970 BC) chose Hebron as the capital of Judah, and was anointed there. Later, David was anointed as king of all of Israel in Hebron, which was also the site of the Ark of the Covenant. He moved his capital to

Jerusalem in c. 1002. Later Hebron became the base of David's rebellious son, Absalom (2 Samuel 15:10). The first Hasmonean king John Hyrcanus captured Hebron in 134 BC. Written references to the burial place of the patriarchs and the matriarchs, dating back to c. 200 BC, suggest that by the time King Hyrcanus arrived in Hebron, there was a structure built around the six cenotaphs. To protect them properly, Roman King Herod the Great constructed a rectangular perimeter of sturdy stone walls, partitioned approximately in the middle and surrounded by pavements. This basic shell remains intact. Over the centuries Byzantine, Crusader and Mameluke structures were built to create a complex that exists today.

The rectangular site, 60 metres by 32 metres – consisting of a subterranean chamber, the original Cave of Machpela, and a superstructure – appears on first sight as a massive fortress, all the more so because of the heavy presence of armed Israeli soldiers.

The waxing and waning of the powers of Jews, Christians and Muslims have left their marks on the oldest revered site of monotheism. Following the failed Jewish Revolt, the city was destroyed in AD 70, and Jews were banished. But as before Hebron came to life again and thrived. The Byzantinian basilica with four rows of columns, initiated by Emperor Justinian I (r. AD 527–65), was completed in AD 570. After Hebron fell to Caliph Omar ibn Khattab in AD 637 he converted the church into a mosque. He allowed the Jews not only to return but also to build a small synagogue within the Herodian precinct. Severe damage done to the premises by an earthquake in 1033 was not repaired when the Crusaders conquered Hebron in 1099.

After expelling the Jews from Hebron, the Crusaders renamed it Castellum, and converted the mosque and the adjoining synagogue into a church and a monastery. Written records show that an exploration of the underground caverns by the monks revealed a circular chamber containing bones, believed to be those of Abraham and Isaac, and another chamber behind the first, holding the bones of Jacob and 15 jars, containing the bones of his sons. The monks constructed a stairway to the caverns to assist pilgrims, who in 1170 included Rabbi Benjamin of Tudela.

Seventeen years later Saladin (r. 1171–93) captured Hebron. In 1191 he furnished the Great Mosque – also called Ishaqiye Mosque (Isaac's Mosque) – with a magnificent wooden pulpit. He allowed the Jews to return to Hebron. During the Mameluke period (1250–1517) the monument became an exclusively Muslim shrine. In 1267 Mameluke Sultan Baybar banned entry of non-Muslims into the Cave of Machpela. However, he let Jews pray through a window into the wall erected at the entrance of the cavern, located near the pulpit of the Isaac's Mosque. In 1318 the Mameluke sultan built the adjoining Jawliye Mosque, erected two towering square minarets capped with domed canopies, and added crenellation on top of the outer Herodian walls. He also added a small mosque containing, according to Muslims, the cenotaph of Joseph,[10] and another small mosque for women in the south-eastern corner of the complex. In a corner is a shrine which, according to Muslim tradition, holds a stone bearing a footprint of Adam which he is believed to have left on his way out of the Garden of Eden. In the 1330s followed the construction of aboveground cenotaphs of marble over the ones that lay subterraneanly – those of Isaac and Rebecca ending up inside the Isaac's Mosque, and the remaining in the courtyard outside this mosque. Each of the later was covered by an octagonal or hexagonal hall, with an interconnecting room, the Mameluke structures looking distinctive due to the use of alternative white and red stones. Once the aboveground cenotaphs were ready, and decorated with embroidered shrouds (green for patriarchs and purple of matriarchs), the Mameluke sultan sealed the passage leading to the subterranean chambers. He then permitted the Jews to go no higher than the seventh step of the outer staircase and pray there. Most such worshippers were foreign pilgrims since the local Jewish population was minimal. Following the expulsion of the Jews from Spain in 1492, some came to live in Hebron – then part of the Ottoman empire (1517–1917) – via Turkey in the sixteenth century. The number of resident Jews increased steadily. At the beginning of the British mandate in 1922, they were about 800 strong in a town of 50,000 people, rising to 900 at the time of the 1929 Arab-Jewish riots, which led to their exodus. Those few who returned in 1931 finally left in 1937 when inter-ethnic violence recurred. The Jewish absence ended three decades later. The Israeli military took charge of the Tomb of the Patriarchs/Haram al Khalil, which had been under the management of the waqfs (Arabic, religious trusts) department of the Jordanian Government since 1948. The IDF implemented the Jewish demand to pray inside the precincts.

Gradually, the IDF institutionalized the intial tentative arrangements, and established separate entrances for Muslims and Jews under heavy Israeli military presence. Once the Kiryat Arba settlement was founded in the early 1970s, followed by the revival of the Jewish presence in downtown Hebron a decade later, the Jewish settlers repeatedly announced their intention to evict the Muslims from the Tomb of the Patriarchs altogether. (A plan map of the site, entitled 'Division of the Tomb of the Patriarchs', I picked up at the public relations office of the Kiryat Arba Municipal Council in March 1995 did not carry the names of any of the three existing mosques.) The Israeli Government used major violent incidents in Hebron, whether against Jews or Arabs, to expand the rights of Jews at the Tomb of the Patriarchs at the expense of Muslims. By installing the ark, containing Torah scrolls, it converted the interconnecting rooms between the cenotaphs of Abraham and Sarah, and Jacob and Leah, into synagogues. It kept the Cave of Machpela shut, but assumed control over a small area in the Isaac's Mosque to make an opening so that written prayers by Jews could be dropped into the Cave of Machpela – a practice similar to the one at the Western Wall in Jerusalem where the pious insert prayer notes into the spaces between the stones of the sacred monument. (Eliakam Haetzini, a pioneering resident of Kiryat Arba, told me that in 1982 the Jewish settlers there had dug a one-kilometre-long tunnel to the Tomb of the Patriarchs to check the authenticity of the Cave of Machpela and its contents, and were reassured by what they found.) Following the Palestinian massacre in February

1994, the site was closed to improve security arrangements. When it reopened in November, Muslims, who had been the victims of premeditated violence by a Jewish settler, discovered that their access to the cenotaphs and the right to pray anywhere within the precinct had been curtailed further. Earlier, on 26 June, the official inquiry commission had concluded that Baruch Goldstein had acted alone, and that 'We cannot accuse anyone of negligence'.

My unique experience of visiting the sacred site from the Jewish and Muslim sides on different occasions gave me an understanding denied to most other visitors. In mid-February 1995, after interviewing Badran Jaber, I took a local taxi for a general run of the city, ending with a visit to the Haram al Khalil. My taxi-driver, Khadam, a plumpish man in his late-30s, wearing the compulsory moustache of a Palestinian male, gave me basic information in passable English as he drove past the city's landmarks.

At the Muslim entrance of the Haram al Khalil, Khadam and I went past a heavy entrance barrier and metal detector, followed by a search of my camera bag by young armed IDF soldiers. We went up many steps along the Mameluke stairway, to be met at the top by more soldiers with Uzi sub-machine-guns. Another metal-detector check. We followed a man in a black and white *kiffayeh* to whose enquiry – 'Are you a Muslim?' (a standard question both at the Haram al Sharif, Jerusalem, and here) – I replied, 'No'. Past a passageway, we were into the prayer hall of the Jawilye Mosque, furnished with small overlapping carpets under a vaulted, whitewashed roof with hanging lights. I then peeped into the Isaac's Mosque to have a glimpse of the shrines of Isaac and Rebecca. As the time for the afternoon prayer approached I, a non-Muslim, had to leave.

Intent on visiting the cenotaphs of the remaining two patriarchs and their wives, I asked Khadam to try the Jewish side. I was equipped with a press card issued in Hebrew and English by the Government Press Office, Jerusalem, a document that had proved invaluable so far. Unlike the cramped feeling one gets on the Muslim side, this approach was altogether spacious and pleasant, taking the visitor first

to a vast, gently rising courtyard, leading to a staircase. At
the outer checkpoint one of the three soldiers understood
the worth of a government press card, and let both of us
proceed to the inner checkpoint. Here the three soldiers
were standing against the background of rooms marked
'Armoury' and 'Weapon Loading' – white lettering against
a blue background – in Hebrew and English. A discussion
ensued in Hebrew, with Khadam explaining to the young,
fair-skinned soldier with a mobile phone that that he needed
to take me around to explain in English what was what.
The serviceman asked Khadam if he was a Muslim. Yes,
he replied. The soldier contacted his superior on his mobile
phone, saying something like a Muslim wanted to enter from
the Jewish side. 'Lo, lo (No, No)!' The decision was swift and
brusque. It was too late for me to ask: 'Can I, a non-Muslim,
go in on my own, without Khadam?' The 'Lo, lo!' from
the soldier was too persistent and loud, even threatening,
to contemplate anything other than a quick departure.

A few weeks later I was back there. This time I was in the
company of Rafi and Naom Arnon, the spokesman for the
Kiryat Arba settlement. It was as if we were visiting long-lost
friends. Arnon was a familiar figure to the soldiers, and Rafi's
embroidered shoulder-bag, bought in India, became a subject
of friendly enquiries. Arnon acted as our guide briefly before
leaving us to join an after-wedding party gathered in a special
room in the complex to sing appropriate songs communally.
We entered the semi-dark room connecting the multi-sided
halls over the cenotaphs of Abraham and Sarah. Though
officially a synagogue, with a Torah ark in a corner, the
ambience of the place was palpably Islamic. There were
Quranic verses in Arabic on the tiles along the plinth in
the room. To our right, behind a walled grille I saw a
cenotaph covered with an embroidered shroud with a small
carpet pinned to it in the middle, carrying an inscription in
Arabic: 'This is the tomb of the Prophet Abraham/May peace
be upon him.' (Behind it was a small sign in Hebrew, which
was hard to read.) On the floor, in front of the cenotaph, lay
a few objects covered in embroidered cloths, and another row
of several vases and copper pots between the colourful covers

and us. The farther objects seemed to be the Holy Qurans resting on folding wooden book-rests. But I was puzzled by vases. 'What are these for?' I said to Arnon. He made a dismissive gesture – just what Rabbi Shlomo Aviner at a yeshiva in the Muslim Quarter of Jerusalem's Old Town had done when I asked him the name of the 'good Arab' of his anecdote. 'I don't know,' Arnon replied. 'They are Arab.' Just as we left the room, I saw a middle-aged Arab – a religious functionary, judging by his relaxed gait – go past the cenotaphs. Arnon could have stopped him, and directed my question at him, in Hebrew, a language in which most Muslim Hebronians are fluent. As someone who conducted tours of the site, the information would have been useful to Arnon. But he did not.

When Israel set up an inquiry commission after the massacre by Baruch Goldstein, the local Muslim religious trust, which manages the Haram al Khalil, boycotted it. Instead it co-operated with the committee appointed by the PLO Chairman, Yasser Arafat, and headed by the local mayor, Mustafa Abdul Nabi Natsche.

'Our conclusions were different from those of the official inquiry conducted by the Shinkar Committee,' he told me. 'We found that many of the IDF soldiers did not report for guard duty that [early] morning. There were only a few present when the shooting happened. Later, IDF men were involved in the shooting inside the Ibrahimi Mosque. We sent the report to Chairman Arafat. He did not publish it.' Natsche spoke the last sentence in a neutral tone. In any case, it was difficult to read the bloated face of Natsche, a Chinese Buddha lookalike, but with a moustache. A small, plump, fair-skinned man in his mid-50s, he was dressed in many colours: a blue striped shirt, red sweater, a dark blue business suit, and a black and white tie. A large ring on a left-hand finger shone in his cold, ill-lit office, furnished with a dozen chairs, upholstered in dark brown and stacked against the walls, four coffee tables, and a carpet portraying birds and animals in a jungle setting. On the wall facing him was a verse from the Quran. Behind his chair on the wall were a map of Palestine (as under British mandate), pictures of Hebron, and a large, framed map, entitled 'Hebron City' in Hebrew and English. The office windows were covered with metal grilles, a precaution against an explosion.

'After the massacre by Goldstein the Israelis put a partition in the Ibrahimi Mosque,' Natsche continued. 'They are committing a violation of our mosque. They have limited the number of Muslims who can pray.' But that was not all, I discovered. 'The Israelis closed the [nearby] wholesale vegetable market for security reasons, because it is adjacent to the Jewish settlers in the city centre. There are 1,500 soldiers in the city mainly to protect some 400 settlers. That is, four soldiers for every Jewish man, woman or child. The Palestinians are not allowed to travel in their cars in the city centre. They are harassed by soldiers and settlers. Palestinian youths are stopped at random, made to raise their hands against the wall, and beaten by soldiers. This has severely hurt the economy of the city. All this for the security of some 50 Jewish families and 120 yeshiva students.' He got up and faced the wall-map of Hebron. 'All the local streets leading to the main road to Kiryat Arba have been blocked with concrete drums so that the Jewish settlers can move freely,' he said, pointing out the streets. 'The Palestinians living there have to leave their cars some distance away and walk to and from their homes.' In the dim light it was hard to see. 'Could you mark this up on a small map I can take with me?' I suggested. He looked askance. 'There must be a city map somewhere in the building,' I remarked. 'You can give me a photocopy.' Pause. 'There is no map here, not in this building,' he murmured. 'But this is the town hall, the centre of local government,' I said. Natsche shrugged his shoulders. Finding his assistant approach him with a bunch of cheques to sign, he excused himself.

Leaving the building, I crossed the crumbling King Abdullah Road, and took a good look at the decrepit two-storey building carrying a sign in red 'Municipality'. It was hard to believe that this was the local powerhouse of the capital of the southern West Bank. But then the town hall was typical of the run-down state of the city itself: the pot-holed roads, the leaning electric poles, a general air of shabbiness. This state of affairs in turn was reflective of the decline in the economy, and the dependence, political and economic, on Israel.

'There is no industry in Hebron, aside from the traditional crafts of pottery, glass and leather-tanning, so people live on agriculture,' explained Natsche. 'Most people here depend on work in Israel, mainly construction. But due to the closure [ban on entry into Israel] since 22 January [1995], following a suicide bomb explosion [in Beit id], there is a lot of unemployment here.' His mayoral position derived from appointment by the Israeli authorities in late 1985, and not an election. But he had been a deputy to the popularly elected mayor, Fahd Qawasmeh, from April 1976 to May 1980, when they were both sacked following the killing of six Jewish settlers in downtown Hebron.

As it happened, Fahd Qawasmeh's close relative, Fayaz, a rich scion, had impinged earlier on Jewish Israelis. For he was the owner of Nahar al Khalil (Arabic, [Eternal] River of the Friend [Abraham]) which, for mysterious reasons, acquired currency as the Park Hotel in Israeli medias. 'I built the hotel in April 1965 [when the West Bank was part of Jordan] with 20 rooms,' Fayaz Qawasmeh began. 'After the June 1967 War, when the Israelis came, it was practically empty, there was no business. Everything was depressed in the West Bank.' He lit his second cigarette. A small, neat man with a slight paunch and a white moustache, Qawasmeh, aged 61, had an expressive face. He was alert and lively, his English fluent, and his recall swift and assured. We sipped delicious cardamom coffee in dainty cups in a bright reception room, tastefully furnished – an unobtrusive extension to the ground floor of his two-storey, buff-coloured stone villa, elegant, with a porch on each floor, capped with a slanting red-tiled roof, and sealed from the busy, dusty road by a vast vineyard behind a high stone wall. Before departing, I entered the main building to use the toilet, and found an enormous hall, dimly lit, with the areas for sitting, dining, and watching television subtly demarcated, and furnished with a gallery on three sides. On the wall leading to the reception room hung a framed photograph of the portraits of Qawasmeh and Yasser Arafat.

'In April 1968 Moshe Levinger and some other persons came to my hotel, and said that they worked at Kiryat Gan [near Tel Aviv] and wanted to spend their Passover [holiday] in Hebron,' Qawasmeh went on. 'I didn't ask why; maybe it was hot and humid in Kiryat Gan and the weather was nice in Hebron. They took six rooms with two beds each for one week at 5 [Israeli] liras per room. They had arrived with small pieces of luggage and appeared like travellers. On the second day they said that another group was coming. They took four more rooms. Then another group came, and they took six more rooms. I had very few [other] guests, and the rooms had been empty. They spent three days like that. On the fourth day they put up a sign in Hebrew and English, "Hebron Settlers". I threw out the banner. The moment they said they were settlers I started quarrelling with them. Then they said they wanted to cook. Until then they had been bringing food from outside. I refused them permission. Then they wanted to remove chairs from the hall of the hotel and use it as school for their kids. I refused. They wanted to put up an Israeli flag. We began disputing and quarrelling. After eight days of this we went to the military governor, and told him "If you don't take them out of my hotel there will be trouble". After two days the military governor came and took them to the military base. Then the IDF put it about that the owner of this hotel was a Fatah supporter, which was a criminal offence. After a month or two Levinger and company approached us to rent some space in the hotel to open a restaurant. We refused to discuss anything with them. I've closed the hotel since then, and it has remained shut. On 14 March 1969 I was arrested and put under administrative detention which lasted 9 months.'[10] Since the defunct hotel was nearby, almost next door, accompanied by Qawasmeh's young nephew, I went over, and took pictures of an empty, elegant building along a busy road leading northwards to Jerusalem.

There has been an organic link between Jerusalem and Hebron since ancient times – with Hebron, situated at a higher altitude and endowed with ample water resources, quenching the thirst of the inhabitants of Jerusalem, a settlement deficient in water. And both have attracted the pious of the monotheistic persuasion. With the advent of Islam, Hebron, the site of the tombs of the founding patriarchs of monotheism, emerged as a deeply Islamic and conservative city. In the twentieth century, for instance, it never succumbed to the lure of cinema, perceived by its residents as a corrupting medium. Today it boasts 40 mosques, one for 300 Muslims. It also harbours an Islamic university, the only one of its kind in the West Bank.

This institution, recognizable from a distance by an entrance gate capped by a dome of white stone, decorated with a Quranic verse, is an example of self-help. Unlike Birzeit and Al Najah (Arabic, success) Universities, founded by rich local families, it was set up by numerous small donors in 1971. They established a college of the Sharia (Arabic, lit. Way; fig. Islamic Law) and religion, with 50 students, and then expanded it. Now there are more than 1,400 students, and the university provides courses in Arab history, education and psychology, besides the Sharia. Ever since the Student Council was established, it had been controlled by the Islamic Bloc, except in 1986 when the secular, nationalist Fatah triumphed. The Islamic influence is apparent in a series of powerful murals that cover half of the perimeter wall facing the entrance: skilfully designed and executed colourful images of science and technology, and religion, a Palestinian peasant woman holding up a model of a vast Islamic monument and a large banner, inscribed with 'Bismallah Rahman al Rahim: Aqr Bassam Rabak al Dhi Khalq (In the name of God the Merciful: Read in the name of God, who created you)', unfolding over a book.

The overall modesty of the university is well captured by its small, threadbare cafeteria – a far cry from its counterpart at Hebrew University or even at Birzeit University near Ramallah. Here, assisted by Saida, my Arabic interpreter, I conversed with a group of female students – Amani Jaabari, Nabila Isnaineh, Sabiha Ahmad and Khadija Hafiz. Clad in jeans and shirts underneath white shrouds, their faces enclasped by spotlessly white scarves, they were all soft-spoken, but far from shy.

On the Ibrahimi Mosque: 'The prayer space for Muslims has been reduced to take only 300 instead of the 1,500 before the massacre,' said Sabiha Ahmad, pursing her thin lips. 'Sometimes Muslims are forced to pray in the street. And the place for Jews has been expanded.' None of them had been to the Ibrahimi Mosque in the year since the slaughter. Nabila Isnaineh, with almond-shaped eyes, said: 'I am afraid to go there to pray [in the women's mosque] because I think the massacre will happen again.'

On the Jewish settlers in the city centre: 'When the fancy takes them they rampage through the fruit and vegetables and upturn stalls,' said Khadija Hafiz. 'They go about the town with sub-machine-guns. At night they deliberately play loud music and make the situation difficult for the Arab neighbours to drive them away. The same happens in the neighbourhood of the Ibrahimi Mosque, where the IDF joins in. The Arabs in the area cannot sleep and are late for work. These settlers in Hebron's centre are a provocation [to Arabs] and a source of conflict. They must leave.'

On the Jewish settlers in the Kiryat Arba group of settlements: Amani Jaabari, an aquiline-nosed student of Arab history, lived in the village of Al Shuab, which is circumscribed by this complex. 'To get to my own home in Al Shuab I have to go past an IDF checkpoint,' she said. 'It is like living in one country and studying in another.'

The parsimony of the university was obvious in the semi-dark registration hall, buzzing with activity (we had arrived on registration day), and in the claustrophobic room, furnished with bare desks and chairs, used as its office by the Students Council. Here, I interviewed Bassam Mutaweija, the secretary-general of the Council. A bearded man of medium height and build, fair, he was dressed in khaki, and had the impatient energy of a 20-year-old. 'Our university has contributed many martyrs to the struggle,' he began. 'In July 1983 Zionist terrorists attacked our university with assault rifles and hand grenades, and martyred four Muslims. In 1987 as soon as the intifada erupted, the Israelis closed our university. It stayed shut until 1991. Lots of our students were arrested, including seven of the nine Students Council members. One hundred and twenty students belonging to the Islamic Bloc were imprisoned, and a minority of them are still inside. And some students were martyred.' Can you give me names? 'Yes, Amjad Momeini and Amjad Abu Khalif.'

Were any university students killed in the Ibrahimi Mosque massacre in February 1994? 'Yes, some, I don't know the exact number. After that massacre we had three days of mourning at the university. We utterly reject the new arrangements the IDF has made at the Ibrahimi Mosque. This is an Islamic mosque, and Jews have no right to be there. The Israelis have taken the first step to controlling our mosque completely. They have limited the number of Muslim worshippers. They have turned our mosque into an Israeli military base.' What have you done in protest? 'As we are under military occupation, we cannot protest properly,' he replied. 'All we can do is to send letters to the UN and other international organizations. But they achieve nothing, because the UN treats Israel as its spoilt baby. Look, who controls the UN Security Council? America, the god-mother of Israel. Our main weakness is that we are not an armed people like the Jews [of Israel].'

Some days later at an exhibition organized by the Islamic Bloc at the Al Najah National University in Nablus, I saw sets of enlarged colour pictures of individual Palestinians, always young and bearded, displaying a machine-gun, loading and unloading it, posturing bravely. It was at once a symbol and a reality, the possession of a powerful gun – an act of defiance – but also an attempt to assert a right which their occupier, the Israel Defence Forces, conferred automatically on the Jewish youth, male or female, the day they turned 18. Young Palestinians, encountering daily the Israeli Jews of the same age in their scores, carrying sub-machine-guns in the way businessmen carry briefcases, felt deprived, and eyed them with envy. Next to these images of daring in a spacious, high-ceilinged, rectangular hall, with a gallery, on the first floor of the sleek main building of the university lay pictures of several martyrs – those who had sacrificed their lives in the struggle for the liberation of their homeland – not far from an assortment of hand-crafted items, often clothing, made by the 'Islamic prisoners of Israel'.

Saida and I had arrived at the university, erected on top of a hill, on 11 March, the beginning of the spring semester, the day the Islamic Bloc unveiled its book exhibition. The walls of the hall were draped with flowing green banners, inscribed in Arabic: 'Bismallah al Rahman al Rahim/ Kushah al Mujahid al Shaikh Izz al Din al Qassam (In the name of Allah the Merciful/Congratulations to Holy Warrior Shaikh Izz al Din al Qassam)'; and 'Qut al Islam, Jamaa al Najah/Alslamwah alhil (Islamic Bloc, Al Najah University/Islam is the solution)'. On long, sturdy tables, covered with tablecloths, thousands of books, many of them with gold-embossed covers, were neatly laid out. The display was an impressive example of precision combined with meticulous organization. Omar Mahmoud (a pseudonym), a tall, square-shouldered student in his early 20s, with a thick wavy beard and curly black hair, in a checkered sweater, told me that he and his comrades had worked four days and nights around the clock to organize the display. 'For every copy sold the Islamic Bloc will get a certain percentage,' he said. The commissions, so earned, would strengthen the Bloc, which had won elections to the Students Council for three years running in the early 1990s (the university had been closed by the Israelis from 1988–91). In 1994, following the Israeli-PLO Accord, the Islamic Bloc fell one percentage behind Fatah (at 46 per cent), the mainstay of the PLO, and lost control. The rivalry between the Islamic Bloc and Fatah sharpened, especially after Fatah became the chief party in the Palestinian Authority which assumed powers of autonomy in the Gaza Strip in 1994. The administration of Al Najah University, I was told, played to the tune of the Palestinian Authority. When it discovered an impressive book exhibition by the Islamic Bloc on the day the university reopened for registration, it objected, saying the Bloc had not gained specific permission for the event. But, instead of escalating tension by attempting to shut down the display, it closed the whole institution for a day.

Like Hebron Islamic University, Al Najah started as a

college, a status it had on the eve of the Israeli occupation of the West Bank. Later, when its management applied for a license to function as a university, the Israeli authorities took two years to issue it, and then only for a year at a time. In the late 1970s it had 750 students and 75 teachers, and now with a student body of 5,000 students and a teaching staff of 400, it was the largest university in the West Bank. Though it drew students from all over the territory, both the students and staff had a reputation for upholding Palestinian nationalism, which was nurtured for long in Nablus. With a population of 200,000, Nablus is now the largest city of the West Bank, including the Palestinian East Jerusalem, and the unofficial capital of the northern sector of the territory.

Like Hebron, its southern counterpart, Nablus is a strategic place. Established by Roman Emperor Flavia Vespasian (r. AD 69–79) in AD 72, it thrived as an east-west gateway between north-facing Mount Jerizim and south-facing Mount Ebal because it was endowed with an abundant water supply from springs. The mountains appear in Deuteronomy 11:27–29: 'A blessing, if ye obey the commandments of the Lord thy God that I command thee this day. And a curse, if ye will not obey the commandments of the Lord thy God ... When the Lord thy God hath brought thee in unto the land whither thou goest to possess it, that thou shalt put the blessing upon Mount Jerizim and the curse upon Mount Ebal.' Nablus is a twin of the nearby Shechem (Hebrew, neck/ridge), an Old Testament settlement, where Abraham and his family, having left their native Ur in Iraq, arrived on their first entry into the land of Canaan. Captured in AD 636/637 by Muslim Arabs, who changed Neapolis (Greek, New City) to Nablus, it remained under Muslim rule until 1967, except between 1099 and 1187 when it was ruled by the Crusaders, who suffered defeat at the hands of Salah al Din Ayubi. A severe earthquake destroyed much of Nablus in 1927. In the 1930s it was a leading centre of Arab resistance to the Jewish immigration into Palestine, and the birthplace in 1936 of the Arab Higher Committee, which led the Arab Revolt of 1936–9. Following the 1948–9 Arab-Israeli War, it became part of Jordan, and later a centre of Palestinian guerrilla activities against Israel, initially directed by Yasser Arafat from the Casbah, the Old Town.

Visiting the Casbah, it was plain to see the advantages it offered for clandestine activities. A maze of narrow lanes and by-lanes, arched bridges, tunnels and cul-de-sacs, buzzing with the ceaseless activity of a thriving bazaar, the Casbah was an ideal place for hide-and-seek, and a nightmare for IDF and Shin Beth personnel, especially after their informer network had collapsed in the course of the Palestinian intifada. At the one-room sawmill of a pleasant-faced carpenter, Adnan Hawash, in the midst of an odd mixture of smells – baking pitta bread, chicken shit and grilled kebab on skewers – we met a middle-aged, bespectacled printer, Khalid Nabulsi. He proudly gave us a calendar he had printed, a pictorial catalogue of the 54 Palestinians killed during the first three years of the intifada, mostly young men, some of them teenagers. The ageing walls of the Casbah were plastered with fliers displaying a picture of Imad Nasser, a tousle-haired youth with intense eyes, and announcing his fifth death anniversary. Killed by the IDF in December 1989 in a raid on a local barber shop, Nasser, a creature of the Casbah, was the founder in 1988 of the Ninjas of the Casbah, an armed group, which soon split into the Black Panthers (led by Nasser), affiliated to Fatah, and the Red Eagles, affiliated to the Popular Front for the Liberation of Palestine. However, both factions concentrated on assassinating suspected Palestinian collaborators.

In the square outside the Casbah, the fruit and vegetable trade was in full swing, Saturday being the weekly market day. As in Hebron, the local industry has not progressed beyond the traditional making of soap and olive oil. A match factory, marking the city's shaky advance in modern manufacture, closed down in the face of tariff-free Israeli imports. In the absence of an emerging industrial bourgeoisie, the city's leading families continue to dominate the region's agricultural economy, based on wheat and olives, control wholesale trade, and own much real estate. Among them is the Shakaa clan, whose senior member, Bassam Shakaa, born in 1930 and elected city mayor at 46, made news headlines, worldwide, in mid-1980 as a victim of the Jewish terrorists' bomb explosion, when he lost both his legs, and was confined to a wheelchair.

The attack on him was a reprisal for a terrorist operation against the Jews in Hebron which in turn was a retaliation for the settlement of Jews in downtown Hebron which had been allowed by the Israeli Government after a group of Kiryat Arba women, led by Miriam Levinger, had occupied the old Beit Hadassah (Hadassah House) building in April 1979. Following the establishment of the Beit Hadassah enclave, Kiryat Arba settlers had taken to praying at the Tomb of the Patriarchs on Friday evenings and then visiting the well-guarded Beit Hadassah for a communal meal. On the first Friday in May 1980, three Palestinian gunmen, having climbed on to the roofs of the buildings across the street, and another, concealing himself in a doorway, fired their automatic rifles and threw hand grenades at the party of the Jews, some of them armed, as they approached Beit Hadassah. Six Jews lay dead, and another 16 were injured. The attackers made a quick getaway. The military governor of the area imposed an indefinite curfew, and deported not only the elected mayor of the city, Fahd Qawasmeh, but also the head of the Muslim religious trust, responsible for the management of the Ibrahimi Mosque/Tomb of the Patriarchs, Shaikh Rajab Tamimi – to Lebanon. 'The first day the Israeli army came to Hebron [in June 1967] they flew the Israeli flag over the Ibrahimi Mosque, and they have continued Judaizing the Haram [al Khalil] until it is virtually a synagogue now,' said Shaikh Tamimi. 'They [the Israelis] come into the Haram ... in their boots and shoes. Twice they brought a dog with them as a provocation for they know Muslims consider dogs to be unclean. They tore up the Quran there.'[11] Once the 30-day period of mourning for the Jewish dead had ended, a group of Jewish terrorists struck at three important leaders of the (Palestinian) National Guidance Committee, among them Bassam Shakaa.

'After that explosion in my car, I spent five months in Stanmore Hospital in the [Greater] London suburb to recover,' Bassam Shakaa said. He was a surprisingly cheerful-looking man, with a ruddy face and a greying moustache, balding, dressed in dark grey clothes, wearing a black wristwatch with white hands. 'The welcoming procession [for me] took three hours to cover one kilometre from the mayor's office to the Nablus Library.' He turned to a large black-and-white photograph of the marchers, carrying him on their shoulders under a fluttering Palestinian flag, hanging from the wall behind his wheelchair. His beady eyes brightened up as a smile spread over his avuncular face. 'In those days my house was in the valley near Elam Ridge by Rafidiya Hospital,' he continued. 'We moved to this house [on top of a hill] in 1986, five years after I was sacked as mayor by the Israelis.' (When Prime Minister Shimon Peres decided to nominate a mayor in late 1985 his choice fell on Ghasan Shakaa, a junior member of the same family.)

Unlike a fellow patrician, affluent and enjoying local esteem, Fayaz Qawasmeh, a confidant of Yasser Arafat, Shakaa was resolutely opposed to the Israeli-PLO Accord of September 1993, popularly called the Oslo Accord. 'The division among Arab countries shown during the [1991] Gulf War, the weak situation of Arabs due to the collapse of the Soviet Union; all that helped the US to impose the Oslo Accord on the Palestinians,' Shakaa explained. 'The Accord is a framework which will not lead to a Palestinian state and independence. It will lead to a more complex clash in the future because it has complicated the ongoing conflict between Zionism and Palestinians. The bottom line is that Palestinians cannot forget themselves, cannot cancel themselves. Israel already controls 55 per cent of the land in the West Bank. Its confiscation of more Palestinian land continues. The Israelis do not have the right to be here. They are an occupation force. They have changed our laws, demography, geography and established Jewish settlements against the international law. Since their actions are illegal, they must face the consequences at some point.' Why does the PLO not take Israel to the International Court of Justice? 'Ours is not only legal but also a political and humanitarian struggle. Due to the force used by Israel, backed by the US, we have suffered. If you go to the [Israeli] High Court, the IDF blows up your house. Due to this, we have not gone to courts. The international legal institutions failed to stop Israel to establish more and more Jewish settlements. When it comes to the crunch at the UN Security Council America uses its veto in favour of Israel. And Yasser Arafat failed to get Israel to stop activities against the international law.'

Leaving Shakaa's vast stone mansion, I surveyed the scene on that fine sunny morning in March. Covered with a green carpet speckled with wild flowers, the surrounding biblical mountains were a stunning sight. Nature's bounty contrasted with the mean-spiritedness and aggression of humanity.

A strong sense of history permeated the discussion I had during my next trip to Nablus with a few academics in the courtyard of Al Najah University by a marble water-fountain. I posed the question: Why did Israel come about?

'A Christian-Zionist alliance supported the Jews in their idea of a homeland in Palestine,' said Dr Mansour Abu Ali, head of the geography department. Plump, dark and clean-shaven, Dr Abu Ali, in his early 40s, was dressed in a white shirt with blue stripes, black sweater, light grey trousers and a black and white tweed jacket, and carried blue plastic worry beads. 'The roots of this alliance can be traced to the nineteenth century. During the Ottoman period [1517–1917] there was no conflict between Jews and Muslims. The Jewish idea of a homeland was supported and developed in Europe. Without western support Israel would not have come into existence.'

'The conflict is not between Israel and Palestinians or Jews and Arabs since its roots go beyond modern times, into pre-Christian times,' stated Jamal Joudeh, professor of political science. He was a neat-looking man in his early 50s, with grey hair and a moustache who, like Dr Abu Ali, was dressed in a white shirt with blue stripes, light grey trousers and a black and white tweed jacket, but was wearing a dark tie. 'You cannot overstate the strategic importance of this part of the eastern Mediterranean. The commercial routes of the area became apparent when the Greeks occupied the land. Look at the effort Alexander the Great [r. 336–23 BC] made to capture Tyre [in south Lebanon]. Later Palestine became the centre of leading religions. Then in AD 637 Islam came and took over the region, and got rid of the European occupation. Then Crusaders. Salah al Din finally got rid of the Europeans. Then renassiance and industrial revolution in Europe, and the emergence of nationalism there. Britain carried "civilization" to "barbaric" countries around the globe. Palestine became more important than before. Jews were encouraged to think of their ancient homeland because it suited western interests. The emergence of the Zionist theory can be understood only in that context. Zionists had a European way of thinking. They used it to convince fellow Europeans of the value of setting up a Zionist state in Palestine, and how it was in western interests to do so. Israel was established here in 1948 as a representative of the West. It remains a representative and protector of the West in this region. Israel became all the more important once Britain and France had lost direct control over the region after World War II. Palestine is the centre from where you can control the whole region: Lebanon, Syria, Jordan and Egypt. The coast of Palestine is strategic since it leads to Sinai as well as Lebanon and Syria and Jordan. The strength of the Jews in the West forms a supporting element in this nexus. The Zionist lobby in Europe and America is strong. Initially the West had tried to control Palestine directly and on its own; now Israel is an additional power for the West in the region. The awareness by the Arab leaders of this western political strategy at that time was very low or non-existent.'

'The leadership of Palestinians and Arabs failed to understand the full political implications of the establishment of Israel in 1948,' said Dr Iyad Barghouti, a social scientist. A youngish-looking man, immaculately dressed, clean-shaven, Dr Barghouti was soft-spoken. 'Due to their social and political background the Arab leaders failed to deal with the problem. They too were linked with the West. And Israel stood for the West. The present situation is that the Arab leadership does not represent the people; that is, it lacks democratic credentials. The West trusts Israel partly because it practises democracy.'

'There is the importance of Israel as a spiritual, religious state to the Jews,' Dr Abu Ali said. 'Secondly there is the political and strategic importance of Palestine. Israel is the front of the West into the East. The third dimension is economic. The Third World is a vast consuming block of the world. The West wants to keep markets open for the western manufacturing industries and needs a foothold in the countries like Palestine and Egypt. Fourthly, there is a confrontation now between Islam and the West. Islamic fundamentalism is the leading enemy of the West and Christianity. People in the the West don't trust Muslims. This is not surprising because there has all along been conflict between western culture and oriental religions like Islam. Finally, Israel is the silk glove of the West. Through Israel the West wants to exert influence over the Arab world. As US Defence Secretary, Dick Cheney, said on the eve of the [1991] Gulf War, there are two American aims: protect Israel; and preserve the West's oil supplies.'

Having studied the capitals of the northern and southern zones of the West Bank, it was essential to pick a lacklustre place in the central sector, preferably a refugee camp, home to one West Banker out of nine.[12] My choice fell on the Jalazoun refugee camp, 6 kilometres north-east of Ramallah, where 8,000 Palestinians lived. Set up in 1950 under the Jordanian rule, it held 7,000 residents on the eve of the 1967 War, which pushed a substantial minority across the Jordan River into the East Bank (of Jordan).

The immediate and overall impression that Jalazoun conveys to a visitor is of a transient place, where exiled people rested, temporarily, expecting to return to their native abodes in the near future. That was why the United Nations Relief and Work Agency for Palestinian Refugees in the Near East (UNRWA) – established by the United Nations' office in Vienna, Austria, following the resolution by the United Nations General Assembly in December 1949 to care for those Palestinians who had lost their homes and means of livelihood during the 1948–9 Arab-Israeli War – erected two-room shelters of breeze blocks for them. But as months turned into years, and years into decades, and families multiplied, with no prospect of a return home, the camp dwellers took to adding rooms and porches haphazardly on the ground floor, and building upwards. The local UNRWA director, himself a refugee and a camp resident, turned a blind eye. Streets and roads emerged, unplanned, pot-holed, without pavements, giving the settlement an appearance, as seen from an aircraft – or an IDF base established on top of an overlooking hill to keep the refugee camp under constant surveillance, part of the military strategy applied all over the West Bank – of a spreading skin disease.

Traversing the camp, accompanied by Saida, I found most dwellings low, single-storey breeze blocks, the rest two storey, made of stone. But they were all covered with graffiti in the colours of the Palestinian flag – red, black, green and white – espousing Palestinian nationalism. Many of the slogans acclaimed Fatah, others Hamas, and still others smaller groups such as the Popular Front for the Liberation of Palestine. There were occasional leaflets on the walls bearing the sad-looking face of Shaikh Ahmad Yasin, the Hamas leader. The first hint of rain, I was told, and streets turn into mud lanes, and sewers overflow.

Luckily for us, it was a dry crisp morning in February. We called on Habib Shaheen, the director of the camp. His office, built on a raised platform near the entrance gate, was a small single-storey structure with doors painted in sky-blue (the UN colour), and a tiled floor. Behind a large steel desk with a wooden top, sat Shahin, a heavy shouldered, middle-aged man, moustached, in a woollen jacket and *kiffayeh*, tapping his cigarette in an Air France ashtray. Acting as the middle man between the UNRWA and the refugees, he looked after the UNRWA property, supervised the services provided by the agency, decided who should live in his camp, and distributed food and welfare benefits. The rest of his office, illuminated by strip neon-lights and heated by a struggling two-element electric heater, was occupied by nine chairs with chrome tubing body and brown plastic seats.

Soon these chairs were occupied by Walid al Bayed, Riyad al Safi and Abu Jamil al Safi. Lightly bearded, small and slim, with a sensitive face, Walid al Bayed was clad in a brown shirt, an orange-coloured sweater with a dirty golden-yellow border, dark brown trousers, white socks and brown shoes. Next to him sat the short, plumpish and moustached Riyad al Safi, in a polo-neck vest, blue jeans and white trainers. He held blue worry beads in his right hand. His neighbour was his 50-year-old father, Abu Jamil al Safi, unshaven and cross-eyed, a man of medium height, wearing a black-and-white woollen cap, ill fitting grey jacket and trousers, and black boots. Presently Nasr Mahmoud Zubaidi arrived. He was a thin-eyed, good-looking, sinewy man, clean-shaven (a rarity), in a brown-red jersey and black boots. He was followed by Hamad Mahmoud Adaibe. Sporting a salt-and-pepper beard and a receding hairline, and looking older than his age, 39, he was clad in a coloured check shirt, black trousers and dirty shoes.

Despite the difference in their ages they had two things in common: smoking and imprisonment. Soon a cigarette-smoke cloud filled the office.

Though only 22, Walid had been arrested three times, and had served 26 months behind bars. 'I participated in a Day of the Land demonstration on 30 March 1986,' he began. 'But they arrested me in December for that. Two months, in a jail near Jenin. The second time was in January 1988, soon after the intifada, for throwing a Molotov cocktail. Eighteen months, spent in Darie detention camp near Hebron. The third time was administrative detention in July 1990. Spent six months in Ansar III detention camp in the Negev. On my release I was given a green ID, which meant that I could not leave the Jalazoun camp. Three years like that. Only after the Oslo Accord [September 1993] was I given the regular orange ID. I am now a first-year student at Birzeit University [located three kilometres away]. I am doing history and political science, and enrol for a course when I've earned enough [as a construction worker].'

Twenty-four-year-old Riyad was a veteran of five imprisonments and detentions. 'The first time was in October 1984 when I was 13,' he said. 'A Shabak [Hebrew acronym of Sherut Beitkhon Klielat, General Security Service] man in civilian clothes arrived with an IDF unit at about 10 p.m.

They broke into our house. I was in bed. A soldier pulled my hair, and asked me my name, and then ordered me to wear my clothes. My parents tried to stop him, and they hit my father who had himself served a jail sentence. They handcuffed and blindfolded me and put me in a Jeep. They drove around for a while. Then they took me to the Ramallah jail, actually a tent outside the jail. They abused me and threw me around like a piece of luggage. Then six soldiers came and beat me. I was in prison for 10 months. The next time was in November 1986, for two months. The third time was in 1988, for eight months. In May 1990 there was a demonstration in our camp after the murder of seven Palestinians in Rishon LeZion [near Tel Aviv]. They imposed a curfew. But people were throwing stones. Shabak men shot at the demonstrators. A bullet hit me in the stomach. I was in hospital for 20 days. One week after I had left hospital an IDF death squad wearing masks broke into my home. They made me run from my home to a gathering area for prisoners. I fell down, and they caught up with me, five of them. They deliberately hit me on the stomach. It hurt badly. They removed their masks, and I could see them clearly, the Israelis. In July 1990 I was arrested along with six others, all of us under administrative detention. Each of us was interrogated by the Shabak man, Captain Maher. "I didn't mean to shoot you in the stomach," he told me. "I meant to shoot you in the neck, to see you die." So I replied: "It is in the hands of God. If he wishes then I'll die, if not, then not."' Riyad lit a cigarette, and offered me one. A non-smoker, I made an exception, and accepted it. 'I was out after the six month detention ended,' he continued. 'But they arrested me again under administrative detention in November 1991. Another six months.' What had he been doing since his release? 'Work as a labourer and study. I enrolled at Birzeit University to study political science and social sciences. I take courses when I have saved enough.' Abu Jamil, Riyad's father, who was incarcerated for two years in 1969 for his membership of Fatah, looked visibly proud of his son.

Hamad Adaibe had three stints in jail, starting in 1977, when he was 23. 'The first time was for three and a half years; then in 1983 for a fortnight, for interrogation. The last time was in December 1990 for 20 months.'

Nasr Zubaida, now 34 and employed as a sanitary worker by UNRWA, had his first imprisonment when he was half that age. 'For throwing stones and Molotov cocktails,' he said. 'Two years in Beersheba prison. Then in 1982 I was jailed for eight years for threatening local collaborators, and for throwing a Molotov cocktail which injured an Israeli soldier. I spent most of the time in Jneid jail near Nablus. Soon after I got out I married, in April 1990.'

I noticed tittering and nervous laughter as my interviewees described their experiences of arrest, jail, beatings and shootings. They had, it seemed, developed a sardonic sense of humour as part of their survival kit.

How were the conditions in prison? 'In 1977, quite awful; no mattress, no radio,' Nasr replied. 'If you talked politics you were punished, including solitary confinement. Everything was oppressive. We struggled. We went on hunger strikes, first for eight days, then 12 days, and finally 23 days. Drank only water. This was just to get a mattress and a pillow. First I was at Beersheba jail. Two of my colleagues in Beersheba – Jaafari and Rahman – died during a hunger strike in 1980.'

What was the daily routine? 'Wake up, exercise, breakfast,' replied Riyad. 'While eating we always talked politics. We are a political people, inside prison and outside. All our experience is politics. Then different political factions had discussions among themselves. We gained this privilege through struggle. Then exercise for half an hour. From 2 to 4 p.m. read books, read and write; from 4 to 6 p.m. a general meeting of all prisoners, political analysis. But the routine during my administrative detention in the Negev was different. There were 30 prisoners in each tent. We played cards, chess. At the end of my detention we got radio and TV. Dinner was at 6.30 p.m., and bed at 11 p.m.'

Had imprisonment weakened or strengthened their convictions? 'I'm the same, before and after,' came the reply from Nasr. 'I'd do it again what I did.' I turned to the younger men. 'The living conditions in a prison are such that they harden you, make you strong,' said Walid. His friend, Riyad, nodded in agreement. 'Even if I were to be imprisoned 50 times I would not give up the struggle for the Palestinian national rights,' replied Riyad. 'Jail has a great effect on your personality when you are young. It made me stronger.'

If one were to think of the PLO as a regular army, the men in the room would be counted as its combatants. They were not atypical. Indeed, as Shaheen, the director, pointed out: 'At the height of the intifada in August 1990 there were 480 males [aged 15 to 50] in prison. Now [in March 1995] 70 are still in jail.' This meant that at least one out of every three Palestinian males aged 15 to 50 had endured imprisonment, a remarkable statistic. However, they had survived the long intifada. But there were eight camp dwellers who had perished in the struggle, victims of numerous army firings. Nasr recited their names: Amin Raja, Amjad Badawi (aged 19), Awad Tabsin, Mustafa Sharaka (aged 17), Tahrir Arayshe, Ahmad Shankl, Hussein Musaaid and Marouf al Safi. There was an eight-sided memorial pillar in their honour, decked by a Palestinian flag and lights at the ends of eight spokes branching out from the flagpole, at the centre of the main square, the commercial hub of this indigent settlement of refugees.

Once again the Jalazoun camp was typical. Indeed it was less militant than Deheisheh near Bethlehem, with 9,000 residents. 'During intifada,' its director, himself a Palestinian refugee, told me, '16 people were killed, seven were deported, four houses were demolished and two were sealed.' For a people who have been thrown out of their native land, losing a house is a particularly traumatic experience.

Like the deprived people elsewhere in the world, these refugees and their progeny had long memories. Nasr said that his family was originally from Lod, now the site of Israel's sprawling international airport. Walid's family was from Dawayma village near Hebron. 'The IDF entered the village in July 1948 and killed some people,' he said. 'The rest fled out of fear. My family fled to Jericho, then Taiba village near Ramallah, and finally ended up in the Jalazoun camp.'

What were the reasons for the Palestinian defeat in 1948? 'No Arab country helped the Palestinians,' explained Riyad. 'This happened because the Arab leaders could not take decisions on their own: they were under the control of Britain and France. Israel was superior militarily. The Arabs did not have good weapons. Israel had much better weapons. Also Britain was a superpower in those days; and its policy was to keep the Arab governments weak. The Iraqi and Egyptian soldiers fought well on the battlefield, but their leaders were the pawns of Britain. So when they captured some areas, as in Jenin, their army generals got orders to withdraw.' His father, Abu Jamil, agreed, and added: 'The Jews did not have the power on their own to occupy Palestine. Without the British help they would not have been able to do what they did.'

Why did Israel come about? 'It was in the mutual interest of the Jews and the European governments to enable the Jews to come here and occupy us to fulfil their aim in this part of the world,' replied Walid. 'Helped by Britain, the Zionist movement found a rationale, and built up world opinion that the Jews should have their homeland here. What happened to them in World War II also helped them. But the Arabs had nothing to do with what happened to the Jews in Europe. Yet we have been forced to pay the price for the crimes of the Germans.'

Why were the Arabs defeated again in 1967? The reasons given could be summarized as follows. There was a lack of military supplies and weapons in the Arab camp. Israel attacked the Egyptian air force on the ground and destroyed it. Israel was determined to take the Old City in Jerusalem which was important to the Jews. The Jordanian military was under King Hussein who was under the British influence. The Jordanian army had been rough on the Palestinians in Jordan during 1948–67. The Palestinian revolution had just started (after the establishment of the PLO in 1964). Yet the Palestinian commandos fought well in the West Bank and Gaza.

Would they accept the pre-1967 borders as a permanent solution? 'I would accept that the West Bank, Gaza and

East Jerusalem are enough for us,' said Riyad. 'But there must be complete Israeli withdrawal from there.' All the eight Jalazoun residents present endorsed Riyad's position – except Hamad Adaibe, a member of the Islamic Jihad. 'We claim sovereignty over the whole of the British mandate Palestine,' he said. 'This is our land. The Jews took our land, our assets. We have to struggle to recover what is ours. Each phase of the struggle has its own methods. We do not know how long the struggle will go on. But I know that the Muslims throughout the world will support us. I used to be a member of Fatah, but I left in 1980.'

There was vigorous disagreement with Hamad's views from the rest of the assembly. Why? 'Islam would exclude other religious groups like Christians and Druzes to participate in the Palestinian nationalist struggle,' was one reason offered; 'The anti-Israeli struggle is about Palestinian nationalism, a subject which the Islamic Jihad ideology does not address,' was another; 'The Islamic Jihad wants to internationalize the struggle, but we want to keep it as our struggle limited to Palestine,' was still another; and finally, 'Under secularism everybody speaks up, Muslim or not, and gives vent to his opinion, but not so under a religious ideology.'

What they were unanimous about was that there had been no economic spin-off from the 1993 Oslo Accord. Indeed with frequent sealing of the Israeli borders to West Bankers and Gazans, heavily dependent for their livelihood on work in Israel, the economic situation had deteriorated.

Within the Jalazoun camp the UNRWA was the chief employer, providing such public services as garbage collection, road maintenance, sanitation, health clinics and education (which is compulsory up to 15). In the private sector jobs were available in metal workshops, groceries and garages. These activities provided employment to about a third of the job-seekers. The rest were dependent on work inside Israel, behind the Green Line, mostly in construction, sometimes as manual labourers in factories. The average wage was NIS (New Israeli Shekel) 60 or $20 a day, about half of what a Jewish labourer earned, they said. In other words, when the Israeli border was closed to West Bankers and Gazans, the jobless rate in Jalazoun shot up to 65–70 per cent. Again Jalazoun was typical. At the Deheisheh camp unemployment, normally at 40 per cent, doubled when the Green Line was sealed off.

The inequality in the living standards of Israelis and the inhabitants of the Occupied Territories was stark. At $2,067, the per capita GNP of West Bankers (in 1992) was one-sixth that of Israelis; and at $1,622, the per capita GNP for the Occupied Territories' residents was only one-seventh.[13]

This state of affairs is the end result of the policies Israel has followed in the Occupied Territories regarding land confiscation, land use and planning, water resources, agriculture, industry, commerce, employment, taxation and financial services.

Ever since its occupation of the Palestinian territories, Israel has pursued a strategy concerning land designed to yield a dual result. Large scale confiscation of Palestinian land has not only advanced the Israeli policy of 'redeeming' the soil of Eretz Israel, but has also severely weakened the close link that Palestinians have traditionally maintained with agriculture and land, thus undermining their nationalist feelings rooted in soil. The success of this policy is illustrated by the fact that between 1967 and 1985 the percentage of West Bankers engaged in agriculture declined from 46 to 27. (The corresponding figures in the Gaza Strip were 32 and 18.)[14] The displaced Palestinian labour had to find alternative means of livelihood. With the non-agricultural sectors of the economy in the Occupied Territories rigidly controlled by the Israeli military regime, unable to expand and absorb the surplus Palestinian workforce, the latter had no choice but to seek employment at below market rates as unskilled or semi-skilled workers in Israel in its agriculture and construction and catering industries. Not surprisingly, by 1985, as much as 54 per cent of West Bank wage labourers were employed in Israel. (The corresponding statistic for the Gaza Strip was 67 per cent.) That explained why a half of the workforce in the Israeli construction industry was Palestinian.[15]

Within a year of its occupation of the Palestinian territories in 1967, Israel had consolidated its economic stranglehold over the West Bank and Gaza Strip. It was the source of 75 per cent of the Palestinian imports, and the destination of 40 per cent of the Palestinian exports. By the end of the 1980s these statistics had risen respectively to 90 per cent and 66 per cent.[16] The trade imbalance was equally striking. In 1986 Israel's exports to Occupied Territories amounted to $780 million, and its imports to $289 million, giving it an annual trade surplus of $491 million.[17]

By issuing some 200 military orders, Israel so mutilated the inherited Jordanian taxation law that a Palestinian living in the West Bank ended up paying more in taxes than a person with the same income resident in Israel, a country known for its high taxation. And, despite their dramatically lower living standards, West Bankers found themselves subsidizing Israelis. According to Meron Benvensiti, the Israeli director of the West Bank Data Project, in 1987 more than $80 million collected from the Palestinians in the Occupied Territories were channelled into the Israeli public exchequer.[18] And the flow continued.

Following its capture of the West Bank and Gaza in June 1967, Israel immediately closed all Palestinian as well as other Arab and non-Arab banks, and froze their assets and liabilities. While it allowed the Jordanian dinar as joint legal tender with Israeli Lira (later Israeli Shekel, and New Israeli Shekel), it specified exclusive control by the Bank of Israel in all banking activities. Because of Israel's insistence on this condition for the reopening of the closed banks, and because of Jordan's insistence that the West Bank-based banks must function under the supervision of the Jordanian Central Bank, West Bankers were for all purposes deprived of normal banking facilities until September 1986, when Military Order 1180 modified the Jordanian Bank Law, and permitted the opening of the Cairo-Amman Bank in the territory. Further relaxation came in 1992 when tight restrictions on receiving foreign funds were eased. Dependence on private, expensive banking and credit arrangements for two decades damaged the West Bank economy badly.

The cumulative effect of stagnant output, high taxation, restrictions on import of foreign currencies, and the long absence of proper banking and credit facilities was to reduce funds for investment in industry and other capital projects. The industrial backwardness of the Occupied Territories could be judged by the fact that in 1987 the value of the annual industrial output in the territories was a mere $85 million, equal to the production of one medium-sized Israeli company.[19]

'The Israeli Government's policies are designed to increase the structural integration of the Palestinian economy into that of Israel at the expense of all indigenous economic development initiatives so as to prevent the possibility of any economic competition,' state the authors of *Israeli Obstacles to Economic Development in the Occupied Palestinian Territories*. 'The occupied Palestinian territories are thus captive repository markets for Israeli goods against which they have no protection. Israeli restrictions are designed to work for the benefit of the Jewish Israeli state and exclude the Palestinian economy from world markets. The majority of Palestinian workers are [now] dependent on external demand for their cheap, flexible labour; and Palestinian industrialists and manufacturers are restricted to local markets and demand lest they [should] compete with their Israeli counterparts.'[20]

The overall situation was much worse in the tiny Gaza Strip, which was home to almost half of the Palestinians in the Occupied Territories.

10

GAZA:

The End of the Line

'We had to do guard duty in the observation post overlooking the [Palestinian] refugee camp in Gaza,' said an Israeli soldier, a reservist in a highly decorated unit, in an interview with the *Kol HaIr* (The City Voice), a Hebrew weekly, in mid-1992. 'Every day . . . children would come and start shouting for us to throw some food. At first, we thought this was a game. Later, we saw that they would jump on everything we threw, even if the bread was full of sand.' Once, he continued, he had witnessed a group of Palestinian teenagers kill a pigeon with a slingshot. After grabbing it, 'they . . . started arguing who would get what piece. They ate it raw.'[1] Earlier, in an interview with the *Jerusalem Report*, Yossi (a pseudonym), a member of Israel's Golani Brigade, a combat unit, had remarked: 'Gaza is the end of the world, and Rafah is the pit at the end of the world.'[2]

Nothing has changed since then either in the Gaza Strip or in Rafah.

Rafah, the name borne both by a town and a refugee camp, is home to 120,000 Gazans, about an eighth of the total living in the territory in the mid-1990s. For me, a photograph of a back alley of low breeze-block dwellings with roofs of corrugated sheet – bisected by an open sewer of stagnant, malodorous liquid in the foreground – with a tattered Palestinian flag, limp on its pole, in the middle distance, aptly captured the squalor and degradation of Rafah. Having emerged from a maze of alleyways of unremitting filth, Abdul Hakim al Samra, my Gazan interpreter, and I found ourselves stomping on a wide sandy road, lacerated once again by open sewers, much wider than before but equally revolting, its otherwise smooth surface gnarled with sundered cinderblocks, plastic bottles, broken bricks, polythene sheets, stones and pieces of cement. Single storey shelters, screened from the gaze of pedestrians by a wall of uneven, rusting metal sheets, straight and corrugated, held together by unseen devices, demarcated both sides of the sandy road without pavements. Relief came when, in our wanderings, we chanced upon a football match in progress: the open, orderly space, the smartly dressed players, the youth and enthusiasm of the spectators, all male, erupting every so often in cries and shouts of support, applause or denigration.

Not far from there, shouts of another kind filled the warm air of the desert. Many men and women, dressed in black or grey cloaks, and standing close to a high metal-wire fence held up by thick round wooden poles, were conversing loudly with their interlocutors across a no-person's land 50 metres wide. The people on the other side, the sovereign soil of Egypt, too were clawing the fence as they shouted. An IDF Jeep, mounted with guns, went past slowly. The Gazans and Egyptians continued talking loudly, uninterrupted.

In a different context, unaffected by the 1948–9 Arab-Israeli War, Rafah, a border town along the Egyptian-Palestinian border during the British mandate, had kept on expanding, a process which continued unchecked, since the Gaza Strip later became an Egyptian-administered territory. The situation changed in June 1967 when the Strip was occupied by Israel. The demarcation of the boundary between Egypt and Israel that followed in the aftermath of the 1978 Camp David Accords left the hugely enlarged

Rafah sliced into two parts, one Egyptian, the other Gazan. The partition, however, left intact filial connections, which continue, and are renewed through public dialogue – across the international fences. The talk, Abdul Hakim told me, was as much about family matters as the property left behind by the interlocutors. A freelance journalist, Abdul Hakim al Samra had brought many foreign reporters and authors to this site, a Middle Eastern version of the Berlin Wall. In his mid-30s, an urbane looking man, courteous, clean-shaven, with close cropped jet-black hair, he was dressed in a dark blue shirt and blue jeans and black shoes. A graduate of the American University in Cairo, he was at ease with the English language.

The town of Rafah provides entry into the Rafah salient of Egypt leading to the port of Al Arish (the terminus of an abandoned railway from Palestine, during the British mandate, whose tracks are still intact), which connects overland with Port Said at the northern end of the Suez Canal across which lies mainland Egypt. As a gateway between west Asia and north-east Africa, Gaza has had a long and turbulent chronicle. The repeated conquests and pillages by foreigners made the native people all the more determined to resist alien rule and, in case of failure, suffer the consequences. Having subdued them in 332 BC, Alexander the Great penalized them for their fighting spirit by selling into slavery some 10,000 Gazans. History repeated itself when, following their occupation by Israel in 1967, Gazans struggled against the Israelis vigorously, and were severely repressed. Following the adoption in AD 313 of Christianity by their political masters, the Romans, the Gazans, loyal to the pagan god Marnas, fought the Christians long and hard, but yielded in the end. Like the rest of the region, Gaza fell to Muslim Arabs in AD 635. It changed hands during the Crusades, which ended with the rise of the Mamelukes. In 1517 it was incorporated into the Ottoman empire, and stayed there, except in 1799 (Napoleon Bonaparte) and during the revolt by Muhammad Ali during 1831–40. In World War I it was the site of major battles between the Ottomans and the Allies, principally the British. The Ottoman offensive

in 1915 mounted from Gaza to capture the Sinai and the
Suez Canal, which the British managed to repel at great
cost, made London realize the strategic importance of the
Palestinian region as a buffer to safeguard Egypt and the
Suez Canal, Britain's lifeline to its empire in India. It led to
British resolve to acquire control over Palestine after victory
in the war, an objective it attained primarily because it was
the British forces under the command of General Edmund
Allenby who expelled the Ottomans from the region in late
1917. The vicious fighting in Gaza, the target of heavy British
bombardment, left the area devastated. Indeed Gaza city was
so badly damaged that nothing of historical value survived.
The famous Omar Mosque was revived properly only after
it had been repaired in 1925.

Travelling from Jerusalem, one overcast March morning
70 years later, I mused over the long chronicle of strife in
Gaza. Little did I know that I was heading for a battle
frontline, at least in appearance. As our shared taxi, known
locally as a *sheroot*, a sturdy white Mercedes-Benz, bearing
the white license plates of Gaza, neared the military checkpoint at Ezer, I saw a whole battery of concrete barriers on
both sides of the road. Young soldiers with machine-guns
abounded. Artificial sand dunes scattered over a large area
indicated an ambitious construction project in progress – to
transform the transient checkpoint into a solid fortress. We
stopped behind a monstrous-looking IDF truck – the type
which, by killing and injuring several Gazans in late 1987,
had triggered a six-year-long uprising.

Each of us, five male and two female passengers, was
given a thorough check-up, with the young IDF soldier
looking carefully at each document and also at the face
of the passenger: an unflinching eye-to-eye contact. It was
the first time since my arrival in Israel 10 weeks earlier
that I had encountered such treatment. The light-skinned,
smooth-faced soldier with bushy eyebrows asked a passenger,
a bearded man in his early 30s, to get off the vehicle, and pass
through a metal-detector. He detained a young Palestinian
with a long narrow face wearing a flimsy windbreaker. Past
the IDF checkpoint, we reached a set of barriers manned

by a joint force of Israelis and Palestinians, then finally a checkpoint which was (notionally) fully Palestinian. Here an older policeman in khaki trousers and a khaki sweater was standing leisurely between two vertical cement concrete barriers with tea glasses on top. He waved us through, the way I remember the IDF soldier doing when I had returned to Jerusalem in the car of a Jewish settler from Beit El.

The eight kilometre ride to the centre of Gaza city was along a narrow road bounded by low buildings, an unpainted derelict house of cement concrete here, a half filled shop there. Donkey carts were a common sight. When the thoroughfare widened, its spine – demarcated by a line of wooden poles, holding up electric wires sagging above a pavement – appeared in the middle. When our vehicle approached the Palestine Square, the hub of the capital, the lively chaos of an Arab city, made worse by the rain and mud, dictated that we be disgorged some distance from the normal destination.

Struggling to safeguard my hold-all from the muck that motorized vehicles were splashing on the pedestrians, I allowed myself to be dragooned inside a rickety car with an opaque windshield by its driver, a young, bright-faced, chirpy Palestinian in his early 20s. It was clear from his expression that he had never heard of Cliff Hotel. The inevitable enquiries from passers-by gave him a clue. Despite the discomfort of a rough ride over crumbling, choked roads in a car which lacked springs, I could sense that we were heading for the Mediterranean. The face of the city improved. The buildings became steadily higher and newer. Finally, the newly built Cliff Hotel, its restaurant being lapped by sea waves, lifted my sagging spirits.

The next day Abdul Hakim proved quite methodical. 'From head to toe the Gaza Strip is 46 kilometres,' he said. 'For most of its length it is six kilometres wide, rising to 10 when you reach Rafah. The total area is 360 square kilometres. There are 16 Jewish settlements. Then there are the closed IDF areas. Finally, there is the security perimeter running along the border between the Gaza Strip and Israel. All told Israel and its 3,000 Jewish settlers control some 40 per cent of the Gaza Strip.' That gave a population density of

19 square kilometre for the Jewish settlers and 5,000/square kilometre for the Palestinians, a ratio of 1:260.

The population explosion had started in 1948 due to the Arab-Israeli War, when 160,000 native Gazans found themselves living next to 180,000 refugees from the rest of Palestine. The trebling of the inhabitants of the Gaza Strip since then was well encapsulated by the Jabaliya camp to the north-east of Gaza city. Here 77,000 people were crammed into an area of 1.5 square kilometres. The adjacent village of the same name and roughly the same area was home to a mere 10,000 Palestinians.

Abdul Hakim took me to the camp in his modest car with its peculiar starting and stopping habits. The refugee settlement is situated in a sandy depression about one kilometre from the coastline. One of its landmarks is the Suleiman's Pool, filled with raw sewage, near an elementary school, a watery grave for several of the pupils. Abdul Hakim drove me to the site of the first demonstration of the intifada, on 9 December 1987: an open sandy ground littered with the usual debris in front of a motley of single- and double-storey cinderblock dwellings built at right angles, with a couple of cars parked outside, a few men lounging and many children loitering – an eminently forgettable place – except that it was near a school from where students had emerged in their hundreds shouting slogans on their march to the local IDF base, a demonstration that had ended with a loss of four lives, victims to army firings.

The immediate trigger for the protest was an accident on 8 December at a petrol station near the Ezer checkpoint, in which an IDF truck hit two Palestinian vehicles transporting Gaza workers from the Jabaliya camp, killing four and injuring more. When the news reached the camp its dwellers perceived the accident as a deliberate act, a revenge for the stabbing of a 45-year-old Jewish trader, Shlomo Sakal, in Gaza city's Palestine Square the day before, with the rumours describing the IDF truck-driver as a close relative of the dead man. Accompanied by Abdul Hakim, I visited the PAZ petrol station near the Ezer checkpoint. An orderly, spacious site, its concrete floor well swept, four tall steel poles holding up a metal-sheet canopy over yellow pumps, it was signposted boldly: large black letters in Hebrew against a yellow background, with one concessionary sign in Arabic: *musfah al betrol* (Arabic, place for petrol). Nothing memorable here, either.

There were of course deeper causes for the eruption of the intifada. Its roots could be traced to the 'iron fist' policy towards the Palestinians announced by Yitzhak Rabin in August 1985, then Defence Minister in a national unity government. This policy resulted, in the words of Ziad Abu Amr, a tall, suave, soft-spoken professor of political science at Birzeit University, in 'loss of life [by army firing, 115 in three years], imprisonment, detention, house or town arrest, demolition of dwellings, deportation, fines, interrogation, travel restrictions, curfews, closure of educational institutions, unjust taxes, economic hardships, and the like'.[3] The figures for the West Bank, collected by Meron Benvenisti, showed that between April 1986 and May 1987 there was a weekly average of 56 violent demonstrations, involving stone-throwing, raising of the banned Palestinian flag, distributing of leaflets, and daubing of walls with nationalist graffiti. There was also an average of four incidents a week involving use of firearms, knives, explosives and petrol bombs. And each week 81 West Bankers were arrested for participating in a demonstration or engaging in terrorist activity.[4]

Tension began rising steadily from mid-1987, especially in the Gaza Strip. In early summer six members of the Islamic Jihad escaped from Gaza central jail. Soon after they assassinated Captain Ron Tal, head of the IDF military police in Gaza. In the early autumn there was an armed confrontation between the Jihad activists and Israeli security forces in which four Jihad militants and one Shin Beth officer were killed. On 25 November, the news that a member of the Popular Front for the Liberation of Palestine-General Command, armed with an assault rifle, a pistol and hand grenades, had landed at the Gibor army camp near Kiryat Shimona in northern Israel by using a hand-glider from south Lebanon, and killed six Israeli soldiers, electrified the Palestinians. It made them realize that despite its over-whelming military might, sophisticated weaponry and tight security measures, Israel was still vulnerable. This feeling was bolstered when, following the fatal stabbing of Shlomo Sakal on 7 December, foreign minister Shimon Peres said that the Government should seriously consider demilitarizing Gaza. Before these events the 14th Arab League summit, meeting in Amman from 8–11 November, had focused on the Iran-Iraq War, and paid scant attention to the Palestinian problem. This made West Bankers and Gazans resolve to take their fate into their own hands.

The intifada, which lasted nearly six years, went through the following phases: December 1987 to early August 1990 (Iraqi occupation of Kuwait); August 1990 to February 1991 (the end of the Gulf War); March to October 1991 (convening of the Middle East Peace Conference); November 1991 to June 1992 (Labour's electoral victory in Israel); and July 1992 to September 1993 (signing of the Israeli-PLO Accord).

'The intifada started small, became more violent, and then settled down to a pattern of big or small demonstrations,' said Dr Adel Manna, an Israeli Arab academic. 'It became a state of mind for Palestinians. Once they realized that they could not get liberation through intifada they started a war of attrition from 1990–91 onwards which went on until the Oslo Accord.'[5]

Dr Mahdi Abdul Hadi of the Palestinian Academic Society for the Study of International Affairs (PASSIA), based in East Jerusalem, described the opening year of the intifada as the 'Palestinian Year', when the inhabitants of the Occupied Territories, acting on their own, put their problem back on the international agenda, and rid themselves of the remnants of Jordanian control. During this period the local intifada leadership, enjoying complete freedom, devised such inno-vative tactics as refusal to pay taxes to the Israeli authorities or accept the magnetic tape identity document. Then came the 'PLO Year', when the PLO, representing both Palestinian communities, inside and outside the Occupied Territories, and headquartered in Tunisia, took the centre-stage, and imposed strict control over the local leadership in the West Bank and Gaza. This period culminated with the Palestine National Council declaring a Palestinian state, thus preparing the ground for a diplomatic solution. The third year, ending in December 1990, was to have been the 'Israeli Year', with bridges to be constructed between the two camps.[6] But it got sidetracked when Labour quit the national unity government (March 1990), the PLO-US contacts were suspended following the raid on the Israeli beaches by the Palestine Liberation Front, led by Abu al Abbas (the *nom de guerre* of Muhammad Abbas Zaidan) in retaliation for the earlier killing of Palestinians in Rishon LeZion (May 1990), and the occupation of Kuwait by Saddam Hussein (August 1990).

Within 10 days of the massive demonstration in the Jabaliya camp on 9 December 1987, the intifada had spread to all parts of the Gaza Strip, the West Bank and East Jerusalem, with predominantly young protestors attacking the Israeli security forces with stones and petrol bombs, and the latter responding with tear gas and live ammunition. On 19 December East Jerusalem experienced the worst violence since the June 1967 war. By the end of the month, when the Israeli forces had shot dead 24 Palestinians, both the PLO, headquartered abroad, and the Islamic Centre, the front organization of the Muslim Brotherhood, based in the Occupied Territories, had lent the spontaneous uprising their support.

On 8 January 1988, the day the PLO-sponsored United National Leadership of the Uprising (UNLU) issued its first communiqué, Israel shut down all universities and schools in the Occupied Territories. The UNLU communiqués were printed and distributed clandestinely, and were then broadcast by the Al Quds Palestinian Arab Radio, based in Damascus, and the Voice of the PLO Radio, operating in Baghdad.

Its Communiqué Number 1 called for 'a general and comprehensive strike until Wednesday evening, 13 January 1988', and included specific instructions to 'Brother workers', 'Brother businessmen and grocers', 'Brother owners of taxi companies', and 'Brother doctors and pharmacists'.

Containing a 'General warning' – 'Walking in the streets will not be safe in view of the measures that will be taken to make the comprehensive strike a success . . . [T]he strike groups will be deployed throughout the Occupied Homeland' – it ended with the slogan of the strike: 'Down with the occupation; long live Palestine as a free and Arab country.' (Later, unable to stop or intercept this highly effective means of communication, the Israeli Shin Beth resorted to issuing its own forged communiqués in order to sow dissension in the Palestinian ranks. An example of this was the Communiqué 38 put out in late October 1988 on the eve of the Palestine National Council session in Algiers. The genuine communiqué and excerpts from the Shin Beth version are reprinted in *Intifada* edited by Zachary Lockman and Joel Beinin.[7] At about the same time Hamas, established by the Islamic Centre, issued its own communiqué. In order to maintain the intifada's popular character, both the PLO and Hamas advised use of 'popular weapons' by the Palestinians, such as stones and petrol bombs (later knives, axes and stone cutters), and not firearms or explosives.

In response, Israel's Defence Minister, Yitzhak Rabin, declared on 19 January that the 'first priority' of the IDF was to 'use force, might and blows' to squash the rioting. The result was a series of 'aberrations (according to the IDF)'/'atrocities (according to the Palestinians)' by Israeli soldiers, including the live burial of four Palestinians in a West Bank village who were saved from death by asphyxiation in the nick of time. Two days after Israeli chief of staff, General Dan Shomron, declared on 23 February that the soldiers were allowed to resort to beating as a device for dispersing the rioters, and not as punishment, the New York-based Columbia Broadcasting Service Television showed Israeli soldiers beating bound Palestinians in order to break their bones. Responding to the international criticism, the IDF unveiled a specially designed device for dispersing crowds: a mechanized stone thrower, equipped with a machine to break a large rock and spit hundreds of medium-sized stones at high velocity at demonstrators through its revolving turret. When the intifada showed no sign of subsiding, the Government tried to protect Israelis from its effects by sealing off the Occupied Territories. It did so on 28 March 1988 after nearly 21 years of occupation and 11 years of issuing a map of Israel without the 1949 armistice lines.

Believing that the evil genius of the PLO's military chief, Khalil Wazir with the *nom de guerre* of Abu Jihad (Arabic, Father of Struggle) was responsible for the continuing uprising, the Israeli Government decided to eliminate him. In a well-planned commando action, Israel's death squad assassinated Wazir at home in Tunis in the early hours of 16 April 1988. The shocked Palestinians protested violently, and 16 of them lost their lives, victims to IDF shootings. However, to the consternation of the Israeli authorities, the loss of Wazir made little difference to the intensity of the intifada. In any case, Islamic Hamas, functioning outside the PLO, had become a major, independent player, and had been so recognized by UNLU.

Furthermore, the intifada had infected the Palestinian teenagers. 'No [Palestinian] child, no teenager is immune from the politics of the intifada,' noted Helen Winternitz, an American researcher, based in rural West Bank. 'Throwing a stone, and thereby joining the makeshift army of the intifada, is a rite of passage into manhood. Every boy knows this dictate. To do less is to be a weakling; to do more is to be a hero.'[8] Along with stone throwing went two other major protest activities: the raising of the Palestinian flag, and spraying the walls with political graffiti, often in one of the four colours of the Palestinian standard. Red in the flag signified blood of the martyrs, green for fertility of the Palestinian plains, white for peace, and black the oppression of occupation (to be removed when Palestine had been liberated).[9] 'Bits of green, black and red cloth, the PLO colours, hang from telephone lines, like torn laundry,' noted Yossi Halevi, a journalist, serving his reserve duty in the Gaza Strip. 'Walls on the main streets are scarred with white streaks of paint blocking out political slogans; sometimes several layers of black- or green-lettered slogans alternate with whitewash. But on the alley walls the slogans and fantasy images of the intifada have not been erased.'[10]

These jobs were done by the youthful ranks of the PLO and Hamas.

The function of the graffiti was twofold: to express nationalist, anti-Israeli sentiment, and to convey information about forthcoming strikes or demonstrations, commemoration of martyrs and nationalist days, boycott of Israeli products, and assisting specific groups of Palestinians (such as employing those under town or village arrest). Graffiti were spray-painted or stencilled at strategic locations for maximum exposure. In the Jalazoun refugee camp, for instance, the wall near the coffee shop in the main square was the favourite spot, and in downtown Gaza city Omar al Mukhtar Street was popular. The size varied from a scrawl to a wall mural, covering a whole building, often in villages where IDF patrols were infrequent. The most popular slogans in the UNLU camp were: 'Yes, yes to the blessed Intifada; Yes to the United National Leadership of the Intifada'; 'Revolution, revolution against the occupier'; 'No to the Zionist entity'; and 'O Jews, leave our land'. The map of mandate Palestine, the Palestinian flag and a gun were frequent images, and often appeared together. In a similar vein the word 'Fatah' was incorporated into a Kalashnikov assault rifle, an exercise simplified by the fact that Arabic script is easy to transform into illustrations. Also popular with Fatah activists was the combined image of an eagle and a picture of Arafat embracing (the assassinated) Khalil Wazir. No great artistry was needed to spray garbage bins of all sizes with 'Israel' or '[Israeli Premier] Shamir's Office'. Shamir was consistently drawn as a donkey, (defence minister) Rabin as a monkey, and (industry minister) Ariel Sharon as an elephant. Other popular anti-Israeli images were: a machine-gun firing bullets at an Israeli flag, and a sword slashing the Star of David. Besides paint spray guns other means were used to deploy graffiti as an effective political tool. 'We cut the shape of symbols and slogans out of a newspaper, placed them against the wall, and applied paint,' Adil, a young Palestinian activist, told Paul Lalor, a British researcher. 'If there was an order to put up a certain slogan in Manara [downtown Ramallah] there would be three or four people involved – some to do it, others to keep watch. It was usually done at night, and sometimes we would barricade the road to give us time to get away in case an army patrol came.'[11] When they failed to escape on time, they sometimes paid a heavy price. During the first two and a half years of the intifada seven Palestinian graffiti writers were shot dead by IDF patrols. The IDF combined this tactic with a policy of fining the person who failed to remove graffiti from his property.

As for the leading figures, many of those involved in the intifada were young educated Palestinians, fluent in Hebrew and familiar with Israeli norms, who took over the communal leadership from the older generation of Arab notables, professing peaceful co-existence with the Israelis. Both UNLU and Hamas urged the Palestinians to resign from all posts of the Government, stop using public services, withdraw money from Israeli banks, boycott Israeli products, cease paying taxes, and join the strikes they called periodically. UNLU and Hamas committees issued circulars containing instructions in these matters, and urged all Palestinians to share the sacrifices required by the intifada. The Palestinians used charity funds, religious and secular, to support the large number of families where husbands or brothers were jailed. Actions by the Israeli security forces, involving firings, curfews, harassment, beatings, arrests and house searches and demolitions severely disrupted Palestinian life.

By the time the intifada entered its second year in December 1988, Palestinians could claim substantial achievements. In late July King Hussein of Jordan relinquished the last vestiges of legal and administrative ties between Jordan and the West Bank, thus laying to rest any prospect of Israel exercising its 'Jordanian option' to resolve the Palestinian problem. On 15 November the Palestine National Council, meeting in Algiers, proclaimed an independent State of Palestine, and accepted the United Nations Security Council Resolutions 242 and 338. Addressing a specially convened session of the United Nations General Assembly in Geneva on 14 December, Yasser Arafat renounced all forms of violence, and recognized Israel's right to exist in peace, thus paving the way for substantive dialogue between the PLO and the United States.

On the Israeli side, according to the head of the IDF's budgetary office, the intifada cost the IDF more than $750 million during the first year. And, according to the Bank of Israel, the Israeli economy suffered a loss of $500 million due to a decline in tourism, construction and exports to the West Bank and Gaza.[12] In mid-May 1989, Prime Minister Yitzhak Shamir proposed elections to choose Palestinians to negotiate with Israel. Both UNLU and Hamas leaders rejected the offer, seeing it as a ploy to defuse the intifada.

However, continued defiance and protest by Palestinians took its toll on the community. For instance, in 1989 the residents of the Jabaliya camp, where the intifada originated, had to endure 156 days of curfew, cooped up in their homes day after day with brief releases to do essential shopping. The cumulative effect of army firings and beating and long curfews – enforced to immobilize youths and eliminate stone throwing – manifested itself *inter alia* in a rise of clinical depression and schizophrenia, up from 189 cases to 226 between April 1989 and February 1990, according to Dr Muhammad Abu Sweieh, the head of the camp's health clinic.[13]

The vital importance of the curfew in the military's counter-intifada strategy was highlighted by an account of his reserve duty in the IDF by Yossi Halevi of the *Jerusalem Report*. '[In the Nuseirat camp, between Gaza city and Khan Yunis, at 11 p.m.] the unpaved, sandy streets are dark and totally still. Like the rest of Gaza, Nuseirat is under nightly curfew, from 9 p.m. to 3 a.m. We park in the central square . . . lit by the sporadic streetlamps that illumine only scattered patches, like spotlights . . . Rows of political slogans have been painted on to a concrete wall, and our job is to find someone to erase them. We come at night because the curfew allows us to operate freely, without the crowds of stone throwers that follow us by day . . . Alon [the unit commander], a university student, chooses a house at random. He bangs on the door and the whole sleeping camp seems to reverberate. "*Iftah, jeish* (Open, army)!" he shouts.

Our few Arabic phrases are all imperative . . . Alon shows them [Ahmad, the head of the household, and his two sons] the wall, then sends them home for paint and brushes.'[14]

The Israeli politicians' fear that the intifada would spread among the Arabs of Israel was fulfilled in May 1990. Early morning on 20 May Ami Popper, a young Jewish resident of Rishon LeZion, 12 kilometres south of Tel Aviv, took his elder brother's rifle and drove to the site – an intersection of two main roads on the outskirts – where Palestinians from Gaza gathered daily as casual labourers to be hired by Israeli contractors. Brandishing his weapon, he forced the Palestinians to squat on the ground in three rows. He then began firing at them. As the Palestinians ran helter-skelter, he reloaded his rifle, and fired again. He then jumped into his car and sped away. His carnage left seven dead and 11 injured. The news of the murders caused outrage not only among West Bankers and Gazans but also among Israeli Arabs, especially in Nazareth, and resulted in rioting in which 15 more Palestinians lost their lives. However, the retaliatory action by the Palestine Liberation Front, a pro-Iraqi group, thwarted by the Israelis, had far more serious consequences. During the early hours of 30 May, the Jewish holiday of Shavout, the PLF's 16 commandos, operating in two batches, tried to land separately on the Nitzanim and Gaash beaches of Tel Aviv, the city where the Defence Ministry was based, with a plan to attack a military officers' camp. But one team was intercepted on the high seas by the Israeli navy, and the other on land by the border police. Together they killed four guerrillas, and captured the rest. When Yasser Arafat refused either to dismiss the PLF leader, Abu al Abbas, from the PLO's executive committee (something he was not authorized to do) or condemn the planned PLF's operation – arguing that the PLO's agreement with the United States exempted attacks on military targets inside Israel – Washington suspended dialogue with the PLO. This pleased the right-wing Israeli Government of Yitzhak Shamir.

Several weeks later a far more shattering event shook the region. On 2 August Iraq invaded and occupied Kuwait. Ten days later the Iraqi president, Saddam Hussein, made a linkage between Iraq's evacuation of Kuwait with Israel's evacuation of Occupied Arab Territories. This made him a hero among Palestinians. By integrating the Palestinian national demand into the wider regional conflict, Saddam Hussein lifted the intifada from its recent doldrums and infused new life into it.

'[During the first heady year] a festive violence lit the streets of Palestinian neighbourhoods and villages with burning tyres whose acrid black smoke tasted of success,' noted Helen Winternitz. 'When the IDF, border police and Shin Beth countered with bullets and truncheons, tear gas, tax raids and mass arrests, the violence was checked superficially, but smouldered underground like coals ... And when Saddam Hussein rose against the established order in the Middle East, the winds from Iraq blew an ideological oxygen that inspired Palestinians. The coals were rekindled into pro-Saddam flames.'[15]

Saddam Hussein's proposal was rejected summarily by US President George Bush, who took the lead in rallying the international community against Iraq. During the ensuing Gulf crisis, the Palestinian problem caught world attention on 8 October. On that day the Israeli border police shot dead 17 Palestinians and injured another 150 during rioting at the Haram al Sharif/Temple Mount in Jerusalem, which was triggered by the plans of the Temple Mount Faithful to lay a foundation for the Third Jewish Temple on the mount. The immediate rioting that followed in the commercial district of Greater East Jerusalem led to three more deaths, making it the highest one day Palestinian fatalities since the start of the intifada. Iraq ordered three days of mourning. The United Nations Security Council unanimously adopted a resolution which expressed alarm at the violence, called on Israel to abide by the Fourth Geneva Convention, and instructed the UN Secretary-General, Javier Perez de Cuellar, to dispatch a mission to the region to submit a report on the situation there by 30 October. But Israel refused to receive the UN mission. On 24 October the Security Council unanimously called on Israel to reconsider its decision. Shamir's Government in Israel remained obdurate. Perez de Cuellar recommended

Rabbi Moshe Levinger, the first Jewish settler in the West Bank, at home in downtown Hebron, February 1995

A wall mural in Gaza city shows Palestine (written in Arabic) as a boat about to sail, watched by Abu Jihad, a Palestinian leader assassinated by the Israelis in Tunis

One of the many empty villas in the Beit El Jewish settlement near Ramallah, the West Bank

יידיעות אחרונות

הילדים שלא ישובו

The front page photographs of 18 of the 21 Israeli soldiers killed in a suicide bombing attack at Beit Lid on 22 January 1995 in the *Yediot Aharonat* on the wall of a school in Beit Vagan, West Jerusalem

A typical Palestinian refugee house, Jalazoun camp near Ramallah, the West Bank

Pictures of 17 Palestinians killed by the Israeli security forces on the Noble Sanctuary/Mount Moriah on 8 October 1990 at the Islamic Museum near the Al Aqsa Mosque, Old City, Jerusalem

The memorial to six Fatah activists killed by an Israeli death squad in March 1994, Gaza city

Kiryat Arba residents paying respects to Dr Baruch Goldstein – who massacred 29 Palestinians inside the Ibrahimi Mosque and was killed on the spot – at his tomb in Kiryat Arba on top of a hill overlooking Hebron

The inscriptions on the banner on the wall at a book exhibition, organized by the Islamic Bloc of Al Najah University, read (from top to bottom): 'Al Mujahid al Shaikh Izz al Din Qassam Brigade'; 'There is no god but Allah, and Muhammad is the messenger of Allah'; 'The Islamic Bloc of Al Najah University'; and 'Islam is the solution'

The Palestine Mosque, Gaza city, a stronghold of Hamas

Harb Abu Namous (in traditional Arab dress) with a daughter-in-law and two grandsons, with some of their children at their three-room house, Gaza city

Open sewerage, Rafah, the Gaza Strip

A Palestinian woman from Rafah in the Gaza Strip shouting across the fence and no-man's land, patrolled by the Israeli military, to a relative in the Egyptian part of Rafah

President Anwar Sadat of Egypt, watched by Shimon Peres and Israeli Premier Menachem Begin, delivers a speech at the Lod international airport, November 1977 – as depicted at the Wax Museum, Tel Aviv

Watched by US President Bill Clinton, Yitzhak Rabin and Yasser Arafat shake hands on the White House lawn, Washington D.C., 13 September 1993. (G.P.O., Jerusalem)

Shimon Peres and
Yitzhak Rabin confer
with Yasser Arafat
and Ahmad Qrei at
the Erez checkpoint,
Gaza Strip, January
1995. (G.P.O.,
Jerusalem)

Binyamin
Netanyahu, the first
directly elected prime
minister of Israel,
June 1996.
(G.P.O., Jerusalem)

that a special session of all 164 UN members be called
to discuss the measures to be taken to make Israel comply
with the Fourth Geneva Convention. Following the release of
Perez de Cuellar's report on 2 November, the Gazans rioted
so intensely in its support that the IDF caused injuries to
300 people in three days, and imposed an indefinite curfew.
But nothing happened at the Security Council. In its next
communiqué, Number 65, issued in December, UNLU urged
Palestinians to use 'all means' in their anti-Israeli struggle,
thus going beyond its policy of limiting protest action to
stone throwing.

By the time the intifada completed its three years in
December 1990, the Palestinian death toll was put at 930
to 1,104, including 76 to 161 children below 14 to 16 years.
Of these 307 to 310 were suspected Palestinian collaborators
murdered by Palestinians. The number of Jews killed, military
and civilian, was 21 to 23. More than 119,000 Palestinians,
a sixth of them children, were seriously wounded. 2,050
Palestinian houses were demolished or sealed. At any given
moment Israeli prisons and military detention camps held
some 14,000 Palestinians, about 4 per cent of the total
male population of the West Bank and Gaza Strip aged
above 14. 'Almost every Palestinian family has paid a
price for the intifada – be it a relative dead, a house
demolished, a friend crippled, a job lost, a sentence endured,
an education interrupted, a business ruined,' reported Helen
Winternitz.[16]

Some Palestinian households suffered more than others.
The family of Muhammad Harb Abu Namous and Baraaka,
originally from Beersheba now living in Gaza city, was an
example. Abdul Hakim and I ran into a young son of the
family, Jamal, by accident in Gaza city as we talked to people
near the memorial to six Fatah militants assassinated by Shin
Beth agents. An oval-faced man of 24, in dark brown trousers,
and a green, short-sleeved T-shirt and sandals, Jamal was
taciturn. His mother, Baraaka Abu Namous, whom I met in
a back alley near their home, was a contrast. A sprightly,
articulate woman of 41, with high cheekbones and an
aquiline nose, she was dressed in a black skirt touching

her sandalled feet, and a long-sleeved yellow blouse covered by a white shawl, bordered with flowers, which took in her head and neck, leaving only her face exposed. She delivered her first child, a boy named Ahmad, when she was 15, and has since then borne nine more – five male and four female – the youngest, a boy, aged three and a half. Ahmad and the next son, Nidal, aged 24, were married, with children, and lived with their parents. Altogether an extended family of 20, they occupied three rooms, each five metres by five metres, with a corridor and a small courtyard in the back. A glance at the main room, used as a bedroom at night, revealed no furniture, only rolls of striped woollen rugs stacked in a corner. On the fading, sky-blue wall facing the tiny window by the alley, there was a picture of the Dome of the Rock next to a framed verse from the Quran, its gold letters meekly reflecting the sun, the only cheer inside the hollow cube formed by cinderblock walls, an asbestos roof and a floor covered with a ragged carpet.

Muhammad Harb had been too ill to work. Of the four grown-up sons only one, Ahmad, a father of four, had a job. He was with the Palestinian Authority police, and earned $263 a month. He was away on duty when we called. The second son, Jamal, arrested for throwing a petrol bomb at an IDF patrol in 1988, had spent nearly seven years behind bars – in Ashqelon, Ansar I, Ansar III and Gaza central prisons. It was hard to imagine a man looking so shy and withdrawn doing such a daring thing as lobbing a Molotov cocktail at soldiers. 'Ansar III was the worst,' he said. 'I was there for three years. We went on a hunger strike there. We got some rights. But there is no Israeli promise that you can trust. In jail it was just eating and sleeping. They gave us just enough food to keep us alive. They treated me like a monkey. They would throw food at me as if I were an animal.'

The third son, Ziad Muhammad, a serious-looking man of 22, with jet-black close-cropped hair, in black trousers and a flowery bush-shirt, appeared less introverted. He, too, had suffered in the course of the intifada. He was injured in a leg by IDF shooting when he was three years younger. So, too, was his younger brother, Imad, aged 18, twice: once in an arm by IDF firing when he was only 12 years old, and then again in a leg when he was 15. 'I still have a bullet inside my leg,' he told me matter-of-factly. Dressed in black trousers with red and green patches – colours of the PLO flag – and a long-sleeved white jersey imprinted with a psychedelic design, Imad, flashing a posturing smile, seemed more suited for a career as a pop singer than a stone-throwing subversive in the rag-bag ranks of the PLO. The remaining two brothers were too young to challenge the Israeli occupation.

But the mother, Baraaka, too had suffered. 'I remember the first time the soldiers came, in the middle of the night,' she recalled. 'I opened the door. They put a gun against my breast. I was so frightened I went dumb. Couldn't speak, couldn't even cry. Terrible. The next time was in 1991. Again in the middle of the night. This time I would not open the door. So they jumped over the front wall [which does not join up with the roof]. They had torches which they flashed. Then they switched on the lights. Suddenly in the middle of the night we had Israeli soldiers with guns all over the house. I protested. They hit me and kicked me. I was pregnant, and lost my baby. I travelled to Amman for hospital treatment. The PLO paid for it. Bless them!'

Her description of the night raid by the IDF, and my view of the room used for sleeping at night, reminded me of the passage in *The Yellow Wind* by David Grossman, an Israeli journalist and writer. 'Whoever has served in the army in the "territories" knows how such rooms look from the inside during the night. Whoever has taken part in searches, in imposing curfews, in capturing a suspect at night, remembers. The violent entry into rooms like this one [in the Deheisheh camp, West Bank], where several people sleep, crowded, in unaired stench, three or four together under scratchy wool blankets, wearing their work clothes still in their sleep, as if ready at any moment to get up and go wherever they are told. They wake in confusion, squinting from the flashlight, children wail, sometimes a couple is making love, soldiers surround the house, some of them – shoes full of mud after tramping through the paths of the camp – walking over the sleep-warm blankets, some pounding on the tin roof above.'[17]

Despite all the suffering and trauma the Abu Namous family had endured, they showed no self-pity. They all seemed to have been steeled by the experience, not demoralized. With her (covered) head held high, Baraaka had lost none of the high spiritedness that I imagined her possessing when she was younger. Nor was there any sign that she or other Gazans were prepared to accept anything less than a fully-fledged sovereign state of Palestine.

Equally remarkable was the (historical) fact that by the end of 1990 the intifada had drawn level in its longevity with the Arab Revolt during the British mandate, which had lasted from April 1936 to March 1939. There was as yet no sign that the intifada was faltering.

The military-political assessment of the intifada on the Israeli side was mixed. There was quiet satisfaction among civilian commentators that the earlier IDF tactics of firings and beatings had given way to a systematic escalation of response – tear gas, gravel throwing by machine, rubber and plastic bullets, capped finally by live ammunition – in order to reduce Palestinian fatalities. But feelings in the IDF ranks were turning increasingly sour. 'Going to the Territories just stinks,' said Yossi. 'You dislike the Arabs. You don't believe in what you're doing ... Patrolling the streets of Rafah, [you are] nervous to take each step, knowing that a petrol bomb or bullet can come at you from any direction. You're worried that you're going to get it in the face.' These were the words of a 21-year-old soldier who, having served his three-year conscription, had volunteered for a combat unit. Another draftee, serving his reserve duty in the Gaza Strip, described an early-morning foot patrol in the Bureij camp of Gaza thus: 'We walk slowly through back alleys that curl around main streets, listening for distant whistles and howls that alert the camp to our presence. We scan the rooftops for falling cinderblocks, intersections for flying stones. On main streets we eye passing cars, to make sure no one tries to run us down.'[18]

Summing up the general mood prevalent among the young conscripts, David Horovitz of the *Jerusalem Report* wrote: 'The initial excitement at getting "some real action after all the training" has long since paled into a mixture of revulsion for the Palestinians, a sense of humiliation at having to carry out regulations that leave him [the Israeli soldier] impotent in the face of stone throwers, and frustration with the Government for failing to initiate a political solution that could free the army from the West Bank and Gaza.'[19]

Mixed response also prevailed in the political arena. The rightists, whether in the Government or outside, became more convinced than before that Israel must keep the West Bank at all costs, and based their argument on military and security grounds rather than ideology. The leftists took a contrary view. 'Israelis like "invisible Arabs" – those who do the menial work, then disappear without a trace,' stated Zeev Schiff, a leading military commentator, and Ehud Ya'ari. 'But many by now understand that security is not just about territory and strategic depth. It also has to do with this increasingly embittered population that interacts with Jewish society.'[20] The failure of the Israeli Government, in the eyes of the liberal left, was that it had been dealing with the symptoms rather than the causes of the intifada.

The general mood in West Bank villages that Helen Winternitz had been studying since the eruption of the intifada was summarized by her thus: 'In the most hidden place of all, in the mind of many Palestinians, the intifada has wrought irrevocable change. Although many are desperately depressed about its lack of concrete results, they still believe there is no alternative to their struggle for statehood ... To one carpenter in a village north of Jerusalem, the intifada is "like climbing a ladder whose rungs are burning beneath your feet. You cannot go back down".'[21]

Little wonder that most Palestinians came to see Saddam Hussein as their liberator. They were behind Yasser Arafat when he embraced the Iraqi leader, physically and ideologically. When the Gulf War started on 16 January 1991 they waited with bated breath to see whether Saddam Hussein would, as promised, hit Israel. And, when two days later 12 Iraqi Scud ground-to-ground missiles landed in or near Tel Aviv and Haifa, their trust in the Iraqi President rose.

'The Occupied Territories were under curfew during the 44 days of the Gulf War,' said George Hintlian, a Christian Palestinian intellectual. 'So people would go up at night to their terraces despite the wintry weather, and watch the skies. Every time they saw a Scud in the sky, they would start dancing and shouting "Allahu Akbar! (God is Great!)". This made the Israeli soldiers mad. They didn't know what to do. So in desperation they would just fire in the air.'[22] In mid-February 1991 Arafat had a meeting with Saddam Hussein in a Baghdad bunker. Later, in an interview on the Jordanian (state) television, he said: 'By Allah, by Allah, by Allah, I tell you that the day when I and my brothers Abu Uday [Saddam Hussein, father of Uday] and Abu Abdullah [King Hussein, father of Abdullah] will pray at the Al Aqsa [Mosque, in Jerusalem] is very soon.'[23]

When on 28 February, having already evacuated Kuwait, Baghdad accepted the ceasefire conditions of President Bush, the leader of the anti-Iraq coalition, including the uncondi- tional acceptance of all 12 United Nations Security Council resolutions on the subject, many Palestinians wept openly, and some angrily broke their televisions sets. However, once they had recovered their equilibrium a few weeks later, they realized that the situation in the region could not return to the *status quo ante*. 'We made absolutely no mistake by support- ing Saddam, because we will soon begin to reap the fruits,' said Faizeh Jayousi, a Palestinian teacher in Tulkarm. 'Now the entire world knows that the core of the Middle East crisis is the Palestinian issue, and that without solving it there will be no stability in the region.'[24] Among those who agreed with this assessment was James Baker, the US Secretary of State, who had played a vital role in devising and implementing the American policy during the Kuwait crisis and the Gulf War.

His untiring endeavour led to the convening of the inter- national peace conference in Madrid in late October 1991. The decision of the PLO leadership not to boycott the confer- ence caused dissension among its constituents. Until then they had all been united around the Palestine National Council's two-year-old resolution declaring the establishment of the State of Palestine.

The fourth year of the intifada, ending in December, added a further 368 Palestinians to the growing list of the dead, a large majority of them killed by the IDF. However, the proportion of the suspected collaborators murdered by the Palestinian militants began to rise from the previous 30 per cent of the total Palestinian fatalities. This was due to three main reasons – strategic, economic and psychological. There was a growing realization among intifada leaders that unless the Shin Beth's 20,000-strong intelligence network, which underpinned the Israeli military regime, was totally demolished, the IDF would succeed in reimposing its control. The worsening economic condition of the Palestinians was another major reason. The economy of the Occupied Territories suffered sharply due to the pro-Iraqi stance of the 400,000-plus Palestinians who lived and worked in the six Gulf monarchies, with more than three-quarters in Kuwait. The devastation of the emirate's economy due to the Iraqi invasion and occupation hurt badly the Palestinians resident there. The situation deteriorated when, following the restoration of Kuwait to the ruling al Sabah family, most of the remaining Palestinians were expelled from the emirate. Finally, the Palestinian community had begun directing inwards the anger and frustration it felt at the defeat of Saddam Hussein, seen briefly as the modern-day Salah al Din, and the expulsion of the Palestinians from the Gulf states.

Another major outcome of these developments was that confrontations between the young protestors and the IDF acquired a ritualistic air. 'Except for an occasional hand grenade or Molotov cocktail, the intifada has become a sport, a mutual hunt with well-defined rules,' noted Yossi Halevi of the *Jerusalem Report* in his diary, published in October 1991. 'Our patrols are stalked, then his with stones and bottles. When we get angry enough, we chase stone throwers and exchange roles with them, becoming hunters instead of prey. Each side has its advantage: We wear helmets, they outrun us and know the terrain. We have guns, but everyone knows that [that] only seems to be an advantage: We are forbidden to shoot stone throwers. One day some teenagers break the rules of the hunt. Instead of running for cover after throwing stones, they stand in the middle of the street, taunting us with their fearlessness. A soldier aims their gun at them, hoping they'll flee. One of the teenagers extends his arms as though holding a gun, and mimics the soldier's pose. Our job is to "demonstrate a presence" in the army phrase, and prevent the masked terrorists from taking over the camps. The stone-throwers' job is similar: To prove that we don't rule the streets. As we mount our trucks after a foot patrol and drive away, they follow at a safe distance as though they are expelling us, throwing rocks and shouting taunts about our mothers' promiscuity. We have demonstrated our presence, they have proved their audacity.'[25] Yet there was another interpretation of this well-worn exercise; and it came from Yossi, a member of an IDF combat unit, with long experience of service in Gaza. 'It's their [Palestinians'] victory when we shoot them dead; the families get money, there's world attention,' he said. 'And it's our victory when we allow ourselves to be humiliated.'[26]

On the Palestinian side, the Madrid peace conference split UNLU and Hamas, which opposed participation in it in any form. Within the PLO, the sponsor of UNLU, the radical Popular Front for the Liberation of Palestine (PFLP) and the Democratic Front for the Liberation of Palestine (DFLP) hardened their position as Fatah (Arabic, Victory; reverse acronym of Harkat al Tahrir al Falastini, Movement for the Liberation of Palestine), led by Arafat, actively backed the idea of co-operating with the participants in the conference. Indeed, much to Fatah's satisfaction, as talks between the Israelis and the joint delegation of the Jordanians and Palestinians progressed, the latter split into two, with each side negotiating with the Israelis separately. It was not long before Arafat was able to puncture the claim made by Shamir's Government that it was not dealing with the PLO since many of the Palestinian delegates openly declared that they were taking their orders from the PLO. The subsequent embarrassment of Shamir's Likud bloc benefited Labour in the June 1992 parliamentary election. It won. But this had no impact on the intra-Palestinian politics. Indeed tension between Fatah and Hamas escalated into street fighting in

the Gaza Strip in early July 1992, which lasted for three days
and resulted in three deaths and injuries to 100. It ended when
neutral Palestinian leaders intervened, successfully. The two
sides pondered the idea of reviving the intifada once the newly
formed Government under Yitzhak Rabin, who also became
the Defence Minister, had settled down.

Soon after Israeli officials had briefed the media in September that the intifada was finished, the Fatah Hawks, the
armed militants of the party, in the Rafah refugee camp had
a five-hour gun battle with the IDF, in which two Palestinians
were killed. When the seventh round of the Israeli-Palestinian
talks opened in Washington in mid-October, Gazans and
West Bankers showed their disapproval by staging strikes
and demonstrations, which left five Palestinian youths dead.
A month later the PFLP's Red Eagles engaged in a gunfight
with the IDF in the Gaza Strip, which resulted in three
Palestinian deaths.

Not to be outdone, Hamas in Gaza greeted the eighth
round of the Israeli-Palestinian negotiations on 7 December
with an ambush of an IDF Jeep, which left three Israeli
soldiers dead. The Government responded by imposing an
indefinite curfew and sealing off the Strip. Two days later
the West Bank and Gaza commemorated the fifth anniversary
of the intifada – the last year increasing the total death toll
by 136 – with a general strike. A depressed Rabin told a
visiting American Jewish delegation: 'I wish Gaza would
detach itself from Israel and sink into the [Mediterranean]
sea.'[27] Hamas militants ambushed another IDF Jeep, this
time in Hebron, killing two soldiers, on 12 December, and
topped their operations the next day by kidnapping an Israeli
border guard officer, Nissim Toledano, in the Israeli town
of Lod, and demanding the release of their leader, Shaikh
Ahmad Yasin. The Government responded by imposing an
indefinite curfew in Gaza, the hotbed of Hamas. When
Toledano was found dead on 15 December, Rabin went
all out to suppress Hamas. He ordered the arrest of 1,200
Palestinians suspected of membership of Hamas or Islamic
Jihad, and expelled 413 of them to the no-man's land in
south Lebanon on 18 December.

When the indefinite curfew in the Gaza Strip was lifted the next day, there was severe rioting in Khan Yunis, the second largest city. The IDF shot dead six Palestinians, and over the next three days killed five more. A mood of despair descended on Israelis. The public debate on the future of the Gaza Strip, initiated by a petition to the Government by 36 army reservists in June, urging withdrawal from the territory, intensified. An increasingly popular view held that the principal culprit responsible for terrorist activities against Jews was Hamas, a group with a strong base in Gaza, and therefore severing Gaza from Israel would lead to a dramatic decline in terrorism. Among those who advocated evacuation from the territory was (former) Brigadier Yitzhak Pundak who, as the military governor of Gaza in 1970–72, had played a leading role in repressing the Palestinian resistance. 'I see no alternative to a unilateral Israeli disengagement from Gaza's rebellious population,' he now declared. 'The gravity of events in Gaza does not stem from the [Palestinian] resort to firearms, rather from thousands of children who take a hand in throwing stones and burning tyres.'[28]

With Hamas emerging as the main force behind the intifada, the Rabin administration decided to confer an air of respectability on the PLO. Acting on its initiative, the Knesset lifted the long-established ban on contacts with the PLO on 19 January 1993. This was to be a preamble to Israel entering into clandestine talks with the PLO. But the revelation came seven months later.

Meanwhile, Rabin, now Premier and Defence Minister, continued the iron fist policy he had pursued as Defence Minister during 1984–90. The only difference was that Rabin was acting against the background of some 400 Hamas and Islamic Jihad leaders, now banished to makeshifts camps in south Lebanon, mounting an effective public relations campaign against Israel, with Hamas activists inside the Occupied Territories showing no sign of laying down their arms.

'With the [Palestinian] deportation issue dragging on, unresolved, and despair taking root among Palestinians in the face of mounting Israeli repression, there has been a sharp increase in the cycle of violence between Palestinians and Israelis,' noted Daoud Kuttab, a Palestinian journalist, based in East Jerusalem, in mid-March 1993. 'The shootings of Palestinians correspond with a marked increase in the number of Palestinian assaults on Israelis . . . It is hard to pinpoint how the latest escalation of violence began and where it is going: revenge, random shootings and stabbings, house demolitions, curfews and closure of the Gaza Strip, more stabbings and shootings of Israeli settlers and soldiers, another closure of the Gaza Strip etc. . . . The most convincing explanation is that there is little hope for a peaceful solution in the near future. In fact Palestinians are more sceptical today with a Labour Government in Israel than they were during the days of Likud.'[29]

The situation became so critical in the Gaza Strip in mid-March that Rabin, then visiting the United States to meet the newly elected President Bill Clinton, cut short his trip. In repeated clashes between the protestors and the IDF during 20–23 March, 16 Palestinians lost their lives. In an unprecedented move, Rabin ordered checkpoints along the Green Line, the pre-1967 border of Israel, and at the entrances to Jerusalem, allowing West Bankers and Gazans to enter Jerusalem only if they had special permits. He thus redrew *de facto* the 1949 armistice line (except in the case of Greater East Jerusalem), which Israel under the Begin administration had officially removed 16 years before. Later, responding to terrorist actions against Israelis, Rabin would order the closure of the Green Line, thus denying entry into Jerusalem even to those Palestinians who possessed special permits.

Gazans and West Bankers showed their disapproval of the hitherto futile Israeli-Palestinian peace negotiations by staging a general strike on 27 April on the eve of the ninth round of talks held in Washington. The continuing violence pushed the number of Palestinians killed by the IDF and Jewish settlers in May to 34, a figure reminiscent of the early, intense days of the intifada. In an unprecedented action, the IDF fired an anti-tank missile at a residential block in Gaza city in June, killing two residents. The periodic murdering of the suspected Palestinian terrorists by IDF death squads, belonging to the Samson Unit, continued.[30]

There was no formal end to the intifada, just as there had been no official launching of it, since it had occurred spontaneously on 9 December 1987. However, once PLO Chairman, Yasser Arafat, had in his letter to Rabin on 9 September 1993 renounced the use of violence against Israel, and assumed responsibility over 'all PLO elements and personnel in order to assume their compliance, prevent violations and discipline violators', the PLO-UNLU wrote itself out of the intifada.

But since, in his reply to Arafat's letter the next day, Rabin made no mention of the cessation of his Government's efforts to apprehend and punish those it considered responsible for terrorist actions in the past, the undercover assassinations of the IDF's Samson Unit continued. A dramatic example was its killing in broad daylight of six Fatah militants on 28 March 1994. A modest pillar of white stone was soon erected at the spot of their murder – a road junction in the Barke (Arabic, Lake) Abu Rashid neighbourhood of Gaza city – to commemorate the dead. What lifted the unassuming memorial, with the names of assassinated men engraved on it under the appropriate Quranic verse – Martyr Ahmad Mualim aged 30; Martyr Jamal Abdul Nabi aged 27; Martyr Anwar Muhammad aged 24; Martyr Majid Yusuf aged 28; Martyr Juwazim Sayyid aged 28; Nahiz Muhammad Oudieh aged 30 – was the large four-colour Palestinian flag fluttering in the afternoon breeze against the background of a sturdy white-stone minaret of a mosque in the distance.

As I took pictures of the memorial column, a dark, bespectacled man of medium height, about 35, moustached and unshaven, wearing a white shirt, dark brown trousers and sandals, approached Abdul Hakim to enquire about the purpose of my activity. Once reassured, the man, called Mufeed Abu Aied, working in the United Nations Relief and Work Agency's eligibility department (to decide who gets free rations and who does not) told us the tale. 'The six Fatah activists were in a car, and were distributing leaflets,' Mufeed said. 'They stopped at this intersection to get gasoline.' I looked at a corner shop with its shutters open on both sides, and saw drums of gasoline. 'They were surprised by Israeli undercover agents dressed like Palestinians,' Mufeed continued. 'Sixteen of them came in three cars from three directions. They used Uzi sub-machine-guns to kill the Fatah men. They killed them instantly, but one of them, Nahiz Muhammad Oudieh, was still alive. So the undercover agents repeated the shooting. My brother, Jibril, saw this with his eyes. Since then he has gone crazy. He is still in trauma and is unable to get a job. The Israeli agents did not allow ambulances to come through. So a woman bystander who was injured was denied immediate medical treatment.' Mufeed asked me if I could help his brother, Jibril, in some way. His request baffled me. Before then he had mentioned his master's degree in business administration from Colorado State University in Fort Collins. I imagined his life on and off a university campus in the United States, and looked around the squalor that surrounded us: the unpaved streets, the stink from open drains, the rusting shacks of corrugated sheets.

Mufeed Abu Aied was the first English-speaking Gazan I had interviewed during my stay, a member of the local middle class who, by Abdul Hakim's reckoning, formed about 30 per cent of the population. There was of course Abdul Hakim himself, who was well-qualified to be included in my sample of interviewees.

Born in the village of Beit Lahiya in northern Gaza, in a well-to-do family, he was sent to the American University in Cairo. 'It was not our first choice,' he told me. 'Lebanon was closed and there were no places at Jordan University in Amman. In Egypt all local universities were closed to Palestinian students after Sadat's Peace Treaty with Israel [in 1979]. The AUC was mighty expensive. It cost $300 a month for nine months a year for three years. A lot of money. I got a degree in computer programming in 1983. When I returned to Gaza after graduation, I was picked up by the IDF at the [Rafah] checkpoint. They threw me in jail, and interrogated me for two months. I was surprised by how much they knew of my political activity in Cairo. They said you met so and so on such and such a day etc. How did they know all this?' Following the Peace Treaty, Israel set up an embassy in Cairo, I said matter-of-factly. Abdul Hakim paused, took in what I had uttered, and nodded. 'However, I denied everything,' he continued. 'Back in Gaza and Israel, I applied for a job. NCR [National Cash Register] in Tel Aviv selected me for a job. When they saw that I lived in Gaza they said, "Get a clearance letter from the Interior Ministry". Forget it, I said to myself, with two months in an Israeli jail my chances were zero.

'Then I got into the restaurant business in Tel Aviv mainly because I liked Italian food. I was employed by an Israeli who lived in Europe and had a chain of Italian restaurants in Israel. His Tel Aviv restaurant was near the US embassy. The chef was Palestinian, also all the waiters. It was hard work, running the restaurant until late in the evening, rushing back home, a ride of 75 minutes by car, and up early in the morning. So we rented an apartment in Tel Aviv – broke the law about the Palestinians not staying in Israel overnight. Somebody reported. So we were all arrested, then released after two months. I was re-employed by the same Israeli. Soon after the intifada started, I was arrested under administrative detention. Served six months in jail. My Israeli boss, who lived abroad, didn't care. He re-employed me, and appointed me manager of a new restaurant he opened in Haifa. I had seven people working under me. This went on until I was arrested [for the third time] in late 1990 for being a leader of Fatah in my village. Spent four months in prison. So all-told three political arrests, and one for staying overnight in Israel. Now there is simply no question of having a proper job in Israel. At most I could expect to be employed as a casual worker on a daily basis.'

He took me to his village of Beit Lahiya, about 2 kilometres south-west of the Ezer checkpoint. After the overcrowded refugee camps and Gaza city, Beit Lahiya felt like a half-abandoned habitation. Responding to my wish to meet more of the territory's middle class, Abdul Hakim introduced me to Abdul Qadir Ealin, the owner of a store selling groceries, soft drinks and hurricane lanterns. An avuncular man of medium build and intelligent looks, 66, his alert eyes twinkled behind tinted glasses. Dressed in grey trousers and jacket, and a light green checked shirt with a breast pocket bearing a pen, he wore a white *kiffayeh* held down by a black *igal* (Arabic, rope).

'Under the Israeli occupation the situation was very bad,' he said in fluent English. 'Much better now under the Palestinian Authority. But we have no freedom of movement, and the economic situation is worse. One million Gazans live in an area of 45 by 8 kilometres almost half of which is still occupied by the Israelis. Because agricultural produce is cheap, Gazans working on land do not make enough money, and so they, too, seek work for wages. And that sort of work is available mostly in Israel. In the past 60,000 Gazans used to work in Israel, now only 5,000 are allowed in. The unemployment is high. Because people have no jobs they have no cash. Ninety per cent of my sales are on credit. In the past our vegetables and fruit used to go to Saudi Arabia, Jordan and Kuwait through Israel, but now that is closed [because the Israeli authorities discovered that the Islamic groups were using these trucks to smuggle explosives].' What was the solution? 'Israel must leave the Jewish settlements in Gaza and the West Bank,' replied Abdul Qadir. 'Donor countries should provide funds for factories to create jobs. Palestinians should be re-employed in the Gulf states. Loss of their jobs there has caused a problem here.'

As I brought Abdul Qadir, standing against the half-empty shelves of his wares, into the view-finder of my camera, I noticed a framed photograph of a younger man, crouching on the soil of a garden, above a line of hurricane lanterns. Who was he? 'My son, Hassan, assassinated by the Shin Beth,' said Abdul Qadir. 'In 1978 he was sentenced to 20 years in jail as a leader of the Popular Front [for the Liberation of Palestine] in Gaza. He was released in 1985 in the prisoner exchange [between Israel and the Popular Front for the Liberation of Palestine-General Command, formed by Ahmad Jibril after he split from the PFLP in late 1968]. In September 1986 he got a telephone call, and the caller told him to go and pick up something, a package, in the back garden of his house. When he did, he got blown up by an explosive. He was gone!'

Abdul Qadir sat down. He struggled to hold back tears. The murder had occurred nearly nine years ago, but so severe was the blow to his psyche of the sudden, dramatic loss – the body of his beloved son blown to pieces – that he still found it a wrench to recall the deathly account.[31] 'After murdering my son, they arrested me!' Abdul Qadir continued, having regained his composure. 'I was so distraught that I couldn't eat. "How can I eat when my son has just been killed?" I'd say to my jailers. So they put me in solitary confinement for three weeks.' That was his second imprisonment, the first one being in 1979, for two and a half months. Yet, like his son, Abdul Qadir remains loyal to the Popular Front, of which he is the acknowledged leader in the village.

What explained the strength of the Popular Front in the Gaza Strip? The roots of the Popular Front for the Liberation of Palestine (PFLP) lay in the Arab Nationalist Movement (ANM), which came into being in 1952 as a result of the merger of two groups, composed chiefly of the students and staff of the American University in Beirut. Its main slogan was: 'Unity [of Arabs], Liberation [of Palestine], Revenge [against the Zionist state].' It placed much hope in the coup by nationalist military officers in Egypt in July 1952, especially as a vehicle to effect Arab unity. Since Gaza was administered by Egypt, ruled by radical President Gamal Abdul Nasser from 1954, the Gaza branch of the ANM found itself in a congenial environment. Acting in conjunction with the Egyptian army, it participated in guerrilla attacks on Israel. Nasser was pleased at the resistance Gazans offered to the Israeli occupiers, from November 1956 to March 1957. He established a Palestinian battalion within the Egyptian army. In 1958 he appointed an executive committee, composed of local notables, and convened a legislative assembly partly nominated and partly elected by a small electoral college. After the Palestine Liberation Organization was formed in 1964, he allowed it to post its military wing, the Palestine Liberation Army, in Gaza, where male secondary school students were imparted compulsory military training.

When the Egyptian military departed from the Gaza Strip during the June 1967 War, it left behind its arms and ammunition depots as well as its underground bunkers. These were inherited by Palestinian militants. Those belonging to the ANM, which transformed itself into the Popular Front for the Liberation of Palestine in December 1967, became particularly active against the Israeli occupation, especially in the refugee camps. By 1969 the Palestinian guerrillas held sway in the refugee camps at night and harassed the Israeli army during the day. Later that year when General Ariel Sharon became commander of the Southern Command, he decided to tackle the problem systematically.

By appointing a local scion, known for his moderate, pro-Jordanian views, Rashid Shawwa, as mayor of Gaza city in 1970, Sharon tried to divide the Gazan community politically. Then in mid-1971 he began to implement the military part of his counter-insurgency plan with a ruthless resolve. To improve IDF patrolling he had the densely populated refugee camps criss-crossed with wide roads. To facilitate access for IDF armoured vehicles he had entire sectors of refugee camps bulldozed. He dispatched the displaced refugees to the abandoned barracks of the United Nations Emergency Force (which had departed on the eve of the June 1967 War) near the Egyptian frontier, thus hugely bolstering the size of Rafah town and refugee camp. He punished stone throwers with deportation to Jordan. He banished the families of suspected guerrillas to the IDF detention camps in the Sinai. He ordered the IDF to carry out house-to-house searches while he placed whole towns and camps under long curfews, and resorted frequently to blowing up the houses of suspected terrorists. By February 1972, the IDF had killed 104 Palestinians and arrested 742 more. This weakened the Palestinian resistance but did not destroy it. The riots that erupted in the Shaati (Arabic, beach) camp, adjacent to Gaza city, in September spread throughout the Strip, and continued for two months. Sharon quelled them with an iron hand. In the process he lost Rashid Shawwa who, responding to the popular outcry, resigned. During the following summer Sharon left the IDF to enter politics. But before then he had implemented another part of his plan in the Gaza Strip.

He secured the approval of the Labour-led Government,

headed by Golda Meir, to establish five military-agricultural settlements at strategic places in order to split the Palestinian communities and prevent the emergence of a large contiguous swathe of the Palestinian population. Thus in 1972 five military-agricultural settlements at Erez, Netzarim, Nahal Qatif D, Kfar Darom and Morag came into being. The land confiscation by Israel that started the colonization process continued relentlessly for more than two decades. By the time the Israeli-PLO Accord was signed in September 1993, over one-third of the Gaza Strip had been seized by Israel, and the number of the original colonies had more than trebled. Two of the settlements were in the north, one (Netzarim) in the centre, and the rest, collectively called the Gush Qatif (Hebrew, Qatif Bloc), in the south, all of them along the Mediterranean, except two, Morag and Kfar Daroma, which were inland. The settlements were safeguarded by high barbed-wired fences, land mines and IDF troops. The size of the ultra-nationalist settler community reached a peak of 4,500 when the Oslo Accord was concluded, and then began to decline steadily.

As Abdul Hakim and I drove southward on a cloudless but windy day in March 1995 along the main north-south highway bisecting the Gaza Strip, past the Palestinian village of Deir al Balah, we travelled a short distance buttressed by the Jewish settlements – the Gush Qatif on the Mediterranean side and Kfar Daroma on the opposite – green fields, separated from the road by a razor-wire fence, decked with skull and bones signs in red, and guarded by soldiers in watch-towers, their machine-guns pointing outwards. 'Kfar Daroma and the northern part of the Gush Qatif is accessible from Israel through the Kissufim checkpoint by a road that bypasses the Palestinian villages and refugee camps,' Abdul Hakim explained. 'The southern end of the Gush Qatif and Morag are accessible from Israel by the Sufa checkpoint.' What about the Netzarim settlement? 'The problem there is the junction of the access road from Israel and the north-south highway. It is supposed to be patrolled jointly by the IDF and Palestinian Authority police.' What about the northern settlements? 'These hug the Gaza-Israel border,' he replied.

'You enter directly into them through the Elai Sinai and Erez checkpoints.' The principle of the Jewish settlements having direct road access to Israel was later to be applied to all of the 128 Jewish colonies in the West Bank before the IDF troops were redeployed on the eve of the elections to the Palestinian Council in January 1996.

The Gush Qatif settlements remains a world unto itself, a Garden of Eden in the hell-hole of the Gaza Strip. It includes the HaShalim Beach (for the exclusive use of the settlers and Jewish Israelis), a tourist village and a beach hotel with a restaurant offering a panoramic view of the Mediterranean Sea. Here Jewish settlers live in the midst of water-sprinkled lawns, fragrant trees, orange groves and greenhouses. However, a resort hotel catering specially to Orthodox Jews, constructed at the cost of $9 million in the mid-1980s closed in 1989 as a direct consequence of the Palestinian intifada.

The insularity of the settlers, physical and psychological, was well captured by Robert Friedman, a Jewish American journalist, in his account of a visit in November 1990, in the midst of the intifada, to the head office of the Gaza Regional Council in the Neve Dekalim settlement of the Gush Qatif, and an interview with the elected head of the Council, Zvi Hendel, 41-year-old Romanian Jew, 'a big muscular man with a knitted *yarmulke* and an easy smile'. Like all other settlements in the Gaza Strip, Neve Dekalim was surrounded by 'barbed wire, watch-towers and heavily armed Israeli soldiers'. Across the road was the Khan Yunis refugee camp with 50,000 Palestinians crammed into an area of 1.5 kilometres, living in grinding poverty. 'We have two reasons for being here,' Hendel explained to Friedman. 'First, it's our land. Secondly, our presence enhances Israel's security. We're the eyes and ears of the army.' When the subject of the intifada came up, Hendel's analysis was simple and direct. 'Our good Jewish hearts have exacerbated the intifada,' he said. 'If we had killed 200 Arabs at the beginning of the intifada, it would be over. If we expel 7,000 troublemakers now, everything would be okay.' At the same time Hendel's view of the recent past was uncommonly rosy. He told Friedman that before the outbreak of the intifada, 'the settlers tried to build a "harmonious" life with the Arabs', and added: 'But even during the intifada, I have maintained friendships [with the Arabs]. I'm sorry I can't take you with me to visit my Arab friends . . . But they are afraid.' He went on to claim: ' "99 per cent" of the Arabs oppose the intifada, but they are terrorized into rebelling against [the] Israeli rule by a small number of Palestinian activists.' But this did not square up with what Friedman discovered at the nearby Atzmona settlement. When he saw a group of Ethiopian Jews loading sacks of potatoes on to a truck there, he requested an interview with them, but this was brusquely rejected by the Jewish American settler who was supervising the loading. 'Before the intifada, the settlements in the Gaza Strip had employed Palestinian refugees to do most of the manual work,' wrote Friedman. 'No longer. The settlers are afraid to allow Palestinians into the settlements, despite Hendel's claims of good fellowship.'[32]

In early 1995, welcoming the Israeli Deputy Defence Minister, Mordechai Gur, at the Netzarim settlement, Hendel once again harked back to the 'good old days' when they could travel freely through Gaza. Reporting the encounter in the *Jerusalem Post Magazine*, Steve Rodan wrote: 'Gur cut them [Hendel and others] off. "Don't tell me it used to be wonderful," he said. "Terror never ended. There have been periods when it was up and when it has been down. [But it never disappeared.]" '[33]

Following the implementation of the 1993 Israeli-PLO Accord in July 1994, when Palestinian Authority took charge of administering limited self-rule in the Gaza Strip – with the Jewish settlements remaining under the exclusive control of Israel – the significance of the Netzarim settlement rose sharply. Situated on the fringe of Gaza city's southern suburb of Shaikh Ijleen, it overlooked the capital, and its location allowed the IDF to slice the Gaza Strip into two. It was described variously as 'a bone stuck in our throat' (the Palestinian Authority), 'an obstacle to peace' (the left-wing ministers of the Israeli Government) and 'a ball bearing' (Prime Minister Rabin). Measuring 700 hectares (seven square kilometres) and housing a mere 30 Orthodox Jewish families, it became, in the words of a reporter of the *Jerusalem Post Magazine*, 'perhaps the most heavily protected spot in the Middle East'. This came about after the junction of the access road from Israel and the north-south highway attracted the attention of Gaza's bombers, who wanted the settlement to be closed. In November 1994 a Palestinian suicide bomber blew himself up and killed three IDF officers, and another Palestinian gunned down an Israeli army officer.

To highlight the sacrifices made by the Israelis to maintain control over the Gaza Strip, the Netzarim settlers swiftly built temporary commemorative monuments, in honour of the dead, at the entrance to their colony, little realizing that by so doing they were underlining the dangers to Israelis of living in or patrolling Gaza, thus isolating themselves further. 'Many residents acknowledge their isolation,' reported Steve Rodan of the *Jerusalem Post Magazine*. 'Even their parents [in Israel] don't want to chance a visit.'[34]

But the tenacity to hold on was not limited to the settlers, it extended to the Government as well. Why were the Israeli authorities so keen to keep the Jewish settlements in the miserable Gaza Strip, I asked Abdul Hakim. 'To bargain about the cost of giving them up just as they did in the case of Sinai [in 1982] with the Egyptians,' he replied. 'For the present the rumour is that the settlers are pumping out water from Gaza to Israel. So they need these settlements to carry out this theft.'

11

THE PALESTINE LIBERATION ORGANIZATION:

Armed Resistance to Red-Carpet Respectability

There is no mistaking where you are in the Gaza Strip village of Beit Lahiya when you see a line of short steel poles on both sides of a steep bend in a dusty road leading to the main north-south highway – an accident prevention measure – painted red and white: the colours of Fatah, the leading constituent of the Palestine Liberation Organization. You are outside the two-storey office of the local branch of Fatah. At the end of an outside staircase, built in two sections, the higher one backing on the lower as it rises at an angle, you find yourself on the top floor facing a hall, flanked by two large rooms. In one of the rooms, furnished with a desk, a few chairs, and a large logo of Fatah – two crossed machine-guns protecting the Palestine of the British mandate era – I met Muhammad Talouli. A shy, clean-shaven man of 27, slim, good-looking, he was wearing a white open-neck shirt, and a grey jacket to match his trousers of the same colour. He was a member of Fatah's central committee of the northern district, and it was his turn that day to attend to the party business. In many ways, I thought, he epitomized the up-and-coming image of Fatah, the ruling party of the future in the Palestinian territories.

Muhammad Talouli was a true Gazan in the sense that his parents came from the village of Dimra just north of the IDF's Erez checkpoint. During the 1948 War they set up home in the Jabaliya refugee camp. It was there that Muhammad was born a year after the 1967 War. 'I became a member of Fatah when I was 14,' he told me in hesitant English. 'I was put in jail in 1985 because I threw a petrol bomb at an IDF patrol. Six years. I spent much of my time studying in the prison. I was released in 1991. I applied for a place in the Al Azhar University [in Gaza city] and was accepted. I am now in my final year, doing education.'

How typical was he as a Fatah member to undergo incarceration? 'Well,' he replied, 'during the intifada more than 10,000 Fatah members were jailed in our northern district.' What was the population of the district? 'Something like 300,000, or about 40,000 families, with the average family having seven members.' Taking into account other political groups participating in the intifada, would he reckon that every other family had a male member in prison? 'Yes, definitely. And all parties tried to help the families of those who were jailed or wounded or martyred. Fatah used to pay an outright sum to the family of a martyr. But then we had a financial crisis. Now the party is recovering slowly. Recently we gave $100 each to the families of the martyrs.'

Fatah and other secular groups were particularly strong in the refugee camps, I discovered. Since Fatah's philosophy was simple – resistance to Israel, with no debate about what would follow once the Israeli occupation was ended – it was popular. That is why it became the main force in the refugee camps.

Indeed the Al Bureij refugee camp in central Gaza Strip had provided two of the three co-founders of Fatah: Salah Khalaf with the *nom de guerre* of Abu Iyad (Arabic, Father of Festivities), and Khalil Wazir. The third, and the most famous of them, Yasser Arafat, also known by his *nom de guerre* of Abu Ammar (Arabic, Father of Construction), had ancestral links with Gaza. He belonged to the al Husseini clan of Gaza – no relation of the al Husseini clan of Jerusalem. His father, Abdul Raouf al Qudwa, died there in 1953 while Arafat was at university in Cairo.

The reason for the Gaza Strip to emerge as the seedbed of Palestinian nationalism lay in the divergent policies followed by Jordan, which annexed the West Bank after the 1948 Arab-Israeli War, and Egypt, which merely administered the Gaza Strip. Whereas the monarchical regime in Amman actively pursued a policy of inculcating Jordanian identity among West Bankers as well as the Palestinian refugees in Jordan, the regime in Cairo, whether headed by King Farouq (r. 1936–52) or nationalist military officers, kept the flame of Palestinian identity flickering in the Gaza Strip.

Due to the absence of universities or colleges in the Strip, hundreds of Palestinian students joined Egyptian universities, particularly those based in Cairo. Among them was Salah Khalaf, a strongly built, obstreperous young man of 19, who enrolled in a teachers' training college in Cairo in 1951. Born in 1932 into a middle-class household in Jaffa, Khalaf and his family had fled at the time of the establishment of Israel. In the Egyptian capital he met Yasser Arafat, who was in the second year of the civil engineering degree course at Cairo University. In 1952 they prepared a joint list for the officials of the Palestine Students' Federation. It won. Khalaf became a member of the executive committee of the PSF, and Arafat its chairman. Born Muhammad Abdul Raouf Arafat al Qudwa, nicknamed Yasser (Arabic, care-free), to a merchant father who was originally from Khan Yunis in the Gaza Strip, but later ran a shop in Jerusalem, (Yasser) Arafat was born in Cairo during his father's tem-porary residence there. When his mother died in 1933, his father, Abdul Raouf al Qudwa, sent him to live with close relatives in the Old Town of Jerusalem near the Western Wall. After his father had remarried in 1937 he recalled (Yasser) Arafat to the Egyptian capital, where he was later to join Cairo University, then called King Fuad University.

As part of his higher education he underwent compulsory military training. Growing up in Cairo had left him speaking the Egyptian dialect of Arabic.

After graduating from a teachers' training college in Cairo, Salah Khalaf worked as a teacher in the Gaza Strip. He maintained his position as a member of the executive committee of the PSF. In August 1956 he and Arafat travelled to Prague to attend the International Students Congress, which accepted the PSF as its member. By then Arafat had met another Palestinian refugee, Khalil Wazir, a 20-year-old, with a neatly-clipped moustache, an intense gaze and a sharp mind. The trio became life-long personal and political friends. There was a particular chemistry between Arafat and al Wazir, the former being hot-tempered and impetuous, given to acting before thinking, and the latter cool, rational and given to deliberating before acting.

Born in a middle class household in Ramle, Palestine, Wazir and his family fled after the town had fallen to the IDF in mid-July 1948. He grew up in the Al Bureij refugee camp in the Gaza Strip. In 1954 he was selected by the Egyptian military first for commando training and then further military instruction in Cairo, where he met Yasser Arafat at a demonstration by Palestinian students against the Israeli attack on an Egyptian military base in Gaza in February 1955. Wazir was later commissioned as a lieutenant in the Gazan brigade of the Egyptian army.

During the Suez War in October–November 1956, as a reserve officer in the Egyptian army, Arafat was called up and assigned to a bomb disposal unit. With the Gaza Strip and the Sinai falling to the Israelis, Wazir and the Gazan unit retreated to Cairo. Before the fall of the Strip, Khalaf left the territory for the Egyptian capital, and then Egypt. He enrolled as a student in Stuttgart, Germany, and so did Wazir.

Having graduated as a civil engineer in 1956, Arafat worked for the Egyptian Cement Company. Two years later he got a job with the public works department of Kuwait. He was soon joined there by Wazir. Together they floated the idea of setting up a Palestinian organization committed to liberating Palestine. They backed it by producing, periodically, a journal, *Falastinuna: Nida al Hayat* (Arabic, Our Palestine: The Call of Life). They won the backing of Khalaf when he arrived in Kuwait in March 1959. They decided that Fatah, the reverse acronym of *Harkat al Tahrir al Falastini*, Movement for the Liberation of Palestine, should be a movement, not a party.

Later that year, with the assistance of an influential contact in Lebanon, they secured a license to publish *Falastinuna: Nida al Hayat* as a monthly journal in Beirut, and distribute it throughout the Middle East. This enabled them to start establishing secret cells of Fatah not only in Kuwait but also in the Palestinian refugee camps in Jordan, Syria and Lebanon. By then the basic Fatah ideology and tactics had crystallized thus: revolutionary violence, practised by the masses, was the only way to liberate Palestine and liquidate all forms of Zionism. In short, Fatah believed in a people's war.

Wazir returned to Stuttgart to organize the Palestinian students in West Germany. He also established contacts with the National Liberation Front of Algeria which succeeded in ending French imperial rule and assuming power in the country in July 1962. Wazir and other Fatah leaders travelled to Algiers in December and secured an official recognition for their movement. When Fatah opened its bureau in Algiers in 1963, Wazir became its head. In the Algerian capital he set up a network of contacts with other radical states and liberation movements. The following March he and Arafat visited Peking and then Hanoi, North Vietnam. In the summer he helped organize a military training camp for some 100 Fatah recruits in Algeria.

1964 was an eventful year for Palestinians in general and Fatah in particular. In January the first summit of the Arab League meeting in Cairo, called primarily to 'struggle against the robbery of the Jordan River waters by Israel', directed Ahmad Shuqairi – a Palestinian lawyer who had served as under-secretary for political affairs at the Arab League headquarters in Cairo during most of the 1950s – to consult fellow Palestinians and present a plan for the creation of a

Palestinian body to enable them to play their part in liberating Palestine and determining their own future. The summit did so by virtue of an annex to its founding charter which gave the League the right to select an Arab Palestinian to take part in its work.

Born in 1908 into an eminent religious-political family in Acre, Palestine, Shuqairi trained as a lawyer at the Jerusalem Law School and the American University in Beirut. He served as a member of the Arab Higher Committee from March–June 1946. After the 1948 Arab-Israeli War he moved to Damascus. He was a member of the Syrian delegation to the United Nations, 1949–50, and then joined the Arab League headquarters in Cairo as an under-secretary. After leaving the League in 1957, he served Saudi Arabia as a Minister of State of UN affairs and ambassador to the United Nations, 1957–62. At the United Nations he espoused the cause of Palestinians. Within a few months of a directive from the Arab League summit to present a plan for the creation of a Palestinian entity, he produced a document entitled the Palestine National Charter.

The Charter demanded the founding of a democratic and secular state in a Palestine as constituted under the British mandate. It was adopted by the delegates, chosen by the Palestinians living in several Arab countries, who assembled at the Ambassador Hotel in East Jerusalem, then under Jordanian control, in late May 1964. It was a momentous event, inaugurated by King Hussein of Jordan, and attended by the luminaries of the Palestinian Diaspora scattered across the Middle East and elsewhere. Wazir and a few other activists of Fatah, now past its phase of a clandestine existence, attended the assembly, but insisted on calling themselves independent. Their argument for unleashing a people's war on the Zionist entity fell on deaf ears.

The conference established the Palestine Liberation Organization as an umbrella body. Each of the affiliated bodies, which did not include Fatah, was represented on the 350-member Palestine National Council,[1] which elected a central council, which was to meet every three months, and an executive committee. It chose Shuqairi as the Chairman of the

PLO executive committee. Under Shuqairi, the PLO had the full backing of the Egyptian President, Gamal Abdul Nasser, who allowed its chairman to run a radio station in Cairo.

1964 was also the year when the Syrian regime, run by civilian and military leaders of the radical, pan-Arabist Baath Socialist Party, decided to assist Fatah leaders in their plans to mount guerrilla actions against Israel from Syria and elsewhere. Aware of the Arab summit resolution on the stealing of the Jordan River waters by Israel, Fatah's military wing, Al Assifa (Arabic, The Storm), headed by Wazir, attacked the Israeli Water Carrier at Beit Netopha in the Galilee on 1 January 1965 from Ein Hilwa Palestinian refugee camp in south Lebanon. The plan to blow up the water pipes was far from successful. None the less 1 January has now become an important date in the official calendar of the Palestinian Authority, with Fatah activists proudly citing the Al Assifa Communiqué Number 1: 'Let the imperialists and Zionists know that the people of Palestine are still in the battlefield and shall never be set aside.'

Also the use of *noms de guerre* by Fatah leaders can be traced to this event. Arafat, Wazir and Khalaf, who were involved in the operation, were arrested by the Lebanese authorities, and jailed for two months. In prison they decided to adopt *noms de guerres*. Arafat chose Abu Ammar, Father of Construction, signifying his profession as a civil engineer, and Wazir, Abu Jihad, Father of Struggle, due to his military background.

On their release Arafat and Wazir moved to Damascus, where the Syrian Government continued to provide military training facilities for Fatah recruits. From there they travelled together to the Palestinian refugee camps on the West Bank, then part of the Jordanian kingdom, to enrol recruits for Fatah. Khalaf concentrated on the Gaza Strip and Jordan proper, where almost half of the refugees from the pre-1948 Palestine were based either in camps or Jordanian towns and cities.

By mid-1966 Fatah and its guerrilla actions against Israel had become an element in the Byzantine politics of the region. The Syrian forces bore the brunt of Israel's fierce retaliatory response. But Jordan was not spared. Indeed in late 1966 Israel struck heavily on the West Bank village of Samu. These skirmishes proved to be the preamble to the June 1967 Arab-Israeli War.

The humiliating defeat of the Arabs in the six-day conflict was a political-military earthquake which radically rearranged the pieces on the Middle Eastern chess-board. Among its principal Palestinian losers was Shuqairi. On the eve of the hostilities, Shuqairi, then heading a small Palestinian militia, indulged in hyperbolic rhetoric on his radio station, creating a war psychosis that was out of proportion to the military muscle he possessed. Not surprisingly, he was compelled to resign his chairmanship of the PLO in December 1967, and was followed by Yahya Hamouda, another Palestinian lawyer, who acted more as a caretaker than a lasting fixture.

Like much else in life, though, the Six Day War was not an unmitigated disaster for the defeated. It had its silver lining, at least for the Palestinians. So said Albert Aghazarian, a native of Jerusalem's Old Town and lecturer on Middle Eastern history at the Birzeit University on the West Bank. While the trade mark of Arafat is a starched black and white chequered *kiffayeh* folded in a way to replicate the daggerlike shape of Palestine, that of Aghazarian, sporting a goatee beard and flashing almond-shaped eyes of an Armenian, is a perpetually lit briar pipe, the pungent smell of the tobacco burning the nostrils and lungs of his interviewer. 'The positive aspect of the 1967 War was that it gave birth to Palestinian nationalism,' he told me at his university office. 'I should know because I went through a phase when I was indoctrinated to believe that I was Jordanian.'[2]

If Aghazarian took a reflective view more than a quarter century after the event, to his credit Arafat reached the same conclusion in the heat of the moment. Unlike most of his colleagues in the Fatah executive committee, who were paralysed by the crushing defeat inflicted on the Arab neighbours by Israel, Arafat saw a welcome opportunity for Palestinians to become self-reliant and initiate an armed liberation struggle against Zionist imperialism, represented by Israel, on their own. Having participated in an acrimonious meeting of the executive committee, which decided to reconstitute itself, at the house of Wazir in a Damascus suburb, Arafat, given to the doctrine of 'doing something', crossed the Jordan River in the company of his aide, Abu Ali Shaheen, and disappeared behind the Israeli lines. Basing themselves in a village near Jenin, they set up an infrastructure for launching a guerrilla campaign. Arafat then secured the consent of the party's new executive committee before ordering an attack on an Israeli target in September 1967, hoping it would trigger an escalating series of armed assaults. In practice, the result was neither a dramatic success nor an abject failure. To Arafat's disappointment, though, it was not enough to shake the Israeli military. Drawing on the information from the files of the defeated Jordanian administration, the IDF repressed the Palestinian resistance, killing over 60 guerrillas and arresting 320 by the end of the year. Among their prisoners was Abu Ali Shaheen.

But Arafat, always quick on his feet and blessed, it is said, 'with nine lives', escaped. He made his getaway from the back window of his hideout, a spacious house in Al Bireh, wearing women's clothing – so the story runs – as the Israeli soldiers entered from the front door. Twenty-eight years later, I arrived at the said residence one breezy afternoon, hoping to check the veracity of the account. It was a large house, just off Ein Jaloud Road, well kept, with a stone platform in the back. I saw the large windows, and imagined the small, stocky figure of Arafat, then 38, dressed like a woman escaping. Disappointingly, the house was empty. The owner had migrated to the United States; and, being affluent, had not bothered to rent it.[3]

Within three months of this close shave, Arafat and his Fatah guerrillas achieved a military success that firmly established them as the prime force among Palestinians. This was the military confrontation between the IDF and Fatah guerrillas at the Jordanian border town of Karameh (Arabic, dignity) on 21 March. By early 1968 the Israeli-Jordanian frontier was buzzing with guerrilla activity, with Palestinian commandos crossing the Jordan at night, placing land-mines or throwing hand grenades, and then returning to base. On 18 March a land-mine exploded under an Israeli schoolbus, and killed two. In the early hours of the morning of 21 March an IDF armoured column, along with some 7,000 infantry, advanced into Jordan to destroy the guerrilla infrastructure. The Israelis, who had expected the Palestinians to flee, instead faced stiff resistance from the 400 commandos who were covered by artillery fire by the Jordanian army. By the time the battle ended at sunset, 28 Israelis were dead and 34 of their tanks damaged against the death of 98 Palestinian guerrillas. Such a loss inflicted on the IDF by the Arabs was unprecedented.

Since Jordan could not officially claim direct involvement and invite a punishing Israeli retaliation, Fatah and Arafat took most of the credit, with the smaller Popular Front for the Liberation of Palestine garnering the rest. Overnight the Karameh confrontation turned Fatah into a popular organization, which thousands of Palestinians volunteered to join. With this, it became incumbent on the Fatah to abandon its collective image, and project the image of a single personality – a role now assigned to Arafat.

Little wonder that in the area under the control of the Palestinian Authority today, 21 March is an important day in the official calendar. I got a whiff of this when I arrived at the oldest high school in the middle-class district of Al Rimal in Gaza city on 20 March to interview the headmaster. With the premises festooned in a sea of multicolour Palestinian flags and the portraits of Arafat and Wazir, the mood was festive. It did not require much imagination to guess the tone and content of the speeches that would be delivered the next day by the teachers and Palestinian Authority officials to the future citizens of Palestine from the podium of an impressive-looking theatre hall. One story told me by a middle-aged teacher with salt-and-pepper eyebrows about Force 17 – the elite security unit of the Palestinian Authority – well known for its fierce loyalty to Arafat, was bound to be related in a highly embroidered fashion. 'During the Battle of Karameh,' the teacher began with a twinkle in his eyes, '17 *fedayeen* (commandos) took up positions in the trenches along the Jordan River, armed with RPGs [rocket-propelled grenades]. As the Israelis crossed over they stayed put. They fired their weapons at point-blank range and made a hash of the Israelis. In the end all of them were killed, except one. But they will live as long as there is Force 17!'

As it was, for the next two and a half years after the Battle of Karameh the Palestinian resistance rode an unprecedented wave of popularity at both public and official levels. 'From March 1968 to September 1970, the Palestinians appeared to have seized the moral leadership and attained enormous influence over almost the entire Arab world – despite the fact that they still lacked a secure territorial base and possessed only a minuscule fighting force (not more than 15,000 guerrillas) and a rudimentary political infrastructure,' noted Professor Michael C. Hudson, an American specialist on the Middle East. 'Syria provided sanctuary; Egypt provided diplomatic support; Algeria supplied [military] training and material; Saudi Arabia and the Gulf states provided money; Jordan and Lebanon almost provided a state.'[4]

The role of Egypt, the single most important Arab state, and its president, Nasser, who, notwithstanding the drubbing he got from Israel in 1967, retained most of his earlier popular appeal in the Arab world, was crucial in the rise of Fatah and Arafat. Nasser received Arafat in April 1968 at his home in a Cairo suburb. 'I would be more than glad if you could represent the Palestinian people and the Palestinian will to resist [Israel], politically by your presence and militarily by your actions,' Nasser told Arafat. He then advised Arafat to preserve Fatah's independence from Arab regimes, but to co-ordinate with them in the same way that Jewish guerrilla groups did with the mainstream Zionist movement before the founding of Israel.[5] Nasser complemented his counsel with a pledge to arm and train Fatah recruits. In reality Fatah emerged as the mainstream party of Palestinians in the way Mapai did among Zionist pioneers in Palestine, and Arafat as a latter-day David Ben Gurion of Arab Palestinians, who came to embody Palestinian nationalism.

In retrospect it can be said that in 1968 Nasser, the towering leader of the Arab world, anointed Arafat as Mr

Palestine, a label which, despite the sharp vicissitudes of the Middle Eastern politics, stuck firmly.

Rise of Radical PLO

At the fourth session of the Palestine National Council in July 1968 in Cairo, Fatah and other smaller guerrilla groups affiliated to the PLO. The first task of the PNC was to alter the Palestine National Charter substantially. The modified Charter declared: 'Armed struggle is the only way to liberate Palestine [Article 9].' Of the 33 articles in the rewritten Charter the other important ones were: 'Palestine, with the boundaries under the British mandate, is the homeland of Palestinian Arabs, and is indivisible' (Articles 1 and 2); 'the Jews who lived in Palestine before the Zionist immigration are considered Palestinian' (Article 6); 'the partition of Palestine and the founding of Israel are illegal since they violated the will of Palestinians and the principle of self-determination included in the United Nations Charter' (Article 19); 'the Balfour Declaration and the British mandate for Palestine are null and void' (Article 20); 'the Palestinians reject all solutions which are substitutes for total liberation of Palestine' (Article 21); and 'Zionism, associated with international imperialism, is racist, expansionist and colonial, and Israel is the instrument of the Zionist movement' (Article 22). The PNC rejected the United Nations Security Council Resolution 242 since it made no specific mention of Palestinians.

The next congress of the PNC, convened in February 1969 in Cairo, festooned with the red and white logo of Fatah for the occasion, reflected the overwhelming strength of the guerrilla groups, with Fatah, claiming a force of 15,000 commandos, far ahead of others. At a session attended by President Nasser, the PNC elected Arafat Chairman of the PLO's executive committee, which included three more Fatah figures, including Wazir and Khalaf. But Arafat ensured that the leaders of all other commando groups, irrespective of their political views, were included in the executive committee. Taking his cue from the elected assembly of the Yishuv, the Jewish community in Palestine, which represented all hues of Zionism, Arafat was keen to have all those who believed in Palestinian nationalism and liberating Palestine through any means affiliate to the PLO. Also, aware of how rivalry among Arab Palestinian leaders during the Arab Revolt of 1936–9 had undermined the effectiveness of the uprising, he wanted to gather every Palestinian faction under the PLO umbrella.

Among the smaller parties the Popular Front for the Liberation of Palestine (PFLP), led by George Habash, was the most important. Born in 1925 into a Christian family in Lydda (later Lod), Palestine, Habash moved to Amman along with his parents during the 1948 Arab-Israeli War. A brilliant student, a dashing young man and extraordinarily eloquent, he graduated in medicine from the American University in Beirut. While at university, he co-founded in 1952 the Arab Nationalist Movement. Under his leadership the ANM's Palestinian members formed a 'Preparatory Committee for Unified Palestinian Action' in early 1966. Overall, though, Habash put his faith in Egyptian President Nasser as the leader who would liberate Palestine through a conventional war with Israel. But the Arab defeat in the June 1967 War destroyed this possibility. In December Habash merged the Palestinian section of the ANM with the Syria-based Palestine Liberation Front led by Ahmad Jibril, to form the Popular Front for the Liberation of Palestine. It immediately undertook guerrilla operations against Israel, and participated in the much-celebrated Battle of Karameh in March 1968.

Arafat inherited the infrastructure of the PLO, which included not only the bureaucracy, running among other things a finance directorate, but also the Palestine Liberation Army, trained by Egypt and stationed in the Gaza Strip, and popular organizations – the unions of artists, doctors, engineers, farmers, journalists and writers, lawyers, students, teachers, women and workers – that had been founded in the Arab countries where Diaspora Palestinians lived and worked. He gained direct control over the Palestine National Fund, modelled on the Jewish National Fund, which was set up by the PLO to meet its financial requirements. The contributions were in the form of grants from Arab and other friendly countries, a general Palestine tax collected by certain Arab states, an income tax on the Palestinians living in the rest of the Diaspora, and personal donations from affluent Palestinians. It shared its headquarters with the Palestine National Council, based in Cairo (until 1979).

In the early days of Fatah in Kuwait, Arafat had started a construction company in order to finance the movement, and had shown considerable business skills, an attribute which was to stand him in good stead in his political career, where he came to manage the finances of not only Fatah but also the much bigger PLO. At the first Arab League summit he was invited to attend in Rabat, Morocco, in December 1969, he appealed, successfully, to fellow leaders, especially the oil-rich rulers, for substantial contributions to the PLO.

With Jordan providing home to almost half of the Palestinians who had fled their native land in 1948, the 10 Palestinian refugee camps in the kingdom emerged as important centres of Palestinian commando presence. The three camps around the capital and the one, Baqaa, near the border of the Occupied West Bank, were particularly active. The presence of a large body of trained armed men, functioning as private militias and flexing their muscles, posed a threat to the regime of King Hussein. When the monarch imposed restrictions on the commandos in February 1969 they protested violently. The subsequent compromise between the king and Arafat proved fragile. While the monarch quietly prepared to have an armed showdown with the Palestinian guerrillas, the PFLP, and its breakaway, the Democratic Front for the Liberation of Palestine, headed by Nayif Hawatmeh, adopted increasingly radical policies. As Habash graduated from a radical Palestinian nationalist to an internationally-oriented Marxist-Leninist, wedded to bringing about global revolution, he added international Zionism, world imperialism and Arab reaction to Israel as the enemies. To him 'Arab reaction' included the monarchical regime of King Hussein. Equally, Hawatmeh, born in 1934 in the Jordanian city of Salt into a Christian family, perceived the liberation of Palestine and

Jordan as inseparable. Believing that hijacking an airliner was more effective in drawing world attention to the plight of Palestinians than killing Jewish Israelis, Habash had begun organizing hijacks – his first target being an Israeli aircraft at Athens airport in December 1968, which resulted in the release of 16 Palestinian prisoners.

Periodic clashes between armed Palestinians and the 55,000-strong Jordanian army started in the spring of 1970. Fatah, then based in Amman, had 20,000 armed men in its Al Assifa militia. The party leadership was evenly divided between right and left, with Arafat often acting as a mediator between Salah Khalaf and Farouq Qaddumi, a former member of the Baath Socialist Party, on the left, and Khalil al Wazir and Khalid Hassan, close to the conservative Saudi royal family, on the right.

The truce between the Palestinian commandos and Jordan, brokered by the Arab League in June 1970, became tenuous in early August when King Hussein accepted an American peace plan, aimed initially at securing a truce in the War of Attrition between Egypt and Israel. Since the monarch's action contradicted the uncompromisingly rejectionist stance adopted by the latest Arab League summit held three years earlier in Khartoum, Sudan, relations between him and the PLO soured. Tension heightened following the blowing up of three emptied western airliners (American, British and Swiss) on 12 September after they had been hijacked by PFLP guerrillas to an abandoned airstrip in the Jordanian desert, named Dawsons Field, once Israel refused to free Palestinian prisoners.

Though Arafat and other Fatah leaders were in two minds about confronting King Hussein, they got swept into the maelstrom that followed in the aftermath of the destruction of the airliners. Fighting erupted between the Palestinians, who were joined by radical Jordanians, in Amman and northern Jordan on 15 September. Four days later, the tank units of the Syrian-based Palestine Liberation Army crossed into northern Jordan and captured Irbid. Assured of US and Israeli backing, Hussein deployed his air force against the Palestinians in the Irbid zone. The Palestinian armoured units withdrew to Syria. A ceasefire, mediated by the Arab League, went into force on 25 September. Since Palestinian militia units were often posted inside refugee camps and used them as their base, there was much fighting in the overcrowded camps. The casualties included about 4,000 dead. The Palestinians called the event 'Black September'.

The net gainer was Israel. The number of Palestinian guerrilla actions against it fell steeply, from a monthly total of 300 to about 50.

The chances of the truce, solemnized on 27 September by a handshake between Arafat and Hussein in the presence of Nasser, leading to a lasting reconciliation faded when the Egyptian President died of heart failure three days later. Slowly, the Jordanian forces began to tighten the noose around the bases of the Palestinian commandos, isolating some 4,000 of them in the hilly areas of Jarash and Ajloun in the north-western corner of the country. When the efforts of Arafat, hiding in the hills with his men, to seek a rapprochement with Hussein in late April 1971 showed little promise, he escaped to Syria. His fighters were decimated by the Jordanian military in July, thus finally ending the PLO's armed presence in Jordan.

King Hussein tried to make amends for the iron fist he had wielded against the PLO by proposing a United Arab Kingdom, with the federated provinces of Jordan and Palestine, after Israel had withdrawn from the West Bank. The tenth Palestine National Council assembly, meeting in April 1972 in Cairo, rejected the proposal, and instead adopted a resolution to establish a Palestinian-Jordanian National Front – an idea that had been developed by the PLO's Planning Centre, based in Beirut and run by Nabil Shaath, who two decades later was to emerge as a leading aide of Arafat. However, this resolution remained unimplemented.

Having lost its main base of operation in Jordan, the PLO had to relocate itself. Syria, with 10 Palestinian refugee camps, half of them in the Damascus area, was one choice; and Lebanon, with 13 refugee camps, chiefly in the southern and central zones, was another. But Syria under the iron hand of President Hafiz Assad, who had seized supreme power in

November 1970, was hardly a place to give the PLO the freedom of action it needed to mount guerrilla assaults against
Israel. So the choice fell on Lebanon, a multi-confessional
country, with a long record of parliamentary politics, and the
least centralized state in the region. Already the hilly terrain
of southern Lebanon had proved ideal for the Palestinian
commandos to mount periodic attacks on Israel.

State Within State

Without much fanfare the PLO gradually relocated itself in
the Fakhani district of (west) Beirut in 1972. The comparatively free atmosphere of the Levantine port allowed the PLO
and Arafat the diplomatic impact it had not made before.
During the decade it functioned from the Lebanese capital,
the PLO emerged as a state-within-state.

The October 1973 Arab-Israeli War altered the balance of
force in the region in favour of the Arabs. Besides restoring
Arab unity, it underlined the immense power of an economic
weapon – oil – which the petroleum-producing Arab states
had only used marginally, and ineffectively, during the 1967
conflict. This diminished the desperation which Fatah and
other PLO constituents had felt after the débâcle in Jordan
in 1970–71, and which had led them increasingly to mount
dramatic terroristic actions such as the killing of 11 Israeli
athletes in September 1972 at the Olympic Games in Munich,
covered by some 6,000 print and broadcasting journalists.
The retaliatory air strikes by Israel on the Palestinian targets
in Lebanon and Syria killed 200 to 500 people, most of them
civilian.[6] Indeed, the pioneer in this field, the PFLP, at its
party congress in December 1973 suspended actions against
Israeli targets abroad, thus ending a chapter which included
16 such operations since July 1968. Fatah followed its lead
two months later. However, Israeli targets inside the Jewish
state and the Occupied Territories of the West Bank and Gaza
were still regarded as legitimate.

A renewed confidence made Palestinian leaders edge
towards realism and moderation. The initiative came from

Nayif Hawatmeh, a broad-shouldered, garrulous Marxist intellectual, with a hawk nose and a luxuriant moustache, who maintained good relations with the Communist Party of the Soviet Union. He was instrumental in persuading the Kremlin, in the aftermath of the October 1973 War, to recognize the PLO as 'the sole legitimate authority, representing the Palestinian people', and invite Arafat, Habash and himself to Moscow in mid-November, a mutually fruitful exercise. In early 1974, addressing an audience at the American University in Beirut, which has a long history of spawning thinkers and intellectuals in the Arab world, Hawatmeh proposed the idea of setting up a national authority in the West Bank and Gaza as the first step towards the liberation of all of Palestine. Participating in the ongoing public debate, Salah Khalaf (Abu Iyad), an eminent Fatah leader, said: 'The question we must ask ourselves is whether, by refusing to accept anything less than the full liberation of all Palestine, we are prepared to abandon a portion of our patrimony to a third party.' He pointed out that the Zionists had obtained their state of Israel in the late 1940s by accepting only a portion of the land they claimed whereas the Palestinians, by consistently saying no, had ended up with nothing.[7]

Echoing these sentiments, the twelfth Palestine National Council assembly, meeting in June 1974 in Cairo, called for the establishment of 'the independent combatant national authority for the people over every part of the Palestinian territory that is liberated', and that 'Once it is established, the Palestinian national authority will strive to achieve a union of the [Arab] confrontation countries, with the aim of completing the liberation of all Palestinian territory.'[8] This indicated that the PLO was ready to accept the ministate of the West Bank and Gaza, if only as a (theoretically) transient stage, a stance rejected by the PFLP's Habash, who could muster only about a quarter of some 250 PNC members present. Speaking in favour of the resolution, a delegate said: 'Remember, remember what [David] Ben Gurion told the 22nd Zionist Congress at Basle in 1946: that the Zionists would accept a state within a reasonable part of Palestine without forgoing their historic rights to it all.'[9]

The PNC resolution provided Arafat with a means to win broader diplomatic recognition. The first sign of success came in mid-October when the United Nations General Assembly decided by 115 votes to four to hold a special discussion on the question of Palestine, something it had not done for the past 22 years, and to invite the PLO 'as representative of the Palestinian people' to participate in the debate. The subject had been on the UN agenda since 1947. And it was the predecessor of the United Nations, the League of Nations, formed in 1920, which had allocated the mandate over Palestine to Britain two years later.

In late October the seventh Arab League summit in Rabat, Morocco, declared the PLO to be 'the sole and legitimate representative of the Palestinian people' with 'the right to establish the independent State of Palestine on any liberated territory', and conferred full membership on it. (Arafat had attended the 1969 and 1973 summits on an *ad hoc* basis.) It was with great reluctance that King Hussein of Jordan, who had claimed special interest in the West Bank, accepted this resolution, which implied that he would have to give diplomatic recognition to the PLO and allow it to open a mission in Amman. At the conference's closing session on 2 November, Arafat declared: 'Today is the turning point in the history of the Palestinian people and the Arab nation. I vow to continue the struggle until we meet together in Jerusalem with the same smiling faces as we see here tonight.'[10]

On 13 November 1974 Arafat arrived in New York surrounded by the most stringent security the city had witnessed, the sort that had been accorded earlier only to such heads of state as Fidel Castro of Cuba and Nikita Khrushchev of the Soviet Union. Just before noon Arafat entered the headquarters in the glass and steel skyscraper on the left bank of the East River in Manhattan. To his fatigues of a commando – an open-neck shirt, baggy trousers, an oversize jacket – topped by his trademark chequed *Kiffayeh*, he had added dark glasses. But, for a change, he had taken care to shave off his usual stubble. He received a standing ovation as he entered the General Assembly hall on the ground floor. Everybody joined, except the American delegates. Two banks of seats were empty in the spacious hall, those of Israel and South Africa. As Arafat responded by raising his arms to give a revolutionary salute, he inadvertently exposed a holster at his side which, UN officials insisted later, was empty of its normal content: a Beretta pistol.

In his 100-minute speech, he covered a vast ground, dwelling on the past (drawing parallels between western imperialism and Zionist colonization of Palestine); describing the present (the anti-colonial nature of the struggle being waged by the PLO and the sufferings of the Palestinians under Israeli occupation); and portraying the future of his dreams ('I may return with my people out of exile, there in Palestine to live . . . in a democratic state where Christian, Jew and Muslim live in justice, equality, fraternity and progress'). He ended his address thus: 'Today I have come bearing an olive branch and a freedom fighter's gun,' he said. 'Do not let the olive branch fall from my hand. I repeat: do not let the olive branch fall from my hand.' It would be another 14 years before Arafat would be invited again to address the United Nations General Assembly, convened especially in Geneva due to America's refusal to grant him a visa.

The significance of the PLO's diplomatic victory in 1974 could be judged by the vehemence of Israel's denunciation of the event. Its ambassador to the United Nations railed against Arafat's 'band of murderers and cut-throats' who had plunged the UN into a 'Sodom and Gomorrah of ideals and values', and went on to attack the international community which, during its 'days of degradation and disgrace, of surrender and humiliation', had allowed them to do it.[11]

On 22 November, at the end of a nine-day debate, with 61 out of 81 speakers backing the PLO, the United Nations General Assembly adopted Resolution 3236, which described the PLO as 'the representative of the Palestinian people', and reaffirmed the Palestinian right to self-determination and national independence, and the right of the Palestinian refugees to return to their homes and property, by 89 votes to eight with 37 abstentions. By adopting another resolution by 95 votes to 17 with 19 abstentions, the General Assembly gave an observer status to the PLO at the UN.

In December, Zehdi Terzi, the PLO's representative to the UN, was invited to participate in the United Nations Security Council debate on the Palestinian issue. On 22 January 1975 the Council endorsed the General Assembly stand by adopting a resolution affirming the Palestinian right to establish an independent state. But it was vetoed by the US administration of President Gerald Ford (r. 1974–6).

The PLO scored another diplomatic victory when on 10 November 1975 the United Nations General Assembly passed Resolution 3379, which defined Zionism as 'a form of racism and racial discrimination', by 72 votes to 35, with 32 abstentions.[12]

The enhanced status of the PLO abroad rubbed off on its management of internal affairs. Khalil Wazir became more active, ordering numerous guerrilla operations against Israel. He emerged as the right-hand man of Arafat, Chairman of both Fatah and the PLO, which besides Fatah now included the Arab Liberation Front (pro-Iraq), Democratic Front for the Liberation of Palestine, Palestine Communist Party, Popular Front for the Liberation of Palestine, Palestine Front for the Liberation of Palestine-General Command, Popular Struggle Front, and Saiqa (pro-Syria). Wazir assisted Arafat in his continuing endeavours to impose PLO discipline and a centralized military command on the various PLO constituents without alienating any of them. Arafat applied his powers of mediation and consensus-building he had developed as the foremost leader of Fatah to keep together a motley crowd of Palestinian groups – some Marxist-Leninist, others pan-Arabist, still others funded by such Arab states as Iraq, Syria and Libya. Inside the West Bank, the PLO-sponsored Palestine National Front won most of the mayoral posts in the local elections that Israel held there in 1976.

When a civil war between left-leaning Lebanese Muslims, headed by Kamal Jumblat, and rightist, mainly Maronite Catholic, Lebanese Christians, led by Camille Chamoun, erupted in April 1975, the PLO could not avoid taking sides. Expectedly, the PLO allied with the Lebanese National Movement, headed by Jumblat, and set up a joint military command, against the rival Lebanese Front, which insisted on the expulsion of the armed Palestinians from Lebanon before discussing political and constitutional reform in Lebanon. By early April 1976 the LNM-PLO alliance controlled two-thirds of the country. In desperation the Lebanese Front turned to Syria through (Maronite Christian) President Suleiman Franjieh, who had friendly relations with his Syrian counterpart, Hafiz Assad. Afraid that radical Lebanon, by giving the PLO a wide berth in its armed struggle against Israel, would provoke the Jewish state into an all-out invasion of Lebanon, which would draw Syria into the conflict at an inopportune time, Assad decided to aid the Lebanese Front in June. The next month, after Syria and the Lebanese Front had gained the upper hand, there was a ceasefire, except in south Lebanon, where the PLO's anti-Israeli activities were being hampered by an Israeli-backed Christian militia. In late October the eighth Arab League summit meeting in Cairo decided to station a 30,000-strong Arab Deterrent Force, consisting mainly of Syrian troops, in Lebanon to maintain peace.

The May 1977 electoral victory of Likud, led by hardliner Menachem Begin, in Israel introduced a new factor into the regional politics. An equally dramatic event occurred on 19 November when Egyptian President Anwar Sadat addressed the Israeli Knesset in Jerusalem in pursuit of peace. When his gesture culminated in the signing of the Camp David Accords in September 1978, Arafat and the PLO were shattered. By agreeing to make peace with Israel unilaterally, Sadat broke the Arab ranks, hitherto committed to a multilateral peace with the Jewish state under the UN auspices, and deprived the Arab League of the option of war with Israel to settle the Palestinian problem. These Accords laid out the framework for a Peace Treaty between Egypt and Israel, and a resolution of the Palestinian problem. The latter objective was to be achieved by granting autonomy to the West Bank and Gaza for an interim period of five years, but the autonomy was to be granted to the people not to the territory, which was to remain under permanent Israeli sovereignty.

Arab leaders responded swiftly and unanimously. Condemning the Camp David Accords at the the ninth Arab

League summit in Baghdad in November 1978, they decided that pan-Arab sanctions against Egypt, including suspension of its League membership and severance of diplomatic relations, should go into effect if and when it signed a peace treaty with Israel. When this happened in March 1979, the Arab League moved its headquarters from Cairo to Tunis. The PLO shifted its Palestine National Council headquarters from Cairo to Damascus.

Another major decision taken at the Baghdad summit concerned funding of the PLO, which had by now won the recognition of over 100 countries, far more than Israel. The oil-rich Gulf states promised it $250 million annually for the next 10 years. This sum, together with another $100 million received from Iraq, Libya and Algeria, formed about 70 per cent of the PLO's annual budget of $500 million. The rest came from the taxes that the Arab states, mainly in the Gulf, collected from the Palestinians working there and channelled into the Palestine National Fund. The other source of revenue for the Palestinian movement was the Samed Foundation, the commercial-industrial arm of Fatah. During the PLO's stay in Lebanon, the activities of Samed, directed by Ahmad Qrei (Abu Alaa), a banker by training, mushroomed – encompassing not only manufacturing plants in Lebanon but also farms and factories in other Arab states, and trading in equities and commodities in international markets. Its fairly secure financial base, combined with the unifying experience of fighting the IDF during its invasion of south Lebanon in March 1978, enabled the PLO to consolidate and strengthen its fighting forces. Its military arm, functioning under Wazir, now consisted of 23,000 armed commandos, and 8–10,000 troops of the Palestine Liberation Army. The virtual break-up of the Lebanese military in early 1976 enabled the PLO to build up its arms arsenal which now included tanks. It had also begun to purchase arms and ammunition from Moscow. Indeed, equipped with Soviet weapons, some 3,500 Palestinian commandos had offered spirited resistance to the invading IDF in south Lebanon, causing (in their estimation) 450 Israeli casualties.

All this was of grave concern to the Begin administration in

Israel. And, having won a fresh mandate from the electorate in July 1981, it set out to cut the PLO and Arafat to size. This task, to be performed by the hawkish Ariel Sharon, the new Defence Minister, was best accomplished after the final phase of the peace treaty with Egypt had been implemented in late April 1982.

Israel used the unsuccessful assassination attempt in London on Shlomo Argov, the Israeli ambassador to Britain, on 3 June by a member of the Palestinian group led by Sabri al Banna (Abu Nidal) – who had been expelled from the PLO in 1974, and subsequently sentenced to death *in absentia* by a Palestinian court in Beirut for trying to murder a leading PLO official, Mahmoud Abbas (Abu Mazen) – as a pretext to mount a fully-fledged invasion of Lebanon on 6 June.

Though Arafat and his security and intelligence chief, Salah Khalaf, did not expect the Israelis to advance to Beirut, they had made contingency plans – including storing ample supplies of food and ammunition – to withstand an IDF siege for about three months. In reality, the PLO stood its ground for two months, from 13 June to 13 August.

Taking advantage of the absence of Premier Begin, visiting the United States from 20 June onwards, Sharon, whose forces had reached Beirut a week earlier, unleashed intensive artillery fire, naval gunfire and aerial bombardment against West Beirut, which harboured the PLO. His intention was not only to secure an unconditional surrender of the PLO but also to decimate Arafat. He failed on both counts. The only way he could defeat the PLO was by deploying his soldiers in the streets and alleys of West Beirut to wage guerrilla warfare, thus incurring high casualties, a politically unacceptable option. On 3 July he cut off all food, water and fuel into West Beirut, and subjected it to intense artillery bombardment. But he had to reverse his decision four days later under pressure from US President Ronald Reagan (r. 1981–7). The spirit of PLO fighters was high. On 9 July they attacked IDF units. Sharon responded with intense artillery fire and bombardment for three days. Then came a brief truce which lasted until 21 July. That day the PLO took the audacious step of attacking the IDF behind its lines. From 22–9 July Sharon staged more intense bombing of West Beirut. Yet the morale of PLO commandos remained high, with Arafat, surrounded by journalists, freely travelling around West Beirut. By refusing to surrender unconditionally, Arafat demonstrated that the PLO was capable of withstanding savage pounding by the enemy. By now it had done so for a sufficient period to merit a claim to have retrieved its honour from the jaws of an imminent military defeat.

Finally, from 1–12 August, Sharon subjected West Beirut to unprecedentedly intense bombing from air, land and sea. On 1 August he ordered 14 hours of non-stop air, naval and artillery pounding of West Beirut. Two days later, when the PLO-Israel talks conducted through Philip Habib – the American envoy who had been active since the early days of the Israeli invasion – seemed to be stalling, the IDF opened up heavy artillery fire all around West Beirut. Since the Israeli siege imposed in mid-June, nearly half of West Beirut's half a million residents had departed, the rest being either too poor or too rich (who feared losing their posh apartments to squatters) to leave. The IDF attempted to seize the PLO headquarters in the Fakhani district, but failed to advance due to strong resistance by the Palestinian commandos, who showed a surprising degree of cohesion under adverse circumstances. The attackers lost many of their men; and the failed attempt brought home to Sharon the cost Israel would have to bear if it engaged in house-to-house fighting.

While the modalities of the evacuation of the PLO and its commandos were being devised through negotiations, Sharon tried to sever the Palestinian refugee camps of Sabra, Chatila and Burj al Barajina, located south of Fakhani, from the northern part of West Beirut. He failed.

On 12 August, later to be called Black Thursday, Sharon ordered saturation bombing on the scale of the Allied attacks on Dresden, Germany, during World War II. From dawn all areas south of Corniche Mazraa boulevard along the seafront were subjected to non-stop air, artillery and naval bombardment for nearly 12 hours by the Israelis, who cut off water supplies and let the city burn. When the onslaught, which caused the deaths of at least 500 civilians, finally ceased, the IDF units rushed to man the roadblocks, making sure that no food or fuel entered West Beirut. Sharon's action sent shock waves not only through the Arab world and outside, but also through the Israeli Government. The fierce attack ended on 13 August. Six days later Israel accepted the PLO's evacuation plan.

Summing up the long ordeal West Beirutis had endured, Sandra Mackey, a resident American journalist, wrote: 'For 70 days, the Israelis pounded Beirut with bombs and mortar rounds. Shelling came from the north, from the hills, and from the sea. Night after night, the skyline exploded in flashes of orange and yellow by ascending spirals of white smoke from exploding munitions. Israeli gunners, known for their precision, landed rounds on hospitals marked with red crosses and crescents as well as on the headquarters of the International Committee of the Red Cross. Hysterical people piled into basements they knew would become tombs if the building above were hit.'[13]

Along with Sharon's general destruction of West Beirut went his specific plan to eliminate Arafat, which never quite succeeded, and which in its train caused hundreds of deaths. Israeli agents, equipped with portable radios, constantly supplied information about Arafat's whereabouts to Sharon's command centre, which deployed artillery or warplanes to hit the area. In the process eight buildings, including apartment blocks, were razed to the ground. Arafat, working in conjunction with Khalaf, head of Fatah's security apparatus, resorted to operating from, and even sleeping in, his car, which was constantly on the move. Another important precaution that Arafat took was not to speak over his radio phone for more than 10 minutes at a time, aware that the Israeli radio-direction finders, being used to trace his movements through his telephone conversations, took less than 15 minutes to locate his position.[14]

Ever since his rise in the firmament of Palestinian politics in the late 1960s, Arafat had been a target of assassins. But this was the first time that he had endured a sustained assassination campaign by Israel with its powerful military and intelligence machine. It was therefore not surprising that when he left Beirut on 30 August he decided to sail to Athens, the capital of Greece, with which the PLO had friendly diplomatic relations, by a Greek merchant ship, escorted by a Greek warship, under an air umbrella furnished by the US Sixth Fleet.

Pushed to the Margin

Taking stock of the situation on his arrival in Tunis in September 1982, Arafat found the overall picture distinctly bleak. Both the PLO and his own Fatah movement had been yanked out of the core of the Middle East and thrown to a peripheral Arab capital, 2,400 kilometres from Israel. The over 8,000 PLO commandos, evacuated from Beirut, had been scattered to the camps in Syria, Iraq, North Yemen, Libya, Tunisia and Algeria.

The all enveloping darkness was soon to be relieved by a chink of light. It came from Amman. With a view to reviving the old idea of confederation between Jordan and a future Palestine, King Hussein began courting Arafat. He allowed Wazir, the commander of the PLO's western sector since 1981, to establish an office in Amman. From here Wazir set out to renew his contacts with the PLO activists in the West Bank who had earlier, under his guidance, successfully penetrated such Palestinian institutions as student and trade unions, chambers of commerce, women's organizations and the Arabic press.

Unlike Fatah, most of the radical constituents of the PLO, including the PFLP and the DFLP, moved to Damascus, which had been home to the Palestine National Council for the past three years. The Syrian capital now emerged as the hotbed of the Fatah militants – led by an artillery officer, Muhammad Said Musa Maragha (Abu Musa) – who were dissatisfied with the leadership of Arafat who, they said, rewarded loyalty rather than performance, and had spawned bloated bureaucracy. They rebelled and took over a PLO brigade-base in eastern Lebanon in May 1983.

Seeing the hand of the Syrian leader Hafiz Assad behind this, Arafat flew to Damascus to meet him. Their talks yielded little of substance. Fighting between the Arafat loyalists and opponents erupted in eastern Lebanon in June. When Arafat sought the assistance of Rifaat Assad, the influential younger brother of Hafiz, to curb the power of Fatah rebels, the Syrian leader was enraged. He ordered a summary expulsion of the PLO chief on 24 June. Hafiz Assad's move angered the Palestinians in the Occupied Territories. The feeling was expressed dramatically two days later by Shaikh Saad al Din Alawi, the mufti (Arabic, one who issues religious decrees) of Jerusalem. In his Friday prayer sermon at the Al Aqsa Mosque, the mufti issued a fatwa (Arabic, religious decree) against Hafiz Assad: 'It is the [religious] duty of every Muslim to assassinate the Syrian President [Hafiz Assad] for the crimes he has committed against the Palestinian people.'[15]

Since then bad blood between Arafat and Assad has persisted – an exception in intra-Arab relations where heated quarrelling between leaders is sooner or later followed by warm hugs and lofty declarations of eternal friendship and brotherliness.

Apparently, by backing Abu Musa the Syrian President wished to topple Arafat, and take control of Fatah, and thus the PLO. Arafat, committed to maintaining the independence of the PLO at all costs, was determined to resist Assad. The power game between the two leaders had yet to be played out.

The withdrawal in early September of the IDF from the mountains facing south-eastern Beirut to the banks of the Awali River to the south opened up opportunities for the Palestinian fighters to play a role in the unfinished Lebanese civil war. In mid-September Arafat resurfaced in the port city of Tripoli, northern Lebanon, and set up bases in the nearby Palestinian refugee camps of Beddawi and Nahar al Bared located along the coastline. Soon he and his 4,000 commandos found themselves besieged by the Fatah rebels and the Syrian ground troops, with IDF naval gunboats blocking their exit by sea. Once they had been expelled from their bastion in the Beddawi camp on 17 November their fate seemed doomed. 'Already crippled by Israel, Yasser Arafat has [now] been finished off by Syria,' stated the *New York Times* in its editorial on 18 November. 'Such is the bizarre ending of a movement that, for all its daring, never found a political vision.' Like the rumoured death of Mark Twain (1835–1910), the eminent American humorist, such comments about Arafat and the PLO proved premature.

This time, the Saudi King, Fahd ibn Abdul Aziz, came to Arafat's rescue. His foreign minister, Prince Saud al Faisal, flew to Damascus. A compromise plan combined an orderly evacuation of Arafat and his armed militia with a Syrian promise not to try replacing Arafat as the PLO head. But it was another month before the modalities of the evacuation were devised and implemented. Meanwhile, Ariel Sharon, now a minister without portfolio in the Israeli Government, bayed for Arafat's blood, declaring that 'he should not be allowed to leave Tripoli alive'. So while the pro-Damascus forces observed a truce, the IDF gunboats began raining shells indiscriminately, hoping thus to decimate the PLO chief. It was US intervention which silenced the Israeli guns, and allowed five Greek merchant ships, hired by the UN and carrying its flag, and escorted by a French warship, to take on board Arafat and his loyal troops. Before embarking upon his second outward journey from Lebanon on Christmas Eve 1983, aboard *Odysseus Elytis*, a defiant Arafat said: 'The struggle is not over. We will continue until we reach Jerusalem, the capital of our Palestinian state.'[16]

These were brave words from a leader whose liberation movement was damaged seemingly beyond repair. Indeed from December 1983 to December 1987 Arafat floundered in the same way that the Palestinians in the Occupied Territories did.

Having failed to make any tangible gains by following an essentially left-of-centre line, Arafat now leaned rightwards, for reconciliation with the pro-western leaders like King Hussein and President Hosni Mubarak (1928–) of Egypt, still a pariah state in the eyes of the Arab League, hoping thus to win the recognition of Washington. He appeared unaware of the secret written commitment the United States had made to Israel in September 1975, as part of the Sinai II Agreement between Egypt and Israel, not to recognize or negotiate with the PLO until it abandoned terrorism against Israel and recognized its right to exist in tranquillity.[17]

In November 1984 Arafat called a Palestine National Council assembly in the Jordanian capital, Amman. It was boycotted by all the radical Palestinian groups, based either in Damascus, also the base of Al Quds Palestinian Arab Radio, or Baghdad, also the base of the Voice of the PLO Radio. Its proceedings were thus dominated by moderates. By threatening to resign as PLO Chairman, Arafat consolidated his position. Among other things the assembly decided to move the PNC headquarters from Damascus to Amman.

Arafat then went on to sign a five-point accord with King Hussein in February 1985, meant to ease the PLO's way into an international conference on Middle Eastern peace. 'Palestinians will exercise their inalienable right of self-determination when they and Jordanians will be able to do so within the context of the formation of the proposed confederated Arab states of Jordan and Palestine,' stated the operative Article 2. This raised more questions than it answered since the State of Palestine had not graduated beyond an idea and a hope.

Equally seriously, Jordan and the PLO executive committee later began arguing about the PLO's position on the crucial United Nations Security Council Resolution 242. Jordan said that the PLO had accepted it whereas the PLO executive committee insisted that it had not. In the event this proved to be the breaking point. When top US officials, using King Hussein as the intermediary, urged Arafat to accept Resolution 242, which implies recognition of Israel within secure borders, to overcome Israeli objections, the PLO Chairman agreed provided Washington said in writing that it endorsed self-determination for Palestinians. But US President Reagan was not prepared to go beyond 'Palestinian self-rule'. This led to friction between Hussein and Arafat. In February 1986 Hussein announced the annulment of the year-old Jordan-PLO accord. He then closed down all PLO offices in Jordan, including that of the Palestine National

Fund, and expelled many PLO functionaries, including its military chief, Wazir.

Aside from the United States, Israel was unimpressed by Arafat's professed drift towards pragmatism. Its intelligence reports showed that, having lost their capacity to mount attacks on Israel from the soil of Lebanon, Arafat and his military chief, Wazir, had devised a maritime strategy to hit Israeli targets. In this the southern Cypriot port of Larnaca, situated 220 kilometres west of Beirut, played a key role as a waystation. It had become a hotbed of international spies specializing in monitoring maritime and air traffic. Inevitably Israelis and Palestinians were part of the motley crowd, interested as much in watching ships and airplanes as one another. A three-member hit team of the PLO, belonging to Force 17, an elite unit of Arafat, attacked an Israeli yacht moored at Larnaca's marina on 25 September 1985, and killed three people on board, claiming that they were Mossad operators who were doing more than merely monitoring sea traffic in the Mediterranean. Outraged, the Israeli national unity government, headed by Shimon Peres, known to be holding clandestine meetings with King Hussein to advance the peace process, vowed retaliation.

It came on 1 October morning. Six Israeli F-15 fighter-bombers flattened three PLO offices, including the one used by Arafat, at Hammam Shatt, located 20 kilometres south-east of Tunis, on the Gulf of Hammamet. (The PLO then moved its offices in villas scattered across the middle class district of Al Manzeh in Tunis.) Had Israel wished to limit the damage to the PLO buildings and documents and several night-watchmen, its air force would have struck at dawn. But the raid occurred around 10 a.m. when the administrative offices were buzzing with activity, and took a heavy human toll: 56 Palestinians and 17 Tunisians. But it missed its prized target: Arafat. This time it was pure chance that saved the PLO Chairman. Having returned the previous night from one of his endless foreign travels, this time to the neighbouring Morocco, and dallied over a late-night dinner at the seafront villa of the PLO's envoy to Tunisia, Abdul Hakkam Balawi, Arafat had fallen behind his schedule the next morning and was not in his office when the Israelis staged their air raid.[18] The fact that the United Nations Security Council issued a condemnation of Israel by 14 votes to none, with the United States abstaining, was a poor consolation to Arafat. He interpreted Israel's action, authorized by Peres, as running counter to the Israeli premier's public declarations of seeking peace. Among other things this reconciled Arafat with radical Habash and Hawatmeh, from whom he had been estranged for a couple of years.

This reconciliation was consolidated in April 1987 when the 426-strong Palestine National Council, meeting at the conference hall of Club des Pins, 30 kilometres west of Algiers, finally buried the PLO-Jordan accord of 1985. Amidst much show of renewed solidarity between Arafat and his radical rivals within the PLO, the PNC decided to form multi-party co-ordinating committees for the Occupied Homeland.

The latest PNC session at the Club des Pins fitted well the general pattern of Palestinian and Arab politics. 'I don't believe that Arab history has ever known a final estrangement,' remarked Khalid Hassan, the plump, fleshy-faced former foreign minister of the PLO, in a radio interview. 'Our Arab history is full of agreements and differences. When we differ and then grow tired of differing, we agree. When we grow tired of agreeing we differ, and so on. After every agreement or difference we pass through a time that changes things . . . [T]his is the Arab nature.'[19]

Time was about to change the situation radically in the Occupied Palestinian Territories.

Intifada: A Kiss of Life

The eruption of the intifada, a grass roots movement, in the Occupied Territories on 9 December 1987 ended the debilitating phase into which PLO politics had been forced in the aftermath of the movement's expulsion from Beirut in September 1982.

Always keen to exercise power and retain initiative, Arafat

– who gave currency to the term intifada, uprising, by using it in his address on the Voice of the PLO Radio, broadcasting from Baghdad, on 10 December – felt uneasy when in early January the leaders inside the Occupied Territories decided on their own to form the United National Leadership of the Uprising-the PLO, consisting chiefly of Fatah, the PFLP, the DFLP and the Palestine Communist Party.

The intifada emerged as such a powerful movement that it had an impact on the Palestinian leadership in the Diaspora. It made the fractious leaders of the several Palestinian groups affiliated to the PLO really sink their differences. A specific event that accelerated the trend was the assassination of Wazir who, in his capacity as Fatah's military chief, had worked for many years in conjunction with the PLO's Occupied Homeland Directorate to create a PLO infrastructure in the West Bank.

To show that the Fatah leadership in Tunis was doing more than merely applauding the perpetrators of the intifada in the Occupied Territories, Wazir dispatched three Fatah commandos to Israel's Negev desert through the Sinai to attack the Israeli nuclear weapons plant at Dimona. On 7 March 1988 they hijacked a bus carrying the nuclear facility's employees from Beersheba to Dimona. Once the bus had been halted at a roadblock, and the hijackers lured into serious negotiations, the scene was set for a surprise assault by the Israeli police. It came, and left six people dead, including all of the hijackers. Arafat claimed the event a victory since, in his words, it had drawn attention to the clandestine Israeli atomic bomb factory, 'the most dangerous military target in the Middle East'. (With the publication in the (London) *Sunday Times* of 5 October 1986 of a detailed report by Mordechai Vanunu, a former technician at the Dimona nuclear processing plant, along with photographs, this nuclear facility was hardly secret.) As the head of Fatah's military wing, Wazir applauded the martyrdom of his guerrillas. Unsurprisingly, the audacious attempt by Palestinian guerrillas angered Israel, particularly its Defence Minister Yitzhak Rabin. Its inner cabinet of 10 ministers decided to liquidate Wazir.

'Removing a senior commander from enemy ranks would not settle the Arab-Israeli conflict, but the Israelis badly needed some sort of victory four months into the intifada,' explained Dan Raviv, an American reporter, and Yossi Melman, an Israeli journalist, in a book on Israel's intelligence agencies. 'In addition, the experience of the 1970s had taught Mossad that assassinating top terrorist leaders caused severe disruptions in the PLO and its splinter groups. It made them fear the Israelis; it made them hesitate in planning their violence; and it forced them into making mistakes. Perhaps even more than the Israelis needed a triumph, they believed that the Palestinian resistance movement was overdue for a setback.'[20] This turned out to be a gross miscalculation. Indeed the operation proved politically counter-productive.

The Israelis did a professional job, involving the IDF's elite Sayeret commandos as well as the Shayetet 13 (Hebrew, Fleet 13) frogmen, the agents of military intelligence Aman (derivative of Amn, Hebrew acronym of Agaf Modein, Intelligence Branch), and the operators of Mossad. The task of the three Mossad operatives who arrived in Tunis as tourists with Lebanese passports, speaking Arabic with a Lebanese accent, on 12 April 1988 was to rent two minibuses and a station wagon. On the night of 15–16 April they waited at the beach at Rouad to pick up 30 members of the Sayeret unit who were brought ashore in rubber dinghies by frogmen from an IDF missile boat anchored offshore. Just before one a.m. they picked up the Israeli commandos in their vehicles and drove them to the nearby Sidi Bou Said suburb of Tunis. They stopped a block from Wazir's villa, where he lived with his wife, Intissar, a Fatah activist, and their 14-year-old daughter and a two-year-old son, Nidal. Twenty-two commandos in a minibus and a station wagon stayed put, ready to fight PLO men and/or the Tunisian troops, in case things went wrong. The leader of the remaining eight commandos in the other minibus was then led by a Mossad agent to the telephone junction for the area. He plugged the appropriate device into the junction box and short-circuited the system. The Mossad operative then drove the eight-strong unit to al Wazir's villa.

Just after 1.30 a.m. the commando unit, armed with sub-machine-guns and pistols, and operating as two groups of four each, smashed into Wazir's house, shooting dead three men – Wazir's driver sitting inside his car, a Palestinian guard and a Tunisian guard – who came between them and their target. They had done several practice runs on the model of the house that had been built in Israel during their training. Now they headed for the main bedroom upstairs. Khalil Wazir, who had returned home at midnight, was up, and so was his wife, Intissar. He was in the midst of composing a clandestine message to the United National Leadership of the Uprising. Alarmed by the noise downstairs, he picked up his pistol, and moved gingerly to the bedroom door, with Intissar trailing behind. He opened the door and, finding hooded men coming upstairs, fired a shot. That was his last act. He fell in a hailstorm of bullets, 67 to be exact, that poured out of the guns of his Israeli assassins, never to rise again. Intissar watched aghast, expecting to be murdered. But she was not.[21]

Arafat, who was on a tour of the Gulf states, hurried back to Tunis. He was shattered by the news of the murder of his closest ally, someone who had been his confidant for three decades. A psychological profile of Wazir, prepared for Mossad by an Israeli expert on Arabic handwriting, showed him to be 'a highly intelligent man, a good organizer with a precise, analytical mind and great reserves of strength'.[22] His other major leadership asset, that made him a marked man in the inner sanctum of the Israeli political establishment, was his ability to conciliate disputatious factions within the PLO, an attribute much valued in an unwieldy organization like the PLO. Though Arafat in a later interview with his British biographers, Andrew Gowers and Tony Walker, said, 'We [Wazir and I] were one spirit in two bodies', they were in reality complementary to each other – the cool, calculating Wazir balancing Arafat's emotionalism and volatility. Yet Arafat's declaration in the wake of Wazir's violent death came to pass. 'Those who think the assassination of Abu Jihad (Khalil Wazir) will smother the Palestinian uprising are deluding themselves,' he told the *Financial Times*. 'His death will give new life to this heroic revolt.' And it did. On the Israeli side Arafat found an echo in the utterings of Ezer Weizman, then a member of the inner cabinet of Israel, who had opposed al Wazir's assassination. 'It does not contribute to the fight against terrorism,' he told reporters. 'It distances the peace process and will bring greater hostility [towards Israel].'[23]

Instantly the martyr Abu Jihad became a unifying symbol, a legendary figure, revered equally by all PLO factions. His portraits appeared in as much profusion as those of Arafat. Even today this trend continues, the moustached, chubby face of a portly Abu Jihad staring at the visitors to the offices of the Palestinian Authority alongside Arafat's.

Another unexpected development encouraged Arafat to capitalize on the unprecedented unity that Abu Jihad's murder created in the PLO factions. It came from King Hussein who, too, felt the power of the intifada. 'Since there is a general conviction that the struggle to liberate the occupied Palestinian land could be enhanced by dismantling the legal and administrative links between the two banks [of River Jordan], we have to do our duty, and do what is required of us,' he said in an official communiqué on 31 July 1988. 'Jordan is not Palestine. And the independent Palestinian state will be established on the occupied land after its liberation, God willing.' Hussein's statement finally laid to rest the 'Jordanian Option' that Peres and, to a lesser extent, Rabin had been bandying about since the early 1970s. In human terms it meant loss of jobs to 21,000 civil servants and others who had been on Jordan's payroll.

Before finalizing plans for an emergency Palestine National Council assembly on the intifada, Arafat secured a promise from all non-Fatah leaders that there would be no walk-outs. Keenly aware that the policy of the United States, the god-mother of Israel, towards the PLO now mattered most, he called the PNC's nineteenth session on 13 November 1988, five days after the US presidential poll on 8 November. As in the past year, the venue was the circular Club des Pins conference hall near Algiers. It attracted 380 of the 450 PNC members.

On 15 November the PNC unanimously adopted the political communiqué which, while upholding the 'glorious intifada' of the Palestinian people, referred to the favourable United Nations General Assembly's Resolution 21L/43/1 of 11 April 1988 that was passed after the Assembly had debated the intifada. On the more controversial resolution on the establishment of the State of Palestine, Arafat deployed his deputy, Salah Khalaf, to clinch the argument. Khalaf did a superb job. By a large majority the PNC adopted the Proclamation of the Independent State of Palestine. 'The Palestine National Council, in the name of God, and in the name of the Palestinian Arab people, hereby proclaims the establishment of the State of Palestine on our Palestinian territory with its capital Al Quds al Sharif (Holy Jerusalem),' declared Arafat after he had been elected President of the new state and the Palestinian flag had been hoisted inside the marble-floored conference hall. 'The State of Palestine is the state of Palestinians wherever they may be.' The tautology was deliberate, its purpose being to leave undefined the boundaries of the State of Palestine – something the Israeli parliament 40 years before had done at the behest of Ben Gurion by indefinitely postponing the drafting of a written constitution. The PNC's acceptance of two states in the British mandate Palestine was buried in an earlier paragraph: 'Despite the historical injustice inflicted on the Palestinian Arab people, resulting in their dispersion and depriving them of their right to self-determination, following upon UN General Assembly Resolution 181 (1947), which partitioned Palestine into two states, one Arab, one Jewish, yet it is this resolution that still provides those conditions of international legitimacy that ensure the right of the Palestinian Arab people to sovereignty and national independence.'[24] By accepting the United Nations' partition plan of 1947, which had then been rejected unanimously by the seven members of the Arab League, the PNC paved the way for the acceptance of the subsequent United Nations Security Council Resolutions 242 (1967) and 338 (1973), a development which deeply interested the current United Nations General Assembly.

In any event, 15 November became another memorable

date in the Palestinian calendar, on a par with 1 January (the launching of an armed struggle against Israel), and 24 March (the decision to confront the IDF at Karameh, Jordan).

Following the PNC's action, 70 of the 103 countries which had recognized the PLO so far accorded it full diplomatic status. But the state which mattered most, the United States, was not impressed. Indeed its Secretary of State, George Shultz, described Arafat as an 'accessory to terrorism' and therefore 'a threat to US national security', and denied him a visa to address the United Nations General Assembly to spell out the new development. The UN hit back by resolving on 2 December by 154 votes to two (the US and Israel) to hold a single session at its European headquarters in Geneva on 13 December to hear Arafat.

On 7 December Arafat had a meeting in Stockholm, Sweden, with the American Jewish leaders acting as the intermediaries of Shultz, and bearing his letter setting out the lines that Arafat should say in his UN speech in order to get an official recognition by the US. Unable to decide on his own, Arafat signed a 'secret' statement, subject to the approval of the PLO's executive committee. It read: '(1) That it [the PLO's executive committee] is prepared to negotiate with Israel within the framework of the international conference a comprehensive peace settlement of the Arab-Israeli conflict on the basis of UN [Security Council] Resolutions 242 and 338. (2) That it undertakes to live in peace with Israel and other neighbours and respect their right to exist in peace within secure and internationally recognized borders as will the democratic Palestinian state which it seeks to establish in the Palestinian occupied territories since 1967. (3) That it condemns individual and state terrorism in all its forms and will not resort to it.'[25] This statement amounted to a unilateral concession by the PLO, which had hitherto insisted on according formal recognition to Israel (as opposed to implicit recognition built into the United Nations Security Council 242) only in return for Israel's acceptance of the right of the Palestinian people to set up their own sovereign state. Little wonder that Arafat failed to get an unequivocal endorsement of the PLO executive committee of the secret statement he had signed in Stockholm when it met in Tunis.

Like their American counterparts in New York, the Swiss in Geneva provided unprecedentedly tight security to Arafat as he appeared at the old League of Nations headquarters in the Palais de Nations on the banks of Lake Geneva. Fourteen years older than when he had last addressed the United Nations General Assembly, and greying, Arafat appeared in the hall, his facial hair properly trimmed, dressed in battle-green military fatigues, freshly laundered and pressed, and his trademark *kiffayeh*. In a long speech, he scattered his peaceful ideas of co-existence with Israel, and rephrased the points Shultz had prescribed precisely in his letter. But since he did not specifically renounce violence and recognize Israel, the response of Shultz was negative. To make Shultz change his mind, Arafat called a press conference the next day. 'Between Algiers and Geneva we have made our position crystal clear,' he said, reading a prepared statement in English. 'We accept the right of all parties in the Middle East conflict to exist in peace and security. I repeat for the record that we totally and absolutely renounce all forms of terrorism.'[26] A lasting memory of those who watched the press conference on television was hearing Arafat say something akin to 'tourism' rather than 'terrorism'.

Within a few hours Shultz said that the United States was 'prepared' to open 'a substantive dialogue with PLO representatives'. In practice this meant middle level talks between the PLO and the American embassy in Tunis. A week later Yitzhak Shamir, heading a new national unity government in Israel, following a stalemated result in the November 1988 parliamentary poll, indicated his response. He denied Peres, 'the peacenik', the coveted foreign ministry, which he allocated to a Likud hardliner, Moshe Arens.

When Peres brought about the downfall of the national unity government in March 1990 and then failed to form a Labour-led coalition, thus allowing Shamir to rule as the head of the most right-wing administration in Israeli history, Arafat's hopes of successful negotiations with Israel through Washington faded. On top of that he found an Israel on the verge of a rising tide of Jewish immigration from the Soviet Union, with the number of immigrants jumping from 13,300 in 1988 to 199,500 in 1990.

This became a matter of concern throughout the Arab world. The subject dominated the proceedings of the seventeenth Arab League summit held in May 1990 in Baghdad, and hosted by President Saddam Hussein. Its resolution described the emigration of Soviet and other Jews to Palestine and other Occupied Arab Territories as 'a new aggression against the rights of the Palestinian people and a serious danger to the Arab nation as well as a gross violation of human rights, the principles of international law and the Fourth Geneva Convention of 1949'. It called on the United Nations Security Council to prohibit settlement of Jewish immigrants in the Occupied Palestine and Arab Territories, and appoint a UN agency to monitor implementation of such a resolution. By stating that Jewish immigration was a threat to the 'Arab national interest', the summit resolution strengthened the hands of Jordan and the PLO, thus laying the foundation of an incipient alliance between them and Iraq whose president played a leading role in the debate.[27]

Saddam Hussein endeared himself to Palestinians by announcing emergency aid of $25 million to the intifada. As it was, relations between Iraq and the PLO had been cordial ever since Baath Socialist military officers seized power in Baghdad in July 1968. Among other things they allowed the PLO, radicalized in 1968–9, to set up a radio station, called the Voice of the PLO, in Baghdad. When pressured by the Tunisian Government to relocate its military department, following the Israeli air raid on the PLO headquarters in October 1985, the PLO shifted it to Baghdad in early 1987. With this, Arafat became a frequent visitor to the Iraqi capital. The Voice of the PLO Radio played a pivotal role in sustaining the intifada. Part of the reason why Arafat refused to discipline Abu al Abbas (Muhammad Abbas Zaidan) for the failed terrorist action on 30 May 1990 on an Israeli beach was that his group, the Palestine Liberation Front, was funded by Iraq, and based in Baghdad.

Whatever reservations Arafat had about Saddam Hussein's

invasion and occupation of Kuwait on 2 August 1990 evaporated when on 12 August the Iraqi leader offered a peace plan, including 'preparations' of withdrawal of 'Israel from the Occupied Arab Territories in Palestine, Syria and Lebanon; Syria's withdrawal from Lebanon; a withdrawal between Iraq and Iran; and the formulation of arrangements for the situation in Kuwait' in line with the (earlier) United Nations Security Council resolutions.[28] This multi-faceted idea became embedded in the popular psyche as a direct linkage between the issues of the Occupied Kuwait and the Occupied Palestinian Territories, to be settled simultaneously. Many Palestinians came to believe that the strong stand taken by Saddam Hussein in the deepening Kuwait crisis would force the United States and Israel to agree to the linkage he had proposed. This perception prevailed not only in the West Bank and Gaza but also among the Palestinians in Jordan, an important factor which contributed to King Hussein maintaining a pro-Saddam Hussein stance during the Kuwait crisis and the subsequent Gulf War.

All along the popular backing among Palestinians for Saddam Hussein remained consistently high. On the eve of the Gulf War in mid-January 1991, Arafat declared: 'Palestinians will stand alongside Iraqis in the trenches.'[29] This complemented his very warm bear-hug of President Saddam Hussein, the small, tubby Arafat almost clutching to the tall, powerful frame of the Iraqi leader – an image which was screened repeatedly on western television screens. Arafat's prediction that Israel would respond to the Iraqi missile hits with its own attacks, thus joining the US-led anti-Iraqi coalition uninvited, and inadvertently causing the departure of the coalition's Arab members – the Gulf states, Egypt, Syria and Morocco – proved wrong. When some of Arafat's aides questioned the wisdom of his deepening involvement with the Iraqi leader, he replied: 'This is the will of my people.'[30] Given the fevered environment created by the gathering clouds of a major war – which culminated in the assembling of 750,000 troops in the Gulf region and an unprecedented arsenal of weapons, including some 700 nuclear arms – the Palestinian people had expressed their will unequivocally and dramatically.

At the same time Arafat tried to sell the PLO's plan to settle the crisis peacefully. But, with the Arab world deeply divided, he got nowhere. A disappointed Arafat received a shocking piece of news on the eve of the Gulf War. His remaining long-term colleague, Salah Khalaf, the PLO's security and intelligence chief, was gunned down. This happened in the house of Hayil Abdul Hamid (*nom de guerre*, Abu al Hol), head of the PLO's internal security, in Carthage, a suburb of Tunis, on 14 January around 11 p.m. The perpetrator was Hamza Abu Zaid, a bodyguard of Abdul Hamid. Firing his AK-47 Kalashnikov assault rifle, he killed not only his boss, Hayil Abdul Hamid, but also Salah Khalaf and his deputy, Fakhri Omari, all of whom had just finished their late dinner in the ground floor reception room. The young assassin turned out to be a member of the Abu Nidal group. He had infiltrated what was supposed to be the most secure organ of the PLO: its internal security department. It was worth noting that it was the same Abu Nidal group, led by Sabri al Banna (Abu Nidal), whose members – Nawaf al Rosan, Hussein Said and Marwan al Banna – were arrested by the British police in June 1982 for their involvement in the failed assassination of the Israeli ambassador, Shlomo Argov.

Arafat, who heard the news in Baghdad, rushed back to Tunis. He was so aggrieved that he broke down at the wake of Khalaf. Both his long-time friends and confidants, Wazir and Khalaf, were now dead, leaving him to tackle the monumental tasks of the present and the future all on his own, an unnerving prospect even for a man who had been playing a leadership role for a generation.

During the early period of the Gulf War, which started at 23.30 Greenwich Mean Time on 16 January (02.30 on 17 January Baghdad time), Arafat was confident that Iraq would withstand the onslaught by the US-led Coalition of 29 nations for a long time. This was not to be. After an unparalleled non-stop air campaign by the Coalition forces, which resulted in 106,000 air sorties against Iraq and occupied Kuwait, followed by four days of a ground campaign, Iraq completed its unconditional withdrawal from Kuwait by 28 February and accepted a temporary ceasefire. Throughout the conflict the Palestinians in the Occupied Territories were immobilized by an indefinite curfew imposed by Israel, receiving their food and other necessities at home from the United Nations Relief and Works Agency.

Arafat was down but not out. Even in the midst of a devastating air campaign being waged against Iraq, he managed to retain a historical perspective. 'There is something here that the West seems incapable of understanding or absorbing, that the dynamism of our people is not a passing phase,' he told a correspondent of the London-based *Mideast Mirror*, in mid-February 1991. 'The dynamism of our people is deeply rooted in history. Ours is an epic people. It has been struggling since 1917, from the Balfour Declaration until today . . . That is 73 or 74 years, three generations.'[31]

He could have referred to the severe setback the PLO had suffered in Beirut nearly a decade earlier, and survived. But this time what seriously threatened the future of the PLO was the loss of grants from a bankrupt Iraq and the alienated oil-rich Gulf states, which had so far provided a substantial part of the revenue for the PLO. Arafat ordered a belt-tightening which curtailed not only the high living of many senior PLO bureaucrats and diplomats but also the expenditure on such items as schools, hospitals and social welfare. It was estimated that since the 1967 War, the PLO's *Amival al Sumud* (Arabic, The Steadfastness Fund) had channelled an average of $20 million annually into the West Bank and Gaza through the foreign charities functioning there and the Palestinian money-changers. Its welfare department, based in Amman, provided payments to the families where a member was killed as a 'martyr' (a one-off payment of $1,500), wounded, arrested ($120 a month stipend), or deported. This meant providing welfare payments to over 90,000 Palestinian families, a fifth of whom had sacrificed a member to the nationalist cause.[32]

Once President Bush had in his address to the US Congress on 6 March reiterated the need for 'a comprehensive peace [which] must be grounded in the UN Security Council

Resolutions 242 and 338 and the principle of territory
for peace', his Secretary of State, James Baker, actively
tried to convene an international Peace Conference on the
Middle East. In mid-July, once President Assad had made
a dramatic concession on Syria's terms for attending such a
gathering, Israeli consent became most likely. It materialized
on 1 August. Baker's chances of success improved sharply.

But the Shamir government in Israel had extracted a price
which hurt Arafat. And he said as much. 'If Israel has said yes
to the conference, it is because all the conditions which it has
set have been accepted by the US administration,' Arafat complained in an interview to French television on 3 August. 'No
to the presence of the PLO, no to an independent Palestinian
state, no to [Palestinian] representatives from Jerusalem, and
no to the resolution of the status of Jerusalem.'

To overcome the US handicap of suspension of its contacts
with the PLO since June 1990, Baker initiated talks with
Faisal Husseini, living in East Jerusalem, and Hanan Ashrawi,
based in Ramallah – prominent Palestinians officially unconnected with the PLO – who acted as intermediaries. His
queries were: 'Will the Palestinians come to the talks as
part of a joint Jordanian-Palestinian team; will the PLO
forgo a public role in the talks; will the Palestinians forgo
a representative of the Diaspora in the delegation; and will the
Palestinians forgo a representative from East Jerusalem.'

The answers came in the fourth paragraph of the political
resolution adopted by the twentieth PNC assembly on 28
September. 'The PLO, as the sole legitimate representative
of the Palestinian people, reserves the right to make up the
Palestinian delegation from the people inside and outside the
Homeland, including Jerusalem, and to define the form of its
participation in the peace process on the basis of equality,' it
read. The resolution was carried by 256 votes to 68.

As before Arafat called the PNC session at the Club des
Pins conference hall near Algiers. Of the 456 members more
than 350 attended. Of these 313 voted for the resolution
which laid down the guidelines for the Palestinian representatives – setting out both a mandate and the limits
which were not be crossed – with only 18 opposing. Equally

significantly, the PNC replaced the troublesome Abu al Abbas on the executive committee with his deputy, Abu Ismail. It expanded the executive committee from 14 members to 17, with the additional seats going to moderates.

Later the PLO's 99-member central council, a standing body bridging the PNC and the executive committee, approved the 14 non-PLO Palestinians (eight of whom had either been jailed by Israel, put under house arrest or subjected to a travel ban) to join the Jordanian-Palestinian delegation, and appointed an 11-member steering committee to guide the Palestinian negotiators according to the principles laid down by the PNC. Headed by Faisal Husseini, the steering committee included Hanan Ashrawi, a Christian, then a lecturer in English literature at Birzeit University.

Though kept out of the official proceedings of the Middle East Peace Conference, which opened on 30 October 1991 in Madrid, Spain, in the Royal Palace's grand Hall of Columns, under the joint chairmanship of President Bush and President Mikhail Gorbachev of the Soviet Union, the PLO's steering committee – represented by Husseini and Ashrawi – made a palpable impact on the international media, represented by nearly 4,700 accredited journalists.

Faisal Husseini, a balding, clean-shaven, broad-shouldered man with gravitas, came from the illustrious family of the al Husseinis who had arrived in Jerusalem from Mecca in the thirteenth century. In recent times the family had had the distinction of providing the local mayor and the mufti of Jerusalem, a position occupied by Haajj Muhammad Amin Husseini, an uncle of Faisal, from 1922 to 1937, when in the course of the Arab Revolt of 1936–9 he escaped to Syria and then Iraq. Born in 1940 in Baghdad, where his family had taken refuge, Faisal grew up in Cairo. His father, Abdul Qadir, was the field commander during the Arab Revolt. Following the United Nations partition plan of November 1947 Abdul Qadir Husseini took up arms against the Zionist forces, and died in the Battle of Kastel near Jerusalem in 1948, and was buried on the Haram al Sharif, an honour of the highest degree. Among the visitors to the Husseini household in the Cairo suburb of Heliopolis in the 1950s was Yasser Arafat. After his university education in Cairo, Faisal returned to his family home in East Jerusalem, then under Jordanian control. He worked in the Jerusalem office of the PLO after its founding in 1964, and then enrolled at the military academy in Homs, Syria, for an officer's course for the Palestine Liberation Army. After the June 1967 War he found his way back into Jerusalem. There he was contacted by Arafat during the latter's sojourn in the West Bank to set up a guerrilla infrastructure. After Arafat's escape from Al Bireh, the IDF arrested Faisal Husseini, and sentenced him to a year in jail for concealing two of Arafat's guns. He remained politically active. In 1979 he opened the Arab Studies Centre, a research organization, which, in Israel's view, was a front for co-ordinating PLO activities in the Occupied Territories. The Israeli authorities soon closed down the Centre and put him under administrative detention. After his release he was placed under city arrest, which lasted for five years. In the spring of 1989 came another spell of administrative detention. Though he was not a formal member of Fatah, he was widely considered to be close to it, and its leader, Arafat. A highly intelligent and likeable man, soft-spoken, moderate in behaviour and pragmatic in his views, he emerged as an ideal bridge between Baker and Arafat. At the Madrid conference, even though Dr Haidar Abdul Shafi was the head of the Palestinian section of the Jordanian-Palestinian delegation, the insiders knew that it was Husseini who was the real leader of the Palestinians.

The Palestinian case was brilliantly presented in English to the international media by Hanan Ashrawi, the official spokesperson for the PLO's steering committee. An eloquent woman with soft features, short black hair, piercing eyes and discreet make-up, self-assured and lucid – at ease with the English language and explaining the complexities of the situation with an occasional shaft of wry humour – she was a dramatic contrast to Arafat, with his stubbled face surrounded by the *kiffayeh* which fell to his shoulders, his halting English, and his tendency to speak in slogans and catchphrases in television interviews. In the minds of television viewers, worldwide, nothing encapsulated the transition of the PLO from armed resistance to respectability better than the supplanting of Arafat with Ashrawi. The insatiable demand of the US media for Ashrawi showed that at last the Palestinian cause was getting a fair hearing before the American public, whose opinion mattered a great deal in the formulation of US domestic and foreign policies. She had honed her persuasive skills by participating in the periodic briefings that a group of her colleagues at Birzeit University began giving to foreign journalists at her home in Ramallah after their university had been closed down by Israel in early 1988 due to the intifada (and remained shut until early 1992). Born Hanan Mikhail in 1946 into a well-to-do Christian doctor's family in Nablus, she was at the American University of Beirut studying English literature in 1967, when the West Bank was occupied by Israel. She pursued her post-graduate studies at the University of Virginia in the United States, where she took an active interest in Palestinian politics, associating herself with Fatah. On being allowed back into the West Bank in 1973, she began teaching at Birzeit University near Ramallah. She married Emile Ashrawi, a photographer and a former rock musician, and a resident of East Jerusalem.

Having thus infiltrated the Middle East Peace Conference through the back door with the assistance of Ashrawi and Husseini, Arafat concentrated on expanding his area of manoeuvre. This, he concluded, could best be done by undermining Likud Premier Shamir's repeated claims that he was not dealing with the terrorist PLO; and by establishing contacts with opposition Labour leadership with a view to improving its chances of success at the parliamentary poll to be held in 1992.

As for Shamir, having conceded separate talks between the Israeli delegation and the Palestinian section of the joint Jordanian-Palestinian delegation, he pursued his (as yet) unpublicized strategy – summarized by him after his defeat in the June 1992 poll – of dragging out the talks with the Arabs for the next 10 years while ensuring that the Jewish settlement of Judea and Samaria went ahead at full speed.[33] As a result the Israeli delegates consistently limited their negotiations with the Palestinians about the structure and legislative powers of the Palestinian Authority during the interim period, and refused to discuss the weighty subject of transition from the interim accord to the final agreement or the application of the principle of land for peace embodied by the United Nations Security Council Resolution 242.

During this stalemate the one dramatic news that flashed across the world concerned the crash on 8 April 1992 of Arafat's private airplane – a Soviet An-26, in the Sahara desert near the Sudanese-Libyan border – caused by a severe sandstorm during the aircraft's flight from Khartoum to Tunis. The fate of the PLO chief remained unknown for several hours. But the old survivor emerged alive from the crash while the pilot and co-pilot perished. To the joy of his supporters and acolytes, the incident reconfirmed not only his personal indestructibility but also that of the Palestinian people and their nationalist aspirations.

However, Arafat had not emerged unharmed by the accident as he thought at first. He realized later that he needed brain surgery for a blood clot. He underwent an emergency operation at the Hussein Medical Centre, Amman, on 1 June. At the end of a long convalescence, on 19 June, he invited Haidar Abdul Shafi, Faisal Husseini and Hanan Ashrawi to Amman for a much publicized meeting. In the presence of journalists and television cameras the three Palestinian representatives congratulated Arafat on his speedy recovery. The objective of the stage-managed exercise was to give a lie to the repeated assertions by Shamir that his delegation was dealing with the representatives of the West Bank and Gaza who had no direct ties with Arafat's terrorist PLO. When Shamir's rival, Yitzhak Rabin, declared his intention to negotiate with the West Bank and Gaza Palestinians, irrespective of who they in turn consulted, he was charged with having devised a secret plan to deal with the terrorist PLO if he won power. In return, the Labour Party's communiqué baldly stated: 'Despite the Likud declarations and despite the fact that it is sticking its head in the sand, this government has ongoing direct negotiations with the PLO.' With Shafi, Husseini and Ashrawi hugging and kissing Arafat in public on their television screens, Israeli electors knew who to believe. The overall result was a Labour victory on 23 June.

The memoirs of Mahmoud Abbas (Abu Mazen), the second most important official of the PLO, entitled *The Road to Oslo*, published in September 1994 and excerpted in the *HaAratez*, provided details of the clandestine contacts between the two leading Israeli political parties and the then outlawed PLO. In his chapter 'Indirect Contacts with the Labour Party', he stated that Labour leaders, including Yitzhak Rabin and Ephraim Sneh (later to become health minister), discussed what strategy the PLO should pursue in its (indirect) negotiations with the Likud-led Government of Shamir. They advised the PLO to slow down progress in the peace talks, and also to strive to mobilize the Israeli Arab voters for Labour and leftist groups. Mahmoud Abbas also said that PLO officials and Likud politicians met in Europe in December 1991, but nothing came of this as the two sides were too far apart.[34] In an article he published in February 1993 in the *Hadashot* (Hebrew, News), Yehoshua Meiri, a staff reporter, described how while having coffee at the Hilton Ramses Hotel in Cairo on 19 January 1992 he had seen Yossi Beilin, a close aide of Shimon Peres, pass him and enter a nearby room, guarded by an Egyptian security guard, followed several minutes later by Nabil Shaath, a long-time aide of Arafat. The outcome of that Beilin-Shaath encounter was summarized to Meiri by a PLO official thus: 'Beilin promised that if Labour won the election, it would stop [Jewish] settlements, lift the ban on meetings with the PLO, and agree to [Palestinian] autonomy on the basis of the UN Security Council Resolutions 242 and 338.' When, following the formation of a Labour-led government in July 1992, Premier Rabin dragged his feet on lifting the ban on contacts with the PLO, a PLO official leaked a story about a clandestine meeting between the PLO leadership and a 'senior Labour Party personality' in late October.[35] But the ploy did not work. It was only after Arafat had conducted fruitful talks in Tunis in the last week of December with the long exiled leaders of Hamas in the wake of Rabin's expulsion of over 400 Islamists to southern Lebanon, and set up a joint

PLO-Hamas committee on the deportations, that the Israeli premier acted.

Ironically, the single most important thing that unbanning the PLO legitimized immediately was the clandestine dialogue between the hitherto terrorist organization and the Israeli Government.

Secret Diplomacy and the Handshake of Reconciliation

Once the Knesset had legalized the PLO on 19 January 1993, the unofficial, clandestine talks between Professors Yair Hirschfield and Ron Pundak and Ahmad Qrei (Abu Alaa), arranged earlier by Norwegian mediators Terje Rod Larsen and Mona Juul in Norway, became official. Arafat had chosen Qrei for this delicate operation for two reasons. As the only PLO official who besides Arafat knew almost all about the finances of Fatah and the PLO, he had proved beyond any shadow of doubt that he could keep a secret. Secondly, Qrei was the author of a policy discussion document in which he reasoned that economic integration of the West Bank and Gaza and Israel underpin any peace settlement between Palestinians and Israelis. This paper, presented by Larsen to Yossi Beilin – now Deputy Foreign Minister under Shimon Peres – met with the approval of the latter, who dispatched an academic friend, Hirschfield, to London in December 1992 to meet Qrei for exploratory talks. On his side Qrei worked under the supervision of Mahmoud Abbas, who reported directly to Arafat.

Against the background of a worsening crisis in the Gaza Strip, and lack of progress in talks being conducted under the Madrid conference formula, Peres added his ministry's director-general, Uri Savir, to the Israeli team on 20 May. Then came the addition at the next meeting on 11 June of Joel Singer, the legal adviser to Israel's Foreign Ministry. Singer was experienced and a hardliner. He had participated in the talks that had culminated in the 1978 Camp David Accords. As the legal adviser to the defence ministry under Rabin for five years he had the confidence of Rabin, and shared his obsession with Israeli security. Singer and Savir bargained hard, and had their way on most of the contentious issues.

On the length of an interim agreement they stuck firmly to the time frame of five years, a period first specified by Begin in 1978. The PLO had publicly insisted on one year, with the expectation of compromising on three years. Now its secret negotiators gave in fully to the Israeli demand. Having conceded that the highly disputatious subjects of the right to return of the Palestinian refugees, the final borders of Israel and the Palestinian territories, and the status of Jerusalem be postponed to the final phase, the PLO representatives yielded completely on the running sore of the Jewish settlements. When their Israeli interlocutors reminded them that it was only after their Government had stated in August 1992 that there would be no more 'public funding' for the Jewish settlements that Washington had reversed its previous stance and agreed to provide a guarantee for the $10 billion credit that Israel wanted to raise abroad, their Palestinian counterparts seemed satisfied. The result was the absence of any mention of the Jewish settlements in the draft accord. The Palestinians' failure to see the loopholes that the Israeli declaration implied, especially concerning the term 'public funding', which became depressingly clear to them after the Oslo Accord had been implemented, illustrated dramatically how poorly they had bargained. In return for such vital concessions, all Qrei got was Israel's recognition of the PLO as 'the representative' (not 'the sole representative' as Arafat wanted) of the Palestinian people. Once this was conceded in late July by Rabin, who had the last word, the deal was virtually done.

The final draft, the result of 14 clandestine meetings, entitled 'Declaration of Principles on Interim Self-Government Arrangements', was initialled secretly in Oslo on 19 August by Peres and Qrei, followed by a public announcement to this effect 11 days later. Then came an exchange of letters on 9–10 September between Arafat and Rabin – with Arafat recognizing 'the right of the State of Israel to exist in peace and security' and accepting 'the United Nations Security Council Resolutions

242 and 338', and Rabin stating that 'the Government of
Israel has decided to recognize the PLO as the representative
of the Palestinian people and commence negotiations with
the PLO within the Middle East peace process'.

The signing of the document by Peres and Mahmoud
Abbas, the second seniormost official of the PLO, on the
sunlit lawns of the White House on 13 September came
after a dramatic intervention by Arafat only hours before
the ceremony. He proposed that since Rabin in his letter of
10 September had recognized the PLO as the representative
of the Palestinian people this fact should be reflected in
the Declaration of Principles (DOP). Accordingly, Arafat
insisted that the first sentence of the document reading 'The
Government of the State of Israel and the Palestinian team
(in the Jordanian-Palestinian delegation to the Middle East
Peace Conference) (the 'Palestinian Delegation'), representing
the Palestinian people, agree that . . .' be modified to read:
'The Government of the State of Israel and the PLO team (in
the Jordanian-Palestinian delegation to the Middle East Peace
Conference) (the 'Palestinian Delegation'), representing the
Palestinian people, agree that . . .'. Rabin was hesitant, but
Peres persuaded him to comply with Arafat's suggestion.

The dramatic difference in the treatment afforded to Arafat
by the United States – the unfolding of a red carpet in contrast
to the denial of a single day visa to address the United Nations
General Assembly in December 1988 – neatly encapsulated
the metamorphic change that the PLO chief had undergone,
from a guerrilla leader to a world statesman. Yet he retained
his military fatigues and his chequed *kiffayeh* when he
appeared at the signing ceremony at the White House; and he
delivered his speech in Arabic (whereas Rabin addressed the
gathering in English). His offering of the hand of friendship to
Rabin, dressed in a business suit, to solemnize the Declaration
of Principles just signed by their designated deputies, and the
latter's grasping of the hand after some hesitation, thrilled not
only the over 3,000 American and other dignitaries who had
assembled on the White House lawn but also the hundreds
of millions of people worldwide who watched the event on
television. Despite all the aura of spontaneity, which assured

the Handshake a place in the list of the Historic Moments of a Generation, the exercise had been pre-arranged by President Bill Clinton, who had escorted the two leaders from the White House reception hall to the table where the accord was to be signed.[36]

Each side had its own reasons to clinch the deal. The Labour Government realized that if it did not negotiate with the PLO it would be forced to talk to Hamas and the Islamic Jihad. 'The rising strength of the Iranian-backed [Islamic] fundamentalist movement in the territories administered by Israel, and in the Middle East as a whole, influenced the Israeli leaders to explore the possibilities of a deal with the PLO,' wrote Chaim Herzog, President of Israel from May 1983 to April 1993. 'It became clear that apart from Mr Arafat, there was no other valid interlocutor and that without him, the peace talks might collapse.'[37]

At home, Rabin was more down to earth. 'I prefer the Palestinians to cope with the problem of enforcing order in the Gaza Strip,' he told the mass circulation *Yediot Aharonot* on 7 September. 'The Palestinians will be better at it than we were because they will allow no appeals to the Supreme Court and will prevent the Israeli Association of Civil Rights from criticizing the conditions there by denying it access to the area. They will rule by their own methods, freeing – and this is most important – the Israeli army soldiers from having to do what they will do.'

Moreover, Israel realized that it would get a better deal from the ageing leadership of the PLO, which after spending nearly two generations in exile felt weary, rather than from the much younger and more dynamic leadership, secular or religious, based in the West Bank and Gaza. Having grown up under Israeli occupation, and grasped not only Hebrew but also the fault line of the Jewish Israeli society and politics, these Palestinian leaders knew how to put them to advantageous use.

However, for now, the Israelis had several advantages over the Palestinians which they had exploited fully. Firstly, their Government had chosen the mode of serious bargaining – clandestine talks – and manoeuvred the top Palestinian leadership into it. Historically, both Israel and the Zionists in Palestine had preferred secret diplomacy to public negotiations. They had struck a clandestine deal with King Abdullah of Jordan before the 1948 Arab-Israeli War. Later Israel circumvented the armistice talks in progress in the Greek island of Rhodes to strike a secret deal with Abdullah. In 1991, by succeeding in making its Arab adversaries agree to bilateral talks outside the umbrella of the UN, Israel gained in two major ways. It could play individual Arab parties against one another. Secondly, and more importantly, since in the final analysis the contents of an agreement reflect the balance of power – military, economic, diplomatic – between the bargaining parties, Israel, unmatched individually by any of the Arab parties, stood to benefit. By thus setting the basic framework of negotiations, Israel once again paved the way for the usage of 'back channels'.

Along with this overall diplomatic strategy went its operational tactics, which focused on intelligence-gathering. In its dealings with the Palestinians, whether in the Occupied Territories or Diaspora, Israel had all along laid great stress on recruiting agents and spies. Its success in this field could be judged by the accuracy with which its bombers flattened the PLO headquarters in October 1985, and the chilling efficiency with which its operators carried out the assassination of Khalil Wazir in April 1988. But the Israeli intelligence apparatus, whether Shin Beth or Mossad, constantly strived higher. In 1990 Mossad had a great success. It recruited Adnan Yasin during one of his trips to Paris for the medical treatment of his wife, suffering from cancer. Its research had shown that 44-year-old Yasin, fond of drink, was a high spender, and the treatment for his ailing wife was eating rapidly into his modest savings. He was deputy to Abdul Hakkam Balawi, who was both the PLO's ambassador to Tunisia and the head of the PLO's internal security. Since Balawi and Yasin had been posted in Tunis before the PLO's expulsion from Beirut in September 1982, they played a leading role in smoothing the way of the PLO into Tunisia. In the process they acquired open access, day or night, to the top leadership of the PLO as well as their administrative offices. Obviously, by recruiting someone like Yasin, who had taken to travelling frequently to a European capital, Mossad stood to reap a rich harvest of top level information. Its officials approached Yasin posing as businessmen from a West European country, so as not to scare him – a 'false flag' operation. They paid Yasin handsomely, and declared their true identity only after they had compromised him to such an extent that he could not quit. They now made bigger demands on him, providing him with sophisticated radio transmitters, invisible ink and a secret codebook. Finally they made Yasin place bugging devices in the offices of the top officials of the PLO, including Mahmoud Abbas and Ahmad Qrei, both of them involved in the ultra-secret talks with the Israelis, and possibly Yasser Arafat. The signals from Yasin's transmitters were picked up by the receivers at the Mossad stations in the Israeli embassies in Paris and Rome. From there the information passed to the Mossad headquarters in Tel Aviv.[38] Thus Mossad came to know instantly the intimate goings-on at the PLO headquarters in Tunis. Such a damaging breach of security went undetected until November 1993, three months after the crucial Declaration of Principles for the interim self-rule for Palestinians had been settled. In other words, the Israelis had struck the most important accord with the PLO armed with a most powerful tool: the highly secret details of the strategy and tactics of Arafat and Abbas.

Among the important factors that drove the PLO to reach an agreement with Israel was its poor financial state and a crisis of confidence in the top leadership. In mid-July 1993, after the tenth round of talks with the Israelis had proved as sterile as the preceding nine, Haidar Abdul Shafi, head of the Palestinian delegation, publicly called for a radical reform of the Palestinian hierarchy and decision-making. Three weeks later, disgruntled at the way the negotiations with the Israelis were being directed by Arafat, Husseini and Ashrawi, accepted by Israel as members of the main Palestinian delegation since April, arrived in Tunis with their resignations in hand. Arafat pacified them by promising an emergency meeting of the executive committee to discuss his leadership and the PLO's acute financial straits.

By now the PLO's cash crisis had deepened to the point that the employees of the educational institutions, clinics, hospitals and newspapers maintained by it (through such organizations as the Palestine Red Crescent) had gone unpaid for up to six months. The PLO's welfare fund for the families that had suffered variously under the Israeli occupation, operating under Intissar Wazir based in Amman, had shrunk from $8 million a year to $2 million. On top of this came an Israeli move which hurt the fragile Palestinian economy badly. In March 1993 Premier Rabin ordered the closure of the pre-1967 Israel from the Occupied Territories, thus depriving tens of thousands of Palestinians, dependent on work in Israel, of their livelihood.

The aggregation of these factors produced an environment in which criticism of Arafat came to the fore to an unprecedented extent. His detractors now openly accused him of paranoia, autocratic behaviour, egotism, sheer love of power, refusal to delegate authority, and rewarding personal loyalty rather than competence. On policy issues they were critical of his chronic overreaction, swinging from one extreme to the other: to the right after his two expulsions from Lebanon, flirting with King Hussein and President Mubarak; and then to the left, warmly embracing President Saddam Hussein. They also condemned the corruption that had set in at the upper echelons of the PLO, although they never accused him of being personally corrupt. They could not. Arafat continued to live frugally, as he had always done, neither drinking nor smoking, happy to be sharing meals with his bodyguards. His admirers highlighted Arafat's capacity to inspire devotion, his manic dedication to the cause, indefatigability, and exemplary personal courage in mortal danger or emergency. Most significantly, they pointed out that against heavy odds, Arafat had held together the PLO, and that he had successfully frustrated attempts at different times by the leading Arab powers – Egypt, Syria and Iraq – to co-opt the PLO, and maintained the PLO's independence. By any standards, they argued, these were outstanding achievements.

The debate on Arafat's leadership had hardly got going when the news of the secret deal between Israel and the PLO broke. The initial popular reaction to the DOP, formally signed in mid-September, was positive. Those who marched with Palestinian flags aloft in the streets of the Occupied Territories felt that liberation was near. But once they studied the document carefully they realized, depressingly, that all it contained was a road map to peace and a mere possibility of liberation, if that, nothing more. Modelled on the September 1978 Camp David Accords, it offered only limited autonomy, in two instalments, the first one covering the Gaza Strip and a small West Bank town (Jericho), and the second the rest of the West Bank minus Greater East Jerusalem. The interim agreement was to last five years after the modalities of the operation of the first stage had been implemented.

Of the 18 PLO executive members (including Arafat), seven either resigned in protest at the DOP or refused to attend the meeting called to discuss it. Of those present only eight voted for it, with the opposing group including Farouq Qaddumi, a Fatah stalwart and the PLO's Foreign Minister who, as the counterpart to Peres, should in normal circumstances have signed the DOP in Washington. And of the 10 groups affiliated to the PLO, only Fatah, the Democratic Palestinian Union (leader Yasser Abd Rabbo), the Palestine People's Party (leader Suleiman Najab) and the Palestine Struggle Front (leader Samir Ghoshe) accepted the accord. Prominent among those who opposed it was George Habash of the Popular Front for the Liberation of Palestine. He referred to his meeting of minds with Arafat before the 1991 Madrid conference. 'Our friendship was based on the condition that we work according to our PLO National Charter program: (a) the right to return [for Palestinian refugees], (b) self-determination for the Palestinians, and (c) the right to an independent state,' he said on 8 October 1993. 'The Oslo agreement makes no rules on these subjects. On the contrary, it does not include an Israeli withdrawal and the Jewish settlements will remain where they are.'[39] The most telling criticism of the DOP was that there was no mention in it of Israel as the occupying power, which meant that the (indisputably) Occupied Territories had in effect been turned into the Disputed Territories.

Condemning the DOP on these grounds, Hamas rejected the Oslo Accord.

At the PLO central council meeting on 12 November, among those who had second thoughts on the DOP was none other than Mahmoud Abbas who had signed the document in Washington amidst much fanfare. 'This agreement carries in its bowels either an independent state or the consecration of the [Israeli] occupation,' he warned. 'It all depends on our mentality as we deal with it, on our instruments and on our preparations.'[40]

Part of the reason for the unease of Abbas, who played a role comparable to Peres on the Israeli side, and who had a follow-up meeting with him in the Egyptian resort of Taba, on 13 October – the first high level official encounter between the two sides since the legalization of the PLO – was the discovery of Adnan Yasin as an Israeli mole.

Abbas's suspicion was aroused when he realized how knowledgeable Peres was about the Palestinian tactics he had discussed only once in a secret session with Arafat. On his return to Tunis, Abbas contacted Arafat, who recalled how Dennis Ross, the visiting US State Department official dealing with the Middle East peace process, had insisted on meeting him not in the PLO office but at his hotel in Tunis. Arafat ordered a sweep of all PLO premises while the internal security chief, Balawi, conferred with his Tunisian counterpart. The discovery of bugging devices in the offices of Abbas and Qrei confirmed the worst fears of the leaders. But they had no clue who the culprit could be.

Their break came from the Tunisian intelligence. Tipped off by their counterparts in Paris, where the signals being sent by Yasin were being received (and apparently monitored by the French intelligence), the Tunisians intensified their investigation. The radio transmissions emanating from Yasin's house led them to their quarry, on 2 November. They handed him over to the PLO and its justice department. The embarrassed Arafat confiscated the passports of all PLO employees to ensure that none of them fled. He also imposed a news blackout on the investigation of the two alleged moles, the other one being Muhammad Faisal, a radio operator at the PLO's telecommunication centre, who was arrested by Balawi, the PLO's internal security chief.

A doctored report of the PLO's investigative committee, headed by Balawi and including Amin al Hindi (a top intelligence official), Abdullah al Ifranji (former PLO ambassador to Bonn) and Majid al Agha, published later, was an exercise in damage limitation. Its conclusion was that the desk, chair and lamp in Abbas's office that were discovered to be bugged had been placed there only on 10 October after these pieces of furniture, supplied by a 'French businessman', had been picked up in Marseilles by Adnan Yasin's son, Hani (who was found not to be implicated).[41]

It is most likely that, urged by their political boss, Premier Rabin, engaged in the most delicate and important clandestine talks with the PLO leader from January 1993 onwards, Mossad officials had pressed Yasin hard to plant bugging devices and use other means to let them into the counsels of the five PLO leaders who masterminded the negotiations in Tunis: Arafat, Abbas, Qrei, Yasser Abd Rabbo and Hassan Asfour (of the Palestine People's Party).

Little wonder that Asfour's party and Rabbo's Democratic Palestinian Union were vocal in their support for the Oslo Accord. So were Fatah and the Palestine Struggle Front. An opinion survey of Palestinians showed that roughly half of those polled, professing loyalty to one of these groups, accepted the Oslo Accord, while about a quarter, backing either Hamas or secular radical groups, rejected it, with the rest undecided.

On the Israeli side, the same ratio of 2:1 prevailed in favour of the Oslo Accord, with 63–6 per cent for, and up to 30 per cent against. In the Knesset, the accord won a comfortable majority, with three defecting Likud MKs (out of 32) voting for it. Opposing the agreement, Likud leader, Binyamin Netanyahu, spelled out five principles on which peace should be based: preventing the creation of a Palestinian state; preserving the unity of Jerusalem; maintaining the IDF's responsibility for security in the Palestinian territories; offering guarantees for the Jewish settlements in the territories; and a ban on the return of Palestinian refugees.

He volunteered to form a national unity government with
Labour to advance peace 'in the way the majority of Israelis
would like to see it go', but Prime Minister Rabin rejected
his offer.[42]

A majority of Israelis backed the Oslo Accord primarily
because it promised an end to the bloody strife they associated with the Palestinian intifada. Almost half of Palestinians
supported the agreement because they felt that it would result
in the Israeli military relaxing its grip over the Occupied
Territories, and among other things ease draconian travel
restrictions on them.

In the immediate aftermath of the Accord, both sides were
disappointed. There was no change in the behaviour of the
Israeli soldiers on patrol and at roadblocks. They continued
their hardline policy. The end result was 20 Palestinians
dead in the first two months of the Accord. Equally, a rising
number of Israelis became sceptical about Arafat's call to his
followers to abjure violence. Their doubts were confirmed
when on 13 November the Israeli Government announced
that the five Palestinians suspected of killing a Jewish settler,
Chaim Mizrahi of Beit El, belonged to the Fatah movement.
They were unimpressed by the sight of Arafat sharing that
year's Nobel Peace Prize in December with Rabin and Peres
in Oslo.

The situation changed when Baruch Goldstein massacred
the Palestinians at prayer in the Ibrahimi Mosque/Tomb of
the Patriarchs in late February 1994. The PLO suspended
its talks with the Israelis and demanded an armed UN
presence to protect Palestinian civilians in the Occupied
Territories from the Jewish settlers and Israeli soldiers.
But due to the strong opposition of Israel and the United
States, it did not get very far. America's foot-dragging at
the United Nations Security Council meant that it was not
until 18 March that the Security Council passed Resolution
904 which condemned the Hebron massacre and called for
measures to guarantee the safety of civilians in the Occupied
Territories, including Temporary International Presence in
Hebron (TIPH) as part of the Israeli-PLO peace process (not
as part of the UN operations). The Resolution called on Israel

and the PLO to implement the resolution, thus pressuring the PLO to return to the negotiating table. It did, on 30 March. As a result, Mustafa Abdul Nabi Natsche, who had been dismissed as mayor by the IDF in 1983 for 'incitement' against Israel, was reinstated in the Town Hall. On taking office, he declared that 'the precedent of allowing foreign observers to be stationed in the Occupied Territories signalled a qualitative change in long held Israeli policies and practices *vis-à-vis* the Palestinians.'[43] This proved to be a highly unrealistic view. It was not until 8 May that a contingent of 135 lightly armed men from Denmark, Italy and Norway – forming the Temporary International Presence in Hebron (TIPH) – arrived in the city on a renewable three-month mandate to 'provide adequate protection' to the local Palestinians. The IDF billeted them in a northern suburb of Hebron, far away from the tense city centre. During their stay there were clashes between the Palestinians and the Jewish settlers, but the TIPH was unable to intervene. The IDF would declare the disturbed neighbourhood 'a closed military zone' and bar the entry of the TIPH. And when the IDF imposed a curfew it applied not only to the Palestinians but also to the TIPH. As a result the TIPH aroused more sympathy among Palestinians than respect, especially when it failed to get the Ibrahimi Mosque reopened by the time it left on 8 August.

However, by then the Declaration of Principles had been transformed, slowly and meticulously, into a working document, and signed by both parties in Cairo on 4 May 1994. Among other things it gave rise to the Palestinian Authority – *Al Sulteh al Falastiniya* in Arabic, and *HaFalastinit HaRashut* in Hebrew – an executive and legislative body.

12

THE PALESTINIAN AUTHORITY:

An Embryo

'Mansion House.' Abdul Hakim al Samra said the words in passing as he drove slowly by an impressive complex in Qasr al Hakim Street a few blocks from the beach in Gaza city one cloudy morning in March 1995. The name sounded familiar to me, a Londoner. The Mansion House underground station named after the official residence of the mayor of the City of London, the financial heart of the metropolis. Built in 1752, it has a long history. The same could not be said of the Mansion House in Gaza city. It was constructed by the British during their mandate in Palestine to accommodate the office and residence of the regional administrator of Gaza. In the red-tiled slanting roofs of the sprawling, multi-storey structure – decked in more recent times with a slim transmission tower – I saw an unmistakable stamp of the British. The Mansion House, now in its eighth decade, had witnessed a succession of powers come and go: the British followed by the Egyptians, then briefly (in 1956–7) the Israelis, reverting back to the Egyptians, and then again the Israelis. 'It was the residence of the IDF governor,' said

Abdul Hakim. 'During the intifada he set up the Ansar I [detention] camp in tents here, in the compound, when the central jail got too full. Now the Palestinian military uses it as a training camp.' I looked out of the car, and saw smartly dressed Palestinian recruits lined up for a drill.

'I was here on 18th May last year,' intoned Abdul Hakim. What for? 'The last day of the IDF in the Gaza Strip.' Not all of the Strip? 'No, of course not,' he said wearily. 'The Mansion House was the last facility the IDF vacated according to the Cairo Agreement [of 4 May]. A historic moment, as they say.' He smiled his rare smile. 'Worth witnessing. It was like the hot days of the intifada. The Israelis were scared shit that they would be buried in stones. So they tossed tear-gas canisters in the air as they fled, chased by us. But there was one difference, one big difference.' Like what? 'Among their chasers were Palestinian policemen in uniform, with machine-guns. In fact they were running ahead of us all. Quite a sight, I tell you. And the moment they entered the Mansion House they went wild, firing their machine-guns in the air. We had never heard such a racket before, and never will.' Sounds like the Chinese setting off their firecrackers to chase away the devilish dragons, I remarked. 'Something like that.' His face was wreathed in smiles as he relived the boisterous event of May 1994.

For a few weeks, these policemen, some 3,000 of them, operated in a judicial vacuum. It was not until 21 May that Arafat – working from his Tunis office notable for the vast picture of the Dome of Rock on the wall behind his chair – instructed civil and religious courts in the Gaza Strip and Jericho to begin operating according to the laws valid before the 1967 conquest by Israel. These included the laws that had been operational during the days of the Ottomans, the British, the Egyptians and the Jordanians (in the case of Jericho). The Israeli Foreign Ministry was swift to call Arafat's move 'meaningless and invalid', stating that all military laws and orders issued by the IDF since June – more than 2,000 – remained in force and were binding on 'all of the parties'. Its legal adviser, Joel Singer, who had participated in the clandestine talks culminating in the Oslo

Accord, said: 'Neither Arafat nor the Palestinian Authority is able unilaterally to abrogate Israeli military obligations.' He was right. For Clause 9 of Article VII of the Cairo Agreement stated: 'Laws and military orders in effect in the Gaza Strip or the Jericho Area prior to the signing of this Agreement shall remain in force, unless amended or abrogated in accordance with this Agreement.' More ominously for Palestinians, Major-General Matan Vilnai, commander of the IDF's southern command, added that if the peace process did not work Israel would consider all its options. 'In the extreme sense that means Israel returning to Gaza.'[1] There was no mincing of words on the part of Israel, which knew exactly what sort of accords it had signed in Oslo and Cairo, and what powers it had agreed to vest in the Palestinian Authority.

By mid-June, Arafat had appointed 20 members of the Palestinian Authority executive that he headed, providing a judicious mix of insiders (West Bankers and Gazans) and outsiders – the former including Faisal Husseini, Mustafa Natsche, Munib Masri and Zakaria al Agha; and the latter, Ahmad Qrei, Intissar Wazir, Nabil Shaath and Nasser Yusuf. Yet he showed no sign of moving to the self-rule Palestinian territories. Involved in raising foreign grants to fund the Palestinian Authority, expected to run up a substantial deficit, on his terms, he tried to pressure the donors by postponing his departure from Tunis. There was an equal measure of uncertainty on whether he would set up the PA headquarters in Jericho (because it was situated in the larger Palestinian territory of the West Bank) or Gaza city (because the Gaza Strip contained 98 per cent of the Palestinians being granted limited self-rule).

It was to be Gaza city. On 1 July, Arafat approached the capital of the Gaza Strip from the bakingly hot Sinai at 3.15 p.m. to a reception which was, by all accounts, subdued. True to his form, Arafat was late arriving, a ploy he had developed over the years chiefly to wrongfoot his would-be assassins. A welcoming assembly of over 1,000 local dignitaries, which had been waiting since morning in the fiercely hot sun in the desert, got no more than a quick wave of arms by the

PLO Chairman, affectionately called Abu Ammar. Among those present for the occasion was Harb Abu Namous – a grandfatherly figure sporting a white goatee beard, a traditional black cloak and white head dress kept in place by two rounds of black rope – of the extended Abu Namous family in Gaza city. He was downbeat about his experience on that afternoon. 'To be frank I should have listened to my family, stayed home and watch Abu Ammar on television,' he said. 'Once Abu Ammar had marched past the [Palestinian] soldiers' guard of honour, he was immediately surrounded by a sea of bodyguards, like whirling sand in a sandstorm. All we could see from a long way off was a black-and-white chequered *kiffayeh* bobbing up and down in the midst of soldiers. I had the vision of hugging and kissing the President of Palestine on our soil, welcoming him properly.' Harb heaved a deep sigh. 'It was a dream, a silly dream.' His several grandchildren, listening in, nodded in sympathy mixed with amusement. 'Then the bodyguards just bundled Abu Ammar into an open-top limousine, and he was off to the highway to Khan Yunis, his family town.' Did Harb then retire to his television set? 'Yes. What else?'

The recently established Palestine Broadcasting Authority meticulously recorded the activities of Arafat for the next few days in the Gaza Strip and Jericho. He made the right moves to present himself as the national leader, above party politics. At a public rally in Gaza city, attended by 70,000, near the Mansion House, he embraced Dr Haidar Abdul Shafi, aged 75, the grand old politician of Gaza, with a long history of unswerving commitment to the Palestinian cause, albeit outside the aegis of the PLO. Addressing Shaikh Ahmad Yasin, the imprisoned leader of Hamas, Arafat said: 'You are the shaikh of us all. We will not rest until you are here by our side.' This was received with thunderous applause by the crowd. At the press conference in the evening at the beachside Palestine Hotel, his temporary abode, he was more reflective. 'The most important challenge for us is to build the new Palestinian Authority which will lead to an independent Palestinian state, our democratic state, a state for free persons, a state for democracy, equality and non-discrimination,' he declared. 'The road from Gaza leads through Bethlehem and Nablus to Jerusalem.' But it was only on the following day that, in the dilapidated environment of the Jabaliya camp, the birthplace of the intifada, Arafat publicly addressed the pros and cons of the Oslo Accord, a subject of much import to ordinary Palestinians. 'Many of you think the Oslo [Accord] is a bad agreement,' he said. 'It is a bad agreement, but it is the best deal we could get in the worst situation.'[2]

In the coming weeks and months these statements would come to haunt Arafat.

The first and foremost concern of Arafat as well as Premier Yitzhak Rabin was security. It was significant that soon after naming the last member of the Palestinian Authority executive, commonly called cabinet, Arafat, both the President of the PA and its Interior Minister, appointed a Higher Security Council.

Rabin and Arafat were concerned that in the period following the conclusion of the Oslo Accord, its popularity among Israelis had declined steadily. Among Palestinians, it was bitterly opposed by Islamists and by radical secular groups. This state of affairs was well mirrored in the death tolls on the opposite sides of the ethnic divide. In the eight months since the White House signing ceremony, 150 Palestinians had been killed by the IDF or its undercover agents, and 45 Jews by Palestinians.

Both the Israeli Government and the Palestinian Authority were anxious to see that there was no security vacuum due to the hand-over of power from the former to the latter. Israel decided to turn a blind eye if the PA exceeded the limit of 9,000 policemen specified by the Cairo Agreement – later to be known popularly as Oslo I – or set up organizations not authorized by the Agreement. According to Annexe I, Article 3 of the Cairo Agreement, the PA was allowed one security force with four operational divisions: civil policing; public order maintenance; emergency services, such as civil defence; and internal/domestic intelligence service, popularly called mukhabarat (Arabic, information-gathering organization).

But so intent was Rabin on safeguarding Israeli security by

co-opting the emerging Palestinian Authority to decimate the Palestinian Islamist forces, that he authorized a clandestine meeting of the chief of Shin Beth, Yaacov Perry (who retired in 1995), and the IDF's deputy chief of staff, General Amnon Shahak (later to become the chief of staff) with Colonel Jibril Rajoub, a top official in the PLO's military department, and Muhammad Dahlan, a leading official in the Occupied Homeland directorate, in Rome five months before the Cairo Agreement. Arafat later named Dahlan and Rajoub as the heads of the Preventive Security Service (PSS), an agency with an essentially political mandate, in the Gaza Strip and Jericho respectively, to work directly under him. In Rome these officials cut a deal with their interlocutors. The PSS would pass on to Israel intelligence on the Palestinian groups opposed to the Oslo Accord, particularly Hamas and the Islamic Jihad, and Israel would give a *carte blanche* to the PSS even in the Palestinian areas outside of the Cairo Agreement to curb any opposition to the Israeli-PLO Accord.[3] How the PSS was to operate was revealed by Ehud Ya'ari, a senior Israeli columnist. 'Fatah-armed bands whose members were wanted [until recently] by the Israeli security services, like the Hawks, will have special tasks,' he stated in the *Jerusalem Report* of 13 January 1994. 'They will be charged with putting down any sign of opposition [to the Oslo Accord]; the intent is for them to administer show punishments at the earliest possible stage, aimed at creating proper regard for the new regime.' Ten months later, in November, something approaching this scenario came to pass in the Gaza Strip, bringing the territory to the brink of a civil war.

By then Arafat, President/Chairman of the Palestinian Authority, had set up the following uniformed and plain-clothes security organizations in the Gaza Strip and Jericho: *Uniformed*: presidential body guard; Force 17, originally set up in March 1968 after the Battle of Karameh to protect Fatah leaders and – later – also to collect information on Israel and carry out certain operations against Israeli targets (head, Sami Abu Samhadana); and police (heads, Major-General Nasser Yusuf, Gaza, and Major-General

Ghazi Jabali, Jericho) – and *Plain clothes*: internal/domestic intelligence, mukhabarat (head, Amin al Hindi, Gaza); Preventive Security Service (heads, Muhammad Dahlan, Gaza, and Jibril Rajoub, Jericho); military intelligence (head, Brigadier Mousa Arafat); and Force 18, special task security force, dealing *inter alia* with Israeli collaborators. When asked why he required so many cloak-and-dagger organizations, Arafat replied: 'The Syrians have 14, the Egyptians have 12. I only have six to help me.'[4]

The uniformed forces, wearing either a blue or camouflage dress, were largely drawn from the Palestine Liberation Army – the PLO's professional armed service, which had been scattered in half a dozen Arab countries since 1982 – with the remainder recruited locally, consisting chiefly of former members of Fatah Hawks or the shabiba (Arabic, youths). In both cases what counted most was faithfulness to Fatah and its leader Arafat. The PLA personnel were retrained for civil police duty in Egypt or Jordan. But, judging by their later actions, it was doubtful if they really learned to give priority to the rule of law over their unquestioning loyalty to Arafat. When the PLA units arrived at the frontier crossing at Rafah (from Egypt) or the Allenby Bridge (from Jordan), they registered their names and serial numbers with the IDF. As expected, these soldiers-turned-policemen moved into the camps just evacuated by the IDF, and then went on to rent additional space as their numbers soared by spring 1995 to twice the ceiling of 9,000. So, while less than a million Gazans were now policed by a force of 18,000, over seven million inhabitants of New York, a multi-ethnic city notorious for a high rate of violent crime, were policed by 38,000 cops. Even during the intifada the number of Israeli soldiers in the Gaza Strip did not exceed 12,000.

Though the uniformed men were the visible segment of security in the PA territories, an equally important, if not more important, function was performed by the plain-clothes agents of the Preventive Security Service. The word 'Preventive' could be interpreted in one of two ways: prevent actions damaging to security; or prevent expression of passive or active opposition to the peace process – that is,

surveillance, harassment or elimination of the opponents of
the Oslo and Cairo Agreements – often in conjunction with
the IDF and Shin Beth. In practice it was not a question of
enforcing either/or but both. The 4,000-strong force was
divided evenly in the Gaza Strip and the West Bank. It
consisted almost wholly of 'insiders', residents of the West
Bank or Gaza, mostly young Fatah members, who had been
active either in the party's Hawk or shabiba units, or among
political prisoners.

At 30, Muhammad Dahlan, a dapper, clean-shaven man
with a crew cut and an earnest expression, became probably
the world's youngest chief of a security organization. A
native of Gaza, he was a political activist and a natural
leader. 'I headed the shabiba movement in the Gaza Strip,
and I have struggled along with my brethren against the
[Israeli] occupation,' he told the Jerusalem-based *Al Quds*
newspaper. '[For this] I was expelled to Jordan, and arrested
[there]. I then left for Cairo where also I was arrested. I
went to Iraq where I had the opportunity to work with
Abu Jihad [Khalil Wazir], God bless his soul. I learned
a lot politically and socially from him, and from President
Arafat himself . . . [Now] I have a good relationship with
President Arafat developed through my work in Tunis where
I was responsible for the military operations in the Gaza Strip
during the intifada.'[5]

In contrast to the neat figure of Dahlan, 41-year-old Jibril
Rajoub looked roly-poly, despite his military uniform. A
balding, chubby-faced man with thin eyes and thick moustache, he operated from a large, tastefully furnished office,
its marble floor well scrubbed and its walls resplendent with
hand-woven carpets. Born in Hebron, he became embroiled
with Fatah and its armed struggle against Israel in his
mid-teens. He was arrested in 1970 and convicted to a
20-year prison sentence. In jail he set out on a course of
self-improvement, and taught himself Hebrew and English,
'the languages of the enemy'. His leadership qualities won
him the chairmanship of the Fatah prison committee. He was
freed in May 1985 in the prisoner exchange between Israel
and the Popular Front for the Liberation of Palestine-General

Command. He immediately plunged into political activity, and became the chief of Fatah, an outlawed party, in the West Bank. Within a couple of months of the start of the intifada in December 1987, the Israeli Government expelled him to southern Lebanon. From there he went to Tunis, where Arafat appointed him an assistant to Khalil Wazir. Following the latter's assasination in April 1988, Rajoub began performing several of Wazir's tasks. Soon after the PLO had signed the Oslo Accord, Arafat created the Preventive Security Service, and appointed Rajoub as one of its two heads. He arrived in Jericho in June 1994.

Besides establishing the West Bank headquarters of the PSS near the small, deserted Palestinian refugee camp of Aqabat Jabr south of Jericho – prominently signposted (in Arabic) 'The Palestinian Command for Preventive Security in the West Bank' – in an area rich in bananas, Rajoub started a PSS academy there. He planned to put 200 cadets through a two-year course, exposing them as much to the techniques of gathering and transmitting information as complexities of politics, history, religion and psychology as well as civil law, human rights, legal procedures and the gathering of evidence. At the PSS Academy he decided to accept as cadets only West Bankers because, in his words, 'they know the towns, villages and alleyways of the West Bank like the back of their hands'. He had applied the same criterion in recruiting PSS agents. 'When you are talking of the PSS, you're talking about Fatah,' he told the *Jerusalem Report*. 'And they are everywhere, in every [refugee] camp, town and village.'[6]

As it was, in the West Bank still under the IDF control, the PSS operated as a long arm of Fatah. And since the PSS was not established by Arafat as the PA chief, it functioned outside the reach of judicial scrutiny.

Equally controversially, the PSS went about strengthening the peace process through means which were at best questionable and at worst illegal. It performed this function through such positive, but unethical, means as news management. It set about disciplining the press. Those who persisted in their foolhardy views were persecuted. In March 1995 the Jerusalem offices of the PFLP weekly *Al Umma* (The

Community) were burned down after it had ignored warnings from the PSS about giving 'hostile coverage to the Palestinian Authority'. Even the Fatah loyalist *Al Quds*, owned and published by Mahmoud Abu Zuluf, felt the wrath of the PSS and Arafat when it showed any sign of independence. In August the daily was banned from the Gaza Strip and Jericho to discourage it from carrying a statement by the dissident PLO leader Farouq Qaddumi describing the Oslo Accord as 'a surrender of Palestinian rights'. But what caught the attention of the world media was the detention and interrogation at the PSS headquarters in Jericho of the *Al Quds* editor Maher Alami after Christmas. His 'crime' was that he did not splash on the front page the complimentary comparison that the Greek Orthodox Patriarch in his Christmas sermon in Bethlehem made of Arafat and Caliph Omar ibn Khattab regarding their favourable treatment of Christians, but instead published it on page 8. Alami's ordeal ended after six days only because of the interest the international press took in his fate.[7]

Since Hamas and the Islamic Jihad had rejected the peace accords, and since the IDF and Jewish settlers still controlled two-fifths of the Gaza Strip, the bitter conflict between them and Israel was still on. While the IDF and its hit squads targetted Islamist militants no matter where they were, the latter struck at the Jewish targets both inside Israel and the Palestinian territories.

The Rabin government had made a deal with the PLO in the expectation that it would join forces to squash Islamists. But there was a red line which the PA and Arafat could cross only at their peril: an open armed alliance with Israel to combat an organization like Hamas, enjoying very substantial grass roots support especially in the Gaza Strip, would escalate into a civil war and thus play into the hands of the Jewish state to the detriment of all Palestinians. As the events from mid-August to late November 1994 were to demonstrate graphically this was not an exercise in academic speculation but a real probability.

Intent on decimating radical Islamists, Israel pursued them relentlessly. On 12 August Israeli undercover agents killed two Hamas activists in East Jerusalem after a car chase. Two days later the military wing of Hamas, the Qassam Brigade, mounted two attacks near the Gush Qatif settlement in the Gaza Strip, killing one settler and injuring five. The PA police chief, Nasser Yusuf, arrested 20 Hamas activists. On 27 August the Qassam Brigade members killed two Jewish builders in the Israeli town of Ramle. This angered Rabin. 'The entire agreement with the PLO is predicated on the understanding that the PLO must combat terrorism and its perpetrators,' he said. 'If Yasser Arafat is unable to fulfil his part, why should Israel continue implementing agreements when there is no certainty that he could later comply with them.'[8]

Besides responding to Israel's actions against its members, the Qassam Brigade also pursued its own agenda. At the top of it was the release of Hamas prisoners, especially Shaikh Ahmad Yasin, from Israeli jails. On 11 October 1994 it kidnapped an IDF soldier, Nachshon Waxman, and offered to exchange him for 200 Hamas prisoners including Yasin. When Rabin confidently announced that Waxman was being held in Gaza, the Israeli media offered Arafat a stark option: choose peace with Israel, or peace with Hamas. Arafat made his choice clear when the PA police rounded up some 400 Hamas loyalists without charges, set up roadblocks, conducted identity checks and shut down the pro-Hamas Islamic University – the actions associated with the IDF in most Gazan minds. Through the back channels the Palestinian PSS supplied intelligence to the Israeli Government. Acting on it, Rabin ordered a rescue operation on 14 October in Bir Nabala, a village located two kilometres from Jerusalem, where Waxman was being held. The operation went wrong. Waxman and his three captors were killed. The next day the Gaza Strip closed down to mourn 'the martyrs of Bir Nabala'. To avenge their deaths, on 19 October a Hamas suicide bomber blew himself up in a bus in downtown Tel Aviv, killing 22 Israelis. This sensational act sent a shock wave through Israeli society. The Government arrested 1,350 Islamists in Israel and the West Bank, and reaffirmed its resolve to strike at the terrorists no matter where they were.

On 2 November morning when Hani Abid, the 27-year-old co-editor of the Gaza-based Islamic Jihad weekly, *Al Istiqlal* (Arabic, The Independence), opened the door of his car, an explosion killed him instantly. The assassination had the hallmarks of an Israeli undercover operation. Nine days later, Hisham Hamad, a young Jihad activist, riding a cycle, detonated himself outside the Netzarim settlement, killing three IDF soldiers. The PA police arrested 120 Islamic Jihad members. But this was not enough to pacify Rabin. He held a crisis meeting with Arafat in Madrid. There the Israeli Premier warned the Palestinian leader that were there to be a repeat of violence against IDF personnel in the territory under his control, the Israeli army would re-enter the PA areas, and take out the terrorists 'regardless of the autonomy and the Palestinian police'.[9] Had Rabin translated his threat into action, he would have been very much within his rights. For Clause 1 of Article VIII of the Cairo Agreement stated: 'Israel shall continue to carry ... the responsibility for overall security of Israelis and [Jewish] settlements [in the areas under Palestinian Authority control], for the purpose of safeguarding their internal security and public order, and will have the powers to take the steps necessary to meet this responsibility.'[10]

Thus chastened, Arafat accepted the advice of his hardline PA police commander in the Gaza Strip, Major-General Nasser Yusuf: crush Hamas. He apparently gave Yusuf a *carte blanche*.

On 18 November, following their Friday prayer and sermon in Gaza city's elegant, newly built Palestine Mosque, a stronghold of Hamas, about 1,000 Gazans prepared to march to the central jail to demand the release of the Hamas members being held there without charges. They found their path blocked by some 200 uniformed Palestininan police and plain-clothes PSS agents. As they tried to force their way through the police lines, a mêlée ensued. Shots were fired. Soon three men lay dead. The word spread fast. In the streets all over the city police and protestors fought pitched battles. By sunset, 13 men were killed, and over 200 injured.

To the rising satisfaction of the Jewish public and politicians, Arafat did what Ehud Ya'ari, an eminent Israeli commentator, had predicted. He mobilized not only his party, Fatah, but also its armed wing, Fatah Hawks, who had supposedly been disarmed and disbanded.[11] The Fatah Hawks mounted an armed demonstration on 21 November which ended with a rally, attended by 10,000, that was addressed by a belligerent Arafat. The rapidly escalating intra-Palestinian tension thrilled most Jewish Israelis. 'The clashes signal that Arafat will no longer tolerate the Islamist opposition,' Yossi Sarid, a Meretz minister known as a peacenik, declared approvingly. 'He now understands that it's either him or them.'[12] The next day a Palestinian policeman was killed. And on 24 November shots were fired outside the residences of Mahmoud Zahar and Shaikh Ahmad Bahar, eminent Hamas figures. While most Jewish Israelis waited expectantly to see Palestinians slide into a civil war the Israeli Arab MKs, belonging to the Arab Democratic Party and the leftist Hadash, joined Dr Haidar Abdul Shafi to cool the situation. They succeeded. Arafat allowed Hamas to hold a public meeting on 26 November, provided there was no display of arms. In return, Hamas secured a promise from him that there would be no presence of (uniformed) police at the gathering. There was none. And the Hamas rally, attended by 15,000, passed off peacefully.

Palestinians and Arab Israelis heaved a sigh of relief while most Jewish Israelis felt disappointed. The denouement that the latter had expected and wished failed to materialize.

The old equation still held though, with Israel and militant Islamists engaged in a deadly battle, and the Palestinian Authority wishing to see total peace prevail but unprepared to confront Muslim radicals all the way for fear of triggering a disastrous civil conflict. In any case, the PA's relations with the Israelis were still tenuous. It was soon reminded of this.

In the early hours of 2 January 1995 an IDF patrol shot dead four Palestinian policemen, injured one and arrested another in a gun battle near Beit Hanoun village in northern Gaza. According to the IDF, when its soldiers at Ezer checkpoint were fired on in darkness, they gave chase to the assailants into the nearby village of Beit Hanoun. There they mistook the (uniformed) Palestinian police unit of six for the armed militants who, they thought, had attacked them. While most Gazans and West Bankers saw the incident as a cold-blooded murder of their policemen by the IDF, the PA and the Israeli Government blamed poor co-ordination and communications for the mishap, and pledged to improve communication.

It was not long before Muslim extremists struck in retribution. On 22 January, Sunday, two Islamic Jihad suicide bombers blew themselves and 20 IDF soldiers and one civilian up at a bus stop in Beit Lid near Natanya. Outraged Israelis reacted with anger and grief. The Rabin Government imprisoned a further 200 Islamists, bringing the total since the Tel Aviv bombing to over 2,000.

The score of violent deaths since the September 1993 Oslo Accord was: Palestinian 235, Israeli 110. Due to the devastating suicide-bomb attacks against Israeli soldiers and civilians, the Palestinian-Israeli ratio, which hovered around 3:1 at the time of the Cairo Agreement in May, was now down to about 2:1.

At the initiative of Egyptian President Hosni Mubarak, whose regime also faced violence from extremist Islamists, there was a mini-summit of the Egyptian, Israeli, Jordanian and Palestinian leaders in Cairo on 2 February. There Rabin pressed Arafat to get tough with the Islamic terrorists. 'After Beit Lid you arrested only seven members of the Islamic Jihad,' he said to Arafat. 'We arrested 200. We arrested 1,350 after the Dizengoff [Square, Tel Aviv] bombing in October [1994].' In reply, Arafat said: 'We arrested many others in the past, but they were acquitted.'[13] The release had occurred because the PA police had either pressed no charges agaist the detainees or produced insufficient evidence to secure conviction in court.

How was Arafat to overcome this barrier to achieving his political aim? By circumventing the normal judicial system. This was the advice proffered to him by President Mubarak, who had established military courts in Egypt to try suspected Islamic radicals. On 7 February Arafat resurrected an Egyptian law of 1962 (when Gaza was administered by Cairo), and set up a State Security Court. Presided over by three judges, it was authorized to try cases referred to it, either by the PA's attorney-general or its Chairman/ President, outside of the civil law. When Raji Sourani, a prominent lawyer and head of the Gaza Centre for Rights and Law, said that setting up State Security Courts was undermining 'the independence of the judiciary', and marked 'the beginning of a trend towards militarization of Palestinian society', he was arrested on 14 February.

Just as Ehud Ya'ari's forecast about Arafat striking out as a partisan militia leader came to pass in November, now it was time for Rabin's prediction in September 1993 about how justice would be dispensed in the Palestinian-ruled Gaza to materialize.

As for his own policy to eradicate Muslim terrorists by all means, Rabin remained firmly committed to it. His pressure on Arafat to do likewise was paying off. To his satisfaction, co-operation between the Palestinian PSS and the Israeli Shin Beth and IDF was increasing. Among other things this led to a thunderous explosion in an apartment in the Shaikh Radwan suburb of Gaza city on 2 April. It left four people dead, including Kamal Kheil, a member of the Qassam Brigade, whom the Israelis held responsible for the murder of an IDF colonel in 1993, and the PA police of killing 16 Palestinian collaborators during the intifada. The PA claimed that the apartment was being used as a bomb factory by the terrorists, who got blown up by accident. Its police refused to hand over the corpses to the relatives, and buried them hurriedly – thus driving the 10,000 Hamas supporters, who gathered the next day for the funeral procession of Kheil, to conduct a 'notional funeral and burial' of him.

The expected reprisal by the Qassam Brigade of Hamas came on 9 April, the anniversary of the Deir Yasin massacre by the Zionist extremists in 1948, involving over 250 Palestinian men, women and children in the village near Jerusalem. On a road junction south of the Kfar Darom Jewish settlement in the Gaza Strip, a Palestinian car packed with explosives hit an Israeli bus, killing seven troops and settlers, and another such vehicle crashed into an IDF convoy, leaving one soldier dead. One attack was claimed by the Qassam Brigade and the other by the Islamic Jihad. The subsequent round of arrests of Islamists by the PA landed 170 Hamas and Islamic Jihad members in jail.

Among other things, this event impeded the progress being made by Dr Haidar Abdul Shafi and Abdullah Hourani, a member of the PLO executive committee, to bring about a rapprochement between the diverse Palestinian groups. They had managed to devise a common platform, demanding full withdrawal of Israel from the Gaza Strip, dismantling of the Jewish settlements, and release of all political prisoners held by Israel and the PA. When the document, called the National Reconciliation Agreement, was ready for signing by all parties in early May, Arafat refused to do so. His objection was that the Agreement did not contain commitment by Hamas and the Islamic Jihad to cease attacks against Israel from inside the Gaza Strip. His critics argued that Arafat's refusal showed that he had succumbed to the pressure by Rabin who had warned Arafat that he would oppose any agreement between him and the Palestinian opposition unless the latter expressly accepted the Oslo Accord.

Such a step by Rabin would have halted progress stemming from the Oslo Accord, which had so far yielded the Cairo Agreement of May 1994. In the year that had passed since then, the Palestinian Authority had fared better than most people had expected.

A major problem of the PA, charged with administering a penurious territory like the Gaza Strip, was lack of funds. For its economic survival, it was heavily dependent on grants from western states, which wanted to ensure that the PA had transparent and accountable institutions in place before they fulfilled their promises of financial aid. They channelled their grants, in equal measure, through the World Bank's Holst Fund (named after Norway's Foreign Minister, Johan Jorgen Holst, who died in 1994) and the United Nations. The World Bank paid wages to public sector employees, some 15,000 of them; and the UN provided for the salaries and running cost of the 9,000-strong police force as well as the public works and bilateral projects.[14] The UN Secretary-General, Boutros Boutros-Ghali, appointed Terje Rod Larsen, 47, a Norwegian social scientist who had arranged secret talks between Israel and the PLO, the United Nations Special Co-ordinator with the status of an under-secretary. Larsen established the head-quarters of the United Nations Special Co-ordinator's Office (UNSCO) in Gaza city. Among other things the UNSCO set up a UN Local Aid Co-ordination Committee to meet the donors' transparency and accountability requirement, chiefly by auditing randomly the receipts of the funds spent.

During the year July 1993–June 1994 the PA had income of $606 million and expenditure of $756 million, leaving it with a deficit of $150 million.

Receipts from direct taxation, which the PA was author-ized to levy, were low due to high unemployment, running at 55 per cent. This had to do with the deep cut the Israeli Government had made in the size of the Palestinian labour force it allowed to work in Israel, and the frequent closure of the Green Line which followed terrorist bombs. Between January 1993 and January 1995, Israel had curtailed the Palestinian total from 120,000 to 45,000, and made up the shortfall by importing 70,000 foreign workers from such countries as Romania and Thailand.[15] When, following the suicide-bomb attack in Beit Lid on 22 January, Israel barred the entry of unmarried Palestinian workers under 30, considered a security risk, the total licensed Palestinian workers from the Gaza Strip and West Bank fell to a mere 20,000. Little wonder that during July 1994–June 1995, the already low living standards of the Gaza Strip fell by 25 per cent. As Abdul Hani, a small, slim, bearded grocer in the main square of Khan Yunis, put it in March 1995: 'Things are worse economically than before. Last year at the time of the Eid al Fitr (Arabic, Festival of Breaking the Fast), in February, I bought 250 pieces of cheese and sold them all. This year I ordered only 35 and sold only 15.' He caressed his scanty beard gloomily. 'You can see the sweets I bought for the Eid,' he continued, pointing out his wares on display on the pavement under an awning. 'Two weeks after the Eid so many are still unsold.'

The only area where there were overt signs of progress was in public works, especially sewerage, electricity and telephones. It was considered sensible to finish laying these facilities before asphalting roads and streets. Also the health service now covered twice as many Gazans as during the Israeli occupation.

In the private sector construction was booming partly to meet the demand by the burgeoning Palestinian Authority both for office space and housing for its employees, and partly to accommodate the affluent Palestinians returning from the Diaspora. Anybody walking along the Al Rashid Street on the beachfront in Gaza city could see the high-rise apartment and office blocks going up. The PA had also cleaned up certain sections of the beach, hitherto strewn with garbage and sewage, and allowed the renting of temporary beachside accommodation erected by enterprising business-men. Overall the Gaza Strip had been sprucing itself up with liberal coats of whitewash, in the process wiping out the graffiti of the intifada. With the end of the nine p.m. to four a.m. curfew, which had become a permanent feature under Israeli occupation, the general atmosphere was now relaxed.

There were many overt signs of a people slowly but surely emerging as a nation and a state. The flying of the Palestinian flag was one such. Another was the arrival of the Palestine Broadasting Authority on radio waves and television screens. Even those who disapproved of the way the Palestinian television boringly recorded every single activity of President Arafat could not help feeling proud that such a service existed and was competing with the long-established broadcasting services of Israel and Jordan for an audience.

The Palestinians' rising self-confidence transcended politi-cal and economic fields, and extended to the socio-cultural sphere. When, for instance, in Muslim relgious affairs, they had to confront Jordan's Hashemite dynasty, aided by Israel, they did not shy away. They successfully challenged King Hussein's authority to act as the custodian of the Islamic shrines in Jerusalem by ignoring his appointment of 66-year-old Shaikh Abdul Qadir Abidin as the mufti of Jerusalem.

Arafat was quick to move on this front. In October 1993, within a few weeks of signing the Oslo Accord, he appointed Shaikh Ekrima Said Sabri, a Jerusalemite, the mufti of Jerusalem and the Holy Land. A bespectacled, broad-shouldered man of 55, with a trimmed beard and plump face, Sabri, dressed in an immaculate grey cloak over a white shirt, beige tie and camel-brown sweater, looked dignified partly because of the red fez, covered with a broad white band, he wore over his balding head. In his office in a medieval building near an entrance to the Dome of the Rock, he sat behind a vast, shining desk of pinewood. The numerous, glitteringly-bound volumes on the wall shelves behind his dark swivel chair added an air of scholarly authority to him. Indeed as a PhD in Islamic law from the oldest university in the world, the Al Azhar, in Cairo, his academic credentials were impressive. His two young, moustached assistants in polo-neck jerseys and sharp jackets sat in chairs by the wall on the mufti's left by a tall, narrow window, making light of their role as bodyguards. The cooing of the pigeons on the ledge of the window merged harmoniously with the humming of the fax machine.

'Before taking up this position, I was for many years the director of preaching and guidance at the Islamic Waqf [Trust, which runs the Noble Sanctuary],' Sabri told me in mid-January 1995. Sipping the aromatic Turkish coffee from a dainty cup, I wondered aloud about the title of Sabri on the business card he gave me. 'Just as the Greek Orthodox Patriarch Diodoros I is the patriarch of Jerusalem as well as Israel, the Palestinian Territories, Jordan, Kuwait and the United Arab Emirates, I am the grand mufti of all of Jerusalem and the Holy Land of Palestine,' he explained. 'And just as the religious pronouncements of Patriarch Diodoros apply to the Greek Orthodox in all these countries, my fatwas [religious decrees] apply to all Muslims living in my area.'

What about Shaikh Abidin, who had been appointed to the same post by King Hussein a few days before Sabri, and who had his office near the Al Aqsa Mosque on the Noble Sanctuary, I asked. 'Once the Palestinian National Authority was established, whatever residual powers had been vested in King Hussein passed to the PNA,' came the reply.

Soon after came a test to prove whose fatwa Muslim Palestinians were going to follow. In the (lunar) Islamic calendar, Ramadan, the holy month of fasting, begins with the sighting of the new moon. Since the sighting depends on the condition of the sky, cloudy or clear, Ramadan begins on different days in the Muslim world. At least it did in 1995. On Monday 30 January at about seven p.m., Sabri announced before a gathering of the religious leaders from all leading West Bank and Gaza cities, that the moon had been spotted and that the first day of Ramadan had begun. (As with Jews, a Muslim day begins with sunset.) At about the same time in Gaza city, Arafat issued a statement. 'For the first time in the history of the Palestinian nation, we announce to the Arab and Islamic world the witnessing of the new Ramadan moon from the Al Aqsa Mosque under the Palestinian National Authority,' he declared.[16] Sabri's rival, Abidin, waited for a signal from Amman, which came 24 hours later. But by then all Palestinian Muslims had already finished their first day of fasting. On 31 January I happened to be at Birzeit University; and its canteen was closed. Indeed, by all accounts, no Palestinian Muslim seemed to consult Abidin on religious matters.

This was an easy win for Arafat and his nominee. Their chief rival was King Hussein of Jordan, and their domain religion. But when it came to Arafat and his Palestinian supporters confronting the Israeli Government on the issue of the expansion of the Jewish settlements in the West Bank, it was an altogether different story.

I witnessed one such instance on 17 January 1995. It was a breezy, cloudy morning, with a chill in the air, when young men in jeans and windbreakers began collecting near the recently finished mosque with an imposing, dome-topped minaret, on the eastern outskirt of Al Bireh. Their leader carried a large Palestinian flag with 'Fatah Movement' (in Arabic) inscribed over the middle white stripe of the standard. They began shouting slogans: 'No Peace with Settlements'; and *'Biladi, biladi* (Land, land)'. Older men arrived, including the mufti of Jerusalem, Shaikh Ekrima Said Sabri. Then a group of women, among them Hanan Ashrawi, wearing her well-dressed short hair and pearl earrings.

On a distant hill I could see a Jewish settlement, its red-tiled roofs and well spaced new houses providing unmistakable clues about its identity. It was called Kokhaf Yaacov (Hebrew, Star of Jacob). But it was not the target of the demonstrators. They were aiming to march along a zigzag route to the top of another hill, the site of the Psagot settlement with some 115 families, protesting at both the expansion of this colony and the seizure of the Palestinian land to construct an access road that would enable the Jewish settlers to bypass Al Bireh on their way to Jerusalem and beyond.

The protestors marched along a road whose surface declined from asphalt to compact stone to freshly levelled hilly soil, with construction machinery busily shaping the gently rising hill on both sides of the prized ribbon. The reddish soil, covered patchily with scrub, glowed gently in the wintry sun. Having traversed a rising U in the road, the demonstrators haphazardly crossed a trickling stream, and embarked on an uphill march which brought them to a plateau. Here they found, waiting, many IDF soldiers, armed with machine-guns, standing next to Jeeps and armoured personnel carriers, liberally fitted with antennas. They stopped, and ended up forming a well-behaved crowd. Speeches followed. Of the four PA ministers, Yasser Abd Rabbo, the Information Minister, was the most lively. His audience consisted of some 300 Palestinians of assorted ages and dresses – from the jeans, windbreakers and trainers of young men to traditional, heavily embroidered ankle-length dresses of middle-aged matrons – and another 75 media people. I looked hard, but did not see the settlement. It stood above the steep embankment that had been cut to make the access road, and was invisible from where I stood. While we listened to speeches, a large band of youths climbed to the heavily guarded gate of the fenced settlement.

Suddenly we heard a volley of shots in the air. Each shot made a loud bang and gave out a flash. We turned tail. A bullet fell by my side. I picked it up, and started running downhill. (In the report on the event, the next day's *Jerusalem Post* carried a statement, 'The IDF denied using arms to disperse the demonstrators'. I held in my hand the heavy bullet I had collected the day before, and gazed at it for a while.) Others did the same, men, women, youths. It was an unseemly sight. I was soon running beside two Palestinian women dressed in skirts and high-heel shoes. One of them stopped, wisely took off her shoes, and resumed her downhill flight faster than before. The Israeli servicemen started chasing us. 'We are safe now,' I mumbled to myself as we reached the threadbare stream. Not really. By now the young soldiers were in hot pursuit of their quarry – the Palestinian youths – running and firing in the air. This made me revise my assessment: I thought the purpose of the firing outside the settlement was to disperse the crowd, and once that aim had been achieved, the troops would stay put. But no, the rules of the game were different here.

I was now on a level road, asphalted, walking briskly, not running. Ahead of me were three Palestinian matrons, bulky, in gaudy, embroidered long dresses and shawls, mumbling angrily in Arabic. Three young Israeli soldiers, all of them Ashkenazi, in their late teens, went past the women. One of them, with a crew cut and florid face, stopped. Slowly, he raised his machine-gun in a gesture of shooting one of the Palestinian women, all of them now stationary, then lowered the muzzle. I stopped. The soldier did the same with the second woman: he pointed his gun at her, then raised it a few inches above her head, and fired. Only a few metres away, I watched, petrified. So petrified that I let pass a telling moment which richly deserved to be captured on my film. The woman stood straight, unflinching. The young soldier turned, broke into a trot, and joined his comrades, all of them now running, a group among several, chasing their prey, the Palestinian youths.

Later I saw the battle continuing near the mosque, our assembly point in the morning. When a serviceman caught up with a stone-thrower, his mate shouted: 'Give him to me. I want to kill him.' (The words, spoken in Hebrew, were translated to me by a lean, craggy-faced local journalist who had, like me, returned to the assembly point.) Still more soldiers came running, and disappeared in their chase of their stone-throwing enemies. 'It is like *West Side Story*, a street gang warfare,' I said to my interlocutor. 'Except that one side has machine-guns, and the other stones,' he said. 'It's an unequal fight.' It was hard to disagree.

In the final analysis, though, the Al Bireh demonstration was a futile act. (Within a year of the protest, the number of families at the Psagot settlement rose from 115 to 140.)[17] Arafat tried belatedly, and in vain, to recover what he had conceded in the Oslo Accord, which contained not a word about the Jewish settlements in the West Bank and Gaza.

More disappointingly for Palestinians, Arafat did not seem to have learned from his past mistakes, or alter some of his methods of operating in the light of the changed situation, from running a guerrilla organization to creating a state. Such characteristics as secretiveness, deviousness and skilful manipulation, which had been his assets in maintaining the PLO as a single entity and balancing the diverse trends it contained, now became liabilities. For a state with democratic credentials to emerge, there had to be less and less secretiveness. And there had to be a sharing of power, and delegation of authority, to a degree to which Arafat was unaccustomed. After all he had achieved and maintained his prime position in the PLO by showing repeatedly that he was indispensable, and that he possessed an uncanny sense of survival. Part of his success in emerging as the first among equals lay in his skill in engendering tensions between different PLO factions (up to a certain point) and even among his Fatah colleagues, and then intervening as a mediator. Equally importantly, he had used his exclusive control of PLO and Fatah funds as an important tool in his manipulatory game.

Continuing the old pattern in a changed environment – where fighting Israel had given way to talking with it – he resorted to nominating delegates to several negotiating committees at the eleventh hour, and then providing them with insufficient guidelines. When the inevitable stalemate ensued, he would enter the scene, bargain directly with

Rabin, and reach agreements, thus boosting not only his ego but also his public image as a statesman actively and innovately pursuing 'peace of the brave'.

To obfuscate his failures in the talks, he would release piecemeal the details of the agreements he had concluded with Israel. Even Abdul Hakim al Samara, who had braved imprisonment for his membership of Fatah, had turned critical of Arafat. 'When Rabin reaches an agreement he immediately gives the Hebrew translation to all MKs in parliament,' he said. 'As for Arafat, even PA ministers do not fully know what has been signed. So then you find in the Arabic press the PA spokesman says so and so. And then the Israelis say, "Read the agreement". And always the Israelis are right. Every day we find more and more "secret" parts of the agreements.' Arafat also made a poor choice of negotiators. 'The Palestinians he appointed to negotiate the implementation of the Oslo Accord were no match to Haidar Abdul Shafi, Hanan Ashrawi and Faisal Husseini,' Abdul Hakim added. 'To put a novice like Nabil Shaath, a man trained in business administration, against Amnon Shahak, an experienced general and deputy chief of staff of the IDF, to negotiate security was a disaster. No wonder the full details of the Cairo Agreement came out in the Arabic press only in bits and pieces.'[18]

As weeks and months passed, the realization of the grave flaws in the Oslo Accord and the Cairo Agreement seemingly dawned on Arafat, and made him alter his strategy and tactics in the subsequent talks. These pertained chiefly to IDF troop redeployment in the West Bank as a prelude to holding elections to the Palestinian (Legislative) Council and the presidency of the Palestinian (Executive) Authority. He took direct charge of the negotiations, partly because what was being devised was so complex that repeated deadlines, starting with 1 July 1995, were not met.

It was only on 22 September, after thousands of hours of tortuous talks between the teams, led respectively by Arafat and foreign minister Shimon Peres, that the final draft was initialled in the Egyptian sea resort of Taba. The formal signing took place in Washington at the White House's

East Room under ornate chandeliers six days later. Hosted by President Bill Clinton, the two-hour-long ceremony was attended by 200 guests, including President Mubarak and King Hussein.

The Taba Agreement, popularly entitled Oslo II, containing 31 Articles, seven Annexes and nine maps, was 314 pages long. Its salient points were the division of the West Bank into A, B and C Areas; the provisions for elections to the Palestinian (Legislative) Council and the PA presidency, and the description of their powers; a phased programme of Palestinian prisoner release; and a timetable for the implementation of the Agreement.

In Area A, the PA was to exercise full control over civil affairs (covering 40 spheres) and security; in Area B, the PA was to exercise control over civil affairs and public order, with Israel taking charge of overall security; and in Area C, Israel was to exercise full control over security (including Palestinian public order), territorial jurisdiction and Jewish settlers, with the PA taking charge only of Palestinian civil affairs.

Area A consisted of seven Palestinian cities – Jenin, Nablus, Tulkarm, Qalqilya, Ramallah, Bethlehem and Hebron – and covered 6 per cent of the West Bank. The PA's control over civil affairs and security was not unqualified. It was required to guarantee freedom of movement to Israeli civilians and settlers through these urban centres, and provide joint Palestinian-Israeli escorts for their vehicles. Area B included 465 villages, occupying 23 per cent of the territory and accommodating 63 per cent of its population. Here the IDF had the power to intervene at its own discretion to maintain overall security. The rest of the West Bank, taking up 70 per cent of the territory, was labelled Area C. After the Palestinian Council had been elected, it was authorized to take over Palestinian territorial jurisdiction and public order partially. Finally, Oslo II spelled out the executive and legislative powers respectively of the Palestinian (Executive) Authority and the Palestinian (Legislative) Council, which were subject to review and final approval by Israel.

As for the timetable, in Area A, full IDF evacuation of

the cities, except Hebron, was to be accomplished between mid-November and end-December 1995, followed by the IDF's withdrawal from 85 per cent of Hebron by 28 March 1996. The elections to the legislative and executive organs of the PA were to be held on 20 January 1996, with the elected representatives holding their office until 4 May 1999, at the latest. Within two months of the inauguration of the Palestinian (Legislative) Council, the Palestine National Council had to amend those articles of its National Charter which called for the destruction of Israel. On 28 March 1996 the IDF was required to carry out the first of its three six-monthly redeployments, during which additional areas of the West Bank were to pass into PA jurisdiction. Finally, in line with the (Oslo) Declaration of Principles, the latest date for the start of talks on final settlement was 4 May 1996, and the five-year period of the interim agreement was scheduled to expire on 4 May 1999.

The IDF's evacuation of the West Bank cities, starting with Jenin on 13 November, reached a climax with its withdrawal from Bethlehem on 21 December, leading to a four-day open-air party there, thus inadvertently combining the birth of Palestinian nationalism with the birth of the founder of Christianity. Since Arafat was required to dissolve his cabinet before the election campaign began officially on 1 January, he held the last ministerial meeting in Bethlehem on 23 December in the office of the Greek Orthodox Patriarch dominated by a painting of the 'Last Supper' on a wall.

Thus, by chance or design, the run-up to the Palestinian poll started in a mood of euphoria generated by the IDF withdrawal from six of the seven West Bank cities. The 88 members of the Palestinian Council – West Bank 44, Gaza 37, Greater East Jerusalem seven – were to be elected from 16 multi-seat constituencies by 1.45 million voters. Six of the Council seats were reserved for Christians and one for Samaritans. The poll was to be conducted by the Central Election Commission, chaired by Mahmoud Abbas, an appointee of Arafat.

Having allowed Fatah activists to choose candidates for the Palestinian Council in primaries, Arafat cancelled the results because the 'insiders' with a record of active participation in the intifada emerged strong at the expense of the 'outsiders'. He issued his own list which included such outsiders as Ahmad Qrei, Nabil Shaath, Abdul Hakkam Balawi and Intissar Wazir. He reasoned that the outsiders had fared badly in the primaries because they were unknown at home, being in exile, where they had fought for the same cause albeit in a different way. Arafat had another (unexpressed) motive behind his move. The Oslo II required that four-fifths of the cabinet be chosen from the members of the Palestinian Council. So Arafat wanted most of his former cabinet colleagues to get elected to the Council.[19] But in his selection of the insiders, Arafat preferred local affluent grandees to leaders of the refugee camps. Therefore, many of the rejected Fatah activists decided to run as independents.

Both the Islamist and secular opposition parties boycotted the poll since participation in it would have implied accepting the Oslo Accord, which they continued to reject. Yet 644 men and 28 women entered the race for the Council seats.

Arafat's rival for the PA's presidency was Samiha Khalil, a 73-year-old leader of the Palestine Women's Movement, from Ramallah. A veteran of social reform, and a woman with a soft, lined face and a receding hairline, she voiced vague opposition to the Oslo Accords, and conducted a lacklustre campaign. Her statements got buried on the inside pages of Palestinian publications while Arafat regularly hogged the front pages.[20] Also, as before, the PA-run television continued to report slavishly the minutiae of Arafat's daily activities. Its task was made easier by the location of its studios – next door to the office of Arafat. They shared a whitewashed, three-storey structure on Al Rashid Street along the beach front. Constructed originally as the office and entertainment centre of the Gaza Sports Club, a haunt of the local elite, the building stood alone, without immediate neighbours. It was therefore easy to make secure, a crucial consideration for Arafat, a prime target for assassination. From his office decorated, as in Tunis, with a vast image of the Dome of the Rock, and providing a view from its windows of the Mediterranean, with its rolling waves lapping against the sand, Arafat frequently addressed his constituents through Palestinian television.

The PA-run television was openly partial towards the Fatah candidates running for the Palestinian Council seats. It was left to the less effective and glamorous PA-run radio to give access to non-Fatah candidates. Inclement weather – hail and sleet – in the West Bank conspired to abort the non-Fatah candidates' plans to stage marches as part of their electoral campaign.

Whereas Fatah hopefuls put a rosy gloss on the Oslo Accord of September 1993 and the subsequent events, arguing that they were leading to the founding of an independent, sovereign Palestinian state, their opposition rivals highlighted the many flaws of the agreements with Israel. Such independent stalwarts as Haidar Abdul Shafi also demanded that the Palestinian (Executive) Authority should be made accountable to the Palestinian Council, which should also have a say in reaching the final settlement with Israel.

Many of the complaints by non-Fatah contestants about intimidation, including beatings, by Preventive Security Service agents went unchecked by the Israeli authorities, or by the teams of observers from 13 countries and regional and international institutions (such as the European Union), who had arrived to monitor the poll. Both Israelis and other foreigners chose to overlook most of the pre-election irregularities. This was a measure of the goodwill that the Palestinian Authority enjoyed with the international community.

An outstanding instance of foreign, chiefly western, interest came on 9 January. The 30 donor countries, meeting in Paris, announced a further aid package of $865 million for 1996–7 for the Palestinian Authority which, when added to $460 million that had been pledged earlier but not disbursed, came to a total of $1,325 million, or $564 per capita, which amounted to 46 per cent of the per capita Gross National Product. Obviously the Paris meeting was timed to boost the electoral chances of Arafat and his party. And, as expected, the Palestinian Authority-run radio and television milked the story.

The Oslo II allowed the Palestinians living in Greater East Jerusalem to participate in the Palestinian Council elections but on strict conditions. It specified the Jerusalem electoral district with seven seats in such a way that half of it lay outside the Greater East Jerusalem area, into the West Bank proper. It treated the Greater East Jerusalem-based Palestinians as 'absentee electors' entitled to exercise their voting right by mail from a post office. Since the post offices in this section of the city were unable to handle all the voters, a vast majority of the 55,000 Palestinians, who registered to vote, were directed to use the post offices outside the city limits as polling stations. The Israeli Government outlawed public meetings for electioneering, or public display of any electoral material, and swiftly arrested those who broke the bans. To discourage the Palestinians from voting, the Jerusalem municipality under the mayorship of Ehud Olmert, a Likud leader, plastered the walls of Greater East Jerusalem with posters warning that the Palestinians voting for a 'foreign government' would lose their residency status in Jerusalem, and with it, their health care and social welfare benefits. The Israeli Foreign Ministry kept silent. It was only two days before the poll that the Ministry stated that voting in the election would not affect the right of the Palestinians to live, work and have health insurance in Jerusalem. The end-purpose of this multi-faceted strategy, in which the local Likud administration actively backed the central Labour Government, was to depress the Palestinian voter turn-out, and prove that Greater East Jerusalem Palestinians did not want to share the Palestinian Authority rule along with West Bankers and Gazans.

To intimidate the Palestinians on election day, the Israeli Government deployed an extra 4,000 soldiers chiefly around the post offices in Greater East Jerusalem where only 5,000 Palestinians were allowed to vote. It justified the army presence as a measure designed to prevent disruption of the election by Jewish or Muslim extremists. But the official videotaping of the Palestinians casting their vote told a different tale.

Little wonder that the voter turn-out in the Jerusalem district was only 40 per cent versus 68 per cent in the West Bank and 86 in the Gaza Strip. The overall percentage of 68 was quite impressive for a people largely untutored in balloting for political and demographic reasons. Indeed, in the Gaza Strip all of those voting were doing so for the first time. For under the Israeli occupation, unlike in the West Bank, there had been no election for municipalities in the Strip; and under the rule of Egyptian President Gamal Abdul Nasser, the legislative council for the Strip, set up in 1958, consisted of members who were nominated by Cairo or elected indirectly.

Arafat won by 87 per cent to 12 per cent for Khalil. In the Council, Fatah and its allies secured 57 seats (Fatah 50, pro-Fatah independents six, and the Democratic Palestinian Union one), and opposition 31 – consisting of 21 independents including four pro-Islamists, and 10 Fatah dissidents. Among the independents was Haidar Abdul Shafi, who obtained the highest votes by any candidate, and Hanan Ashrawi, one of the six Christian members.

The overall assessment of the poll by international monitors was summed up by James Zogby, an Arab-American member of the United States team. 'Having observed elections in the US over the last 30 years, I can honestly say that I saw nothing in Gaza that I had not seen in Philadelphia, Chicago, New York or Detroit,' he said. 'This is not to excuse such behaviour, but rather to put the irregularities in context. Overall, the Palestinian elections were free and fair.'[21]

Undoubtedly, the 20 January 1996 poll was a landmark in Palestinian history. Among other things it conferred legitimacy on the Palestinian Authority and Arafat. Premier Peres described it as 'a positive endorsement of the peace process', while Arafat perceived it as 'a foundation for a Palestinian state'. In the words of Ashrawi: 'It was a commitment by the Palestinian people to the democratic process, a vote for the democratic state and the rule of law.' A grander and highly optimistic view was taken by a senior Fatah leader. 'This is the end of Greater Israel or Greater Jordan,' he said. 'This is the most important result of the election. It is not possible now for Israel to absorb or expel the Palestinians, or return them to Jordan.'[22] But, unrealistically, he did not refer to the possibility of the Israeli military retaking control of the Palestinian territories, which it was entitled to do under the Oslo I and Oslo II Accords.

On 12 February, Arafat took the oath of office – President of the Palestinian National Authority, *Al Rais al Sulteh al Wataniyeh al Falastiniya* (as the Authority is inaccurately called by Palestinians at official and popular levels) – on the Quran before Salim al Zaadoun, the acting chairman of the Palestine National Council, and Qusai al Abadleh, the chief justice of the Palestinian Authority. Among those who were present at the ceremony in the Mansion House, Gaza city, were the religious and civic leaders of the West Bank and Gaza Strip, and the newly elected members of the Palestinian Council.[23]

The swearing in of the Council members had to wait until 7 March. This had as much to do with the PA's failure to refurbish on time the chambers for the Council, occupying part of the Mansion House, as with the polling date of the impending Israeli elections: 29 May. The Oslo II Accord required that the Palestine National Council (of the PLO) remove the references to Israel's destruction in the Palestine National Charter within two months of the inauguration of the Palestinian Council. To help the electoral chances of Peres and his Labour Party, Arafat decided that the PNC session should be near, but not *too* near, 29 May. So, as in the 1992 Israeli election, Arafat meant to play a part.

But this time around there was another Palestinian faction which also wanted to have an impact on the Israeli poll: the Qassam Brigade of Hamas. Deeply opposed to the Oslo Accord, which it regarded as unjust, it wanted to hurt Peres's chance of success by showing that Israelis were still vulnerable to random acts of violence by militant Palestinians. It did so by carrying out three suicide-bomb attacks in Jerusalem and Ashqelon in a week, two on 25 February, and the third on 3 March. The next one on 4 March, the day of the Purim festival, in Tel Aviv was claimed by both Qassam Brigade and the Islamic Jihad. Following this carnage, which resulted in 59 instant deaths, Israel imposed the most stringent siege of the West Bank and Gaza since the Gulf War in early 1991. This meant *inter alia* that West Bankers could not travel within the territory.

As a result 51 Palestinian Council members, based outside the Gaza Strip, were held overnight at several IDF checkpoints on 6–7 March, and then taken to the Strip under IDF escort. This was hardly a propitious inauguration of the world's youngest parliament.

Its opening session was held at the spacious auditorium of the Shawwa Cultural Centre, a bland, modern building, in downtown Gaza city. Here the members had to make do with chairs without desks, and improvise. Once they had been sworn in, they elected the Speaker. The Fatah candidate, Ahmad Qrei, defeated his independent rival, Haidar Abdul Shafi, by 57 votes to 31. Since the Oslo II Accord specifies that in the case of death, incapacitation or resignation of the PA President, the Council Speaker becomes the acting PA President, Qrei now assumed the second highest office in the Palestinian territories. In contrast to the often dishevelled appearance of Arafat, the bald, clean-shaven Qrei, dressed in a well-cut dark business suit with a matching tie, and wearing dark-tinted glasses, looked decidedly spruce, with a professional air about him. Born in 1941 into a well-to-do household in Abu Dis near Jerusalem, Ahmad Qrei and his family fled as a result of the 1967 Arab-Israeli War. An economist, with an undergraduate degree from Birzeit University, he became a banker in Beirut. When the PLO moved its headquarters to Beirut he grew close to Arafat who, among other things, supervised the economic activities of Fatah, started in Jordan in 1964 to give employment to the martyrs' families. On Qrei's advice, Arafat reorganized the Fatah's economic wing as the Samed Foundation, and put Qrei in charge. Under his directorship, the Samed expanded its manufacturing activities in Lebanon, producing garments, footwear, processed food and furniture. Qrei invested Samed funds into international stock markets as well as industry and agriculture elsewhere in the Middle East and Arab Africa. When the PLO was expelled from Beirut to Tunis in 1982 he moved there, and was appointed economic adviser to Arafat. After being elected to the central committee of Fatah in 1989, he was elected to the central council of the PLO. He was also a member of the Palestine National Council. When the economic condition of the Occupied Territories deteriorated sharply due to the Kuwait crisis and the Gulf War, instructed by Arafat, he produced a plan to revive the territories' economy. Not surprisingly, following the 1993 Oslo Accord, he was appointed secretary-general of the Palestinian Economic Council for Development and Reconstruction by the World Bank.

At their session in Gaza, the Palestinian Council members also elected the legal committee, and charged it with drafting a document which would provide the constitutional framework of the Palestinian entity until the interim period ending in May 1999. Among other things the constitution was expected to delineate the legislative, executive and judicial powers of the Palestinian entity and spell out the rights and duties of citizens.

In his speech to the Council, Arafat, the chief executive, combined his condemnation of the terrorist actions perpetrated by 'the enemies of peace' with his criticism of Israel for its sealing of the Palestinian territories which, he said, 'was decimating our economy and undermining our achievements'.

The closure was becoming a depressing way of life, at least for Gazans. In the 22 months, 669 days that had passed since the Cairo Agreement in early May 1994, the Gaza Strip had been shut off from Israel for 295 days – that is, almost every alternate day. The daily loss to the economy of the Strip amounted to $4 to $5 million. This time the Israeli Government had compounded the ban on the outward movement of goods and workers from Gaza with an additional ban on the imports of materials from Israel, thus creating severe shortages of basic necessities, such as food and medicine, as well as much needed building materials.

By engendering such conditions, the Israeli authorities were undermining the popular standing of Arafat, and making his task of convening the PNC to modify its Charter doubly arduous.

It seemed that, through a strange combination of events, both the PA and the Israeli Government of Peres had willy-nilly become hostages to the military wings of Hamas and the Islamic Jihad.

13

ISLAMIST OPPOSITION:

Hamas and the Islamic Jihad

The sleek, well-varnished benches and desks in the neat classroom, painted pastel camel-brown, reflected the sunshine that filtered through the semi-opaque glass of the wall window facing east. In the right-hand corner, next to the folded black curtain, the glass-fronted print of a lifesize skeleton captured two squares of the sunlight penetrating through the horizontal windows, an unintended example of a natural X-ray. The long, dark, bordered board, with a chalk duster resting on its lower edge, covering the wall from the skeleton to the lightswitch near the door, quietly announced the religio-political affiliation of the educational institution. *Bismallah al Rahman al Rahim* (In the name of God, the Merciful, the Compassionate) – read the inscription at the top of the board. I was at the Islamic University in Gaza city, waiting to interview Dr Mahmoud Zahar, a surgeon with a degree from the Ain Shams University of Cairo (1971), who taught nursing students there.

Dr Zahar's office was in one of the several low, buff-coloured stone buildings scattered around the campus. What made this building distinctive was a vast square sign in bronze against a dark-green background – 'The Islamic University Gaza 1978–1398'[1] written in Arabic and English in an arc under a logo of rounded cotton-buds encompassing a book carrying the inscription, *waql rab zadini ilma* (God increases knowledge and wisdom), resting on waves – installed over its entrance at the end of a wide staircase of a dozen steps. Inside, in his neat office, Zahar rose to shake my hand. A small, squat man, powerfully built, Zahar, 50, wore a black beard laced with white hair. He was dressed in a well-pressed grey suit, a dark green sweater and a blue striped shirt. An energetic, eloquent man, his slow, deliberate movements invested him with gravitas, an important consideration for the political leadership of Hamas when appointing him the official spokesman.

'The Oslo Accord has made things worse for us,' Zahar said. 'With its control of 45 per cent of the Gaza Strip, Israel continues its illegal occupation. And this has been accepted by the international community which thinks that peace has been achieved. It thinks that the Israelis have given us our freedom, which is untrue.' What alternative did Hamas offer? 'Our action plan stems from our analysis,' he began. 'This land is our land. Israel is here as a new kind of imperialist. We propose to neutralize this imperialism. That can be accomplished through an ongoing struggle by the believers both inside and outside Palestine, which is holy land to every Muslim in the world. Once an Islamic state comes into being [in the region] Israel will be demolished. God's Second Promise will be implemented.' Could he elaborate on this Divine Promise, I enquired. Zahar opened a drawer, took out his copy of the Quran, and opened the page. 'Chapter 17, the Night Journey, verse 7,' he replied. ' "If you do good . . . and to destroy utterly that which they ascended to." '[2] Looking up from the Quran, Zahar added, 'The Temple equals Jerusalem. The First Promise was kept by God: the Jewish state fell due to corruption and deviation from the true path. So the First Temple was destroyed. If Jews again fall into corruption then God will fulfil His promise through the hands of His Servants, those who are true to Islam. That is, true Muslims from outside and inside Palestine will demolish the existence of the Jewish state and establish a new situation. Signs of corruption and deviation from the true path among Jews are manifest: killing of innocent people, spreading robbery and expropriation, illegal confiscations, drugs, illegal affairs, bribes etc. The Jews are actively preventing the establishment of an Islamic regime in this region. The manifestations of injustice against Muslims by Israelis can be seen in every walk of life.' How long would it be before 'The Promise of the Second' came to pass, I asked. 'Nobody can tell exactly how long it will be for the prophecy to come true. Nobody before the intifada knew that it would happen. But it did. Likewise the Second Promise will be shared by the people under occupation, and they will establish a Palestinian state and expand the borders of Islam.' When I wondered aloud if I could take a photocopy of the Quranic verse, Zahar was quick to oblige. Instead of calling an assistant to do the job, as I expected him to, he left the office with the Quran. He soon returned with a photocopy of the appropiate page. But before giving it to me, he picked up a pair of scissors and cut the xerox sheet where it had picked up part of the facing page of the Quranic verse in question. Instead of throwing the strip printed with the Quranic text in the dustbin, he caressed it, and gently deposited it in his desk drawer.

Zahar's optimism about the rise of an Islamic Palestine stemmed from the rapid advance that Hamas had made since its founding by Shaikh Ahmad Yasin and six other leaders of the Islamic Centre in the Occupied Territories soon after the oubreak of the intifada in December 1987.[3] The Islamic Centre was the name of the religious charity that the Muslim Brotherhood was allowed by the IDF to operate. The Brotherhood was led by Yasin. Born in 1936 in a land-owning household in Jora village near the northern border of the Gaza Strip, Ahmad Yasin and his family sought shelter in a refugee camp in the Gaza Strip during the 1948 Arab-Israeli War. He joined the clandestine Muslim Brotherhood, in the mid-1950s, a few years after suffering crippling injuries in a sporting accident, which were to leave him wheelchair-bound in subsequent years. He worked as a schoolteacher in Gaza from 1957 to 1964, when he enrolled as a student of English at Ain Shams University, Cairo. His studies were interrupted when, following repression of the Brotherhood in Egypt and Gaza in 1966, he was imprisoned. After the Israeli occupation of Gaza, he was released. He resumed teaching as well as leading the reorganized Muslim Brotherhood.

A pan-Islamist party originating in Egypt in 1928 under the leadership of Hassan al Banna, the Muslim Brotherhood started as a moral-social reform movement, and then acquired political overtones in 1939. It set up branches in British mandate Palestine between 1942 and 1945. The doctrine of the Brotherhood was that Islam, based on the Quran and the Hadith (Arabic, lit. Narrative; fig. Sayings and Doings of Prophet Muhammad) was a comprehensive, self-evolving system, applicable to all times and places. Under al Banna's leadership, besides being a politico-religious body, the Brotherhood was also an athletic group, a cultural union and an economic enterprise. After the 1948 Arab-Israeli War, the fate of the Brotherhood in Gaza became intertwined with its Egyptian counterpart, and that of the Brotherhood in the West Bank with its Jordanian counterpart. Following the ban on the Brotherhood in Egypt in 1954 by President Gamal Abdul Nasser, the Brotherhood in Gaza went underground. This gave a chance to such newly established, secular political parties as Fatah and the Arab Nationalist Movement to grow. These groups drew most of their support from the Palestinian refugee camps where political consciousness and anti-Israeli sentiment were high. In contrast, native Gazans, many of them possessing arable land or real estate, were less militant in their feelings against Israel. Socially conservative, they were able to maintain their traditions, having been spared displacement from their native villages and towns. So they were more likely to back the Muslim Brotherhood than secular ANM or Fatah.

The situation changed with the Israeli occupation in 1967. The upsurge in guerrilla activities by the secular Palestinian groups induced severe repression by General Ariel Sharon from 1970 onwards. The Brotherhood's leader,

Shaikh Ahmad Yasin, urged his followers to purge society of social-moral ills and lead pious lives, arguing that
Islamization of society was a precondition for the establishment of an Islamic state in a liberated Palestine, thus skirting
the contentious issue of resistance to Israeli occupation. After
Sharon had retired from the IDF in the summer of 1973,
the Israeli Government thought it prudent to allow Gazans
limited freedom of association – in socio-religious matters.
It therefore issued a licence to Yasin in the autumn of 1973
to establish the Islamic Centre as a charity to run social,
religious and welfare institutions such as schools, clinics
and mosques, thus authorizing it to receive zakat (Arabic,
derivative of zakaa, to be pure), religious tax, amounting to
2.5 per cent of income, from the believers. The Israeli move
was in line with its general policy of favouring traditional,
conservative Arab institutions and leaders under its rule.

Following the quadrupling of petroleum prices in 1973–4,
private and official sources in the oil rich Gulf monarchies,
including Palestinian expatriates who had flourished there,
became important funders of the Islamic Centre. With the
PLO emerging as the dominant powerful force in the Occupied Territories from the mid-1970s, Israel decided to encourage the growth of the Islamic Centre. Brigadier-General
Yitzhak Segev, the then military governor of the Gaza Strip,
told David K. Shipler, the Jerusalem Bureau chief of the
New York Times during 1979–84, how 'he had financed
the Islamic movement as a counter-weight to the PLO and
the Communists: "The Israeli Government gave me a budget
and the military government gives to the mosques." '4 The
mosques to which Brigadier-General Segev channelled the
government cash were the ones run by the Islamic Centre.
In 1980, when the Muslim fundamentalists burnt down
the Red Crescent Society in Gaza city (funded indirectly
by the PLO), run by Dr Haidar Abdul Shafi, a pro-PLO
politician, the IDF looked the other way. The IDF-Shin Beth
complicity with the Islamic Centre was confirmed by Moshe
Arens, defence minister from February 1983 to September
1984. 'There is no doubt that during a certain period the
Israeli Governments perceived it [Islamic fundamentalism] as

a healthy phenomenon that could counter the PLO,' he said. 'There even was a certain attempt by the army and Shabak [i.e., Shin Beth] to encourage the Islamic fundamentalists against the PLO.'[5] Towards the end of Arens' tenure as defence minister, the Israeli Government began altering its policy, partly because another, recently established Muslim fundamentalist organization, the Islamic Jihad, had taken to following a militantly anti-Israeli stance.

In April 1984 the Israeli authorities arrested Yasin, now confined to a wheelchair, for illegal possession of arms, and sentenced him to 13 years in jail. But in May 1985 he was freed as part of a prisoner exchange deal between Israel and the Popular Front for the Liberation of Palestine-General Command. On his release Yasin resumed his social work from the head office of the Islamic Centre in the poor Jawrat al Shams district of Gaza city with the focus on turning Palestinians away from secularism. But when the intifada erupted in late 1987, Yasin and his colleagues in the Islamic Centre leadership could no longer resist pressure from their nationalistic grass roots to engage in a political struggle against the Israeli occupiers. The result was the founding of Hamas as the activist arm of the Islamic Centre/Muslim Brotherhood.

In August 1988 the Hamas leadership issued a Charter, which set out its ideology and basic policies, and which deserved comparison with the 1968 Palestine National Charter of the PLO. (At about the same time it set up its clandestine armed wing, the Izz al Din Qassam Brigade.) Describing Hamas as part of the Muslim Brotherhood, an international body, the Charter stated that 'it is a distinctly Palestinian movement that gives allegiance to God, regards Islam as a way of life, and works to raise the banner of God over every inch of Palestine'. The Charter reaffirmed Hamas's allegiance to the Muslim Brotherhood credo: 'God is the goal; the Prophet is the model; the Quran is the constitution; the jihad is the path; and death in jihad is our most sublime aspiration.' More specifically, it stated: 'The Land of Palestine is an Islamic waqf (trust) for Muslim generations until the Day of Judgement. It is inadmissible to abandon whole or part of it, or to concede it wholly or partly . . . No organization, whether Palestinian or Arab, has the right to concede Palestine wholly or partly.' Indeed, the Charter added: 'Abandoning any part of Palestine is an abandonment of a part of religion. The patriotism of Hamas is part of its religion. Only a jihad can solve the Palestinian issue.' In the liberation of Palestine, it stated, each of the three factors – Palestinian, Arab and Islamic – had a role to play. While describing the PLO 'as a father, brother, relative or friend' of Hamas, the Charter distanced Hamas from its secularism: 'Secular thought is incompatible with religious thought, completely incompatible . . . [W]e cannot abandon the present and future Islamism of Palestine in order to endorse secular thought. The Islamism of Palestine is a part of our religion.' The Charter assigned a role to the Arab and Muslim countries. 'The Arab states surrounding Israel should open their borders to the *mujahedin* (those conducting jihad) of the Arab and Muslim peoples so that they play their role and add their effort to the effort of their brothers, the Muslim Brotherhood in Palestine,' read the Charter. 'As for other Arab and Islamic nations, they should facilitate the *mujahedin* movement.'[6]

These abstract statements had practical implications. For example, the Muslim Brotherhood in Jordan came to play a pivotal role in the life of Hamas. During his visits to Jordan (then Transjordan) between 1942 and 1945, Hassan al Banna set up Brotherhood branches in many Jordanian towns. When the Brotherhood was dissolved in Egypt in 1954, hundreds of its activists went into exile in other Arab states, including Jordan. Since King Hussein of Jordan was one of the Arab leaders Nasser tried to overthrow, the Jordanian Brotherhood turned increasingly pro-Hussein. When his throne was threatened by opposition demonstrations in 1956, it actively sided with him. In return Hussein's ban on political parties in 1957 exempted the Brotherhood on the ground that it had been registered as a religious charity. During the decade after the 1967 Arab-Israeli War, with the star of Saudi Arabia ascendant in the region, King Hussein grew closer to Riyadh for financial and ideological reasons, and began co-opting Brotherhood leaders into his regime. Their freedom of action enabled them to provide organizational and other backup to the Muslim Brotherhood/ Islamic Centre in the West Bank and Gaza. Since then the Jordanian and Palestinian sections of the Muslim Brotherhood have worked together closely even when their assessments of the Palestinian situation have been far from identical.

In practical terms, the programme of the Hamas Charter could be summarized thus: a short-term aim of reversing Israel's occupation of the West Bank, Gaza and Greater East Jerusalem, and founding an Islamic state there, approved by a referendum; and a long-term objective of establishing an Islamic state in all of (mandate) Palestine. Thus there was a parallel here with the June 1974 resolution of the Palestine National Council which accepted the idea of a mini-state in the West Bank and Gaza, albeit as a transient entity, to be used to liberate all of mandate Palestine.

When it came to participating in the intifada, Hamas used the same methods for mobilizing its supporters – leaflets, communiqués, graffiti, demonstrations and strikes – as the PLO's United National Leadership of the Uprising. It distributed official communiqués as leaflets, 100 of them between early 1988 and mid-1993. But unlike their PLO counterparts, Hamas communiqués started with the Islamic invocation of 'In the Name of God, the Merciful, the Compassionate', and contained Quranic verses as well as allusions to Muslim practices and events in Islamic history. Similarly, the Hamas graffiti, often written in green, were different from those of the main PLO factions. They concentrated on three major themes: (a) Islam and Palestine, (b) Jews and Israel, and (c) responses to events and/or calls for action. The most popular slogans in (a) were: 'Our land is Islamic, this is the identity'; 'Islam is the solution, jihad is the way'; 'The Land of Palestine is an Islamic waqf; the Islamic Law forbids its abandonment or bargaining over it'; and 'Revolution, revolution against the occupier; there is no solution except the Quran.' And the most frequent slogans in (b) were: 'No to the Zionist entity'; 'O Jews, leave our land'; 'The destruction of Israel is a Quranic inevitability'; and 'Khaibar, Khaibar, O Jews,

Muhammad's army will return' – a reference to the Battle of Khaibar when Prophet Muhammad defeated the Jewish tribes in the region of Medina.[7]

What further distinguished Hamas from the PLO was its use of the mosque, an ubiquitous institution. In the Gaza Strip there were some 600 mosques: that is, one mosque for every 1,600 Muslim Palestinians. The proportionate figure for the West Bank was half as much. The Gaza Strip was dotted with newly built mosques, their glittering white minarets like powerful sentinels, an antithesis to the dereliction often surrounding them. Many of these places of worship, especially in Gaza, became known as the strongholds of Hamas or the Islamic Jihad. Hamas turned these venues of prayer and religious learning into places of political activity and assembling points for marches and demonstrations. Also Hamas often combined street protest with religious anniversaries or events in Islamic history. Thus it had an advantage over the PLO factions which, being secular, were averse to using mosques or churches, or religious anniversaries, to political ends. Furthermore, as a religio-spiritual movement, Hamas provided a balm for the confused, agitated minds of Palestinian youths. 'Since June 1988, scores of people from all walks of life (religious and non-religious, poor, well-to-do, educated and non-educated, merchants, businessmen, and even some Christians) visited the home of Shaikh Ahmad Yasin, seeking his good offices, on a daily basis,' noted Professor Ziad Abu Amr. 'During the intifada, most of the Israeli-controlled government institutions, including courts, were practically shut down. The secrecy of the [banned] PLO factions and the fact that they do not enjoy spiritual authority increased the demand for the arbitration of the Hamas leaders. While resort to Hamas undermined the authority of the Israeli occupation, it also undermined the authority of the PLO and nationalist institutions.'[8] Also the influence of young Hamas activists in the Islamic hierarchy began rising at the expense of the old, traditional leaders who in the West Bank depended on Jordan for their salaries. Alarmed at this, Israel formally banned Hamas in May 1989.

A year earlier on 1 June, Israeli defence minister, Yitzhak

Rabin, had a meeting with Dr Mahmoud Zahar. The latter proposed a three-stage solution to the Palestinian problem: (1) Israel to declare its intention to evacuate the Occupied Territories and restore Palestinian rights, with the withdrawal to be completed within a few months, and the Palestinian territories to be transferred either to the United Nations, European Community or Arab League; (2) Palestinians to choose their representatives by means to be decided to the satisfaction of all parties, with no input by Israel; and (3) the final settlement to be negotiated by the Palestinian representatives and Israel.[9]

In early April 1989, Premier Yitzhak Shamir, in consultation with Rabin, offered elections in the Occupied Territories, but without any mention of Israel's intention to withdraw from the territories, followed by a handover to an international or regional body, as Zahar had proposed. Therefore Hamas's Communiqué No. 40, dated 17 April 1989, stated: 'Our enemy will not concede anything to us except by force. We call on our sons to be fully on guard against anything our crafty enemy proposes. Let our slogan be "No!" to the initiatives of Rabin and Shamir, and "No!" to elections until the occupation is banished.'[10]

Hamas combined its opposition to Israel with a critical stance towards the PLO. When the PNC proclaimed the founding of the State of Palestine at its session in Algiers in November 1988, Yasin regarded the declaration premature. 'We have not liberated any part of our country upon which we could found our state,' he said in an interview with *Al Islam wa Falastin* (Arabic, Islam and Palestine) magazine. 'We must have land upon which we can stand in freedom and establish our state without prior conditions and without concessions.'[11]

With the intifada intensifying, and Hamas acquiring a solid constituency of its own, the Israeli authorities decided to act against this fast emerging Islamist force. In mid-May 1989 they arrested more than 250 Hamas activists, including Yasin. He was charged with conspiring to abduct and murder two IDF soldiers, and attack the Palestinian collaborators with Israel. Replying to the charges against him in the Gaza military court, Yasin reasoned that the Palestinian people preferred non-violent means to achieve their liberation, and that they resorted to violence in self-defence and only after having concluded that their Israeli occupiers understood nothing but force and violence. As a people under occupation, Palestinians had no choice but to resort to any and every means, violent or peaceful, to offer resistance, and participate in the intifada with the aim of ending oppression and corruption, and instituting justice. He cited chapter 57, entitled Iron, verses 25–7 of the Quran:

Indeed, We sent Our Messengers with clear signs,
and We sent down with them the Book and the Balance
so that men might uphold justice.
And We sent down iron, wherein is great might,
and many uses for men,
and so that God might know who helps Him and His
    Messengers,
in the Unseen.
Surely God is All-strong, All-mighty.
And We sent Noah, and Abraham,
and We appointed the Prophecy and the Book to be
    among the seed;
and some of them are guided,
and many of them are ungodly.

Since Islam required the believer to struggle for justice, and fight those who defended and perpetrated oppression (occupation in the case of Palestinians) with weapons, no matter what their faith or belief, Yasin continued, he and other members of Hamas had no choice but to resort to arms. Yasin was convicted and sentenced to 15 years imprisonment. This raised the eminence of Yasin among his followers. The image of 53-year-old Yasin, a sad-eyed, hawk nosed, figure with a sparse salt-and-pepper beard and a round white-cloth cap covering fully his balding head, became a frequent feature of Hamas leaflets and other literature as well as wall graffiti.

The presidency of Hamas passed to Dr Abdul Aziz Rantisi,

a plump paediatrician, whose bearded, bespectacled face, topped with a furry cap, would become a familiar image on the newscasts of international television channels in late 1992–early 1993, after he had been elected the leader by the 400-plus Islamists deported by Israel to Marj al Zuhur in south Lebanan. Born in the village of Javne south of Jaffa in 1947, his family took shelter in the Khan Yunis refugee camp during the 1948 Arab-Israeli War. Having joined Alexandria University in Egypt on a scholarship during the period of Egyptian administration of the Gaza Strip, he continued his studies there after the Strip had fallen into Israeli hands in 1967. He came under the influence of the (banned) Muslim Brotherhood in Egypt. After his return home, he worked as a paediatrician at the Khan Yunis hospital, and was also involved with the Islamic Centre's health care programmes. He was close to Shaikh Yasin. As a result of his arrests and detentions, which started in 1984, he spent three years behind bars. After dismissal from his job at the Khan Yunis hospital for encouraging fellow doctors not to pay taxes to the Israeli military government in 1984, he opened a private clinic, and became head of the medical department of the Islamic University, Gaza, in 1986. During the intifada he served two periods of administrative detention.

Like his predecessor, Rantisi continued close co-operation with the Muslim Brotherhood in Jordan. During the 1990 Kuwait crisis, followed by the Gulf War in early 1991, the Jordanian Brotherhood, deviating from its traditional pro-Saudi stance, supported Iraqi President Saddam Hussein. In this it had the overwhelming backing of the Palestinians in Jordan. The support for Saddam Hussein among the Palestinians of the Occupied Territories was almost unanimous. This enabled Hamas and the Jordanian Brotherhood to strengthen their traditional ties, and lessened tensions between Hamas and the PLO to the extent that the former expressed interest in joining the Palestine National Council. Ibrahim Ghoshe, the official spokesman of Hamas in Jordan, met Arafat in the Yemeni capital of Sanaa in early September 1991. But nothing came of it since Arafat regarded Hamas's demand of 40 per cent of the PNC seats as excessive.

However, going by the number of prisoners and detainees in Israeli jails, Hamas was second only to Fatah, the predominant constituent of the PLO. 'With Hamas in the forefront, the [Muslim] Brotherhood could achieve, in less than four years [since its founding], the kind of credibility, popularity and legitimacy the PLO had earned over two decades,' wrote Professor Ziad Abu Amr.[12] Though Hamas constantly reiterated its religious ideology what swelled its ranks had more to do with its radicalism *per se* rather than its Islamism. Shaikh Yasin was more of a political figure than a religious luminary who had made an original doctrinal contribution to Islam like Ayatollah Ruholla Khomeini (1902–89) or Shaikh Sayyid Qutb (1906–66) of Egypt.

Once the PNC at its session in late September 1991 had sanctioned the Palestinian participation in the international Peace Conference on the Middle East in Madrid, the scene was set for a confrontation between the PLO's dominant faction, Fatah, and Hamas. The denouement came in mid-1992 in the Gaza Strip with bloody clashes between the two parties. Mediation by local leaders and Arab Israeli MKs helped to cool tempers. But the basic contradictions remained, with Hamas now engraved as a more radical and more ideological group than any secular faction.

Hamas used the period around the fifth anniversary of the intifada, 9 December 1992, observed by a general strike by Palestinians, to rekindle the uprising. Between 7 and 13 December, the members of its Qassam Brigade attacked IDF patrol Jeeps in Gaza and Hebron, killing four soldiers, and kidnapped a border police officer, Nissim Toledano, in Lod. They offered to exchange him for their leader, Shaikh Yasin. When Premier Yitzhak Rabin refused, they killed Toledano. Rabin, who was also defence minister, arrested some 1,200 members of Hamas and the Islamic Jihad, and expelled about a third of them to the no-man's land in south Lebanon. Most of the deportees were professionals – doctors, engineers, schoolteachers, journalists, lawyers and university professors. Among those who condemned this action, and demanded the immediate return of the Palestinians to their homes, was the United Nations Security Council, which

reaffirmed the applicability of the Fourth Geneva Convention of 1949 to the Palestinian territories occupied by
Israel since 1967. As it had done numerous times before,
the Israeli Government ignored the unanimously adopted
Security Council resolution. However, later Rabin and his
cabinet colleagues came to regret the deportations which,
unwittingly, did more to swell the ranks of the Islamist
organizations than any of their own recruiting drives.

Among the expellees was Shaikh Bassam Jarrar, a resident
of Al Bireh in the West Bank. A slim, tallish man in his
mid-40s, he sported a dense black beard and dashing good
looks. In his dark corduroy trousers and a black polo-neck
sweater, he could be mistaken for an Italian or French movie
director, filming on location. But Jarrar was more bookish
than artistic. An impressive collection of leather-bound volumes neatly stored inside locked, glass-fronted cupboards in
his drawing room was a testimony of his scholarship. Son of
a shopkeeper in Ramallah, he grew up as a brilliant student,
with an avid interest in religion. He pursued his inclination at
Damascus University, where he graduated in Islamic studies
in 1973. On his return home, he began teaching religious
studies first at a secondary school, and then at the Ramallah
Teachers' Training College. Like most educated Palestinians
of his generation, he was intensely political, and started out
by backing the PLO at a time when the occupying Israeli
authorities considered it as their foremost enemy. But once
the PLO was expelled from Beirut to Tunis in 1982, his
loyalty to it began to wane. He turned increasingly to the
Islamic Centre/Muslim Brotherhood, which was allowed to
function in the Occupied Territories. His tentative backing
for the Islamic Centre solidified into a commitment once
the intifada erupted in late 1987 and Islamic Centre leaders
founded Hamas.

For Jarrar, the intifada meant five periods of administrative
detention. 'The last time was in April 1994, and I was
freed four months later,' he told me. 'My deportation to
south Lebanon along with 400 others lasted a year. With
administrative detention you know you'll be released after
six months. But deportation is a leap in the dark. When you

are deported you know that you'll be away from your country and your family for several years, or even for ever. It is only because our deportation caught international attention, and the western media followed our fate, that the Israelis relented. They let us back home.'

How would he describe his experience in south Lebanon, I asked. 'We were in the Lebanese mountains in the middle of winter, and in difficult physical conditions, facing the prospect of never returning home. But the overall experience was enriching to us. We felt like we were in the middle of a war, war of the media. In it we achieved a lot. The media gave us a chance to express our thoughts to the whole world. We told the world what was going on in the Israeli Occupied Territories. That way we got in touch with the Lebanese people, with the Arab people and other peoples. More than 1,100 foreign delegations came to see us near Marj Zuhur in one year of our detention – that is three every day. This gave a boost to the Islamic movement throughout the Arab world and the Muslim world.' What was your message? 'We gave a clear picture of the Palestinian cause, what this conflict meant to them. We had useful dicsussions among ourselves. We set up classes, and many of the detainees took courses in subjects they did not know before. Overall, Israel's attempts to portray Palestinians as hardline fundamentalists failed miserably.'

Indeed later, General Danny Rothschild, the military governor of the Occupied Palestinian Territories, admitted publicly that the expulsion of 400 Muslim fundamentalists in December 1992 was meant to help the PLO, and that it was a total failure.

Actually, the Israeli action proved counter-productive. It brought the PLO and Hamas together. The Hamas leaders based in Jordan (Ibrahim Ghoshe), Syria (Dr Musa Abu Mazruq and Muhammad Nazal) and Iran (Imad al Alami) – as well as the leading figures of the secular radical Palestinian groups, based in Damascus – flew to Tunis for a meeting with Yasser Arafat. Together they formed three committees to deal respectively with the fate of the Islamist expellees, and intra-Palestinian relations inside the Occupied Territories and outside. The Hamas team then flew to Khartoum, the capital of Sudan, ruled by an Islamist military regime, to discuss the possibility of Hamas joining the Palestine National Council. However the Hamas delegation's demand that it be allocated 40 per cent of the seats in the 483-member PNC was once again judged to be unreasonable.

Israel's lifting of the ban on the PLO in January 1993 made Hamas, still outlawed, a distinctly radical organization. Its appeal increased as the Gaza Strip slid deeper into violence in March. Opposed to talks between the Palestinian and Israeli delegations in Washington, it actively supported a general strike call on the eve of the ninth round of negotiations in late April. Israel intensified its repression of Hamas. In early August the Qassam Brigade, the military wing of Hamas, killed three IDF soldiers in attacks near Jerusalem and Tulkarm.

After the Oslo Accord

Expectedly, Hamas rejected the Oslo Accord, which resulted in the virtual break-up of the PLO, with six of its 10 constituents opposing the agreement. These secular factions, most of them based in Damascus, decided to ally with Hamas under the umbrella of the Palestinian Forces Alliance. At the same time a determined effort was made to avert intra-Palestinian violence. The initiative came from Hamas and Fatah prisoners who issued a statement against the resort to violence by those who had responded differently to the Oslo Accord. It was backed among others by Dr Rantisi, the Hamas leader, from his mountainside exile in south Lebanon.

After this agreement with the PLO, the IDF intensified efforts to decimate Hamas and Islamic Jihad militants, and even Fatah Hawks. On 24 November the IDF's undercover Samson Unit killed Imad Aql, a 24-year-old resident of Jabaliya camp, in a Gaza city suburb. Regarded as the commander of the Qassam Brigade in the Gaza Strip, he had been accused of killing a dozen Israeli soldiers and four Palestinian collaborators. Premier Rabin publicly praised his assassination. But the Samson Unit did not stop at eradicating radical Islamists. It went on to settle scores with Fatah Hawks, even though, in accordance with the Oslo Accord, they had been turning over weapons to the IDF under an amnesty plan, a policy which had revived friction between them and the Qassam Brigade of Hamas.

But the massacre of Muslims at Hebron's Ibrahimi Mosque by Dr Baruch Goldstein on 25 February 1994 reversed the divisive trend in the Fatah-Hamas relationship. The Hebron event made all Palestinian factions close ranks. Due to the constraints of the Oslo Accord, Fatah Hawks could not threaten vengeance against Jewish Israelis, at least publicly. But Hamas was under no such restraint. It promised to avenge the Hebron killings by carrying out five operations against Israeli targets.

Its first attack came on 6 April. A Qassam Brigade member, with explosives strapped to his waist, blew himself up in a bus in Afula, north Israel, and left seven Israelis dead. The second Hamas suicide bomb explosion occurred a week later at the bus station of Hadera, central Israel, killing five. According to the Israeli intelligence, both these bombs had the imprint of Yahya Ayash. Born in 1966 in the village of Rafat near Ramallah, Yahya was a son of a well-to-do farmer, Abdul Latif Ayash. After his secondary education he went to Birzeit University where he combined his electrical engineering course with chemistry, a combination which turned him into an innovative bomb-maker, and earned him the nickname 'The Engineer' for his skill in detonating unsual cocktails of chemicals. He became active in the intifada in 1990–91, and went underground in 1992. Pursued relentlessly by the IDF's undercover unit for the West Bank, codenamed 'Cherry', since 1993, he escaped death or arrest several times. After the Cairo Agreement of May 1994, he slipped into the Gaza Strip, thus putting himself, technically, out of the reach of Israel. However, since his parents and his two brothers – as well as his wife, Ayisha, and their two sons – continued to live in Rafat, which was under Israeli control, the security and intelligence agencies kept them and their farmhouse under constant watch. Once when an IDF unit searched the house in the middle of the night, but failed to find Ayash, it smashed all the furniture. The Israeli interception of the family members' telephone conversations and 24-hour surveillance continued, an exercise which in the coming months was to prove fruitful.

The Gaza Strip in which Ayash found a niche was now a place where, chastened by the Hebron killings, and the assassination of six of their comrades by the IDF's Samson Unit in March 1994,[13] the Fatah Hawks had signed an amity pact with the Qassam Brigade in April. They agreed to co-ordinate the strike days, stop defaming one another, and halt assassinating Palestinian collaborators.

More importantly, though, once the PLO had established the Palestinian Authority in Gaza in July 1994, Hamas had to grapple with defining its relationship with the PA which, being an instrument of the PLO, was committed to 'a peaceful resolution of conflict between the two sides'. From then on, Palestinian-Israeli relations were determined not merely by what the PA and Israel did, but also by what Hamas did.

Indeed by kidnapping an IDF soldier, Nachshon Waxman, and exploding a suicide bomb on a bus in downtown Tel Aviv, in October 1994, Hamas acquired the initiative it did not possess before. The Tel Aviv bombing was the most violent attack in Israel for the past 16 years. Whereas Jewish Israelis condemned the terroristic outrage unanimously and unequivocally, Palestinians were divided in their opinion. PA officials expressed sorrow and condemnation, but the prevalent view among young Palestinians was altogether different. 'The Hamas gunmen are wildly popular, particularly among the young who see the underground guerrillas as role models,' reported Said Ghazali of Associated Press from Gaza. 'The Israeli occupation for 27 years has left deep scars, and many Palestinians still remember humiliations at the hands of the Jewish soldiers. The Izz al Din Qassam Brigade's guerrillas are seen as heroes who stand up to the hated occupiers and right past wrongs.' Faraj Dababesh, a 20-year-old student, told Ghazali: 'The children here are taught the songs of the Qassam Brigade. Don't forget people here learn the tactics of Hamas in the mosques.' Since two-fifths of the mosques in the Gaza Strip were under Hamas influence, the implication of the above statement could not be overstated.

With the internal security of Gaza now in the hands of the PA, Israel felt hidebound. So it intensified its anti-Islamist efforts in the West Bank and Greater East Jerusalem. As described earlier, the tit-for-tat between the Qassam Brigade and the Israeli administration translated into a violent confrontation between Hamas and the PA in mid-November.[14] But as before in the case of Hamas and Fatah, now Hamas and the PA pulled back from the abyss of a civil war. In the complex relationship that had developed between the PA, Hamas and Israel, the PA faced a grave dilemma. 'We made peace with our enemy of 47 years, not to make enemies of our own brothers,' said Nabil Shaath, Minister of Planning and International Co-operation in the PA cabinet, and a senior aide to Arafat. 'Once we really resist them [the Islamic radicals] on the street, they're willing to kill us too . . . If we arrest them, we look like human rights violators, Uncle Toms and lackeys of the Israelis.'[15]

While the PA and Fatah had to grapple with this intractable problem, Hamas consolidated its position as the leading constituent of the 10-member Palestinian Forces Alliance based on the rejection of the Oslo Accord. In late December 1994 its representatives attended the PFA meeting in Damascus. They did not shed many tears when the participants concluded that their earlier plan to launch an alternative Palestine Liberation Organization had proved still-born due to lack of funds from Libya or Iran. They concurred with the PFA's decision not to participate in the election for the Palestinian Council to be established under the Oslo Accord. But they found the PFA's resolution of no talks with the PA Chairman, Arafat, puzzling. Indeed, the headquarters of the Popular Front for the Liberation of Palestine and the Democratic Front for the Liberation of Palestine had already dispatched much of their personnel to the Gaza Strip, who had contacted Arafat. However, popular backing for these secular, rejectionist groups was minimal. Hamas was by far the leading opponent of the Oslo Accord, followed way behind by the Islamic Jihad.

The Jihad impinged strongly on the popular psyche on

22 January 1995 when two of its young activists, Anwar Sakura and Salah Shaker, both Gazans, blew themselves up at a bus stop at Beit Lid near Natanya, killing 19 Israeli soldiers instantly and two later.[16] The bombers and their planners had chosen their target and timing carefully. On Sunday mornings, all over Israel, thousands of young IDF personnel use buses to return to their bases after spending the Sabbath at home.

'The Islamic Jihad only aims at Israeli military targets,' stated Fathi Abdul Aziz Shikaki, the exiled Jihad leader based in Damascus. 'We are freedom fighters resisting Israeli occupation.' Responding to the carnage caused by the Beit Lid bombs, he said, 'We want Israelis to share our pain'.[17] In other words, in the view of Shikaki as well as other militant Palestinian leaders, terrorism was an effective tool of the oppressed because it was a leveller of the oppressor's superiority. In the Shajaiye neighbourhood of Gaza city, the preacher at the main mosque, Shaikh Abdullah Shami, an Islamic Jihad leader, who had known Anwar Sakura, a neighbour, for several years, said: 'The Israelis have caused immeasurable suffering to the Palestinians, and deserve to be attacked until all the [Palestinian] refugees have returned to their homes in Palestine.' With his thick black beard, thin-framed glasses, intelligent looks, a skullcap and a black cloak, 40-year-old Shami might be mistaken for a Jewish zealot. In his interview with the *Jerusalem Post* – popular with the English-speaking Jewish settlers in the Palestinian territories – after the Beit Lid bombings, he was surprisingly candid. When asked by the reporter, Jon Immanuel, why Islamic Jihad attacks had become more violent while the suffering imposed on Palestinians had declined from what it had been during the intifada, Shami replied: 'First we had knives, then we got guns, then bombs, now car bombs.'[18]

Actually, in the region it was the Lebanese Muslim militants who were the first to resort to suicide bombing. On 18 April 1983 they used suicide truck-bombing against the United States embassy in West Beirut, killing 63 people, including 17 Americans, several of them employees of the US Central Intelligence Agency. A more sensational attack followed on 23 October when the truck-bombing of the US and French military headquarters in West Beirut left 300 American and French troops dead. The person who killed himself/herself in the process was regarded by Islamists as a martyr in the path of God, a lofty ideal, described in the Quran (Chapter 3 'The House of Imran': verse 164) thus:

Count not those who were slain in God's way as dead,
but rather living with their Lord, by Him provided,
rejoicing in the bounty that God has given them,
and joyful in those who remain behind and have not
    joined them,
because no fear shall be on them, neither shall they
    sorrow,
joyful in blessing and bounty from God,
and that God leaves not to waste the wage of the believers.

The method of being killed in 'God's way' varied. Since suicide committed by the blasting of explosives, either strapped to the body of a person or carried in a vehicle driven by him/her, was a recent phenomenon it had caused debate in religious circles. An article, entitled 'A Reading in the Islamic Law of Martyrdom' – printed in a Cyprus-based Arabic weekly, *Al Islam wa Falastin*, in mid-1988 – gave an exposition of the subject. 'Perhaps it is a blessing of God Almighty bestowed upon one *mujahid* [one who conducts jihad] or two *mujahedin*, enabling him or them to charge against the enemy's position, or against a concentration of enemy military forces on a martyrdom mission, assaulting with explosives, smashing down everything around them, inflicting the heaviest losses, breaking down the enemy's morale and determination in the face of this Islamic spirit of martyrdom which cannot be resisted,' wrote the anonymous author. 'At the same time it increases fear of Muslims after a long period of weakness and humiliation, and it increases the volunteers for martyrdom who seek jihad in the way of God.'[19]

Since the suicide bombers had come from the Gaza Strip, the fledgeling Palestinian Authority in Gaza had to respond to this terroristic action. Its police picked up many Islamic Jihad activists in the Gaza Strip, including Ala Siftawi, the editor-proprietor of *Al Istiqlal*, a weekly founded in September 1994. It banned the magazine. Siftawi spent six weeks in jail, and his weekly remained closed for nearly two months.

In Gaza city I picked up the 12-page *Al Istiqlal* of 17 March, the first issue after it had been unbanned. ' "No" for killing words and breaking the pen' read the defiant headline of its front page editorial. I met Siftawi at his modest, ground floor office in Luzone Building on Al Wahidi Street, a busy thoroughfare. Above his neat desk, a large black-and-white photograph of a dashing, young man stared at me. He was Shaheed (Martyr) Hani Abid, the Islamic Jihad activist killed by the Shin Beth four months before, who still appeared as the *rais* (Arabic, chairman/managing editor) of *Al Istiqlal* along with the editor and the proprietor. In his mid-30s, the bespectacled, bearded Siftawi was wearing a white shirt and jeans. It was hard to believe that this mild-mannered man had planned a successful jailbreak, along with five other Islamic Jihad activists, from Gaza central jail six years before – an achievement which had turned him and others into overnight heroes. He escaped to Damascus where he became a journalist, slipping back into the Gaza Strip soon after the Palestinian Authority was installed there. His Islamic orientation was a divergence from the politics of his father, Assad, a school headmaster, who was a co-founder of Fatah and the PLO in the Gaza Strip, and a contemporary and friend of Arafat. But Ala came under the influence of Dr Fathi Abdul Aziz Shikaki, a co-founder, with Shaikh Abdul Aziz Audah, of the Islamic Jihad in the early 1980s.

As it was, Dr Shikaki, a bear of a man, bearded and bespectacled, started out as a pan-Arab nationalist, with President Gamal Abdul Nasser as his hero, but became disillusioned with him after the 1967 Arab defeat, and joined the Muslim Brotherhood. Born in 1942 into a poor family in Zarnuqa village near Ramle in Palestine, his parents fled to the Gaza Strip in 1948, and lived in Rafah refugee camp. After obtaining an undergraduate degree in mathematics from Birzeit University, he worked as a teacher. In the mid-1970s he joined Zigazig University in Egypt for a medical degree. He came under the influence of Shaikh Sayyid Qutb, a radical Islamic thinker. In his *Signposts along the Road*, published in the early 1950s, Qutb divided social systems into two categories: the Order of Islam and the Order of Jahiliya (Arabic, Ignorance), which was decadent and ignorant, the type which existed in Arabia before Prophet Muhammad had received the Word of God, when men revered not God but other men disguised as deities. He argued that there was an irreconcilable contradiction between the two systems, between 'the rule of God and the rule of man', and that the existence of one required the destruction of the other. He believed that change came only through the overthrow of authority in the Order of Jahiliya, the current state of Egypt under President Nasser, and that only a 'believing elite', a new generation imbued with Quranic teachings, was capable of leading 'the society of belief' against 'the society of unbelief'.[20] As someone who strongly believed in action, Shikaki admired Ayatollah Ruhollah Khomeini, who led the successful Islamic revolution in Iran against the secular, pro-western regime of Muhammad Reza Shah Pahlavi in early 1979. Later that year Shikaki, still pursuing his medical studies in Egypt, published *Khomeini: The Islamic Solution and Alternative* in Cairo without using his family name. But that did not protect him from arrest. After serving two brief stints in jail, and securing a medical degree from Zigazig University, he returned home. His co-founding of the Islamic Jihad was truly secret. When Shikaki was arrested and sentenced to a year in jail in 1983, it was for incitement against the Israeli occupation and not also for belonging to an illegal organization.

After launching a guerrilla operation against Israel, the organization did not claim responsibility. But the throwing of hand grenades by three Jihad activists at the IDF graduation ceremony at the Western Wall in October 1986 was so sensational that the group could no longer remain anonymous. Following this incident, Shikaki was sentenced to nine years' imprisonment, with five years suspended, on charges of smuggling weapons into the Gaza Strip and belonging to the unlawful Islamic Jihad. While he was in jail, Jihad activists killed Captain Ron Tal, commander of the IDF military police, in August 1987. And in early October they engaged in a gunbattle with an IDF patrol in Gaza city's Shajaiye district, where the main mosque was a Jihad base. It left one IDF officer and three Jihad militants dead. Later Islamic Jihad leaders would claim that their dare-devil actions in the summer and autumn of 1987 created the conditions for the eruption of the intifada. In any event, once the intifada had got going, and the jailed Jihad activists had taken to using prisons and detention centres as recruiting grounds, Israel deported Shikaki to Lebanon in August 1988. From there he moved to Damascus.

By then the Islamic Jihad, a small, cohesive group, had become known for its organizational skills, ideological clarity, tight discipline and strict secrecy. Its icons were Hassan al Banna, Sayyid Qutb, Izz al Din Qassam (with the group's armed wing called the Izz al Din Qassam militia), and Khomeini. It was beholden to Iran, a source of its foreign funds.

In his book on Ayatollah Khomeini, Shikaki quoted approvingly the Ayatollah's call to all Muslims 'to eliminate the core of corruption, Israel', and declared it to be their religious duty to do so. In his pamphlet, *After the Two Catastrophes* (in Arabic), published after the 1967 Arab débâcle, Tawfiq al Tayib, an Islamic ideologue, interpreted the 1948 and 1967 catastrophes as defeats respectively for liberal Arab thought and socialist-revolutionary Arab ideology. 'The Zionist presence in Palestine is an embodiment of the modern western challenge, and an evidence that this challenge still exists,' he wrote. 'The natural reaction to the challenge lies in the Islamic trend which constitutes the defence line. And despite our harsh criticism of this trend, it has played a historic role in the restoration of the psychological balance of both the Islamic community and of the educated Muslim.'[21] Like Tayib, Shikaki and other Jihad theoreticians perceived the implanting of the Zionist entity in the Arab Muslim world as a deliberate western attempt to split the Islamic umma (community) and westernize it with a view to subjugating it materially and spiritually, and paralysing its will.

A story splashed on page seven of the *Al Istiqlal* I had with me fitted the above Islamist thesis: 'Israeli travellers in Jordan: Dancing in Jordanian hotels.'

Just across the road, up a few flights of stairs, in the company of Abdul Hakim al Samra, I was in the offices of *Al Watan* (Arabic, The Nation), the Hamas mouthpiece, established in December 1994. At 16 pages an issue, and a circulation of 10,000, it was more substantial and popular than *Al Istiqlal*. And its young proprietor, Imad Faluji, turned out to have a more colourful background than Siftawi. A man of medium height, richly bearded, his determined face softened by a sensuous mouth, Faluji, 33, looked dapper in his well-pressed dark green trousers, a black shirt with white buttons, and a black jacket with a hint of a white handkerchief in the breast pocket. Behind his large desk was a map of Palestine – identical in layout and scale to the standard map of Israel, issued by the Israeli Tourist Ministry, with the long, tapering Negev Desert, drawn to a reduced scale, tucked into the left-hand bottom corner – with the Dome of the Rock and other Islamic shrines floating in the Mediterranean, and the Palestinian flag aloft in the left-hand corner at the top of a column of information on Palestine printed outside the map.

'After my secondary education I went to the Soviet Union – to Kharkov, Ukraine – to study civil engineering,' he began. 'It was cheaper to study there than anywhere else. I was there from 1981 to 1987. Spent a year learning Russian. Towards the end I began setting up Islamic groups among foreign Muslims and Soviet Muslims. I travelled through seven Soviet republics during holidays, trying to set up Islamic groups. The authorities did not like what I was doing. So in 1987 they put me on a plane to Prague. It was later in that year that the intifada started here. I was involved. I was close to Shaikh Yasin. After his arrest in 1989 I became more involved with Hamas. I was arrested in 1991 and sentenced to six years' imprisonment. I was kept in Gaza central jail. In the course of the prisoner release programme

that followed the Oslo Accord, I was freed in June 1994.'
Did that moderate his opposition to the Oslo Accord? 'No.
The Hamas policy is clear. It wants Israeli withdrawal –
not military redeployment – from the Occupied West Bank,
Gaza and East Jerusalem and from the Jewish settlements, as
a prelude to the founding of a Palestinian state in the West
Bank and Gaza, with East Jerusalem as its capital. That is the
minimum position of Hamas. Actually, nothing more radical
than the [King] Fahd Plan adopted by the Arab League in
September 1982.' What was Hamas's position *vis-à-vis* the
Palestinian Authority, a creature of the Oslo Accord? 'The
PA is Palestinian, and we cannot be against a Palestinian
organization. I went to meet Arafat when he arrived in
Gaza last July. I went as a Hamas leader. The permission
to establish our weekly magazine, *Al Watan*, was given by
Arafat himself, as a paper of the Palestinian opposition.'

But when *Al Watan* began performing its role as an
opposition organ, Arafat hit back hard. In mid-May it
printed a story stating that the PA authorities had tor-
tured and unduly detained Nidal Dababesh – a Hamas
activist injured in a mysterious explosion on 2 April in
an apartment in the Shaikh Radwan suburb of Gaza city
– in order to prevent him from contradicting the PA version
of the event. (It was widely believed that the Palestinian
and Israeli intelligence services had colluded to cause the
explosion in order to kill suspected bomb-makers.) As Interior Minister, Arafat ordered *Al Watan*'s closure for three
months. The PA attorney-general, Khalid Kidre, accused it
of publishing 'seditious material and libelling the PA and
its security apparatus'. Following his arrest, its managing
editor, Sayyid Abu Musammeh, was tried and convicted by
the State Security Court within 24 hours – the trial, held at
midnight, barely lasting a few minutes. He was sentenced to
three years' imprisonment. 'Trials in this Court are grossly
unfair, violating minimum requirements of international
law,' concluded Amnesty International, a London-based
human rights organization, in August 1995. 'State Security
Court trials have been held secretly in the middle of the night.
Many started around midnight, some reportedly lasted only

minutes. Those presiding are security officers who have never before served as judges.'[22] Defendants were not permitted to select their own attorneys, and the court-appointed attorneys were invariably employees of the PA's security forces.

The charges of torture by the PA were borne out by the report published by BeTselem (Hebrew, In the Image [of God]), an Israeli human rights group, in September 1995. It concluded that during July 1994–August 1995 in the Gaza Strip six Palestinians in custody had died of torture, which included beatings, sleep deprivation, lack of medical attention, tying-up and hooding. 'Veterans of Israeli jails make up the rank and file of the PSS [Preventive Security Service],' reported Shyam Bhatia in the *Observer*. 'Palestinians say it is no coincidence that the interrogation methods used by PSS agents mirror the tactics employed by Israel's secret police, the Shabak. Hooding, or covering the victim's head with a sack as he is beaten or questioned, is a trademark of the Shabak. In Arabic this form of torture is known as *shabah*, a word also used for ghosts or ghouls.'[23]

This uncanny parallel between the behaviour of the security forces of Israel and the PA was a symptom of the growing co-operation and co-ordination between the powerful, established state of Israel and the fledgeling Palestinian Authority. 'It is clear to us that the Palestinian Authority is a weak tool in the hands of Israel,' said Faluji. 'So the more Israel puts pressure on the Authority, and in turn on Hamas, the more pressure Hamas will put on Israel. Our rifles can never be trained on the Palestinian Authority. Israel will pay the price for anything the Authority does to us . . . Our jihad is against the Israeli occupation.'[24]

In that jihad, suicide bombs had come to play a central part. It was not accidental that the *Al Watan* of 9 March 1995 carried on its page 6 a glowing report on Yahya Ayash, known by his *nom de guerre* of The Engineer, who had become a legend. Israel's most wanted terrorist had by then become the most elusive. Always one step ahead of the Israeli intelligence and security agencies, he was reported to have successfully passed himself off as an ultra-Orthodox Jew driving a car pasted with ultra-nationalist stickers. Before disguising himself as a woman, it was said, he had mastered a female gait.

The suicide bomb on 24 July on a bus in Ramat Gan, near Tel Aviv, which killed seven Israelis, was attributed to Ayash. Regarding the next such attack, carried out by a female Hamas activist, on a bus number 26 in Jerusalem on 21 August, which left five Israelis dead and another 107 injured, the Shin Beth was unable to decide conclusively whether it was Ayash or one of his star pupils, Muhyi al Din Esharif, a 29-year-old resident of East Jerusalem who, like Ayash, was an electrical engineering graduate.

Since Arafat was anxious not to jeopardize a successful outcome to his talks with Israel on the IDF redployment in the West Bank, as a prelude to elections to the PA's legislative and executive organs, he seriously negotiated a deal with Hamas leaders, encouraging them to cease their violent campaign against Israel. He reached an (unannounced) understanding with them in September that they would suspend their armed acts against Israel while they debated their stance on the forthcoming PA elections. The signing of the Oslo II with Israel in late September strengthened Arafat's hand. He could convincingly argue that Israel was serious about extending self-rule to the West Bank. On 10 October he released such prominent Hamas figures as Mahmoud Zahar and Ahmad Bahar, whom he had jailed in late June. To facilitate the reconciliation process, Israel permitted a Hamas team to leave for Khartoum for consultations with the exiled Hamas leaders, who gathered there from Damascus, Amman, Beirut and Tehran. Since Hamas was open to the Palestinians in the Diaspora, its branches had sprung up in Jordan, Syria and Lebanon. And because of its Islamist ideology it was allowed to open offices in Iran and Sudan, where Islamic fundamentalist regimes were in power. Though Hamas remained a single movement with political and military wings – as was the case with Fatah before the establishment of the Palestinian Authority in July 1994 – its overall leadership came to be viewed as consisting of 'insiders' and 'outsiders'. Among the latter, those based in Amman were still the most important. They were in day-to-day touch with their counterparts from the Muslim Brotherhood of Jordan, the ultimate point of reference for Hamas. But in June, under pressure from Israel and America, King Hussein had expelled Dr Musa Abu Mazruq, head of Hamas's political bureau, to Tehran, thus making the Iranian capital appear more significant than it really was in the case of Hamas. The meeting in Khartoum ended with a decision to explore the details of an agreement with the PA.

In late October Israel allowed Imad Faluji, son of a businessman, to attend the multilateral economic conference in Amman. On 29 October Israeli intelligence sources released the news that three days earlier the Islamic Jihad leader, Dr Fathi Abdul Aziz Shikaki, was assassinated by five bullets in his back, outside a hotel in the Mediterranean island of Malta, fired by two hitmen who escaped on a motorcycle. Shikaki, using a false name and a forged passport, was returning to Damascus after a visit to Libya via Malta. The gleeful hints by Rabin and Peres, attending the economic conference in Amman, of the Mossad's involvement were schizophrenic. While keen to impress Israeli citizens that their campaign against terrorism, conducted energetically and innovatively, was succeeding, they did not wish to confirm official involvement in a murder committed in a foreign country. (It was ironic that Rabin was to fall victim to an assassin's bullets within a week of this event.) The Israeli Government's action reminded the Hamas negotiators with the PA, anew, of the relentless energy with which it pursued its prey. They regarded this a bad omen, but continued their talks with Arafat.

In their consultations with the exiled leadership, the Hamas team seriously considered the idea of Hamas establishing an electoral wing, as a counterpoint to its military wing, to participate in the forthcoming PA poll. As Israel began implementing its military withdrawal from the West Bank cities from mid-November onwards, the climate for a PA-Hamas accord improved. Yet at the meetings held between the two parties in Cairo, away from local pressures, a stalemate ensued. In return for Hamas's acceptance of all the agreements the PLO had signed with Israel, and an undertaking to cease its armed attacks against Israel, its negotiators demanded that Hamas be treated on a par with the PLO, and it should be allowed to retain the right to revive its military struggle against the Jewish state should a radically altered situation in the future so demand. Furthermore, they wanted a cast-iron guarantee that Israel would not pursue the Hamas fugitives it held responsible for past guerrilla operations. Arafat was not in a position to give such an undertaking on his own nor did he expect to receive such a promise from Israel. With this, any chance of Hamas participating in the PA elections under any guise evaporated. As for the Islamic Jihad, committed exclusively to waging an armed struggle against the Israeli occupiers, there was no question of participating in any poll in which there was even the faintest involvement of Israel.

Hamas's position on the PA poll, scheduled for 20 January 1996, remained as Zahar had described it to me in March 1995. 'We say yes, when it comes to electing our representatives at the local and non-governmental organizational [students unions, professional syndicates etc.] levels among Palestinians, living inside and outside Palestine, without any preconditions. As for national elections, if the Israelis are aiming for autonomy for Palestinians under their aegis, then we will not participate.' Why? 'Because we reject the whole idea of autonomy contained in the Oslo Accord. We want national independence. Also because in any such elections "outsider" Palestinians will not be able to participate. If the national level elections are for independence, and not autonomy, and are held by an international body like the United Nations, then we will participate.'

Any lingering hope that Hamas would soften its stance disappeared on 5 January 1996. At about nine a.m. that day there was a call for Yahya Ayash on a mobile phone number (050) 507487 in the Gaza Strip. His host and a friend from his university days, Osama Hamad, picked up the phone, and gave it to Ayash, because the call was from his father, Abdul Latif, in Rafat. Hamad left the room. Five minutes later when he returned, he found Ayash lying in a pool of blood, with his head blown off.

When Ayash had first approached Osama Hamad in June 1995 for refuge in his house in Beit Lahiya village, the latter was then employed by his 43-year-old uncle, Kamal, an affluent building contractor in Gaza city. Osama Hamad reportedly warned Ayash that his uncle was not 'clean', that is, he had contacts with the Shin Beth. Yet, inexplicably, Ayash chose not only to ignore the warning but also, contrary to the practice by fugitives, stayed on in the same house for a long time. After Osama had finished working for his uncle, the latter gave him a mobile phone to keep in touch. On 4 January, Osama Hamad was to recall later, his uncle asked for the phone, which he later returned the same day. It was during this period that the Shin Beth agent(s) either planted a miniature 56-gramme bomb inside the old telephone, or replaced it with a rigged phone. The bomb was detonated while Ayash conversed with his father the next morning by a signal broadcast to it over the mobile telephone network. This was made possible by the fact that the cellular phone networks in the Gaza Strip and West Bank were owned and operated by Israeli companies. The disappearance of Kamal Hamad, who left behind his luxurious Mercedes-Benz and cream-coloured stone house, confirmed his involvement as an Israeli collaborator. Reports in the Hebrew press mentioned a fee of $1 million for his services and a forged passport with a United States visa. Many Palestinians were shocked to discover that the Islamic movement had been so deeply penetrated by the Shin Beth.

As soon as the news of Ayash's murder broke, shops and businesses in the Gaza Strip and West Bank closed down in mourning. The two-storey farmhouse of his parents in Rafat was draped with a green Hamas flag. It was a Friday, the holy day of Islam. Soon the air was filled with readings of the Quran broadcast over the loudspeakers attached to the minarets of the mosques. The preachers delivering their sermons after the Friday noon prayers focussed on Ayash's life, portraying him as a hero of resistance against the oppressive Zionist occupiers, who had repeatedly outwitted the mighty intelligence-security apparatus of Israel and carried the fight to the Israeli heartland. By introducing the suicide bomb –

a weapon of fiendish power against which there seemed no protection – into the Palestinian struggle, and proving himself also to be an adept bomb-maker and a recruiter of martyrs, he had single-handedly changed the power equation, where hitherto the Palestinians had been almost powerless, they told their grieving congregations. In short, Palestinians regarded Ayash as a folk hero primarily because he frightened the mighty Israeli state and society. Later that day Arafat called on Mahmoud Zahar, and told him: 'We came here to share your loss.' In his later statements he condemned Israel for violating the PLO-Israeli peace deal which had put internal security of the Gaza Strip into the PA's hands, adding that the killing of Ayash ran counter to 'the spirit of reconciliation'.[25]

To Jewish Israelis, Ayash was an evil incarnate, a demon, responsible for the deaths of 68 human beings.[26] They viewed him as a psychopathic mass murderer, who dispatched his own acolytes to certain death alongside their victims. They felt angry and scandalized at the behaviour of Arafat, whose popular standing among them had all along been very low. On his part, using his earlier engagement to attend the ceremonies of Eastern Orthodox Christmas (on 6 January) in Bethlehem, Arafat excused himself from joining the funeral procession of Ayash.

On that day the Gaza Strip witnessed an unprecedented outpouring of grief and homage to Ayash. An estimated 300,000 people joined the funeral procession from the Hamas-run Palestine Mosque in Al Rimal district of Gaza city to the Martyrs Cemetery on the outskirts of the city. 'Peres, prepare your coffin; Ayash's ghost will appear before you', chanted the mourners; 'We want buses [to be blown up]! We want cars!' Those selling Ayash posters did roaring business. The image of a handsome young man with a luxurious thatch of black hair and an intense look, his neck enwrapped by a red and white chequered cloth (normally used as head dress), was everywhere. Within days, it was to be found all over the Palestinian refugee camps of Jordan, Syria and Lebanon. A later rally in his honour in Nablus drew 100,000 people, half of the city's population.

'Ayash is a link in the chain of the holy jihad,' declared the Hamas leaflet. 'Let the occupying invaders and their stooges await the response to the Zionist crime.' It did not spare the Palestinian Authority, calling it 'the Trojan horse of the Zionists', and accusing it of 'failure to protect its own people against Israel'.

During this emotional period two persons were to prove prescient. One was Yahya Ayash's mother, Ayisha, a sturdy woman of 53, chubby-faced and outspoken; and the other was an unnamed Israeli security official. 'Yahya taught his students, you know, so he will be avenged,' predicted the mother confidently. 'We may have got even with "the Engineer", but his legacy will claim a lot of blood,' warned the Israeli expert.[27]

The acolytes of Ayash struck on 25 February 1996, the second anniversary of the massacre of Muslim Palestinians in Hebron by Dr Goldstein. On that day, Sunday, at about 6.45 a.m. Majid Abu Wardeh – a 20-year-old youth from Al Fawwar camp, four kilometres south of Hebron, studying at the UNRWA-run Teachers' Training College in Ramallah, disguised as a uniformed IDF soldier of Ashkenazi origin, his hair dyed blond and ears pierced (fashionably) with rings, stepped on to bus number 18 on Jaffa Road in downtown Jerusalem. He detonated 15 kilograms of explosives, mixed with nails and ball bearings, strapped to his waist, instantly killing 24 people, three of them Palestinian, and injuring 80. The bomb wrecked the red and white bus, reducing it to a blackened skeleton, blasting its metal body and upholstery to smithereens, the shrivelled sides torn apart, and the roof blown sky-high. About half an hour later, 26-year-old Ibrahim Hussein Sarahneh, a thin-eyed, tousle-haired resident of Al Fawwar camp, also disguised as an IDF soldier, joined a crowd of conscripts waiting for lifts at a road junction outside the coastal city of Ashelon, and blew himself up, instantly killing one soldier.

The communiqué by the Qassam Brigade that followed referred to the Students of Yahya Ayash which, in the estimation of the Palestinian and Israeli sources, consisted of 70 to 80 ultra-militants within the Qassam Brigade. It was established later that they received their orders from the Hamas leadership in Damascus. 'If Israel is serious about peace then it should release Hamas prisoners and stop hunting down Hamas *mujahedin* (those who conduct jihad),' it said. 'If this were done then Hamas would worry about every drop of bloodshed.' It gave Israel one week to consider its offer of a ceasefire on these conditions.

This was in line with the statements made earlier by the supreme leader of Hamas, Shaikh Ahmad Yasin, and Imad Faluji. In his interview with the *Ma'ariv* in June 1995, Yasin had repeated his 'earlier offer' of a truce with Israel that 'could last 10 to 15 years'. And in July 1995 Faluji told the *Jerusalem Report*: 'We haven't recognized Israel yet. But we are ready to accept a ceasefire, through a third party, for a set period of time that would be renewable.'[28] Yet there were persistent reports of a split in Hamas. It centred around the tactic of using suicide bombers to kill innocent civilians, an act which many religious figures, including some in the Hamas movement, considered unIslamic.

Obviously, there was a lack of centralized control within the movement; and there were differences on tactics which, in the view of insiders, stemmed primarily from varied perceptions due to the fractured nature of the Palestinian community. 'In Palestine we are living in different situations militarily, politically and socially,' said an official close to the Hamas high command. 'There is a big difference between the West Bank and Gaza Strip. There is no split, but you could say there are different tactics.'[29] Apparently the population in the Gaza Strip, the birth place and nerve-centre of Hamas, was more radical than in the West Bank; and this was mirrored in the thinking of the local leadership. Equally, the perceptions of the insider Hamas leaders and the outsiders did not coincide. Mahmoud Zahar alluded to this, albeit indirectly. 'The assessment of those of us who are living here is different from the people outside,' he said. 'The people outside receive their information from television reports or telephone calls. We live the fine details and our assessment is much more realistic.'[30] The sub-text of this statement could be read thus: The insider Hamas leaders wanted accommodation with the

PA and suspension of attacks on Israeli targets whereas the outsiders want to continue the military struggle.

Though the outside elements were weak on a realistic analysis of the situation, they were strong on providing funds. Given the penury of the Palestinians in the (now) partially occupied territories, particularly Gaza Strip, Hamas was heavily dependent on funds from abroad to run its kindergartens, schools, health clinics, mosques and social welfare agencies, its socio-cultural infrastructure which was the the bedrock of its popular support. Among those who had conceded this was none less than Shaikh Ahmad Yasin. When asked by the reporter of *Ma'ariv* in mid-1995 about foreign funding of Hamas, he denied that Hamas received money from any Arab or Muslim government, and added: 'Financing comes mainly from the Palestinian donors around the world.'[31] Most of these contributors were resident in Jordan, Lebanon, Syria and the oil-rich Gulf states. But there were also many among some 500,000 Palestinians settled in Europe and North America who made donations to Hamas through the Muslim religious charities set up in such western countries as Britain, Canada and Germany.

Despite the differences between pragmatists and militants within the Hamas movement, the Qassam Brigade ensured that the suicide bombers came from West Bank villages or refugee camps under the overall (security) control of the IDF so as not to violate the understanding Hamas's political leaders had reached with Arafat not to embarass the PA by launching attacks on Israelis from the PA-controlled self-rule areas. (This understanding did not extend to the Islamic Jihad, which showed scant interest in devising a *modus vivendi* with the PA.)

Given the acute despair and deprivation, material and spiritual, that prevailed in the West Bank refugee camps, there was no dearth of volunteers for suicide missions. A Shin Beth investigation in Al Fawwar camp, housing less than 1,000 families, including those of Majid Abu Wardeh and Ibrahim Sarahneh, the bombers of 25 February, revealed that 30–40 youths were willing to carry out suicide attacks.[32] Now the homes of their parents were spray-painted with the

Qassam Brigade's newest slogan: 'More Jewish blood will be spilled until Palestine is freed from its occupiers.'

This became more likely when the Israeli Government did not take the Qassam Brigade's offer of a conditional truce seriously. Part of the reason why the Qassam Brigade had struck was to demonstrate to the Israeli Government that killing Ayash did not damage its capacity to strike. There was an unintended parallel here between the assassination of Khalid Wazir of the PLO in 1988 when Israel had hoped that eliminating him would end the newly started intifada, which was not to be the case. When its deadline of a week passed without any response from the Peres administration, the Brigade struck again – on the same day (Sunday, the start of the Jewish week), the same bus (number 18), the same city (Jerusalem), and about the same time and place (6.30 a.m., and roughly one kilometre from the previous site). The suicide bomber this time was Riad Karim Sharnoubi, 24, a sad-looking, moustached man with bushy eyebrows and thick lips, a student of the Ramallah Teachers' Training College. Of the 18 people he killed instantly, two were Palestinian and six were Romanian contractual workers. Unlike Abu Wardeh and Sarahneh, Sharnoubi came from a village, named Burqah, in the northern West Bank, under the overall security control of the IDF. That he had accomplished his mission despite the closure of the West Bank from Israel, constant helicopter surveillance of Jerusalem, and the provision of a uniformed guard on every bus, showed that Israel's security measures were far from foolproof. Indeed, it was fairly easy to walk into Israel from the West Bank if a person did not use a car.[33] Since a suicide bomber, once equipped with explosives attached to his/her waist, needed no further expertise, assistance or backup, his/her bomb became the most lethal weapon in the arsenal of terrorism so far.

Behind this campaign by the Qassam Brigade lay a political strategy whose end-purpose was to raise the popularity of Hamas at the expense of the PLO and the PA. The best way to achieve this was by discrediting Arafat, by showing that he could gain nothing further from the Israeli administration, which would be the case if Likud and its leader, Binyamin

Netanyahu, won the forthcoming elections, so argued the Qassam Brigade strategists. The most effective tactic to boost the electoral chances of Likud was to demonstrate that the Peres Government was incapable of providing security to its citizens. The sharp drop in the 15–20 per cent lead that Peres had hitherto enjoyed in opinion surveys showed that the Qassam Brigade plan was yielding the expected result. Hamas militants also wished to so outrage the Jewish settlers in the West Bank by their attacks as to trigger similar actions by the settlers, thus setting the scene for a bloody confrontation between them and the Palestinians, and the derailing of the Israeli-PLO peace process.

However, the attribution of the next bomb, on Monday, 4 March, which killed 12 persons instantly and wounded 100, was problematic. This time both the Qassam Brigade of Hamas and the Qassam militia of the Islamic Jihad claimed responsibility. The carnage occurred on the Jewish festival of Purim, the second anniversary of the Muslim massacre in Hebron according to the Jewish calendar. Since the Islamic Jihad had a score to settle with the Israeli Government regarding the assassination of its leader, Fathi Shikaki, it had the motive to commit this act of terror. Also, unlike on the previous three occasions, this time the suicide bomber – later identified as Ramez Obeid, a 23-year-old university art student from a refugee camp in the Gaza Strip – did not strap explosives to his waist, but carried them in a holdall, the major reason why he was denied entry into the Dizengoff Square shopping mall, full of children in fancy dress for Purim. His holdall contained land-mines filled with TNT (Trinitrotoluene), bottles of benzene and nails. It was discovered later that he had been smuggled out of the Gaza Strip by an Israeli Arab driver, carrying scrap metal from the Strip to Israel, through the eastern Karni checkpoint (less stringently monitored than the popular, northern Ezer checkpoint), for a fee of $1,100. The driver had dropped him off in Tel Aviv at Dizengoff Square shopping mall a minute before the blast.

Israel's emergency measures on 3 March included internal closure of the West Bank, banning travel between population centres, and ending the employment of Palestinians not only in Israel but also outside of their own village or town. 'No one goes in, no one comes out,' declared Major-General Ilan Biran, the IDF commander of the West Bank. The total ban on cross-border traffic meant severance of food and cooking-gas supplies to the West Bank and Gaza Strip.

'It is the tightest closure and sealing of borders Israel has imposed on Palestinians since 1967,' said Abdul Hakim al Samra. 'The worst thing to do is to seal the borders like this, or to impose a long-term curfew, when people cannot work. Lack of work leads to acute frustration and anger which turns ultimately into violence. When people work, they have to get up early and return home late and go to sleep. So they have no time or energy for planning [violent] actions, or doing anything against the authorities.' What was the feeling in the Gaza Strip? 'We feel like being inside a jail while the Jewish settlers are allowed to come and go as they please. We are not permitted to go to Israel or the West Bank, or go sailing over the waters of the Mediterranean, or fly into the sky. We used to be controlled by one authority, the Israelis; now we are controlled by two, Palestinian and Israeli. It is worse, much worse.'

The feelings of Gazans and West Bankers did not figure in Peres's plan of action. Following the second explosion in Jerusalem on 3 March, he angrily urged Arafat to act. The latter immediately banned six Palestinian militias, including the Qassam Brigade of Hamas and the Qassam militia of the Islamic Jihad. With another bomb going off in Tel Aviv on 4 March, the pressure on Arafat from Israel and the United States mounted. 'I will co-operate fully with Israel to wipe out terrorism,' he declared. That night he convened an emergency meeting of PA officials and Hamas's political leaders in Gaza city. He told the Hamas representatives bluntly: 'Either you assert control over the military wing or I will ban Hamas as a political organization.' The next day, 5 March, the Hamas political leadership called on 'our brothers in the Izz al Din Qassam Brigade to halt their military operations . . . to fortify national unity'. They responded positively and swiftly. 'We will stop our armed activities for three months [until after the Israeli elections] to give the Israeli Government and the Hamas political leadership . . . a chance to reach a ceasefire,' said their communiqué issued late on 5 March. 'But should Israel hurt Hamas fugitives in the West Bank and Gaza, the ceasefire will be violated.'

But by the night of 5–6 March the die had been cast. The PA and Israel had agreed to carry out co-ordinated action against the Hamas movement. 'There is no dialogue either with Hamas's political or military wing,' said Mahmoud Abbas, a top PLO official, in Gaza on 6 March. 'We will go after Izz al Din Qassam [Brigade], root out every bit of its infrastructure and demolish its vicious organization.'[34]

Starting early morning on 6 March, the PA police raided Gaza's Islamic University and 30 other Islamist institutions. 'All mosques in the Gaza Strip are under the control of the PNA,' declared Khalid Kidre, the PA's attorney-general. In the West Bank towns under its control, the PA acted likewise. Tipped off by the Israeli intelligence, it raided the Ramallah Teachers' Training College, and arrested 21 students, including Muhammad Abu Wardeh, who allegedly recruited Majid Abu Wardeh and Ibrahim Sarahneh to become human bombs. A serious-looking man of 22, with a large nose and sensuous mouth, thinly moustached, Abu Wardeh was tried immediately, found guilty and sentenced to life imprisonment. In the joint-control areas on the West Bank, where Israel was in charge of overall security, the IDF shut down all schools, colleges, clinics and charitable bodies functioning under the Hamas aegis. It re-entered the villages it had vacated in December while, in the words of an Israeli liaison officer, 'the PA police stepped out of the way', and arrested 170 Islamists. To break completely links between the West Bank and Gaza, the IDF ordered that some 1,200 Gaza students studying in the West Bank must return home forthwith.

The next day, 7 March, addressing the inaugural session of the Palestinian Council in Gaza city, Arafat called for an international campaign to combat terrorism, an idea originally aired by President Hosni Mubarak of Egypt. The White House clutched at the suggestion, and organized a summit of the peacemakers in Sharm al Shaikh, Egypt, within a week.

Both the PA and Israel widened their nets to catch Islamists. While widespread arrests of Islamists in the PA areas on charges of 'incitement against the PA' – amounting to 600 in the Gaza Strip alone by 9 March, and including all of Hamas's political leaders (Mahmoud Zahar, Ahmad Bahar *et al*) and some of the Qassam Brigade's officers (deputy commander Abdul Fattah Satari among them) – won Arafat public praise from Peres and US Secretary of State, Warren Christopher, the Qassam Brigade issued its tenth communiqué in the series starting on 25 February. Blaming the Israeli and PA crackdown for its decision, it stated: 'The Qassam Brigade has decided to resume its martyrdom attacks against the Zionists . . . The Palestinian National Authority's [continued] arrest of Hamas fugitives will completely destroy any understanding or future agreement between Hamas and the PLO.'

Meanwhile, ordinary Palestinians suffered. It was the hope of the Peres Government that they would blame Hamas and the Islamic Jihad for their current woes, and turn against these organizations. But Palestinians, who had suffered immeasurably under the 27-year-long Israeli occupation – which continued, albeit in a reduced and disguised form – showed scant signs of holding the Islamist factions solely responsible for the current situation. 'I blame both the Islamic groups and Israel,' said Abdul Hani, a shopkeeper in the main square of Khan Yunis. 'The Islamic guys for not realizing that border closure hurts Palestinians, and the Israelis for doing nothing. The Israelis hold the key to solving the Palestinian problem, but they are not sincere. See how they are co-operating with Jordan after the Peace Treaty. But for Palestinians they are always putting impediments. They ruined our economy, and made us dependent on jobs in Israel. Now they have shut us out of their labour market. What is more, they are not even allowing flour into the Gaza Strip. How can I run my grocery without bread?'

Abdul Hani was one of the Palestinians in Gaza city who demonstrated against the sealing off of the Gaza and West

Bank on 17 March, a strictly controlled protest, flaunting the officially sanctioned slogan: 'Yes to peace, No to the siege.' Addressing them, Arafat accused 'Iran and some Arab countries' of the recent explosions in Israel in order to make Palestinians despair about the peace process. By naming Iran directly and publicly, Arafat obliged Peres, who had for some years been leading a campaign against Iran as a terrorist state. The next day Peres allowed flour into the Gaza Strip. Earlier, on 15 March, he had ended the unparalleled internal closure of the West Bank. But on the eve of the end of the one-month-long closure of the Israeli border, 24 March, he extended it by another month. The only concession he made was to let West Bankers work in the West Bank's Jewish settlements.

With the unemployment rate in the Palestinian territories running at an unprecedented 60 per cent, there was growing alarm at the PA headquarters, Peres's office, and President Bill Clinton's White House that an economic collapse would ensue unless urgent remedying action was taken. As a result, many UN-supervised emergency labour-intensive projects, lasting until June (past the Israeli elections) and costing $100 million, were initiated.

The relief was widely welcomed, but was not enough to dispel the despair that had descended particularly on the Gaza Strip. 'People ask, "What are we left with?"' said Abdul Hakim al Samra. 'They can suffer for a long time. They have much capacity for suffering. Then they reach a breaking point. Then nobody knows what will happen. This is what happened with intifada in 1987. And it lasted six years.'

Before being arrested, in March 1996, for the third time by the 21-month-old Palestinian Authority for 'incitement against the PA', Dr Mahmoud Zahar said: 'If this [repressive] policy continues, I fear it will only drive people underground.' His warning deserved to be taken seriously. Like Zahar, those being driven underground drew their inspiration from the Islamic scriptures, especially the Quran, Word of God. Such people could sustain their faith and belief in their righteousness for a very long time. Indeed, they could point to the tenacity with which Zionist Jews, religious and secular, had stuck to their beliefs and succeeded in their mission.

There was, to put it simply, much in common between religious fundamentalists of Islam and Judaism. And they did not fade away merely because they were described as cranks, fanatics, zealots or religious fascists by those who regarded themselves as rational and secular. In the case of Muslim Palestinians and Jewish Israelis, they both made their case on the ground of divine promises. No matter how arcane such an argument may seem to secular westerners, it is very real in the lives and thoughts of hundreds of thousands of ordinary Jews and Muslims living in Israel and the Palestinian territories today.

14

DIVINE PROMISES:

The Disputing Inheritors

Just as post-1967 Israel, with its rule extended to the West Bank and Gaza Strip, provided an environment in which ultra-nationalist Zionism, religious and secular, flourished, so the Palestinian entity, stemming from the 1993–4 Oslo Accords, is set to create, willy-nilly, conditions in which the proponents, religious and secular, of the liberation of all of mandate Palestine will thrive. Since the Palestinian secularists – inspired by their antagonism to the nexus of American imperialism, Zionism and Arab reaction – subscribe to a waning ideology, and since they have little grass roots support, the task of retrieving all of Palestine has now fallen almost wholly on Islamic fundamentalists.

Besides beards and skullcaps that Jewish and Muslim fundamentalists often share, there are more significant points where the two groups intersect. 'As Muslims we believe in the Torah,' said Shaikh Bassam Jarrar. 'We believe in Ibrahim [Abraham], Ishaq [Isaac] and Yacoub [Jacob], later called Israel, as prophets. But the Torah was written 900 years after Moses had died, peace be upon him, and so it deviated from the original.' When was the Quran compiled, I asked. 'Within 12 years of the death of Prophet Muhammad, peace be upon him. We believe that the Torah is partly true and partly not. But I am prepared to take the Torah as it stands.'

That seemed a common enough ground for Islamic and Judaistic fundamentalists to engage in a debate. Under the present circumstances, though, this was a non-starter. On the other hand, I had spent much time with erudite members of both camps. So, instead of reporting their arguments separately, I will present them jointly, dialectically – in the form of dialogue between two opposing proponents, the Jewish one called 'Amnon' and the Muslim 'Zaki'.

AMNON: The starting point is Genesis 12:1 and 2. 'Now the Lord had said unto Abram, 'Get thee out of thy country, and from thy kindred, and from thy father's house, unto a land that I will shew thee. And I will make of thee a great nation, and I will bless thee, and make thy name great; and thou shalt be a blessing.' Then you have Genesis 12:6 and 7: 'And Abram passed through the land unto the place of Shechem/Sichem, unto the plain of Moreh. And the Lord appeared unto Abram, and said, "Unto thy seed will I give this land".'

ZAKI: When it comes to 'Abram's seed', we Arabs are his descendants through his son, Ishmael.

AMNON: You are moving ahead of the story. Look up Genesis 12:8. Abram moved south to a place between Beit El on the west and Hai to the east, where he built an altar to the Lord. Then in Genesis 12:13 you have Abram and his wife Sarai returning from Egypt with a lot of cattle, gold and silver to his earlier place between Beit El and Hai. Abram now lived in the Land of Canaan. In Genesis 12:15 you have the Lord saying unto Abram, 'For all the land which thou seest, to thee will I give it, and to thy seed for ever'. And then Genesis 12:18: Abram moved to the plain of Mamre, which is in Hebron, where he built an altar to the Lord.

ZAKI: Once again you see a reference to Abram's seed,

and the land in question is Canaan. Since we Arabs are descendants of Abram, we have as much historical claim to this land as anybody else.

AMNON: But the covenant that the Lord made with Abram covered a much larger area. See Genesis 12:18 to 21: 'In the same day the Lord made a covenant with Abram, saying, "Unto thy seed have I given this land, from the river of Egypt unto the great river, the river Euphrates. The Kenites, the Kenizzites and the Kadmonites. And the Hittites and the Perizzites and the Rephaims. And the Amorites and the Canaanites and the Girgashites and the Jebusites."'

ZAKI: That's roughly the region where the Arabs are living today. The phrase Abram's seed was meaningless until he had a son. And that is what Genesis Chapter 16 is all about. After Abram and Sarai had lived in Canaan for 10 years, and Sarai had borne no children, you have 16:3 where Sarai 'took Hagar her maid the Egyptian, and gave her to her husband Abram to be his wife'. Then you have 16:15: 'And Hagar bare Abram a son, and Abram called his son's name, which Hagar bare, Ishmael.' Abram was then 86 years old.

AMNON: But Sarai took care of the relationship between Abram and Ishmael in Genesis 21:10 to 12: '[Sarai] said to Abraham, Cast out this bondwoman [Hagar] and her son [Ishmael]: for the son of this bondwoman shall not be heir with my son, Isaac. And the thing was very grievous in Abraham's sight because of his son. And God said unto Abraham, "Let it not be grievous in thy sight because of the lad, and because of thy bondwoman: in all that Sarai hath said unto thee, harken unto her voice: for in Isaac shall thy seed be called."' That settles it.

ZAKI: Except that the Lord's speech continues . . . Genesis 21:13: 'And also of the son of the bondwoman will I make a nation, because he is thy seed.' This ties in perfectly with what is described in all of Genesis 17, when Abram was 99, and the Lord appeared to him. [17:4] 'The Lord said unto Abram: "Behold, my convenant is with thee, and thou shalt be a father of many nations."' Please note 'many nations'.

AMNON: You are ignoring what happened in Genesis 15:13 and 14: 'And the Lord said unto Abram, "Know of a surety that thy seed shall be a stranger in a land that is not theirs, and shall serve them; and they shall afflict them 400 years. And also that nation, whom they shall serve, will I judge. And afterward shall they come out with great substance."' Now isn't that clear enough? Isn't that about the Jews, in servitude in Egypt, and all that? Isn't it?

ZAKI: Let us return to the basic points: the seed of Abram, and the land offered to it by the Lord. Genesis 17 is the key. It is here that the Lord reveals himself as 'the Almighty God', renames Abram and Sarai as Abraham and Sarah, amplifies on his covenant with Abram, and prescribes circumcision for the male progeny of Abram 'as a token of covenant betwixt me and you'. See especially 4 to 8, and 24 and 25. In 5 to 8 the Lord said unto Abram, 'Thy name shall be Abraham; for a father of many nations have I made thee. And I will make thee exceeding fruitful, and I will make nations of thee, and kings shall come out of thee. And I will establish my covenant between me and thee and thy seed in their generations for an everlasting covenant, to be a God unto thee and to thy seed after thee. And I will give unto thee, and to thy seed after thee, the land wherein thou art a stranger, all the land of Canaan, for an everlasting possession; and I will be their God.' And 24 and 25 read: 'And Abraham was ninety years old and nine, when he was circumcised in the flesh of his foreskin. And Ishmael his son was 13 years old, when he was circumcised in the flesh of his foreskin.' Remember that when the covenant of circumcision was made with Abraham, and the land of Canaan was promised 'as an everlasting possession', it was the 13-year-old Ishmael who was circumcised – along with Abraham. Isaac was not born yet.

AMNON: Maybe so. But God made a clear distinction between Ishmael and Isaac, who was yet to be born, and between Sarah and Hagar. It's all in Genesis 17 to which you keep referring. Genesis 17:16 says: 'God said unto Abraham, "I will bless Sarah, and give thee a son also of her . . . She shall be a mother of nations; kings of people shall be of her".' But God said nothing of the sort about Hagar. As for God's covenant, again He was explicit. Genesis 17:21: 'And God said, "But my covenant will I establish with Isaac, which Sarah shall bear unto thee at this set time in the next year."'

ZAKI: Ah . . . you're skipping the earlier verse, Genesis 17:20. It reads: 'God said, "As for Ishmael, I have heard thee. Behold, I have blessed him, and will make him fruitful, and will multiply him exceedingly; 12 princes shall he beget, and I will make him a great nation."' And when Abraham died it was both Ishmael and Isaac who buried him. That's Genesis 25:9. Anybody with the tiniest shred of objectivity would agree that the descendants of Ishmael have every right to consider themselves of the seed of Abraham.

AMNON: They may say what they like, but there is no divine sanction behind it. The basic question is: How did God treat Isaac and Ishmael? Did He treat them on a par? No. Here is Genesis 26:2 to 4. 'And God appeared to Isaac, and said, "Sojourn in this land [of Gera], and I will be with thee and bless thee; for unto thee, and unto thy seed, I will give all these countries, and I will perform the oath which I sware unto Abraham thy father. And I will make thy seed multiply as the stars of heaven, and will give unto thy seed all these countries."'

ZAKI: Go on. Why do you stop? God's speech doesn't end there. It continues: 'and in thy seed shall all the nations on the earth be blessed'.

AMNON: What exactly does that mean?

ZAKI: You tell me.

AMNON: Whatever I say, or anybody else says, can only be speculation. What I can tell you – for sure – is what God said to Jacob. Genesis 28:13 and 14: 'And, behold, the Lord stood above it [the ladder between the earth and heaven], and said, "I am the Lord God of Abraham thy father, and the God of Isaac: the land whereon thou liest, to thee I will give it, and to thy seed. And thy seed shall be as the dust of the earth, and thou shalt spread abroad to the west, and to the east, and to the north, and to the south; and in thee and in thy seed shall all the families of the earth be blessed."'

ZAKI: Again there is a reference to the blessing of 'all the families of the earth'. Think for example of Esau, the elder brother of Jacob. He was deprived of his status as the successor to Isaac by Jacob through trickery. This same Esau, the eldest son of Isaac, was married to Mahalath, a daughter of Ishmael. So Ishmael and his seed were very much into the mainstream of Abraham's descendants.

AMNON: But God sanctified the position Jacob had acquired by whatever means. Why else would God change Jacob's name in the way He had done with Abram? Look up Genesis: 9 to 13 – after Jacob had returned from Mesopotamia to Beit El, God appeared to him again, and said unto him, 'Thy name shall not be called any more Jacob, but Israel shall be thy name'. And God said unto him, 'I am Almighty God. Be fruitful and multiply; a nation and company of nations shall be of thee, and kings shall come out of thy loins. And the land which I gave Abraham and Isaac, to thee I will give it, and to thy seed after thee will I give the land.'

ZAKI: Once again a reference to 'company of nations'.

AMNON: Only this time Jacob had 12 sons: Reuben, Simeon, Levi, Judah, Zebulin, Issachar, Dan, Gad, Asher, Naphtali, Joseph and Benjamin – in that order.

ZAKI: Mind you, four of these were by maidservants:

Gad and Asher by Zilpah, the maidservant to Leah; and Dan and Naphtali by Bilhah, the maidservant to Rachel.

AMNON: A common practice in those days, it seems. Anyway, there you have the Twelve Tribes, or Nations, if you like.

ZAKI: We call them and their descendants Beni Israel, Children of Israel.

AMNON: Or the Israelites – as in the Old Testament.

ZAKI: So even if we accept your argument that presentday Palestine was promised by God to Abraham and his descendants, you must limit yourselves to Beni Israel, Children of Israel.

AMNON: Fair enough.

ZAKI: Then how do you explain all the Jews in Israel today? Are they all Beni Israel?

AMNON: What do you mean?

ZAKI: How is it possible that Falashas, Ethiopian Jews, have the same ancestry as Arab Jews, what you call Mizrachim, those born in the Middle East and North Africa – and European Jews, many of them with blond hair?

AMNON: Intermarriage.

ZAKI: Impossible to get pure Africans like Falashas through intermarriage.

AMNON: So what's your theory?

ZAKI: I have no theory. Only God's promise. His promise applies to a certain family, the family of Israel – and not to Jews as a religious group. There was no such group as Jews in those days.

AMNON: Were there Muslims then?

ZAKI: No, not in the way we use the term today. After Solomon's death in 930 BC the United Kingdom of Israel broke up into two. Ten of the 12 tribes lived in the north, then called Israel, and the remaining two in the south, Judah. Israel lasted until 722 BC when it fell into the hands of the Assyrians. Lots of Israelites were killed, and others were enslaved and taken to Assyria. Judah continued to exist. But from 605 BC the people of Judah, called Jews, were taken into exile by the Babylonians. Today's Jews acknowledge that the 10 Israelite tribes got lost.

AMNON: I know all that. Come to the point.

ZAKI: My points are in history itself. In 586 BC Nebuchadnezzar of Babylonia inflicted a defeat on the ruler of Judah, populated by two Israelite tribes. He enslaved some of the Israelites and took them to Babylonia. Some of those banished to Babylonia returned to Palestine during the rule of Korush, and that of the Greeks and Romans. Among them some became Christian, especially after AD 70 when the Second Temple was destroyed, and again in AD 135. Later, when Islam came to Greater Syria and Iraq in the seventh century, a large majority of these Isrealite tribes became Muslim. The process continued. In the sixteenth century, under the Ottomans in Palestine, the Jewish Shakhseer, Muslmanee and Mukhtadi families converted to Islam.

AMNON: That's the most distorted view of Jewish history I've ever heard.

ZAKI: Most of the Beni Israel adopted Islam or Christianity. But many pagans embraced Judaism. Reading history you see that certain nations, which were not Beni Israel, adopted Judaism. Some of them were Arab, like the Kinda tribe. There was a Jewish kingdom in Yemen. Seif bin Deyazan, who died in AD 570, ruled a Jewish kingdom in Yemen. During Prophet Muhammad's time in the seventh century in Arabia some tribes were Beni Israel and others had adopted Judaism. Then there was the Kingdom of Khazar, a Jewish kingdom – not Beni Israel – near the Caspian Sea in the tenth century.

AMNON: Yes, the Kingdom of Khazaria, ruled by the Khazar dynasty. It ended in AD 965, defeated by Prince Sviatoslav. Its Jewishness went back to AD 740 when Bulan, the military king of Khazaria, converted to Judaism.

ZAKI: Converted, that's the word. So he was not a Beni Israel.

AMNON: You talk as if Jews and Beni Israel are different groups.

ZAKI: They are. Every Beni Israel is a Jew, but not every Jew is a Beni Israel.

AMNON: What kind of proportions are we talking about?

ZAKI: Experts estimate that about one-tenth of today's 14 million Jews are Beni Israel. And God's promise applies only to them. Not to the nine-tenths of today's Jews who are converts, and have nothing to do with the lineage of Jacob/Israel.

AMNON: Which means nine-tenths of the Jews who are in Israel today have no right to Return.

ZAKI: It depends. Most of the Mizrachim or Sephardim living in Israel today probably are Beni Israel. But worldwide Sephardim are only one-fifth of the Jewish population.

AMNON: What about me, an Ashkenazi?

ZAKI: Most of you are definitely not Beni Israel; you are converts to Judaism.

AMNON: So I can't claim Eretz Israel as my Promised Land?

ZAKI: You said it. (Pause) But what's your definition of Eretz Israel? What are its boundaries?

AMNON: Those of the Hebrew kingdom under King David and King Solomon during the period—

ZAKI: You keep calling David and Solomon kings. They are more than kings. To us they are prophets like Abraham, Isaac, Jacob and Moses. We don't separate our belief in them from that in Prophet Muhammad. So the holiness of Palestine to us comes from our belief in all these prophets *before* Muhammad, who lived here, preached here and ruled here. The most mentioned name in the Quran is Prophet Moses.

AMNON: That's news to me.

ZAKI: He appears in the Quran 136 times.

AMNON: That many. Well, he was our law giver. He gave definition to Judaism.

ZAKI: To monotheism. That's why we have a prayer niche for him in our Al Aqsa Mosque. And for centuries we celebrated the Festival of Moses at the Tomb of Moses.

AMNON: Where?

ZAKI: At Nabi Musa [Prophet Moses], about 12 kilometres south of Jericho. The site has been there since Salah al Din's conquest although most of the buildings were built by [Mameluke] Sultan Baybar about a century later. The annual pilgrimage used to be around April, and the Grand Mufti led the pilgrims from Jerusalem. The festival lasted a week. It was a great event in the Muslim calendar, you know. Muslims came from all over Palestine and abroad.

AMNON: Were Jews allowed?

ZAKI: I don't know. Do the Jews accept the Muslim tradition that Prophet Moses is buried there?

AMNON: We know of no authenticated grave of Moses anywhere. But why don't we hear much about your festival nowadays?

ZAKI: There is none. It was banned by the British in 1937, during the Arab Revolt.

AMNON: The British were like that. They banned the settlement of Jews in Transjordan even though it was part of Eretz Israel under David and Solomon. In fact half of Eretz Israel lay to the east of River Jordan, around 20,700 square kilometres.

ZAKI: But then you didn't have the Negev desert. Now you do.

AMNON: We're entitled to something in return for the land lost east of River Jordan; aren't we?

ZAKI: I question the very basis of your entitlement, the right to Return.

AMNON: Why?

ZAKI: To start with, the Divine Promise was not unconditional. The Beni Israel were required to obey the Lord and his commandments and laws individually and collectively.

AMNON: And if they did not, then God's wrath would be

upon them. The Fifth Book of the Torah, Deuteronomy – the addresses of Moses to the Isarelites before entering Canaan – chapter 28, verses 63 to 66. 'And it shall come to pass, that as the Lord rejoiced over you to do you good, and to multiply you; so the Lord will rejoice over you to destroy you, and to bring you to nought; and you shall be plucked from off the land wither thou goest to possess it. [64] And the Lord shall scatter thee among all people, from the one end of the earth even unto the other; and there thou shalt serve other gods, which neither you nor thy fathers have known, even wood and stone. [65] And among these nations shalt thou find no ease, neither shall the sole of thy foot have rest; but the Lord shall give thee a trembling heart, and failing of eyes, and sorrow of mind. [66] And thy life shall hang in doubt before thee; and thou shall fear day and night, and shalt have none assurance of thy life.' Haven't we been through this? Haven't we suffered?

ZAKI: Yes, not just in modern times, but in ancient times. Because the Beni Israel committed collective apostasy, they were punished. The population of Israel was captured and removed by the Assyrians, and the people of Judah by the Babylonians.

AMNON: But the prophets told the Israelites that a section of the exiles would return.

ZAKI: They did. And they built the Second Temple, in 515 BC. Finally, they enjoyed a period of political independence under the Maccabbees, from 166 BC to 63 BC.

AMNON: That's all we have tried to recreate ever since, most recently with the founding of the Zionist Congress in Basle in 1897.

ZAKI: But that has nothing to do with the prophecies in the Torah. There is no prophecy of another return after the one from the Babylonian exile. In any case the last of the prophets passed away long before the devastation of Jerusalem in AD 70.

AMNON: The prophecies mentioned not only restoring

of the temple and religious life of the Israelites but also heralding of a golden era when the lion would lie down with the lamb, and the desert would blossom, and swords would be changed into ploughshares.

ZAKI: The second part hasn't come to pass yet.

AMNON: That won't happen unless the first part materializes.

ZAKI: Again?

AMNON: The first part is the precondition for the second. The return of the Jews to their Promised Land and the re-establishment of a religious Jewish state is a precondition for the arrival of the Messiah and the beginning of a golden age.

ZAKI: You must get the facts right about the Promised Land. Since Ishmael became the progenitor of Arabs, God's promise to Abraham applies to Arabs as well. We can't accept your elimination of all the children of Abraham except Isaac. We Arabs have as much right to Palestine as our Promised Land as you have.

AMNON: Two peoples claiming the same inheritance. Who settles the conflicting claims?

ZAKI: Time will tell. But one thing is certain: you can't have it all.

AMNON: That's the way it appears – for now.

ZAKI: That sounds like a temporary acceptance.

AMNON: Nothing is for ever.

ZAKI: Except a Divine Promise.

15

SUMMING UP THE PAST,

Surmising the Future

An extraordinary combination of geography, geopolitics and history has made part of the hinterland of the eastern Mediterranean a unique place on earth. As the region, where much of the chronicle described in the Old Testament and the New Testament occurred, the Holy Land/Palestine/Israel is by far the most widely discussed subject – politically, culturally and religiously – in the western world.

At the heart of the Holy Land lies Jerusalem. Much time and space have been devoted in western literature, religious and secular, to this especial city. The Talmud (Hebrew, Learning) – the multi-volume compilation of the Jewish Oral Law, codified around AD 200, and the successive commentaries – cites a medieval sage thus: 'Ten measures of beauty alighted upon earth; nine were possessed by Jerusalem, and the tenth was shared by the rest of the world;/Ten measures of sorrow alighted upon earth; nine were possessed by Jerusalem, and the tenth was shared by the rest of the world.'

Overall, there has been more sorrow in Jerusalem, with

a recorded history dating back to c. 1900 BC, than beauty, more agony than ecstacy. It has been captured and lost by 40 different armies. In the twentieth century alone it has witnessed battles by the Ottomans, British, Jordanians and Israelis. Strife, hatred, bloodshed and holiness have gone hand in hand here, as have religion and politics. 'Our city has always suffered for its holiness,' said 77-year-old Arif al Arif, a former mayor of (Jordanian) Jerusalem, in the late 1960s. 'Holiness is its tragedy. Perhaps that is why our people . . . can remember nothing but struggles. Blood. They have been harmed by this sanctity more than they have benefited.'[1]

In the late nineteenth century, to the continuing historical, religious argument among Jews and other monotheists was added a new, secular dimension: nationalism. (The ongoing debate on whether Jews are a religious or an ethnic group can be traced back to this development of a century ago.) Among the Jews of Europe nationalism manifested itself as political Zionism – a term coined by Nathan Birnbaum in 1893, and applied to the Jewish nationalist movement that aimed to create a Jewish state or national centre in Ottoman Palestine (Greek, Palaistina, derivative of Pleshet, Land of Philistines in Hebrew), the historic homeland of the forebears of Jews. Until then the aspiration to return to Zion – the Canaanite name of the hill on which Jerusalem stood – to recreate it as a spiritual-religious centre of Jews, had been couched in religious terms and expressed in the liturgy, with the ideology underlying this yearning called 'religious Zionism'. Political Zionism emerged formally as the Zionist Organization (later renamed World Zionist Organization), which the first Zionist Congress, held in Basle in 1897, established, and which defined Zionism thus: 'Zionism strives to create for the Jewish people a home in Palestine secured by public law.'

Between then and 1948, the birthdate of the State of Israel, representing a compendium of religious and political Zionism, a series of events, coupled with ceaseless lobbying by European Jewish leaders, contributed towards the realization of the Zionist aim. The principal ones in the chain were the failed Ottoman offensive from Gaza in 1915 against the Allied Powers during World War I (June 1914–November

1918), the 1917 Balfour Declaration, the League of Nations mandate to Britain in 1922, the discovery of oil in Iraq in 1927, and the genocide of some six million European Jews by Nazi Germany during World War II (September 1939–August 1945). Interlinked with these crucial events were instances of convergence of interests of leading world powers: Britain and the United States in 1916–17; Britain and France in 1920 at the League of Nations (which the United States did not join); and the United States and the Soviet Union in 1947 at the United Nations, the successor to the League of Nations.

At the beginning, in 1897, when the Ottoman empire extended over most of the Arab Middle East, there was no administrative-political unit called Palestine. The term had gained currency among the western travellers to the Holy Land in the nineteenth century, and was used, notionally, to mean the geographical area roughly between the eastern Mediterranean Sea and the desert. In the Ottoman empire, this territory was scattered over the *sanjak* (Turkish, administrative unit) of Jerusalem and the *vilayat* (Turkish, province) of Beirut, with Jerusalem and suburbs ruled directly from Istanbul.

As it happened, (notional) Palestine was, and remains, the most strategic territory in the Middle East – the meeting point of Africa, Eurasia and the Mediterranean region – providing access not only to Egypt via the Sinai Peninsula but also Jordan, Syria and Lebanon. In the Middle East, the Red Sea, an extension of the Indian Ocean, and the Mediterranean Sea, an extension of the Atlantic Ocean, are set apart only by the narrow isthmus of the Suez. And the distance between Gaza, the most south-eastern point of the Mediterranean Sea, and Aqaba, at the head of the Gulf of Aqaba, an extension of the Red Sea, is not very much longer than the Suez isthmus. The land between the Mediterranean Sea and the head of the Persian Gulf too can be seen as an isthmus. While being longer than the isthmus of Suez or Gaza-Aqaba, ancient traders found it short enough to develop it as a thriving trading route between the East and the West. Among the early conquerors who realized the potential of the region as a commerical crossroads was Alexander the Great. His occupation of Palestine in 333 BC underlined the economic importance of the area. During his occupation of Egypt, from 1798 to 1801, the French general Napoleon Bonaparte (1769–1821) chose the Palestinian path, unsuccessfully, to advance towards India.

Once the Mediterranean Sea and the Red Sea were connected directly by the Suez Canal in 1869, the Middle East regained its position as the foremost intercontinental highway. By occupying Egypt in 1882, Britain ensured control of the Suez Canal, now its lifeline to its empire in India.

The outbreak of World War I between the Allied Powers (Belgium, Britain, France, Italy, Japan, Montenegro, Russia and Serbia) and the Central Powers (Austria-Hungary, Bulgaria, Germany and the Ottoman empire) opened up unprecedented opportunities for Zionist dignitaries, who had been lobbying their cause in the leading European capitals and in Washington. They reasoned that the colonization of Palestine by European Jews would create a western outpost in the Middle East which would be immensely beneficial to the West. This was a convincing enough argument, as the Balfour Declaration would show.

The Balfour Declaration arose out of the convergence of Zionist aspirations with Britain's imperial aims, which came to the fore during World War I. The January 1915 Ottoman offensive against the Suez Canal across the Sinai Peninsula, which was repelled by the British, made London realize anew the strategic importance of Palestine in defending the Suez Canal, its lifeline to India, and caused it to resolve to control Palestine after winning the war. In a memorandum to the Cabinet in March 1915, Sir Herbert Samuel, a senior civil servant of Zionist persuasion (later appointed British High Commissioner for Palestine), proposed establishing a Jewish homeland in Palestine as a cornerstone of British policy in the Middle East. Until then the world Jewry, concentrated in Germany, Austria-Hungary and America, had by and large remained neutral in the war. With the United States joining the conflict in April 1917 on the Allied side, the role of American Jewry became important.

In order to gain its active co-operation, the pro-Zionists in the British Government, led by Premier David Lloyd George and Foreign Minister Arthur James (later Lord) Balfour, proposed backing the Zionist cause in September 1917, but failed to win cabinet approval. They then sought the advice of US President Woodrow Wilson, known to be a pro-Zionist. Wilson replied that the time was inopportune for anything more than a statement of general sympathy for the Zionists. But next month, responding to Zionist pleas and rumours of Germany wooing the Zionist movement, Lloyd and Balfour broached the subject again with Wilson. After some hesitation, he approved a draft statement which, following minor editing, was issued by Arthur James Balfour on 2 November 1917 in the form of a letter to Lord Rothschild, a British Zionist leader.[2]

Endorsed by the chief Allied Powers, the Balfour Declaration was included in the San Remo Agreement of 1920 – the title given to the decisions on the Middle East taken by the Supreme Council of the League of Nations, consisting of major Allied Powers. According to the San Remo Agreement, Britain and France were authorized to decide the nature of the League of Nations mandates for the region and submit them to the League for debate and voting. The Balfour Declaration was incorporated into the British mandate over Palestine authorized by the League of Nations in July 1922. The freshly demarcated, sword-like Palestine disrupted the geographical continuity of the Arabic-speaking world extending from Mauritania along the Atlantic to the Persian Gulf. Among those who noted the geopolitical importance of this development was Joseph Stalin (1878–1953), the leader of the Soviet Union. Instructed by him, in 1924–5, the national delimitation commission, while dealing with the Caucasian region, allocated the sword-like Zangezur strip, inhabited by Azeri Turks, to the Republic of Armenia, thus hiving off the Nakhichevan region, bordering Turkey, from mainland Azerbaijan, the land of Azeri Turks. Stalin thus broke the territorial continuity of Turkic lands from the Balkans to China, and eliminated a potential bridgehead for a regional enemy.[3]

The second prong of the British strategy in the Middle East was the Emirate of Transjordan, its protectorate. Its ruler, Emir Abdullah al Hashem, nurtured ambitions to annex the whole or part of Palestine.

Britain had thus created enough tensions and contradictions in the region to assure itself an ongoing lead role as the occupying power as well as the protector and the sole arbitrator, with a large area for manoeuvre and manipulation between the competing interests of Palestinian Arabs, the immigrating Jews from Europe and Transjordanian Arabs.

The discovery of commercial quantities of oil in Iraq in 1927 increased the strategic and economic value of Palestine since it provided a gateway to the Iraqi oilfields through Transjordan. Following the decision of the British navy, which underpinned the superpower status of Britain, to switch from coal to oil in 1913, the military-strategic importance of petroleum had risen sharply. With the Iraqi oilfield in Mosul turning out to tbe world's largest, the prospect of the British quitting Palestine after assisting its people to become self-governing – as was its plan in Iraq, its other mandate territory – evaporated.

As it was, in 1922, the familiar argument of an occupying or imperialist power that if it departed the local people, divided into hostile groups, would drag the country down into a bloody confrontation, had little chance of winning popular conviction in the case of Palestine. At 8 per cent of the population Jews were hardly in a position to initiate or sustain a civil strife. By introducing an external element – European Jews – into Palestine, Britain meant to create a new factor which would have veto over the future of native Arabs. The only way to make the Jewish community a viable opponent of the Arabs was by letting itself expand dramatically. And that is what the British actively encouraged, leading to the Jews becoming 18 per cent of the population in 1931, enough to withstand a sustained assault by the local Arabs. Once their proportion reached a third of the total population, as it did in the spring of 1939, the Jewish community was large enough to sustain a civil war; and this provided the British with a convincing rationale to stay on as the mandate power 'to keep the peace between hostile communities'. It is worth noting that in the Hindu-majority Indian empire of Britain, Muslims, the largest religious group, were a quarter of the total population, and succeeded in thwarting Indian progress towards independence unless the sub-continent was partitioned into India and Pakistan, which happened in August 1947. In Cyprus, another British colony, a *de facto* partition came about after independence in 1960, primarily because the minority, (Muslim) Turks, being about one-fifth of the island's population, could not be made to accept the overweening dominance of the majority (Christian) Greeks.

After World War II, fearing expulsion from the Suez Canal zone by Egypt, the British moved their troops and weapons to Al Arish in the Sinai. This showed they were determined to hold on to Palestine as a gateway to the crucial Iraqi oilfields. It was only after the fear of a forced withdrawal from the Suez had passed that London finally decided that Palestine had become ungovernable, and referred the problem to the United Nations.

In the region, though, Britain was intent on maintaining the hegemony it had enjoyed for over three generations. And Stalin, the leader of the emerging Soviet bloc, was equally intent on expelling British imperial power from the geostrategic Middle East. He reckoned that the best way to achieve this was by depriving London of any rationale to stay on in Palestine, if only to contain the murderous conflict between Arabs and Jews. This meant having to back the United Nations Partition Plan. He did. And, but for the eight-strong Soviet bloc vote, the Palestine Partition Plan, needing two-thirds majority, would not have been passed, by 33 votes to 13, at the United Nations General Assembly on 29 November 1947.

Almost half a century later, my conversations with several post-graduate Jewish students of history and international relations at the Hebrew University of Jerusalem revealed that none of them was aware of the vital role performed by the Soviet Union in the creation of Israel. Nor were they aware of the crucial part played by the supply of arms, including fighter aircraft, by Czechoslovakia, under the orders of Moscow, to the Zionists in Palestine which began arriving from March 1948 onwards, two months before the establishment of Israel, which was accorded *de jure* recognition by the Soviet Union (in contrast to a *de facto* recognition by Washington).

In any case by 1948 the centre of Zionist activty in the Diaspora had shifted from Britain to the United States, which had emerged as the uncontested leader of the West. The discovery of the unprecedented scale and gruesomeness of the Holocaust that European Jews suffered at the hands of Nazi Germany produced a groundswell of sympathy for Jews and Israel in the United States and elsewhere in the West.

Once Israel had materialized, its links with America strengthened rapidly. These became all the more important as the Suez War of 1956 sounded the death-knell of British and French imperialism in the region.

Over the next decade American commitment to the survival and strengthening of Israel became so strong that by the time of the spring 1967 crisis in the Middle East, the US intelligence efforts in Egypt had been tailored to Israeli needs. The Jewish state's total alignment with the United States in the international arena had its parallel in domestic politics: the centre of gravity of Israeli politics moved steadily rightwards. A milestone was reached in mid-1967 when ultra-nationalist groups, including Menachem Begin's Gahal – hitherto considered untouchable by the Labour establishment – were invited to join a national unity government.

The stunning victory that the Jewish state scored in the June 1967 War with the Arabs left such a strong imprint on state and society that neither Israel's stand-off in the October 1973 armed conflict nor its ignominious withdrawal from Lebanon three years after attacking it in 1982 wiped it off. 'For the new generation of Israeli Jews, born after the 1967 War, it feels that the West Bank belongs to Israel,' said Professor Moshe Ma'oz of the Truman Institute at the Hebrew University. 'It does not see any difference between Jaffa and Hebron.'[4] So thorough has been the success of the Israeli state, aided by the mass media, in this case that even the map printed in *In the Land of Israel* by Amos Oz, an eminent liberal-leftist writer and journalist, active with the Peace Now group, labels the West Bank and the Gaza Strip as territories 'Held by Israel since 1967', not 'Occupied by Israel since 1967', which is how the world at large, including the United States, regarded them in 1983 when the English translation of the book was published.

The endeavour, official and unofficial, to give an ultra-nationalist spin to contemporary history continues hand in hand with a sustained effort to do the same with distant chronicles, both at popular and intellectual levels. 'Historian Yaacov Shavit has produced a series of academic books, including *History of Palestine, Volumes VI-VII*,' said Ilan Pappe, a Jewish Israeli historian at the Haifa University. 'In Palestine the Jews were only 1 per cent of the population from the eleventh to the late nineteenth century. There were small Jewish communities in Jerusalem, Hebron, Tiberias and Safed. They were all Ottoman subjects until the collapse of the Ottoman empire in 1918. But reading Shavit's books you would think they were the only people living in Palestine. This is typical of the official literature and other literature in Israel. It is the traditional Israeli view: Palestine was an empty, arid land where nomads attacked the settled population.'[5] This may seem a clear-eyed, objective view to most non-Israelis, but in mainstream Jewish Israel, academics such as Pappe are often dismissed as anti-Zionist, self-hating Jews.

Israeli authorities are used to implementing their decisions with such thoroughness that sometimes they end up as victims of their own success. After the 1967 occupation of the West Bank and Gaza, they damaged the economies of these territories so effectively that they made a very substantial proportion of the Palestinians dependent on casual work in the Jewish state. By so doing, they created a host of problems, not least of which was weakening the security of Israel, an issue of paramount import. For some 30 years the Israeli media and Government invariably described the Palestine Liberation Organization as a terrorist outfit, and Yasser Arafat a bloodthirsty, terrorist leader, not even a guerrilla leader, much less the chairman of a national liberation organization. Then, one day in September 1993, the Israeli public found its Prime Minister, Yitzhak Rabin, shaking the hand of the arch terrorist of all times, Arafat, before a world audience. Part of the reason why Labour leaders today find it an uphill task to swing a convincing majority of Jewish Israelis in favour of peace and reconciliation with the PLO – and maintain that position for any meaningful length of time – is that month after month, year after year, they and other politicians presented the PLO as the evil incarnate, devoid of any saving grace.

Just as in Northern Ireland, so in Israel and the Palestinian territories, perceptions on terrorism vary. On the Jewish Israeli side today there is an unqualified condemnation of terrorism as a political weapon, despite the fact that during the decade leading to the founding of Israel in 1948, first the Irgun and then both Irgun and Lehi – committed to terroristic means against Palestinian Arabs and the British – used terrorism quite effectively, and, in strictly objective terms, played a significant role in the emergence of the Jewish state. The existence of an impressive museum in Tel Aviv dedicated exclusively to Irgun, and the naming of an important thoroughfare in that city after Lehi, are just two of the numerous examples of the official recognition conferred on the Jewish terroristic organizations of the recent past. It is worth noting, too, that the respective leaders of Irgun and Lehi – Menachem Begin and Yitzhak Shamir – went on to become Prime Ministers of Israel, and together held that supreme office for as many years as did David Ben Gurion, the towering Labour leader and the prime founder of Israel.

A slight stretching of one's historical perspective should make plain the fact that today most Palestinians and Israeli Arabs are equivocal about the role of terrorism in politics in the same way that most Jews in Palestine were before the founding of Israel.

'Today Israelis have official terrorism,' said Dr Adel Manna, an Israeli Arab historian. 'They terrorize with laws. They demolish houses, they arrest you arbitrarily, they humiliate you at random, they parade you in handcuffs at your workplace. They deport you. They send death squads. They have laws of occupation, the Law of the Dominant Party. Whatever Israel does is "official". The Palestinians have only the weapon of resistance which they use as much as they can. Each day they see more and more of their land confiscated and turned into Jewish settlements, despite the Oslo Accords. They feel desperate. They choose the only effective weapon they have, suicide bombing.'[6]

On the Israeli side, most politicians take a narrow view of security, focusing almost exclusively on its military and law and order aspects, and sidelining the larger political context. Military security of a state is best assured within the framework of political security; and that in the case of Israel and the Palestinians means a peace settlement which is seen by a vast majority of the Palestinians, by far the weaker party in the conflict, as just and equitable. The United Nations Security Council Resolution 242 of 22 November 1967, on which the current Middle East peace process is founded, refers to 'a just and lasting peace' in the region.

The Israeli state and media have reared two generations of citizens on the promise of creating an environment that is absolutely free of any threat of Arab terrorism, an unrealistic aim in the presentday world. The reality, deplorable though it is, remains that today no Government, not even that of the United States – which witnessed an explosion in Oklahoma City in April 1995 which killed 168 people – can offer 100 per cent protection to its citizens from random bombs and bullets. The examples of Britain and Spain, both western nations, are pertinent. The violence stemming from the conflict between Protestant and Catholic Christians in Northern Ireland – rooted in the antagonism of the Catholic natives to the Protestant settlers brought in from Scotland during the rule of Oliver Cromwell (1599–1658) – has since 1969 made London, universally regarded as a peaceful metropolis, a bomb-prone city. In Spain, the violence linked to the nationalist aspirations of the Basque minority continues to be expressed in bombs and assassinations. No Briton or Spaniard realistically expects its Government to put a definite and final end to such random violence which mainly maims and kills innocent civilians.

While diligently and rightly pursuing those Palestinians who perpetrate terrorism against its citizens, the Israeli administration has not been evenhanded in meting out justice to proven terrorists *per se*, irrespective of their ethnicity. Among others BeTeslem, the Israeli human rights organization, pointed out that following the massacre of Muslim Palestinians by Dr Baruch Goldstein in early 1994, his house in Kiryat Arba was not demolished by the IDF, a punishment which is invariably meted out to the family of a Palestinian terrorist. The life sentence of Menachem Livni, involved in the plot to blow up the Dome of the Rock and in the killings of Palestinian students at Hebron's Islamic University, was commuted to seven years in jail. After the assassination of Premier Yitzhak Rabin in November 1995, it was revealed by official sources that the intelligence agencies had concentrated so much on the scenario of an extremist Palestinian murdering Rabin and other Israeli leaders that they had neglected to take seriously the proposition that Labour politicians might be targeted by Jewish zealots.

'Not even the Sabra [Palestine-born Jews] establishment – of which Rabin was a founding member – can escape blame for the murder [of Rabin],' wrote Zeev Chafets in the *Jerusalem Report*. 'The Shin Beth (the quintessential Sabra security force), which was under Rabin's own command, failed to protect him from the gunman. But that failure was the last link in the chain. None of the country's agencies of law and order, including the army, the police and the courts, have been willing or able to effectively stand up to the [Jewish] zealots. Instead, they indulged them. They allowed the leaders of Kach and Kahane Hai movements to roam the country giving interviews with impunity . . . They stood by while settlers flaunted court orders, and rabbis incited to sedition and murder. Partly, this was the result of political calculation by the Labour Party (yes, and Rabin himself) who didn't want to alienate potential Orthodox support. But more profoundly, it was a lack of will, a show of weakness and irresolution by a liberal, secular Zionist establishment that seems to have lost faith in itself and its ideals . . . Yitzhak Rabin paid for that failure with his life.'[7]

It was the self-same political opportunism which led the Israeli Government to support the rise of the Muslim Brotherhood/Islamic Centre, especially in the Gaza Strip. So intense was its hostility towards the PLO, a secular, nationalist body, that it encouraged the rise of a rival religio-political movement from 1973–84 on the expeditious principle that any group which reduced the PLO's influence among Palestinians was a positive development for the Jewish state. This short-sighted policy was to prove extremely harmful to Israel in the middle term.

As if to live down that self-damaging record, in recent years Israeli politicians have taken to crusading against Islamic radicals among Palestinians and other Arabs with a zeal that can only be counter-productive.

It is understandable that, having lost a long-standing ideological foe in the form of the Soviet Union and leftist Arabs, following the collapse of the Union of the Soviet Socialist Republics in late 1991, Israel felt a need to fill the resulting vacuum, and found Islamic fundamentalism a credible and viable ideology to target.

But at the popular level distrust and hatred of Israel in the Arab world remain so entrenched that any railing against a Muslim group or country (such as Iran) by Israeli leaders induces the response which can be summarized thus: if Jewish Israelis are rabidly against something, then there must be something beneficial for Muslims and Arabs in it.

It needs to be noted that Israel's unrelenting pressure on the Occupied Territories increasingly made Palestinians turn to religion for succour. The number of mosques rose sharply, and the influence of preachers and prayer-leaders grew. The example of the Deheisheh refugee camp was typical. Before the intifada it had only one jami (Arabic, major) mosque. During the intifada the residents constructed another such mosque with their own meagre resources. And a third jami mosque went up soon after the intifada. So, while the indigent refugees built two impressive, new mosques with voluntary contributions, a hospital, funded

by outside sources, remained unfinished because the money
ran out.

The rising interest in Islam provided one key to understanding the growing popularity of Hamas. The other key lay in
the analysis that once the PLO had compromised heavily on
its basic tenets contained in the Palestine National Charter
in its Oslo Accord with Israel, an alternative organization
was bound to arise if only to fill the political vacuum created
by the PLO's retreat. So even if six-year-old Hamas had not
existed in 1993, some such party would have emerged in the
aftermath of the Oslo Accord.

Shorn of its references to Islam, the 1988 Charter of Hamas
was not much different from the one the PLO had adopted
in 1968. In any event, the idea of Zionism as imperialism
is not the monopoly of the likes of Dr Mahmoud Zahar of
Hamas but is shared by a Christian intellectual such as Albert
Aghazarian, a resident of the Old City of Jerusalem. 'An
imperialist power always likes monopoly,' he said. 'Zionists
and Israel take a monolithic view of history, not pluralistic.
They constantly stress only four key elements – the First and
Second Temples in ancient times, and kibbutzim and the 1967
War in recent times – and ignore all others. This applies as
much to the excavations carried out by the Israelis. There are
many layers there, many successive empires have called the
shots here. The Jewish layer pertains to only 120 years when
they had their own leum, peoplehood; and before that were
the Israelites, for about 450 years. Applying all its power,
determination and stamina, the State of Israel is demolishing
all other mirrors at the expense of its own. The mounting
of the Jerusalem 3000 festival in September [1995] will be
a perfect example of that monopolistic policy.'[8]

Such perceptions are not limited to Palestinians, and are to
be encountered widely among Israeli Arab intellectuals. 'Like
other imperialists Israelis look down upon the local people as
retarded,' said Dr Manna. 'They know what's good for the
natives. We will make progress, economic development, in
their land, and show them. Even when Zionists were a tiny
minority [in Palestine] their attitude was not to recognize
natives as people, to deal with them directly. Instead they

tried to make deals with Arab "leaders" – to make peace with the Hashemites in Transjordan, the Egyptian regime, and so on. They wanted this country without the people. This was the end objective. This land belongs to the Jews. You know the Jewish National Fund does not buy land here, it "redeems" land; the same with the IDF when it confiscates Palestinian land. It is all "redemption". This is how they teach history in Israeli schools.'

Yet not every Jewish Israeli ends up parroting the conventional, mainstream views. There are notable exceptions. Historian Ilan Pappe is one such. 'The [pioneering] Zionists thought of Arabs as they thought of swamps, mosquitoes, stones and other negatives of nature around them, never as human beings with their own rights and own dignity,' he said.

However, misconceptions and myth-making are not the monopoly of one side. In the Palestinian camp the tendency to indulge in hyperbole and rose-coloured analyses, however comforting in the short term, proved damaging in the medium-to-long term. 'In the 1948 War, because the Jews did not capture East Jerusalem, it allowed the Palestinians to create myths about their fighting prowess,' said Aghazarian. 'Those fighting at the Jaffa Gate, Old City, would say: "We put sewer pipes in the barrels of our guns, and the Zionists thought we had cannons." Then we had the inane statements like "If every Arab spat on Israel it would drown in spit", and "If every Arab threw an orange at Israel it would drown in oranges", and so on. This enabled the Israelis to manufacture the myth of facing the colossal power of five Arab countries.' But the Arab propensity for exaggeration persisted. Even a slight chink in the armour of Israel was perceived as bearing a potential for the ultimate demise of the Jewish state. 'Before the 1967 War the thinking among Arabs was that contradictions between Ashkenazim and Sephardim would be able to destroy Israel from within,' said Emile Habibi, the veteran Israeli Arab writer-politician. 'This was mere fiction. But the bogey of extermination which was developed by Israel, using the sensationalist Arab slogans, helped in bringing together

Ashkenazim and Sephardim, especially under the threat of war in 1967.'9

Sometimes myths are created instantly. Palestinians today invariably use the term *Al Saliteh al Wataniye al Falastiniye* (the Palestinian National Authority) which is not the term mentioned in the Cairo Agreement that the PLO signed with Israel. The correct, official term mentioned in the Cairo Agreement is the Palestinian Authority; and the title the Palestinian National Authority has more to do with the term used in the main Palestine National Council resolution passed in 1974 than what happened between the PLO and Israel nearly 20 years later.

In a different, but more profound, context, Israeli text-books state that the Zionist Jews migrated to the Eretz Israel, which did not exist – and not to the Ottoman Palestine, which existed, albeit in a fractured form.

In the everyday lexicon the almost universal Jewish Israeli habit of using the terms 'terror' and 'terrorism/terrorists' end-lessly – without lacing them with such variants as 'guerrilla operation', 'violent action', 'bloody explosion' etc. – has the inadvertent effect of robbing the word 'terror' and its derivatives of the shock value they contain. As if in retaliation to this Jewish Israeli norm, Palestinians often say 'the Sunday event' or 'the event on Monday', instead of uttering even such terms as 'killings on Sunday' or 'the massacre on Monday'.

Then there is the sociological fact of Jewish Israelis being news-junkies, and reacting instantly to the latest develop-ment, behaving in a mercurial fashion. '[Jewish] Israelis are obsessive listeners to the radio news,' writes Amos Elon, an eminent Israeli historian and commentator. 'It is almost a druglike addiction. Few try to kick the habit; even fewer succeed . . . Israeli buses are often equipped with radio sets . . . The loudspeaker, attached above the luggage racks, emits mostly pop music, lost in the general commotion. But every hour on the hour comes the NEWS. It blares out over the noise of the traffic, and the entire bus falls silent . . . No people in the entire world tunes in to the news as often, as regularly, and with such fervour. Seven or eight times a day, at the sound of the news beep, most Israelis pause at whatever they are doing, to hear whether there has been another air battle or artillery exchange across the Suez Canal or some new act of sabotage by Arab terrorists. Not infrequently the names of the latest casualties are read out. (My God, isn't that so and so's son?) Modern Israelis turn to their radios like their ancestors once turned to prayers.' But there is more to this Jewish Israeli ritual today – which oddly parallels the prayer calls to Muslims five times a day – than merely keeping abreast of what is going on. 'The habit of following the news so often and so closely partly explains the sudden shifts in the public mood, which can be as sharp as they are frequent,' continues Elon. 'Israelis easily fall from heights of exhilaration to dark abysses of gloom; from glowing hope for imminent peace to bleak depression that the war will never end and that they may be crushed by it.'[10]

'Crush, or be crushed': that has been the leitmotif of the politics of Palestine/Israel for the past many decades, the two nations locked in an intimate embrace, unable to disengage, unable to devise a means of co-existence, even a tentative one – until 1993. 'Palestinians were the first to understand that solving the national conflict through one people's annihilation of the other is not possible in our time,' said Habibi. 'But the scenario of getting rid of Palestinians is still persistent in the Israeli public opinion much more than the idea of getting rid of Jews is amidst the Palestinian public opinion. That is the main hindrance to real peace. We Palestinians dared to drink our bitter cup and come to the conclusion that there is no other way but reconciliation with Israel. But we say to [Jewish] Israelis, "You have not drunk your bitter cup. Hence the recurrent crises in the peace process. You cannot run away from drinking your bitter cup. Without your leaders telling you this, you will not comprehend the scope of the price extracted from Palestinians to have your State of Israel."'

To a non-partisan outsider, the price seems plain enough: three-quarters of the British mandate Palestine. But most Jewish Israelis do not see it that way, nor do their leaders.

Yet the past must be addressed, and a reasonably objective balance sheet drawn. For, in the words of Dr Manna,

'The past, present and future are interlinked; and unless you change your attitude to the past you cannot connect correctly with the present and the future.' Specifically, he would like Israeli textbooks to address two central questions, something they now omit: Why did Palestinians resist Jewish immigration? And what caused the Arab Revolt of 1936–9?

As for Israelis drinking their bitter cup, Habibi did not bring out and address the question: *why* does a community drink 'a bitter cup'? The short answer is: only when it finds itself in dire straits. That is what happened to Palestinians, or at least to the PLO. After the 1991 Gulf War, it found itself beset with a host of crises – ranging from loss of funds from the oil-rich Gulf states and, equally damagingly, depletion in popular support as more and more Palestinians turned to Hamas. In contrast, Israel and Israelis today are hardly in dire straits. Certainly, IDF soldiers got weary of controlling the Palestinian intifada, especially in the Gaza Strip. But there are four other vital dimensions to the Jewish state – the rate of Jewish immigration, the economy, Israel's links with the Diaspora Jews, and its ties with the United States – which show no sign of slackening or fatigue. A steady inflow of Jews from the former Soviet Union at about 70,000 annually is assured until the turn of the century. Israel's economy remains buoyant, helped partly by the surge in its diplomatic recognition following the Oslo Accord, and the new trade opportunities that have ensued. Thirdly, Israel continues to pay top priority in tapping into the tremendous goodwill it enjoys among Diaspora Jews. Its highly-developed and effective programmes in this field ensure that every Diaspora Jew gets the opportunity to visit Israel at least once before he/she is in his/her mid-20s. For instance, all Israeli universities have well-tailored programmes for Diaspora Jewish students which run from three weeks to six months. The thinking behind all this is simple: even if the Diaspora Jew decides not to emigrate to Israel, he/she must have a first-hand knowledge and experience of the Jewish state, since that would enhance the chance of his/her financial contribution to Israel through the Jewish National Fund, which owns 93 per cent of all land in Israel. Finally,

Washington's unqualified support for Israel – military, economic, diplomatic – remains firm. This has strong bi-partisan backing not only in the US Congress but also public opinion. As the US is the sole superpower today, its stance on Israel carries immense weight, regionally and globally.

In sum, Israel remains powerful economically, militarily and diplomatically. It therefore negotiates with both the Syrians and the Palestinians from a position of strength.

This will be the case during the final round of the Israeli–Palestinian talks which would take place *only* if the newly elected Premier Binyamin Netanyahu decides to soften his hardline position, and honour fully the Oslo Accord signed by the Labour government. These will cover: (a) Palestinian refugees, (b) Jewish Settlements, (c) final borders, and (d) Jerusalem. Given the complexity of the issues, compounded by Netanyahu's uncompromising stance, the negotiations will be arduous and long.

(a) *Palestinian Refugees.* Since the Madrid peace process is based on the United Nations Security Council Resolution 242, which pertains to the June 1967 War, at best Israel will limit the discussion only to those Palestinians who became refugees as a result of that conflict even though the Resolution refers generally to 'achieving a just settlement of the refugee problem' – an issue which has been with the UN since the 1948–9 Arab-Israeli War, and on which the UN has repeatedly called for the return of the Palestinian refugees to their homes and livelihood. But the chances are that when the Palestinian delegation raises the subject of the three-quarter million Palestinians who lost their homes in the 1948–9 War, and who now number over 2.5 million, it will get short shrift from the Israelis. It is most unlikely that Israel will pay heed to the argument of the PLO – which, unlike the Palestinian Authority, represents both the home-based and Diaspora Palestinians – that it is morally wrong for Jews to insist on exercising their right to Return based on ancient history while denying the same right to the recently uprooted Palestinians. As a compromise, the Israelis may discuss the possibility of a token number of post–June 1967 Palestinian refugees returning home on very strict terms. Deeply concerned about the deomographic trend in the area covering the British mandate Palestine, which is running against Israel, despite the recent upsurge in immigration from the former Soviet Union, the Jewish state wants to minimize the number of Palestinians returning to their native homes.

An agreement, which denies some 40 per cent of the overall Palestinian population of more than 6.5 million the right to return home, will plant seeds of discontent which will, going by past history, sprout in the future.

(b) *Jewish Settlements*. The break-neck speed with which the Labour-led Government began building 20 bypasses at the cost of $100 million in the West Bank to minimize contact between the Palestinians and the Jewish settlers in order ostensibly to prepare the way for the Palestinian Authority to assume greater control over the territory had a more insidious aim. The unstated objective was to do to the West Bank what Israel had done earlier to the Gaza Strip:[11] to establish a road network which severs the Palestinian urban centres. The end-purpose is to ensure that in case of an armed conflict between Israel and a future Palestinian entity, Palestinian civilians and soldiers are trapped into enclaves which the IDF can easily surround and overpower.

Regarding the Jewish settlers, it has been calculated that some 70 per cent of them are concentrated in 10 per cent of the West Bank which is continguous with Israel, and covers that bit of the Jewish state where it is at its narrowest, 14 kilometres wide. In the 'best case' scenario for the Palestinians, Israel will propose annexing 10 per cent of the West Bank in return for cash while ensuring that the remaining 30 per cent of the settlers retain their Israeli citizenship and protection. In the 'worst case' scenario for the Palestinians, the final talks will start against the background of Israel establishing new Jewish settlements in the C sector (as defined by Oslo II) of the West Bank, occupying 70 per cent of the territory.

With Netanyahu in office until 2000, and Ariel Sharon running an important super-ministry, the Jewish settlers will play an important role in the forging of Israeli policy on the settlements. Netanyahu's election victory conferred respectability to the ultranationalist credo, summed up by Eliakim Haetzni, a settlers' leader, thus; 'Judaism's central pillar is the Return [to Zion] and the Eretz Israel, which includes the Land of the Patriarchs, where I am based now [in Givat Mamre, Kiryat Arba]. If you don't believe in this, then you're not a Jew.[12]

Netanyahu's opposition to conceding sovereignity to the Palestinians means that Israel will continue to control two-thirds of the West Bank land, most of it being 'state land' – a right Israel arrogated to itself, having declared itself the 'state' that ruled (not occupied) the territory, the earlier 'states' being Jordan and Britain.

(c) *Final borders.* The subject of the final borders is linked with the Jewish settlements. Security concerns remain paramount among top Israeli decision-makers. According to the military doctrine first enunciated by Yigal Allon in 1970, and then adopted by one of his leading protégés, Yitzhak Rabin, the eastern security border of Israel lies along the Jordan Valley. After Rabin's assassination in late 1995, there was no indication that Shimon Peres had disavowed his doctrine. Nor is it likely to be discarded by Netanyahu, were he to enter into serious negotiations with the Palestinians on the future of their territories. The second salient Israeli security concern remains the narrow neck of the pre-1967 Israel 16 kilometres north of Tel Aviv: it is particularly vulnerable to artillery and rocket attacks by hostile forces from the West Bank. Both these issues will have to be resolved. If the past is any guide, they will be – to the satisfaction, basically, of the stronger party, Israel.

On the other hand, the erection of a border fence equipped with surveillance equipment, that is constantly patrolled by the IDF, must go a long way to satisfy Israel's security needs, and lessen pressure on the Palestinians to concede territory to Israel.

(d) *Jerusalem.* Netanyahu's insistence on maintaining a united city need not clash with the Palestinian proposal that Jerusalem should become the joint capital of both Israel and Palestine. But the Israeli position on Jerusalem has been so uncompromising, and the subject so emotionally charged, that negotiations on the subject will be particulary tough and acrimonious. Among the points to be settled will be the new borders of Jerusalem, acceptable to both sides.

Though, strictly speaking, Jerusalem is a subject that concerns only Israelis and Palestinians, it has much wider implications. It was the arson attack on the Al Aqsa Mosque in August 1969 which acted as a trigger for the establishment of the Islamic Conference Organization, the first official pan-Islamic institution of inter-governmental co-operation, at the initiative of King Faisal of Saudi Arabia. By establishing a committee on Jerusalem under the chairmanship of King Hassan of Morocco, the ICO signalled that the fate of the Holy City concerned all Muslim states. This position remains unaltered.

More specifically, the country which is likely to have an impact on the future of Jerusalem, albeit indirectly, is Syria. Once the strategy of its President, Hafiz Assad, to have all the Arab negotiating parties co-ordinate their positions before each round of talks with Israel had been undermined by the secret 1993 PLO–Israeli Accord, he began wishing that Syria's talks with Israel would enter a serious phase about the same time as the final round of Palestinian–Israeli negotiations. Due to various developments, most of which were not of Assad's making, this timing came to pass. But Assad, whose delegates had been negotiating with their Israeli counterparts during the run-up to the May 1996 Israeli elections, found himself shut out of the peace process after the poll, when Premier Netanyahu declared that Israel would not withdraw from the Golan Heights at all, thus reversing the position taken by his predecessor.

Faced with this situation, Assad turned to Hosni Mubarak, president of Egypt, the leader of the Arab League, and the Saudi monarch. The summoning of the Arab summit in Cairo on 21 June, and its adoption of a resolution calling for Israeli withdrawal from 'all' Arab territories occupied after 4 June 1967, showed the extent of Assad's diplomatic success.

Beyond that, he had other cards, including the presence in Damascus of hardline Hamas leaders. According to the Israeli and Palestinian intelligence agencies, they were the ones who ordered the hardline members of the Qassam Brigade to detonate suicide bombs in Israel during February–March 1996.

These bombings were directed as much against the Israeli Government of Peres as at the Palestinian Authority of Yasser Arafat. The message to Arafat was that Hamas would not tolerate any compromise on such issues as Jewish settlements, final borders and Jerusalem in the final round of talks, and that the Israeli withdrawal from the Occupied Palestinian Territories, including (Jordanian) East Jerusalem, must be total, and that all Jewish settlements must be evacuated.

Though the final Palestinian-Israeli talks will be conducted independently of what has been agreed in the interim accords, called Oslo I and Oslo II, the earlier agreements have created certain precedents in procedures and institutions which would be hard to ignore. Among other things they have engendered numerous joint Israeli-Palestinian committees, and set ground rules for tackling every conceivable crisis. This was particularly true of Oslo II concerning the West Bank, which benefited from the experience of implementing Oslo I.

But all this was agreed under the general supervision of Israel, which retained the ultimate authority. 'If Oslo II does [work], fantastic,' an unnamed top Israeli official told the *Jerusalem Report*. 'If not, well, we gave it our best shot, we really tried, the other side wasn't up to it. The army will retake control.'[13] Under the current accords, Israel has the right to 'retake control' of the territories run by th PA. Netanyahu reiterated this by stating that the IDF would protect the Jews no matter where they were settled in Eretz Israel.

In reality, though, the IDF's attempt to do so would meet armed resistance by the PA police and security forces, and lead to massive bloodshed, and result, most likely, in the posting of UN peace-keeping forces in the Palestinian territories. However flawed the progress of the peace talks between the PLO and Israel has been so far, Palestinians of all political hues will fight tooth and nail to prevent the situation reverting to the pre-September 1993 period. Any

Israeli attempt to put the clock back will boost the fortunes of radical Islamists locally and regionally.

Barring this scenario, and assuming that a satisfactory final accord has been struck by the deadline of May 1998, the resulting peace will need steady nurturing. How well or badly consolidation of peace proceeds will depend on how Israeli Arabs and Mizrachi Jews play their bridge-building part, and whether the Palestinian entity emerges as a democratic polity, or dictatorial, or something in-between.

History has imbibed Israeli Arabs with assets that are uniquely suited to strengthen rapprochement between Israelis and Palestinians. 'Israeli Arabs are Palestinian and are also Israeli citizens,' explained Dr Manna. 'They know Israeli Jews, their language, culture, day-to-day life. Yet they are also Palestinian themselves. At the same time they see things much more clearly whereas the major contending groups cannot. Israeli Jews are directly involved. Palestinians are directly involved. Only Israeli Arabs can see the story from both sides.'

The assets of Israeli Arabs can be useful to the country's leaders beyond the borders of British mandate Palestine. 'Jewish Israelis think they don't need Israeli Arabs; that is an illusion,' said Habibi. 'They will not be able to build bridges with the Arab world without Israeli Arab intellectuals. For example, the only force inside Israel which can end the current anti-Israeli wave in Egypt are the Israeli Arab intellectuals.'

A vital bridge-building role awaits Mizrachi Jews, especially intellectuals in the community, once Palestinians and other Arabs have ceased to be Israel's foes. What had been a liability – looking like your enemy and sharing his culture – for Mizrachim could be transformed into an asset. 'Peace [with Arabs] may open Israel to Arab culture and may make relevant the Mizrachim's cultural affinity with the Arabs,' writes Professor Sammy Smooha. 'Israel's cultural orientation may become a real issue which could divide Israeli Jews ethnically, the Ashkenazim tending to consolidate Israel's western orientation in order to prevent the danger of "Levantization", or assimilation into the Arab world, and some of the Mizrachim wanting to benefit from fostering cultural and other ties with the Arabs.'[14]

As stated earlier, Mizrachim with university education, who have regained confidence and pride in their Arab origins, are more dovish than hawkish on the issues of peace and security.[15] 'We know very little of Islam and Islamic culture in Israel,' said Dr Meir Buzaglo, a researcher at the Hebrew University of Jerusalem. 'Understandably we [Mizrachim] have much sympathy for Arab culture. We'll teach Arabic at the high school level in our [special] Kedma schools. We do not see Arabs as a Black Hole. We don't see Arab countries as "all bad".'[16]

How Mizrachi Jews evolve over the next generation will shape the socio-cultural future of Israel. A survey in 1988 revealed that 38 per cent of Jewish Israelis favoured 'a distinct western culture' for Israel; 44 per cent preferred either a 'western culture in which Arab elements are incorporated' or 'a mixed culture consisting of western and Arab elements' in almost equal proportions; and nearly six per cent 'an Arab culture in which western elements are incorporated', with the rest rejecting both cultures.[17] Interestingly, twice as many Mizrachim as Ashkenazim backed the idea of a combination of western and Arab cultures. Incorporating Arab elements into its culture will assist Israel to win acceptance in the Middle East at the popular level.

The question of Israel's cultural identity will move up the national agenda as the implications of the demographic trends begin to take hold of the public imagination. Though overall Israeli Arabs are about one-sixth of the Israeli population, in the under-20 age group they are a quarter of the total. In the mid-1990s, in the British mandate Palestine, there were 4.3 million Jews and 3.2 million Palestinians (including 0.9 million Israeli Arabs). The fertility rates among Palestinian and Jewish women were: 7.4 children to 2.9 children. Given this, and the return to the Palestinian entity of some of the refugees by the early 2000s, it will not be long before the Palestinians catch up with the Jews in numbers. Indeed, even without the return of the Palestinian refugees, the estimated date for the Palestinian community to be as large as the Jewish is 2015.

At present, besides the IDF, and the universal conscription of its Jewish nationals, what holds Israel, a multi-ethnic and multi-sectarian society, together is the sharing of democratic values by all its citizens. What will help consolidate its peace with Palestinians will be the emergence of a Palestinian entity as a fully-fledged Democratic Republic of Palestine.

A democratic Palestinian entity offers a more lasting and secure future for Israel than a dictatorship, weak or strong, or semi-dictatorship. Though a Palestinian strongman may be able to muzzle the Islamic opposition, and thus make Israel more secure, his success is likely to be temporary rather than permanent, if the problems of Palestinian land and sovereignty as well as economic deprivation are not resolved satisfactorily. If repressed severely by a Palestinian dictator, radical Islamist activists will seek refuge in the neighbouring Arab states and bide their time. After all Islamic fundamentalism is a regional phenomenon, not local.

In any case, it will be hard to write Hamas out of the script. For it was the rise of Hamas which drove Israel to strike a deal with the PLO in the first place. Later, had Arafat succumbed to Israeli pressure and drastically repressed Hamas, he would been judged as an agent of Israel, and lost popularity among Palestinians. Also, in the absence of having won office through elections, he had no such mandate from his voters. Finally, Arafat found it expedient to have Hamas around in order to extract concessions from the Israelis that he would otherwise not have been able to do.

As it is, during the next few years the fate of Hamas and the Islamic Jihad will be shaped largely by the kind of final peace settlement Arafat signs with Israel. If he concedes too much to Israel, then the Islamist opposition will grow. Unlike its opposition to participation in the 20 January 1996 poll which, in its view, legitimized Palestinian autonomy, not national independence, Hamas is committed to contesting local elections in the Palestinian territories as well as ballots for such non-governmental organizations as the chambers of commerce, students unions and professional associations – something its parent body, the Islamic Centre, always did.

And keeping Hamas out of these contests would strike at the very root of democracy.

Current signals about the democratic behaviour of the Palestinian Authority are mixed. Relentless Israeli pressure to ensure security for its citizens at any cost forces Arafat into a dictatorial stance. His egotism and past behaviour do not augur well for democracy; old habits die hard. And his political icons still remain Presidents Hosni Mubarak and Saddam Hussein.

But, on balance, the chances of democracy taking root in the Palestinian entity are higher than not. There are several internal and external reasons for this.

The manner in which a Palestinian polity is being created has no parallel in the region. Due to historical circumstances, a Palestinian entity is being engendered from the bottom up, an aggregation of dispersed power, which is dramatically different from the phenomenon of a political or military leader inheriting an ongoing centralized state such as Egypt, Syria or Iraq. Political-administrative power is being gathered through free and fair elections from citizenry which is the most politicized in the Middle East. It is also highly literate. 'It is not possible to set up an authoritarian state in Palestine even if Arafat wanted to,' said George Hazboun, a Palestinian Council candidate in Bethlehem in January 1996. 'From the first years of the intifada, every Palestinian has been interested in politics. We are a much more political people than the Syrians and the Iraqis. It can't be done.'[18]

Politicization of Palestinians expresses itself in different ways. How it shapes their attitude towards the police and military, a vital element in the success or failure of a dictatorial system, was explained by Abdul Hakim al Samra, a journalist in Gaza, thus: 'If the IDF says something to me I keep my distance and do it. If the Palestinian National Authority police stops and checks the boot of my car, I argue with them, "What are you looking for, alcohol? If I wanted to drink I'd do so in your presence, here, and so on." While dealing with Palestinian policemen I feel equal to them, even better. An Israeli is my enemy so I never get into thinking whether I am equal to him or not. If a Palestinian policeman kills my brother we will get into our traditional mores: I will kill his brother or father or uncle; eye for eye, our tradition.'[19]

The Palestinian Authority is dependent for its economic survival on donations from 30 foreign countries, most of them western democracies, committed to upholding civil and human rights. Any persistent or severe violation of these rights will result in the foreign aid being suspended or stopped, a powerful leverage.

Finally, the presence of the international media based in Jerusalem will aid democratic forces among Palestinians. The manner and speed with which the irascibility of Arafat regarding the *Al Quds* editor, Maher Alami, and the human rights activist, Bassam Eid, was exposed, illustrated the power of the media and the arduous task the dictatorial forces in the Palestinian ranks faced.[20]

Still, constant vigilance will be needed on all sides to let the seed of democracy strike roots in the Palestinian soil. The most conducive climate for the growth of this plant is peaceful co-existence between Israel and the Palestinian entity.

Taking a historical view, Emile Habibi said: 'It so happened that there arose in Palestine two nations in conflict with each other, the Israeli versus the Palestinian nation. The Israeli nation is different from the world Jewish heritage, and the Palestinians have special local characteristics and are different from the old Arab nations. Only after the [1993] Oslo Accord were these facts recognized mutually. This phenomenon of the appearance of two nations has affected both sides. So long as conflict persisted it brought out negative characteristics in both sides. Now peace will bring out positive aspects of both sides. There is no way out of living together, peacefully.'[21]

A long-term sharing of the Promised Land by Palestinians and Israelis seems in prospect. But, given the current imbalance in power between the two peoples, the framework for a peaceful co-existence and its terms will continue to be set by Israel.

EPILOGUE

The electoral victory of Binyamin Netanyahu on 29 May 1996 albeit by a thin margin, caught by surprise not only the Arab countries but also the United States, whose Secretary of State, Warren Christopher, had visited the Middle East 24 times in three and a half years to advance the peace process.

However, President Bill Clinton, who had backed Shimon Peres's candidacy for premiership, urging him to complete 'the cycle of comprehensive peace in the region', and cold shouldered Netanyahu, was quick to accept publicly the result of the 'democratic process' in Israel, and congratulate the winner.

Regionally the greatest loser was Yasser Arafat. Since he had prepared no contingency plan to deal with the defeat of Peres, he was lost. As in the past, faced with a crisis, he conferred with the leaders of Egypt and Jordan.

Alarmed by Netanyahu's repeated assertions, following his electoral success, that Israel would not vacate the Golan Heights, President Hafiz Assad too sought regional support. Following a discussion on the Israeli poll with President Hosni Mubarak in Cairo on 3 June, he hosted a meeting with Mubarak and Crown Prince Abdullah of Saudi Arabia in Damascus. They decided to convene an Arab League summit on 21 June in Cairo, and invited all the 22 leaders except President Saddam Hussein of Iraq. The last such gathering had taken place on 9 August 1990, a week after the Iraqi invasion and occupation of Kuwait. Since then differences between member states had proved so irreconcilable that no attempt was made to hold a summit which, until 1990, had been an annual event.

The summit's final communiqué, issued on 23 June, stated that the Arabs remained committed to the process of peace which they had embarked upon at the Madrid conference in October 1991, and reiterated the Arab positions: total Israeli withdrawal from the occupied Arab lands for total peace, based on United Nations Security Council resolutions 242 and 338; an end to Jewish settlements on the Arab soil; and a sovereign state for the Palestinians with its capital in Jerusalem. 'If Israel abandons basic principles like return of occupied land for peace, or reneges on existing agreements', it continued, 'the resultant setback to the negotiations would oblige all Arab states to reconsider the steps they have taken towards Israel in the context of the peace process.'

Assad's proposal that the Arab states currently normalizing ties with Israel should suspend contacts and freeze relations in the absence of progress in the peace process was diluted in deference chiefly to Mubarak's eagerness not to upset Washington,[1] which did not want the Arabs to foreclose any options at this stage, and give time to Netanyahu to spell out his policies.

The Israeli premier was quick to respond to the Arab summit's communiqué. 'The peace process cannot be made hostage to any prior conditions,' he said. 'Preconditions that hinder security for Israel are incompatible with peace negotiations. For the quest for peace to continue, for it to achieve success and move forward, such preconditions must be removed.'[2] Describing the Arab call for Israel's re-commitment to the concept of swapping occupied land for peace as 'an unacceptable precondition', he said that this principle was nothing more than 'a general guideline'.

This was not so. In his seminal statement, contained in his address to the US Congress on 6 March 1991, a week after the end of the Gulf War, President George Bush stressed the need for 'a comprehensive peace [which] must be grounded in the United Nations Security Council Resolutions 242 and 338 and the principle of territory for peace.'[3] This was the seed which seven months later yielded the Middle East Peace Conference in Madrid.

While opposing preconditions by the Arabs, Netanyahu reaffirmed his own set. It could be summarized as Five Nos: No to the withdrawal from the Golan Heights; No to a Palestinian state; No to a Palestinian capital in East Jerusalem; No to the return of Palestinian refugees (as that would constitute a threat to the 'demographic security' of Israel); and No to freezing the Jewish settlements.

It was widely expected that in the course of his first official meeting with President Clinton on 9 July in Washington, Netanyahu would soften his stance somewhat. He did nothing of the sort.

At a joint press conference after the meeting, while Clinton remarked that setting up new settlements would 'do more harm than good,' Netanyahu said: 'I cannot preclude new West Bank settlements, but their pattern has yet to be decided.'[4]

On the Palestinian front, he complemented his uncompromising stands on the subjects to be settled during the final round of negotiations – the status of Jerusalem and the Jewish settlements, and the return of Palestinian refugees – with hardline statements on current issues: the evacuation of Hebron and the easing of the closures of the West Bank and Gaza Strip. 'I'll let Palestinian workers back into Israel only if the Palestinian Authority sustains its crackdown on Hamas, the Islamic Jihad and other militant organizations operating from its territory,' he stated. Apparently, the continued incarceration of nearly 1,200 Islamists in PA jails, most of them without charge or trial, was not enough to convince Netanyahu of the PA's seriousness about suppressing the Islamic opposition.

On evacuating seven-eighths of Hebron, agreed by Premier Peres, Netanyahu said: 'I'll fulfil the agreement to withdraw the IDF from Hebron only if I am assured of the security of the Jewish settlers in the city.' But certainly his predecessor, working in conjunction with top military and intelligence officers, had made provisions for the settlers' security, and fixed 28 March as the deadline for evacuation. Arafat protested. 'We cannot agree to retreat from what has already been attained and agreed upon, as this would mean a return to the unknown whose results cannot be foreseen by anybody,' he stated.[5]

The Arabs were not the only ones to criticize Netanyahu. The mainstream Israel opposition did the same. 'I fear, my friend the Prime Minister, that you will quickly discover that the platform on which you were elected cannot serve as a recipe for success and progress in the peace process,' warned Peres in his main speech in the Knesset. 'Petty slogans will be no substitute for policy, and coalition formulas will not forestall the need for brave and fateful decisions.'[6]

This had no effect on Netanyahu. For instance, as in the past, he continued to use the term 'the Palestinians', and never 'the Palestinian Authority' or 'the Palestinian Liberation Organization'. In contrast, Arafat came through as a pragmatic realist. 'The election results in Israel have created a new reality which cannot be ignored,' he said. 'Despite all the slogans and extreme declarations, we are still interested in negotiating with the elected government.'

On the Syrian front, while Clinton in Washington urged 'an attempt to re-engage Syria' in the peace process, Netanyahu declared: 'I rule out further talks with Syria until it ends all support for terrorist organizations based either in Syria or southern Lebanon.' Before flying to Washington, he publicly told the leaders of the 15,000-strong Jewish settler community in the Golan that they could go ahead with ambitious development plans stretching beyond 2000.

Part of the reason for Netanyahu's aggressive confidence was the imminence of the US presidential poll, due in early November. He knew that a pro-Israeli Democrat President like Clinton would not pressure him for fear of alienating the crucial Jewish funding of his election campaign. During his visit to Washington, Netanyahu held a much-publicized meeting with Robert Dole, the Republican candidate for president. Both Dole and Clinton were conscious that between a quarter and a third of contributions to their parties came from Jewish citizens.

While Arab–Americans have no impact on the domestic political scene in the United States, the role of the Arabs in the Middle East peace process remains vital. The latter had comprehended the importance of Netanyahu's electoral success and acted swiftly. 'We must thank Netanyahu for bringing us together,' said Colonel Muammar Qadafi of Libya. 'Without him [winning the election], there could have been no such summit.'[7]

By the same logic Netanyahu's intransigence could only spawn hardening of policies on the Arab side. 'We cannot allow ourselves to be moderate,' said the Syrian spokesman at the Arab summit in Cairo. 'Netanyahu will stick to the Likud's platform, will expand the settlements and will not withdraw from the Golan Heights. Then we shall convene a new Arab summit, and take much more interesting decisions.'[8]

On the Palestinian side, the phlegmatic Ahmad Qrei, Speaker of the Palestinian Council, and the second-in-command at the Palestinian Authority, warned in mid-July that if Netanyahu persisted in his hardline policies, there would be another Palestinian intifada. There were reports of fragmentation within the Fatah Hawks and the Qassam Brigade, which increased the chance of the breakaway members acting independently of the leadership, and carrying out terroristic attacks, thus triggering an unpredictable chain of events. (After all, it was the murderous act of a lone Jewish fanatic, Yigal Amir, which altered Israeli history. Had Rabin been alive, he would have defeated Netanyahu in the prime ministerial contest.) These extremist elements are unlikely to wait around until the US presidential poll is out of the way, and Netanyahu, yielding to the newly elected US President's pressure, resumes serious negotiations with the Palestinians and the Syrians in a spirit of compromise. The worsening economic condition in the West Bank and Gaza, where living standards have fallen a further 20 per cent over the past year, provides a fertile environment for desperate actions by desperate men.

Given this, it is hard to disagree with Peres's words after the 29 May Israeli poll: 'There could have been four wonderful years ... But four very difficult years – very difficult – are in store for us.'[9] The term 'us' should include not only Israelis but also Palestinians, Syrians and Lebanese.

NOTES

Introduction

1 Colin Thubron, *Jerusalem*, Century Hutchinson, London, 1986, p. 177.
2 The detailed information on 'Immigration and Absorption' in *Statistical Abstract of Israel, 1994*, a volume of 947 pages, does not break down the figures into 'Jews' and 'non-Jews' as it does in all other sections dealing with people. It assumes that all immigrants are Jewish.
3 Yossi Melman, *The New Israelis*, Carol Publishing Group, New York, 1993, p. 132.
4 Edward W. Said, *The Question of Palestine*, Pantheon, New York/Routledge & Kegan Paul, London, 1980, p. 174.
5 Ibid, p. 175.

Chapter 1 *The Walled Heart of Jerusalem*

1 All biblical quotations are from *The Holy Bible: The Old and New Testaments*, conformable to the edition of 1611, commonly known as the Authorized or King James Version, World Publishing Company, Cleveland and New York, 1960.
2 Michael Romann and Alex Weingrod, *Living Together Separately: Arabs and Jews in Contemporary Jerusalem*, Princeton University Press, Princeton, N.J., 1991, p. 4.
3 Cited in Colin Thubron, op. cit., p. 58.
4 Cited in Shirley Eber and Kevin O'Sullivan, *Israel and the Occupied Territories: The Rough Guide*, Harrap Columbus, London, 1989, p. 83.

5 Amos Elon, *The Israelis: Founders and Sons*, Holt, Rinehart & Winston, New York, 1971/Adam Publishers, Jerusalem, 1981, p. 182.

6 Graham McNeill, *An Unsettling Affair: Housing Conditions, Tenancy Regulations and the Coming of the Messiah in the Old City of Jerusalem*, Birzeit University, Birzeit, 1990, p. 4.

7 Meron Benvenisti, *Jerusalem: A Study of a Polarized Community*, Research Paper 3, The West Bank Data Base Project, Jerusalem, 1983, p. 12; and Shirley Eber and Kevin O'Sullivan, op. cit., p. 81. Muhammad Burqan built a new house outside Jerusalem on land owned by his relatives. When the Israelis constructed Pisgat Zeev, the third in the suburban settlement rings to the north of Jerusalem, in 1980, his house ended up in the middle of a traffic roundabout.

8 There is an old, established neighbourhood in West Jerusalem called the German Colony. No attempt has been made yet to rename it.

9 Cited in Robert I. Friedman, *Zealots for Zion: Inside Israel's West Bank Settlement Movement*, Random House, New York, 1993, p. 98.

10 The breakdown was 70 properties by 1987 for an estimated $10 million, and another 53 between January 1988 and the June 1992 general election. Some of the real estate bought by the JRP had belonged to the Jews who had lived in the Muslim Quarter before 1936. Robert I. Friedman, op. cit., pp. 98–104; and the author's interviews in the Old Town, February 1995. Buying the remaining properties in the Muslim Quarter was estimated to cost $100 million. Friedman, op. cit., p. 98.

11 Graham McNeill, op.cit., pp. 6–7.

12 Interview in February 1995.

13 David K. Shipler, *Arab and Jew: Wounded Spirits in a Promised Land*, Penguin Books, New York and Harmondsworth, 1987, p. 377.

14 Robert I. Friedman, p. 104.

15 *Jerusalem Report*, 30 January 1992, p. 5.

16 Its other uniqueness is that it is the only major Muslim shrine open to non-Muslims.

17 Yehuda Etzion, *The Temple Mount* (in Hebrew), E. Capsi, Jerusalem, 1985, pp. 2 and 5.

18 Cited in Gerald Kaufman, *Inside the Promised Land: A Personal View of Today's Israel*, Wildwood House, Aldershot, 1986, p. 32.

19 Menachem Livni, *Interrogations* (in Hebrew), Court documents, Jerusalem, 18 May 1984.

20 David K. Shipler, op. cit., p. 107.

21 *Village Voice*, 12 November 1985, p. 22.

22 See also *Time*, 16 October 1989, p. 32.

Chapter 2 *Jerusalem*

1 Cited in Dilip Hiro, *Desert Shield to Desert Storm: The Second Gulf War*, HarperCollins, London/Routledge, New York, 1992, pp. 554–5.

2 The last of the four Conventions – developed by an International Red Cross conference in Stockholm in August 1948 and ratified by United Nations members in Geneva on 12 August 1949 – was entitled The Geneva Convention Relative to the Protection of Civilian Persons in Time of War, 1949. It forbids the Occupying Power doing the following to the Protected Civilians: collective punishment and reprisals; deportation of individuals or groups; hostage-taking; torture; unjustified destruction of property; and discrimination in treatment on the grounds of race, religion, national origin or political affiliation. Article 47 states: 'Protected persons ... shall not be deprived of ... the benefits of this Convention by any changes introduced, as the result of the occupation of a territory, into the institutions or the government of the said territory, nor by any agreement concluded between the authorities of the occupied territories and the Occupying Power, nor by the annexation of the whole or part of the occupied territory.' Article 49 (6) states: 'The Occupying Power shall not deport or transfer parts of its own civilian population into the territory it occupies.' Cited in Dilip Hiro, *Dictionary of the Middle East*, St Martin's Press, New York/Macmillan, London, 1996, p. 91.

3 *Financial Times*, 12 May 1995.

4 Michael Romann and Alex Weingrod, op. cit., pp. 46–7.

5 In late 1993, the Palestinian population of Greater East Jerusalem was estimated to be 150,000, and the Jewish population 155,000.

6 *Guardian*, 5 September 1995.

7 Michael Romann and Alex Weingrod, op. cit., p. 54.

8 *Jerusalem Report*, 17 June 1993, p. 10.

9 *Ibid.*, 12 June 1993, p. 12.

10 The full title of Histadrut is HaHistadrut HaKelalit shel HaOvedim be Eretz Israel, the General Federation of Workers in Land of Israel.

11 Graham McNeill, op. cit., pp. 153–4.

12 12 June 1993, p. 10.

13 Michael Romann and Alex Weingrod, op. cit., p. 48.

14 *Jerusalem Report*, 17 June 1993, p. 12.

15 *Mainstream*, 20 May 1995, p. 29.

16 Interview in March 1995.

Chapter 3 *Mea Shearim*

1 See p. 25.

2 Rabbi Dow Marmur, *Beyond Survival*, Darton, Longman & Todd, London, 1982, p 53.
3 Interview in Jerusalem, March 1995.

Chapter 4 *Mizrachim/Sephardim*

1 Cited in Sammy Smooha, *Israel: Pluralism and Conflict*, Routledge & Kegan Paul, London and Boston, 1978, p. 88.
2 Interview in Tel Aviv, March 1995.
3 Stephen Brook, *Winner Takes All: A Season in Israel*, Picador, London, 1991, pp. 238–9.
4 Cited in Sammy Smooha, op. cit., p. 88.
5 *HaAretz*, 21 May 1978.
6 *Kedma* means going East; and *kidma* means going forward. That is, 'going East' means 'going forward', say Kedma's founders, intent on infusing pride among Mizrachim.
7 Amos Elon, op. cit., p. 245.
8 Keith Kyle and Joel Peters (eds), *Whither Israel? The Domestic Challenges*, I.B. Tauris, London and New York, 1993, pp. 170–71.

Chapter 5 *The Secular Centre*

1 The Elected Assembly, elected by the members of the Yishuv, (Jewish) Settlement/Community in Palestine, consisted of 170 to 300 members. It elected the National Council, *Vaad Leumi*, of 23 to 42 members.
2 See pp.83–4.
3 Westview Press, Boulder, COLO/Dawson, England, 1979, p. 148.
4 Cited in Dilip Hiro, *Inside the Middle East*, McGraw-Hill, New York/ Routledge & Kegan Paul, London, 1982, p. 236.
5 *The Paratroopers' Book* (in Hebrew), Ministry of Defence, Tel Aviv, 1969, pp. 157–8, cited in Dilip Hiro, ibid, p. 204.
6 Seymour M. Hersh, *The Samson Option: Israel's Nuclear Arsenal And American Foreign Policy*, Random House, New York/Faber & Faber, London, 1991, pp, 225–8 and 231; and Dilip Hiro, *Dictionary of the Middle East*, p. 198. During his first meeting with President Sadat on 7 November 1973, Kissinger reportedly explained the sudden American airlift to Israel as a decision aimed at avoiding a nuclear escalation.
7 Dilip Hiro, *Dictionary of the Middle East*, p. 198.
8 *Sunday Times*, 22 May 1977.
9 The full title of the Tehiya party was Tenuhat HaTehiya – Brit Ne'emanei Eretz Israel, The Renaissance Movement – Covenant of the Land of Israel Faithful.

10 Dilip Hiro, *Dictionary of the Middle East*, p. 141.

11 See p.94.

12 Cited in Dilip Hiro, *Desert Shield to Desert Storm: The Second Gulf War*, p. 332.

13 Seymour M. Hersh, op. cit., p. 318.

14 Cited in Ehud Sprinzak, 'The Israeli Right', in Keith Kyle and Joel Peters (eds), op. cit., p. 136.

15 Here are two examples. When a friend asked him why he was wearing only one trainer shoe, David Levy turned over the shoe, and pointing at the embossed sign on the sole – 'TAIWAN' – said, 'TIE ONE'. As a member of an Israeli delegation Levy arrived at a White House reception. He soon disappeared. His colleagues found him standing on the roof of the White House, holding a drink in his hand. 'What are you doing there?' asked an Israeli aide. 'Down there they said "Drinks on the House",' Levy replied.

16 According to the unpublished part of the Shamgar Commission's inquiry into Yitzhak Rabin's assassination, among those who provided posters portraying Rabin as a Nazi SS officer at an opposition rally was Avishai Raviv, an agent of the Shin Beth, who had been planted into Kiryat Arba after Baruch Goldstein's killings of Palestinians, and instructed to establish two extremist groups, Eyal and the Sword of David, with the aim of 'hunting down Jewish traitors'. When these posters were distributed at the rally against the Oslo II Accord in October 1995, which was addressed by Binyamin Netanyahu, his action was widely criticized. *Observer*, 31 March 1996.

17 Of the 44 Labour MKs two were Arab, and of the 12 Meretz MKs one. The Rabin Government had the backing also of two Jewish MKs who had split from the opposition Tzomet party. Of the remaining Arab MKs, two belonged to Hadash, two to the Arab Democratic Party, and one to Likud.

18 *Jerusalem Report*, 30 November 1995, p. 17.

19 *Observer*, 3 March 1996.

20 Ibid.

21 *Independent*, 28 February 1996.

22 It was not until 12 July 1996 that the representatives of these five countries, meeting in Washington, agreed on procedural matters.

23 See pp. 573–4.

24 Cited in *Observer*, 28 April 1996. The next day the Labour Party Central Committee voted to remove the clause in its election manifesto which opposed the establishment of a Palestinian state.

25 *New York Times*, 2 June 1996.

26 A mini-crisis ensued when Netanyahu refused to give any of the important ministries of Defence, Finance or Housing, to Ariel Sharon, whom he regarded 'a persistent dissident'. This angered Sharon, who

had played a crucial role in keeping the secular right-wing united behind Netanyahu, and courting the religious right; successfully. It was only after David Levy had publicly threatened to resign if Sharon was not appointed a minister that Netanyahu relented. It was not until 8 July that Sharon was put in charge of the newly created Ministry of National Infrastructure which – besides railways, ports and military industry – included 'bypass roads in the West Bank'.

27 *New York Times*, 19 June 1996, and *Middle East International*, 21 June 1996, p. 11.

Chapter 6 *The Israel Defence Forces*

1 Zahal, Hebrew acronym of Zvai Haganah LeIsrael, Defence Force for Israel.

2 Yossi Melman, *The New Israelis*, Carol Publishing Co., New York, 1993, p. 136.

3 *Davar* (Hebrew, Word), Tel Aviv, 1 April 1994.

4 Interview on Israeli Television, 13 January 1988. It soon proved to be an ineffective gesture.

5 'How did the intifada affect the IDF?' in *Conflict Quarterly*, Vol. 14, No. 3, University of New Brunswick, New Brunswick, Canada, Summer 1994, p. 12.

6 Druzes are members of a heterodox Muslim sect which does not feel bound by two of the five pillars of orthodox Islam: fasting during the holy month of Ramadan, and the pilgrimage to Mecca.

7 *HaAretz*, 1 May 1992.

8 Cited in *Jerusalem Report*, 29 December 1994, p. 13.

9 Interviews in Jerusalem and Haifa, January–March 1995.

10 Ilan Pappe *The Making of the Arab-Israeli Conflict, 1947–51*, I.B. Tauris, London and New York, 1992.

11 Susan Hattis Rolef (ed.), *The Political Dictionary of the State of Israel*, Jerusalem Publishing House, Jerusalem, 1993, pp. 313–16.

12 Amos Elon, pp. 191 and 192.

13 Ilan Pappe, op. cit., p. vii.

14 Ilan Pappe, op. cit., pp. 110–11; and Benny Morris, *The Birth of the Palestinian Refugee Problem, 1947–1949*, Cambridge University Press, Cambridge and New York, 1987, p. 22.

15 Walid Khalidi (ed.), *From Haven to Conquest: Readings in Zionism and the Palestinian Problem until 1948*, Institute of Palestine Studies, Beirut, 1971, p. 861. In addition, the estimates for the 'Dissident Groups' of Irgun and Lehi are put respectively at 3–5,000 and 2–300. Ibid., p. 863.

16 Walid Khalidi, op. cit., p. 685; and Benny Morris, op. cit., pp. 21 and 22.

17 Walid Khalidi, op. cit., pp. 865 and 867–8.

18 Ibid., pp. 866 and 868.
19 See p. 137.
20 Benny Morris, op. cit., p. 291. Though it was in May 1946 that, following the independence of his country, Emir Abdullah of the Emirate of Transjordan changed the name of his realm to the Hashemite Kingdom of Jordan, with himself as king, it was only after March 1948, when he had signed a revised 20-year treaty with Britain, that international recognition of the new status of him and his country followed gradually.
21 Ilan Pappe, op. cit., p. 271.

Chapter 7 *The Double Marginals*

1 Interview in Jerusalem, February 1995.
2 Interview in Haifa, February 1995.
3 Interview in Nazareth, February 1995.
4 Interview in Haifa, February 1995
5 Benny Morris, op. cit., p. 1.
6 Ibid., pp. 288–9.
7 Ibid., pp. 289, 290 and 291.
8 Ibid., p. 292.
9 Ibid., p. 294.
10 Interview with Said Barghouti, February 1995.
11 The PLO publicly appealed to Israeli Arabs to vote for the Democratic Front for Peace and Equality. Dilip Hiro, *Inside the Middle East*, p. 197.
12 Said Barghouti, *History of the Middle East, Vol. II*, p. 210.
13 The eight Arab MKs were divided thus: the ADP 2, the DFPE 2, Labour 2, Meretz 1 and Likud 1. Of these two MKs, one Labour and the other Meretz, were deputy ministers.
14 *Jerusalem Report*, 2 July 1994, p. 19.

Chapter 8 *New Frontiersmen*

1 Cited in *Village Voice*, 12 November 1985, p. 22.
2 Cited in Gideon Aran, 'A mystico-messianic interpretation of modern Israeli history: the Six-Day War as a key event in the development of the original religious culture of Gush Emunim', *Studies in Contemporary Jewry*, No. 4, 1988, p. 268.
3 See p. 154.
4 *Jerusalem Report*, 3 October 1991, p. 7.
5 See p. 184.
6 *Jerusalem Report*, 3 October 1991, p. 8. It is worth nothing that it cost Israel $300 million in 1982 to resettle the 6,000 Jews settled

earlier in Sinai – that is, $50,000 per settler – following its Peace Treaty with Egypt.

7 *Jerusalem Report*, 9 February 1995, p. 14. The Jewish construction activity used up 763 hectares, or 7.6 square kilometres, of the Palestinian land.

8 Cited in *Newsweek*, 16 June 1980, p. 18.

9 *Jerusalem Report*, 3 November 1994, p. 14.

10 See p. 35.

11 Cited in *Village Voice*, 12 November 1985, p. 17.

12 Cited in David K. Shipler, op., cit. pp. 86 and 503.

13 El Sayyid Nossair, a 35-year-old Egyptian-American, arrested as the suspected murderer, was found not guilty of murder, but was convicted of possessing an illegal weapon.

14 On my return journey at night from Kiryat Arba to Jerusalem in March 1995, our bus was stoned. The shatterproof windshield was damaged, but nobody was hurt.

15 Whereas most Jews believe that God is sanctified through martyrdom, Rabbi Meir Kahane argued that the final expression of *kiddush HaShem* for the Jews is to decimate their enemies, thus revealing the power of God. 'Goldstein did what is written: "Whoever comes to kill you, rise up to kill him,"' said Rabbi Ido Alba of Kiryat Arba. 'This is a simple Halacha . . . The Arabs are not afraid of the army, and one of the ways to protect our lives is to make them afraid of us.' *Jerusalem Post*, 18 January 1995.

16 *Jerusalem Report*, 3 November 1994, p. 15.

17 See pp. 34–6.

18 In 1989 some 70,000 settlers were using 40 per cent of the water in the Occupied Territories. Danny Rubinstein, *People of Nowhere: The Palestinian Vision of Home*, Times Books, New York, 1991, p. 112. Since the early 1980s the IDF had not allowed the Palestinians to dig a new well, banned by a military order, in the West Bank. Robert I. Friedman, op. cit., p. xxiii.

19 *Jerusalem Report*, 9 February 1995, p. 13. Three-fifths of the Jewish settlers were secular, most of them living within commuting distance from Tel Aviv and Jerusalem. Many of them were reportedly more interested in larger and cheaper housing than in claiming the historic rights of the Jews in Eretz Israel. Ibid., 18 November 1993, p. 11.

20 9 February 1995, pp. 4 and 14.

Chapter 9 *The West Bank*

1 Zachary Lockman and Joel Beinin (eds), *Intifada: The Palestinian Uprising Against Israeli Occupation*, I.B. Tauris, London and New York, 1990, p. 108.

2 'Membership in, contact with, or expressed support for the aims of

a proscribed organization (e.g., the Palestine Liberation Organization or its constituent elements) is grounds for arrest [in Israel or the Occupied Territories].' The US State Department, *Country Reports on Human Rights Practices for 1982*, pp. 1158–9. 'Educational materials, periodicals, and books originating outside Israel are censored for alleged anti-Jewish or anti-Israeli content and for perceived encouragement of Palestinian nationalism. The occupation authorities maintain a list of forbidden publications ... Possession of such publications, many of which are legal in Israel and East Jerusalem, by a West Bank or Gaza Arab is a criminal offence, frequently resulting in fine or imprisonment; however, according to Israeli press reports, the list of forbidden publications is not made public.'

3 Zachary Lockman and Joel Beinin (eds), op. cit., p. 108.

4 The title Ansar for a detention camp, which contained Palestinians and Lebanese, was first applied by the Israeli military to a camp in south Lebanon. The name Ansar II was given to the detention camp Israel set up in Gaza city.

5 For an account of the intifada, see Chapter 10.

6 Responding to Palestinian guerrilla attacks, an Israeli armoured column with air cover crossed into Jordan at Karameh on 21 March 1968. Instead of retreating, the Palestinians, backed by Jordanian artillery, fought a 12-hour battle, destroyed many Israeli tanks and halted the IDF advance into Jordan. See further p. 377.

7 Though Kiryat Arba today is the second most populous Jewish settlement in the West Bank, after Ariel, an air of defiance remains. As you enter it from Hebron's Ein Bani Salim Road past a white-painted, electronically-controlled steel gate, the large sign in Hebrew reads: 'Kiryat Arba/ Zionist-Political Settlement/The more you harass us, the more we will expand.'

8 See pp. 383–4. This was a reference to the fighting between the Palestinian commandos and the Jordanian army in September 1970 in which the Palestinians lost.

9 With an altitude of 930 metres, Hebron and its environs are suitable for growing almonds and pistachios.

10 Though, as the owner of the hotel in question, Fayaz Qawasmeh was one of the two parties involved in this historic event, in all these years he had been interviewed only once before on this subject – by a British Broadcasting Corporation television researcher. I was the second researcher to interview him on this matter. All accounts so far have originated solely from Rabbi Moshe Levinger or other members of his group in April 1968. In addition to the two versions of the event provided in Chapter 8, here is another, published in the *Jerusalem Report*, a Jerusalem-based fortnightly, on 3 October 1991. 'On Passover 1968 ten families led by Rabbi Moshe Levinger checked

into Hebron's Arab-owned Park Hotel,' reported Yossi Halevi. 'They claimed to be Swiss tourists, on pilgrimage to Hebron, the city where Abraham and Sarah are buried. When the holiday ended they refused to leave.'

11 Cited in *The Middle East*, June 1980, p. 18.
12 Of the 1.2 million Palestinians in the West Bank in 1994, some 42 per cent were registered as refugees with the United Nations Relief and Work Agency for Palestinian Refugees in the Near East (UNRWA). Of these about a quarter lived in refugee camps, and the rest outside.
13 Central Bureau of Statistics, *Statistical Abstract of Israel, 1994*, Jerusalem, 1995, pp. 201 and 791.
14 Zachary Lockman and Joel Beinin (eds), op. cit., p. 225.
15 Ibid.; and *Jerusalem Report*, 13 December 1990, p. 15.
16 Jerusalem Media and Communication Centre, *Israeli Obstacles to Economic Development in the Occupied Palestinian Territories*, Jerusalem, 1994, p. 89.
17 Zachary Lockman and Joel Beinin (eds), op. cit., p. 225.
18 Meron Benvenisti, *Demographic, Economic, Legal, Social and Political Developments in the West Bank*, The West Bank Data Project, 1987, Jerusalem, p. 32.
19 Zachary Lockman and Joel Beinin (eds), op. cit., p. 225.
20 Jerusalem Media and Communication Centre, op. cit., p. 160.

Chapter 10 *Gaza*

1 Cited in Robert I. Friedman, op. cit., p. 199.
2 *Jerusalem Report*, 13 December 1990, p. 16.
3 Ziad Abu Amr, *Islamic Fundamentalism in the West Bank and Gaza*, Indiana University Press, Bloomington and Indianapolis, 1994, p. 53.
4 Meron Benvensiti, *Demographic, Economic, Legal, Social and Political Developments in the West Bank*, p. 18.
5 Interview in Jerusalem, February 1995.
6 Cited in *Jerusalem Report*, 13 December 1990, p. 14.
7 Zachary Lockman and Joel Beinin, op. cit., pp. 286–91.
8 *Jerusalem Report*, 13 December 1990, p 14.
9 This standard was originally adopted by the Arabs in 1916 after they had revolted against the Ottoman sultan during World War I. In pre-Islamic poetry in Arabia, white signified good deeds, green fertility, black the enemy who fights, and red the enemy's blood.
10 *Jerusalem Report*, 24 October 1991, pp. 22–3.
11 *Middle East International*, 8 November 1991, p. 18.
12 Cited in Robert I. Friedman, op. cit., p. 205.
13 Cited in *Ibid.*, op. cit., pp. 193–4.

14 *Jerusalem Report*, 24 October 1991, p. 22.
15 Ibid., 13 December 1990, p. 13.
16 The lower figures were provided by the IDF, and the higher by BeTselem, an Israeli human rights monitoring group. *Jerusalem Report*, 13 December 1990, pp. 13 and 19; and Robert I. Friedman, op. cit., p. xxvi.
17 David Grossman, *The Yellow Wind*, Dell Publishing, New York, 1989, pp. 14–15.
18 *Jerusalem Report*, 13 December 1990, p. 16, and 29 October 1991, p. 22.
19 Ibid., 13 December 1990, p. 16.
20 Ibid., p. 8.
21 Ibid., p. 13.
22 Interview in Ramallah, March 1995.
23 Cited in *Jerusalem Report*, 14 March 1991, p. 26.
24 Ibid., p. 26.
25 *Jerusalem Report*, 24 October 1991, p. 23.
26 Ibid., 13 December 1990, p. 16.
27 Graham Usher, *Palestine in Crisis*, Pluto Press, London, 1995, p. 8; and *Middle East International*, 18 December 1992, p. 4.
28 Interview with *HaAretz*, cited in *Middle East International*, 18 December 1992, p. 4.
29 *Middle East International*, 19 March 1993, pp. 8–9.
30 During the Philistine era Gaza was the site of the Temple to pagan god Dagon, which was destroyed by Samson, the jilted strongman.
31 Hassan Ealin was one of the seven leaders of the Popular Front for the Liberation of Palestine in the West Bank and Gaza to have been assassinated by the Shin Beth. Having agreed to release them in 1985 as part of a prisoner exchange, the Israeli Government reckoned that they were too dangerous to be allowed to live as free men and decided to kill them.
32 Robert I. Friedman, op. cit., pp. 197–201.
33 *Jerusalem Post Magazine*, 17 February 1995, pp. 15–16.
34 Ibid., p. 16.

Chapter 11 *The Palestine Liberation Organization*

1 Anybody born of a Palestinian father, irrespective of his place of residence, was entitled to become a Palestine National Council member.
2 Interview at Birzeit University, Birzeit, January 1995.
3 Yasser Arafat kept on making brief clandestine visits to the West Bank until early 1969, just before being elected Chairman of the Palestine Liberation Organization in February.

4 Michael C. Hudson, *Arab Politics: The Search for Legitimacy*, Yale University Press, New Haven, CT., and London, 1977, p. 302.

5 Andrew Gowers and Tony Walker, *Arafat: The Biography*, Virgin Books, London, 1994, p. 83, citing Mohamed Heikal, a confidant of President Nasser, who was present at the meeting.

6 David Hirst, *The Gun and the Olive Branch: The Roots of Violence in the Middle East*, Faber & Faber, London, 1978, p. 314.

7 Abu Iyad (with Eric Rouleau), *My Home, My Land: A Narrative of the Palestinian Struggle*, Times Books, New York, 1981, pp. 135–6.

8 Cited in Dilip Hiro, *Inside the Middle East*, p. 55.

9 *Guardian*, 10 June 1974.

10 Cited in Moshe Shemesh, *The Palestinian Entity, 1959–1974: Arab Politics and the PLO*, Frank Cass, London, 1988, p. 259.

11 Cited in David Hirst, op. cit., p. 335.

12 On 16 December 1991, at the American initiative, the United Nations General Assembly revoked Resolution 3379 by 111 votes to 25, with 13 abstentions.

13 Sandra Mackey, *Lebanon: Death of a Nation*, Congdon and Weed, New York, 1989, p. 178.

14 Dilip Hiro, *Lebanon, Fire and Embers: A History of the Lebanese Civil War*, Weidenfeld & Nicolson, London/St Martin's Press, New York, 1993, p. 89; and Mohamed Heikal, *Secret Channels*, Harper Collins, London, 1996, p. 355.

15 Cited in E. Sahliyeh, *The PLO after the Lebanon War*, Westview Press, Boulder, CO., 1986, p. 165.

16 *Washington Post*, 25 December 1983.

17 The Sinai II Agreement between Egypt and Israel, primarily concerning disengagement in the Sinai, brokered by Washington, was signed on 4 September 1975. It consisted of three published and four secret documents. Of the latter, three concerned the United States and Israel, including reaffirmation of America's earlier commitment to help Israel maintain military superiority over its Arab neighbours, and a guarantee of oil deliveries to Israel from Iran, then ruled by a pro-western monarch, or mainland US. Dilip Hiro, *Dictionary of the Middle East*, op. cit., p. 302.

18 Andrew Gowers and Tony Walker, op. cit., pp. 337–8.

19 *Foreign Broadcasting Information Service*, Washington DC, 11 December 1984.

20 Dan Raviv and Yossi Melman, *Every Spy a Prince: The Complete History of Israel's Intelligence Community*, Houghton Mifflin, New York and London, 1991, p. 394.

21 Ibid., pp. 395–7.

22 *Sunday Times*, 24 April 1988.

23 Dan Raviv and Yossi Melman, op. cit., p. 397.

24 Zachary Lockman and Joel Beinin, op. cit., pp. 396 and 397. George Habash of the Popular Front for the Liberation of Palestine, while opposed to the political communiqué and the declaration of the founding of the State of Palestine, stated that he would abide by the decision of the majority.
25 Cited in Mohamed Heikal, op. cit., pp. 394–5.
26 *Washington Post*, 15 December 1988.
27 Cited in Dilip Hiro, *Desert Shield to Desert Storm*, p. 79.
28 Cited in ibid., p. 505.
29 Cited in *Jerusalem Report*, 28 March 1991, p. 10.
30 Cited in Andrew Gowers and Tony Walker, op. cit., p. 444.
31 *Mideast Mirror*, 11 February 1991.
32 *Jerusalem Report*, 11 March 1993, pp. 24–6; and Walid Khalidi, *At a Critical Juncture: the United States and the Palestinian People*, Centre for Contemporary Arab Studies, Georgetown University, Washington DC, 1989, p. 23. The PLO also paid compensation to those whose houses were demolished by the IDF.
33 *Guardian*, 1 July 1992.
34 Cited in *Jerusalem Post*, 13 January 1995.
35 Ibid.
36 It was the same table on which the Camp David Accords were signed in September 1978.
37 *The Times*, 14 September 1993.
38 *Guardian*, 8 and 12 November 1993, *Middle East International*, 19 November 1993, p. 3; *Jerusalem Report*, 30 December 1993, p. 20, and *Observer*, 20 March 1994. Adnan Yasin's wife died soon after his arrest in November 1993.
39 *Independent*, 9 October 1993.
40 Cited in *Guardian*, 12 November 1993. Of the 107 central council members, 25 radicals boycotted the meeting. The rest split thus: 63 for the accord, 8 against, with 11 abstentions. *Guardian*, 13 October 1993.
41 *Ibid.*, 8 and 12 November 1993; *Middle East International*, 19 November 1993, p. 3; and *Jerusalem Report*, 30 December 1993, p. 20.
42 *Los Angeles Times*, 28 September 1993.
43 Cited in *Middle East International*, 26 August 1994, p. 6.

Chapter 12 *The Palestinian Authority*

1 *The Times*, 26 May 1994. For the text of the Cairo Agreement, see Graham Usher, *Palestine in Crisis*, pp. 104–15.
2 *Guardian*, 2 July 1994, and *Middle East International*, 8 July 1994, p. 3.
3 In reply to a question at a cabinet meeting Rabin confirmed on

18 September 1994 that 'Palestinian Authority security personnel' operated throughout the West Bank with 'Israel's knowledge and in co-operation with Israel's security forces to safeguard Israel's security interests'. Cited in *Middle East International*, 1 March 1996, p. 16.

4 *Observer*, 3 September 1995.

5 *Al Quds*, 12 January 1995.

6 *Jerusalem Report*, 18 May 1995, p. 34.

7 A few days later Force 17, acting on Yasser Arafat's orders, abducted Bassam Eid, an Israeli Arab human rights activist resident in East Jerusalem who had led the campaign for Maher Alami's release, and took him to the Force's Ramallah headquarters for interrogation. Eid's ordeal lasted a day.

8 Cited in Graham Usher, op. cit., p. 69.

9 Cited in *Middle East International*, 14 April 1995, p. 3.

10 See Graham Usher, op. cit., pp. 109–10.

11 In a similar partisan move, soon after his arrival in Gaza city in July 1994, Arafat had dismissed the local council – consisting of all PLO factions, Islamists and the representatives of refugees, landowners and professionals – nominated by mayor Mansour Shawwa, his appointee, and replaced it with a council consisting exclusively of six Fatah members.

12 Cited in Graham Usher, op. cit., p. 71.

13 *Jerusalem Post*, 5 February 1995.

14 Funds for the policemen above the 9,000 limit fixed by the Cairo Agreement, and other security organizations such as the PSS, came most probably from the accounts of Fatah, which were managed secretly by Arafat.

15 *Jerusalem Post*, 20 February 1995.

16 *Al Quds*, 31 January 1995.

17 *Jerusalem Report*, 2 November 1995, p. 17.

18 Interview in Gaza, March 1995.

19 Commenting on Arafat's inclusion of Nabil Shaath, a millionaire, in the Fatah list for Khan Yunis, Ziad Saleh, a local unemployed engineer, said: 'What's Shaath's revolutionary background? When our children were throwing stones, his children were shopping in London and Paris'. *Observer*, 14 January 1996.

20 When Samiha Khalil tried to hold a rally at Al Najah University in Nablus, the guards acting on 'orders from high up', barred the entry of her supporters as well as reports. Ibid.

21 Cited in *Middle East International*, 16 February 1996, p. 7.

22 Cited in *Independent*, 20 January 1996 and *New Statesman and Society*, 27 January 1996, p. 6.

23 The team 'Palestinian national authority' can be traced back to the June 1974 resolution by the Palestine National Council. See p. 386.

Chapter 13 *Islamist Opposition*

1 1398 was the Islamic year.
2 See the last Quranic verse in Chapter 1, p. 39. All Quranic verses are from Arthur J. Arberry, *The Koran Interpreted*, Oxford University Press, Oxford and New York, 1964.
3 The other co-founders of Hamas were Abdul Fattah Dukhan, a teacher; Isa Nashshar, an engineer; Dr Abdul Aziz Rantisi, a physician; Muhammad Shamaa, a teacher; Shaikh Salah Shihada, a professor; and Ibrahim al Yazuri, a pharmacist.
4 David K. Shipler, op. cit., p. 177.
5 Cited in Rony Shaked and Aviva Shaby, *Hamas* (in Hebrew), Ketter Publications, Jerusalem, 1994, p. 87.
6 Cited in Ziad Abu Amr, *Islamic fundamentalism in the West Bank and Gaza: Muslim Brotherhood and Islamic Jihad*, Indiana University Press, Bloomington and Indianapolis, 1994, pp. 80–3.
7 *Middle East International*, 8 November 1991, pp. 17–19; and Ziad Abu Amr, op. cit., p. 78.
8 Ziad Abu Amr, op. cit. pp. 69–70.
9 *Al Sirat* (Arabic, The Path), June 1988, p. 23.
10 Cited in Ziad Abu Amr, op. cit., p. 74.
11 *Al Islam wa Falastin*, 30 December 1988, p. 10.
12 Ziad Abu Amr, op. cit., p. 89.
13 See p. 358.
14 See p. 442.
15 *Jerusalem Post*, 27 January 1995.
16 The explosions occurred a few hundred metres from the Beit Lid jail where Shaikh Ahmad Yasin of Hamas was held. 'It caused me pain,' he told the mass circulation Hebrew daily, *Ma'ariv*, on 2 June 1995. 'However, the Israeli occupation and violence against Palestinians are the cause, not the effect, of Palestinian violent resistance. Don't ask me to denounce violence as long as I am under your occupation and persecution. The end of violence would have to be bilateral, not unilateral.'
17 *Jerusalem Times*, 26 January 1995, and *Jerusalem Post*, 27 January 1995.
18 Interview in Gaza, March 1995.
19 5 June 1988, p. 14. By the early 1990s suicide bombing had been adopted by Sri Lanka's Tamil rebels, Hindu by religion, fighting for an independent state. One of their activists assassinated Indian Prime Minister Rajiv Gandhi in May 1991 this way. And in early 1996 a suicide truck-bombing in front of the Central Bank of Sri Lanka in downtown Colombo killed 72 people and devastated a large area.
20 Sayyid Qutb, *Signposts along the Road* (in Arabic), Dar al Mashriq, Beirut, 1986, p. 21, cited in Dilip Hiro, *Islamic Fundamentalism*,

Paladin Books, London, 1988/*Holy War: The Rise of Islamic Fundamentalism*, Routledge, New York, 1989, p. 67.
21 Al Mukhtar al Islami, Cairo, 1979, p. 13.
22 Cited in *Observer*, 3 September 1995.
23 Ibid.
24 *Jerusalem Report*, 27 July 1995, pp. 32–3.
25 *Guardian*, 8 January 1996.
26 The figure of 68 included 21 Israelis killed at Beit Lid by the explosions caused by the activists of the Islamic Jihad, to which Yahya Ayash did not belong, the remaining 47 consisting of the victims in Afula (8), Hadera (5), Tel Aviv (22), Ramat Gan (7) and Jerusalem (5).
27 *Observer*, 28 January 1996; and *Sunday Times*, 7 January 1996.
28 *Jerusalem Report*, 27 July 1995, p. 33.
29 Cited in *Observer*, 10 March 1996.
30 Cited in *Sunday Times*, 10 March 1996.
31 *Maariv*, 2 June 1995.
32 *Independent*, 6 March 1996.
33 During the border closure in early 1995, for instance, many Palestinian cars and communal taxis from Ramallah entered Jerusalem either via a long, circuitous asphalted route or backroad pedestrian tracks.
34 Cited in *Middle East International*, 15 March 1996, p. 4.

Chapter 15 *Summing Up the Past, Surmising the Future*

1 Cited in Colin Thubron, *Jerusalem*, p. 163.
2   Foreign Office
                                                                2nd November 1917

        Dear Lord Rothschild:
        I have much pleasure in conveying to you on behalf of His Majesty's Government the following declaration of our sympathy with Jewish Zionist aspirations which has been submitted to, and approved by, the Cabinet. 'His Majesty's Government view with favour the establishment in Palestine of a National Home for the Jewish people, and will use their best endeavours to facilitate the achievement of this object, it being clearly understood that nothing shall be done which may prejudice the civil and religious rights of existing non-Jewish communities in Palestine, or the rights and political status enjoyed by Jews in any other country.' I should be grateful if you would bring this declaration to the knowledge of the Zionist Federation.

                                                                Yours sincerely,
                                                                (Arthur James Balfour)
3 See further, Dilip Hiro, *Between Marx and Muhammad: The*

Changing Face of Central Asia, HarperCollins, London and New York, 1994, p. 305.
4 Interview in Jerusalem, January 1995.
5 Interview in Haifa, February 1995.
6 Interview in Jerusalem, February 1995.
7 *Jerusalem Report*, 30 November 1995, p. 14.
8 Interview in Jerusalem, February 1995.
9 Interview in Haifa, February 1995.
10 Amos Elon, op. cit., pp. 243–5.
11 See pp. 363–4.
12 Interview in Kiryat Arba, March 1995.
13 *Jerusalem Report*, 2 November 1995, p. 18.
14 Sammy Smooha, 'Jewish Ethnicity in Israel', in Keith Kyle and Joel Peters (eds), *Whither Israel? The Domestic Challenge*, p. 168.
15 See pp. 125.
16 Interview in Jerusalem, March 1995.
17 Cited in Keith Kyle and Joel Peters (eds), op. cit., pp. 274–5.
18 *Guardian*, 20 January 1996.
19 Interview in Gaza, March 1995.
20 See p. 440 and p. 562, note 7.
21 Interview in Haifa, February 1995.

Epilogue

1 None the less, Egypt was one of the eight Arab countries – six Gulf states, Egypt and Syria – which threatened in mid-July to freeze their relations with Israel if it did not accept the principle of exchanging occupied Arab land for peace. Of the Gulf states, Oman and Qatar had established commercial links with Israel.
2 *Independent*, 24 June 1996.
3 See pp. 411–12.
4 *The Times*, 10 July 1996. Without waiting for an official go ahead, on 14 July the Council of the Jewish Communities in Judea, Samaria and Gaza announced plans to expand 15 existing settlements and set up eight new ones, and double the settler population over the next four years.
5 *HaAretz*, 24 June 1996.
6 *New York Times*, 19 June 1996.
7 *Independent*, 24 June 1996.
8 Ibid., 25 June 1996.
9 Cited in ibid., 21 June 1996.

APPENDIX I

United Nations Security Council Resolutions 242 (1967) and 338 (1973):

United Nations Security Council Resolution 242
22 November 1967

The Security Council,

Expressing its continuing concern with the grave situation in the Middle East,

Emphasizing the inadmissibility of the acquisition of territory by war and the need to work for a just and lasting peace in which every State in the area can live in security,

Emphasizing further that all Member States in their acceptance of the Charter of the United Nations have undertaken a commitment to act in accordance with Article 2 of the Charter,

1. Affirms that the fulfilment of Charter principles requires the establishment of a just and lasting peace in the Middle East which include the application of both the following principles: (i) Withdrawal of Israeli armed forces from territories occupied in the recent conflict; (ii) Termination of all claims of states of belligerency and respect for and acknowledgement of the sovereignty, territorial integrity and political independence of every State in the area and their right to live in peace within secure and recognized borders from threats or acts of force;

2. Affirms further necessity (a) For guaranteeing freedom of navigation through international waterways in the area; (b) For achieving a just settlement of the refugee problem; (c) For guaranteeing the territorial inviolability and political independence of every State in the area, through measures including the establishment of demilitarized zones;

3. Requests the Secretary-General to designate a Special Representative to proceed to the Middle East to establish and maintain contacts with the States concerned in order to promote agreement and assist efforts to achieve a peaceful and accepted settlement in accordance with the provisions and principles of this resolution;

4. Requests the Secretary-General to report to the Security Council on the progress of the Special Representative as soon as possible.

Adopted by unanimous vote

United Nations Security Council Resolution 338
22 October 1973

The Security Council
1. Calls upon all parties to the present fighting to cease all firing and terminate all military activity immediately, no later than 12 hours after the moment of adoption of this decision, in the positions they now occupy;

2. Calls upon the parties to start immediately after the ceasefire the implementation of Security Council resolution 242 (1967) in all of its parts;

3. Decides that, immediately and concurrently with the cease-fire, negotiation shall start between the parties concerned under appropriate auspices at establishing a just and durable peace in the Middle East.

Adopted by 14 votes to one with
one abstention (China)

APPENDIX II

*Letters of Mutual Recognition by Israel and the
Palestine Liberation Organization, exchanged
through Norwegian Foreign Minister, 9–10
September 1993*

From Yasser Arafat, Chairman, Palestine Liberation Organization to Israeli Prime Minister Yitzhak Rabin (on 9 September 1993)

Mr Prime Minister

The signing of the Declaration of Principles marks a new era in the history of the Middle East. In firm conviction thereof I would like to confirm the following PLO commitments:

The PLO recognizes the right of the State of Israel to exist in peace and security. The PLO accepts the United Nations Security Council Resolutions 242 and 338.

The PLO commits itself to the Middle East peace process and to a peaceful resolution of the conflict between the two sides and declares that all outstanding issues relating to a permanent status will be resolved through negotiations.

The PLO considers the signing of the Declaration of Principles constitutes an historic event, inaugurating a new epoch of peaceful co-existence, free from violence and all other acts which endanger peace and stability. Accordingly, the PLO renounces the use of terrorism and other acts of violence and will assume responsibility over all PLO elements and personnel in order to assure their compliance, prevent violations and discipline violators.

In view of the promise of a new era and the signing of the Declaration of Principles and based on Palestinian acceptance of Security Council Resolutions 242 and 338, the PLO affirms that those articles of the Palestinian Covenant which deny Israel's right to exist and the provisions of the Covenant which are inconsistent with the commitment of this letter are now inoperative and no longer valid. Consequently, the PLO undertakes to submit to the Palestinian National Council for formal approval the necessary changes in regard to the Palestinian Covenant.

Sincerely,
Yasser Arafat, Chairman,
Palestine Liberation Organization

From Mr Yitzhak Rabin to Mr Yasser Arafat (on 10 September 1993)

Mr Chairman

In response to your letter of September 9th 1993 I wish to confirm to you that, in light of the PLO commitments included in your letter, the Government of Israel has decided to recognize the PLO as the representative of the Palestinian people and commence negotiations with the PLO within the Middle East peace process.

Yitzhak Rabin,
Prime Minister of Israel

From Mr Yasser Arafat to Mr Johan Jorgen Holst, Norwegian Foreign Minister (on 10 September 1993)

Dear Minister Holst

I would like to confirm to you that, upon signing of the Declaration of Principles, I will include the following positions in my public statements: In light of the new era marked by the signing of the Declaration of Principles, the PLO encourages and calls upon the Palestinian people in the West Bank and Gaza Strip to take part in the steps leading to the normalization of life, rejecting violence and terrorism, contributing to peace and stability and participating actively in the shaping of reconstruction, economic development and co-operation.

Sincerely,
Yasser Arafat, Chairman,
Palestine Liberation Organization

SELECT BIBLIOGRAPHY

Abu Amr, Ziad, *Islamic Fundamentalism in the West Bank and Gaza*, Indiana University Press, Bloomington and Indianapolis, 1994.

Alwash, Naji, *The Arab Resistance in Palestine, 1917–1948* (in Arabic), Dar al Mashriq, Beirut, 1973.

Arberry, Arthur J., *The Koran Interpreted*, Oxford University Press, Oxford and New York, 1964.

Benvenisti, Meron, *Demographic, Economic, Legal, Social and Political Developments in the West Bank*, The West Bank Data Base Project, Jerusalem, 1987.

Benvenisti, Meron, *Jerusalem: A Study of a Polarized Community*, Research Paper 3, The West Bank Data Base Project, Jerusalem, 1983.

Brook, Stephen, *Winner Takes All: A Season in Israel*, Picador, London, 1991.

Central Bureau of Statistics, *Statistical Abstract of Israel 1994*, Government Publishing House, Tel Aviv, 1995.

Eber, Shirley, and O'Sullivan, Kevin, *Israel and the Occupied Territories: The Rough Guide*, Harrap Columbus, London, 1989.

Elon, Amos, *The Israelis: Founders and Sons*, Holt, Rinehart & Winston, New York, 1971/Adam Publishers, Jerusalem, 1981.

Etzion, Yehuda, *The Temple Mount* (in Hebrew), E. Capsi, Jerusalem, 1985.

Friedman, Robert I., *Zealots for Zion: Inside Israel's West*

Bank Settlement Movement, Random House, New York, 1993.

Gowers, Andrew and Walker, Tony, *Arafat: The Biography*, Virgin Books, London, 1994.

Grossman, David, *The Yellow Wind*, Dell Publishing, New York, 1989.

Heikal, Mohamed, *Secret Channels*, HarperCollins, London, 1996.

Hersh, Seymour, *The Samson Option: Israel's Nuclear Arsenal And American Foreign Policy*, Random House, New York/Faber & Faber, London, 1991.

Hiro, Dilip, *Desert Shield to Desert Storm: The Second Gulf War*, Routledge, New York/HarperCollins, London 1992.

Hiro, Dilip, *Dictionary of the Middle East*, St Martin's Press, New York/Macmillan, London, 1996.

Hiro, Dilip, *Inside the Middle East*, McGraw-Hill, New York/Routledge & Kegan Paul, London, 1982.

Hirst, David, *The Gun and the Olive Branch: The Roots of Violence in the Middle East*, Faber & Faber, London, 1978.

The Holy Bible: The Old and New Testaments, conformable to the edition of 1611, commonly known as the Authorized or King James Version, World Publishing Company, Cleveland and New York, 1960.

Jerusalem Media and Communication Centre, *Israeli Military Orders in the Occupied Palestinian West Bank, 1967–1992*, Jerusalem, Second Edition, 1995.

Jerusalem Media and Communication Centre, *Israeli Obstacles to Economic Development in the Occupied Palestinian Territories*, Jerusalem, 1994.

Kaufman, Gerald, *Inside the Promised Land: A Personal View of Today's Israel*, Wildwood House, Aldershot, 1986.

Khalidi, Walid, *From Haven to Conquest: Readings in Zionism and the Palestinian Problem until 1948*, The Institute of Palestine Studies, Beirut, 1971.

Kyle, Keith, and Peters, Joel (eds), *Whither Israel? The Domestic Challenges*, I.B. Tauris, London and New York, 1994.

Lockman, Zachary and Beinin, Joel (eds), *Intifada: The Palestinian Uprising Against Israeli Occupation*, I.B. Tauris, London and New York, 1990.

McNeill, Graham, *An Unsettling Affair: Housing Conditions, Tenancy Regulations and the Coming of the Messiah in the Old City of Jerusalem*, Birzeit University, Birzeit, 1990.

Melman, Yossi, *The New Israelis*, Carol Publishing Group, New York, 1993.

Morris, Benny, *The Birth of the Palestinian Refugee Problem, 1947–1949*, Cambridge University Press, Cambridge and New York, 1987.

Nasser, Jamal and Heacock, Roger (eds), *Intifada: Palestinians at the Crossroads*, Birzeit University & Praeger, Birzeit and New York, 1991.

Pappe, Ilan, *The Making of the Arab-Israeli Conflict, 1947–51*, I.B. Tauris, London and New York, 1994.

Peretz, Don, *The Government and Politics of Israel*, Westview Press, Boulder, COLO./Dawson, United Kingdom, 1979.

Qutb, Sayyid, *Signposts along the Road* (in Arabic), Dar al Mashriq, Beirut, 1986.

Raviv, Dan, and Melman, Yossi, *Every Spy a Prince: The Complete History of Israel's Intelligence Community*, Houghton Mifflin, New York and London, 1991.

Rolef, Susan Hattis (ed.), *The Political Dictionary of the State of Israel*, Jerusalem Publishing House, Jerusalem, 1993.

Romann, Michael and Weingrod, Alex, *Living Together Separately: Arabs and Jews in Contemporary Jerusalem*, Princeton University Press, Princeton, N.J., 1991.

Rubinstein, Danny, *People of Nowhere: The Palestinian Vision of Home*, Times Books, New York, 1991.

Said, Edward W., *The Question of Palestine*, Pantheon, New York/Routledge & Kegan Paul, London, 1980.

Schiff, Zeev and Ya'ari, Ehud, *Intifada: The Palestinian Uprising – Israel's Third Front*, Simon and Schuster, New York, 1990.

Shaked, Rony and Shaby, Aviva, *Hamas* (in Hebrew), Ketter Publications, Jerusalem, 1994.

Shemesh, Moshe, *The Palestinian Entity, 1959–1974: Arab Politics and the PLO*, Frank Cass, London, 1988.

Shipler, David K., *Arab and Jew: Wounded Spirits in a Promised Land*, Penguin Books, New York and Harmondsworth, 1987.

Smooha, Sammy, *Israel: Pluralism and Conflict*, Routledge & Kegan Paul, London and Boston, 1978.

Sprinzak, Ehud, *The Ascendance of Israel's Radical Right*, Oxford University Press, New York and Oxford, 1991.

Thubron, Colin, *Jerusalem*, Century Hutchinson, London, 1986.

Usher, Graham, *Palestine in Crisis*, Pluto Press, London, 1995.

INDEX